Desegregation from Brown to Alexander

An Exploration of
Supreme Court Strategies

By
Stephen L. Wasby,
Anthony A. D'Amato, *and*
Rosemary Metrailer

With a Foreword by Victor G. Rosenblum

SOUTHERN ILLINOIS UNIVERSITY PRESS
CARBONDALE AND EDWARDSVILLE

Feffer & Simons, Inc.
London and Amsterdam

Library of Congress Cataloging in Publication Data

Wasby, Stephen L. 1937-
    Desegregation from Brown to Alexander.

    Includes bibliographical references and index.
    1. Afro-Americans—Civil rights—United States.
2. United States. Supreme Court. I. D'Amato,
Anthony A., 1937- joint author. II. Metrailer, Rosemary,
1944- joint author. III. Title.
KF4757.W38   342'.73'08502643   76-30792
ISBN 0–8093–0805–3

We dedicate this book
to
all those who do not believe
    that keeping the Supreme Court's processes
      shrouded in mystery
is essential
   to the Court's efficacy
     in a democratic system.

Contents

Foreword

by Victor G. Rosenblum

THIS collaborative enterprise by a renowned law professor who is also a skilled political scientist with a distinguished political science professor who is also a brilliant analyst of legal affairs and with an able law student and researcher who majored in political science has produced a uniquely broad-gauged and insightful probe of the use of strategy by the Supreme Court as a policy-making body.

Utilizing the racial desegregation decisions from the enunciation to the demise of "with all deliberate speed" as their primary base, Professors D'Amato and Wasby and Ms. Metrailer dig deeply and lucidly into the norms and nuances of Supreme Court decision making.

With precision and sophistication they examine judicial techniques of case selection, choices of language and reasoning, criteria for deference and delay, uses of summary disposition and per curiam rulings, and the general judicial preference for incremental actions. They explore and explain judicial options and tactics in policy making ranging from "broad brush strokes" to "salami slicing" and "hit 'em where they ain't." They carry out their complex task without pedantry, cavil, or obfuscation by jargon. A pervasive concern for the practicalities and realities of judicial choice is evident throughout the volume.

Their incisive analyses of options and strategies in doctrinal development and articulation by the justices are models of integrative application of legal and social science skills. In addition to the clarity and ease with which they delineate the patterns and processes of judicial policy making, the authors achieve a major breakthrough in research into judicial behavior by correlating arguments before the justices with the contents of ensuing judicial decisions. What the justices said in their opinions is thus viewed in relation to what counsel urged in their briefs and oral arguments and what the justices inquired into and commented about in the course of oral arguments. This enables them to construe the cases as products of systemic development rather than as spontaneously generated, isolated fragments of judicial policy making.

The reader can't help but become intellectually aroused and extensively informed by this innovative, integrative volume that Professors D'Amato and Wasby and Ms. Metrailer have given us. The authors have carved a new bench mark for interdisciplinary collaboration that combines professional breadth and sophistication with easy to understand "situation sense."

Northwestern University
Departments of Law and
Political Science
September 1976

Preface

THIS book, which examines the Supreme Court's strategies in handling race relations cases from the 1954 decision in *Brown v. Board of Education* to the end of the 1960s, has two premises. The first is that shedding more light on the crucial American institution of the Supreme Court may dispel myths about it, but surely will not destroy its effectiveness.[1] We are convinced that the study of the Supreme Court has been hindered by scholars' unwillingness to probe very deeply into the Court's workings, thereby reinforcing the Court's own secretiveness about how it operates. Those persons who still believe that the Court acts only to find and not make the law have difficulty thinking about the nation's highest court in terms of strategy, a concept which seems to them to suggest crass politics rather than principled judging. To elucidate the components of the Court's strategies, or even to try to infer them from often obscure data, seems to those persons to be highly indelicate. Even those who realize that the Court is a policy-maker, not merely a discoverer of preexisting law, often hold back from examining the Court openly. Our second premise is that, operating in a complex political environment, the Supreme Court cannot avoid politics in the broadest sense. The Court has at least a rough idea of what it wants to do and where it is going, and to be effective must undertake the difficult task of reacting to its environment. Thus, recognizing that the Court does not avoid politics entirely does not make the Supreme Court into something it is not; it remains a court.

Because attorneys' positions may serve as a limit on what judges can do, we look at the lawyers' arguments, but that attention is subordinated to the judges' strategies. Thus we have not devoted time to detailing the activity within the NAACP or the Department of Justice as the desegregation cases were argued.[2] This does not mean that lawyers' strategies are unimportant; because of the NAACP's involvement in many cases, such strategies obviously were significant in the desegregation cases. Lawyers' strategies are especially critical as to the decision whether to bring a case initially or to appeal a lower court ruling. Even so, the cases brought to the Supreme Court are often a function of the types of cases the justices have recently accepted or rejected. This fact suggests the importance of the judges' strategies, which become even more important once the decision to proceed has been made. Furthermore, even in cases producing major constitutional doctrine, the lawyers did not necessarily pursue the case in order to achieve that doctrine but rather to win for their clients.[3] They allow the judges much freedom of action by offering all possible arguments in the effort to win a case, something done frequently even by lawyers (such as NAACP attorneys) who are seeking a particular doctrinal result.

With respect to judges' strategies, external rather than internal strategy primarily engages our attention. We are more interested in the means the Court used to achieve its stated goals than in the ways by which judges dealt with each other. Our analysis stresses ways in which the Court planned—or at least the ways in which it appears to have planned—its strategies and the effectiveness of the various strategies which the Court has adopted to achieve its goals. Mindful of Hans Linde's comment that "criticism of a court's performance on instrumentalist grounds . . . depends on the attribution to the court of pragmatic goals beyond the normative premises stated in the ruling itself,"[4] we have tried not to attribute to the Court goals it has not adopted; wherever possible, we have taken the Court's announced goals at face value. Thus when the Court said that "separate but equal" had no place in public education, the question for us was whether the Court did what it could have done to achieve that stated goal. While it is true that "political realism in assessing the effects of a decision and the responses of other institutions and of the public is a luxury of critical hindsight that is most problematical as a premise of adjudication,"[5] there must be some *ex post facto* examination if the Court is to be understood better. Hence we must run the risk of analysis through hindsight.

Our analytical approach affords, we think, a perspective for describing and analyzing Supreme Court behavior which can cast a new light upon the role of the nation's highest court. Although attorneys who argue before the Court undoubtedly have at least some intuitive—and sometimes a highly educated—idea of the strategic direction in which the Court may be expected to move, our analytical approach has not been applied heretofore to a broad area of law over an extended period. Very little is known about the Court's strategy; few of the scattered studies of the subject are extensive; and what is known is principally about the strategy of individual justices—as in Murphy's discussion of a "policy-oriented judge."[6] Some attention has been paid to the links between the individual judges' strategy and the Court's collective acts, but the primary concern of scholars has been with matters of internal strategy, such as David Rohde's work on the establishment of a "minimum winning coalition."[7] External strategy—strategy vis-à-vis other actors in the political system—has received even less attention, although some scholars such as Martin Shapiro and Arthur Miller have urged that the Court utilize a "jurisprudence of consequences,"[9] and Rohde has touched on the Court's response to external threats. Such threats, although rarely discussed by

the Court, have exerted a powerful and very conservative influence over
the justices' decision-making. In any event, apart from attorney Jack
Greenberg's comparison of the Court's treatment of some school desegregation and sit-in cases from an external strategy perspective,[9] few
attempts have been made to look systematically at the range of alternatives open to the Court in a given policy area.

   The approach used here differs from that found in studies of community conditions or of the impact of decisions of the Supreme Court,[10]
but it can be seen as part of the increasing literature on "law and change"
in which scholars have attempted to portray changes which have
followed—and perhaps resulted from—statements of law or in which
they have tried to identify conditions attending such change-inducing
statements of law.[11] Quite different are the many studies of the doctrinal
basis of the justices' opinions, the backgrounds and political attitudes of
the justices, and the way the justices came to be selected for the Supreme
Court. Our approach also differs from studies which have focused upon
the voting behavior of the justices, and differs as well from various
attempts which have been made to predict the Court's decisions.[12] Taken
together with these other approaches, we hope this volume adds an
important dimension to the study of judicial—especially Supreme
Court—behavior.

ii

   The period under examination—from before *Brown v. Board of Education* through the end of "all deliberate speed"—was selected because it
seemed to provide a natural unit for analysis of the Court's strategies.
Brown marked the beginning of what Arthur Larson has called "the
modern law of race relations."[13] The scope of this field is not obvious; it
does not include every case arguably connected with race or all cases
involving blacks.[14] We focus upon areas in which we judge the racial issue
to have been dispositive, whether or not that issue was openly discussed by
the justices. In some cases—for example, demonstration cases decided in
free speech terms, anti-NAACP cases decided in terms of the right of
association, and the sit-in cases disposed of on procedural grounds (lack
of evidence to sustain a conviction for breach of the peace)—the racial
issue was not at the core of the Court's discussion and even seems to have
been avoided. That this avoidance of explicit treatment of the issue was
part of the Court's strategy can be seen in the effort by Justice Frankfurter, who had been an NAACP counsel, to get his brethren to play down
race aspects in their decisions. According to Murphy, "He consistently
cautioned his colleagues to play down anti-racist rhetoric on the ground
that 'this Court should avoid exacerbating the very feelings which we seek

to allay. And if I myself at times betray this wisdom,' he added, 'so much the worse for me.' "[15]

Our primary interest is in *Brown v. Board of Education,* which was central to the "social revolution" started by the Court in its 1954 and 1955 rulings and which continued, perhaps more consciously, thereafter. Yet this is not simply another book about the School Cases of 1954 and 1955.[16] The cases before *Brown* are summarized in an early chapter. Then, after dealing with *Brown,* we proceed topically to explore the Court's rulings in other areas of race relations in order to provide the larger strategic context in which *Brown* and its progeny were decided. Such areas as housing, voting, transportation, public facilities, public accommodations, and protest are examined. Although we move in essentially chronological fashion within each topical area, we are not writing another history.[17] We have a different focus and a different purpose; we use a chronological approach within categories because the Court's strategy becomes more evident as we watch the justices' actions over time.[18] More important is that while we deal with much of the same material as would a legal historian, we encompass matters such as denials of review to which others have paid insufficient attention. In addressing the practical question of Supreme Court behavior in a long line of desegregation cases, we look at the entire pattern of the Court's behavior, not only the cases the Court decided with full opinions but also its summary actions and its refusals to grant review. The public is accustomed to hearing mostly—or only— about major doctrinal decisions of the Supreme Court, not about the trend of decisions, the incremental pattern of growth, the amount of time it takes the Court to reach a major result, the many intermediate sorts of decisions, and the denials of review which collectively extend the time frame for resolution of major issues. It is to such matters that we pay considerable attention.

Desegregation in education through 1964—both higher education (graduate school and college) and lower education (primary and secondary schools)—is the subject of the first portion of the book. Included here are the cases dealing with efforts to restrict the NAACP's activities. This section is followed by a discussion of cases involving issues of cemeteries, mixed marriages, and gifts of land (the donation by a white person, through his will, of a building or park for use "by whites only")— issues put aside during consideration of *Brown.* Housing—intimately related to school desegregation because of the effect of residential patterns—and the right to vote—the most basic element of citizenship— are examined next. In both areas, the Court relied heavily on statutes in sustaining rights. (Employment rights, also heavily based on statutes, are not treated here because they came either before the Court's post–World War II race relations involvement or after 1969.) Transportation, public facilities, and places of public accommodation, along with voting at the heart of the modern civil rights movement, are then examined. Transportation is included because the transportation cases provide a follow-through from pre-*Brown* decisions and because the "Freedom Rides" and the "sit-ins" were intimately related. The public facilities cases, used by the Court to make known that *Brown* was intended to have a reach broader than education and to show the justices' impatience with the slow pace of desegregation, also provided a means for solving some of the early cases in the public accommodations area. Moreover, the public accommodations cases provide a pattern of behavior by the Supreme Court quite different from that which occurred in school desegregation. Ending this section is an examination of the Court's separate treatment of protest activities, which while intended to bring about changes in the substantive law often were also more general in purpose. Our analysis closes with a return to school desegregation for the Court's positive action in 1968 and 1969, followed by a brief discussion of the "stock-taking" which occurred twenty years after *Brown* and a recapitulation of the strategies examined in this study. In the line of cases examined in this period, the massive evidence of the written opinions and the justices' questioning at oral argument make clear their result-orientation. By and large they behaved pragmatically and strategically; they perceived a social result that was badly needed and adapted the wide variety of judicial means at their disposal to bring it about.

iii

In our investigation of the Court's strategies we use a source often overlooked by students of the Supreme Court: the oral argument before the Court, particularly the questions asked by the justices.[19] Our procedure was that in cases decided by the Supreme Court with full opinion, the lawyers' briefs were read first. Transcript of oral argument was then read when it was available; otherwise, summaries were used. For the last few cases, tapes of the recorded argument were used. Lower court opinions were also examined, particularly where the Supreme Court disposed of a case in summary fashion, including denial of review. The Court's decisions, both those issued with full opinion and per curiam dispositions, were of course used.

The legal briefs and oral arguments of counsel are the most immediate factors commanding the attention of the justices as they proceed to deliberate the outcomes of the cases to which they have decided to give full-dress treatment; they provide the foreground of the judges' environment. Recent testimony makes clear the fundamental importance of oral argument. Responding in 1972 to proposals for reducing or eliminating oral argument, Justice Brennan stated that he had had "too many occasions when my judgment of a decision has turned on what happened in oral argument, not to be terribly concerned for myself were I to be denied" it. And Justice Harlan said that for him there was "no substitute" for this "Socratic method of procedure in getting at the real heart of an issue and in finding out where the truth lies."[20] More recently, Justice Powell asserted that "the quality of advocacy—the research, briefing and oral argument of the close and difficult cases—does contribute significantly to the development of precedents."[21] Oral argument may not always be determinative, but when one finds new doctrine urged on counsel by the justices, forcing the lawyers to broaden the position they adopted in their briefs, one cannot doubt its importance.[22] Furthermore, it is one of the best sources of information from which observers might infer judicial strategies. In particular, judges' questions often reveal basic strategic concerns which do not make their way into the final opinions— drafted in more "legal-like" terms—and which thus tend to be overlooked by those who analyze the Court only on the basis of the reported opinions. In oral argument, lawyers' basic positions on the law become inextricably tangled with the justices' questions; this is particularly true when several cases appear together or there are multiple rounds of argument. Because the school desegregation cases—*Brown v. Board of Education* and its companions—are especially complex and difficult to comprehend without close study, we have rearranged material from oral argument for presentation, with the lawyers' basic statements and some crucial responses to questions separated from most of the justices' questions. For the reader's benefit, we have also tried to present the arguments made and questions asked in a more coherent fashion than may have occurred at the oral argument itself.

Oral argument fulfills a number of important functions for the Court. For one thing, it forces the lawyers to focus on the arguments the lawyers consider most important. The need to condense a case into a half-hour or a full hour of oral communication forces counsel to emphasize which of his arguments are the important ones. This lexical ordering of arguments in terms of importance is often not discernible from the briefs, which are organized point after point in correspondence to the facts and statutes involved in the case. Indeed, counsel may avoid emphasizing importance in their briefs, on the theory that you try to convince the court in as many ways as possible, never knowing which argument or which arguments might be persuasive. However, in oral argument most judges soon ask counsel which arguments are being relied upon most heavily. Thus along with such direct questions the very choice of arguments highlights relative importance. Oral argumentation is a very effective way to put counsel on the spot, forcing him to convey to the court which of his many arguments he deems central and thus necessary for the court to consider and which are collateral issues which might provide the court with an opportunity (or excuse) for remanding the case so that they might be explored. If counsel makes little or no mention of one (or more) of the arguments he has set forth in his brief, he has little cause to complain when the court makes short shrift of those matters in its opinion.

Another function oral argument serves for lawyers—and through them, for the litigants—is to assure that the Court has actually heard the case. The mere submission of briefs does not accomplish this; one never knows whether the justices actually read the briefs. Even a resulting opinion of the Court does not necessarily mean that the justices have read the briefs, for often the detailed reasons given in opinions have been at least initially drafted by the judges' law clerks. Thus the oral argument serves as a uniquely helpful and encouraging part of the communications process between counsel and the court, in which both sides can feel that their case was heard by real people. As Albert Sacks remarked, setting the *Brown* case for reargument "not only assured full and fair consideration of the issues, but made it clear to all that such consideration had been given."[23]

Just as oral argument is important for lawyers and the public, it also fulfills crucial functions for the judges, important from our perspective. Oral argument helps to legitimate the justices' judicial function. While briefs can deal with matters in great detail and lawyers can communicate with and challenge each other through them, oral argument "provides an opportunity for communication between bench and counsel," and has been said to be "at its best, and most useful, when the judges are questioning the lawyers."[24] Oral argument helps provide the judges with information. Sometimes they simply want a clearer picture of what the lawyers are saying, a point particularly evident in the several rounds of oral argument in *Brown v. Board of Education*. Obtaining clarification is not all that is involved. Examination of the three rounds of *Brown* argument indicated that the justices' questions "gave highest priority to three criteria . . . *clarity, adaptability* and *strategy*."[25] As stated by Leon Friedman, "The Justices' purpose in oral argument is to force the lawyers to think out the political, social, and constitutional implications of their arguments." Making even clearer that oral argument is relevant to judges' strategic concerns, he adds, "The Justices constantly seek to relate the immediate problem to analogous situations . . . and try to cut through the rhetoric of the lawyers to see the concrete result of any argument advanced."[26] They want the lawyers to tell them where they might be heading.

Oral argument can also be used by the justices to obtain support for their own positions. In fact, the sessions are often a means by which the judges communicate with each other, even if as a matter of form they are addressing the lawyers. If a justice hammers on a particularly difficult point, he may be intending to persuade his colleagues that they will have to deal with that point and resolve it if they want to decide the case in a certain direction. Or a question to counsel can in reality be an argument, not thought of or pressed by counsel but which the justice, knowing his colleagues, has decided to bring out in the open. As the amount of time devoted to collegial discussion of cases prior to decision in the Supreme Court is necessarily very limited, it is not surprising that the judges would naturally use part of the oral argument time for getting across obliquely to their colleagues on the bench arguments regarding the eventual disposition of the case.

Even though the functions performed by the oral argument are many, of greatest importance for our study are the questions and comments which punctuate oral argument and which may indicate the justices' strategic concerns. That we are not without some basis for using the questions in examining strategy is shown by the strong parallels which exist between justices' questioning and their ultimate positions. While identical strategic questions asked by different justices do not invariably lead them to the same result, our observation of the record suggests that the questions are far from being irrelevant. While parallelism between oral argument questioning and final result may be coincidental, resulting from the justices' personal convictions or from other influences on them, "Nevertheless a comparison of the oral argument with the decision suggests that the relative weight of the oral argument may be heavier than most people suspect."[27]

iv

This book requires of the reader a minimal amount of legal background, but does presume some familiarity with the Constitution and constitutional terminology. It is intended to offer something for both the general reader and the more avid and scholarly "court-watcher"—by helping the former appreciate the particular type and quality of institution which is the Supreme Court of the United States and by providing the latter evidence of the additional dimensions of the richness and complexity of the high court's individual and collective decision-making. Although our focus is upon strategy, we do not exclude doctrinal arguments based upon the meaning of constitutional provisions, inasmuch as any attempt to divorce "pure law" from strategy would only result in seriously distorting the latter. Yet we have tried not to do more than indicate doctrinal arguments as a necessary background for appreciation of judicial strategy considerations.

Whatever our ultimate success in establishing the Court's desegregation strategy, we think that race relations is an intrinsically rich issue-area which commends itself for examination. Despite the issue-area's special characteristics, the Court does not change its character totally in dealing with other areas of political concern, and therefore our approach could be extended to other subjects as diverse as interstate commerce or obscenity. To disembody the Court's strategy from the cases would be a mistake, as we believe that illumination of Supreme Court strategic behavior can only come from an examination of what the Court was trying to accomplish substantively in a given issue-area and whether it succeeded. Thus, although we do not and cannot promise a set of strategic theories which could be applicable to any issue-area, we hope that our mode of analysis itself can be used with respect to other topics.

In focusing upon the Supreme Court's role in the engineering of desegregation in American society, we deal with an area whose active history is in transition.[28] The period of the Warren Court, characterized by "all deliberate speed," is completed. The Court's environment has changed, and its membership has also been altered from the period we have examined. Having stated that de jure segregation must end "at once," the Court now has to face the remaining complex problems of the mechanics of desegregation, such as the permissible extent of busing and the merger of central city school districts with surrounding suburbs, problems which merge inextricably with the problems of de facto segregation resulting from neighborhood housing patterns. Yet these complexities seem of a different order from the issues of the Warren Court period when the justices were staking out the basic ground rules regarding constitutional protection against racial discrimination. At this point, however, we are at least in the position to take an overview of an era.

WE WISH TO THANK the many people who have helped at various stages of the project, which has had a long and involved history. It originated in Professor D'Amato's teaching of political science at Wellesley College in the mid-1960s and ended with Professor Wasby's association with the project in the early 1970s. We wish to acknowledge with particular gratitude the assistance of the Walter E. Meyer Research Institute of Law, which provided a grant covering Ms. Metrailer's expenses in Washington, D.C., while she tracked down manuscripts of oral arguments and developed the "working documents" which became the basis for this volume, and of the School of Law, Northwestern University, for a summer research grant to Professor D'Amato and for typing assistance.

Of considerable help were the discussants for Professor D'Amato's paper on "Schools, Cemeteries, and Mixed Marriages: The Supreme Court and Desegregation Strategies," presented at the 1968 meetings of the Midwest Political Science Association. Carol A. Welch, University of

Wisconsin-Milwaukee, was an excellent sounding board and editorial revisor at an early stage of the manuscript. We also wish to thank Susan Crain and Jesse Brown, who found and checked many case citations, and Professors Milton Dickens (Speech Communications, University of Southern California); Jeanne Hahn (Political Science, Evergreen State College); Hans Linde (Law, University of Oregon); Randall Nelson (Political Science, Southern Illinois University); and S. Sidney Ulmer (Political Science, University of Kentucky) for their communications and helpful suggestions. Lucille Grimes, Terry Nelson, Susan Ritch, Bonnie Sheehan, and Tina Saylor all helped substantially with the preparation of the manuscript.

Writing this book has been stimulating and exciting work, even when we were quite unsure of ourselves, a not infrequent phenomenon. Now that our words are in cold (or, for McLuhan, "hot") print, we can only hope that we have been in some way persuasive. For that, taking responsibility for our errors, we await the readers' verdict.

Desegregation from Brown to Alexander

Chronology

1960   *Bates v. Little Rock*
       Thompson v. City of Louisville
       Hannah v. Larche
       Shelton v. Tucker

1961   *Boynton v. Virginia*
       Burton v. Wilmington Parking Authority
       Garner v. Louisiana

1963   *Watson v. City of Memphis*
       NAACP v. Button
       Goss v. Board of Education of Knoxville
       Peterson v. City of Greenville
       Edwards v. South Carolina

1964   *Griffin v. County School Board of Prince Edward County*
       Bell v. Maryland
       Heart of Atlanta Motel v. United States/Katzenbach v. McClung
       Hamm v. City of Rock Hill
       McLaughlin v. Florida
       NAACP v. Alabama

1965   *Bradley v. School Board of Richmond*
       Cox v. Louisiana

1966   *Evans v. Newton*
       Brown v. Louisiana
       Adderly v. Florida
       Harper v. Virginia Board of Elections
       South Carolina v. Katzenbach
       Georgia v. Rachel/City of Greenwood v. Peacock

1967   *Walker v. City of Birmingham*
       Loving v. Virginia
       Reitman v. Mulkey

1968   *Jones v. Mayer*
       Green v. School Board of New Kent County

1969   *Alexander v. Holmes County*

1970   *Evans v. Abney*

Chapter 1

Introduction:
The Supreme Court and Strategy

THAT the Supreme Court initiated a social revolution in race relations in 1954 is beyond debate. During the 1940s there had been some forward movement on civil rights, particularly by President Harry Truman, and the 1948 split in the Democratic party over a civil rights plank indicated increasing activity. Yet, not very much had happened when President Eisenhower took office. In the midst of his complacent administration, the Court issued its famous decision in *Brown v. Board of Education** that "separate" education for blacks and whites in elementary and secondary schools was not "equal" education under the Equal Protection Clause of the Fourteenth Amendment to the United States Constitution. A year later the Court held that the schools must desegregate "with all deliberate speed." The modern era in civil rights in this country had begun, ninety long years after the Civil War.

No reasonable observer can claim that the *Brown* decision was a success in the area of elementary and secondary school education. Certainly, it was not an immediate success; ten years elapsed after the *Brown* implementation decision with almost nothing happening in much of the South. The pace of southern desegregation accelerated only as a result of the Civil Rights Act of 1964, which provided for cutting off funds to government agencies that discriminated, and as a result of the HEW Desegregation Guidelines which followed the act. To be sure, *Brown* had helped create the tone which allowed the Civil Rights Act to be passed, but it was the act and the guidelines, far more than *Brown* itself, which produced desegregation. An entire generation of black students went through school and became adults before the Supreme Court made clear in its 1969 ruling in *Alexander v. Holmes County* that there had to be an end

*Where the name of a case is indicated in the text, no citation will be provided in a note; the citations for all the cases are available in the Table of Cases Cited at the end of the volume.

to "all deliberate speed" and that desegregation had to come "at once." Moreover, twenty years after *Brown* vast de facto segregation in the North remained largely untouched. The busing used to eliminate northern segregation that was caused or abetted by school officials had created massive and increasing hostility. The Supreme Court raised expectations of equality, but inferior education in overcrowded, under-funded all-black schools continued as usual. By doing little to implement the expectations that *Brown* had engendered, the Court had added to America's extended failure to resolve the "American dilemma."

The *Brown* decision put the Court in a central position in the race-relations area. Although 1957 and 1960 saw the beginnings of congressional action on voting rights, for a decade after *Brown* the president and Congress deferred to the Court, thereby avoiding their own responsibilities. If law is as Pound has stated the "science of social engineering,"[1] the question is, did the Court use its position to engineer desegregation in this country? Furthermore, did the Court do what it could to see to it that its desegregation ruling was implemented? To ask these questions is to raise the more fundamental questions of whether the Court can get involved in "administering" a rule of law it has enunciated and of whether it should do so.

We often hear that a court should simply interpret the law and leave to the other branches of government the function of administering the law. Whatever the other branches of government do, the Court cannot help being involved in administering the legal doctrine it enunciates. Charged with the responsibility of interpreting a "living" Constitution, the Court is no ordinary body of judges but, rather, is a special court among the world's tribunals. Through its power of judicial review, the Supreme Court of the United States can and does attempt to ensure compliance with the Constitution. It necessarily interprets the Constitution in light of present-day circumstances and engages in the political task of safeguarding this "living Constitution" in all walks of American life.

The Supreme Court does not engage in such political tasks by personal lobbying. Because it is a court, different from other governmental institutions, and because it must remain so if it is to function effectively, the Supreme Court must rely upon the legal compulsion and the broader political force of its opinions in particular cases. Yet, even full compliance with all the Court's rulings would not be enough for the Court to achieve its broad goals, for cases come before the Court somewhat haphazardly, often reflecting the short-run demands of particular litigants. As members of a political body, the justices of the Supreme Court realize that the Court must manipulate its docket so that appropriate cases will be before it for decision and so that the Court will not issue the wrong decision at the wrong time. Also, the Court must frame its own decisions narrowly or broadly, depending upon its perception of what is politically feasible or necessary at a given time. In addition, the Court engages in legal-political tactics to see to it that its efficacy is not endangered in the real world. There are thus several facets of strategy—the questions asked by the justices, the decision to handle certain cases and not others, the type of disposition to be rendered, and the grounds of the opinion. Among the many and varied specific strategies used by the Court in the race relations area were docket manipulation, procrastination, reduction or expansion of issues in a case, incremental decision-making, and decision of race relations cases without discussing their racial context.

In order to be effective, the Court must depend upon the cooperation and consent of those to whom its rulings are addressed and upon those to whom it must turn for assistance in enforcing those rulings. Like any other organization, the Court is concerned with maintaining its options, getting others committed to what it is doing, and gaining the confidence of those on whom it relies.[2] In so doing, the Court departs from dispensing exact justice to the litigants. Judges must remain concerned about individual litigants if they are not to act like any other policy maker.[3] Yet individual justice to the litigants may be compromised in light of the judicially perceived "larger" social necessity to select some cases rather than others or to frame decisions so as to accomplish broad social objectives. For example, the Supreme Court refused to decide the sensitive miscegenation question in the case of an Alabama woman convicted for marrying a white man, although the result was that she went to jail.[4] Similarly, though many cases were raised in the federal courts by soldiers contesting the constitutionality of the Vietnam war, the Supreme Court refused to review all such cases throughout the duration of the conflict. Here again, in the eyes of the Court, a social issue overrode the individual soldiers' claim to adjudication.[5]

Traditionally, the Court is viewed as an expounder of constitutional doctrine and developer of statutory interpretation, following the rule of stare decisis, or precedent, a major element in our legal tradition. This rule tends to explain the Court's unwillingness to move very far from its past decisions. It is also helpful when judges wish to conceal policy-making activity and useful in explaining some adjustments the Court makes in explicit doctrine. However, adherence to precedent cannot explain other actions, such as the summary disposition of appeals from those lower court rulings which go a step beyond the Supreme Court's own earlier rulings. Seeking to explain such actions, and looking for similarities between the work of the courts and that of other governmental bodies, those individuals unwilling to accept the conventions have found that for courts as for other bodies policy is made a bit at a time, at the margin (to use the economist's language), by increments. Such a theory, which minimizes the number of explanations of the behavior of separate institutions, e.g., the use of stare decisis in the legal system,[6] is based on a rejection of the idea that judicial decisions, "legal" in nature, are reached in ways different from the ways other "political" decisions are reached and that "legal reasoning" is quite different from other modes of political thinking.

Judicial rulings do not lead in an upward linear path. Moreover, in a "line" of cases there is much wavering and many breaks from straight-forward development. And many major decisions of the Supreme Court have departed sharply from precedent, indicating that other factors play some part in the Court's action. Although the opinion in *Brown v. Board of Education* did far less than it might have done, the ruling in that case can be seen as a jump from the baseline created by the *Plessy* "separate but equal" precedent; this is true even though *Plessy* was not specifically overruled. Even though each new departure from precedent creates a new base line, there are other more-or-less abrupt departures from a norm. Although much of the Supreme Court's activity is incremental in character, movement away from the line traced by past doctrine, and the important instances in which the Court has been decidedly nonincremental, require us to know when, why, and how the Court departs from the incrementally dictated result. With respect to desegregation, the "when" seems to have been shaped and modified by the "why" and the "how." Such instances also mean that incrementalism cannot provide a full explanation for the Court's behavior. Nevertheless, the concept is important for exploring the Court's strategies. Other things being equal, the Court strives for smooth, evolutionary, and accommodation-oriented management of the nation's law.[7] The Court discerns the need to make its decisions appear incremental. If each new decision seems to deviate minimally from past decisions, the public tends to view the judges' function as "finding" and not "making" the law—the result the judges seem to want. Too many sharp deviations and departures, too many unpredictable results—in short, too heavy a dose of nonincrementalism—would disturb the general feeling of the law's stability and lead to criticism of the Court for usurping the functions of a legislature.

2

Attention to the Court's role as a court has obstructed examination of other aspects of its work. Thus relatively little attention has been paid to Supreme Court decision-making as a function of its strategy. There has always been tension between the idea of law as a fixed, certain set of doctrines—to be discovered by the justices and handed down—and the idea that the law changes and is adaptable and purposive. Most scholarly attention has been paid to the first idea, despite the fact that the concept of law as social engineering goes back at least to Roscoe Pound.

Certainly, the Supreme Court is not completely isolated from the surrounding world. The justices do not become hermits upon donning the robes. In addition to its own past decisional law and what the justices bring to the Court, the Court's environment consists of a set of general events, attitudes and opinions, and an audience to whom the Court's messages are directly addressed: interested individuals, including, among the most important, national executive and legislative officials, various state and local government officials, and other political persons who may want to enforce or counteract the Court's rulings. Their and the general public's good will, on which the Court might later draw, is affected by current rulings. If the rulings are well received, the Court gains more freedom to hand down other, less popular rulings. Conversely, an angry public incensed over past rulings will constrain the Court's future activity. As Ulmer has remarked, "Support for civil liberties, as provided by the Supreme Court, is a commodity for which buyers' markets alternate with sellers' markets in some kind of cyclical pattern. Courts of law can be expected to 'read' their markets as well (hopefully) as any other producer of consumables."[8]

The justices often show their awareness of their environment, and it is clear that their decisions are based in some measure on such practical considerations. In fact, the justices themselves have provided adequate evidence that they are concerned with the external implications of what they do. The justices' comments in the Warren Court's criminal procedure retroactivity cases—which Fahlund suggests can only be explained as a strategic response to negative reaction to substantive Court rulings[9]—indicate how careful they were in adding to the "burdens" of the criminal justice system. Recently the justices provided official evidence of such considerations. At the session of the Court memorializing Mr. Justice Byrnes, Chief Justice Burger stated: "When *Taylor v. Georgia* was unanimously decided in 1942, Chief Justice Stone assigned the writing of the opinion to Justice Byrnes for the very sound reason that an opinion by a leading figure from the South gave added force to a holding that the Georgia statute violated federal prohibitions against peonage."[10] Other evidence, such as the indication that the decision in *Brown* was delayed to get a more nearly unanimous vote, is available in the papers of former justices.[11]

Even when the justices do not discuss their strategies, and even when they do not necessarily intend particular effects, their actions often have strategic effects or relevance and the justices may act so as to protect persons affected by the Court's decisions. In the early 1940s, the justices became aware of the effect their support for the compulsory flag salute had had on the lives of Jehovah's Witnesses. Their awareness may have caused the Court to reverse its position.[12] In the period covered by this book, the justices, knowing the country's racial situation and fearful of potential violence, may have been hesitant to use the sit-in cases to uphold the right to service in places of public accommodation or to uphold the sit-in device directly, and therefore chose to use more technical means of upsetting many sit-in convictions.

Just as the justices' awareness of the Court's effects did not mean they always planned to have those effects, to say that the Court is engaged in strategy is not to say that strategy governs all its actions. Like actions of other governmental bodies, much of what the Court does may be unintended or may result from its normal routines or, in Allison's words, from "compromise, coalition, competition and confusion."[13] Yet strategy indeed is there, leaving us with the complex question of the degree to which the Court engages in strategy. One of the most important aspects of that question is what one means by strategy. Most persons distinguish between strategy and tactics. Murphy has proposed the following distinctions: "*Tactics* . . . refer to maneuverings designed to obtain advantages in dealing with colleagues, lower court judges, other governmental officials, interest groups, or the public at large. *Strategies* . . . refer to the overall plans under which such maneuverings against specific obstacles are co-ordinated and for which scarce resources are allocated in order to further the accomplishment of the broad policy objective."[14] Instead of maintaining such a distinction, we find the definition developed by Jeanne Hahn in her discussion of the NAACP closer to our interests. For her, strategy "is used . . . not to mean a concerted, well-developed blueprint that is only waiting to be operationalized. Rather, strategy refers to over-all plans, co-ordination and direction developed for a major area of litigation, general enough to allow for flexibility and adaptability to changing circumstances."[15]

Put another way, to talk of "strategy" is to imply that a certain result was perceived as being desirable and that means were selected which appeared to be the most effective in achieving that result. Result-orientation, in other words, is very close to the meaning of "strategy." An investigator seeking to discover what is true, right, or just is not literally acting "strategically"; with no particular result in mind that he is seeking to validate, he will go wherever truth and justice lead him. Quite different is a group decided upon a specific goal; they then select the means to achieve that goal most efficaciously, and one may speak of a strategic selection of means to accomplish that goal. The means selected need not be individually true, right, or just in any abstract or universal sense, yet if they comport with the achievement of a goal they can be said to be rational. And if the goal itself is a just goal, the rational means to achieve it may also be said to be derivatively just. Thus, once the Supreme Court determined that desegregation was the goal required by the Constitution, the means selected to achieve that goal could be defended in terms of the importance and justice of the goal itself, but they also had to be judged in terms of whether they contributed to that goal.

Strategy implies conscious activity and planning. Even if one recognizes that strategic effects or strategy-relevant actions may at times occur without conscious consideration by the justices, one can see that there are several senses in which the Court's decisions are planned. First, there is a conscious decision to accept a case for consideration. Once the Court has accepted a case, there is a norm that the justices will decide it. The constraint imposed by such a norm can be escaped if the Court then dismisses the case on the ground that certiorari was "improvidently granted," but criticism will result if this device is used often. Second, the justices vote on how to dispose of a case. Third, the existence of the opinions themselves is not fortuitous; they are released on specific days. At the opinion-writing stage, all the justices have seen—and had the opportunity to comment on—all the opinions before they are released. This increases the planned nature of the Court's work because each justice knows, and can take into account and try to affect, what the others are doing.

Perhaps strategy is most consciously involved at the time the decision is made whether or not to grant review. The sheer numbers of petitions for certiorari or jurisdictional statements in appeals cases make it difficult for the justices to ponder all cases as fully as they might like, and the justices often delegate authority to the Chief Justice to indicate which cases will (or will not) be discussed in conference. But conscious consideration does occur, no matter how rapidly, and on important cases decisions result after collective discussion.

This process of controlling what comes before the Court is a major part of the Court's administration of the law. Because the Supreme Court is not presented with a prepared agenda, it must develop one from cases it is requested to hear, something not done absent-mindedly. The large volume of cases filed must be reduced to manageable proportions by rejecting some of them (a principal method) and by delegating authority for some of them to the lower courts, state and federal. With a number of matters with which to be concerned, and a limited number of hours in which to work, the justices, like the leaders of any organization, cannot solve everything themselves, nor can they devote exclusive attention to one particular aspect of the Court's work—except perhaps for very short periods of time. Instead, the justices must develop methods of operation to allow them to deal with the whole range of concerns with which the Court is charged, although many of the standards used are unstated and implicit. The methods used by the Court include disposing of cases other than through a full, signed opinion of the Court, summary actions, and refusals to grant review—denials of certiorari or dismissals of appeals "for want of a substantial federal question;" other methods are more closely tied to doctrine, for example, the doctrine of procedure, particularly the question of who will be allowed to bring cases—standing—or to assert particular sets of rights. Hence, there are two different basic dimensions of the Court's strategy—the dimension that occurs between cases (manipulation of the docket) and the dimension that occurs in the range of choices in a given case (for example, between deciding it summarily or issuing an opinion or between writing a very narrow opinion or a broad one). The Court may even exert a creative role in fashioning cases that come to it for review. This is accomplished by the indirect process of hinting in a judicial opinion that a certain issue "awaits further resolution by this Court," or "is not squarely presented by the facts of the present case." Such hints encourage lawyers to pursue the new questions all the way to the Supreme Court.

To what extent are the justices constrained by the positions urged upon them by the lawyers? Lawyers start with goals in mind, ranging from simply winning for a particular client to establishing broad policy, and work toward them within the constraints of the Court's past decisions and the justices' known positions. Other courts, such as the International Court of Justice, feel less constrained by the parties' positions than do our courts. In an adversary system of justice such as ours is supposed to be, courts are supposed to make decisions on the basis of material submitted by the parties, not by going "outside the record." This is most true with respect to factual matters at trial, but it applies also at the appellate stage, where judges seem to feel freer to explore matters on their own. Certainly at high appellate levels, because of the broad effects their cases are to have, the justices need the freedom.[16] Yet even at this level the judges cannot depart totally from the materials, which at least provide a starting point and often far more.

That judges work within the range of positions established by the parties does not, however, mean they are always severely constrained. Freedom is provided when the justices can group several cases for argument and thus manage the docket. They also have the authority to approve the participation of "friends of the Court," particularly in instances in which both parties have not granted it. Lawyers accustomed to pleading multiple claims and defenses sometimes give the justices extraordinary latitude. Such a situation may occur when the contending sides are trying to force a case back and forth between the substantive and procedural aspects of a case. For example, a Negro complainant may press for a doctrinal output and the white opponent may seek a pro-

cedural limitation on the determination of the case.* Procedural arguments presented to the Court give the judges particular freedom because
the Court almost invariably invokes procedure in order to leave an issue at
a lower level of the court system for resolution. It is far more acceptable
for the Court to go outside the record to decide a case on procedural
grounds than on substantive doctrinal matters.

Often arguments are presented simply because the lawyers think the
justices want to hear them. Many of the strategy-relevant arguments used
in the race relations cases may have stemmed from counsel's perception
that such arguments had the best chance of persuading the Court. There
are other reasons for presenting strategically relevant arguments. The
most obvious is that those attorneys taking the longer view want more
than a narrow win in a particular case. Lawyers may also try to keep the
judges "in bounds" by their arguments. They may press matters narrowly.
Or both parties to a case may come close to saying the same thing, making
it more difficult for the justices to obtain their goals within the confines of
party-urged positions. At times the justices may be happy that they have
not been pushed harder to deal with broader, more encompassing questions, or they may claim to be constrained by the positions urged upon
them by the lawyers, but the Supreme Court is not at the parties' mercy.

There is a question of the extent to which one can talk of a strategy of
the Court. If we mean that nine justices explicitly agree on specific goals
and set out to accomplish them, we are in trouble before we begin. Even if
all the justices are concerned about strategy, they may not give attention to
strategic considerations simultaneously or, if they do, they may focus on
different aspects of a case or prefer different strategies. Yet it is not at all
clear that all the judges concentrate on strategy for extended periods of
time. Murphy has effectively pointed out the problem: "Probably relatively few justices have had a systematic jurisprudence; more but probably
still relatively few have been so intensely committed to particular policy
goals as to establish rigid priorities of action that dominated their entire
lives; probably few have been able to act only rationally in seeking to
achieve their aims."[17] And even if the justices were so committed, their
human limitations would constrain the attention they give to strategy;
since "every Justice has only a finite supply of time, energy, research
assistance, and person influence, he would not be able even under op-
timum conditions to accomplish all that he wanted."[18] Thus, from the
actions taken officially in the Court's name, even when all join in the result
or decision or opinion of a case, we must be careful not to attribute that

---

*Our interchangeable use of "Negro" and "black" throughout the text, rather than the
exclusive use of "black," reflects in part the prevailing terminology used by the Supreme
Court in the 1950s.

strategy to all the justices in equal measure, because all the justices may not
have participated in developing it or may not have joined in it for identical
reasons.

There are other problems in talking of a strategy of the Court. For one
thing, there are changes in the Court's personnel. During the period
under study here, after Chief Justice Warren replaced Chief Justice
Vinson in 1953, President Eisenhower made several more appointments
(Justices Brennan, Stewart, Harlan, and Whittaker), President Kennedy
appointed Byron White, and Lyndon Johnson appointed Arthur
Goldberg and Abe Fortas. Each change in personnel would require that
the "strategy of the Court" be reworked as the new justice began service.
Even when the Court's membership is stable, there may be few goals on
which there is any explicit agreement, and these may be only the general
ones of "upholding the Constitution" or "being good judges"; even then,
the justices may differ as to the best means of achieving those goals. It is
unlikely that nine judges working closely together feel the need to articulate the more-or-less generally understood and habitual strategies by
which they proceed. Problems may be on the minds of some justices but
not brought to the level of collective consciousness. One can easily have a
situation in which each justice individually is aware of a situation but no
justice takes responsibility for doing anything about it. Understandings
between the judges are likely to be implicit, reinforced by the fact that the
justices do much of the Court's work alone. Consideration of the Court's
major cases results in regular interaction both between individual pairs of
judges and the whole assemblage in conference, such as the discussions in
chambers and over lunch which took place from the first conference on
Brown after Warren took his seat on the Court through the time *Brown I*
was announced. However, consideration of certiorari petitions and
opinion-writing, particularly on concurring and dissenting opinions, is
pretty much individual work, even when the signatures of colleagues are
welcomed. If considerations of strategy remain implicit, the chance that
different justices will be operating from different strategies increases,
since agreement is more difficult to reach implicitly than explicitly.
Therefore the Court should be treated as a "mixed-motive" or "mixed-
strategy" group.

Despite these problems, there are instances which can clearly be designated as the "strategy of the Court." For example, self-preservation for
the Court would seem to be a goal shared by all members of the Court.
Agreement on means of institutional preservation may be great enough
to enable one to see the Court's response to external threat and to other
external events as collective strategic moves. The Court no doubt was
aware of the massive resistance to *Brown,* and its awareness may have
contributed to its withdrawal from the education area. Nor, after its

1956–57 internal security decisions, could the Court have been unaware of congressional efforts to limit the Court's jurisdiction severely, as could be seen by its far more cautious rulings of 1958–59. In order to reinforce the point we need only mention the "switch in time that saved nine," the Court's abrupt reversal, in reaction to Roosevelt's "court-packing" scheme, of its trend of holding Roosevelt's New Deal legislation unconstitutional.

The Court's collective action can also be seen in its voting patterns. In a recent study, David Rohde distinguished between threats to the Court's power (e.g., attempts to limit the Court's jurisdiction) and more frequent and longer-lasting threats to its authority (resistance to its mandates). He noted that the Court's available options for dealing with such threats included deciding in favor of the threatening side, refusing to decide more cases on the issue over which the threat arose, using per curiam rather than full opinion rulings, and persisting in the path which produced the threat. The Court also could respond by deciding cases with larger majorities. Rohde found that majorities were indeed larger in the face of threats than would have been predicted from the idea that, in multi-member bodies, only "minimum winning coalitions" are likely to form.[19]

The "strategy of the Court" is basically external strategy—that is, strategy vis-à-vis other actors in the political system or attention to the means used to achieve the Court's goals. There is also internal strategy, strategy within the Court, as justices deal with each other to build coalitions. The two are intimately related. Matters of internal strategy certainly affect both individual and collective external strategy. Because he is in a bargaining relationship with his colleagues and does not know how far they will agree with him, a judge may give more ground than he would prefer to in seeking agreement. Majority justices may accept a broader or more ambiguous opinion in order to pick up "hold-outs," as may have occurred in *Brown* in order to achieve unanimity. A judge may "come on too strong" and lose votes from a potential majority. A persuasive dissent may attract votes and reverse the Court's position. Former Attorney General Kleindienst noted that Justice Byrnes once drafted a dissenting opinion in a Fair Labor Standards Act case and persuaded Justice Jackson to change his vote, the Byrnes draft being issued as the Court's majority opinion.[20] Where we have evidence of internal strategy (as from a justice's memoirs), it may throw some light upon external strategy. However, in the normal situation internal strategy is quite effectively hidden. We often have to infer it from external strategy, and since the latter itself is usually the product of an inference, the former is doubly inferred. As a result, it is not helpful (except in cases where we have direct evidence) to look at internal strategy as a means to identify or explain external strategy.

Just as internal strategy affects external strategy, the reverse is also true. The judge trying to achieve certain goals may begin his work from the Court's collective strategy, at least as he perceives it. In dealing with a case falling in an area with which the Court has dealt before, a judge will know at least the general outlines of policy or the thrust of the Court's decisions, such as the "salami-slicing" in which the Court engaged in the sit-in cases prior to Congress's passage of the 1964 Civil Rights Act. However, when the Court begins a new line of cases, as in the 1957 *Roth* obscenity ruling, or makes a break with the past, there is no previous group strategy from which the individual justice can work. Even here, while he cannot proceed from even an implicit external strategy to internal strategy, he knows his colleagues' general orientations, giving him some referents as he begins his own deliberations.

3

Essentially two concerns face the Court: whether to decide a case and how to decide it. The first concern constitutes docket-management. It includes the matter of selectivity—reducing the number of cases to a manageable figure so that the Court may give sufficient attention to them, the timing involved in picking cases on particular issues, and the grouping of cases for argument and decision. It also includes sending cases back to the lower courts by vacating and remanding lower court rulings, sometimes with specification of required further action.

Some courts must hear all cases brought before them. Their jurisdiction is mandatory, as long as procedural guidelines established for bringing the cases are followed. Courts such as the Supreme Court are allowed to exercise discretion over much of their jurisdiction. And choose the Supreme Court does, accepting only about 5 percent of the cases brought up on certiorari and about 50 percent of the cases brought up on appeal. Some choices would have to be made simply for reasons of work load. The Court must operate as a single Supreme Court, with all justices participating in all cases. It cannot divide into departments or divisions as some state supreme courts do. Yet if the justices are giving thought to strategy, there may be reasons other than work load for the Court's choices. If the only important issue were that of numbers, the Court could pick cases at random or have them selected by some previously adopted formula.

We can see the strategic implications when we look at the arguments over what is meant when the Court grants or denies review in a case.[21] The official judicial interpretation of turning down a petition for certiorari—or the equivalent, turning away a supposedly mandatory appeal "for want of a substantial federal question" is that the Court has not decided the case. Such a position was held even by Justice Douglas, the most frequent dissenter from such denials. Citing Justice Frankfurter, Douglas re-marked recently, "Our denial of certiorari imparts no implication or inference concerning the Court's view of the merits."[22] Yet Chief Justice Warren, after leaving the Court, pointed out that "denials can and do have a significant impact on the ordering of constitutional and legal priorities. Many potential and important developments in the law have been frustrated, at least temporarily, by a denial of certiorari."[23]

In Rule 19 of its rules of procedure, the Court itself indicates some of the reasons which might be considered in granting the writ. The list of reasons which, the Court makes clear, is not exhaustive, includes the importance of the case, conflicts between the circuits in interpreting the law, departure by a federal court from "accepted canons of judicial proceedings," and interpretation of an important federal law question in conflict with the Court's own precedents. Beyond the announcement in the Court's rules, in various off-the-bench statements individual justices have indicated what the Court is supposedly looking for. Chief Justice Vinson once said that the Court does not grant certiorari merely to correct errors of the lower courts but, rather, to deal with cases with broader effects, "questions whose resolution will have immediate importance far beyond the particular facts and parties involved."[24] Justice Harlan once stated from the bench, "The certiorari jurisdiction was not conferred upon this Court 'merely to give the defeated party in the . . . Court of Appeals another hearing,' . . . or 'for the benefit of the particular liti-gants,' . . . but to decide issues, 'the settlement of which is of importance to the public as distinguished from . . . the parties.' "[25] And Chief Justice Warren stated that certiorari jurisdiction was "designed by Congress for a very special purpose . . . not only to achieve control of its docket but also to establish our national priorities in constitutional and legal matters."[26] Yet for all this emphasis upon importance, throughout the Vietnam war the Court consistently denied certiorari to every case contesting the con-stitutionality of the war, a striking "negative fact" substantiating the thesis of docket-manipulation by the Court for its own strategic purposes.

The most impressive evidence of the policy meaning of denial of review comes from examination of dispositions of cases actually accepted. The evidence suggests that the Court's refusal to hear a case is not merely indifference but approval of what is left undisturbed. In a study of the mid-1950s Glendon Schubert showed consistently high reversal rates for cases accepted on certiorari. The chances for affirmance or reversal in formal certiorari dispositions (those decided with opinion) were about even, but there were high reversal rates for per curiam dispositions of certiorari cases from both state and federal courts. Schubert also found a higher ratio of state court than federal court appeals reversed. Federal appeals decided per curiam were affirmed at high rates, but those decided with formal opinions resulted in a high reversal ratio.[27] More recently, the patterns found by Schubert have also been found in the cases for the 1967 through 1972 Terms,[28] providing a even firmer basis for Schubert's assertion that "the patterns of affirmances and reversals in the various types of cases are too definite to have arisen by sheer happenstance."[29]

If choosing some cases out of the total number presented is one part of docket-management, another is taking one case rather than another to obtain the right case at the right time with the right content.[30] Timing is often particularly critical; accepting or refusing cases for review in relation to major doctrinal rulings can be of considerable strategic importance. While all such decisions are important, accepting or turning away cases after the Court has begun to take action in an area may have greater strategic implications than similar action coming prior to the Court's initiatives. If after having decided a major question of law the Court declines to hear further cases on the subject, it may be showing it wishes to avoid the issue, thus "depressing the market" for that issue. Studies of the impact of judicial decisions suggest that "continued denial of certiorari with respect to a given subject will decrease the number of cases filed concerning that subject."[31] This result may also be achieved through summary affirmances and reversals, which serve to reinforce the Court's ruling as well as to confirm its unwillingness to make more new law on the subject at least for the time being. When people see many cases dealt with peremptorily, they tend to decrease their litigation on those questions. Also, summary actions leave the justices future flexibility by making it less clear what was intended, even though, as Justice Brennan has complained,[32] such rulings are a disservice to lower court judges.

Docket-management may also involve selection of more than one case for argument or decision at the same time. Grouping of cases not only provides the justices with a broader range of strategic alternatives but also emphasizes the broad policy implications of the subject under review. Although the Supreme Court can choose from the flow of certiorari petitions, it may have considerable difficulty ignoring some. Examples would be instances of extreme resistance to its own past rulings such as that which occurred in the Little Rock situation. Here the Court not only departed from the pattern of not taking lower education cases after *Brown* but held a special session to hear and rule on the case. Challenges to major new federal statutes like the public accommodations section of the 1964 Civil Rights Act and the 1965 Voting Rights Act would also have been hard to ignore, because both the executive and legislative branches of the national government as well as the protesting parties in the states wanted an answer. As these cases suggest, the other branches of government help set the Court's agenda.

Another possible constraint on the Court's selection of cases is that it must avoid concentrating its efforts disproportionately in a few areas of case law. Although certain types of litigation may be in vogue at particular times, giving a certain "tilt" to the Court's docket content, no one issue ever dominates the cases from which the Court may choose. Even when the number of cases accumulated on a specific point is rather large, it will usually be small in percentage terms. The Court can dispose of many of these cases after a major decision by vacating lower court rulings and remanding them for reconsideration in light of the Court's principal action, thus clearing away considerable backlog.

There is an expectation, reinforced by various interests whose cases are on the docket, that the Court will deal with a variety of problems and not get "stuck" on one or some of them. When the Court takes up and decides one or more major cases from a particular area in a given term, its doing so may impose limits on how many more the Court will take from that area. For example, if the major civil rights cases accepted for decision in a Term of Court were outside the education field, there could be further delay in dealing with pressing education issues. On the other hand, the wide variety of issues available for choice means that the Court may be able to avoid certain fields completely for at least a term or two.

The second of the Court's two primary concerns—how to decide a case—involves a decision by the Court whether to utilize a method of summary action like those just noted (not helpful when full explanation seems needed) or to issue an opinion, either per curiam or signed by a justice. Some per curiams set forth the Court's reasons in only a few sentences. Some of them give no reason whatsoever except perhaps for a case citation or two, the application of which may not be clear. Occasional per curiams are lengthy.[33] When an opinion is to be written, the Court must decide whether it is to be broad or narrow and whether the grounds to be used and the tone to be adopted should be deferential to lower authorities or forceful and impatient. By its handling of all these matters, the justices can reach or avoid issues in varying degrees with varying degrees of visibility. Although the media may pay more attention than before to the Court's summary actions, low visibility is characteristic of anything short of a full opinion of the Court.

The Supreme Court's full opinions play a special role in the Court's strategy. Charles Miller has observed that "because of their political significance, constitutional opinions and their language may exert influence well beyond the specific legal holdings."[34] They are "the chief demonstration that reasoning is the essential element of the judicial process" and serve "to convince the judge, the parties, and the public that cases are rightly decided," thus reinforcing the Court's moral power. If they are to serve this end, they "must ultimately be accepted by and make sense to the people to whom they are addressed."[35]

The Court is not without felt constraints in developing its opinions. There are multiple audiences: the media, "court watchers," lawyers, judges, legislators, administrators, the "general public." These audiences may differ in their levels of knowledge about the law and in their expectations about what the Court should do, but generally they expect to hear law from the courts. The Court must educate if its decisions are to have an effect, but it generally avoids performing its teaching function explicitly. In other countries the law's educational function is given greater emphasis, but in this country it runs against our grain when we feel we are being "taught" by a court which sounds like a "super-legislature."[36]

In the long run, the Court must operate with people's expectations in mind, but the justices can fashion their opinions to fit the interests of particular audiences. Ambiguous language, allowing many possible results, may subsume much, and is thus at times advantageous. However, if the Court wishes to have the greatest substantive effect, it must speak with a relatively clear voice. "Repeater" cases—those showing up more than once—result not only from earlier remands and willful failure by the parties to hear but also from the Court's failure to clarify. The less clear the Court is, the more it will have to contend with at a later date.[37]

Because it is difficult for the Supreme Court to determine whether or not its decisions have been complied with unless the winning party complains in new litigation, the justices must try particularly hard to do what they can to produce compliance. However, most administrative and judicial decisions are rarely tailored to facilitate monitoring.[38] Although clear opinions make it easier for the executive branch, for example, or others such as "private attorneys general" like the NAACP to carry out the monitoring, ambiguous decisions, which complicate the work of lower court judges, in a way facilitate monitoring because they make it extremely likely that the cases will return to the Supreme Court. Even when its decisions are clear, the Court can be sure it will have opportunity to monitor developments in the law because of lawyers' tendency to develop new doctrine in cases they take to the Court on appeal. Experience with the lower court rulings would point toward the best way to deal with the issue and would also serve to warn the Supreme Court of any difficulties.[39]

Whether or not they are clear, the Court's opinions vary considerably in their breadth. Any judicial opinion is a justification for the decision reached upon the particular facts of the case. The opinion can be framed very narrowly, making it seem applicable only to those facts and any future similar configuration of facts—or it can be framed broadly, departing from the particular facts to embrace other situations that are only similar in some respects to the particular facts of the case. Judges tend to view their role as deciding cases narrowly, since the broader the opinion seems the more "legislative" the judge's role appears. Yet opinions that are too narrow do not illuminate the law, for they do not provide sufficient guidance for those whose cases entail different fact situations. Thus judges are sometimes inclined to strike out on broader lines, to wax philosophical, to indicate that the law is using the particular facts of the case as a mere launching pad. In recent decades the Supreme Court has had a decided tendency to breadth. Justice Fortas's writing perhaps exemplified the broadest possible opinions; he seemed to regard a case as an opportunity to expound his own personal judicial and political philosophy in the large. He not only told what he felt the law was with respect to the particular facts of the case before him but he also went on to indicate what he felt the law was with respect to other types of factual situations not present in the particular case or only vaguely, if at all, suggested by it. A contrast is provided by Justice Brandeis, who strove for precise factual adjudication of the issues raised by the contesting parties and the avoidance when possible of constitutional determinations. This approach, of confining an opinion as much as possible to the particular facts of the case and, even more, to the particular arguments of counsel, is one toward which the Court has been leaning since the departure of Chief Justice Warren—who also wrote in broad-brush strokes—and the arrival of the Nixon appointees. Some of the most recent Court opinions seem to be moving in still another, more complex direction—a brief "majority" opinion followed by seven, eight, or even nine "concurring" opinions of the individual justices. Whatever the style of the justice writing a majority opinion, it is usually the case that opinions of individual judges concurring or dissenting tend to be broader than the opinion of the Court, since the latter is often the lowest common denominator produced by the justices conferring together. Sometimes they can agree only on an ambiguously worded opinion, into which each justice reads what he wants. In such cases, even a unanimous opinion can be broad due to ambiguity.

The grounds the Court chooses—the Constitution, statutes, regulations, or procedural rules—help to determine breadth or narrowness of an opinion. An opinion can be kept narrow by confining it to a statute. The issues tend to get broader if the Constitution is involved, since that document itself is framed in broad and somewhat ambiguous language. Sometimes the Court strains to avoid the constitutional ground by stretching the statutory language. The degree to which the Court takes pains to avoid deciding on constitutional grounds is sometimes a good indicator of the way the Court wants the Constitution to be interpreted. In the "sit-in" cases, for example, the Court went out of its way to decide cases on narrow procedural grounds, thus indicating to any reasonably intelligent observer that a certain interpretation of the Constitution itself hovered in the background and thus dictated the result, although not the explicit grounds, of the decisions. Such techniques may make for narrow opinions against a background of broad immanent constitutional interpretation.

An opinion's breadth can be examined in relation to the parties' positions. The Court can be said to have acted broadly if it goes outside the grounds the attorneys have urged even if it does so to rely on a narrow doctrinal point. Yet, where the range of positions offered the Court is wide, an opinion can be broad even when the justices do not go outside those positions. The Court's usual practice is to reach only those questions necessary to achieve some result; therefore, the relatively infrequent opinion which answers completely all the questions posed for the Court may be said to be broad. When the justices do not decide all the issues tendered, we say the ruling is narrow. We should note that in connection with their rulings the justices sometimes specify what has not been decided. Determining what the Court means strategically in doing this is difficult as the Court's intent is highly dependent on the circumstances connected with the particular ruling. By focusing attention on those matters, the justices may make their comments to encourage others to raise undecided points in new litigation, but disinclination to see the Court as other than a passive body makes it difficult for people to accept that argument. Alternatively, the Court may simply be making an effort at precision, or the justices may be expressing denial of a desire to act because they may not know how to decide the issue.

When the Court is writing its opinions, it is concerned with more than breadth. Content is paramount, and content includes the opinion's grounds and the type of materials used. With respect to the latter, there is an expectation, deriving from our Anglo-American legal tradition, that precedent will be used and even heavily relied upon. History and social science are other elements in the "mix" of materials used in the Court's opinions, though the use of social science is often counter-productive for the Court because of the reluctance of many people to accept social science findings, particularly in a legal context. However, history, like precedent, helps achieve continuity.[40] Of particular relevance to this study is the Court's mention of race. Explicit treatment of that subject results in opinions which are narrow and of less precedential value than if the Court had kept quiet on the subject. However, forthrightness about race may enhance the Court's moral leadership;[41] conversely, if the subject is never mentioned in a case the facts of which clearly involve race, people puzzle as to why the subject has been avoided.

Choosing the grounds of an opinion is of particular strategic importance. Sometimes only one type of ground is used. The principal grounds are the Constitution, statutes, and facts. Sometimes they are intimately related, as when statutory interpretation hides certain constitutional issues which might be revealed if the statute were interpreted differently.

When constitutional issues are reached, the particular constitutional provision used is also quite important. A Thirteenth Amendment "badge of slavery" argument, one based on the Fourteenth Amendment Equal Protection Clause, and, in voting cases, the Fifteenth Amendment may all be available.

Use of any constitutional provisions may require attempts to interpret the framers' intention. Such efforts are not often satisfying. Charles Black notes that the "textual method . . . forces us to blur the focus and talk evasively"[42] because we may feel bound by the intent of the amendment's authors, even when such intent is ambiguous, out-of-date, or plainly unintelligible. Such is particularly likely to be the case, he states, when the text is "of that high generality and consequent ambiguity which marks so many crucial constitutional texts."[43] Black's specific suggestion is that instead of trying to find "state action" to satisfy Fourteenth Amendment requirements we should use the structure of the federal union and the relation of the federal government to the states as a source of certain national rights, because there is a "national citizenship" or "general citizenship" carrying with it certain basic rights and because "the creation and protection of individual rights is the highest function of any government."[44] Yet it is not entirely clear that the "structure" Black advocates is any more specific or determinative of particular results than the "ambiguous" constitutional provisions themselves.

Black's proposal, which has not been adopted by the High Court, directs our attention to the need for the Court to consider the "federalism variable" in its environment when developing strategies. The United States Supreme Court is the highest court in the land, the capstone for both federal and state court systems. The Court is mandated to supervise the national judiciary, but its relations with state judicial systems are far from specific. Controversy over federal court intervention in state court proceedings during the Burger Court led to a line of cases limiting the situations in which federal courts could deal with state laws once state prosecutions had been initiated.[45] In dealing with state courts, the Supreme Court does use the principle of comity, and shows considerable deference to the acts of state judges. The justices' approach to the acts of other state officials is also careful or cautious. They have suggested that it would be better if state law enforcement officers enforced criminal statutes so that certain federal laws would not have to be invoked.[46] Yet the High Court is willing to reverse state court judgments, indicating there are definite limits to its accommodation with the states. The Court is not hesitant to intervene to rebuff defiance, although such a response is by no means usual.

At the national level, the Supreme Court has to pay attention to its own supposed subordinates, the lower federal courts, as well as to the executive and legislative branches of the government. Here, as with the states, the question is not whether deference is to be extended, but how much and what form it is to take. The Supreme Court will try to accept lower courts' views of appealed litigation, and may even allow the lower courts to stake out new positions in advance of the High Court's own past ones. Once the "coordinate" branches have acted, the Court, generally extending deference to its "co-equals," will try to validate statutes and uphold executive branch orders. However, when Congress or the president do nothing, the justices will not always sit idly by. Continued inaction will often produce judicial initiative. That was the case in the race relations area, in which Congress had done nothing until 1957 and nothing substantial until 1964. Except for some action with respect to desegregating the armed forces, the executive branch also had done little until some time after *Brown*. While the Court treats both legislative and executive branches favorably, the executive branch's enforcement powers, which the Court must enlist where possible, also require the Court to deal with the executive with particular care. There is frequent contact between Court and executive branch, a result of the government's appearances before the Court either as a party or as amicus curiae. This makes the executive one of the most prominent, if not the most prominent, actor in the Court's immediate strategic environment.

Evidence from desegregation and other policy areas that the justices of the Supreme Court use strategy in their efforts to achieve their own and the Court's goals as an institution has been noted here. The types of strategies used—particularly manipulation of the Court's docket and options in the types of opinions written and the language used in those opinions—have also been suggested. Those strategies should be kept firmly in mind as the reader moves to our extended treatment of the Court's actions (and non-actions) in the field of race relations. Attention is turned first to pre-*Brown* history, to the cases from the end of the nineteenth century in which the Court undercut Congress's efforts to achieve civil rights and established the "separate but equal" doctrine and to the cases prior to the 1950s, in which the Court laid the groundwork for the *Brown* rulings. Later chapters present the argument and opinions in *Brown*, the post-*Brown* education cases, and the strategic process in other areas of race relations—housing, voting, transportation, public facilities, public accommodations, and protest—and the education cases of the late 1960s, which bring the book to a close.

Chapter 2

Before *Brown*

THE Supreme Court has been involved in resolving race relations controversies for a long time. Many of the cases which
were decided from the end of the Civil War up to 1900 provided the basis
for what was to come in the mid-twentieth century. In that earlier period,
the Court narrowly defined the meaning of the post–Civil War amendments to the Constitution, limited Congress's ability to legislate on matters
of discrimination, and affirmed the doctrine of "separate but equal."
Although *Brown* may seem to stand out from the rest of the Supreme
Court's race relations decisions, one can argue that what the justices did in
Brown was only to erase what it had done earlier in imposing disabilities on
racial minorities.

That the Court was not writing on a blank slate in the 1950s is shown
by a number of key cases of high doctrinal importance. They are: the jury
selection cases; the *Civil Rights Cases* (1883), critical for the public accommodations area and which established the "state action" doctrine;[1] *Plessy
v. Ferguson* (1896), along with *Cumming* (1899), and *Gong Lum* (1927),
through which the *Plessy* "separate but equal" doctrine was eased into
education; the "white primary" cases leading to *Smith v. Allwright* (1944),
in which some major state action questions were raised; and the housing
discrimination cases of *Buchanan v. Warley* (1917), *Corrigan v. Buckley*
(1926), *Shelley v. Kraemer* (1948), and *Barrows v. Jackson* (1950), all of which
were crucial in establishing the "state action" doctrine's boundaries. Of
these cases, *Shelley* and *Barrows* stem from the post–World War II or
"modern" period, as do some cases following up *Smith v. Allwright;* the two
transportation cases, *Morgan* and *Henderson,* which provided the Court
with unused opportunities to dispose of *Plessy;* and the line of graduate
education cases from *Gaines* (prior to the war) through *Sipuel* to *Sweatt* and
McLaurin, which provided the immediate legal and strategic context in
education in which the *Brown* set of cases was brought. We examine all the
older cases primarily to indicate the doctrine the Court announced; with
the more recent cases, we are interested both in doctrine and in the
Court's strategies prior to *Brown*; and in several of the cases we introduce
portions of the oral argument before the Court.

1

The first cases raising questions about the jury selection section of the Civil Rights Act of 1875—which outlawed race as a basis for jury disqualification and made it a misdemeanor so to exclude someone—reached the Supreme Court in 1880. In three cases handed down on the same day, the Court upheld the act, sharply defined the nature of the right guaranteed, and set the tenor for future decisions. In the first case, *Strauder v. West Virginia,* the Court invalidated a West Virginia statute expressly excluding Negroes from serving on juries as a violation of the Fourteenth Amendment and as imposing "a brand upon them, affixed by law, an assertion of their inferiority, and a stimulant to that race prejudice which is an impediment to securing to individuals of the race that equal justice which the law aims to secure to all others." The justices pointed out that the question facing them was not whether a Negro, when indicted, had a right to a grand or petit jury composed in whole or in part of persons of his own race but only whether, in the composition or selection of jurors by whom he is to be indicted or tried, all persons of his race may be excluded by law solely because of their race or color. In the second of the cases, *Virginia v. Rives,* the Court found that even in the absence of a state statute a state officer could not constitutionally deprive blacks of the right to jury service. It ought to be presumed, the justices said, that the lower court itself would redress such a wrong.

The third case, *Ex parte Virginia,* involved a county court judge who excluded Negroes from grand and petit juries. The attorney general of Virginia contended that the state had not authorized or directed the county judge to do what he was charged with having done and had not denied to the colored race the equal protection of the laws. Consequently, he argued, the act of the judge must be considered his own individual act, in contravention of the will of the state. Even though the laws of the state did not authorize or permit the judge to make such discrimination, the Court, showing its willingness to enforce prohibitions against persons under specific conditions, found violations of the Fourteenth Amendment and the Act of 1875. The Court defined as state action the action by any state agency or action by officers or agents by whom the state's powers are exerted, done in the name of and for the state. Congress had power to enforce the provisions of the amendment by appropriate legislation, the Court noted, and added that "such legislation must act upon persons, not upon the abstract thing denominated a State but upon the persons who are the agents of the State in the denial of the rights which were intended to be secured."

These early decisions were clearly the most egalitarian opinions in the

Court's early handling of civil rights cases, and contained language which provided the material out of which the *Brown* doctrine was later carved. However, they were soon to be deprived of their force, initially in the *Civil Rights Cases* of 1883, involving challenges to the public accommodations sections of the Civil Rights Act. There the Supreme Court, while not overruling them, distinguished them—a favorite device for disposing of disliked cases while still in some way not frontally attacking them. In the *Civil Rights Cases,* the Solicitor General made a strong argument, based on both the Thirteenth and Fourteenth Amendments, that innkeepers and theater owners had restricted Negroes' freedom of "locomotion" and had done so while operating a private establishment for the public use. Nevertheless, the Court invalidated the challenged sections of the act because the Fourteenth Amendment merely permitted Congress to pass corrective legislation directed at the states, as in the jury selection statutes, not legislation which attempted to lay down rules for social conduct aimed at individual persons violating the claimed rights. Justice Bradley assumed that there were adequate remedies under state law for anyone denied rights under existing state laws requiring innkeepers and public carriers to furnish proper accommodations to all unobjectionable persons who in good faith applied for them. In dissent, Justice Harlan argued that the Court's decision would allow discrimination to be continued under the states' tolerant eyes, thus imposing a badge of servitude on the Negro even though Congress had sought to secure for Negroes a *legal* right to equal enjoyment of public accommodations by enforcing an express prohibition upon the states.

2

The facts of the *Plessy* case, as well as its doctrine, are generally well known. Plessy, who was seven-eighths Caucasian and one-eighth Negro but refused to admit he was in any sense or proportion a colored man, was a passenger on a purely local line between two stations within Louisiana. He had seated himself in a coach designated for whites. Acting under a Louisiana statute requiring the separation according to color of passengers on all railway carriers in the state, the conductor adjudged him a Negro and assigned him to the appropriate coach. When Plessy refused to move, the conductor had him forcibly ejected and imprisoned for having violated the state law. Plessy argued that the law was unconstitutional on Thirteenth and Fourteenth Amendment grounds and claimed that he had been denied the "property" of having the reputation of belonging to the dominant race by the conductor's decision.[2]

Although almost twenty years earlier the Court had invalidated a Louisiana statute forbidding segregation on steamboats,[3] it was now willing to sustain the law requiring such segregation. The Court dismissed the Thirteenth Amendment "badge of servitude" argument by saying that a legal distinction based on color neither destroyed the legal equality of the races nor reestablished slavery. With respect to the Fourteenth Amendment, Justice Brown said that its purpose was to enforce only legal, not social, equality. As to Plessy's property claim, if Plessy were improperly classified and placed in the colored coach, he could sue for damages; otherwise, he had been deprived of nothing as he was not entitled to the reputation of being white. Looking at the legislature's power to pass the statute, the Court found the central question in the case, the "equal but separate" requirement (which we have come to know as "separate but equal") to be a reasonable regulation, quite within the state's police power. In upholding such laws, Brown alluded to separate schools as another example of the exercise of this power, thus showing the applicability of the rule to education even though it was not a part of this case. In sustaining the forced separation of the races, Justice Brown's sociological language—ignored in the 1950s by those accusing the Warren Court of a sociological result in *Brown*—spoke of the meaning of separation between the races:

We consider the underlying fallacy of the plaintiff's argument to consist in the assumption that the enforced separation of the two races stamps the colored race with a badge of inferiority. If this be so, it is not by reason of anything found in the act, but solely because the colored race chooses to put that construction upon it.
. . . .
The argument also assumes that social prejudices may be overcome by legislation, and that equal rights cannot be secured to the negro except by an enforced commingling of the two races. We cannot accept this proposition. If the two races are to meet upon terms of social equality, it must be the result of natural affinities, a mutual appreciation of each other's merits and a voluntary consent of individuals.

In dissent, Justice Harlan predicted the decision would prove quite as pernicious as the judgment in *Dred Scott* and not only stimulate aggressions but also encourage the belief that by means of state enactments it is possible to defeat the beneficent purposes of the amendments so recently fought for by the people of the United States.[4] "The Constitution is colorblind," he argued.

Only three years after *Plessy,* the Court decided a controversy in which the Board of Education of Richmond County, Georgia, had temporarily closed the separate Negro high school on grounds of economic necessity.[5] Negro parents asked for an injunction to reduce the expenditures for the white high school or to compel its closing. In *Cumming v. Board of Education,* the Supreme Court upheld the action of the school board. The board's action was not due to racial discrimination, the Court held. No one had been denied equal protection of the laws or any privileges of citizenship. The Court added that education in schools maintained by state taxation was a matter into which federal authority could intrude only in the case of unmistakable disregard of rights secured by the supreme law of the land. Because the requirement of separate schools for each race had not been raised in the pleadings below, it was not before the Court despite its mention at oral argument. The Court thus managed not to rule directly on the *Plessy* doctrine, and Harlan's *Plessy* dissent did not prevent his writing for the unanimous Court. The Court's failure to provide a direct ruling on *Plessy* created a problem later when people argued whether *Plessy* had been applied in the education field and thus needed to be specifically overruled there.

The other early school case, *Gong Lum v. Rice,* involved a Chinese girl living in Mississippi. She was prohibited from attending the only high school in the county solely on the ground that she was of Chinese descent and not a member of the white or Caucasian race. Writing for a unanimous Court, Chief Justice Taft, noting the availability of a school in a separate colored school district, rejected her father's contention that his daughter was entitled to an education at the only available school in the district. Citing *Plessy* and *Cumming* and several other state school cases, the Chief Justice concluded that the question of whites creating a privilege for themselves and thus discriminating was an old question many times decided to be within the constitutional power of the state legislatures. Although there was no clear head-on ruling on "separate but equal" in education in *Cumming* and *Gong Lum,* the Court had indicated that the *Plessy* doctrine did apply to education.

3

The question of voting rights for Negroes occupied the Court frequently after the end of Reconstruction because of persistent attempts to disenfranchise those who had received the right to vote through the Fifteenth Amendment. Questions before the Court in the early days included such matters as whether Congress could outlaw all interference with the right to vote or only interference by government officials (held: only the latter); what the federal government had to show in prosecuting private conspirators who had interfered with the right to vote (an intent to prevent the vote on account of race had to be shown); and whether protection existed against private interference with voting in federal elections, such as those for Congress (answered in the affirmative).[6] After the turn of the century, the Court also had to deal with the "grandfather

clause" subterfuge, which it voided in 1915 in the *Guinn* case. The principal recurring question before the Court was that of the right of Negroes to
vote in primary elections, which were clearly determinative in the Democratic one-party South. In 1921, the Court decided *Newberry v. United States,*
a Michigan case involving campaign expenditure limitations. Four justices said that primaries were not "elections" in the constitutional sense,
with a fifth reserving judgment on the question because the events of the
case preceded the ratification of the Seventeenth Amendment (direct
election of senators). The Court did not examine the "white primary"
directly for another six years, but this ruling indirectly safeguarded the
practice.

The first white primary case, *Nixon v. Herndon,* was brought under
NAACP sponsorship. In it the Court struck down a Texas statute which
declared that no Negroes under any circumstances were eligible to participate in the state's Democratic party primary election. The controlling
question in the decision was state action. The Court found that the statute
did indeed violate the Fourteenth Amendment guarantee of equal protection, so much so that the Fifteenth Amendment need not even be
considered: "States may do a good deal of classifying that it is difficult to
believe rational, but there are limits, and it is too clear for extended
argument that color cannot be made the basis of a statutory classification
affecting the right set up in this case." Although any statement about
positive Fifteenth Amendment rights had been carefully avoided, reducing the immediate importance of the case, the ruling did open the way for
future litigation once the Court brought primaries under federal surveillance and control. The case also shows that when one ground rather than
another is chosen early in a line of cases on a certain subject, there tends to
be a compounding effect which makes it even more difficult to get to
other issues on which people were seeking a ruling.

The practical effect of the judgment was merely to invalidate the
racially based law, not to assure the Negro of his vote in the primary. New
methods of evasion were promptly devised. The Texas legislature repealed the invalid law and substituted for it one giving the executive
committee of the state Democratic party the power to determine party
membership. The committee immediately barred Negroes, and the Supreme Court was soon faced with the question of the constitutionality of
the new Texas device in a suit brought by NAACP lawyers. By a vote of
only five-to-four, in *Nixon v. Condon* (1932) the Court voided the new
party membership statute as state action in conflict with the Fourteenth
Amendment, since the committee's discriminatory action was state-
authorized. Because a state law governed by the Fourteenth Amendment
was at issue, again the Fifteenth Amendment question of federal power to
regulate primaries as elections did not have to be answered. This necessar-

ily diminished the significance of the decision, and deprived the Court of a basic tool for later invalidating discriminatory action by the parties in the primaries they ran. The force of the ruling was further weakened both by the close vote and by a statement in the majority opinion which clearly indicated the next step for those wishing to continue excluding Negroes from the primary: "Whatever inherent power a state political party has to determine the content of its membership resides in the State Convention."

The Texas Democratic party in its state convention promptly passed a resolution whereby only white citizens otherwise qualified would be allowed to be members and participate in the party's deliberations. With the white primary thus still intact, the Court now had to pass on the validity of a subterfuge virtually recommended in its own handwriting. Just three years later, in 1935, the Court upheld the party's action in *Grovey v. Townsend,* finding no violation of Fourteenth or Fifteenth Amendment rights in a county clerk's refusal to furnish an absentee ballot for the primary election to a Negro because of his racial ineligibility for party membership. Observing that no statute authorized the state convention's action, the Court found that discrimination by this party organ could not be considered state action controlled by the Fourteenth Amendment. A party is a voluntary association, the Court ruled, so that although the primary was held under statutory compulsion it was a party primary; similarly, although the state convention was also regulated by state statute its policy-making was still not state action. That the nomination by primary is tantamount to election was ruled of no importance as confusing the privilege of party membership with the right to vote; the former is not the state's concern. The Court also said that discrimination against Texas Negroes by their state's Democratic party could not be proved from the fact that the national Democratic party had never acted to exclude Negroes. The only consolation in the ruling was the reiteration of the doctrine that denial of the vote in a general election on the ground of race or color by the state would be violative of the federal Constitution.

The Court went through a period of change during the years after 1937, and the first evidence of a new and more realistic approach to the problem of voting rights came in 1939 in another NAACP case, *Lane v. Wilson.* The case took up again the old grandfather clause of Oklahoma which had been outlawed back in 1915, but for which had been substituted a hardly less satisfactory requirement that persons previously barred from qualifying as voters could do so only by registering during a twelve-day period in 1916. This new statute did not reach the Supreme Court until twenty-three years later, when it was contested by a Negro who had not registered during the prescribed period. Promptly voiding the provision, Justice Frankfurter, speaking for the Court, agreed that the twelve-day registration period had been so inadequate that the grand-father clause was in actuality still in effect, and held that the Fifteenth Amendment "nullifies sophisticated as well as simple-minded modes of discrimination." Of particular interest was Frankfurter's discussion of certain sociological factors which made this attempt at disenfranchise-ment disallowable. "We are dealing," he pointed out, "with a body of citizens lacking the habits and traditions of political independence and otherwise living in circumstances which do not encourage initiative and enterprise." The decision firmly reinforced the older *Guinn* grandfather clause case. More important, *Grovey*'s foundations were somewhat sha-ken because without taking a very large step legally the Court had indi-cated that it was more willing to take a realistic look at discriminatory schemes.

Two years later, in 1941, the Court moved even further in this direc-tion in a case which, while it did not directly concern racial matters, had important implications for the still unsolved white primary problem. In *United States v. Classic,* the Court upset the general assumption, based on *Newberry*, that the federal government had no power to regulate state primaries. Specificially involved were indictments against New Orleans election officials for perpetrating fraud in a primary to nominate candi-dates for United States representative, brought under two provisions of the Criminal Code (18 U.S.C. 51, 52) making it an offense to deprive a citizen of any right or privilege under the Constitution. Primaries in Louisiana were regulated by state law, and candidacy in the general election was restricted by law to those who had received a certain percen-tage of votes in the primary election. The Court ruled that interference with the voter's choice here was interference at the only stage where it could have any effect on the election's outcome. The Court admitted that the Constitution had not specifically mentioned primaries because noth-ing had been known about them, but held that where state law had made the primary an integral part of the election procedure, or where the primary in fact effectively controlled the choice of the elector for his United States representative, the vote in the primary was then subject to constitutional protections (Art. I, Sec. 2). The Court also made quite clear that the election official's acts were state action prohibited by the Constitu-tion and subject to statutory punishment.

This official recognition, based on political realism, that the Constitu-tion's protection had to be extended to primaries to be effective seemed further to undermine the Court's *Grovey* position. With the stage thus set, that 1935 ruling was challenged by a Texas Negro who had been excluded from the state's Democratic primary. In 1944, the Supreme Court de-cided his claims in *Smith v. Allwright*, the most important of the white primary cases. In an opinion by Justice Reed over Roberts's lone impassioned dissent, the Court overruled *Grovey* and held the practice of the state Democratic convention in excluding Negroes from the primary tantamount to state action in violation of the Fifteenth Amendment.[7] Because of the unitary character of the electoral process found in *Classic,* a reexamination of the *Grovey* decision was compelled, said Justice Reed, declaring that the right to vote in a primary election which is an integral part of the election process is secured by the Constitution and cannot be abridged on the basis of race. A detailed examination of the Texas statutes regulating primaries and directing the selection of party officers led him to conclude that the statutory system made the party an agent of the state, with the state endorsing the discrimination against Negroes practiced by the party. It was this prohibited state action which required that *Grovey* be overruled.

In brief, the Court had said that when the privilege of membership is also the essential qualification for voting in a primary to select nominees for a general election, then the state makes the action of the party the action of the state and is subject to constitutional limitation. The Court did not openly discard the doctrine that a political party was a "voluntary association," thus encouraging some states to engage in "fooling around" to avoid the thrust of the Court's ruling. The Court also did not inflexibly limit the right of a party to determine its own membership. Nor did Justice Reed rely too heavily on the *Classic* decision, using only the test formulated there that the primary was an "integral part" of the election machinery by law. The status of the voters in the two cases was certainly quite different—one was fully qualified to vote in a state-conducted primary but was victimized by vote fraud while the other was not qualified for membership in the party and thus could not vote in the party-conducted primary—but *Classic* was invoked as indicative if not controlling. Use of that ruling, however, allowed the Court to avoid appearing as if it were overruling *Grovey,* a unanimous decision only nine years old, for no reason at all; it permitted the appearance of as much consistency with precedent as was possible.

After *Smith v. Allwright,* the Court did not hand down an opinion on voting rights until 1953, when it reinforced its position on the white primary. In the interim, reinforcement came through denial of review. When South Carolina tried to avoid the thrust of *Smith v. Allwright* by repealing all her primary laws, the lower federal courts invalidated the action and the Supreme Court merely denied certiorari.[8] In *Terry v. Adams* in 1953 the Court faced perhaps the last and least vulnerable contrivance for preserving the all-white primary. In Fort Bend County, Texas, the Jaybird Democratic Association conducted its own primary before the official nominating primary, with the winner of the Jaybird primary almost invariably winning the official party nomination without opposition. Although after *Smith* no legal bar prevented Negroes from voting in this all-white "private club's" primary the plaintiff brought a class action suit charging the Jaybird Association with violation of Fifteenth Amendment rights.

The Jaybirds contended their primaries were merely "straw votes" with no bindng nor legally enforceable results, in no way adopted by nor acquiesced in by the state, but the Supreme Court, over one dissent, ruled in favor of Terry. However, the majority was badly divided, with one justice—Frankfurter—particularly concerned with the relief which courts could properly order, and the seven remaining justices split into two groups differing in the breadth of their position. Black, writing for himself, Douglas, and Burton, said that the Jaybird primary had become an integral part, indeed the only effective part, of the elective process that determined who would rule and govern in the county, making the association's exclusion of Negroes tantamount to state action in violation of the Fifteenth Amendment. Such flagrant abuse of the Constitution occurred only because the state had permitted the action of improper duplication of its election processes. Justice Clark, in a concurring opinion for himself, Chief Justice Vinson, and Justices Reed and Jackson, urged setting the case under the broad principle laid down by *Smith* whereby any part of the machinery for choosing officials becomes subject to the Constitution's restraints. Despite this doctrinal division, the Court's promise to outlaw sophisticated as well as simple modes of discrimination had been made good in confronting the white primary.

4

The first housing case to reach the Supreme Court was *Buchanan v. Warley* in 1917. Buchanan, a Louisville, Kentucky, white homeowner, had signed a contract for the sale of his city home to Warley, a Negro. Warley refused to go ahead with the purchase because a city zoning ordinance prohibited a Negro from moving into a residence in any block containing a greater number of whites than Negroes, and vice-versa. Buchanan brought suit in the state courts for enforcement of the contract, but lost on the ground that the city ordinance was constitutionally valid and a complete defense for Warley. Louisville sought to justify its ordinance before the Supreme Court as a measure enacted under the state's police power to promote the public peace, to maintain racial purity, and to prevent the deterioration in value of white-owned and white-occupied property. The Supreme Court rejected this argument, and ruled unanimously that this exercise of the police power violated the Fourteenth Amendment right of the white owner to dispose of his property by prohibiting occupancy solely on the basis of race or color. The police powers of the state, the Court emphasized, could not be exercised in any manner which denied constitutional rights. The Court distinguished *Plessy* on the grounds that no attempt was made to deprive persons of color of the principal object involved—transportation—whereas in *Buchanan* a basic right—to acquire, enjoy, and dispose of property, a right accruing under the Fourteenth Amendment and civil rights statutes—was being removed.

One of the very earliest cases presented by NAACP lawyers, *Buchanan* allowed the Court to enter the field of racial discrimination in housing very cautiously and yet assure the public that it was doing so. By stating its first invalidation of a segregation law in terms of the civil rights of a white property owner, the Court protected the right of the Negro while cloaking the protection in terms which appealed to Caucasians. The Court's citation of a number of cases, particularly the early jury cases, made the decision seem to fit into a logical pattern. But the applicability of *Buchanan* was restricted by the fact that it involved an explicit ordinance discriminating against Negroes. Towns and counties removed explicit racial discriminations in their ordinances and relied on a general understanding that state officials would continue discrimination in their decisions in particular cases. Furthermore, private contracts, such as land covenants and wills, explicitly continued to discriminate against Negroes. The first challenge to these private agreements reached the Supreme Court in 1926 under NAACP sponsorship in a case arising in the District of Columbia. Buckley, a partner in a 1921 covenant to prohibit sale of properties to any person of the Negro race or blood for twenty-one years, brought suit to enjoin Corrigan from carrying out her 1922 contract of sale to Curtis, a Negro, or conveying the lot to Curtis during twenty-one years from the date of the covenant and to enjoin Curtis from taking title to the lot or from using or occupying it during that period. Corrigan moved to dismiss on the grounds that the covenant was contrary to the Constitution and to public policy, as did Curtis on the grounds that it attempted to deprive her and others of property without due process of law and was contrary to the equal protection afforded them by the Fourteenth Amendment and federal laws.

When the lower court judgment enjoining the sale on the basis of the restrictive covenant was appealed, the Supreme Court avoided altogether the constitutional issues by declaring that there was no state action constituting a basis for its jurisdiction but, rather, a private agreement to which the white seller had covenanted. The Fifth, Thirteenth, and Fourteenth Amendments apply only to limitations on state and federal government action and thus do not prohibit individuals from establishing contracts controlling the disposition of their own property; the Thirteenth Amendment, while denouncing slavery, did not in other matters protect the individual rights of persons of the Negro race. The Court also held that if the contention that the court decrees in themselves deprived the defendants of property without due process had been properly raised it would still have been lacking in substance, because the defendants were given a full hearing in both lower courts and were not denied any constitutional or statutory right, and because the decrees were not so plainly arbitrary and contrary to law as to warrant reversal. By requiring state action before the Fourteenth Amendment could be applied, the Court followed the line of reasoning in *Plessy* and was consistent judicially with the *Buchanan* case which involved overt action by Louisville. However, the Court refused to follow its own initiative in *Buchanan* in eliminating racial discrimination in housing. The presence of a willing white seller and a willing Negro buyer would have allowed the Court to appeal to white sentiment once more by couching its opinion in terms of Caucasian property rights, but evidently there were circumstances which made the Court reluctant to enter the area of private contracts with a broad interpretation of state action. Because the case had attracted nationwide attention for the bearing it might have on the segregation laws in operation in many states, the practical effect of the Court's implication that restrictive covenants were enforceable inevitably encouraged the use of those covenants and other means of racial and ethnic segregation in housing, as well as indicating that the Court had backed off from support of Negroes' attempts to achieve freedom of choice with respect to housing.

The question of enforcement of restrictive covenants, avoided in *Corrigan,* was bypassed again several times before the Court finally reached the issue in 1948. There were cases which would have allowed the justices to reach the issue while favoring white sellers, but in one the case was distasteful because the white seller wanted to get out of an increasingly black area in the District of Columbia, and in another case from the District at the end of the war only two justices (of the necessary four) voted to grant certiorari.[9] In a third case the Court did reverse the judgment of the Illinois Supreme Court on the ground that white Chicago property owners had been denied due process in being prevented from challenging the validity of a covenant upheld earlier in a case to which they were not party. They claimed that the covenant was defective because the required 95 percent of the property owners in the area had not signed the agreement. The Supreme Court held that the state court did not have to repeat the error of the earlier state court ruling enforcing the covenant, thereby giving open-housing advocates a limited victory.[10]

By the time of the Vinson Court, the NAACP had determined upon an all-out effort to reverse restrictive covenant decisions. The postwar general housing shortage posed particularly acute problems for Negroes, and the steadily mounting roster of appellate court decisions upholding restrictive covenants made the necessity of securing both a hearing and a favorable judgment in the United States Supreme Court even more imperative. In mid-1945 in Chicago and then again in early 1947 at Howard University in Washington, conferences on racially restrictive covenants were held to bring Negro leaders together to decide upon a strategy.[11] Three main considerations resulted from these conferences: litigation from the states and not just the District of Columbia should be proffered; enough time should be allowed to elapse so that there were a number of cases from which to choose before a single one was attempted; and the publication of articles and books denouncing restrictive covenants from all angles should be encouraged in order to have an impressive list of supporting publications in the briefs.

Nevertheless, in early 1947 a St. Louis Negro attorney unilaterally decided to file a petition for certiorari in *Shelley v. Kraemer*, involving covenants which restricted use and occupancy of the covered land for a period of fifty years to persons of the Caucasian race. When the white owner of one of the covenanted houses conveyed her property to a Negro couple, the adjoining landowners obtained an injunction preventing the purchasers from taking possession. The NAACP responded to the *Shelley* certiorari petition weeks later in the Michigan case of *McGhee v. Sipes*, which it had entered initially as amicus curiae but for which it was principal architect in the Supreme Court proceedings. At the same time the Court of Appeals for the District of Columbia handed down two more adverse decisions in *Hurd v. Hodge* and *Urciolo v. Hodge*. These two cases carried detailed and forceful dissents by Judge Edgerton, arguing that the Supreme Court had not considered the validity of enforcement by injunction in *Corrigan* but had held only that neither the Civil Rights Act of 1866 nor the Constitution prohibited private parties from agreeing to covenants. For Edgerton, judicial enforcement of such covenants was unquestionably unconstitutional. One month later, at the very end of the 1946 Term, the Supreme Court granted the petitions in *Shelley* and *McGhee*, and early in the 1947 Term did the same with the two cases from the District of Columbia.

It is certain that the justices were aware of the views of Judge Edgerton and of those of a growing number of lower federal court judges who agreed with him. By 1947 the FHA finally had responded to NAACP pressure to the extent of eliminating from its manual a recommendation for the use of restrictive covenants. Furthermore, in that same year the first report of the president's newly created Committee on Civil Rights was issued. It contained recommendations covering restrictive covenants and advocating that states act to outlaw them, that, furthermore, Congress act to outlaw them in the District of Columbia, and that the courts refuse to enforce them. When President Truman made civil rights a major issue in his 1948 campaign for reelection, it was clear that all other branches of government were at long last beginning to concern themselves openly with the problems of Negroes. Hence, the strategic value in taking up the covenant issue lay more with the Court than with the interest groups presenting the suits. Furthermore, although petitions for certiorari were received over the intervening summer and autumn in three other cases (one from Ohio and two from California) which raised some peripheral issues such as church-state relations or the rights of aliens, the Court did not accept them.[12] By agreeing to review only the two state and two federal cases which put the issue of judicial enforcement of racial covenants directly before it, the Court set the stage for consideration of the constitutional questions long avoided.

The four cases, grouped together and allotted two days of oral agrument,[13] were all based on the assertion that the action of state or federal courts in enforcing racial restrictive covenants constituted state action prohibited by the Fourteenth Amendment. Diversity of argumentation was assured by the fact of four separate cases and approximately twenty amicus briefs for the "Shelley" side and one-fifth as many for the white homeowners. Important also was the fact that the argument before the Court opened with a one hour statement by Solicitor General Perlman for the United States as amicus curiae, urging that racial restrictive covenants were unconstitutional, contrary to public policy, and inimical to civil rights. Such property agreements, he said, should be relegated to the limbo of other things as dead as slavery. However, in answer to a Frankfurter question, Perlman said the government did not question the rule of the *Civil Rights Cases,* holding that the Fourteenth Amendment applied only to state action.

George L. Vaughn and Herman Willer argued for the Negroes in *Shelley.* Vaughn claimed that enforcement of the Missouri court decree would violate the Civil Rights Act of 1866 by violating laws on liens, conveyances, and recording. Using the Thirteenth and Fourteenth Amendments, he argued that enforcement of the covenants was involuntary servitude.[14] Willer asserted that a party seeking judicial aid in enforcing a private agreement calls on the state to act, and the deliberate, conscious decree of the court carries with it governmental sanction and force. He maintained it makes no difference when the government steps in, whether authorizing discrimination (by statute) or ratifying it.

Defending the covenants, Gerald L. Seegers asserted that the state court was following its established rule equally applicable to any contract. But in response to questions from Justice Frankfurter he also claimed that no offense against the Fourteenth Amendment would occur if Missouri statutes allowed citizens to restrict transfers of property on grounds of race or to exclude Negroes from a neighborhood by two-thirds vote: the statutes would be permissible because permissive.[15] Since the Negroes had admitted that the contracts themselves are not contrary to the Constitution, Seegers argued, and since Missouri had said that the contracts are not against public policy, there was no basis on which the lower courts can be reversed. Petitioners were really protesting against state inaction—failure to enact a statute prohibiting enforcement of the covenants. Seegers further asserted that there was no difference between a price covenant (preventing construction of houses under a certain price) and a racial restrictive covenant. If the covenant in *Shelley* were impermissible, he said, the price covenant would also collapse, because it discriminated against poverty.[16]

In *McGhee v. Sipes*, the Michigan case, Thurgood Marshall said that, while there would have been nothing wrong with the whites asking Negro petitioners to move, going to the courts was another matter. Marshall also stressed the vast amount of sociological material in the briefs (drawn from the articles intentionally written for law reviews and other journals), including references to housing problems, crime, disease, and other claimed results of segregation policies, and defended the material against Frankfurter's inquiries as to its relevance. Commented the justice, "If you are right about the legal proposition, the sociological material merely shows how it works. If you're wrong, this material doesn't do you any good." Marshall said the data, an essential part of the argument, was legally significant, particularly in the District of Columbia cases where matters of public policy were central because the state action theory was not applicable. Marshall did not really answer Frankfurter's objection, but his use of the sociological material was a good argumentative tactic. In essence it said, "Here is *why* you ought to decide in our favor; once you so decide, we are confident you will be able to think up the appropriate legal reasons for doing so."

For the white Michigan homeowners Henry Gilligan based his argument on their right to associate, but James A. Crooks focused on the state action argument, which he said was the heart of the case, and claimed that *Corrigan,* because cited so frequently, had become a "rule of property" on which people had relied. Answering Frankfurter, he said that a court decree enforcing a private contract is not an act of the state enforcing discrimination but a decree enforcing the private rights of citizens. Frankfurter agreed but pointed out that the citizens couldn't enforce the contract themselves: "They need the full strength of the state's judicial power to enforce something which the state could not itself declare as state policy. Is that a fair statement of the case?" Crooks's response: Yes.

In the District of Columbia cases, where arguments were generally similar to those in the state cases, Phineas Indritz, arguing for the Negroes, stressed that *Corrigan* had only the effect of rejecting the claim that the covenant itself was void, thus leaving for present decision the matter of whether enforcement of a covenant by the courts is constitutional. Negro attorney Charles Houston claimed that the owners of the houses had no right with respect to their neighbors' property, but he made the strategic concession that they could sell or refuse to sell their own property.

Gilligan and Crooks, attorneys for the whites, stressed the differences between the District of Columbia and state cases. Congress not only had made no statement of public policy against the covenants but, in addition, had operated separate schools and parks. When Crooks asserted that the problems should have been addressed to the legislature, Black asked, "With what effect?" and Crooks said, "Congress could do what New York has done," that is, bar discrimination in housing. Crooks reminded the Court also that there was no "equal protection" clause in the Fifth Amendment like that in the Fourteenth and hence the District of Columbia, not being a state, was not bound to give its residents equal protection of the laws—an issue which was to arise in the District of Columbia school case only a few years later. Because three justices—Reed, Jackson, and Rutledge—had disqualified themselves, only three votes were needed by the white property owners to produce the tie that would leave standing the lower court decisions favorable to them. However, less than five months later, a unanimous Court declared, in two opinions by the Chief Justice, that judicial enforcement of restrictive covenants could not stand.

Considering the state cases together, the Chief Justice first phrased the question before the Court quite narrowly—the validity of court enforcement of private agreements which have as their purpose the exclusion of persons of designated race or color from the ownership or occupancy of real property. After listing the Fourteenth Amendment rights petitioners urged had been denied them (equal protection of the laws, deprivation of property without due process, and privileges and immunities of citizens), he then demonstrated that the question of whether the Fourteenth Amendment inhibits state judicial enforcement of racially based covenants had never been before the Court. He then showed that the prospective effect of the agreements was purely on the basis of race, not of use, and stated that the rights to acquire, enjoy, own, and dispose of property were without doubt among the civil rights protected under the Fourteenth Amendment. While these restrictions on the right of occupancy clearly could not stand if imposed by state statute or local ordinance, the Chief Justice, citing *Buchanan* and other cases to show the conclusiveness and longevity of this position, stated decisively that the restrictive agreements standing alone could not be regarded as offensive to the Constitution, so long as effectuated by voluntary adherence. Citing the *Civil Rights Cases,* he emphasized that only state and not private action,

however discriminatory or wrongful, is inhibited by the Fourteenth
Amendment. Moving closer to the real issues of the case, the Chief Justice
stated that from the Fourteenth Amendment's adoption to the present
the Court had consistently ruled that the amendment covered the action
of state courts and judicial officials. There was no doubt, he said, that
petitioners would have been free to occupy the properties but for the state
action in these cases, which denied rights subject to Fourteenth Amendment protection and thus could not stand. The state action here was
immunized neither by having been taken pursuant to the state's common
law policy nor because the pattern of discrimination developed initially
from the terms of a private agreement. He added that the Constitution
gave no individual the right to demand action by the state which denies
others equal protection.

The Chief Justice said that resolution of the federal cases did not
require judgment on the constitutional question because other grounds
adequate to dispose of the case were available. The Civil Rights Act of
1866 was held to guarantee certain property rights against discriminatory
governmental action. The interpretation to be given that act in terms of
the courts of the District of Columbia was implied by *Shelley,* and the
conclusion was the same: the action of the courts of the District denied
Negro petitioners and white sellers rights intended by Congress to be
theirs under the protection of the Civil Rights Act, and thus that action
cannot stand. Even in the absence of the statute, enforcement of restrictive covenants would be contrary to the public policy of the United States
and should be corrected by the Supreme Court. In a brief concurring
opinion, Frankfurter saw the grant of injunctions to enforce these racial
covenants as a violation of rights much broader and more basic to our
society than the majority opinion indicated.

The Court demonstrated extreme caution in its wording of both the
preparation for the announcement of the holding and in the holding
itself in these cases. Every effort was made to make the opinion appear
consistent with a long line of previous decisions, and *Corrigan* was distinguished rather than overruled. Not the restrictive covenants themselves
but only their enforcement by the courts was being prohibited. Furthermore, emphasis was placed on the presence of a willing seller and a willing
buyer and on the fact that it was state action, not state inaction, which had
been found, a holding which seemed to rule out any interpretation of
state inaction as state action. The former fact prevented the automatic
application of the decision to a situation in which the white seller was
unwilling to sell his home to a Negro and made the right of the Negro to
buy not an absolute right but one dependent upon the willingness of the
white property owner to sell.

Perhaps the Court could have done no more; judges are generally reluctant to invalidate private agreements, although some are set aside as "against public policy." The distinction gave the appearance that the Court was avoiding total interference with the right to private contract, although any such contract based on racial discrimination would be invalidated if it became the subject of litigation. This argument was probably designed to pacify white segregationists, as was the opinion's stress on the white seller's willingness and desire to dispose of his property. However, the Court's stance meant that citizens would continue to use the covenants privately, supported by the argument that they were constitutionally valid—and perhaps thus ethically proper as well. Although the Court had gone a little farther than *Buchanan* in upholding the right of the Negro buyer rather than that of the white seller, the Court had failed to take a strong direct stand against discrimination in housing. What was involved was a matter of emphasis, but it was an important one.

Instead of concentrating on the enforcement mechanism as it did, the Court could have stressed that it was the racial discrimination, unconstitutional when the government was involved, which led to non-enforcement by the judiciary. It could have taken the position noted during oral argument by Justice Frankfurter, who said that the English tendency is to prohibit a contract if you cannot get a court to enforce it, a position well beyond the Court's ruling. The opinion involved the smallest step possible in eliminating housing discrimination, but its state action aspect could have opened to judicial attack a wide area of discrimination which formerly had been interpreted as private action and thus was potentially quite broad. Had the Court invalidated the agreements themselves, their enforcement would clearly have been invalid, but the doctrine of the invalidity of otherwise valid private discriminatory agreements had a much greater reach, even though the Court was reluctant in the post-*Shelley* years to extend it. The ruling, while narrow in being restricted to the question of enforcement of covenants, was thus broad both in its potential reach and in its answer to all the questions posed. Yet we must keep in mind that because it left unclear just how broadly the concept of state action should be construed, the *Shelley* decision has been extremely difficult for legal scholars to decipher. Some legal scholars have wondered whether the ruling left any limitation concerning the Fourteenth Amendment's "state action" requirement.[17] *Shelley*, however, did not settle such a question; it merely raised it. One of the most cited constitutional law cases of all time, it has been referred to as the "*Finnegans Wake* of Constitutional Law" by those who have tried to make sense of it, many of whom "were not satisfied that the opinion provided a doctrine of decision which governed the case before the Court, dealt rationally with the past, and promised to apply to tomorrow's case."[18]

After *Shelley,* the Court disposed summarily of the Ohio and California cases which had come up at the same time. However, the *Shelley* issue was soon to arise again. By 1953, loose ends from *Shelley* had manifested themselves in cases in which Missouri and Oklahoma state courts had awarded damages to white neighbors who brought suit for breach of contract against white covenant breakers, although courts in the District of Columbia, Maryland, Michigan, and California had refused to award damages in similar cases.[19] Only two of these cases were taken to the Supreme Court; the Court refused certiorari to one in 1949, and then granted review to a California case, *Barrows v. Jackson,* involving restrictions which did not prevent occupancy but allowed compensation for economic loss due to expected diminution of property values from Negroes moving into the area.

Arguing for the white property owners,[20] J. Wallace McKnight tried to distinguish his case from *Shelley* on the grounds that Mrs. Jackson, the white seller, was an original signer of the covenant who, having bought the property feeling the courts would enforce the contract, could not now turn around and disavow such enforcement. McKnight, trying to keep the validity and enforceability of contracts together, stressed that *Shelley* had two parts—state action and denial of rights. Arguing for Mrs. Jackson, Loren Miller stressed the distinction between the contract and its enforcement in the courts, saying that to allow damages would vitiate the sale and would obviously deter future sales. During Miller's presentation, Chief Justice Vinson showed concern about the effect of the *Corrigan* decision. He also indicated his feeling that no non-Caucasian's constitutional right had been impinged upon. For him, there was nothing particularly unusual about an agreement which could be enforced voluntarily as long as people chose to but which they couldn't ask a court to enforce.

Not quite seven weeks after argument, the Court, in an opinion by Justice Minton, ruled that a racially restrictive covenant may not be enforced at law by a suit for damages against a co-covenantor who allegedly broke the covenant. With Reed and Jackson again not participating, only six justices made up the majority. The Chief Justice stood apart in a strongly worded dissent, unusual for him. With no non-Caucasian claiming a denial of rights, the case had presented the question of whether Mrs. Jackson, in defending against the damage suit, could rely on the invasion of their rights. Without a positive answer to this question, the Court would have had difficulty reaching the substantive question provided, although standing might have been based on Mrs. Jackson's economic injury. The Court traditionally had been reluctant to allow any party to invoke third party rights in challenging the constitutionality of state action directed against himself. Yet Minton declared that this case nevertheless seemed to present a unique situation in which it would be difficult if not impossible for the persons whose rights were asserted to present their grievance to any court. They would either have been denied the sale—with such denial not yet held illegal—or have occupancy. Thus the traditional rule of practice was to be relaxed, in order to "close the gap to the use of this covenant, so universally condemned by the courts."

Minton said that to compel Mrs. Jackson to respond in damages would be to allow the state to punish for failure to carry out a discriminatory covenant that according to *Shelley* or *Buchanan* the state could not enforce or which could not be enforced in federal jurisdiction on the basis of *Hurd*. Such a sanction removed the observance of the covenant from the realm of voluntary choice and thus constituted the same state action prohibited by *Shelley*. As to the question whether this state action deprived anyone of protected rights, Minton said that to allow damages would encourage the use of such restrictive agreements and would lead a prospective seller of restricted land either to refuse to sell to non-Caucasians or to require a higher price to cover the damages which might be assessed. Thus solely because of their race, non-Caucasians would be unable to purchase and enjoy property on the same terms as Caucasians, denying them the equal protection of the law contrary to the Fourteenth Amendment.

In an opinion consistent with his questioning of Miller, Chief Justice Vinson said he could not agree that the *Shelley* state action doctrine could be applied because no identifiable non-Caucasian appeared before the Court to assert a denial of rights and because the ruling would affect only future rights, since the non-Caucasians in this case already had obtained the property they had sought. The Chief Justice openly accused the majority of deciding the case on the basis of social policy rather than settled judicial rules. The strength of his dissent reinforced the property owners' feelings and prompted them to petition the Supreme Court to rehear the case. Like most such requests, the petition was denied.

Substantively, the decision in *Barrows v. Jackson* was a logical extension of *Shelley*. The case was more important in terms of the ruling on standing. In one sense, standing had not been expanded greatly, for the white seller would sustain economic injury if forced to pay. However, the precedent established by the Court's relatively expansive reading of standing in allowing Mrs. Jackson to assert the rights of Negroes as part of her response to the suit has had great and continued application. And that position was almost imperative from the perspective of the Court's strategy. The Court might have used traditional standing doctrine to escape from the case, but that would have been difficult in the aftermath of *Shelley*. A ruling on the merits in *Barrows* was needed to reinforce that case, and the ruling handed down clearly provided that reinforcement.

5

The line of restrictive covenant cases ending in *Shelley* and *Barrows* involved the "state action" question. In the area of transportation, in which it had first handed down decisions on "separate but equal," the Court had two chances to consider anew the application of that doctrine. Both the *Morgan* and *Henderson* cases were decided in favor of the Negroes, but the Court did not eliminate separate but equal. It therefore was present to haunt and plague the Court in *Brown v. Board of Education.*

In an earlier transportation case, *Michell v. United States,* a Negro member of the United States House of Representatives had been denied first-class Pullman facilities on an Illinois Central train traveling through Arkansas, in accordance with an Arkansas statute requiring segregation of Negro and white passengers. The railroad made a practice of assigning Negro first-class passengers to the drawing rooms or coaches, defending this action on the ground that it would be financially ruinous to carry separate Negro Pullmans in view of the minimal demand for them. Despite this assertion, the Court ruled against the practice. Following its own doctrine that generally a statutory basis of decision is to be preferred over a constitutional one where it is available, the Court did not consider the question of the constitutionality of the state law. Instead, the justices construed the antidiscrimination clause of the Interstate Commerce Act to require equal accommodations for Negroes. Said Chief Justice Hughes: "If facilities are provided, substantial equality of treatment of persons traveling under like conditions cannot be refused. It is the individual, we said, who is entitled to the equal protection of the laws, not merely a group of individuals, or a body of persons according to their numbers. . . . The Interstate Commerce Act expressly extends its prohibitions to the subjecting of 'any particular person' to unreasonable discriminations."

Morgan v. Virginia, decided in 1946, involved a Negro woman traveling from Virginia to Baltimore through Washington, D.C., on a Richmond Greyhound bus. Acting on the basis of a Virginia segregation law which allowed shifting of seats to maintain racial separation, the bus driver tried to force her to move to the rear of the bus to make room for a white passenger. She refused; a sheriff was summoned; and she was subsequently convicted of violating the state law. When the case was taken to the Supreme Court, Thurgood Marshall and William Hastie argued the case for the NAACP.[21] Marshall, relying on a nineteenth-century Supreme Court ruling, *Hall v. DeCuir,* argued that the racial segregation statute imposed a burden on interstate commerce, and Hastie stressed the

great variety and uncertainty with reference to segregation or nonsegregation policies and laws of several states through which a bus must pass,
including differences in the meaning of colored person. The justices'
questions indicated their desire to find a ruling which would seem the
least possible departure from past decisions and thus least offensive to the
states and the entrepreneurs who had long been left virtually undisturbed
in their practices. Justice Rutledge asked Marshall if a state could prohibit
a carrier's Jim Crow regulation. Marshall said *Hall* still forbade such
interference. Rutledge also pressed Hastie as to whether the case could be
determined without reference to the Fourteenth Amendment. The inter-
relation between the Fourteenth Amendment and the Commerce Clause
was also raised by the justices. Perhaps most important for the ultimate
result was Chief Justice Stone's questioning of the applicability of any
federal statute. Marshall suggested the applicable language of the Motor
Carrier Act of 1935 gave the Interstate Commerce Commission power to
regulate motor carriers. The Chief Justice also asked whether the Virginia statute applied to all interstate vehicles—the answer was yes—and,
in a practical vein, whether there were difficulties in shifting passengers
around. Frankfurter asked about the applicability to night travel, but
Marshall conceded that the trip in question had been during the day.

   Arguing Virginia's case, Attorney General Abram Staples tried to get
rid of the Fourteenth Amendment question by saying it had not been
raised below—in fact, had been specifically disavowed by Morgan—and
thus could not be raised before the high court. Further, he stressed that
the carrier had established the regulation and even initiated the prosecution; the state had not mandated adoption of the policies. The only party
which could claim a burden on interstate commerce, Staples said, was the
carrier, not the passenger; the carrier appears not to have been hampered
by the procedure. Staples was unsuccessful in persuading the justices,
who, with only Justice Burton dissenting, ruled for the Negroes. But
Staples may have succeeded in persuading the judges not to reach the
constitutional dimension in the case, for Justice Reed in his opinion for
the Court avoided any mention of *Plessy* and concentrated solely on the
state burden on interstate commerce. He clearly had found persuasive
Hastie's description of the great variety and uncertainty of state segregation regulations and Hastie's contention that this was not a matter of
substantial local concern when applying a "balancing test" to the statute.
Without a federal act dealing with the separation of races in interstate
transportation on which to rely, Reed ruled that "seating arrangements
for the different races in interstate motor travel require a single, uniform
rule to promote and protect national travel." The opinion was forthright
on this issue, although it avoided reaching the constitutional question.
Short concurring opinions by both Black and Frankfurter and a concur-

rence in the result by Rutledge left even less strength behind the Court's limited grounds.

Morgan presented the Court with a golden opportunity to reverse *Plessy,* mentioned during oral argument. If the Court had repudiated "separate but equal" in the area in which it arose instead of in the schools, there would have been less public clamor. The public would have had an opportunity to accept the idea before the Court applied it in education cases. Then, too, immediately after World War II, despite economic problems in part caused by strikes, we were a mobile nation and we were in an "up" period. In contrast, *Brown* came in a "dead" period in our history, in the end-of-Korea let-down. Although the incremental development of the law had not yet reached the point where the Court was prepared to strike out against "separate but equal" in 1946, by 1954 the law had developed, but the political climate was less supportive and the country had undergone a change from a president who supported civil rights—Truman—to one—Eisenhower—whose lukewarm attitude on the subject was obvious.

Had the Court used *Morgan* to dispose of separate but equal, the lower education cases would have come sooner. The Court could have set them aside temporarily, letting the lower courts work matters out until a clearer picture had developed, just as the Court ultimately did after *Brown II*. Once the Court had spoken directly to segregation in public education, it could have done so not only in a more incremental manner but also with a much stronger opinion. After all, the Court would have been building directly on the transportation area. In other words, *Brown* would have been mere implementation of *Morgan,* not the heavy blow struck in what must have been the most sensitive area of American life except marriage. The American public was forced to get both its philosophy and its education "cold." The Court's reliance on nonconstitutional grounds in the transportation cases, which put off a direct ruling on the modern-day applicability of *Plessy,* simply made it more difficult for it to come to grips directly with the central *Plessy* doctrine. One delay begot another.

Even though it missed the strategic opportunity presented by *Morgan,* the Court could still have disposed of *Plessy* in *Henderson v. United States,* argued at the same time as the graduate education cases of *Sweatt* and *McLaurin* (1950). Because the *Plessy* matter was far more clearly presented to the Court in *Henderson* and in the graduate education cases than in *Morgan,* the narrowness of the Court's opinion in *Henderson* was less justified than was the narrowness of the *Morgan* ruling. In addition, the federal government appeared in support of desegregation in *Henderson,* and submitted an amicus brief in the graduate school cases. The Court had support for separate and equal rulings from a coordinate branch of the government.

Henderson, a Negro passenger on the Southern Railway traveling from Washington, D.C., to Birmingham, Alabama, was unable to obtain food service because of the railroad's dining car practices. He subsequently brought suit against the Interstate Commerce Commission, challenging *Plessy*'s doctrine and the Commission's approval of discriminatory practices in interstate transportation. In oral argument,[22] Attorney General McGrath attacked the "separate but equal" doctrine and argued that segregation is intended to signify inequality. The racial barrier in the dining room was an imposition of legally enforced caste status denoting the separated individual an inferior. Conceding that no act of Congress or Supreme Court decision could eradicate racial prejudice, he pointed out that "ways of thinking and behavior are at least partly shaped by the rules of conduct prescribed by law as interpreted by this Court. Your decision can and may give rigidity and respectability to barriers which have their root in prejudice and thereby solidify these barriers, or your wisdom may to a large degree undermine these barriers and bring them into disrepute." Continuing the argument, Solicitor General Perlman noted that segregation was a violation of the Constitution and that Section 3 of the Interstate Commerce Act prohibited segregation on railroads. He asserted the statutory violation but also said in response to a Frankfurter question that the Court should reach the constitutional question, something it would have to do if the Court affirmed the lower court's ruling that the regulation did not violate the act. Like McGrath, he specifically asked for reexamination of *Plessy,* although he tried to be gentle about the old precedent by saying the Court, closer to slavery at the time, might have had good reason—although not in law—to adopt that rule. Perlman argued that Harlan's dissent in *Plessy* was correct and that the post-*Plessy* cases merely assumed that "separate but equal" was correct with the Court not having fully analyzed or reaffirmed them. In addition to adverting positively to the United States' appearance, Henderson's counsel, Belford V. Lawson, Jr., suggested that *Plessy* was itself a departure from an 1873 case forbidding separate railroad cars.[23] Lawson said he wanted the Court to go beyond the *Mitchell* case on providing equality of service, saying it would be a Pyrrhic victory if the Court did not decide the constitutional question. The Court's decision was, however, foreshadowed by Justice Frankfurter's suggestion that it was not necessary to do so.

According to the Interstate Commerce Commission's counsel, Allen Crenshaw, the basic question was the validity and lawfulness of the Commission's order. The Commission looked for—and the act required—only equal service, Crenshaw said, with racial separation left to the carriers' judgment. Because the Commission had been obedient to the congressional will, Congress, which had refused on more than two dozen occasions to pass a bill abolishing segregation, would be the proper source of reform. This argument brought the response from the bench that such non-action could mean that Congress believed a prohibition was already in the bill, and one justice quipped, "There are more reasons for refusing to pass a bill than for denying certiorari." Ever on the lookout for procedural aspects which would dispose of a case, Frankfurter pointed out that with the railroad's rule changed as a result of Henderson's complaint there might not be a suit, or that Henderson might not be able to challenge the new rule. (Crenshaw: "I hadn't thought of it in that way but you could look at it like that.") Supporting the Commission's position was Congressman Hobbs of the House Judiciary Committee. Congress, he said, had the sole and exclusive power to regulate interstate travel. He claimed that those trying to upset the railroad segregation were "impatient reformers" who couldn't and wouldn't wait for congressional action. Their position, he said, was "but the fitful fever of reformers who have a passion for immediacy."

For the Southern Railroad, Charles Clark said that while the states couldn't burden interstate commerce, the Congress and the railroad could, with the Fifth Amendment the only possible way for Henderson and the government to get to any constitutional issue. On this point Frankfurter suggested the Fifth Amendment could be seen as writing an antisegregation provision into the act. Clark, like Crenshaw, pointed out that Congress, given many opportunities, had not enacted the antisegregation provision and, in further support of maintaining segregation, raised an argument to be used frequently in the District of Columbia desegregation cases—that the Congress which adopted the Fourteenth Amendment also passed legislation for separate facilities in the District schools.

As in *Morgan*, the Court's opinion did not go any part of the distance that had been so vigorously urged upon the justices in argument and did not decide the constitutional question but, in a ruling which really did little more than repudiate the railroad's current policy, instead held that the Southern Railroad's table-allotment policy violated the statute. The decision did not generalize about segregated facilities or address itself to the question of segregation per se, although the segregation practice was criticized obliquely: "The curtains, partitions and signs emphasize the artificiality of a difference in treatment which serves only to call attention to a racial classification of passengers." The Court's opinion in this last transportation case decided before the key lower education cases did make some inroads against "separate but equal," and by redefining the doctrine moved in the direction of repudiating it, but because the holding was particularly cautious, especially in view of oral argument, it was therefore a great disappointment to many Negroes and other civil rights advocates.

The public's reaction to *Brown* in 1954, and particularly the wide-spread criticism of the Court's "legislative" action in repudiating the *Plessy* precedent in that case, indicates that while the Court and some commentators might have thought that the transportation cases were important milestones on the way to *Brown,* they were in fact insignificant in the public mind. The cases indicated to "insiders" but not to the public the direction in which the Court was heading. Had the Court overturned the "separate but equal" doctrine in these transportation cases, *Brown* or cases like it would have seemed far less arbitrary. One can only conclude that the Court made a major strategic error in not "biting the bullet" of *Plessy* in a transportation case because the result was that *Plessy* had to be disposed of in the area of elementary school segregation, far more sensitive for those affected by the ruling.

6

Bearing most directly on *Brown,* and coming shortly before it, were cases from the graduate level of higher education. The way in which the Court chipped away further at *Plessy* in these cases is particularly important because the Court had missed its chance in *Morgan* and in *Henderson.* Before taking up those cases, however, we must go back to a pre–World War II case, the first major graduate-level victory, one brought up frequently in the *Brown* argument.

In 1938, the Supreme Court made its first attempt to clarify what was meant by "separation but equal" in higher education. Brought by NAACP Legal Defense Fund lawyers, the *Gaines* case involved a Negro who had been refused admission to the University of Missouri's law school in accordance with the provision of the state constitution for "separate education of the races." Gaines sued in state court for admission to the state law school because no other facilities for a legal education in Missouri had been made available to him. The lower court and the Missouri Supreme Court denied his claim because Missouri law authorized the curators of the state's Negro college to provide out-of-state tuition grants for qualified Negroes or to establish all necessary schools and universities.

On appeal, the United States Supreme Court found that grants for Negroes to attend law schools out-of-state did not create equal facilities, since whites were afforded law schools within the state. Avoiding any larger discussion of the constitutionality of segregated education per se, the Court held that the obligation of the state to assure equal protection of the laws can be performed only within its own jurisdiction—in other words, only where its laws operate. The state was reminded that limited demand for a particular facility by Negroes did not justify or excuse discrimination in favor of whites. The Court did not question the prestige of state schools and out-of-state law schools or discuss Gaines's possible financial loss. Rather, the Court specifically stated that these matters were beside the point, and ruled on an abstract question of what might be called "constitutional geography."

While the decision was clearly a small step in terms of the needs it met and the results it accomplished, it appeared sweeping and theoretical. While the Court noted that the university curators acted as agents of the state under state statute and thus their refusal to admit a Negro to the law school or otherwise to provide for him equal legal training within the boundaries of the state amounted to state action in violation of the Equal Protection Clause, it tactfully emphasized the powers and rights to be provided by the states, rather than the federal prohibition controlling the states. To argue against the propositions of Chief Justice Hughes's opinion in this case, which included all the premises of a states' rights position, would have been to argue for increased federal intervention and control. Unfavorable public opinion was thus skillfully anticipated.

Much as southern spokesmen disliked the result, they saw that they could not question the law. Hence they began immediately to devise ways to comply with it. Unfortunately, the Supreme Court did not order Gaines's admission to the University of Missouri's law school, but showed deference to the state by offering two additional alternatives. Missouri did not choose the first alternative, that of desegregating its state university, nor did it choose the second alternative, that of discontinuing legal education at state institutions for everyone. In a separate opinion which amounted to a dissent, in which he was joined by Justice Butler, Justice McReynolds feared that would happen. The state chose the third option, that of establishing an "adequate" separate law school for Negroes. Although Gaines's attorneys began at once to challenge the adequacy of the new law school, Gaines himself seems to have disappeared mysteriously, and no one else stepped forward to press the case.

Perhaps some discerning Southerners viewed the *Gaines* result as beneficial. The ruling could cost states money in establishing separate but equal facilities for the education of blacks, but the very establishment of these facilities might serve to affirm the reality of the Court's separate-but-equal doctrine, in the sense that their existence would make it difficult for the Court to say that all the separate schools spawned by its decision were unconstitutional from the outset. Lawyers sometimes adopt a similar strategy in neighborhood zoning cases. If it is unclear whether a commercial building such as a high-rise apartment or a factory can be built in a particular area under a local board's zoning regulations, the decision is often made to build it, under the asumption that the zoning board hardly ever will decide to have the nonconforming building forcibly razed.

Gaines thus helped establish the tradition of "overnight graduate schools" for Negroes in the southern states. Under this practice, as soon as Negroes filed suits for admission to white graduate schools "equal" facilities in the desired field of study were set up, virtually overnight, in existing Negro state institutions. Certainly, it would seem, a more effective strategy for the Court would have been to take a slightly bolder step in rendering a decision for Gaines if the case was to be heard at all. For example, the Court could have distinguished those states that had separate graduate facilities for Negroes from those that did not, ordering Gaines's immediate admission to the University of Missouri on the ground that at the time he sued there was no separate law school. Since there were scarcely any graduate schools for Negroes in the South at that time, the Court could have avoided ruling on the "separate but equal" question and the "quality of equality" issues which inevitably arose in the wake of *Gaines.* The Court did not adopt this approach, and the result, history has shown, was even greater separateness and even less equality for Negro graduate and professional students throughout the South.

Ten years later, the first case in *Gaines*'s wake reached the Supreme Court for decision. *Sipuel v. Oklahoma Board of Regents,* another NAACP-directed case, involved a young Negro woman refused admission to the University of Oklahoma Law School, the only law school in the state, solely because of her race. The Oklahoma Supreme Court ruled against her on the ground that the state had not been given sufficient notice to set up a separate Negro law school for her. Amazingly enough, after its long absence from the subject, the United States Supreme Court reached a decision with remarkable speed, over the weekend following argument. In a broad per curiam opinion, the justices announced that not only was Miss Sipuel entitled to secure legal education afforded by a state institution but also that the Fourteenth Amendment did not allow that it be denied her while provided for others; the state must provide for her as soon as it does for applicants of any other group. The Court's speed and its use of a per curiam order can be seen as reinforcing the need for the state to take appropriate action. However, rather than specifically ordering her immediate admission to the law school, the Court merely reversed the state court decision and remanded the case back to it "for proceedings not inconsistent with this opinion," the same directive as in *Gaines.*

The trial court, interpreting the Supreme Court's order after the state supreme court had said she must have an opportunity to study at a state institution, gave the state the choice of enrolling her in the University of Oklahoma Law School, but only until a Negro law school was established equal to the one afforded whites, at which time she could not be enrolled at the university's law school, or of not enrolling any applicant until such a separate school were established. To comply with the requirement of a separate school, the state opened a one-student law school with three faculty members in the state capital building. Because this school was obviously far below the standards for accreditation, Miss Sipuel, by then Mrs. Fisher, applied to the United States Supreme Court for a writ of mandamus to produce greater compliance with the Supreme Court's earlier mandate. In *Fisher v. Hurst,* the Supreme Court said that the only question before it was whether its *Sipuel* mandate had been followed; the question of whether the establishment of a separate Negro law school satisfied the Equal Protection Clause was not at issue. The Court also ruled that the lower court had indeed not departed from its mandate. Rutledge, in a seeming state of bafflement, dissented, saying that the mandate had quite plainly meant, to him at any rate, that Oklahoma should end its discrimination against Ada Sipuel Fisher at once, not at some later time, near or remote, and that the equality required was equality in fact, not in legal fiction. His bafflement is easily understood: the majority was in effect saying that it was not ready to say anything about "quality" in higher education. The Court further seemed to be betraying its intention in the *Gaines* and *Sipuel* decisions, and seemed to be retreating a few steps from its position in *Gaines* ten years before and its short-lived revival in *Sipuel* just months earlier. The Court was giving the southern states time, opportunity, and an abundance of loopholes to postpone the establishment of at least equal law schools in every state.

The Court's vacillation can probably best be understood as a calculated gamble. The southern states had consistently tried to devise ways to evade *Gaines,* but their response demonstrated that they recognized the force of the decision and that, eventually at least, they would have to improve educational opportunities for Negroes. The post-*Gaines* period was thus marked by significant growth in the number of state-supported Negro institutions and by the establishment of Negro graduate schools in most states. Perhaps in light of this modest success, the Court felt a similar pattern of compliance would emerge after *Sipuel.* By the time of *Fisher* the election of 1948 was close at hand; with civil rights a bitter election issue, judicial restraint may have seemed the better part of political valor. At any rate, if the Court had hoped for voluntary compliance and desegregation, it was not completely disappointed. Between 1948 and 1950, a number of graduate and professional schools in Arkansas, Delaware, Kentucky, and Oklahoma had admitted Negroes. The University of West Virginia had admitted Negroes to its graduate and professional schools even before *Gaines.* Thus only a few states remained immutable in their higher education policy by 1950. Quality was still a problem, however, and many separàte, makeshift graduate programs for Negroes still existed in the South.

Finally, in 1950 the Court chose to refine the realities of "separate but equal" in two emphatic cases. The strength of the Court's action in these cases was particularly noticeable because the two most liberal justices present during the *Sipuel* litigation, Frank Murphy and Wiley Rutledge, had died in 1949; their replacements, Republican former Senator Sherman Minton and Democrat Attorney General Tom Clark, were far less liberal. Instead of leading to the retrenchment in the Court's position on desegregation one might have expected, this change in personnel did not affect the forward movement of the law, perhaps an indication of greater ferment within the Court than was visible to outside observers.

The first of the two 1950 cases was *Sweatt v. Painter,* which involved an experience much like Ada Sipuel's. Sweatt, a Negro, applied for admission to the University of Texas Law School and was refused, although there was no Negro law school. The trial court upheld his claim for a legal education, but allowed the state six months to establish a new law school for Negroes. Sweatt, however, refused to enroll in the new separate law school, and took his case through various Texas courts which found the facilities of the separate law schools substantially equal. Advised by NAACP attorneys, Sweatt sought review in the United States Supreme Court, where another NAACP case challenging further discrimination in Oklahoma graduate schools was being taken simultaneously. That case, *McLaurin v. Oklahoma Board of Regents,* brought slightly different questions for review, particularly the issue of segregation after admission. McLaurin had been successful in his suit for admission to the graduate school in education at the University of Oklahoma, but in light of the new admissions situation the state legislature had amended its segregation statutes to provide that Negroes must attend white institutions "upon a segregated basis." Under this statute, McLaurin was forced to sit in a designated place in the classroom, use a special table in the library, and eat at an assigned table in the cafeteria. He was denied relief at the district court level. His appeal to the United States Supreme Court was argued together with that of Sweatt from Texas. These decisions together represented perhaps the most significant step taken by the Court in direct preparation for *Brown* four years later. They are of particular note because the composition of the Court did not change significantly between these cases and the initial argument in *Brown,* nor did any external events of great possible bearing occur in the interim.

The *Sweatt* case, argued second, was clearly the broader of the two cases and was treated as such by the Court.[24] Here, as Thurgood Marshall pointed out in his part of argument for Sweatt, the separate-but-equal issue had been raised from the beginning. Going to the key argument, Marshall argued that even if the state built an exact duplicate of the original law school, "if it is segregated, it is unequal." Marshall pointed out the inconsistency between the state's argument in the lower court that the "basement law school" for Negroes at Austin was better than that at the University of Texas and its building of a new law school for Negroes at Houston after the state won in the lower court. Although he was clearly attacking "separate but equal," Marshall was doing it on a limited basis, asserting he was not talking about the "common schools" or swimming pools but about admitting qualified Negroes to law schools. Yet he argued broadly that education was not a privilege but the foundation of our rights. He pointed out that the fact was shown by the tremendous sums Texas spends for education and the minute control it keeps over education. Only *Plessy* caused problems, he said, because subsequent cases show that racial classifications are improper.

Marshall tried to limit his argument specifically to law schools, but Attorney General Price Daniel of Texas tried to make the issue broader. He said that what was involved was whether the Court was going to overrule its previous decisions in an opinion not limited to graduate schools. It was public policy, Daniel said, that Marshall was asking for. First Assistant Attorney General Joe R. Greenhill concentrated on the Fourteenth Amendment, arguing that integrated schools were not an objective of that amendment. In rebuttal, Marshall made a point which would appear in *Brown I*: either conclusion could be drawn from the history of the amendment but equality in the amendment meant equality in its normal context.

The crux of the *McLaurin* case at argument was that although the railings around McLaurin's seats had been removed he was still seated separately. Robert Carter, arguing for McLaurin, answered Justice Frankfurter's question about equality of education by saying there was no controversy with respect to the quality of education received but only on the point that "the state has set him apart." The racial base of the distinction was even clearer from the fact that Negroes were assigned specific seats, while whites were not. Although most of his argument was devoted to the factual situation, Carter did bring up *Plessy*. He said the case was bad law and didn't apply here because it was a transportation case which did not lay down a general principle. He also noted that the Court had not specifically upheld segregation in the field of education.

Most of the questioning of Oklahoma First Assistant Attorney General Fred Hansen also revolved around the factual situation, whether there were formal regulations and whether they were made known to Negroes. Noting that segregation had pretty much broken down if McLaurin was attending the white school, Minton asked, "There isn't much point to segregation, is there?" Hansen conceded, "Not, possibly, on the graduate level," but argued for the necessity of maintaining separate but equal as a doctrine because of the impact of its removal at other levels of education. Jackson brought the discussion back to the level of education involved in this case, asking, "When segregation breaks down as it has in Oklahoma, what purpose can it serve in this school before us?" Hansen's response was that trouble might have resulted if segregation had not existed, adding that the school officials were thoughtful and good men doing the best they could under difficult conditions.

The Court's decision in *Sweatt,* like that to follow in *McLaurin,* was unanimous and was written by Chief Justice Vinson. Although we now see the case as marking the beginning of the broad reach toward *Brown,* Vinson began with a lengthy discussion of the narrowness with which the decisions were to be regarded. Acknowledging the broader issues urged for the Court's consideration, Vinson restricted the opinion to the application of the Equal Protection Clause to distinctions between students of different races in professional and graduate education. Much of the excellent research and detailed argument presented by counsel was unnecessary to disposition of the cases, he said. Turning to the fact situation, and noting differences in facilities, Vinson said that the Court could not but conclude that the University of Texas Law School was superior in every one of these ways to the law school provided for Negroes. What is more important, he wrote, "the University of Texas Law School possesses to a far greater degree those qualities which are incapable of objective measurement but which make for greatness in a law school," such as faculty reputation, alumni prestige, and community standing. Because law is an intensely practical profession, no one who has practiced law would choose to study in an academic vacuum, removed from the interplay of ideas and exchange of views with which the law is concerned. But the state had put the Negro student in just such a vacuum, away from those with whom he could come in contact as lawyers, witnesses, jurors, judges, and the like. Sweatt's right, Vinson said, was a personal and present one: he was entitled to legal education equivalent to that offered by the state to students of other races. "Such education is not available to him in a separate law school as offered by the State." But as to *Plessy,* Vinson said that the Court need not reach the argument that *Plessy* should be reexamined.

The Court also decided *McLaurin* unanimously, with a brief opinion also written by the Chief Justice. Setting McLaurin apart operated to impair and inhibit his ability to pursue effective graduate study. This impairment was critical because at this level he was trying to obtain training "to become . . . a leader and trainer of others. Those who will come under his guidance and influence must be directly affected by the education he received." To the extent it is unequal the quality of the counseling given to them would suffer. Again limiting his opinion to the situation before him, Vinson said that once a student was admitted to a state-supported graduate school it was a denial of equal protection to give him treatment at the hands of the state different from that received by students of other races. Removal of the restrictions would at least give the student the opportunity to secure acceptance by his fellow students on his own merits. Vinson's opinion appeared to be broad in requiring equal treatment for those admitted, and it had important implications with reference to quality of education, instruction, and psychological environment, given the short period between it and *Brown*. However, the ruling was limited in not expanding desegregation requirements below the graduate level.

Considerable practical distance may have separated graduate and professional education from primary and secondary education, and hesitation to move from one to the other may have existed in NAACP circles, but the Court had taken action which served to raise for that group the possibility of a direct attack on the *Plessy* rule as applied to education and to shift the legal focus concerning desegregation. In the years immediately preceding *Brown,* desegregation of graduate and some undergraduate state universities seemed to be proceeding fairly smoothly. Before *Sweatt,* southern colleges had been able to evade desegregation by continually trying to equalize separate educational facilities. With the introduction in the *Sweatt* case of intangible factors such as social isolation and prestige, however, separate but equal in education became a legal fiction; the old option was closed. The gradual but continual narrowing of the meaning of "equal," begun quite cautiously by the Court many years earlier, had evolved by 1954 to require a state to provide, within its borders, simultaneously, the same courses of study, educational facilities of the same size, quality, and variety, colleges of the same prestige, and faculties of the same reputation, for both whites and Negroes. In addition, inconvenience of location and cost of traveling could be considered, and segregation within an institution was invalid. For all intents and purposes, then, separate but equal schools in higher education were operationally impossible some years before the Court handed down its decision in *Brown*. The decision to hear the latter was made during the ongoing implementation of the former.

Chapter 3

The School Cases: The First Two Rounds

THE early 1950s could not have made civil right advocates particularly optimistic about the chances of making major strides toward equality. To be sure, there had been important changes. More Americans, aware of Hitler's racism, were concerned about the "American dilemma" so effectively portrayed by Gunnar Myrdal[1] and others who were publicizing the problem. There had been a successful if partial integration experience among servicemen, and a number of racial barriers had dropped after World War II, particularly in the North. Minority groups were becoming increasingly politicized.[2] But Congress continued to turn a deaf ear, and the soon-to-be inaugurated Eisenhower administration would be characterized by a president who never in eight years of office uttered a single word in support of desegregation. The courts, generally more accessible to minority groups than the legislatures, provided a somewhat different picture. However, the NAACP had achieved some partial success in the Supreme Court. This encouraged the organization to continue to use litigation as its primary weapon. As Justice Jackson recognized in commenting during the oral arguments in *Brown v. Board of Education,* "I suppose that realistically this case is here for the reason that action couldn't be obtained from Congress."

Civil rights attorneys had begun the task of assembling and marshaling arguments attacking the "separate but equal" doctrine on a variety of grounds. Seeing the signal in *Sweatt* to focus upon the constitutionality of "separate but equal," and further stimulated to act by constituency pressure,[3] the NAACP turned its attention to segregation in the public schools. "Separate but equal" could—and should—have been overturned in its "logical" context—in cases involving segregated transportation facilities. But these cases were resolved by a cautious Court on narrow grounds abounding in legal technicalities of Interstate Commerce Commission regulations and procedures, making it frustrating for the

NAACP to continue to bring cases in the transportation area. Contributors to the NAACP also could not be expected to understand and appreciate the significance of continuing legal battles against "separate but equal" in areas other than that which constituted the most visible and important application of this doctrine—the public school system. As a result, the NAACP changed its attention. The Supreme Court thus soon had thrust upon it the necessity of confronting the doctrinal question of "separate but equal" in perhaps its most sensitive context—that of segregated public school facilities for impressionable grade-school children.

1

What was the Supreme Court to do when it was finally faced with school desegregation cases? There were a number of options, some of which had several variations. The principal options were to avoid the cases, to rule directly on the constitutional question, or to use precedents to reach a less direct constitutional ruling. Some of these alternatives were raised in the course of oral argument. Others were standard modes of operation for the Court. The range of alternatives open to the Court was greater than those presented by the lawyers or raised by the justices in their questioning of the lawyers.

First, avoiding the cases completely was not a viable option, but one should not dismiss too quickly the possibility of the Court's doing so. Although the Court might not have been able to avoid the area of lower education for very long, it probably could have avoided it longer than it did by continuing to refuse cases. The mere fact that the school cases were being adjudicated below did not compel the Court to handle the problem. Even had the Court waited only until 1954, when it handed down the first *Brown* opinion, to accept cases, there would have been more time for action in the South on which the Court could have drawn in order to frame a better opinion. *Sweatt* would have had more time to "sink in," and there would have been more opportunities for Negro plaintiffs to take *Sweatt*-based complaints to the southern courts and possibly win them. The courts from which the School Cases were brought did not go as far as *Sweatt,* but equalization orders were entered in two instances, and important judicial concessions were made in the others; with more time, other courts might have gone as far as *Sweatt.* Certainly, the application of *Plessy* to less-than-equal facilities for Negroes would have continued in the interim and would have resulted in further equalization of school facilities. As Anthony Lewis has pointed out, it "was only when the trend of Supreme Court opinions beginning in the 1930s and 1940s made it clear that the legal basis of segregation was threatened that the South began spending those vast sums on Negro education that we hear so much about."[4] Although the Negroes were certainly seeking more than education in their quest for equality, such school-building and -equalizing activity would have placed them in at least a temporarily better stead; such equalizing, we must remember, did not continue after *Brown*.

Use of a strategy of avoidance would not have been without great costs. Negro children would have been left in segregated schools, in most instances in the existing facilities. Even if the possibility of longer-term social justice were to be increased by the Court's waiting, individual justice for those children would not have been served. More than that, continuing to deny certiorari to lower court decisions which continued to affirm segregation in education was dangerous because, despite official claims to the contrary, such actions could be interpreted as supporting those decisions. Furthermore, not to intervene in lower education before *Sweatt* was one thing, but it was quite another to avoid cases afterward, particularly if the constitutional question were squarely presented. Once the important step of considering intangibles had been taken, the Court's refusal to deal with the larger problem would have been severely criticized. In short, the Court seemed to have been "overtaken by events," here of its own making. Yet a variety of alternatives was available once a case challenging school desegregation was accepted; accepting the cases did not dictate a particular result or a particular way of reaching that result.

The second option, at the opposite pole from avoiding the cases, was to reach the issue of whether segregated schools offended either the Equal Protection Clause of the Fourteenth Amendment or a more abstract concept of equality. Drawing on the language of the Japanese relocation cases[5] and on the white primary cases, the Court could have suggested that racial classifications were immediately suspect, thus shifting the burden to the states to defend their use. Going further, the Court could have invalidated the whole scheme of school desegregation as based on prejudice. Still other grounds for ruling on the constitutional question were asserting the right to equal treatment as a national right deserving of national protection under the Fourteenth Amendment[6] and use of the Thirteenth Amendment, according to which school segregation might have been considered a "badge of slavery." One must be careful not to assume that reaching the constitutional issue would have required the Court to invalidate segregation. The Court could have held that segregation was constitutionally allowable although the international political climate, including the presence of the United Nations Covenant on Human Rights,[7] might have made such a ruling totally unpalatable politically. Segregation could have been held to be completely within the power of the states, which could require, authorize, allow, or prohibit it as they saw fit. Such a holding, like that urged by the dissenters with respect to the death penalty in 1972,[8] would have been consonant with the deference due the states in our federal system, as well as with the "self-restrained" role some envision for the Supreme Court in our democratic political system. Another option, which would have allowed the Court to decide the cases while avoiding having to deal frontally with the segregation issue, would have been for the Court to turn to Congress for a statement, holding that segregation was allowable until Congress made a specific pronouncement under its power to implement the first four sections of the Fourteenth Amendment as given in Section 5 of that amendment. This option would have required at least a determination that the framers of the amendment did not intend to preclude Congress from dealing with education, but this would have had the advantage of being more limited than a finding that the amendment's framers intended directly to prohibit or allow segregation in education.

A third general option would have been for the Court to avoid direct interpretation of the Constitution through use of precedents. Such use certainly would have had constitutional implications, since constitutional issues had been raised in the earlier cases. Whatever meaning the Court gave to the precedents would be read by the Court's audience into the Constitution itself. However, the "checkered" nature of the precedents posed serious problems. While some of the immediately post–Civil War cases could be used in the Negroes' favor, as could more recent cases (*Gaines* and those following), the *Plessy* generation of cases stood in the way, and they were likely to be used against efforts to extend the *Sweatt* ruling to lower education. Yet the precedents themselves provided the Court with several options. Use of *Sweatt* and *McLaurin* might have allowed the Court to avoid *Plessy*. Despite argument which could be expected over whether it was explicitly considered in the recent cases, *Plessy* would not have to be confronted directly, allowing a decision building incrementally on cases only a few years old. However, we must remember that use of *Sweatt* and *McLaurin* would not have necessarily dictated a pro-desegregation decision if graduate and higher education were differentiated from lower education and if the Court stressed the compulsory nature of the latter and the need to reinforce parents' views. If *Plessy* could not be avoided, it could be explicitly overruled. This was perhaps the Court's most extreme possibility. Had the Court decided no case in the school area for many years, perhaps the issue could have been disposed of sub silentio. That option obviously was foreclosed by the presence of *Sweatt* and *McLaurin*. Or the issue could have been distinguished by confining it to railroad transportation, thus negating the claim that the Court had refused to review *Plessy* in deciding *Sweatt*. At the very least, the Court could have affirmed *Plessy* as applied to lower education, perhaps at the same time demanding real equality of facilities—that is, "qualitative" as well as quantitative equality, returning the cases to the lower courts for

fact-finding as to equality of facilities in each case, and ordering immediate equalization when disparities were found. Despite already-noted
moves toward equalization in the South, this strategy would have achieved
dramatically different results.

2

We now turn to the question of how the School Cases of 1954 came to
the Court. Just before those cases arrived, the Court avoided another
opportunity to deal with "separate but equal" in lower education. The
1951 *Bagsby* case involved a suit by Negro taxpayers in a district where the
Negro elementary school had been gradually abolished. The school authorities had sent the Negro students from the district to adjoining Dallas
by bus, leading to complaints from the Negro parents about the greater
distance their children had to travel. When they brought suit for mandamus to get the school officials to maintain the local school as a full
elementary school and to provide equal educational facilities within the
school district, the lower court agreed to issue the writ, but a state appeals
court reversed, stating it found no evidence of prejudice by the school
officials. Perhaps because it presented a straight "separate but equal" case
too frontally, the Supreme Court refused to take it.

In the 1952 Term of Court, what was to become the original school
desegregation case, *Briggs v. Elliott,* was appealed to the Court. Piloted by
the NAACP legal staff, it was an attack on South Carolina constitutional
and statutory provisions requiring separate schools for children of the
white and colored races. A three-judge federal district court had found
that the physical facilities of the separate schools in Clarendon County
were not equal according to the test set up in the early higher education
cases, and ordered the school authorities to proceed at once to improve
the Negro schools and to report within six months as to what action had
been taken. Judge Parker, for himself and Judge Timmerman, held *Plessy*
directly applicable to lower education, and was unwilling to set it aside on
the basis of limited testimony by experts. He felt that "if public education
is to have the support of the people through their legislature, it must not
go contrary to what they deem for the best interests of their children," and
he urged that the question of desegregation's producing better schools or
simply more racial tension was a matter "not . . . of constitutional right
but of legislative policy." In what turned out to be a courageous dissent,
because he was hounded from the bench and left the state, Judge Waring
drew a clear distinction between railroads and education and also sharply
attacked the racial prejudice which gave rise to segregated schools While
the arguments of Judges Parker and Waring did not constitute the full

range of possible positions, they presented the Court with the first of several options to be provided before the issue was finally decided.

As should be expected, the Supreme Court approached this early case with extreme caution. The case was not given a full hearing which would have enabled the Court to adjudge the larger questions urged before it. Instead, the Court ruled per curiam that the judgment below should be vacated and the case remanded so that the district court might consider the equalization report—which in the meantime had been filed with the court by the school authorities as requested—and take appropriate action. Black and Douglas, in dissent, said that the Court erred in supporting further adjudication along "separate but equal" lines and should instead consider the constitutional questions raised before it by the appeal. The dissent served as a strategic tip-off as to the direction the Court as a whole might take if Black and Douglas could exert leadership. Also notable was the fact that most of the preceding important full segregation decisions had been unanimous. Thus a very small incremental step was taken by the majority, indicating that equal separate facilities should be provided for Negro public school children. The vocal minority gave hope that further challenges would not be completely ignored. When the lower court, on remand, ruled once again only that school authorities should make every effort to equalize facilities, finding from the authorities' plan that such would probably be done by September 1952, the case was again appealed to the Supreme Court on the larger constitutional questions.

Fortunately from the viewpoint of the Court's desire not to be limited by two sides of a single case, other elementary school cases were also available for discretionary review. A Kansas case, *Brown v. Board of Education,* had been initiated by Negro residents of Topeka in protest against the Topeka school board's policy of segregating the race in its sixth-grade elementary schools under a statute authorizing, not requiring, segregation in the elementary schools in cities of the first class (over fifteen thousand) and in the high schools of Kansas City.[9] The complaint contended that the state statute deprived Negro children of equal educational opportunities in violation of the Fourteenth Amendment. The three-judge federal district court which heard the case found that there was no material difference in the physical facilities of the Negro and white schools, that identical courses of study were offered, and that the teachers were equally qualified and therefore rejected the Negroes' plea for an injunction against enforcement of the statute. The district court, however, declared a finding of one difference—that segregation in and of itself created a sense of inferiority in Negro children which affected their motivation to learn and that therefore segregation with the sanction of law had a tendency to retard the educational and mental development of

Negro children. The district court's finding was significant in that it was a determination of fact by a trial court and not a mere legal argument introduced at an appellate level. Feeling bound to follow *Plessy,* however, the court decided that this inequality of opportunity was not a violation of the Fourteenth Amendment. With this background, the case came to the Supreme Court.[10] While Kansas had defended its statute in the lower courts, its posture before the Supreme Court was different. No brief was filed or appearance entered by either the state or by the school board, and the school board's counsel had indicated that the board would not appear at oral argument or file a brief. Although Justice Black was apparently uneasy about such action,[11] the Supreme Court issued an intermediate order requesting that the state present its views at oral argument through the attorney general or otherwise indicate whether such a default constituted a concession of the invalidity of the statute.

The Court, only shortly before, had engaged in some docket-management with regard to the school desegregation cases. With *Brown* and *Briggs* already docketed, the Court was faced with a request to hear the *Davis* case from Prince Edward County, a county with a population of approximately fifteen thousand persons, half of whom were Negro, in south-central Virginia, whose state constitution required school segregation. A federal district court in March 1952 had rejected Negro plaintiffs' claim that segregation in and of itself was invalid, although it did find that the facilities for Negroes in the county were inferior to those for whites and had ordered the school officials to proceed with diligence to correct this inequality. Accordingly, a new Negro high school which had already been planned was ordered completed with all possible speed and was expected to be ready for use by September 1953. In noting probable jurisdiction in *Davis* on June 8, 1952, the Court, over Justice Douglas's objection, simultaneously continued *Briggs* and *Brown* so that they could be heard together as requested by appellees in the three cases. But that was not all. The Court "reached out" to take the District of Columbia case, *Bolling v. Sharpe*, involving issues generally similar to the other cases, with segregation in the public schools being challenged by Negro petitioners whose complaint had been dismissed without even the appointment of a three-judge court. With the *Bolling* case pending in the Court of Appeals, the Supreme Court took the strategic initiative of inviting the filing of certiorari petitions in that case so that it could be heard with the others. Certiorari was then granted on November 10, 1952.

Continuation of *Briggs* and *Brown* seems to have been a play for time because of the complication caused by the distinction between the Fourteenth Amendment, on which the state cases were based, and the Fifth Amendment, at the heart of the District of Columbia case. By adding *Bolling,* the Court was taking on another legal hurdle—that of doctrinally

assimilating the Equal Protection Clause of the Fourteenth Amendment
to the Due Process Clause of the Fifth, which in terms was applicable to the
federal government. Some observers believed this made the barriers to a
legal resolution of the separate-but-equal question even more formidable.
Others, however, were heartened by reasoning that surely the Court
could not eventually come up with one result for the states and a different
result for the federal school system in Washington, D.C. Therefore, by
taking on *Bolling* the Court might be indicating that its intention was to
confront the issue head-on and across-the-board. As Ulmer put it, the
effect of combining the cases was to underscore the Court's concern with
school segregation "as a social rather than a legal problem."[12] Grouping
the cases focused particular attention on the subject's broad policy implications and provided a cross section of situations, thus assuring the
justices that what was before them was not unique.[13]

The last case, *Gebhart v. Belton,* was from Delaware. It was added after
the others were set for December 1952 argument, with the certiorari
petition filed on November 13 and granted on November 24. Because of
the pressure of time, briefs were not required in this case until three weeks
after argument. Also, the case differed from the others in being an appeal
by state authorities from a decree in favor of Negro plaintiffs. Delaware's
supreme court had upheld a lower court's finding that the separate school
facilities for Negroes in New Castle County were inferior to those provided for white children, and on that basis ordered the immediate admission of the Negro plaintiffs into the white schools. As in *Brown,* the claim
that segregation was harmful to Negro children was found valid but was
held to be legally irrelevant. Chancellor Seitz felt that it was up to the
Supreme Court to say that his findings of fact should control the case,
because by allowing "separate but equal" in *Gong Lum* the high court had
accepted the doctrine in a constitutional sense in lower education. Thus
Gebhart not only completed the set of five cases but served to tie them
together in another way. The lower court decisions in *Briggs* and *Davis*
had been decided before the Delaware case had been considered. Chancellor Seitz thought that he had reached a conclusion similar to that of the
Briggs and *Davis* courts in saying that segregation in education was not
inequality in a constitutional sense. However, Chief Justice Southerland
of the Delaware Supreme Court explicitly rejected, as not reconcilable
with Supreme Court decisions, the approach of granting only gradual
relief, despite citation by the Delaware attorney general of such relief in
Davis and *Briggs.*

This grouping of cases, something which the Court has from the
beginning asserted its power to do as it deems appropriate as an out-
growth of its strategic control of its docket, has definite implications for
oral argument. Seeing the cases together and recognizing the NAACP's

involvement in all of them might lead us to overestimate one side's unity of approach. Each case had similarities to the others and we find some arguments repeated from one case to another. There was a central issue, as noted by T. Justin Moore, arguing for Virginia: "There is, of course, one main stream which runs through all of the cases and . . . that is the real question . . ., to test finally, if possible, the issue as to whether the mere fact of segregation by law is a denial of equal protection."[14] But the factors which differentiate the cases cannot be ignored. These include the statutes. In the state cases, some statutes made segregation mandatory while others merely permitted it; there were also differences in local autonomy which could affect implementation of a court order. The District of Columbia case involved both statutory and constitutional bases different from the state cases. Variations in lower court rulings, both as to findings and result, further differentiated the cases. As Spottswood Robinson pointed out, his Virginia case involved refusal of an injunction against continuance of segregation after a finding of inequality of facilities, while the Delaware case reached the opposite conclusion from the same finding. In Kansas there were equal facilities and a finding of injury from segregation, whereas in Virginia there had been a finding of unequal facilities and no finding of harm from segregation.[15]

Perhaps what brings the greatest differentiation in a set of cases is the attempt by each attorney to distinguish his case from others in the set, seeming to take what he can get in the service of his client. For example, Jack Greenberg conceded in the Delaware case, the most favorable to the Negroes below in terms of immediate remedy, that a finding of unequal educational opportunity in one place might not mean the same finding elsewhere. Lawyers are trained to engage in such differentiation, just as they are trained to raise multiple claims even when the claims may seem to the uninitiated to be logically incompatible.[16] However, each element of a lawyer's argument can be viewed as part of a strategy; he tries to appeal to various strains of thought, both legal and more broadly political, in the judge's mind and to provide a hook on which the judge can hang his views. Greenberg's statement, "We are urging all the reasons we can for affirmance of the judgment below," is an indication of this behavior. While such differentiation is at the heart of the lawyer's strategy, the ultimate advantage lies with the Court, which need not accept a party's desire not to have his case lumped together with others. While multifaceted arguments in a single case can provide the Court much freedom of movement, the strategy of grouping the cases allows the justices to see the overriding issue through the thicket of particularistic concerns lawyers might raise, and the lawyers simply have to make the best of the situation.

It would seem that the Court, in consolidating for argument so many diverse cases, was looking either for some approach to the desegregation problem short of deciding that separate but equal was unconstitutional, or was trying to ensure that all arguments could be heard before making an enormously significant constitutional decision. But *Briggs* alone could have served the latter purpose—the Court could have invited amicus briefs to get all the arguments. Perhaps the Court did not have a clear sense of its strategy, and consolidating diverse cases was simply the easiest solution as some justices undoubtedly preferred certain cases while their colleagues preferred to hear other cases. Deciding to hear all of them provided the common ground on which to resolve the bargaining. Whatever the internal strategy explanation, the result was that the Court painted itself into a very conspicuous corner in consolidating five lower court cases for argument on the issue of racial separation in elementary education.

3

At the initial round of oral argument, *Brown* was the first case to be heard. Robert Carter, arguing for the Negro appellants, divided his constitutional argument into two separate contentions: first, that the Fourteenth Amendment outlawed any classification based solely on race or color, and, second, that a segregated school system denied the equality of opportunity guaranteed by the Fourteenth Amendment. Given the later outcry about the "sociological" emphasis of the decisions, it is important to note that it was the first of these two arguments which was stressed. However, Carter did call special attention to the expert testimony presented below on the effects of segregation upon the personality and mental attitudes of Negro children and the district court's finding that segregation deprived Negro children "of some of the benefits they would receive in a racially integrated school system." He maintained that the lower court felt that the *Sweatt* and *McLaurin* decisions applied here but felt bound by *Plessy* and *Gong Lum* to uphold segregation. Giving the Court the broadest opportunity for the narrowest of rulings still in favor of his position, Carter argued that *Plessy* merely upheld segregation in public transportation on the basis of evidence that no inequality resulted, thus not precluding the presentation of evidence showing that segregation will in fact create inequality of opportunity requiring its abolition in the public schools.[17] Carter also stated his willingness to face the full issue of the constitutionality of "separate but equal." Apparently sensing that the Court's mind was receptive to a broader-based constitutional appeal, in his final statement he placed the broader argument ahead of his narrower *McLaurin-Sweatt* approach, claiming that the Court did not even have to deal with the lower court's finding of fact because of his clients' position that the racial classification was unconstitutional by definition.

Kansas Assistant Attorney General Paul E. Wilson further tried to force the issue that *Plessy* was "absolutely controlling." Wilson found no statement in either *Sweatt* or *McLaurin* indicating the Court's intent to reverse or modify earlier decisions. Thus, he said, any Court decision against school segregation would "necessarily overrule" *Plessy*. Furthermore, he claimed that such a decision would amount to a ruling that the legislatures of the seventeen states with compulsory segregation and the four states with permissive segregation, the Congress of the United States, and dozens of appellate courts had been wrong for a period of seventy-five years.

Appearing for the Negro appellants in *Briggs*, Thurgood Marshall contended that this case was basically another attack on a classification statute, but he paid particular attention to the term "equal protection of the laws." He tried to make clear that he was not basing his case on "equality," because "most of the cases in the past have gone off on the point of whether or not you have substantial equality. It is a type of provision that, we think, tends to get us into trouble." His "equal protection" argument was based on *McLaurin* and *Sweatt*, where, he said, the Court held that the only question to be decided was whether or not the action of the state in maintaining segregation was denying the students equal protection of the laws. "Of course," he said, "those decisions were limited to the graduate and professional schools. But we took the position that the rationale, if you please, or the principle, to be stronger, set out in those cases would apply just as well down the line provided evidence could be introduced which would show the same type of injury." He also said that, if because of the weight of *Plessy* he could not win a *Sweatt*-based argument, other racial discrimination cases, including the white primary cases, would support his position. Marshall also argued that segregation in the schools was no more ingrained than the segregated transportation which had been upset in *Morgan*. That Marshall had been engaged in a multipronged attack, using arguments of different breadth, was clear from his statement:

I was trying to make three different points. I said that the first one was peculiarly narrow, under the McLaurin and Sweatt decisions. The second point was that on a classification basis, these statutes were bad. The third point was the broader point, that racial distinctions in and of themselves are invidious. I consider it as a three-pronged attack. Any one of the three would be sufficient for reversal.

John W. Davis, who had argued more cases before the Supreme Court than any other attorney, presented the case for South Carolina. He insisted that if the appellants' construction of the Fourteenth Amendment should prevail, a state would have no further right to segregate its pupils on the ground of sex, age, or mental capacity. Davis then asserted that the district court's decree requiring equalization of facilities had been fully complied with; all the construction and improvements promised the district court had been completed by September 1952. The district court had specifically found in its ruling prior to that date, he observed, that these contemplated improvements would make the separate school systems substantially equal. Moving next to a defense of the state's segregation requirement, Davis called attention to numerous instances of legislative and judicial interpretation supporting the contention that the Fourteenth Amendment had never outlawed segregation of the races. Davis stated that it was inconceivable that the Congress which submitted the Fourteenth Amendment would have forbidden the states to employ an educational scheme Congress itself persistently employed in the District of Columbia. In view of that fact, and in view of the Court's decisions, he said, "It is a little late to argue that the question is still at large." Davis also attacked the testimony of plaintiff's expert witnesses, criticizing their competence concerning southern segregation and the relevance of their information:

Not a one of them is under any official duty in the premises whatever; not a one of them has had to consider the welfare of the people for whom they are legislating or whose rights they were called to adjudicate. And only one of them professes to have the slightest knowledge of conditions in the states where separate schools are now being maintained. Only one of them professes any knowledge of the condition within the seventeen segregating states.

He then extended his attack to social science generally: "It seems to me that much of that which is handed around under the name of social science is an effort on the part of the scientist to rationalize his own preconceptions. They find usually, in my limited observation, what they go out to find."

Spottswood W. Robinson III argued for the Negroes in *Davis,* claiming that the district court's findings of inequality gave them an immediate right to admission to the white school, since their right to equal facilities is "personal and present" according to the higher education cases. A permanent remedy cannot be afforded the Negro children unless segregation is finally abolished, he insisted. Otherwise, the Negro children would be faced with the prospect of coming into court every time the facilities became unequal. If the Negro children were to be admitted to white schools merely until the Negro facilities were brought up to par they would be shunted back and forth between the two school systems. But Robinson, careful not to entangle himself, also said that such a pronouncement was not necessary for the Court to achieve the result he wanted. He also said, in response to a question from Justice Douglas, that the Court had not held that the Fourteenth Amendment required congressional action before it could be put into effect—although there were cases in which such pronouncements had already been made. The Court, he urged, had the power to make the pronouncement on its own. In a further argument, paralleling Marshall's statement about the duration of segregated transportation, Robinson stated, "The duration of the particular practice has not been considered by this Court in the past to prevent reexamination of the problem," and pointed out that the long existence of graduate/law school segregation which "had become a part of the community life, did not, in the judgment of the Court, establish its validity."

T. Justin Moore, Jr., who presented the argument for the county school board, expounded the position that Virginia's segregated school system was not based on prejudice or caprice but upon a "way of life" and pointed out the pertinent fact that about 70 percent of the nation's Negro population was concentrated in the seventeen states which had compulsory segregation in the public schools. Moore called the Court's attention to the fact that in his case, unlike those from Kansas and South Carolina, there was a considerable body of testimony to the effect that equality of opportunity could be provided in a segregated school system. Expert witnesses had testified for his side but, Moore also argued, plaintiffs' expert witnesses had been ineffective: "I say you might as well be asking people whether it is desirable for everybody to live according to the Sermon on the Mount as to ask them the kind of questions that they had put to them." He also suggested that the Appendix to Plaintiffs' Brief submitted by a number of social scientists was "just an effort . . . to try to rehabilitate those gentlemen [who testified in the case] and add to it with some other persons."

Attorney General J. Lindsay Almond, Jr., presented further argument for Virginia in defense of her compulsory school segregation laws. Almond admitted that in the past Virginia had been "grossly neglectful of our responsibility to bring about equal facilities for the Negro," but said that the people of the state had come to feel a moral obligation to afford equal facilities and that a vast program had been initiated to accomplish that goal in the field of public education. A decision by the Court against segregation, he said, would make it impossible to raise public funds in the state through taxation and therefore would "destroy the public school system in Virginia as we know it today" and "stop this march of progress, this onward step."

Adding to the complexity was the Washington, D.C., case, argued next. The Negroes' attorney, George E. C. Hayes, pointed out to the Court that his case did not involve the sensitive area of conflict between

federal and state legislation. More important, there was no authority for
segregation in the District's public schools, Congress not having specifically required or authorized segregation.[18] Hayes admitted that Congress
had in many enactments indicated the belief or assumption that separate
schools might be maintained in the District and certainly had recognized
their existence through appropriations measures for those schools since
the mid-nineteenth century. But, Hayes asserted, Congress had segregated schools in the District both to give the Negroes something and as a
political, expedient act to enable Congress to concentrate on the Civil War
amendments. Intentional racism was not involved. Hayes also offered a
more frontal attack. If the Court were to find that segregation has been
authorized or compelled by Congress, he argued, it should rule that such
authorization 1) violates the Fifth Amendment's Due Process Clause, 2)
violates the public policy of the United States as declared in the United
Nations Charter, and 3) constitutes a bill of attainder by arbitrarily imposing punishment without trial on the basis of past acts.

On behalf of the District of Columbia, Milton D. Korman argued that
Congress had given specific statutory recognition to the existence of
segregated schools. The real purpose of Congress's enactments setting up
a separate school system for Negroes was, he said, to "aid in the elevation
of the colored population of the District and not to stamp them with a
badge of inferiority." He also attempted to refute the argument that
segregation had not been authorized in the District and said that his
opponent was an excellent example of the high quality of the work turned
out by the District's Negro schools.

The last case to be argued was from Delaware. Attorney General H.
Albert Young contended that plans for school improvements which
would equalize the Negro facilities were completed. He tried to argue that
the chancellor's finding that segregation in and of itself creates inequalities was not before the Supreme Court because it had not been
reviewed below. He also tried to force the Supreme Court to decide the
constitutional question by insisting that both the chancellor and the state
supreme court had based their rulings on the Fourteenth Amendment,
not equity discretion. On behalf of the Negroes, Louis L. Redding insisted
that racism was the only basis for the state's segregation statutes. He
pointed out that Delaware had never ratified the Fourteenth Amendment, but instead had issued a resolution stating that the amendment
"would be an attempt to establish an equality not sanctioned by the laws of
nature or of God."[19]

The concerns shown by the justices in their questions and statements
from the bench can be divided into several major categories: the meaning
of Supreme Court cases and of the lower court rulings in the cases before
them, constitutional issues, the interpretation of statutes, factual matters,

and problems of implementation. In examining their questions and statements, we must remember that the justices do not ask questions with the same frequency. Justice Frankfurter was the most frequent questioner, while Justice Douglas, so well known for the outspoken nature of his written opinions, asked few questions. Nor did the lawyers receive equal numbers of questions from the justices. Some of the attorneys made their presentations virtually uninterrupted, while others—for example, George Hayes in the District of Columbia case—seemed to be bombarded with inquiries. Such questioning made delivery of a coherent position difficult, but in Hayes's case the questioning no doubt resulted from his own initial lack of clarity—which led Justice Frankfurter to make a better summary of his argument than he himself made and to put to Hayes's co-counsel, James Nabrit, the same questions he had already asked of Hayes.[20] A notable difference in the rates at which questions were asked of the two sides in a case came in *Briggs,* where Marshall was interrupted by questions or comments 127 times while John Davis was interrupted only 11 times. Among the reasons for this difference were the greater clarity of Davis's statements—Marshall used what Chief Justice Vinson once called an "oral shorthand"—and Marshall's attitude to the questions the justices asked him. He seemed to invite more questions; Davis's attitude discouraged questioning.[21]

In this first round of argument in the School Cases, some of the judges almost immediately showed concern with the meaning of the Court's own past decisions, both individually and collectively. This was a crucial matter if the Court were to use precedent in its ruling. Thus, Robert Carter was met quickly with questions as to whether the *Gong Lum* case involved the basic segregation issue because of the petitioners' concession there of the validity of segregated schools. Frankfurter's concern in effect was whether one could attack *Gong Lum* when "liberal" justices on the Court at the time, like Brandeis, had not raised the issue. Frankfurter also wanted to know whether the "separate but equal" test was involved in *Sweatt* and *McLaurin,* and Reed inquired whether it was involved in *Gaines.* Vinson wanted to know the meaning of Justice Harlan's *Plessy* education references, and Frankfurter went back even further to ask about the meaning of the *Roberts* Massachusetts school segregation case. Turning away from individual cases and conceding that the question of segregation in primary grades had not been specifically adjudicated previously, Frankfurter wondered whether "separate but equal" had not been written into the law in a long series of decisions, thus giving it even more strength. One of the most crucial issues to be raised concerning past cases, seen in a question by Justice Burton, was whether they might have been "overtaken by time"—that is, whether changing social and economic circumstances might lead to a different meaning for "separate but equal" than the Court might have attached to it earlier. Were this so, Burton and his colleagues would have a way of eliminating school segregation without having to overturn precedent or "saying that these courts of appeals and state supreme courts have been wrong for seventy-five years."

With respect to the lower court decisions currently before them, the justices had questions about the opinions in those cases. Vinson wanted to know the meaning of "equality of rights" supposedly preserved to plaintiffs by Judge Parker's decision, and both Justices Frankfurter and Black wanted to know whether the chancellor's finding of inequality resulting from segregation had "survived" the ruling of the Delaware Supreme Court, which had not dealt specifically with it.[22] However, the justices' primary concern with the lower court cases was the reach and validity of the findings, which might allow a decision short of the constitutional question. Chief Justice Vinson wanted to know whether more than physical facilities were involved, and Justice Black, concerned about the effect of findings of fact adverse to the Negroes, asked several times whether the findings applied only to a particular case. When Carter stated that a segregated school system cannot afford educational opportunities "equal in law," Black asked what he would say if another court found strictly to the contrary. When Carter replied that the Supreme Court would reexamine the findings and reach its own conclusions, Black then asked, "Do you think there should be a different holding according to the place where the segregation might occur?" He also inquired whether Carter would have the holding depend on the finding of fact. When he pressed Carter about the breadth of the lower court finding in *Brown,* Carter responded, "I think I agree that the finding refers to Kansas and to these appellants and to Topeka."

Closely related was Justice Reed's question of a trial court's accepting plaintiffs' experts' testimony about injury to Negro children, raised with Moore in the *Davis* case. Here Frankfurter was interested in what to do about competing expert testimony, on which he questioned Marshall. He also asked whether the Court could take judicial notice of authors' writing even when the authors were not called as witnesses. This question perhaps presaged the famed "footnote number 11" with its references to Myrdal and others. In general, Frankfurter made quite clear that he didn't think much of social science materials. As he stated to Greenberg: "The mere fact that a man is not contradicted does not mean that what he says is so. . . . If a man says three yards, and I have measured it, and it is three yards, there it is. But if a man tells you about the inside of your brain and mine, and how we function, that is not a measurement, and there you are. . . . We are here in a domain which I do not yet regard as science in the sense of mathematical certainty. This is all opinion evidence," Certainly he gave the materials a back seat to constitutional arguments.

Wanting to know whether the answer to the question was in the Constitution, he asserted, "If it is written into the Constitution, then I do not care about the evidence. . . . If that is a settled constitutional doctrine, then I do not care what any associate or full professor in sociology tells me."

Another set of the Court's concerns was constitutional, including such matters as the Fourteenth Amendment's meaning, the applicability of various constitutional provisions, the validity of racial classifications, and the basic question of whether "separate but equal" must be faced. As to the "separate but equal" matter, Frankfurter kept pressing Carter on how to decide a case involving equal facilities without reaching "separate but equal." Although this seems to suggest that Frankfurter thought the doctrine unavoidable, in a remark in *Davis* he said that when inequality was present the Court would not "borrow trouble" by deciding the larger issue. And although there was general agreement that the Equal Protection Clause was the one on which four of the cases were based, there was some concern about whether other constitutional provisions could be used and about the relationship between the Fifth and Fourteenth Amendments, with Reed querying both Carter and Robinson about the possible use of the Due Process Clause. Here Carter saw no real distinction between equal protection and due process. The meaning of the Fourteenth Amendment's provisions clearly troubled members of the Court. This is shown by Frankfurter's questions at this round of argument and by the Court's questions in its subsequent order. Directly presaging the first question in that order, Frankfurter wanted to know how one would find out the reach of the amendment's protections. At another time, he asked Marshall whether the prohibition on race as a basis for classification could be found in the Constitution. That he found the matter far from clear is shown in his remark, "We would not be arguing for ten hours if it is clear that this is a violation [of the Constitution]. We do not argue for ten hours a question that is self-evident." Looking ahead to the possible scope of a ruling on school desegregation, Frankfurter also asked whether any legislation based on color, including that dealing with miscegenation, would be invalid. Foreshadowing the Court's avoidance of the miscegenation issue, Frankfurter stated his concern, "I do not want to have trouble tomorrow or the day after tomorrow, but one has to look ahead these days."

It would seem that although the Court was explicitly asking about the force of other precedents and the verbal meaning of the Constitution, the guiding reasons offered to—and accepted by—the Court for making distinctions in the prior cases or adding a meaning to the Constitution were themselves rooted in normative perceptions of public policy. This interest was evident in questions about the basis of state segregation statutes—for example, when Justice Minton asked Carter whether the only basis for classifying the children in Kansas was color—and in questions about congressional action, past and future. For example, the justices wondered what would be the effect if, under Section 5 of the Fourteenth Amendment, Congress were to say that segregation was contrary to national policy. Justice Jackson, who also asked whether the amendment would be sufficient to accomplish desegregation, asked such a question of Moore, who claimed that such a statute would be unconstitutional and that a constitutional amendment would be the only constitutionally acceptable congressional action. When Moore also tried to avoid an answer by saying that a case coming to the Supreme Court after such a pronouncement would be a different case from the one he was arguing, Frankfurter remarked, "That is a good answer." Reed seemed to feel that a congressional pronouncement would not help, saying, "But if segregation is not a denial of equal protection of due process, legislation by Congress could do nothing more except to express Congressional views," an indication that the Court's determination of constitutionality would still be necessary. The meaning of congressional action naturally arose in *Bolling,* where the justices asked about such matters as whether Congress had intended to harm Negroes when it put them in separate schools, what the implications were of legal recognition of a separate assistant superintendent for colored schools, and whether the District of Columbia School Board was compelled to segregate or only authorized to do so. Although focused on the District, such questions had broader implications because of the light they might shed on the Fourteenth Amendment.

In its questions on the state segregation statutes, the Court revealed an explicit concern with the kind of policy that would be desirable for the country. Finding it hard to get Carter to understand that more than "race" could be involved, Frankfurter wanted to know whether matters like willfulness and inhumanity might be behind the Kansas statute. A somewhat different concern he had was whether the "sociological facts" behind the legislation, including the concentration of Negroes in some states, could be ignored. Justice Reed asked whether the South Carolina legislation was intended to avoid racial friction. He was concerned as to whether the legislature had determined that segregation was the best policy, "the greatest good for the greatest number," foreshadowing possible deference to the legislatures. Similar legislative deference could be seen in Frankfurter's bringing in the case in which the Court had sustained a Louisiana statute restricting the occupation of river pilot to first sons of pilots and in his remark that one had to look at the legislature's determination in light of the problem's history.[23]

What could be called "factual" questions covered much ground. Some questions had to do with the effects of segregation on a child's ability to learn, raised by Burton and Reed with Burton asking if the educational process involved more than books. Other questions concerned the number and location of blacks and where they went to school, where Indians went to school, and population shifts and overcrowding. School facilities seemed to be of particular concern to the Chief Justice, who asked about the status of building and improvement programs and new facilities, as well as about the extent of segregation beyond transportation. Still other questions were historical, relating either to the history of a situation in a particular state or to whether schools had been segregated in the District of Columbia prior to the Civil War. These factual questions probably went most to the clarifying function of oral argument, while the others were more directly related to strategic concerns like the possible basis of a decision.

The matter of implementation is the most obviously strategic concern of the justices. In practice, concerns about implementation are frequently linked to other aspects of a case. The rule adopted may require a particular type of implementation, or a particular rule may be adopted because of the limited means of implementation available. The relationship may be even more intimate, seen, for example, in Frankfurter's remark that "the consequences of how you remedy a conceded wrong bear on the question of whether it is a fair classification." Yet implementation is often raised independently, as it was in these cases even before the Court focused on it with the questions of its first order. For the lawyers, Thurgood Marshall had provided the basic statement. He asked not for affirmative relief but only that segregation be removed, with matters left to local school boards to work out—an argument to be used against increased speed in desegregation more than fifteen years later. However, Marshall made clear that while implementation was a tough question the solution was not to deprive people of their rights. He insisted that the southern people would not be lawless, and said, "Every single time that this Court has ruled, they have obeyed it, and I for one believe that rank and file people in the South will support whatever decision in this case is handed down." Marshall felt that the Court could not take judicial notice of noncompliance unless a state attorney general said in court he could not control his own state. However, something almost like this was said by Virginia Attorney General Almond, who stated that if desegregation were ordered whites would cease approving the bond issues necessary for the continued development of education. It certainly was said by the southern attorneys general at implementation reargument. Also with respect to implementation, Spottswood Robinson suggested that equalization decrees be avoided because "at the very best the facilities would only be made comparable or approximately equal" according to the defendant's view, forcing plaintiffs to be in court continuously. More important, both Robinson and Jack Greenberg said, instability for children would result from shifting them around based on changes in equality/inequality—a point later conceded by Delaware's attorney general—with Greenberg arguing that difficulty in lower court supervision of equalization decrees was a reason for abolishing segregation outright. What was needed was the immediate remedy properly granted by the Delaware court. "To postpone relief would be to deny relief," Greenberg emphasized. When Jackson asked Greenberg, "Is it your position that the court, finding a right being denied, has no power to take into consideration the time it will take to correct it?" Greenberg responded, "That is right," thus taking a stronger position than Thurgood Marshall.

Among the justices, possible effects of reversing the lower courts' rulings created greater concern. Frankfurter, who several times during argument remarked on the need to look at "consequences," at "where we are going," wanted to know from Marshall the effect of reversing *Briggs*, and their exchange included exploration of problems created by Negroes wanting to go to one school rather than another and gerrymandering of district lines. Perhaps the most interesting exchange on implementation occurred rather early in the *Brown* argument when Frankfurter asked Kansas Assistant Attorney General Paul Wilson the consequences of Supreme Court reversal of the lower court ruling in *Brown*. Wilson's reply to such a question at this early date seems surprising, since the decree which the Court finally fashioned under Warren obviously anticipated a much more violent or at least negative reaction. "In perfect candor," Wilson answered, "I must say to the Court that the consequences would probably not be serious. Our Negro population is small. We do not have Negro administrators that would necessarily have to be assimilated in the school system. That might produce some administrative difficulties, but I can imagine no serious difficulty beyond that." Justice Jackson then broke in with a most pertinent question. "You emphasize the smallness of the Negro population. Would it affect your problem if there were heavier concentrations?" Wilson replied that he found that question most difficult to answer. "It might," he said, "but I am not acquainted with the situation where there is a heavier concentration." Similarly, Marshall's concession of limited effect may also seem surprising. In response to Frankfurter's query, "You mean that, if we reverse, it will not entitle every mother to have her child go to a nonsegregated school?" Marshall said that no, it would not. Frankfurter then asked what it would do. "The school board, I assume," Marshall said, "would find some other method of distributing the children by drawing district lines."

The justices were interested in more than the immediate decrees. They wanted to know the effect of the litigation on school districts other than those immediately involved. Here Frankfurter indicated his feeling that rulings would inevitably have to be made with respect to individual

districts because of differences in circumstances. The justices also inquired as to whether there had been a problem with desegregation in
Delaware and whether it had taken place in response to the lower court's
decree, and were told that Delaware had decided to appeal the case
because of the lower court decision's terrific impact upon the rest of the
state. Chief Justice Vinson wanted to know whether adequate facilities
were available for a changeover to a desegregated system, and Justice
Reed wondered whether legislatures could consider problems of "law and
order" in dealing with desegregation. Reed also anticipated the problem
of in-school segregation which had given rise to the *McLaurin* case because
there had been no *McLaurin*-type ruling in lower education.

Although as usual the Court did not reveal what transpired at its
internal councils, it now appears that during the justices' deliberations,
Chief Justice Vinson observed that the Court would have to confront the
problem of desegregation if Congress did not deal with it.[24] On the
question of federal versus state segregation, Justices Frankfurter and
Black differed. Frankfurter apparently felt that segregation in the District of Columbia violated the Fifth Amendment Due Process Clause
although segregation in the states was not unconstitutional. Black, on the
other hand, saw the states' power in this area as more limited than the
federal government's. Looking to implementation, he thought serious
incidents would occur if the states' power to segregate were abolished, but
on balance he was prepared to come out with an antisegregation position
because racial segregation violated the Fourteenth Amendment—unless
precedent prevented him from adopting such a position. With respect to
the District, his discomfort about "lawmaking" by judges was apparently
stronger, and he was unsure that Congress was barred from enacting
segregation. However, a concern about consistency in public policy led
him to see "the anomalous results of permitting segregation in the District
of Columbia but not elsewhere."[25] The apparent line-up at the post-
argument conference was Douglas, who saw the cases as presenting a
simple constitutional question, Black, and Minton as favoring overruling
segregation, with the Chief Justice and Justices Reed, Frankfurter,
Jackson, and Clark favoring or leaning to affirmance.[26] However, in the
several months after this conference some change in positions must have
occurred, for in May 1953 Burton suggested a six-to-three vote to outlaw
segregation, with Chief Justice Vinson among the minority.[27]

On June 8, 1953, six months after the argument and at the very end of
the 1952 Term, the Court, adopting a position specifically suggested by
the government in its amicus curiae brief, announced that it would need
more information before final disposition of the cases could be made. For
this reason the cases would be restored to the docket and additional
argument would be presented next Term on five specific questions, three

of which concerned interpretation of the Fourteenth Amendment and judicial power under that amendment and two of which dealt with decrees which the Court might issue. The questions were:

(1) What evidence is there that the Congress which submitted and the state legislatures and conventions which ratified the Fourteenth Amendment contemplated or did not contemplate, understood or did not understand, that it would abolish segregation in public schools?

(2) [If not] was it nevertheless the understanding of the framers of the Amendment: (a) that future Congresses might, in the exercise of their power under Section 5 of the Amendment abolish such segregation, or (b) that it would be within the judicial power, in light of future conditions, to construe the Amendment as abolishing such segregation of its own force?

(3) On the assumption that the [earlier] answers do not dispose of the issues, is it within the judicial power, in construing the Amendment, to abolish segregation in public schools?

(4) Assuming . . . that segregation in public schools violates the Fourteenth Amendment (a) would a decree necessarily follow that, within the limits set by normal geographic school districting, Negro children should forthwith be admitted to schools of their choice, or (b) may this Court, in the exercise of its equity powers, permit an effective gradual adjustment to be brought about from existing segregated systems to a system not based on color distinctions?

(5) [If so] . . . (a) should this Court formulate detailed decrees in these cases; (b) . . . what specific issues should the decrees reach; (c) should this Court appoint a special master to hear evidence with a view to recommending specific terms for such decrees; (d) should this Court remand to the courts of first instance with directions to frame decrees in these cases, and if so, what general directions should the decrees of this Court include and what procedures should the courts of first instance follow in arriving at the specific terms of more detailed decrees?

The direction of the Court's persuasion seemed clear, but the call for reargument and the questions posed for debate gave rise to considerable speculation that more than further information stood to be gained by the newly created time lapse. Opinion ranged from the position that action was delayed because the justices were deadlocked to the interpretation that the time lapse was meant as a reprieve during which the South could study and prepare for changing to a system of integrated public education. In the middle, some southern school officials merely saw the delay as time during which to hurry to equalize the facilities of white and Negro schools.

When reargument took place in December 1953, a slightly new atmosphere was to prevail in the courtroom. It emanated from the new Chief Justice, who was to preside over a change in the course of American history to which we are still reacting. Ironically, the burden of initiative in this revolution was thrust upon the new Chief Justice, appointed by a president uninterested in civil rights, whereas the civil rights attitudes of the previous administration were positive in the face of the more reluctant Vinson Court.

4

Reargument appears in a way not to have been particularly central to the outcome in *Brown v. Board of Education.* All the justices other than the new Chief Justice had heard the first round of argument and had already been sifting the crucial materials presented there. In addition, although the lawyers certainly argued the questions the Court had posed in its 1953 order, the justices did not press them hard about their responses, particularly those to the first three questions. This left the impression that the justices had asked the questions knowing they would not produce determinative answers or had already decided not to use the answers as a basis for their decision. As the Court did not rule on implementation as a result of this reargument, the justices' somewhat greater questioning about the responses to Questions 4 and 5 did not have a direct effect on the substance of its 1954 decision, although counsels' statements and responses must have led to the not unimportant decision to have still further reargument on the subject.

There was at least one significant difference between the first and second rounds of argument: the government was present at the second round to argue its position. The Court had received a request from the Acting Solicitor General for permission to argue for thirty minutes. Despite its earlier refusal to let the Attorney General participate at the first round of argument, the Court now asked the United States Attorney General to join the argument and to file a supplemental brief if he so desired. Although there was no explicit dissent from this order, there was some internal disagreement. Five days after the case had been restored to the docket, Justice Black sent a memorandum to his colleagues suggesting withdrawal of the invitation on the grounds it involved the Court in inappropriate political controversy,[28] and Black was apparently prepared to vote to amend the order if given a chance.

Because much of the time at reargument was taken up with responses to the justices' questions about procedural issues, the central cases were really *Briggs* (South Carolina) and *Davis* (Virginia), argued together.[29] Here Spottswood W. Robinson III argued that the framers and ratifiers of the Fourteenth Amendment intended that the amendment would abolish segregation in public schools and provide complete legal equality of the races. The Radical Republicans wanted both to invalidate the "Black Codes" and to prevent further attempts to impose governmental distinctions predicated upon race. He claimed that the ratifying states, which eliminated any reference to school segregation in their constitutions, must have understood the Fourteenth Amendment as prohibiting such measures, and he noted that those states did not adopt racial segregation in the schools until after the Reconstruction era.[30] Taking a much more direct position than in the first round of argument, Thurgood Marshall stated flatly that it was within the judicial power to abolish public school segregation.

Arguing on behalf of the South Carolina school authorities, John W. Davis told the Court that his opponents were wrong in assuming that the Abolitionists crusaded not only against slavery but against racial segregation in the schools. He also pointed out that the Radical Republicans did not control the Thirty-ninth Congress, which never went as far as they wished. Furthermore, he said, the sponsors of the Civil Rights Act of 1866 in answering criticism had insisted that the law did not outlaw school segregation; his co-counsel argued that suffrage, intermarriage, and non-segregated schools were eliminated from the amendment's coverage, although suffrage was later covered by the Fifteenth Amendment. Davis also attacked petitioners' use of statements by members of Congress, criticizing the way "they take for granted that if they can quote any Senator, Congressman, or other character in favor of racial equality, they can count him down in the column of those who were opposed to segregated schools, which is a clear non sequitur and a begging of the question." Davis attached special significance to Congress's actions creating the District of Columbia public schools, saying these were not merely routine performances. Furthermore, the Freedmen's Bureau, "the pet and child of Congress," had installed separate schools throughout the South. Davis reasoned that since the Fourteenth Amendment was not intended to abolish segregation Congress could not derive the power to do so from that source. Nor did the Court have the power to abolish school segregation because the "separate but equal" doctrine had become fully established. "Sometime to every principle comes a moment of repose when it has been so often announced, so confidently relied upon, so long continued, that it passes the limits of judicial discretion and disturbance," he asserted, adding that the judiciary could not set aside "on a sociological basis" a system that "has stood legally for three-quarters of a century." The Court would also be prevented from abolishing segregation by the "doctrine of reasonable classification," for there was no reason to believe that putting a few white children in a classroom with colored children would make any of the children happier or would help them learn more quickly. Frankly, Davis said, he doubted that white children would be prevented from getting a distorted idea of racial relations if they sat with Negro children, adding that the happiness, progress, and welfare of

Negro children are "best promoted in segregated schools." Also arguing for the school officials, T. Justin Moore urged that the Court should not upset a one-hundred-year-old doctrine followed in seventeen states with 70 percent of the nation's Negroes. "The size and history of this problem make it clear that the solution should be left with the legislature," he claimed.

Several other points of importance were raised by those arguing the Kansas and Delaware cases, both of which touched on matters of relief. Robert Carter, in *Brown,* said the question of the adequacy of relief remained, although he was confident that Topeka would not reverse its policy of abandoning segregation. For Kansas, Paul Wilson said the Topeka Board of Education's plan was purely a policy decision, leaving the constitutionality of the Kansas statute—which authorized school segregation—still at issue. He conceded that the basic question in these cases was subject to resolution by the judiciary, but insisted that the Court must exercise "restraint" in reaching its decision. He also said that the Court need not concern itself with a detailed decree in *Brown,* as the case did not entail most of the problems involved in the other cases.

In the Delaware case, the state's attorney general stated that the state constitution's segregation provisions were thought the most workable method of educating white and colored children. He also argued that abolishing segregation in the schools was a legislative rather than a judicial matter. For the Negroes, Jack Greenberg, urging alternative grounds for affirmance, used the questions posed in the Court's reargument order to get at the constitutional question. He argued that equal protection of the laws would not be given until the separate-but-equal doctrine was finally eliminated. Saying that the state supreme court decree did not give all that the Constitution guaranteed, Greenberg asserted that the Negro children attending desegregated schools were "under a cloud" because they were not in the school on the same basis as white children, their admission having been based on the old doctrine. What was required, he said, was a Supreme Court finding that segregated treatment constituted unequal treatment in and of itself. However, in concluding the argument, Marshall demonstrated greater caution. Agreeing that the remedy point was not involved in the appeal, he conceded that the judgment of the Delaware courts could be affirmed on the narrow basis that in the absence of equal physical facilities the colored children must be admitted to the white schools.

In the District of Columbia case, George Hayes maintained that the statutes, whether permissive or mandatory as to school segregation, violated the Fifth Amendment. He argued that the statutes' authors recognized that freedmen could not generally afford to attend the private schools where white children were enrolled, and thus that their primary motive was not to require separate school systems or even to approve racial segregation for the city of Washington but, rather, to provide public education for Negroes. Hayes's co-counsel, James M. Nabrit, Jr., took a different stance. Because one could read into the statute "an intent on the part of Congress not to segregate Negroes by compulsion," he said, it was not necessary to hold the statutes authorizing segregated schools in the District unconstitutional. Instead, when the District authorities made school attendance compulsory and compelled Negroes to go to segregated schools, they exceeded their statutory authority. In opposition, Milton D. Korman insisted that the board of education was compelled by statute to segregate because the lower courts had interpreted the statutes to require a segregated school system. He also argued that Congress through its appropriation acts showed its intent to separate schools on the basis of race. Korman added that if the board changed the segregation rule and were then sued to compel segregation he would not defend the board because the law would not permit it to change to a desegregated system.

For the government, Solicitor General Rankin argued that the history of the Fourteenth Amendment did not support either side's claim. Because the amendment's framers had never said a single word to indicate they wanted to preserve school segregation, the Court was free to strike down separate schools while remaining within the amendment's broad terms. Rankin also insisted that Congress simply did not consider the relationship to the Fourteenth Amendment of the statutes authorizing segregation in the District of Columbia. On the issue of whether the Fourteenth Amendment permitted the state to legislate segregation in public education, Rankin felt the Court rather than Congress should act. Perhaps because of fear that President Eisenhower would not approve it, the government's brief had been far more hesitant than the government's position in its brief for the earlier round, containing no specific statement asking the Court to declare public school segregation unconstitutional. At argument, however, Rankin went further than the brief while answering a question from Justice Douglas,[31] saying, "It is the position of the Department of Justice that segregation in the public schools cannot be maintained under the Fourteenth Amendment."

As with the first round, the justices' questions tended to fall into certain categories: past cases, the meaning and basis of Congress's action including the District of Columbia statutes, and factual questions. An important new category, however, was that of procedure. The procedural issues were whether the state of Kansas was a party and whether the case had become moot because the state had formulated a plan to eliminate separate schools and had begun to put the plan into effect. Justice Frankfurter was the most insistent questioner[32] on the mootness point, perhaps using it to signal to his colleagues that he thought the foundation of these cases was so shaky that a cautious approach would have to be taken in resolving them. No sooner had Robert Carter stood up to argue *Brown* than Frankfurter asked, "Is your case moot, Mr. Carter?" Carter responded jokingly, "I hoped I would get a little further into the argument before that question was asked," but at a later point he said, "I certainly have no real desire to proceed with an argument." Frankfurter persisted: "They have every intention of giving you what you want, is that it?" When Carter replied that they did, the justice said, "That is what I call a moot case." Then Jackson asked, "Do I understand that the parties you represent are now admitted to unsegregated schools?" When Carter replied that only one of the appellants had been admitted, Frankfurter was at him again: "But by the authorized pronouncement of the appellee, they will be admitted just as soon as it is administratively possible?"—a point Carter conceded. A little later, Frankfurter asked whether the case would be moot if all the children had been admitted. There were also questions on the likelihood of Topeka resuming segregation. When Carter tried to suggest that he had "serious questions" about Topeka's desegregation plan, Frankfurter suggested that the real problem left was merely one of the terms of the decree. When Frankfurter began the same litany of mootness questions with Paul Wilson, who was arguing Kansas's case, Chief Justice Warren was provoked to the point of remarking irritatedly, "I think when both parties to the action feel that there is a controversy and invited the Attorney General to be here and answer these questions, I for one would like to hear the argument."[33]

The mootness issue was also present in *Bolling.* President Eisenhower had said he would use his powers to bring about desegregation in the District of Columbia, and the president had been followed up by the commissioners of the District. These apparent changes in the school board's position led Justice Black to suggest that if the rules were going to be changed the Court should not decide the constitutional question, construing the statute so as to avoid the bigger issue. The changes also led several justices to ask persistently whether Korman was acting under instructions to maintain his position.[34] When Korman said that he had advised the board on what the law is, Frankfurter observed that the board members did not have to pursue their rights but could "take a position in advance of the law." In this context, Frankfurter indicated a strong preference for an out-of-court settlement, which he thought advanced the public good.

Another procedural matter arose in the Delaware case. Here Frankfurter obviously had trouble with Greenberg's position that the broad questions could be argued under the Court's "invitation" to answer the questions put to the participants in the companion cases. Frankfurter made clear he thought Greenberg should have cross-appealed, noting that while it was permissible for Greenberg to urge any ground he wanted to justify the lower court decree, "you cannot go outside the decree." Here Jackson pointed out, "We cannot direct the state court as to what decree it shall enter." "All we can say," he added, "is, 'you shall not go beyond a certain point which we say is the constitutional limit.' "

Once they turned to substantive legal matters, the justices were most interested in the meaning and basis of Congress's actions. Raising a point not raised previously, Justices Jackson and Frankfurter asked whether the Constitution's "necessary and proper" clause might cover Congress's power in this area. The absence of a specific congressional statement on desegregation and congressional action after the passage of the amendments both attracted considerable attention, and Justices Jackson and Reed asked about actions of northern legislatures which had ratified the amendments. The justices asked whether the District of Columbia statutes had been construed by the lower courts and whether their constitutionality turned on whether they were permissive or mandatory. Closely related was Frankfurter's inquiry whether segregation resulted from the school board's discretion or from compulsion on the board.[35] When Nabrit replied that the school authorities said they were compelled, Frankfurter asked what Nabrit would do if the Court told the board there was no compulsion and the board then said they were doing it as a matter of discretion. Nabrit replied, "We would file suit that day." Factual questions related to this case concerned the percentage of Negroes in the District of Columbia in the post–Civil War period, whether the commissioners of the District had expressed themselves on school segregation, and how the District school board was structured as well as whether it was autonomous. Because the District Court for the District of Columbia appointed the school board, Chief Justice Warren asked whether any problems would exist in remanding *Bolling* to that court.

The meaning of past cases received less attention than at the earlier round of argument. Reed inquired of Marshall whether the *McLaurin* case rested on "separate but equal." Frankfurter engaged Marshall in a long exchange about whether Marshall, who had asserted that all racial classifications were invalid, was thus rejecting the basis of the Delaware case and decision based on *McLaurin*.[36] Jackson, however, seemed to want to avoid discussion of past cases. When Marshall began to launch into such a discussion, he remarked, "I do not believe the Court was troubled about its own cases. It had done a good deal of reading of those cases." With respect to the present cases, the justices wanted to know whether any other desegregation cases were pending in the Delaware courts and whether any segregated schools remained in the state. Chief Justice Warren, perhaps feeling his way at this early stage, did not ask many questions although he did ask about the current situation in Delaware.

Implementation took up a much larger portion of this round than it had of the first round of argument. Marshall, making the central presentation, insisted that nothing other than "administrative problems" were "valid for this Court to consider" and said further that it would not take longer than a year to deal with administrative matters. "If they don't have staff enough to do these administrative things, the sovereign states can hire more people to do them." Marshall also argued presciently that allowing a longer period of time for compliance "would get the lower court into the legislative field. The duty and responsibility of the federal courts ends with telling the state what it can't do." Marshall also criticized Virginia and South Carolina for making no effort "to conform to the clear intent of past decisions." In a skillful use of earlier segregationist arguments, he pointed out that in the southern states' *Sweatt* and *McLaurin* amici briefs the Court had been warned that desegregation of the graduate and professional schools would result in the schools being closed. As a matter of fact, Marshall pointed out, there were presently fifteen hundred Negroes in graduate and professional schools in previously all-white universities in twelve different states, and many southern private schools, not covered by the segregation laws, were not segregated. "The truth of the matter is," Marshall declared, "that I have more confidence in the people of the South than the lawyers on the other side have. I am convinced they are just as lawful as anybody else, and once the law is laid down, that is all there is to it."

John Davis disposed quickly of the implementation questions. He said that every court of equity had the right to postpone a remedy, but asserted, "Your Honors cannot sit as a glorified Board of Education for the State of South Carolina or any other state." He found "nothing here on which this Court could formulate a decree." He also thought the lower federal court did not have the power to formulate a decree telling the state what course of action to take. Moore, for Virginia, agreed that the Court as a court of equity plainly had the power and the duty to permit gradual adjustment in situations like this. If there were to be "this unhappy, unfortunate decree," he felt the case should be sent back to the lower court, which could receive new evidence and consider local conditions.[37] Virginia Attorney General Almond buttressed Moore's argument by calling the Court's attention to the vast administrative difficulties which would be occasioned by a decision upsetting the established separate-but-equal doctrine, adding that Virginia had already considered her possible reaction, including repeal of compulsory attendance laws.

In the District of Columbia case, Korman said that a ruling that segregation is unconstitutional would require the entry by the district court of a declaratory judgment to that effect and compliance would be forthcoming throughout the District. The decree would thus not be limited to admission of only the petitioners to the white schools. Following up the suggestion in his brief that the decree recognize "the necessity for proper preparation and changes which appear essential to perfect integration in all jurisdictions," he suggested remand of the cases to the district courts, with instructions for the courts to prepare decrees directing the immediate commencement of such preparation and providing for periodic investigation of progress. Korman said he could not suggest any maximum period of time for completing integration. James Nabrit countered this argument by insisting that no "gradual relief" was necessary. He saw no special administrative problems that would prevent a reassignment of students to District schools on the basis of location instead of race.

In dealing with the problem of phrasing a decree, Solicitor General Rankin took a position which diverged from that of the NAACP. He argued for a gradual adjustment, with emphasis on development of local solutions rather than the imposition of one national timetable. Local school officials should have the burden of satisfying a federal district judge as to the time needed to make adjustments. More specifically, he said, state officials should be given a year for the presentation and consideration of a desegregation plan, with the lower court determining whether it satisfied constitutional requirements. However, responding to an observation by Justice Reed he took a less gradualist position: "It is our position that unless it can be shown by the defendants that immediate integration cannot be accomplished at once in accordance with the precedents of this Court of granting them their present and personal rights when their constitutional rights are invaded, then they should have them."

That the judges were troubled by the implementation problem was quite clear. The vast dimensions of the problem may have even led some justices to wonder whether *Brown* and the related cases were not too big and cumbersome and hence would seem of revolutionary or at least legislative dimensions. Very early, Frankfurter asked how the Court should frame its decree and what guidance it could give the lower courts. The justices also indicated that reaching a constitutional result was far different from getting it implemented; a standard and its application were different. Legislatures might be forced to spend money, and Frankfurter pointed out that the Court could not raise taxes. At the heart of the issue was the degree to which implementation should be decentralized. Jackson, the most skeptical about obtaining enforcement, inquired of Korman as to how the Court could be better informed on a maximum period of time than the local school board, and at another point agreed with Solicitor General Rankin that the Supreme Court should not determine educational policy for individual school districts. "Even if we said that the state segregation provisions are unconstitutional, local custom would still perpetuate it in most districts." When Rankin seized upon this, saying, "We do not assume that once this Court pronounces what the Constitution means that our people are not going to try to abide by it as rapidly as they can," Jackson disagreed with the implication: "I do not think that a court can enter a decree on that assumption, particularly in view of the fact that for 75 years the separate but equal doctrine has prevailed in the cases." Noting that the separate-but-equal rule had not been complied with in many cases, Jackson asked, "If our decision is not acquiesced in, we have to proceed school district by school district, is that right?" When Rankin replied that the Court traditionally handled each case as it came before it, Jackson agreed, but said he did not get from Rankin's statement any criteria which the lower court could be told to take into consideration. Jackson wanted guidance so the Court could "avoid the situation where in some districts everyone is perhaps held in contempt almost immediately because that judge has that disposition, and in some other districts it is 12 years before they get a hearing." Frankfurter, who felt that resistance to or dislike of the result should not affect the implementing court, nonetheless shared Jackson's concern about the lawsuit-by-lawsuit approach and about what the district judges would do. He suggested a difference between having courts establish school district lines and merely having those courts pass on plans submitted by the school officials.

When the justices began to consider the school desegregation cases after oral argument, they had available for their ruling the same grounds of decision which had been available earlier, plus the possibility of disposing of one or more of the cases on the basis of the changes in circumstances which had occurred since the initial round of argument. Certainly, if some parties were themselves settling the cases through the admission of Negro children to previously all-white schools, the need for a decision on the constitutional issue, or for any decision at all, would be less, although mere admission of Negro children would not necessarily solve the larger problem. However, the need to decide the basic issue one way or another now seemed virtually unavoidable, particularly now that the Court had heard further argument after once postponing a decision. The Court thus was very visibly constrained, its choices limited by a sequence of facts stretching at least as far back as its missed opportunity in the *Morgan* transportation case, to invalidate "separate but equal" in the area in which it had started.

The justices discussed the cases in December 1953, but did not immediately take a vote. Years later, Chief Justice Warren said that the

Court's not following its customary procedure of taking an immediate vote helped contribute to the unanimous vote, because the justices "didn't polarize [themselves] at the beginning," but he conceded "some division" on the Court about the case.[38] Justice Burton's notes suggest that Jackson and Reed were "No" votes in December and that Frankfurter, adhering to the position he had taken in conference the previous year, was negative as to the state cases. Thus Warren seems to have started out with a six-to-three majority, although it may have been seven-to-two. In the Court's conference, the new Chief Justice stated his views clearly. He indicated that the issue must be reached and segregation prohibited even if past cases had to be overruled, because "the only basis for segregation and separate but equal rights was the inherent inferiority of the colored race." This statement, including personal feelings about the inability to justify segregation based on race, contained "no reference to the inconclusive history of or the intentions behind the Fourteenth or other Amendments," but did include the claim that the Fourteenth Amendment and the Thirteenth and Fifteenth Amendments were violated.[39] Warren asked for recognition of differences between the states and warned against precipitous remedies which would inflame the situation.

Dealing with a matter which Justice Burton had raised at argument, Justice Reed "conceded that the Constitution of *Plessy* might not be the Constitution of today," but he tended to come down in favor of segregation as an exercise of the state's police power. Justice Clark had apparently switched from the position Burton had earlier recorded, perhaps because of the persuasion of the Chief Justice.[40] He now supported Warren's position contingent on relief varying to fit different situations.[41] Justice Douglas, who had not been helped by the legislative history offered the Court, suggested that *Bolling* be sent back to the Court of Appeals on the question whether segregation was mandatory or permissive in the District of Columbia.[42] The problem for Justice Jackson, perhaps the last holdout as the case neared its conclusion,[43] was the Court's opinion more than its result. According to Ulmer, "Jackson asserted that the *Segregation Cases* required a political decision. This, he said, was no problem for him, but he did not know how to justify the abolition of segregation on judicial grounds. The problem for him was how to create a judicial basis for a political decision."[44] In conference Frankfurter apparently said that the legislative history did lead to viewing school segregation as unconstitutional. On January 1, 1954, he sent his brethren a memo reflecting the concerns expressed in his long exchange with Marshall over whether equalization of facilities should still be considered the Court's doctrine. In the memo he argued "that the inequalities deriving from segregated schools should be eliminated as soon as possible without disrupting school systems or substantially lowering standards for any sizeable group" and suggested that the Court appoint a master to deal with remaining aspects of the cases.[45]

Whatever the alignment of the Court in December, by the time the decision was announced unanimity had been achieved, although apparently only shortly before the opinion was released. On May 7, the Chief Justice, taking upon himself the writing of the opinion, as the Chief Justice often does in the Court's most important cases, suggested in a memorandum that the opinion "should be short, non-rhetorical, unemotional and, above all, non-accusatory,"[46] perhaps echoing Frankfurter on that point. Because the final opinion can be so characterized, it is likely that few changes were made in the ten days between that memo and the issuing of the opinion. Yet it was uncertain as little as five days before the opinion was handed down whether it would receive undivided backing. "The holdouts or doubtful members appear to have been Frankfurter and Jackson, or one of them," Burton noted, with Frankfurter perhaps in doubt on the state cases "until the last possible moment."[47] Another observer has said that Reed, "Right up to the end . . . had considered noting his disagreement with the Court's action."[48] Perhaps the holdouts gave in because the cases could not be avoided through use of the mootness doctrine or use of a master. Perhaps it was because, as Berman has claimed, they were "won over by the Department of Justice's assurance that a modern approach to implementation could be adopted."[49] However, another, more persuasive, explanation of Frankfurter's vote, according to Ulmer, is that "being a member of a minority group, and being acutely aware of that status, [he] would in no event have dissented from a majority ruling condemning racial segregation. At the same time . . . he might have been willing to sustain, along with a court majority, the power of the states to legislate in the area of public education free of the kinds of restrictions imposed by the Brown decisions. In other words, . . . that is where his heart lay but not being able to get support for his position, he was not willing to vote it."[50]

On May 17, 1954, the Court handed down its historic decisions. Chief Justice Warren began with the opinion in *Brown v. Board of Education*, explaining first how the four state cases had reached the Court and describing the common legal questions which they raised. Plaintiffs contend that "segregated public schools are not 'equal' and cannot be made 'equal' and that hence they are deprived of the equal protection of the laws," he explained. Next he discussed the reargument that had been held, largely on questions of constitutional history. The Court's conclusion on that material, he said, was that it was at best inconclusive. There was such great divergence between the most avid proponents and opponents of the postwar amendments, and the system of public education was so embryonic at that time, that "it is not surprising that there should be so little in the history of the Fourteenth Amendment relating to its intended effect on public education." As for the history of litigation involving the Fourteenth Amendment, he explained that the separate-but-equal doctrine did not make its appearance until 1896 in *Plessy*, that the two early education cases, *Cumming* and *Gong Lum*, had not challenged the validity of the doctrine itself, and that in the more recent graduate school cases it had not been necessary to reexamine the doctrine in order to grant relief. Therefore the question had been held in reserve, but "In the instant cases, that question is directly presented." Explaining that in each case it had been shown that facilities had been or were being equalized, at least insofar as "tangible" factors were concerned, he declared that thus the Court's decision could not turn on a comparison of tangible factors but must be based instead on the effect of segregation itself on public education.

After these background statements Warren, here following Justice Burton's question at oral argument, observed, "We cannot turn the clock back to 1868 when the Amendment was adopted, or even to 1896 when *Plessy v. Ferguson* was written." Rather, the justices thought they would have to consider public education in light of its full development and its present place in American life, since it was now "perhaps the most important function of state and local governments." Warren noted that education was compulsory and the object of great expenditures and public concern and said it was doubtful that any child could succeed in life if he were denied the opportunity of education. He then declared, "Such an opportunity, where the state has undertaken to provide it, is a right which must be made available to all on equal terms." Repeating the question presented—whether racial segregation in the public school deprived children of the minority group of equal educational opportunites—the Court concluded that it did. The intangibles on which *Sweatt* and *McLaurin* turned would apply with even more force to younger children and would generate within them a feeling of inferiority as to their status in the community that might never be undone. Rejecting any contrary language in the *Plessy* opinion, Warren noted, "Whatever may have been the extent of psychological knowledge at the time of *Plessy v. Ferguson*, this finding is amply supported by modern authority," and cited a number of social science findings in a footnote. Then came the conclusion, obvious from what Warren had already said, that "in the field of public education the doctrine of 'separate but equal' has no place. Separate educational facilities are inherently unequal." Thus, the Negro children here were found deprived of equal protection, Warren said. This conclusion made unnecessary any discussion as to whether the Fourteenth Amendment's Due Process Clause was also violated. Warren then noted that the formulation of decrees presented particularly complex problems because the cases were class actions and because of the wide applicability of the decision and the great variety of local conditions in these cases. Evidently not satisfied with the discussion of this aspect of the cases during reargument, the Court declared that the cases should be again restored to the docket for further argument of Questions 4 and 5 concerning a proper decree, with the attorneys general of affected states appearing as amici curiae.

In *Bolling v. Sharpe,* the Chief Justice began the Court's opinion by explaining that the case challenged the validity of segregation in the public schools of the District of Columbia on the ground that such segregation deprived plaintiffs of due process of law under the Fifth Amendment. Although the Fifth Amendment did not contain an equal protection clause, Warren said that "the concepts of equal protection and due process, both stemming from our American ideal of fairness, are not mutually exclusive." The first is a more explicit safeguard, and the two may not always be interchangeable phrases, he continued, but this Court has recognized that discrimination may be so unjustifiable as to violate due process. Noting the old rule that classifications based on race must be carefully scrutinized because they are constitutionally suspect, Warren quoted from 1896 and 1917 cases which held that the Constitution forbids the federal government and the states from discriminating against any citizen because of his race and held, further, that a statute limiting the right of a property owner to sell to a person of another race was a denial of due process. Coming to the heart of the opinion, the Chief Justice said that because segregation in public education was not reasonably related to any proper governmental objective, "it imposes on Negro children of the District of Columbia a burden that constitutes an arbitrary deprivation of their liberty in violation of the Due Process Clause." If the Constitution prohibited the states from maintaining racially segregated schools, no lesser duty was imposed on the federal government.

5

The first point to be noted about the declaration handed down on May 17, 1954, is that in a way it did not really decide very much. To be sure, on the basic issue—that of the constitutionality of the *Plessy* rule of separate but equal—the decision was of course conclusive, at least in the direction which it took. The ruling can be, and most often is, viewed as making a major break with the past by "dispatching" *Plessy.* Yet it can also be seen as merely representing developments in society.[51] Furthermore, the ruling did not answer the majority of the five questions which had been presumed to be so important during the preceding year, and it represented far less than the final disposition of the cases before the Court. Further-

more, since the Court did not explicitly overrule *Plessy*, although it was
excluded from application in education, and since the direction of the
decision seems to have been at least generally indicated a year earlier by
the tone of the questions the Vinson Court had posed, its announcement
in two opinions which took less than a half hour to read aloud in the
courtroom seems somewhat anticlimactic. The decision was at once
heralded as momentous, which of course it was, but it might well be
argued that the unanimity of the declaration, not its substance, was its
most significant characteristic.

The Court's decision, which has been called "a sweeping and revolutionary policy statement,"[52] did have an immediate and substantial
effect in the country. It has been said to have "rocked the South, secured
the fame . . . of the Warren Court, and propelled the nation into the
modern era of its on-going revolution in race relations."[53] As Jack Greenberg put it, *"Brown v. Board of Education* proved to be the Declaration of
Independence of its day. Together with the other school desegregation
cases it profoundly affected national thinking and has served as the
principal ideological engine of today's civil rights movement."[54] In the
words of Justice Goldberg, who was to participate in the Court's desegregation activity in the 1960s, the ruling "clarified values and ideals for a
country that had shown itself to be sorely in need of such guidance."[55] Yet
the decision's effect, at least in the short run, was largely symbolic. This is
recognized in comments that the ruling had "symbolically legitimized the
protest against the denial of opportunity to Negroes in general" and had
"signified a permanent change in the Negro's status." By acting in the
field of education, thought to be the principal ladder of social mobility,
the Court had further intensified the symbolic effect.[56] That the Supreme
Court had handed down a ruling with such a substantial symbolic effect
should not be understated. It had transmitted an important signal, particularly that the Supreme Court—and by extension, the government—
cared for minorities.

There were many long-run effects from the decision, across and
through the society as a whole. The "fallout" from *Brown* was substantial,
particularly when it was backed up by legislative action. That, however,
was not to come for ten years; there was little immediate effect.[57] In the
period immediately after *Brown*, little happened with respect to actual
desegregation of the schools. Initial reaction to *Brown I* was relatively
restrained, and some southern newspapers and spokesmen urged restraint against hasty action and compliance with the inevitable on a calm
and reasoned basis.[58] But that did not mean compliance was coming. The
South did not rush to comply, and many statements of opposition could
be heard. Although the violence and "Massive Resistance" which occurred after *Brown II* did not characterize the post–*Brown I* period, the

South perhaps realized, as Reed Sarratt has noted, that "history gave the South ample reason for its general calm reaction to the precedent-shattering decision"[59] because so little effort had been made to enforce the "but equal" provisions of *Plessy*. Thus the South could afford to adopt a "wait and see" attitude, at least until there was an implementation order to which to react more directly. In short, the basic ruling had been made, and the basis for what was later to happen had been established, but the real issues of what to do in fact, not in theory, had only begun.

Here it is important to recognize that that impact of cases is not always in direct proportion to what people immediately think the change will be or what they initially see as the amount of legal change from the past. Indeed, one can argue that there is an inverse relationship: the greater the perceived change, the greater the resistance, and thus the less the actual change.[60] When perceived change is great, the Court's opinion may be crucial in what follows. Yet particularly where large numbers of individuals are affected, as with desegregation, the result may be the only part of the Supreme Court's message that means very much; what the Court approves or rejects is of utmost importance, while how it does so is of less importance, or a least of less immediate importance.

Certainly, southern leaders would have felt "put upon" because of the decision, regardless of what Chief Justice Warren wrote; it might have been impossible to mollify the South, at least in the short run; and northern suburbanites presently opposed to "forced busing" would have been similarly extremely difficult to please in the long run. Yet, while the public wants specific litigation before the Court settled, and while many persons may believe the dictum that "it is more important that some cases be decided than that they be decided right," the manner in which the Court explains what it has done is important, for the public wants not only results but also "symbolic outputs which help in social adjustment and in the projection of anxiety of inner tensions."[61] Here the Supreme Court in *Brown I* did not help itself; it created trouble with respect to the process of implementation in its opinion. Put another way, if *Brown* was a great decision, the opinion, when one looks at it closely, was far less than it might have been.

Criticism of the opinion, not only immediately but also in the decade after the decision—from which much of the commentary for this section is drawn—was considerable. And it came not simply from those who might have been opposed to the result even with a different opinion but from many other places on the political spectrum as well. Conservatives objected to the Court's free-floating reasoning which was said to depart from processes of "constitutional government," but NAACP lawyers were also displeased, because desegregation rights had not been made "personal and present," and "northern liberal jurists who warmly applauded the decision made known their objections and reservations to the Court's conspicuous use of social science."[62] The general tone of criticism which was not directed at the result is seen in Wechsler's statement: "The problem inheres strictly in the reasoning of the opinion"[63] and in Kurland's assertion: "The Warren Court . . . failed abysmally to persuade the people that its judgments had been made for sound reasons."[64]

The criticisms of the opinion in *Brown I* can be divided into several categories. First, the opinion lacked clarity; the Court did not satisfy its audiences. Second, legal and historical continuity were not adequately provided for in the opinion; there was inadequate reference either to precedent or to clearly stated legal principle. Third, the opinion had the appearance of "judicial legislation" enacted by the Court acting like a "super-legislature." Fourth, the Court abused nonlegal materials in its opinion, misusing history and using sociology when it should not have been used at all. Finally, the Court had failed to deal with implementation. Before exploring those criticisms, the reader should keep in mind the recent comment by Harvard law professor Derrick Bell, Jr., that our present problems concerning school desegregation do not result from *Brown's* "analytical inadequacies" or from the Court's "unfortunate failure" to require immediate compliance, but instead stem from "the continuing resistance of many whites who fear that the realization of 'equal educational opportunites' for blacks will mean the loss of economic and status benefits that they or their children now enjoy solely on the basis of race."[65] We do not want to be understood as saying that present problems result solely from the "analytical inadequacies" examined here, as we certainly recognize the problems of racism of which Bell speaks. Our point, is rather, that had the Court done things differently in *Brown,* the future might have been different—a statement about which neither we nor Professor Bell can have absolute certainty.

Justice Frankfurter once remarked that the Court must strive "to be as precise, persuasive, and invulnerable as possible in its exposition" of issues.[66] Professor Paul Freund has quoted Brandeis, for whom he clerked, as saying, "I think the opinion is now persuasive, but what can we do to make it more instructive?"[67] But the question is, "Instructive for whom?" The Court has a number of potential audiences which shift to some extent from issue to issue. Aside from the "general public," the Court may write for a relatively educated, attentive, lay public or for the legal community, with the possibility of writing for a group which is not highly educated, like police in criminal procedure cases.[68] Writing for each audience entails somewhat different considerations, just as such considerations may shift from issue to issue, particularly from highly controversial and emotional ones to far more complex, technical matters like patents, estates, and taxation, where the decision to write for the experts may be relatively easy. However, when the former type of issue is before the Court, a larger audience will be interested, and the Court's potential problem is much greater.

With respect to such issues, there is a disagreement about the audience for whom the Court should write. Some, like Charles Hyneman, think the audience should be the "informed and thoughtful citizen,"[69] while others think it should be lawyers, thought to be the only ones likely to comprehend the legal issues about which the Court is speaking. The first group is likely to attack the second for trying to keep matters from those who are likely to be affected by the Court's work and who are indeed quite able to understand the Court's decisions. Thus, Kenneth Clark has commented that the *Brown* opinion was "sometimes criticized because laymen can understand it,"[70] and Justice Goldberg observed that the Warren Court, trying to breach the gap between the legal community and the public, was "manifesting a growing impatience with legalisms, with dry and sterile dogma, . . . which served to insulate the law and the Constitution it serves from the hard world it is intended to affect."[71] However, the Supreme Court's most important opinion, *Marbury v. Madison,* penned by Chief Justice John Marshall, was both clear in terms of intelligibility to laymen and exceedingly complex, so complex and "legalistic" that it achieved its purpose of asserting the Court's right to strike down unconstitutional statutes without engendering any effective opposition. Some observers commented that what the Court needed in *Brown* was a John Marshall to write the opinion.

In most cases, judges write primarily for lawyers and others trained to look at the justices' opinions before they act. What the Court says in its opinions is extremely important for these informational middlemen or "opinion leaders" from whom the public often learns what the Court has done and particularly how well it has done its job.[72] The public, generally naïve and unknowledgeable about the Court[73] and complicated legal matters, and without direct access to the Court's opinions, tends to take the word of the lawyers and others who do in fact read the opinions. Because these opinion leaders have a different perspective from that of the general public, for the Court not to aim its opinions at them, for example, to write instead for the public, may be counter-productive: the public will not be reached directly, and the opinion leaders will pass their criticism on to the public in any event. Furthermore, while it is possible to write opinions both "technically correct and still intelligible to non-lawyers,"[74] writing for the nonlegal community may not provide the necessary clarity because such writing may decrease moderation and encourage a tendency toward "ideological inflation," which in turn results from "*evangelism,* in which desires to persuade lay publics reinforce tendencies to black-and-white argument."[75]

Particularly in an area of substantial controversy like school segregation, even though more people are likely to have opinions and to hold
them intensely, opinion leaders' views about what they think a poorly
crafted opinion can predispose them to work against implementation and
reinforce rather than offset preexisting negative reaction to the result
among members of the public. A skillfully composed opinion may also
allow lawyers and others knowledgeable on the subject to take over the
argument as to how a ruling should be interpreted or carried out, as often
has occurred in antiobscenity campaigns where lawyers defending civil
liberties interests were able to use the standards established in *Roth v.
United States* to limit attempts to control "smut" even though the Court had
held that obscenity was outside the protection of the First Amendment.[76]
Similarly, the clarity of the Court's stipulations as to regulation of abortion
made it difficult to obtain judicial rulings limiting the thrust of the
Supreme Court's controversial 1973 opinions in *Roe v.Wade* and *Doe v.
Bolton*. Yet in *Brown v. Board of Education*, the Court's supporters had
precious little to which to turn.[77]

One commentator, writing shortly after *Brown I*, stressed the opinion's
"style of straightforward simplicity," which he felt "was especially appropriate to the expression of basic principles governing an historic controversy."[78] Speaking for the critics, on the other hand, Hyneman has
taken the position that the Court's opinion did not meet appropriate
standards of straightforwardness and clarity. If one accepts his evaluation, what are the possible results? Ambiguity is most often thought to
result in noncompliance with the Court's decision. if you don't know what
is required, you cannot comply.[79] Furthermore, variation in lower court
decisions, difficult to eliminate at any time, is quite likely to increase. The
centrifugal pulls in our nation's judicial system can only be offset by broad
and unambiguous constitutional principles. On the other hand, some
ambiguity may assist the Court in achieving its goals. For example, ambiguous doctrine may force people to turn to lower courts for interpretation of the Supreme Court's rulings, preserving future flexibility, at least
if the Court does not allow this to happen frequently or in areas where the
justices will not ultimately spell out what they want. Conversely, departures from clear, unambiguous statements can be detected easily both by
those supposed to be served by the Court's rulings and by appellate
courts, but they also mean that lower courts can administer the law
beyond the eye of the Supreme Court because few people will be inclined
to appeal to the high court to obtain its interpretation.

If new law is to achieve its greatest acceptance, not only must it be clear
but the rationale for the law must be articulated in terms of legal as well as
historical and cultural continuity and compatibility. One of the objections
to the *Brown* opinion is that it lacked adequate reference to precedent.

Both precedent and history were discussed briefly, then dismissed.[80] In
Brown, there was little excuse for avoiding precedent, because the lawyers
for the Negro plaintiffs, by arguing that segregation injury could be fit
into the *Plessy* rationale and by urging that the elimination of school
segregation be fit within the "separate but equal" doctrine, provided the
basis for a precedent-based opinion. A long juristic opinion might well
have blunted much criticism, although it would not have eliminated it
completely. The *Brown* opinion dealt with precedent in a rather offhand
way, as if the Court was saying, "Our recent cases involving separate but
unequal facilities in higher education should have alerted anyone to our
trend toward eventually finding unconstitutional any deliberate attempt
to separate the races for education in our public schools. So do not be
surprised that today we reach that result, anything in *Plessy v. Ferguson* to
the contrary notwithstanding." Even moderate southerners like Hodding
Carter, who read the Supreme Court opinion in this manner, found it
hard to invoke "the law" against reactionaries because "the law" in *Brown*
did not seem to be "law" at all but rather the personal preferences of nine
justices. Quite different would have been a fifty- or one-hundred-page
meticulous opinion analyzing all the precedents, omitting all sociological
references, and concluding that the present case simply affirms what was
the real thrust of the previous cases, that separation based on race violated
the Equal Protection Clause of the Fourteenth Amendment.

In particular, *Brown* could have contained an exhaustive analysis of
the *McLaurin* and *Sweatt* decisions, indicating that *Brown* was simply one
more incremental step following from previous cases. The Court might
have presented a long and scholarly analysis of its previous decisions in
the higher education cases and in other areas of segregation such as
transportation, all pointing to the overwhelming conclusion that by 1954
there was no validity whatsoever left in the idea of "separate but equal"
and that *Plessy* had already been overturned by *McLaurin* and other cases.
The force of precedent could have been held to compel the unsurprising
conclusion that in primary schools, as elsewhere, "separate but equal" was
a fiction that was outmoded in the late 1930s and 1940s. *Plessy* might then
have been dismissed as a Reconstructionist aberration of the nineteenth
century. Or the Court could have written a long essay on the use of
precedent in interpreting a "living constitution," pointing out that
phrases like the Fourteenth Amendment's "equal protection of the laws"
were written deliberately to allow content to change over time. Here the
Court could have said that "equal protection" meant more in 1954 than in
1896 simply because there is more "protection" of the laws in general;
hence to get "equal" protection may mean more than it did in the past
Certainly the development of public school systems was far more advanced in the 1950s than before the turn of the century, allowing the use

of such an argument. In other words *Brown* could have been written to be true to precedent in the dynamic sense.

More directly, *Plessy* could have been finally and irrevocably rejected by a turn which would have absolutely precluded charges of sociology against *Brown*. The Court could have pointed out that *Plessy* deviated from the general intention of the Fourteenth Amendment because there—and not in *Brown!*—the amendment had been discarded for the sake of judically perceived sociology—that separation of the races did not necessarily imply the inferiority of one race to the other—which, although it had little to do with the constitutional issue raised in the case, controlled the result. Alternatively, the precedents could have been distinguished away, as the Court showed an inexorable across-the-board trend against segregation, citing not just *Plessy* and the law school cases but all cases from other areas like housing, including the restrictive covenant cases, and voting rights. We must remember, however, that the Court had a checkered set of precedents with which to deal, with the post–Civil War and more recent precedents inconsistent with *Plessy* and other cases of the "*Plessy* generation."

Even where there is little precedent on which to draw, or where precedents cause difficulty, the absence of precedent does not mean the absence of principle, the importance of which is seen in the criticisms of *Brown* for not "coming to grips with violations by the states of the Fourteenth Amendment" and for "failure to base these decisions on a basic legal interpretation of the amendment."[81] The basic argument about the need for principle, particularly so called "neutral principle," has been made by Wechsler. He called for the courts to use criteria which "can be framed and tested as an exercise of reason and not merely as an act of willfulness or will." Wechsler was searching for an opinion of the Court "that rests on reasons that in their generality and their neutrality transcend any immediate result that is involved." Noting that "the Court did not declare, as many wish it had, that the Fourteenth Amendment forbids all racial lines in legislation," Wechsler was forced to guess or assume the basis on which the *Brown* judgment rested because of the Court's lack of stated principle. He felt the judgment "must have rested on the view that racial segregation is, on principle, a denial of equality to the minority against whom it is directed; that is, the group that is not dominant politically and, therefore, does not make the choice involved."[82]

Important as is the "social importance of an announced principle for its own sake, or the social cost of failure to announce it,"[83] we must not forget that "entirely principled" opinions are likely to be impossible to construct.[84] Disagreement with Wechsler has been substantial. Some scholars have argued that the major race relations cases, including *Brown*, were decided on the basis of neutral principles even though the principles "were hidden below the muddy water of clumsy judicial language."[85] Even Wechsler, who found the issue in *Brown* to be not discrimination but a right to associate which was abridged by the segregation statutes, has said he could not write a school desegregation opinion which would be so based.

Even if the search for fully principled decisions is quixotic, the Court might still be expected, because it is a court, to try to act neutrally and to strive toward principle.[86] In *Brown,* this means that there could have been far greater reliance on and explication of *equality.* Perhaps this has been put most forcefully by former NAACP attorney Lewis Steel:

In 1954, the Court was in a position to serve notice on the American people that equality was an absolute right of all citizens, that this right came before all other rights and that its further subversion could not be tolerated. By taking this stance, the Court could not only have gone a long way toward relieving its conscience but it could also have established itself as a true constitutional court, dedicated to an impartial search for just principles, irrespective of race.[87]

If the state cases required discussion of equality because of the Fourteenth Amendment's Equal Protection Clause, the District of Columbia case, where the Court had to use Fifth Amendment due process language, required enunciation of a different principle or some better assimilation of due process to equality than the Court produced. However, if the Court could say in *Bolling* something as direct as that racial classifications were unreasonable so as to violate due process, the justices could have said something as direct in *Brown,* providing a similar foundation for both. Linde's comment that the *Bolling* opinion "omitted all examination of constitutional premises in a rush toward a realistically inevitable outcome whose apparent inevitability might well have merited closer scrutiny"[88] suggests that lack of principled decision there.

Another issue posed by the presence of the *Bolling* case is whether the Court should have treated it and *Brown* in identical fashion. In the District of Columbia *Hurd* case accompanying *Shelley,* the Court had rested its decision not only on the Fifth Amendment but also on the 1866 Civil Rights Act. That action made it less than "unthinkable"—Warren's word in *Bolling*—that the Constitution might impose a smaller duty on the federal government than the states to abolish discrimination. Linde, saying "the unthinkable often bears thought," pursued the possibility that the Court, reasoning from restrictions Congress had imposed on the states after the Civil War, might have found segregation impermissible in the states, but might not have been able to find comparable grounds for eliminating segregation in the schools of the District of Columbia, which had been segregated at the time of the passage of the Fourteenth

Amendment. Had the Court handed down such a ruling, the decision would have been attacked as "a failure of judicial creativity," but Congress would undoubtedly have righted the omission immediately rather than leave segregation in the District when the Court had banned it in the states.[89] Had the Court done the reverse, banning segregation in the "federal city" but not the states, the effect would have tended in the same direction—to extend the ruling—but clearly the southern states would have been in no hurry to be "consistent."

The Court was vague on whether *Brown* applied only where segregation was intentional—that is, required by law—or whether it also applied when it occurred for any reason—so-called de facto segregation. This problem suggests that clarity is closely related to the issue of principle. *Brown* was generally seen as applying only to intentional segregation, which helps explain its support in the North—which saw the ruling as applying purely in the South. Yet there was no clear statement on the matter. Had the Court dealt with the de facto point, resistance might have been greater—although it is likely it would not have been because the School Cases were southern in origin and segregation was seen at the time as a southern problem. Then when *Brown* came north, the basis for dealing with segregation stemming from other causes could have been reached far more easily.

The *Brown* opinion might have better served the Court's ends by being clearer on the de facto segregation point, but perhaps the Court's strategy—or that of the justices who noticed the problem—was that there was no real need to get into the issue. One need not have dealt with desegregation in the public schools as a whole, but could have learned a lesson from the higher education cases and remained particularistic, saying, "In the cases before us there was deliberate segregation according to race. We do not reach other questions with respect to separation of the races." And we must recognize that even a *Brown* ruling limited to intentional segregation has served the Court reasonably well in dealing with the North, where segregation was often not de facto but intentional, as school districts purposely drew lines and located schools to increase segregation.[90] In any event, had the Court wanted to write a decision which allowed the inclusion of de facto segregation later, it could have done so far more directly.

Closely related to the problem of the de jure-de facto distinction was the distinction between whether *Brown* required merely desegregation—the elimination of explicit segregation by law—or integration, "mixing" of children of different races. By talking about "separation of the races," the Court could be read as saying that education remained unequal as long as there was no mingling of Negro and white children. Yet again, if it were to have said that, it should have done so more clearly. Its failure to do so almost immediately produced a judicial statement by Chief Judge John Parker of the Fourth Circuit: "Nothing in the Constitution or in the decision of the Supreme Court takes away from the people freedom to chose the schools they attend. The Constitution, in other words, does not require integration. It merely forbids discrimination."[91] This statement served to stall effective desegregation for a long time.[92]

We can see from this discussion of areas where principle either did not appear or appeared unclear that the Court could have written an opinion which would have been more persuasive. Its failure to do so led directly to the criticism of the Court for acting not like a court but "extra-constitutionally" or "like a legislature," an attack related to criticism about the Court's lack of principle in *Brown*. As stated in the "Southern Manifesto," the Court "with no legal basis for such action, undertook to exercise their naked judicial power and substitute their personal political and social ideas for the established law of the land." While there is strong support for the position that the Court did not "make law" in *Brown*, or at least no more than in other cases,[93] we also find comments like that by Kurland who has said, "To the extent . . . that the Court's lawmaking is not justified by well-reasoned opinions, it is indulging a privilege that belongs more to a legislature than to an appellate court,"[94] and not requiring of itself what it requires of lower courts. The Court's problem is that although the legal positivists say we should frankly admit that courts legislate, people don't want to admit that courts do so any more than they will concede that courts engage in strategy. Thus if a court must legislate, its opinions need to be couched in nonlegislative terms, something the Court failed to do in *Brown I*. The justices also appear not have seen their failure, for they compounded the problem with the "all deliberate speed" language of *Brown II*. The suggestion that the Court was operating legislatively leads to the idea that the justices could have declined to resolve the desegregation issue by insisting that it was a matter for Congress. Thus treating the issue as a "political question" would have been an option had the Court wanted neither to overrule nor reaffirm *Plessy*. This, however, would have been seen as a "cop-out" and evasive of the Negroes' claims and, in Charles Black's words, "a real innovation, a real break with tradition."[95]

The attack on the Court for "lawmaking" was based in part on the Court's unanimity. This unanimity, coupled with the language of the opinion and the citation of social science materials, led many persons to feel that they were being "put upon" by a super-legislature, not dealt with by a court. The conventional wisdom is that, if possible, a severely divided Court, shown by five-to-four rulings, is to be avoided and unanimity achieved and that unanimity shows the strength of the majority view and dissents encourage noncompliance.[96] Although a five-to-four decision in

Brown would have been catastrophic, because it would have made those resisting even more determined, the wisdom about a divided ruling may not apply well to the *Brown* opinion. Doubts that the justices differed did not vanish simply because they all joined the opinion.[97] A dissenting opinion might even have been a plus. The effect of one or two negative votes is often overestimated. While the Court is often divided in cases involving controversial issues, people usually remember not the division in the Court but the perceived doctrine of the case.[98] More important, dissents are likely to expose weaknesses in the majority's legal argument and make the majority judges "tighten up"; a fragmented Court may thus leave good constitutional results. In *Brown,* opponents of the result might have been somewhat mollified by a dissent, perhaps feeling that someone was listening to them. Readers of the opinion might have felt that contrary arguments had been clearly and effectively presented to the Court and rejected by the majority. This process is institutionalized in the International Court of Justice. Operating with fifteen judges, it has two additional *ad hoc* judges for each case, one appointed by the plaintiff nation and one by the defendant nation. It is thus ensured that there will be at least one dissent in every opinion. The losing nation knows its "voice" has been heard in the *inner* councils, not merely at the argument stage.

Our argument is that Chief Justice Warren gave up too much in his opinion.[99] That does not mean he traded off tough points for the votes necessary for unanimity, because we have seen that his initial memorandum was much like the ultimate opinion. Yet he may have given away matters from the very beginning—matters such as an explicit overruling of *Plessy* and a more clearly stated distinction between intentional and de facto segregation. New to the Court and perhaps less sophisticated than experience would lead him to become about intracourt influence and bargaining, he may have written in part for a justice like Frankfurter with his philosophy of judicial self-restraint instead of letting Frankfurter dissent. Greater sophistication would have made him less hesistant to do that, as the reapportionment case of *Baker v. Carr* suggests. There the Court went on despite Frankfurter's most impassioned dissent in which he predicted the demise of the Court as he had come to know it, to hold that reapportionment complaints could be heard by the courts. When the Court's "activism" did not bring its destruction, Frankfurter's argument was demolished. And when the Court survived even Senator Dirksen's active efforts to revoke the reapportionment rulings, the Court was able to move forward in the late 1960s with the tough language of the later desegregation cases. If Warren was listening closely to Frankfurter in 1954, the resulting opinion did not assist the Court.

The Court's use of nonlegal materials to reach its conclusions and its refusal to pay more attention to history have also been criticized. The

Court's conclusion that the Fourteenth Amendment's history was inconclusive produced the criticism that, particularly after reargument on Court-posed questions, the historical discussion was a fraud, with the Court already having decided that 1954, not the 1860s, was the important time to examine.[100] The Court might have started its opinion with a long and boring inquiry into the background of the Fourteenth Amendment, leading to the conclusion, if possible on the historical record, that it was the purpose of the amendment to reach school segregation. The justices could have argued along with Alexander Bickel that school segregation was not among the rights which the Fourteenth Amendment's framers sought to insure, any more than was jury service, suffrage, or other specific rights subsequently supported by the Court, because the framers, aware they were writing a constitution, not a statute, chose language which was not intended to foreclose the Court from applying it to segregation in public schools or other evils arising in the future.[101] Such specific acknowledgement that the history of the amendment left it open to the Court to determine whether school segregation violated the requirement of equal protection would, we think, have lent explicit legitimacy to the Court's procedure. Using a more positive approach to the intentions of the framers, the Court could have drawn from the formative and interpretive aspects of the Fourteenth Amendment a general intention to eliminate all state-imposed discriminations against persons because of race, an intention commanding equality, and then noted how this command of equality had been extended to jury service, voting, and the like, as the Negro began to assert his rights against state discrimination. Then the Court would have had but a short step to conclude that school segregation supported by law was but another aspect of this state action contrary to the Fourteenth Amendment.

The use of social science materials, particularly those cited in the famed footnote number 11, perhaps brought more criticism from both opponents and supporters of the decision than any other single part of the *Brown* opinion. The states felt cheated because psychological and sociological material, which they had not even considered admissible, seemed to be the controlling evidence for the decision. On the other side, there have been complaints that the cited materials did not support the point for which they were introduced and that, more important, they made it appear as if the Negroes' rights rested on a very slim reed, because if the decision turned on the facts, new facts would require changes in result. As Edmond Cahn put it, "I would not have the constitutional rights of Negroes . . . rest on any such flimsy foundation as some of the scientific demonstrations in the records."[102] Although courts have always used "sociological" data[103] as we have seen in *Plessy*—the use of social science data "had the effect of partially obscuring the real grounds for overthrowing segregation, which were constitutional, political, and moral."[104] Furthermore, the social science data invited further dispute over the central holding in *Brown* by those who thought that by controverting the facts, one could obtain a different judicial ruling.[105] The presence of findings which have challenged the effect of education in providing equality has thus to some extent undermined the decision far more than could have occurred if the Chief Justice had avoided the reference. As Henry Levin has pointed out, because it has been assumed that integrated education would improve the academic performance of black children, people became upset at evidence which seemed to suggest that test scores were not improving as people thought they would. This meant that further attention was drawn away from the basic question—"What kind of educational policy regarding school racial patterns is consistent with our democratic ideals?"—and the "larger moral and human dilemmas raised by segregated public institutions" to which the overall thrust of *Brown* had been directed. To the extent the Court had directed attention to social science findings, its opinion had thus served to weaken the crucial overall constitutional position it had tried to take.[106] Had the Court wished to use social science, it could have relied heavily on the lower court opinion which it cited—indicating the process by which social science testimony had led to the findings of fact, with the district judge "holding back" only because of *Plessy*. The problem of reliance on social science evidence would have remained, but it would have been handled more forthrightly than footnote number 11 was handled. Even better, the Chief Justice could have taken judicial notice of the meaning of segregation in society, as he had done with respect to the importance of education.[107]

At the time, sociology was a relatively new field, its tools and methods far from precise. While we all engage in implicit social science, people were reluctant to accept explicitly offered social science findings. The Supreme Court was also unfamiliar with the sociological data and not equipped to analyze it critically.[108] All of this led to the Court's poor handling of the material, which cast its use in a bad light. That is another unfortunate by-product of the *Brown* decision because sociological data is relevant in determining the Constitution's applicability to particular cases and because such data, properly arrived at and carefully used, is much more likely to reflect social reality than are individuals' intuitive opinions.

The Court's decision to hear further argument on the question of relief was perhaps the most crucial strategic decision it made in these cases and the one most open to criticism. In announcing in 1954 that segregated public education was contrary to the Constitution, the Court knew that in three of the five cases steps had already been taken to remedy existing conditions in the direction such an announcement commanded. The justices also knew that the southern states, from which the greatest opposition could be expected, were not totally unprepared for such an announcement and were taking steps to upgrade inferior Negro schools. Argument solicited by the Court had been heard from both sides on implementation of a decree. All parties seemed to agree that a gradual adjustment supervised by the lower federal courts in the tradition of equity would be proper, although there were differences of opinion about how long gradual adjustment should be expected or allowed to take. Unanimity evidently had been achieved largely on the basis of a moderate approach to implementation. Yet instead of ending its opinion with a ringing declaration that the petitioners had illegally and unconstitutionally been deprived of their rights and that they must be admitted forthwith to the schools in question under the protection of judicial contempt proceedings, or simply issuing an ethical, just pronouncement and let the compliance chips fall where they might, the Court hesitated and stopped in its tracks. Worse still, it had invited the participation of the potential resisters in a full-scale hearing.

If the avoidance of a statement about implementation in *Brown I* was meant to preserve the legitimacy of the basic decision, the Court seems to have misfigured. Though the Court was not criticized by the Negro newspapers in 1954 for its failure to set up immediate implementation, such inaction did not save it from southern criticism, which continued to build. If the Court thought it was being realistic in passing the implementation issue it was again in error, as realism was interpreted by many who followed the Court as extralegal, making the ruling not worthy of compliance. The result was that *Brown I* became a weak opinion tolerable for the South precisely because it did not require anyone to do anything pending *Brown II*. In fact, the incentive to build more southern schools for blacks vanished after *Brown I;* there was simply no more point to building separatist schools.

Albert Sacks has called Warren's separation of the formulation of a decree from the issue of constitutionality "judicial statesmanship," because "present attention was focused on the basic principle which was decisive of the merits, and the problems of enforcement . . . were assigned a subordinate status."[109] Traditional equity practice does involve a separate hearing on the decree. This secures additional time "not only for further deliberation in the Court, but also for adjustment of views outside of the Court."[110] However, for the Supreme Court to have followed this procedure in such a crucial case may have been a mistake, because the public in this country—unlike the British—has never understood equity courts and because this was no time for the Supreme Court to try to teach the public about equity. And certainly in the past the Court had not hesitated to make rights "personal and present," as in the law school cases where it had done so despite the South's *argumentum ad horrendum* concerning noncompliance.[111] Marshall had pointed out to the Court that compliance with both *Sweatt* and *McLaurin* had occurred despite such statements. Even if that compliance was, despite the Court's firm statement, much less than Marshall suggested, the firm ruling itself did the Court no damage and made it appear appropriately principled.

Thurgood Marshall and Spottswood Robinson, arguing before the Court in *Brown II*, were to say that no one before had ever contended that basic constitutional rights should be postponed. If there was a constitutional right for blacks to attend any school without restriction, then how could that right be delayed? How could anyone argue that there would be any justification on the side of those who would deprive black school children of their immediate right to an equal education? The irony of the situation was that the Supreme Court itself was in effect the body that contended that this right could be postponed. By requiring a separate consideration of the implementation decision after *Brown I*, and by asking the questions it did, the Court itself severely undercut the constitutional rights that it had just proclaimed. The opinion in *Brown I* could thus be seen as a strange message from the Supreme Court: an opinion couched in the language of constitutional rights but, because of the postponement of consideration of implementation, an opinion which obviously does not mean what it says. It was like saying, "Segregation is immoral, but you can continue doing it until we figure out a comfortable way for you to ease out of the practice." Surely the public could interpret such a message by concluding that segregation could not be very immoral, illegal, or unconstitutional after all.

The Court may later have learned lessons from what it had done in *Brown I*. However, its errors meant that *Brown* itself was not finished in 1954; indeed, the Court was to compound its problems in *Brown II*. Then, either overreacting or feeling badly burned by the lesson, the justices beat an unseemly retreat from the public school education field which was to last, with a few exceptions, for over a dozen years.

Chapter 4

The Implementation Round and *Brown II*

THE time consumed in the third round of argument was longer than in either of the other two.[1] Because argument was limited to matters of implementation, both the lawyers' presentations and the justices' questions were far better focused. They were also more complex because of emphasis on detail. Yet the basic posture of the parties can be identified. Kansas, Delaware, and the District of Columbia said, in effect, "We've made progress; so leave us alone." The NAACP, looking to past examples, said, "If progress has been made there, it can be made elsewhere." The South's position was that a requirement of prompt desegregation would mean that resistance would be great, that there would be no schools at all, and that desegregation would take many years. The NAACP retorted, "If the South says, 'Never,' there is no need for gradualism." In the deluge of proposals made to the Court, several problems were discussed frequently. They were the uses to which the lower courts should be put, the specifics the Supreme Court itself should enunciate, and the element of time. There were suggestions that the cases be remanded to the lower federal courts, that to supervise implementation those lower courts should retain jurisdiction of the cases, and that a special master be appointed to review lower court rulings and make recommendations to the Court. Suggestions were also made that the Supreme Court say specifically that existing segregation statutes were unconstitutional and that school attendance not be based on race or color. Some persons wished the Court to write a detailed decree, while others wanted no more than a call for action in accord with the opinion. Throughout the disagreement as to what provisions might be included in a decree, were one to be written, ran the recurring theme that the Supreme Court and the lower federal courts were equity courts with wide latitude to fashion remedies. On the question of time, suggestions varied from demands for a "forthwith" decree, perhaps allowing only for "administrative" time to make adjustments, to a decree with no ultimate date established for the end of segregation.

Kansas Attorney General Harold R. Fatzer opened by saying he was not appearing as an adversary but wished to assist in drafting a proper decree. He reported that the Supreme Court's decision in *Brown I* had been received with approval by students, teachers, and parents of both colored and white children. However, he argued, Question 4(a)— whether a decree should provide that within limits set by normal geographical school districting Negro children should forthwith be admitted to schools of their choice—should receive a negative answer. Instead, he suggested that the case should be remanded to the federal district court in Kansas. Fatzer pointed out that the Topeka Board of Education had begun several years earlier to terminate segregation by moving from universal segregation in its elementary schools to a system consisting of twelve integrated schools and two which were partially integrated, with five schools maintained exclusively for white students and four attended only by Negroes. In the next step, to become effective in September 1955, segregation would be terminated in all remaining buildings, but any child affected by a change in districts could finish the elementary grades where he attended school in the 1954–55 year. Thus, he said, the board had complied in good faith with the Court's decision. He suggested that the Board of Education be permitted to carry out its program with a decree, and cited precedent in support of the proposition that where administrative intent is expressed but not yet come to fruition a case is not ripe for equitable intervention. Robert Carter's succinct position was that the Court should specifically invalidate the Kansas statute even though *Brown I* already had that effect. He said that the Topeka School Board should also be told not to base attendance on race or color because the present plan had the effect of continuing segregation through districting. The district court should determine whether the school board had complied.

Because the children in the Delaware case had been attending desegregated schools and because both sides accepted the idea of affirmance of the state supreme court's decision, argument was necessarily narrow. Backing off to some extent from his predecessor's position, Attorney General Joseph Craven suggested that time was needed to make facilities equal because the state was a border state. "I cannot tell the Court that all will be well. We are a divided and troubled people in the face of the mandate of the Court," he said. He did not want an ultimate date set for completion of desegregation, but wanted the cases remanded with a direction that the state authorities submit plans which, when approved, would be supervised by the local courts. He felt that there was a need for orderliness coupled with attention to local needs. For the Negroes, Louis Redding argued that plaintiffs' rights should be declared personal and present. He pointed out that while the Delaware Supreme Court, interpreting *Brown I,* had invalidated the state's segregation provisions,[2] the children had not immediately entered the schools.

George Hayes echoed the call for personal and present rights in the *Bolling* case and suggested some differences between policy and practice in the District of Columbia. Although the corporation counsel had declared the segregation statute unconstitutional and the board of education had acted forthrightly, and although greater speed in desegregation was being made than the administration had thought possible, Hayes said there were transition mechanisms, particularly allowing students to stay in particular schools until they graduated, which slowed down the process. In response to a series of questions from Justice Black, Hayes said also that he wanted to limit somewhat the ability of the child to choose any school he wanted so that such choice could not be used to undercut desegregation. He wanted the possibility preserved of going to court if "flagrant violations" occurred or anything were done "where race was used as a criteria [*sic*]." James M. Nabrit, Jr., also argued that alleged multiple administrative difficulties were not as great as might be expected and that long periods of time were not necessary. A fitting conclusion to this litigation, Nabrit urged, would be a decree that integration shall be effective forthwith. Because there were approximately 104,000 pupils in the District, of whom the majority were Negroes, Nabrit stressed the value and relevance of this case to the situation in the South. Firm administrative and executive hands are most effective elements in bringing about integration, he said, as is a militant stand against ordinary objections. Milton Korman's argument for the other side in the case showed that the government preferred low-visibility integration in Washington, D.C., to any judicial decree. Using a mootness argument in an attempt to persuade the Court to back off, Korman said the only reason for a dispute was the Negroes' desire for a decree directing specific acts. He contended that there was nothing here to enjoin and no chance for a return to segregation. The Court must know, he said, that there was a pronouncement by the District of Columbia commissioners that segregation should be cast out. The school board members wanted integration and had moved fast to integrate. With desegregation already in effect, he argued, the school board members ought not to be placed under an order saying they had to integrate.

Spottswood W. Robinson III opened the argument in the Virginia and South Carolina cases by calling for a decree requiring desegregation as soon as necessary administrative and mechanical procedures could be accomplished. The Court should not formulate a detailed decree, Robinson stated, nor need it appoint a special master to hear evidence. Instead it should remand the case to a court of first instance to frame the decree.

However, he argued, the Supreme Court's decree should contain certain specified provisions. Following the *Sipuel* case in which the Court accelerated the granting of relief and gave relief forthwith, the decree would require 1) immediate initiation of administrative procedures and steps toward integration and 2) admission at the coming September term of the applicants and others to nonsegregated schools. Robinson used the District of Columbia, Kansas, and Delaware cases to support his claim for a short time-period, with September 1955 as "the terminal date of the desegregation process." The burden should be on the state officials to show the necessity for delay, Robinson explained, because the rights involved, the rights of children, are personal and present and must be satisfied while they are still children. Continuance of racial segregation causes irreparable harm to students, he added. Robinson maintained that no case had been found in which, when a constitutional right was involved, the Court had postponed action. It would be strange indeed, he asserted, that enjoyment of fundamental and human rights could be postponed. These rights are secured by the Fourteenth Amendment, he asserted, and such rights should not be "forced to a pace geared down to practices that that Amendment was designed to practice against."

Thurgood Marshall, continuing, told the Court it must issue a forthwith decree, although any decree issued would be subject to ordinary administrative processes. By forthwith, he meant not tomorrow but the school term beginning in September 1955, when the appellants of high school age and the entire class they represent should be admitted. Here Harlan commented that in his brief Marshall had suggested an alternative date of September 1, 1956. "Have you receded from that position?" Harlan wanted to know. Marshall replied that he had felt obliged by the Court's Question 5 to pick an alternative date. But, he contended, the least the Court should do is put in a date certain. The Court should recognize that the present and personal rights are still there and that they are of the type enforced in *Sipuel, Sweatt,* and *McLaurin.* He summarized his position concerning the decree as follows:

The least that would do us any good at all would be a decree which included four items: (1) That this Court make the clearest declaration that not only those statutes but others are in violation of the Fourteenth Amendment. We think it is necessary for that to be put in the decree. (2) That they start immediately to desegregate. (3) File reports. (4) That it must end at a day certain, and that, we take the position, is the minimum that we should expect if we cannot get the decree which will say that as of the next school term.

Pressing his plea for forthwith relief, Marshall alluded to the situation in Kansas, Delaware, and the District of Columbia. The District case was highly significant, he said, for there the authorities desegregated between

May and December, although they must have been working on the problem before the Court's decision. To the argument that the number of Negroes involved made a difference in the relief to be afforded, he pointed out that the District had the largest ratio of Negro to white students of any city in the country—almost 60–40—and yet in the District numbers had proved to be unimportant. Frankfurter then commented "that argument is lost only if all other factors are the same." Marshall agreed, adverting to the good will and other factors involved in the District, but he contended that his argument was not negated. Scientific studies show, he stated, that desegregation needs a firm hand of government but it matters not if the firm hand is legislative, administrative, or judicial. A district court properly instructed by this Court would supply the firm hand, as would the Fourth Circuit. The people in North Carolina and South Carolina would comply when the law was made clear, Marshall said, reiterating that he had "inherent faith in our democratic process." The people in the South are no different from anybody else when it comes to being law-abiding, Marshall said, adding that public opinion polls "don't mean anything—a man can't predict what he will do."

The *Sweatt* and *McLaurin* cases had opened graduate and professional schools in twelve southern states, he said, with only one untoward incident, although the attorneys general of southern states made the same dire predictions that are made here. The same predictions had also been made in the *Henderson* train case many years earlier but were not borne out, he added. Marshall made it clear that no one was more conscious than he that this present problem was a difficult one, but said that the fact that attorneys general have problems doesn't matter—they get paid for handling problems. Marshall also argued that indeterminate delay of relief would not accomplish anything. Had Virginia and South Carolina requested a period of four or five years, it would have been one thing, but Virginia's Commission on Public Education publicly stated that it was going to explore avenues designed to prevent enforced integration and was asking the Court for time to work on that, for a moratorium or local option. There is no local option in the Fourteenth Amendment, and the fact that a state is a southern state or in a border area is no reason to delay relief. In the statement he made after the attorneys for the southern states had completed their argument, Marshall said the case should be seen in its larger context. *Brown I* was the "forthright straightforward position of the law of this country as pronounced by its highest Court." Now because implementation had been left open and because "the whole country has seen in the South that this decision means nothing as of now," it was necessary that the Court must set a time limit—"part of the effectiveness, forthrightness if you please, of the May 17 decision." Stressing that the "strongest type of a decree" would be to "arm the district judge and the court of appeals judge with these necessary high level decrees so that they can operate from then on," Marshall said he had hoped that by now the Court could be told when its decision could be complied with. When some persons said not in their lifetime and others said hundreds of years, nothing before the Court justified gradual adjustment, he said. Despite the protestations, not one state had started to do anything. Characterizing his opponents' argument as one of "if you don't give me what I want, I'll close up the schools," Marshall said he didn't believe that the problem would be solved by increasing ignorance. Without a time limit there would be no effective enforcement of the May 17 decision, because through the South people were being told that the *Brown* ruling meant nothing until a time limit was set and unlawful conduct would continue indefinitely without it. Marshall insisted that the other side should not be allowed to have an advantage brought about by their own wrongdoing. He declared that the Court should not take a middle ground between two positions on the time for enforcement of a constitutional right. The argument that the Court should postpone constitutional rights had never before been advanced and "is never made until Negroes are involved." He added that the enforcement of constitutional rights should be uniform throughout the country and should not "mean one thing in one state and another thing in another state."

First to appear for the South was S. E. Rogers of South Carolina.[3] His opening statements were indicative of the South's position. Asserting that his opponents recognized the magnitude of the problems, he said, "We are not in the position of Kansas or the District of Columbia. Clarendon County is an agricultural community. The people are tied to the land and can't move." He explained that the school district was located in an old plantation section of the county, which consequently had a large Negro and a small white population, 2,559 colored students and 299 white students. If this Court should order immediate integration, instead of the integration most people have in mind, only a few whites would go to colored schools. Agreeing with appellants' statement that desegregation involved problems on the frontier of scientific knowledge, Rogers pointed out that Clarendon County had had a biracial society for over two centuries. Although progress had been made, he said, and the schools had been equalized with Negroes going on to be lawyers, doctors, and teachers, "I do not believe that in a biracial society we can push the clock forward abruptly to 2015 or 2045." A change of attitude must be brought about slowly, not quickly. He pointed out that because desegregation does and will affect the social life of the community, to say that the Court's decision is unpopular would be the understatement of the year. Yet because his clients wanted to work within the framework of the decision, he was asking that the case be sent back without instruction for action in conformity with the decision.

Rogers's position on the result of sending the case back to the district court was, however, unclear. He was obviously unwilling to commit himself to the position that it would work. This was evident from a statement he made toward the close of his argument: "To say we will conform depends on the decree handed down. I am frank to tell you, right now in our district I do not think that we will send—the white people of the district will send their children to the Negro schools. It would be unfair to tell the Court that we are going to do that. I do not think it is. But I do think that something can be worked out. We hope so." He also showed his uneasiness in an exchange with the Chief Justice, who took a more active role than in earlier argument.

WARREN: But you are not willing to say here that there would be an honest attempt to conform to this decree, if we did leave it to the district court?
ROGERS: No, I am not. Let us get the word "honest" out of there.
WARREN: No, leave it in.
ROGERS: No, because I would have to tell you that right now we would not conform—we would not send our white children to the Negro schools.

Next to speak for South Carolina was Robert McC. Figg, Jr. Emphasizing that he was not discussing the May 17 decision, he stated that it was his position that the decree should not order forthwith desegregation and that the Supreme Court had the power to permit effective gradual integration. Adverting to the characterization of the Negro students' rights as personal and present, Figg contended that the power of the Court was not thereby limited. He cited authorities to support the view that the Court has full equitable discretion, and said that Supreme Court decisions did not sustain the suggestion that there might be some limitations on the equity powers of the Court to consider the circumstances. His view was that the case should be remanded in the usual course for a decree in accordance with the opinion. The appellants would then present their difficulties to the lower court, which would have sufficient powers to achieve the Supreme Court's goals. He argued that to set September 1955 as a time limit would mean the end of the public school districts. Forces over which the local authorities have no control would bring about this result, and the local officials would be confronted with the question "of whether you are going to have funds to run a school . . . [and] whether you are going to have the legislation necessary to run the schools." Like Rogers, Figg stressed the length of time during which whites and Negroes had lived in a "biracial society." When a pattern had continued for ninety years, some time was necessary to achieve "community acceptance" of change, particularly if public support for education were to be continued, far more important for the Negroes than for the whites. Acceptance would be advanced by allowing the local courts to handle matters, he said.

Archibald G. Robertson, for Virginia, took an even stronger position than had the South Carolinians. He told the Court, "We cannot foresee any future date when segregation can be solved." Many people, he explained, have indicated a refusal to consent to compulsory integration. No court decrees can be effective if the decree is opposed by a majority of the people. If the Court had reversed and remanded earlier, it practically would have wiped out the public school system of Virginia, he argued. The governor had appointed a legislative commission to study the problem. The commission, having obtained the advice of people in all walks of life, was seeking a solution in good faith, and the state would move with all reasonable speed. Robertson said that because this was an equity proceeding, the Court had the power to—and should—permit gradual adjustment. Virginia is not here as a convicted culprit, he argued, for segregation had been lawful; at the very least the Court should grant Prince Edward County a fair opportunity to adjust. But because without evidence a detailed decree would be based on surmise and the case might require months or years of the district court's time, the Supreme Court could not do the job of writing the decree. He thus noted his agreement with the government's position stated in its brief that no "forthwith" decree should be entered and that there should be effective gradual adjustment. However, he felt that no specific direction should be given the district court and no definite time limit should be set.

Robertson also argued that the sociological evidence presented did not show the emotional or psychological effect of desegregation on white children. To this argument he added a discussion of "racial differences," including the intellectual superiority of whites and the vast differences in morals and health standards. Calling the Court's attention to the fact that in Prince Edward County Negroes made up 55 percent of the population but that the whites supported the schools, he contended that without a favorable community attitude no favorable result could be obtained. He added that because appropriations were made locally, as in South Carolina, the schools might have to close to permit workable plans to be developed. Because the percentage of Negroes varied from zero to 73 percent in different parts of the state, time was needed, and no single pattern under one rule would be appropriate. The Supreme Court can tell Virginia what not to do, he said, but it cannot tell Virginia what kind of schools it should have. He warned that to do so would encourage the bitterness of the Reconstruction era and injure the public school system of the state, with schoolchildren the victims.

Virginia Attorney General J. Lindsay Almond, Jr., a good orator, was to make the strongest statement not only in opposition to immediate action but also in support of resistance, an indication of Virginia's later "massive resistance" in which he was directly involved. Almond said he disagreed with *Brown I,* but "it is the law of the land and I trust we may be given an opportunity to work out a solution at the local level. There is not a shadow of a doubt that the Supreme Court may permit effective gradual adjustment to be brought about." Yet to Virginians, he continued, "that does not mean enforced integration." The decision required merely a changeover "from an existing segregated system to a system not based on color distinctions." If the Court were to adopt the view that the rights of the Negro schoolchildren were personal and present and require immediate enforcement, that "disastrous" position would result in subjugation of the rights of millions, and would be "pre-emptive of the rights of a sovereign people" to promulgate state laws. Our opponents want the power to destroy the most important function of state government, he continued, and a grant of this "unbridled power" would result in the schools not operating. He emphasized that his assertions were statements of fact and not threats. We are facing possible destruction of our public school system, he said, and this Court should afford a reasonable opportunity in good faith to reach a solution by remanding the case to the court of first instance. Shaping a solution "to the dilemma which confronts it" was the state's prerogative. He also said that the Court had authority neither to "legislate" directly nor to delegate such authority to the district courts. "It has no power to give to a state or a local school board affirmative directions as to the operation of its school system." To do so would mean that the southern states "had not had their day in court to test the constitutionality of any solution which they might evolve in an honest effort to save their public school system from destruction." Almond argued further that no consideration had been given to the effect of integration on white children or to the ability of the state to maintain a public school system. These problems do not stem from racial antipathy, he asserted, and those who say so are as "reckless with the truth as Sherman was with fire in some parts of our country." In conclusion, he said, in some of the most emotional language of the entire three rounds of argument: "No blanket forthwith decree entered by any court could possibly do aught but preclude an approach to a solution and not only turn the clock back education-wise, far beyond *Plessy v. Ferguson,* but wreak damage upon the hearts and minds of children . . . in a way unlikely to be ever undone." What the Negroes wanted, Almond said, was "unwarranted and undue force," with the Court being urged "to press this crown of thorns upon our brow, and hold the hemlock up to our lips."

Attorneys general for several southern states also appeared to assert their states' resistance to implementation. Although their tones differed, all but one argued that delay was necessary if the school systems were to be preserved. For example, North Carolina Assistant Attorney General I. Beverly Lake said a decree requiring "immediate intermixing" would replace racial "friendliness and peace" with "bitterness and antipathies" like those of the post–Civil War period and would put the public schools "in the gravest danger of abolition." If a community feels that its school system "does violence to [its] earnestly held conviction," one will be left with "inadequate equipment, shoddy instruction, and irregular attendance." The one exception to the tone of hostility was the "lawyers' argument" presented by Arkansas Attorney General Thomas Gentry. Gentry discussed past cases and admitted that responsibility for enforcing plaintiffs' rights clearly was the Supreme Court's because Congress had not acted under Section 5 of the Fourteenth Amendment. Gentry's proposal was that Congress pass a statute placing penalities on this violation of the amendment, thus bringing to bear on the problem not only the equity courts of the country but also "the full power of the law enforcement of the United States Government" and the criminal courts. Although radical by comparison with the statements from the other states, the proposal was not realistic, because Congress in the 1950s was unlikely to pass any such legislation, and thus Gentry did not materially assist in solving the problem of implementing *Brown*.

United States Solicitor General Simon E. Sobeloff recommended that because the Supreme Court cannot act as "super school board," the cases be remanded to the district courts which, he argued, should consider the facts and apply a measure of discretion. Such discretion would not be used to frustrate the goal of *Brown;* there should be no delay for the sake of delay. This does not mean that segregation "will be erased with one stroke of the pen," but "there is such a great variety of conditions that no single formula can be devised that will fit aptly all cases." The thrust of Sobeloff's argument was that the Supreme Court should give lower court judges guidance and a push, so that desegregation would get started. Rather than giving the district courts "no criteria" or a "blank check," Sobeloff thought it important for the Court to indicate an approach to the problem to reduce litigation. If the states can see what is required, opposition could not be expected to "fold up automatically," but the states would be more likely to do things on their own. Sobeloff said the Court should start with a deadline in the district court of ninety days for the submission of a plan. This provision would strengthen the hand of the district court which at the end of the ninety day period could give more time on a showing of reason for it. The important thing was to make clear that there must be a bona fide advance toward the goal. Sobeloff also suggested that the Court could appoint a special master to review the lower courts' reports and make appropriate recommendations to the Supreme Court, which would retain jurisdiction to make any necessary orders.

The range of questions the justices asked was more limited than at the previous rounds of argument. There was also much more repetition of questions, in part a result of the addition of the southern attorneys general to the argument but also a result of the justices' difficulties in deciding the implementation issue after the simpler issue of whether to call segregation unconstitutional. By far the greatest number of questions dealt with factual matters, primarily the numbers and locations of Negro children and secondarily matters such as the progress of desegregation, the autonomy of local schools, and the authority of state officials to enforce rules. For example, Attorney General Fatzer of Kansas, in addition to being asked the "legal" question of the effect of *Brown I* on the state statute, was asked whether segregation had ended, whether school districts were autonomous, and whether some all-white and all-black schools would remain after desegregation. He was also asked for information on the size of the school population, the basis for districting, the percentage of white and black children in each school, and the schedule for desegregation. Both sides were asked by Justices Frankfurter and Warren when classes were made up—important in terms of timing. Justices Clark, Harlan, and Douglas asked Robert Carter about the effect of the option system, which allowed children to continue where they already were. Carter had difficulty getting the Court to understand that the whites thus had choice but that the Negroes did not.

In the District of Columbia case, Justices Burton, Minton, and Black quizzed Hayes on the same matter of the option plan, but many more questions to him went to the operation of the districting plan as a whole. Justice Reed wanted to know how the children's choice operated under the plan, and Justice Black asked Hayes how the proposed plan could result in discrimination. Justice Black inquired about the amount of choice to be allowed the children. Milton Korman, arguing the District's side of the case, was met with questions on protests under the new desegregation plan and on operation of the "hardship rule." Both Justices Frankfurter and Douglas were particularly interested in reasons for the success of desegregation in the District, and they elicited the response that the nonpartisan character of the school board, the equality of quality of teaching staff between the previously all-white and all-Negro schools, and the president's interest in desegregation had all played a part. In what was a mixed question of law and fact, the justices explored whether they were dealing with class actions, the scope of the class action, and the numbers affected. Here the Court was faced with options ranging from having the decrees affect only the children who were immediate parties to the cases to having the decrees framed to include many more students, not simply those from the affected school districts or states. The Court had also been urged to have the cases binding on others not part of the class action only through stare decisis, as a precedent or guide, thus leaving initiation of desegregation in other areas to suits by Negro parents. And Solicitor General Sobeloff had suggested that if the Court did not see the suits as class actions, and thus was dealing only with the immediate parties, there was no reason why a "forthwith" decree should not issue. Justices Harlan, Frankfurter, and Black all questioned Marshall as to the class action aspect of the suit, with Justice Harlan, the newest member of the Court, particularly attracted by the issue.[4] Closely related was the justices' interest in the Delaware case in finding out to whom the relief ran in the present decree—that is, to the specific Negro children or to others as well.

The wording of the Court's decree received particular attention. Rather early in the argument Carter was asked whether the decree needed to contain specific invalidation of the state statute. Frankfurter, who asked Hayes whether the Court could get into particularities, also asked the North Carolina spokesman whether the Court could state affirmatively what needed to be done rather than merely striking down specific actions. Justice Black wanted to know how broad an effect would result from a decree directed only to particular parties, and Chief Justice Warren asked Attorney General Sybert of Maryland whether guidance should be given to the district courts to help those courts with the cases which would arise. A related question concerned the matter of enforcement—for example, when Frankfurter asked Marshall to describe the post-decree events necessary for Negroes not to be excluded from schools because of their race. Matters of how court orders would be enforced were raised by Justice Black, who by both his questioning and more direct suggestion, indicated the availability of procedures such as contempt and civil actions under 42 U.S.C. 1983.

The question of the time to be allowed was frequently raised by the justices. Frankfurter wanted to know of Robinson whether the Court could take judicial notice of a particular date or whether instead hearings would be necessary to set a date. Justice Reed asked for reasons which might justify delay, and Harlan pursued with Marshall the question of why plaintiffs had proposed alternative dates. Frankfurter seemed to be suggesting gradualism when he referred to the "certain unalterable facts of life" which even the Supreme Court couldn't change; for him, these facts included "districting the accommodations, the arrangement of personnel, and all the complexities that go with the administering of schools." Frankfurter's concern for administrative matters also showed in his question to Marshall as to whether there had been administrative problems under *Gaines, Sweatt,* and the other cases.

There were also questions on whether compliance was going on and, particularly, whether efforts in the direction of compliance could be expected. Thus in the South Carolina case Frankfurter asked Rogers whether attitudes change without action and, later, asked North Carolina's attorney whether the state could close its schools. Chief Justice Warren, whose impatience with noncompliance seemed clear from his questions, was direct in asking Rogers whether the Court could assume an attempt to comply and whether an "open decree" was wanted because of resistance. He asked co-counsel in the same case whether compliance should wait on changed attitudes and asked Texas Assistant Attorney General Waldrep what sort of local autonomy he was asking for—to accommodate to local differentiation or to allow nonconformity.

Writing the decree was far more difficult for the Court than writing *Brown I*.[5] That difficulty had been foreshadowed when the Court had avoided discussing the subject of implementation in its earlier opinion. There seems to have been a "gross uncertainty" as to how implementation should be handled.[6] That the Chief Justice was among those favoring some "go-slow" approach is clear from his own recollections in 1972 and from the notes of both Frankfurter and Burton, both of whom recorded him as opposed to fixing a date for the completion of desegregation. But Warren also was less clear about where to go than he had been about the issues decided in *Brown I*. In conference, Warren indicated he had not formed a fixed opinion on the subject, but went on to state his views on a number of alternatives. He was opposed to appointing a master or having the district courts do so, to fixing a date for the completion of desegregation or indicating to the district courts that they do so, to requiring the lower courts to call for school district-submitted plans, although he was willing to let the courts to do that, and to setting procedural requirements. On the positive side, Warren thought the Court instead of issuing a decree should write an opinion containing the principles of *Brown I,* a statement that the cases were class actions, and a list of factors for the lower courts to consider. Warren included among these factors, which he wanted treated as "oughts" rather than as a checklist, frictions and problems of compliance and the progress represented by submitted plans. The lower courts, he felt, should be given both support and latitude.

Justice Black, also recorded by his colleagues as favoring a "go-slow" approach, took much the same stance as Warren.[7] His stress appears to have been on doing everything that could be done to achieve unanimity on the Court. He wanted to issue a decree without more, "on the ground that the less said the better off the Court would be." He was pessimistic about whether the lower courts could enforce desegregation orders and feared that the courts would be damaged by unenforceable decrees. He differed from Warren in wanting the cases treated not as class actions but as individual cases. Also joining Warren and Black in favoring a go-slow approach was Justice Burton, who in December 1952 had favored a ten-year delay, and who later said that "every year helps."[8] We know less about the other justices' positions. Frankfurter, who had earlier advocated the idea of using a special master, did not press it in conference. Justice Reed and Justice Douglas agreed with Black on the individual-versus class-suit matter, and Reed agreed with Warren in saying it would be permissible for district judges to ask for desegregation plans. Douglas, however, wanted a cutoff date for segregation, at least for those involved in the cases before the Court. Justice Harlan, who generally agreed with Warren, noted that he had not thought the cases to be true class suits, and said the class suit idea was appropriate. Justice Minton's position seems to have been only that he would vote with the majority.[9]

Warren's ideas generally prevailed in the short opinion he wrote for the Court, although he did not state his class action recommendation directly. The idea of gradualness permeated the entire opinion. Its first paragraph linked the decree to the constitutional decision of a year earlier and contained a declaration that any state statutes which conflicted with the May 17 decision were void, thus providing a victory for the government and for Robert Carter. All provisions of federal, state, or local law which required or permitted racial discrimination in public education must yield to the earlier announced principle that such discrimination was unconstitutional, said the Court. The Court then noted that the variance of conditions in the cases and the nationwide importance of the decision on relief had led to the request for further argument and extensive amicus curiae participation. Those presentations had been helpful, the opinion continued, and had demonstrated that substantial steps to eliminate the racial discrimination concerned had been taken already in a number of states and the District of Columbia, although it was also noted that South Carolina and Virginia were instead awaiting the Court's decision.

For full implementation of the case's constitutional principles, a variety of local school problems would have to be solved. School authorities were to have the primary responsibility in identifying, assessing, and solving these problems, the Court declared, although whether their action constituted good faith implementation was a question for the courts. Because further hearing might be needed, the Court said it seemed most appropriate to remand the cases to the courts which originally heard them, as they were closest to local conditions. In fashioning and effectuating their decrees, the courts were to be guided by equitable principles, that is, they were to demonstrate practical flexibility and a facility for adjusting and reconciling public and private needs. Underlying that approach had to be recognition that at stake was the personal interest of the Negro children in admission to public schools as soon as practicable on a nondiscriminatory basis. Their rights might call for elimination of a variety of obstacles, which the public interest required be done in a systematic and effective manner. However, said the Court, "it should go without saying that the vitality of these constitutional principles cannot be allowed to yield simply because of disagreement with them." The opinion went on to state that courts should require that the defendants make a prompt and reasonable start toward full compliance with the May 17 ruling and that, once such a start has been made, the courts should allow additional time only if the defendants are able to establish that such time is necessary, in the public interest, and consistent with good faith compliance at the earliest practicable date. The Court then listed problems which might be considered as justifying delay: administration, the physical condition of school plants, school transportation systems, personnel, revision of school districts and attendance areas into compact units for the purpose of achieving a system of determining admission to public schools on a nonracial basis, and revision of local laws and regulations which might be necessary in solving the foregoing problems. The courts should also consider the adequacy of any plans proposed to meet such problems and to effectuate a transition to a racially nondiscriminatory school system, retaining jurisdiction during this period of transition.

After this brief discussion, the opinion gave explicit directions on the disposition of the five cases. All the judgments below except that in the Delaware case were reversed and the cases remanded to the federal district courts, "to take such proceedings and enter such orders as are necessary and proper to admit to public schools on a racially nondiscriminatory basis with all deliberate speed the parties to these cases." The Delaware case was affirmed on the basis of the principles stated in the May 17 opinion, but the case was nevertheless remanded to the state supreme court for such further proceedings as that court might deem necessary in light of the present opinion.

Brown II, which has been called a disaster,[10] certainly further weakened the Court's position. Although it would have been better to have made such a statement in *Brown I,* there was still a chance for the Court to say, following Marshall, "We have analyzed our position in the past year extensively, and we conclude that since constitutional rights are at stake, there is no course for us but to order that schools must be desegregated immediately. By 'immediately' we mean by a fixed date— the next school term." However, the Court in *Brown II* was obviously not accepting Marshall's argument against postponing rights.[11] Its very decision in *Brown I* to have a further implementation hearing meant that it had already decided that there would be a later implementation opinion that would not be couched in terms of immediate rights but, rather, would

involve the court system in a slow process of supervising school boards so
that desegregation could proceed "with all deliberate speed." Indeed, it
may have mustered unanimity on this premise. The result was that, as
Robert Carter was to write, the Court was "mired in the vexing problems
of progress in school desegregation for the [next] thirteen years"[12] and, as
the Court itself acknowledged in 1968 and 1969, fourteen and fifteen
years and two entire elementary school generations passed after *Brown*
with hardly any implementation in the Deep South.[13]

Some of the criticism of *Brown II* may stem from hindsight, for we now
know the decision did not work, did not produce desegregation, and we
are thus more likely to attack it. But more than that was involved. Had the
year between *Brown I* and *Brown II* produced some specific implementation procedures, the open-endedness of *Brown I* and its avoidance of
implementation might have been a price worth paying. As it was, another
year was lost in which the opponents of desegregation had the opportunity to rally their forces and develop methods of evasion—another year
while people waited and then found they had been waiting for the Court
to say almost nothing. *Brown II* further communicated the idea that the
South could take even more time before acting, if it was to act at all. Robert
Carter has suggested that the formula "aroused the hope that resistance
to the constitutional imperative would succeed,"[14] and Jack Greenberg
has argued, "In the context of the widespread assumption that desegregation would have to be accomplished instantaneously," the decision "was
taken by many school boards to indicate judicial reluctance to upset the
status quo."[15]

The opinion in *Brown II* has been criticized for a variety of reasons.
Among the most central are that the Court allowed too much time for
desegregation, that it failed to establish clear guidelines as to what should
be done, and, most fundamentally, that it was insufficiently moral—that it
paid too much attention to compliance at the expense of principle. In
addition to all the other defects in the opinion, the Court provided a list of
factors which could be considered as reasons for delay—reasons that
resistant school boards could have thought up on their own without the
Court's help, but now could cite as authoritative. If the Court shared
Frankfurter's concern, stated in the first round of argument, that "nothing could be worse . . . than for this Court to make an abstract declaration that segregation is bad and then have it evaded by tricks," the Court
did not show it in indicating some of the "tricks" which might be used.[16]

Before examining some of those criticisms in greater detail, we should
note that immediate reaction to the opinion was not great. Hostility had
been expressed during oral argument, but resistance, particularly of the
type known as "Massive Resistance" when it appeared in Virginia, was not
to come until attempts were made to enforce *Brown*. Even the "Southern

Manifesto," in which southern congressmen attacked *Brown,* did not come until 1956. There are a number of reasons why the immediate post-*Brown* period may have been quiet, even though that calm turned out to be a misleading indication of ultimate public reaction to a constitutional requirement of desegregation. When that reaction, in part a delayed reaction to *Brown II,* occurred, it badly "burned" the Court and taught it to proceed with its desegregation strategies in entirely different ways. One reason for the quiet is that the American public has a habit of taking general policy statements as if they are self-executing; they treat the symbol as the substance.[17] Lack of knowledge that the law is not self-executing tends to reinforce the public's acceptance of rules like that emanating from the Supreme Court in *Brown I* and *Brown II.*[18] In addition, many persons accepted *Brown II* as a proper, moderate, nonextreme sort of statement. "With all deliberate speed" had a nice ring to it; that it would mean more deliberation and less speed was not immediately obvious to those not directly affected. Those who were affected knew what it meant—that the South had won a victory.

Of all the parts of the opinion, the "with all deliberate speed" phrase drew the most attention.[19] Although Robert Carter was later to say that "the formula adopted by the Court was a grave mistake," even he and Thurgood Marshall said at the time that the failure of the Supreme Court to set a compliance date was wise in that states could not complain about unrealistic deadlines. They also said that the remand to the lower courts meant that local judges couldn't claim they were not familiar with the situation on which they had to rule.[20] In defense of the often criticized phrase, the late Alexander Bickel argued that it provided an invitation to the other branches of government to get involved in the desegregation problem. This was important because the participation of those branches was necessary if the decision was to be enforced and if it were to be accepted by those affected. The phrase placed the Court in a position "to engage in a continual colloquy with the political institutions, leaving it to them to tell the Court what expedients of accommodation and compromise they deemed necessary," although there was a risk they might not tell the Court anything.[21] While Bickel argued that Congress and the president would have been uncomfortable with "hard and fast principles calling for universal and sudden execution," in fact the phrase "with all deliberate speed" actually made it easier for them to decline to cooperate than it would have been if the Court had simply held as a matter of law that further segregation was illegal now.

Through use of this phrase, the Court did not make clear to people what was expected of them, and thus failed to follow the advice of Justice Frankfurter, who had remarked to Thurgood Marshall at argument, "I am sure you will agree in this kind of litigation, it is of the utmost importance to use language of fastidious accuracy." Or, as one writer recently said, "We may ask whether it would not have been more fruitful to have been more systematic at that time about what was to be achieved when."[22] The sorts of results which could be expected from such a standard not accompanied by more specific requirements is indicated in the idea that the higher the stakes, "the greater the impetus in regulated persons towards resolving the uncertainties of standard application in favor of the course of action to which they are otherwise committed."[23] That reaction came through very clearly when the Department of Health, Education and Welfare later developed its first set of desegregation guidelines after passage of the 1964 Civil Rights Act fund cutoff provisions. Because those guidelines were also somewhat vague, experience with them provides some useful parallels to the effect of "with all deliberate speed." Failure to make requirements clear resulted in submission of thousands of plans which embodied "an enormous variety of ways to express the necessary promises"[24] and which were not up to the level of then-existing judicial standards. The vagueness of the initial guidelines coupled with the absence of an ultimate maximum to be attained and the manner in which they were explained also led both leaders and ordinary citizens to believe that relatively little was required to achieve compliance.

If *Brown I* has been criticized for containing too much social science, *Brown II* has been criticized for not containing enough—for the Court's failure to recognize the effect of a weak statement on those who would resist the ruling. Psychologist Kenneth Clark, a participant in the cases, claims that a more direct decree would not likely have produced more "tension, procrastination, or evasion"[25] than the second opinion which "in practice . . . seems to have led to more rather than to less disruption." He feels social science would have helped because "prompt, decisive action on the part of recognized authorities usually results in less anxiety and less resistance in cases where the public is opposed to the action than does a more hesitant and gradual procedure." What makes matters worse is that "gradualism or any form of ambiguity and equivocation on the part of those with the power of decision is interpreted by the segregationists as indecision and provides them with the basis for increasing resistance."[26] Once that resistance is developed, it becomes even harder to achieve compliance. Thus had the Court made clear what it wanted before southern politicians took public positions directly resisting the Court— positions on which their political careers then depended— implementation might have been easier to carry out.[27] If those to be regulated can find out about policies prior to acting, they will be more likely to conform to the policy

William Evan has stated conditions necessary for law to perform the function of educating people, so helpful if compliance is to be achieved.[28]

Among the conditions he has noted are requirements that pragmatic models for compliance be identified and that there be a "relevant use of time" to overcome potential resistance. Certainly, no compliance models were provided by the Court in *Brown II,* and "with all deliberate speed" was so open-ended that the condition as to time was also not met. Adoption of Marshall's argument of a year for administrative arrangements would have done so. Adopting that deadline or at the very least setting a time limit for the submission of integration plans, as the government had recommended, would have, in Solicitor General Sobeloff's words, both "strengthened the hand" of the district courts and would have put a greater pressure on reluctant district court judges to comply with the Supreme Court's general directive. Even so, a time limit for plans would have fallen far short of an "explicit decree binding on local school boards," an alternative which had obviously bothered the Court at reargument, and it would still have left the problem of implementation principally in the hands of federal district judges. If the Court had also directed the district courts to set time limits for completion of integration plans once they had been submitted and approved or had been more explicit in its directions to those lower courts, the latters' sense of responsibility in the implementation of desegregation would have been even further increased. As Jack Peltason wrote after studying the implementation decisions of southern federal judges, "What the district judges need—and what most of them want—is not the responsibility of making choices, but rigid mandates that compel them to act."[29] He found it "unrealistic" to think that a southern judge would initiate desegregation action after having to "cut through the Supreme Court's vague instructions." Peltason also argued that the judges, particularly those faced with resistant communities, needed "a hierarchy of scapegoats."[30] The district judges should be able to blame the judges of the courts of appeals, who should in turn be able to blame the Supreme Court—with the school board able to blame the district judge. Without "unequivocal mandates" from the Supreme Court, that was not possible. Those scholars who have studied communities undergoing desegregation have offered a variation on this argument. They have said that *Brown* was a help to southern moderates who had begun to realize that segregation was wrong but who were not able to overcome community pressures and that the ruling also served as a "backstop" to prevent further backsliding.[31] However, we feel it was not a very strong check, in large measure because it provided little in the way of a "model of deportment" equivalent to Evan's required pragmatic compliance models.

The most important issue posed by *Brown II* is whether courts in composing their opinions should pay attention to problems of compliance. The "seemingly rational, statesmanlike" decision[32] in the case seems to have been premised upon the expectation of noncompliance,[33] thus dragging the Court into an area that did not seem to be "judicial" in character and thus detracting from the moral authority of the Court. As Kenneth Clark has observed, "In this decision the Court was stepping outside the limited role of determining the constitutionality of segregation and was assuming the more complex role of establishing guidelines for administrative and social change."[34] Clark's view is reinforced by the Court's invitation to the southern attorneys general to present argument at the "implementation round." That action made it seem almost as if the Court were inviting testimony that noncompliance was likely as an excuse for a limited decree, because southern counsel had earlier threatened noncompliance, and because Marshall had stated that the Court could take judicial notice of noncompliance only if an attorney general said he could not control his own state.

Any authoritative body must consider the possible negative reactions of those to be affected by its decisions. This is particularly true of a body which does not have its own "troops" to enforce its decisions. Bodies such as the Supreme Court must work to achieve a situation in which compliance with its decisions will occur without much question, despite the problem that unreviewed controversies are likely to be resolved on some other basis than the enunciated standards.[35] For this reason, and because respect for the law may decline when new legal rules are stated in the face of knowledge that a significant level of evasion or violation will occur, the question is not whether the Court should pay attention to compliance but the degree to which it should do so. If the Court too frequently follows anticipated reactions, it may find that when it wants to lead it will not be able to do so. And it must be recognized that the Court will be criticized regardless of what it does. If this is the case, perhaps the justices should therefore go forward resolutely without attention to possible public resistance. Perhaps the Court's most unassailable moral posture is simply to declare what is the law. If the law then is not obeyed, people can initiate lawsuits on an individual case-by-case basis to force compliance, and the Court can then intervene to assure that the law will be obeyed. This is to argue that respect for the law and for the Court itself is perhaps best maintained when the Court does not trim its sails to the wind. As former Justice Arthur Goldberg once said, "The Court will . . . continue to have powerful supporters and popular acceptance as long as it steadfastly maintains its determination to decide cases on principle and refuses to temper its application of constitutional guarantees with fears for its own political well-being."[36] When the Court demonstrates its "realism" in its opinions, it does nothing but hurt itself.[37]

Certainly it is often difficult for either an individual justice or the entire Court to see when a straightforward opinion is in order. There are arguments favoring "indirection" when the reception to be given to the opinion is not clear.[38] Yet had the Court ordered "immediate vindication" of the rights specified in *Brown I,* as Carter suggested, "such a course probably would not have resulted in desegregation at a faster pace, but it would have kept the Court's image from being tarnished by first yielding fruitlessly to expedience."[39] This position is in line with Murphy's statement, based on his examination of judicial strategy, that if "indirection" and failure to confront an issue "would allow the Court to acquire a reputation for timidity,"[40] a direct approach would be in order, even in the face of perceived resistance. "The direct approach can by no means be written off," he has written, particularly "when the opposition or uncommitted actors may be questioning the determination of the individual Justice or of the Court." He also indicates that such a posture may be appropriate where the desired change is supported by the political environment—in *Brown,* the favorable response foreseeable in the North.[41] Chief Justice Warren was later willing to write such forthright opinions, but had obviously not done so in *Brown II.*[42]

An example of what the Court could have done came seven years later in the malapportionment cases, perhaps a result of the "negative lesson" of *Brown.* In 1962, in *Baker v. Carr,* the Court was faced with the problem of badly gerrymandered districts and a historical unwillingness of the legislatures to reapportion the districts fairly. The unwillingness of the legislatures was, of course, the logical result of the fact that the individual members of the legislatures owed their jobs to malapportionment; any change would jeopardize their own jobs. Hence there was an inherent conflict of interest in legislatures doing away with malapportionment. Given this fact, it seemed that the Court had to do something about the inequity of a person's vote in one county counting for one-tenth someone else's vote in another county. There seemed to be an equal-protection right of any voter to have his vote count the same way as any other voter's. But what would the remedy be? Although initially faced with only the question of justiciability, the judges took action which was in some sense more immediate than what they had done in *Brown.* They ruled malapportionment claims justiciable and sent plaintiffs to the district courts to have their cases heard. While the Court was quite likely to "drop the other shoe" later in ruling on substantive malapportionment claims, the result was considerable legislative activity toward reapportionment, a subject affecting all the states, even before the Court's substantive one man-one vote ruling in *Reynolds v. Sims* two years later.[43] In reapportionment, the Court provided both a symbolic victory for plaintiffs and a direction as to how to proceed in the very first ruling. In the desegregation issue, by contrast, with no justiciability issue to face, but with considerable prior case law on which to build, the Court took two rounds of argument before issuing even a general statement and another year before ordering plaintiffs back to the district courts. All that time produced only a symbolic act—*Brown I*—and left plaintiffs much farther from the integrated school than they had been. If the vote during the Vinson Court was indeed four-to-five against overruling segregation, as noted earlier, the first *Brown* opinion could not have been written any earlier. But certainly the Warren Court could have issued its own opinion earlier and more certainly there was little need for it to wait another whole year for implementation.

Faced later in the reapportionment cases with having to answer extremely difficult questions—How could the Court redistrict all the election districts in the United States? How could it compel a legislative committee to make a "fair" redistricting? What would be fair? Could the Court appoint a special master to do the work? What if the master fell under the political influence of existing legislatures?—the Court merely invalidated malapportioned legislatures, leaving as the alternative an election in which all candidates would be elected at large. Although there was enormous grumbling about the Court's decision, legislature after legislature—fearing that the worst thing would be an at-large election—set about reapportioning election districts.

In *Brown,* although the Court was without the "lesson" of the reapportionment cases, a similar strategy was available. The Court could have held that separate schools are inherently unequal and that school boards cannot make race a factor in assigning pupils to schools. Any school not complying would be subject to being closed down by order of any court upon the complaint of any citizen adversely affected. The result of failure to comply would not mean contempt of court and other judically imposed penalties but, rather, no schools. If the public wanted public schools at all, they would have to be desegregated schools, although as a practical matter it would take a little time for citizens to complain and for trial courts to act, even on this clear basis. Were the result really to be closed schools, for whatever local reason, citizens might have held off attempting to close the schools on the basis of *Brown.*[44] For the most part, this strategy would have offered a promise of results instead of the "token" integration for two successive school generations resulting from the strategy actually adopted by the Court.

In short, the Court's action in *Brown II* had been costly, both in terms of pragmatics and principle. The ruling had not provided lower court judges what they needed to achieve desegregation, and had in fact provided excuses for those interested in evading or resisting the Court's ruling in *Brown I* that desegregation was unconstitutional. Because the Court had tried too hard to operate "realistically," it had given the appearance of being considerably less than fully principled. This did not help its reputation, already somewhat blemished by the difficulties in the

Brown I opinion. Perhaps the best that could be said in mid-1955 was that the *Brown* litigation had resulted in a basic constitutional ruling and a decision on implementation, although the litigation even in these cases was by no means completed, with the Virginia case to return for another major ruling in 1964. The process of implementation, however, could be started even though, as we shall see, the Court was to stay away from the subject like the cat which stays away from a stove upon which it was once burned. Thus the difficulties caused by *Brown II* were further compounded. Before turning to that process, we need to recognize another cost resulting from the Court's extended attention to the issue of school desegregation in *Brown*. That cost was the avoidance of a number of other important race relations problems—segregated cemeteries, the prohibition on mixed marriages, and land given for public purposes but restricted to use by whites—which had been brought to the Court while *Brown* was being considered and which as a result of the Court's refusal to deal with them were resolved only many years later.

Chapter 5

Issues Avoided: Cemeteries, Miscegenation, Gifts of Land

T HREE areas of law had been put aside during the period of the
Supreme Court's immersion in the *Brown* school desegregation litigation. The first was the question of segregated cemeteries, in-
geniously disposed of by the Court in 1955 and not decided subsequently.
The second was the matter of miscegenation, particularly controversial
because sex was the basis of many of the whites' deepest fears about blacks
and because "race-mingling" challenged the very foundation of the
superior-subordinate relations between the races. The Court finally
reached this issue more than ten years after *Brown*. The third was the gifts
of land by private individuals to government bodies for use on a segregated basis, which came to the Court in connection with a school, parks,
and a hospital. Overall, these three areas of law present the matter of
individual versus collective justice: Should the Court after *Brown* avoid
deciding some admittedly difficult cases involving specific individuals out
of a feeling that avoidance is necessary to preserve the proper atmosphere
in which desegregation might go forward? Put differently, had the
Court's *Brown* rulings so completely exhausted its goodwill that it had
little more on which to draw in the race relations area for several years and
thus had to avoid at least some problems? If the Court were to avoid
specific cases in the "here and now," what would it do later? We shall see
that in two of these areas, the issue was presented with sufficient frequency that the Court was able to reach a ruling in due course, yet in one
area—segregated cemeteries—the issue did not return, leaving a residue
of neither individual nor collective justice.

In the two areas ultimately resolved, we find vastly different strategic
approaches by the Court. In one, miscegenation, the issue was ultimately
decided in a clear and clean straightforward manner, with the justices
anticipating their decision by questions in an earlier case involving interracial cohabitation rather than miscegenation. In the other, gifts of land,
we see the use of a particular strategy—which we have called "hit 'em

131

where they ain't"—in which the Court uses a case with a narrow factual base to apply an important doctrine, thus reducing negative reaction. The cases here also provide glimpses of other aspects of the Court's work, such as what the justices do when they have accepted a case they then find distasteful and how the Court tries to deal with state courts which will not allow it to escape responsibility by resolving cases "properly" when the cases are sent down for reconsideration. It is the strategic importance of these three issue-areas more than their substantive importance which warrants considering them at some length.

1

A basic rule of strategy is not to jeopardize a large goal for the sake of a small issue. The Supreme Court followed that rule in November 1954 when it was under intense southern and right-wing criticism for its decision in the *Brown* case the previous May. The wife of Sergeant Rice, a Korean War hero killed in action, had purchased a cemetery lot for his burial in Sioux City, Iowa. During the graveside ceremony honoring the soldier cemetery officials noticed that many of the mourners were Indians. Inquiry revealed that the deceased was eleven-sixteenths Winnebago Indian and five-sixteenths white. Since the contract that Mrs. Rice had signed with the cemetery contained, in its fine print, a clause limiting burial rights to Caucasians, the cemetery officials interrupted the proceedings and refused burial to Sergeant Rice.

The incident was widely publicized in Iowa. The cemetery officials first adopted a policy of silence, which angered the press. Then the cemetery issued a brochure defending its actions. It included the following statements: "The restriction to members of the Caucasian Race is . . . in probably 90 percent of the private cemeteries in the United States, including Forest Lawn in California and Graceland Park in Sioux City. Private cemeteries have always had a right to be operated for a particular group such as Jewish, Catholic, Lutheran, Negro, Chinese, etc., not because of any prejudice against any race, but because people, like animals, prefer to be with their own kind." Mrs. Rice sued the cemetery for damages for mental suffering and, in addition, for aggravation caused by publication of the brochure. Almost immediately thereafter the Iowa legislature enacted a statute invalidating racial restrictions in all cemetery contracts and covenants except for cemeteries operated by cities, towns, churches, or religious or fraternal societies. The statute exempted any pending litigation; in other words, it applied to everyone except Mrs. Rice. Mrs. Rice lost her case in the Iowa courts. When she filed for certiorari in the United States Supreme Court, the Court decided to hear her case, *Rice v. Sioux City Memorial Park Cemetery*.

In the briefs, counsel for Mrs. Rice argued on the basis of *Shelley, Hurd,* and *Barrows* that the state court was giving a stamp of approval to a racially restrictive covenant when it allowed the covenant to be used as a defense to a damages action. Approval, counsel held, became an act of the state in contravention of the petitioner's Fourteenth Amendment due process and equal protection rights of the United States Constitution and of her rights under the United Nations Charter—a United States treaty—and our nation's public policy. Counsel for the cemetery officials argued that no state action was involved. There was merely a voluntary private contractual action between Mrs. Rice and cemetery association officials, whose contract of sale for her burial lot stated that burial privileges accrued only to members of the Caucasian race. There was no "affirmative enforcement" of the covenant by the lower court, it was argued, and the state's "failure to punish" did not constitute state action. The United Nations Charter did not prevent discrimination by private citizens of the states, nor was there any federal public policy forbidding such discrimination by private citizens. Finally, counsel pointed out that many private and religious schools and cemeteries would be affected by a ruling for Mrs. Rice. The American Jewish Congress submitted an amicus curiae brief to the Court in support of Mrs. Rice, answering the cemetery association's allegations concerning the serious consequences of a decision for religious cemeteries and schools. The brief demonstrated the position that the courts traditionally had accommodated equal protection to the right to religious freedom and that this, together with church-state separation, would prevent the state's interference in religious burial grounds apparently assumed by the cemetery and the lower court.

When it came time to decide the case, the Court, with only eight justices—Justice Jackson had died the month before—was evenly divided on the merits, thus affirming the judgment of the Iowa court without an opinion. On the basis of the justices' questions at oral argument,[1] it seems fair to say that the difficulty was with an apparent attempt to reform or redraw a contract. Some justices indicated concern with the effect a ruling in Mrs. Rice's favor might have on religious cemeteries. There also seems to have been some possible doubt as to whether the Iowa court's ruling amounted to state action at all. Counsel for Mrs. Rice then petitioned the Court for a rehearing before a full Court of nine justices, urging the Court to reconsider the bearing of *Hurd, Shelley,* and *Barrows* on the questions of rewriting the contract and of state action. Mrs. Rice was no more seeking a rewriting of the contract here, it was argued, than were the parties in those cases who were directly or indirectly interested in seeing that no life or force be given to the racially restrictive covenant involved. The question was not so much that of rewriting the contract as of refusing to give judicial sanction to a legally offensive covenant. The petition also urged that if the effect of the case on religious cemeteries had caused any of the justices to vote for affirmance, they should reconsider the meaning and function of the First Amendment and of the cases which indicate that, where there is a possible clash between the First and Fourteenth Amendments, the Court must weigh the conflicting interests. It was also asserted that with religious cemeteries not applicable to Mrs. Rice's case, the guarantee of religious freedom could and should override the guarantee of equal protection.

Before looking at what happened on the rehearing, let us consider briefly what might have been at stake in this case. The plaintiff was asking the Court to strike out a clause in a private contract, thus reforming the contract, even though the defendant stood by the contract in its entirety. The racial clause in the contract was clearly a matter of private discrimination: no one compelled the plaintiff to sign the contract or to use that cemetery's facilities. The Fourteenth Amendment through 1954 had been consistently construed to apply only to state action, not to private discrimination. Counsel for Mrs. Rice relied heavily on *Shelley v. Kraemer,* but the covenant in *Shelley* had not been used for defensive purposes by an unwilling seller. Rather, the *Shelley* holding was that the restrictive covenant could not be used for the purpose of procuring a judicial injunction against a sale entered into by a willing seller, for the very act of judicially enforcing the covenant amounted to "state action." Even thus limited, the *Shelley* case had substantial repercussions in all areas of constitutional law. Had the Court decided Mrs. Rice's case in her favor, the ruling might have out-Shelleyed *Shelley*. Racial restrictions in wills, in deeds of trust, in college charters, in parks, in private homes, and in public facilities might have been invalidated. Apart from this impact, a decision for Mrs. Rice certainly would have upset many people on the narrow issue of cemeteries, since over 90 percent of the private ones were restricted at that time. More important, however, the tangible benefits of holding for Mrs. Rice—desegregated cemeteries—seemed small in light of the recently adopted goal of desegregating the living population and might have meant placing in jeopardy the *Brown* decision.

The Supreme Court reheard Mrs. Rice's case just three weeks before it handed down the *Brown* implementation decision. Justice Harlan was now on the bench, but because he decided to withdraw, again only eight justices participated in the ruling. This time the Court did not divide evenly. As if fully realizing the implications of Mrs. Rice's case, the Court on a five-to-three vote reached the astounding result that it should not have granted certiorari to Mrs. Rice in the first place. Thus Mrs. Rice's efforts were wiped out and the Iowa decision against her was the final disposition in her case.

The extent of the Supreme Court's feeling that Mrs. Rice's case was the wrong case at the wrong time is revealed by an examination of the manner in which its decision was reached. The majority opinion seized upon the Iowa statute that precluded future cases of this kind in Iowa. Writing for the majority, Mr. Justice Frankfurter noted that the Iowa statute had been cited in the first arguments before the Court but that none of the justices had particularly noticed the statute in the heat of the arguments. As Frankfurter put it, in an admission that the Court obviously did not enjoy making but felt that it had to, "The even division of the Court forestalled that intensive study attendant upon opinion-writing which might well have revealed the crucial relevance of the statute." Because the new statute had made Mrs. Rice's case unique in Iowa, Frankfurter argued, well-settled certiorari practice would normally have resulted in a denial of certiorari in the first instance had any of the justices noticed the full import of the statute. For, he added, the Court does not "sit for the benefit of the particular litigants" in a case but, rather, to deal with constitutional problems that reach "beyond the academic or the episodic." He also added that there was nothing unique about a dismissal even after full argument. There had been "more than 60 cases" in which such action had been taken after full argument. But this was the first case, as Frankfurter did *not* point out, where a previous judgment was vacated on rehearing. While Frankfurter stated, "We should not unnecessarily discourage such remedial action by possible condonation of this isolated incident," the basic reason for the Court's ruling came in his remarks that the case had "evident difficulties" and that the Court would not "risk inconclusive and divisive disposition" of the case "when time may further illumine or completely outmode the issues in dispute."

On the other side, Black, writing also for the Chief Justice and Douglas, noted strongly felt dissent. Only very unusual circumstances could justify such dismissal of a case, Black protested. The dismissal left undecided the serious questions the case raised concerning denial of equal protection of the laws. Although the Iowa legislature had now provided that similar petitioners can prosecute similar claims, this petitioner could not. "We cannot agree," he said, "that this dismissal is justified merely because this petitioner is the only one whose rights may have been unconstitutionally denied." The dismissal seemed even less justified, Douglas noted, in that had Harlan taken part in the case he probably would have provided the one more vote needed for certiorari, thus forcing a judgment on the constitutional issues.[2]

Justice Frankfurter's reasoning in this case leaves much to be desired. First, Mrs. Rice's case had already been argued and decided by the Court. By the time of rehearing, there had already been considerable time spent on the action. Thus, part of the rationale underlying the certiorari procedure—saving the Court's time for important cases—was clearly inapplicable. Secondly, while it was true that the issue could not arise again in Iowa, it could very well arise in all the other states. Such a situation is well within the traditional ambit of constitutional inquiry, for the Court sits on behalf of the entire country, not just Iowa.

On this point, the Court was later faced with cases providing some basis for comparison. While *Bell v. Maryland,* one of the sit-in cases subsequent to initial sit-in convictions of Negroes in the state, was on appeal, Maryland had enacted a new public accommodations statute under which the Negroes' behavior would not have been criminal. Although the larger constitutional issue was still to be faced in other states, a majority of the Court seized on the statute in order to avoid ruling on the larger question and remanded the cases to the Maryland courts for consideration in light of the changed legal situation. Yet some years later the Court showed that it was indeed willing to decide cases even when there might be only one beneficiary. A public housing tenant had complained of eviction without notice and an opportunity to challenge the eviction. While her case was on appeal, the Department of Housing and Urban Development issued new regulations embodying the notice and hearing requirements. The Supreme Court first sent the case back to North Carolina for reconsideration in light of the new regulations, but reaccepted it when the state courts persisted in refusing the tenant her rights. In *Thorpe v. Housing Authority of Durham,* the Supreme Court then ruled in her favor on the fairly narrow ground that it should decide the case in view of current law, that is, the new regulations, thus avoiding any larger constitutional due process issue. Thus, despite its action in *Rice,* the Court did deal with cases the effect of which was small in terms of the number of people affected.

The significant question in the *Rice* case is not whether Justice Frankfurter's reasoning is "correct" under some higher law binding on the Supreme Court but, rather, whether the Court was wise in so blatantly avoiding the cemetery issue. In many ways the *Rice* case was ideal for a Fourteenth Amendment ruling extending the recent school decision, for it did not involve a Negro. Rice had been a war hero, and there was some public feeling against the mistreatment of his remains. But *Rice* might have opened up the area of housing discrimination in which for some years the Court had been inactive. Had the Court granted relief to Mrs. Rice, it would have to support her claim under *Shelley,* finding that Court recognition of a restrictive clause constituted state action. Since *Shelley* was a housing case, it is clear that a *Rice* ruling under it would have opened up the whole housing and real estate area to affirmative suits by Negroes. The result of such a decision in *Rice* might have been, for example, that an unwilling seller might be forced to violate a restrictive covenant, because court recognition of his right to abide by his covenant would constitute state action in violation of the Fourteenth Amendment. The Court's continued reluctance to enter the area of real estate after *Shelley* seems proof of its desire to avoid the legal difficulties involved in dealing with "unwilling" sellers. Furthermore, since the president and the Congress had the power to curtail discrimination in the sale of housing, it is possible that the Court awaited action from other government branches. In short, by accepting the case in 1955, the Court might have dispensed justice to Mrs. Rice, but only at the cost of imperiling its entire desegregation strategy in other areas of much greater importance. This is what made Mrs. Rice's case clearly the wrong one at the wrong time from the Court's broad perspective. Whatever judgment is made of the wisdom of the Supreme Court's strategy in *Rice,* one point is clear. The Court will be prepared to do violence to its established certiorari procedures and the rationale underlying them if strategic considerations for disposing of a case commend themselves to the nine justices with greater force.

2

The unusual nature of Mrs. Rice's case should not obscure the normality of the strategic considerations underlying its eventual disposition. In a different area, that of miscegenation, the Supreme Court took much the same tactic of avoiding the issue. Miscegenation was a much simpler, more straightforward area for constitutional litigation than Mrs. Rice's restrictive covenant. Unlike her case, miscegenation clearly involved "state action," since miscegenation statutes prohibited marriage between whites and nonwhites and attached criminal penalties for such violations as cohabitation. Moreover, a decision declaring miscegenation statutes unconstitutional would not have invalidated other kinds of legislation or official acts or private acts of segregation. We should keep in mind, however, that while the constitutional question presented by mixed marriages is straightforward, the right involved —freedom to marry—may in some ways be considered more basic, more a part of the individual's essential freedom, than the right to go to school. Furthermore, the psychological impact of a decision declaring miscegenation statutes unconstitutional clearly would have been greater in the mid-1950s than a decision affecting cemeteries. Myrdal had reported in 1944 that of all the areas of discrimination in the United States the most sensitive to the white man was precisely the question of "intermarriage and sexual intercourse involving white women."[3]

Sexual relations and intermarriage between members of different races is the one issue that has always been of deepest concern to whites in their confrontation of expanding Negro rights and privileges. This very basic concern, called by some persons fear of "mongrelization," has been the underlying force in Caucasian opposition to all kinds of desegregation from earliest times. Thus, it has been in areas such as public facilities, housing, and public school desegregation that barriers have been so slow to fall, and then only in the face of bitter opposition, for it was feared that contacts in these areas could lead to miscegenation. The Supreme Court's reluctance to enter this area provides testimony to this Caucasian sensitivity. Many whites who opposed segregation in other areas could not, and still cannot, bring themselves to sanction Negro-white relationships on this most personal level. From such strong feeling evolved more severe punishments for crimes of rape when committed by Negroes against white women. States with no restrictions on Negroes in other areas maintained statutes forbidding racial intermarriage or providing stronger penalties for interracial cohabitation than for intraracial cohabitation or similar offenses. Those persons supporting such practices could find an early authority, in *Plessy,* which contained the statement, "Laws forbidding the intermarriage of the two races may be said in a technical sense to interfere with the freedom of contract, and yet have been universally recognized as within the police power of the State."

Yet Negroes, unlike whites, had regarded the problem of miscegenation as relatively unimportant. For them, Myrdal puts it at the bottom of the list instead of the top. According to Jack Greenberg, the NAACP apparently had never sponsored an antimiscegenation case nor an active program for repeal of these laws as of the late 1950s.[4] Hence, if the Supreme Court had invalidated miscegenation statutes in the 1940s or the 1950s, a great risk would have been taken of marshaling hostile white opinion against the Court and all its programs while doing little in terms of active Negro concerns.

Even before *Brown,* the Court had heard of miscegenation in a couple of cases involving housing and one involving a will. In *City of Richmond v. Deans*, Negroes contested an ordinance prohibiting purchase or lease of property in a block in which the majority of residents belonged to a race into which the would-be occupant could not legally marry. A Negro purchaser thus barred from occupancy sought in the federal courts to enjoin enforcement on grounds that the ordinance's provisions violated the Fourteenth Amendment. On the other side an attempt was made to distinguish the case from *Buchanan v. Warley* because the ordinance based its interdiction on the legal Virginia prohibition against intermarriage, not on race or color. The lower court ruled that since the legal prohibition of intermarriage was itself based on race the question here was identical with the earlier cases and that the ordinance could not stand. The Supreme Court affirmed per curiam. Despite its use to invalidate the housing law, the Virginia miscegenation statute, ultimately to be declared invalid when the Supreme Court reached that issue, was not touched in this case. Another miscegenation-related case came to the Court in 1942, involving the validity of a will contested on the ground that the marriage was illegal bcause the beneficiary was one-eighth Negro and the state had a miscegenation statute. The Court did not reach the issue, however, peremptorily dismissing the appeal because it did not appear that the appeal was applied for within the proper time limits.[5] Still another case in which the miscegenation question was raised was a housing case which was brought to the Court in 1951; this too was turned aside. As in the 1930 *Deans* case, use or occupancy by a Negro of a building in a white-designated district, and vice-versa, had been made unlawful under a zoning ordinance. When the ordinance was challenged, the city argued that to forego enforcement would be to risk the "clear and present danger" of racial violence and problems of miscegenation. Affirming an injunction against the zoning rule, the Court of Appeals for the Fifth Circuit held the allegation of anticipated violence immaterial. The Supreme Court denied certiorari.[6]

In the first round of argument in *Brown,* Justice Frankfurter had raised a question about the validity of miscegenation laws, asking whether the Fourteenth or Fifth Amendments automatically invalidated all legislation drawing a line based on race, including marriage laws. Despite such a question, the Court had avoided the issue since *Brown I* had been handed down. The first miscegenation case after *Brown I, Jackson v. Alabama,* was that of a Negro woman convicted of miscegenation under a state statute imposing sentences of from two-to-seven years imprisonment or hard labor for white persons and Negroes or a Negro's descendants to the third generation inclusive who intermarried, lived in adultery, or fornicated. The Negro woman claimed the statute violated her rights under the privileges and immunities, due process, and equal protection clauses of the Constitution. The state court of appeals held that the statute did not violate the Fifth or Fourteenth Amendments because the same punishment was prescribed for each party to such crimes, regardless of their race. Because the case had squarely presented the constitutional question as to antimiscegenation legislation to state judges who had rejected the claimed constitutional violations, it was an ideal test case, but the Court turned it away.[7] Perhaps it did so because the direct confrontation with the issue would have made it difficult to choose "modest" grounds on which to rest a decision. As did the *Naim* case the following year, the *Jackson* case also posed the strategic problem of whether to deal with another touchy issue at the same time that *Brown,* not yet fully decided, was very much alive. The case also posed problems from the perspective of individual against social justice, particularly because a conviction had resulted. If the case were avoided in order to smooth the way for school desegregation, Mrs. Jackson would go to jail, whereas if the case were taken and decided in her favor—for it could be decided no other way—

"the fate of integration and the rights of countless hundreds of thousands of Negro children" would be jeopardized, "a high price to pay for freeing one woman."[8]

A much more intricate situation confronted the Warren Court in 1955, but the Court was still determined not to make any decision on miscegenation. The case before the Court, *Naim v. Naim,* was that of a white woman and her Chinese husband who left Virginia, which had a miscegenation statute, to get married in North Carolina. Returning to Virginia, they came under the statute's clause prohibiting residents from leaving the state for the purpose of evading the miscegenation law. The wife then filed for and was granted an annulment. In sustaining this decision, the Virginia Supreme Court of Appeals specifically upheld the validity of the miscegenation statute on three grounds: the state power to control the vital institution of marriage; the distinction in *Shelley* between social legislation and that concerning Fourteenth Amendment rights, of which this was the former; and the inapplicability of *Brown* in that miscegenation is not, like education, "the very foundation of good citizenship." When the husband appealed the case, the United States Supreme Court, per curiam, vacated the judgment and instructed the Virginia Supreme Court of Appeals to remand the case to the trial court to make factual determinations concerning the residency of the parties before and after the marriage in North Carolina. The Court explained that the inadequacy of the record as to the relationship of the parties to the Commonwealth of Virginia at the time of their marriage in North Carolina and upon their return to Virginia and the failure of the parties to bring before the Court all questions relevant to the disposition of the case prevented consideration of the constitutional issue of the validity of the Virginia statute on miscegenation "in clean-cut and concrete form, unclouded" by such problems.

The state court refused to cooperate. As if determined to deny the Supreme Court any way out in this case, the Virginia court noted that under the circumstances there was no Virginia procedure under which the record could be sent back to the trial court to be supplemented. The state court held that the material facts in the case, which it restated, were sufficient for annulment under Virginia law. The case then came back to the United States Supreme Court. Naim asked the Court for a motion to recall the mandate and to set the case for oral argument upon the merits, or, in the alternative, to recall and amend the mandate. The Court thereupon dismissed the appeal altogether as "devoid of a properly presented federal question."

This statement is difficult to accept since the federal constitutional question was squarely presented and the facts as to the issue of residence were conclusively established by the Virginia courts. Because the case fell within the Court's supposedly mandatory appeals jurisdiction, Professor Wechsler has said the case was dismissed "on procedural grounds that I make bold to say are wholly without basis in the law."[9] And the Court itself may have been embarrassed because when the justices finally reached the miscegenation issue, they cited many cases but managed to avoid completely referring to *Naim*. Whether or not there was a reasoned legal basis for disposing of the case, there were good strategic reasons for doing so.[10] At the time of this case, more than half the states had miscegenation statutes. Thus the Supreme Court faced the potentiality of angering a majority of states, arousing public opinion, fostering demagogues who would attack the Court, and endangering the entire desegregation program. The Court's awareness of the "volatile" nature of the problem is shown by the comment of an unidentified justice, made after the Court's conference on the case: "One bombshell at a time is enough."[11]

Nine years later the atmosphere was much different. The cumulative impact of the Court's decisions in various areas of desegregation had changed the climate of national opinion. By this time, only nineteen states still had miscegenation statutes; now the Court could be in tune with the majority. The trend toward voluntary repeal of these statutes made it clear that the miscegenation issue was no longer critical. At the same time, Negroes became increasingly concerned about the symbolic status of inferiority that the statutes represented. In 1963, a Negro man and a white woman were sentenced to thirty days each in a Florida jail for cohabitation. The cohabitation statute made it a crime for a "Negro man and white woman . . . who are not married to each other . . , [to] habitually live in and occupy in the nighttime the same room." Filling in the gap was the Florida miscegenation statute preventing such a couple from getting married in the state. The Florida courts upheld the conviction, and the couple appealed to the Supreme Court.

In *McLaughlin v. Florida*, William T. Coleman, Jr., argued for both defendants that the convictions were obtained under an explicitly racial law which violated the Equal Protection Clause of the Fourteenth Amendment because it forbade acts not prohibited if committed by persons of the same race.[12] Because of Florida's law against mixed marriages, the defendants were also denied the opportunity to have a valid common-law marriage. Coleman also argued that Florida's attempt to define a Negro as "every person having one-eighth or more of African or Negro blood" was unconstitutionally vague and that the state relied on a policeman's opinion but had failed to prove that the male defendant was a Negro by that test. Coleman contended that making a relationship as personal as marriage invalid made this an "easier case" than the school desegregation case of 1954. The right to marry a person of one's choice is more important than the right to attend a particular school, he asserted.

Coleman compared the defense of antimiscegenation laws to Hitler's speeches condemning association between Jews and Gentiles. Louis Pollak, also arguing for the defendants, called the right to marry a most "personal and intimate" right and said that antimiscegenation laws were "less defensible" than segregated schools. "The time has come," he argued, "to remove this stigma from the fabric of American Law."

For Florida, Assistant Attorney General James G. Mahorner stated that the "most important" question was the constitutionality of the antimiscegenation law. Justice Stewart interrupted at once to comment, "You say most important, but not most important in this case." Mahorner clarified his position by stating that the antimiscegenation issue "has the most impact upon the client whom I represent" and suggested that one consequence of holding the law unconstitutional would be that an unestimated number of Floridians—whites married to whites but who had previous relationships with Negroes that other states would consider valid marriages—"who think they're married may find they're not." Trying to distinguish *Brown,* Mahorner said, "Education has developed and it is no longer like it was. It is no longer the same beast," but there has been "no such development" as to marriage. Prevention of "illegitimate offspring" was the legislative aim of the cohabitation statute, not "inferiority." "There is no invidious discrimination," he argued. "There is discrimination, we admit, but it is not invidious." The statute provided only a very light jail sentence and a small fine, he pointed out. Mahorner also argued that for the Court to find the antimiscegenation law unconstitutional, it would have to reject the legislative history of the Fourteenth Amendment and overrule prior cases.

The justices' questions of counsel dealt with several areas. The interrelationship between the cohabitation statute and miscegenation statutes seemed foremost. For example, Brennan interrupted Coleman to ask if it was his position that if the Court agreed that the cohabitation statute was unconstitutional on its face, it would not have to go any farther. When the lawyer agreed, Stewart said, "Of course, if this statute is bad, so are anti-miscegenation statutes." Coleman replied that the Florida antimiscegenation laws would play an "important role" in the decision since the trial judge had told the jury that a common-law marriage would not be a defense to the unlawful cohabitation charge. After Stewart had suggested that Mahorner was defending a law that "allows a man to desert a woman who if of the same race would be his wife," the justice asked directly, "You say this issue [the antimiscegenation law] is not before us in this case?" Although Mahorner said, "Yes," his extended defense of such laws both negated his response and also served to help force the Court toward resolution of the broader issue, as both sides were "bracketing" the Court by taking the same position.[13]

Related to questions on the need to overrule past cases were those on equality under the statute. Harlan asked Coleman if there was discrimination when both parties—a white and a Negro—were equally denied the right to marry, producing the answer that it would be hard to say someone had equality if, because of race, he could not marry the woman of his choice. It was in this context that Coleman told Justice Brennan, asking about the vagueness argument, that the cohabitation statute's reference to race made the Equal Protection Clause the "easiest ground" on which to upset the convictions. A different sort of equality question was posed in connection with the judges' concern about the statute's effect. Thus Warren asked, "Could a state do the same with Jews and Gentiles?" When Mahorner replied in the negative, the Chief Justice asked, "Why not?" Mahorner replied that "the Constitution did not have that intention, and we say that the intention was expressed as to Negroes and whites." Stewart then raised a hypothetical issue with Mahorner, with telling effect. What if a mother and son were living in the same room; the mother was white, but the father was Negro; therefore, the son would be one-half Negro. "Would the statute apply?" Mahorner was taken aback. "That's well reasoned. I can't give an answer." But Stewart insisted. "The statute would apply, wouldn't it?" "The question is well put. I suppose it would."

The Court's decision, written by Justice White, who had not been an active participant in the oral argument, struck down the cohabitation statute as unconstitutional but expressly reserved the question of the validity of Florida's miscegenation statute.[14] Normally, observed White, the legislature is allowed the widest discretion in determining whether to attack a part rather than all of an evil. Here, however, because the classification was based upon the participants' race, it must be viewed in light of the Fourteenth Amendment's central purpose to eliminate official racial discrimination. An exercise of the state police power encroaching upon constitutionally protected freedom from invidious discrimination based on race, even though enacted pursuant to a valid state interest, can be upheld only if necessary and not merely rationally related to a permissible state policy, White asserted. Other Florida statutes dealing with promiscuous conduct engaged in by persons of any race would protect the integrity of state marriage laws generally and neutrally. In addition, the law before the Court had not been shown to be a necessary adjunct to the state's ban on interracial marriage. Justices Harlan, Stewart, and Douglas concurred in the result. Harlan, who had been particularly concerned during argument about the views of counsel on antimiscegenation laws, stressed the reasons why he felt the antimiscegenation statute did not have to be considered for the cohabitation statute to fall. Stewart, who had been similarly critical of such laws during argument, wrote for himself and Douglas, taking sharp issue with the suggestion in the majority opinion that miscegenation statutes might in some manner be defensible.[15] Despite Stewart's criticism, it is clear from the point of view of strategy that the Court had found this case a way to ease into the question of miscegenation statues without expressly reaching them. If the public's reaction were favorable, the Court could finish the job in a later case. That they had laid the groundwork seem clear from commentary in the law reviews. A student commentator for the *Maryland Law Review* reasoned, "When the issue does appear directly before the court in a justiciable controversy, the validity of such patently unconstitutional statutes will be at an end." Even the *Mississippi Law Journal* concurred, in a student note: "No one can gainsay the probability that the life expectancy of these statutes will be short."[16]

The case in which the miscegenation question was finally given ultimate judicial answer was *Loving v. Virginia*. Richard P. Loving, a white man, and Mildred D. Jeter, part-Negro, part-Indian, had both grown up in Caroline County, near Richmond, Virginia. In 1958 they married in Washington, D.C., and returned to Caroline County to live near relatives, but were prosecuted under the Virginia statute challenged earlier in *Naim* making it a felony for a white and colored person to leave the state with the intention to be married and to return and cohabit in the state as man and wife as well as under the state law forbidding such unions. The Lovings were convicted of these felonies upon their pleas of guilty and were given one year jail sentences, suspended for twenty-five years upon the condition that they both leave Virginia and never return together or at the same time during that period.

After a five-year exile in Washington, they had returned to visit Mrs. Loving's mother, and again were arrested. This time they appealed to then-Attorney General Robert F. Kennedy, and the American Civil Liberties Union took up their cause. In a motion in the local court to vacate the old judgment against them and to set aside their sentence, the Lovings argued that they had complied with the terms of their suspended sentences but that the statute under which they had been convicted was unconstitutional, making their sentences invalid. The local court denied their motion early in 1965, commenting that "almighty God . . . did not intend for the races to mix." The Virginia Supreme Court then held that although the state statute was not invalid, the conditions under which the sentence was suspended were unreasonably broad to achieve the end that the defendants not again cohabit as man and wife in Virginia, making the sentence void. The court remanded the case for appropriate resentencing. Thus, although the Lovings could now return to Virginia, they still could not live there as man and wife. They then appealed to the United States Supreme Court contending that miscegenation laws violated the rights of personal choice in the marriage relationship of both whites and

Negroes. When the Court solicited Virginia's views as to whether the case should receive a hearing, state Attorney General Robert Y. Button said that laws against interracial marriage, viewed as exclusively a state function by the framers of the Fourteenth Amendment, were so clearly constitutional that the Court should affirm them without a hearing. The law under attack reflected a policy present in almost half the fifty states and was more than two hundred years old in the Commonwealth of Virginia. Button also urged the Court not to inquire into the scientific basis for miscegenation laws, warning that while the state had evidence to support its view, such an exploration would quickly mire the Court in a bog of conflicting scientific opinions.[17]

A few weeks later, the Court announced that it would hear the Lovings' appeal. Significantly, a group of sixteen prominent Roman Catholic clergymen, all from states with laws prohibiting interracial marriage, then joined the Protestant couple as amici in asking the Court to overturn such laws, arguing in their brief that marriage is a fundamental act of Protestantism, Orthodox Christianity, and Judaism and may not legally be restricted by a state without a showing that it endangers society. Their two main arguments were that such laws also prohibited free exercise of religion guaranteed by the Constitution and unconstitutionally denied the right to have children. They quoted writing by Catholic, Protestant, and Jewish scholars, as well as by a prominent anthropologist, to support their position, and maintained that "the preservation of a racially segregated society is not an interest which the state may lawfully protect."

In April 1967 the Court heard argument in the case,[18] thus exploring the only legal aspect of the race question to which the Court had not previously addressed itself. ACLU attorneys for the Lovings asked the Court to strike down the whole framework of Virginia's antimiscegenation laws, both civil and criminal, involving individual rights ranging from inheritances to taxation and the legitimacy of children. Denouncing the statutes as "white supremacy" and "slavery" laws held over from a bygone era, ACLU attorney Philip J. Hirschkop compared them with the laws of Nazi Germany and South Africa, and argued that they denied Negroes the equal protection of the laws and due process guaranteed by the Fourteenth Amendment. He said the laws were based solely on discriminatory grounds, to "keep the slaves in their place," and that the one issue of the case was, quite simply, whether a state may proscribe a marriage between two consenting adults because of their race and their race alone. He viewed the laws as being concerned with racial supremacy, not racial integrity, as slavery laws, pure and simple, depriving the Negro of his dignity. This required their invalidation. He contended that the Virginia legislature had never been able to define "Negro" or "white person," and pointed out that it had changed the definition of "Negro" from a person with one-eighth Negro blood in 1705 to one-fourth Negro blood in 1785 and to "any trace" of Negro blood in 1930. Conversely, the current definition of a white person was one with "no trace of any blood other than Caucasian." If that definition were to be turned around, Hirschkop said, marriage would probably be altogether banned. Since there is, in any event, no way to determine race by blood, Hirschkop called the Virginia law "ludicrous" and clearly violative of due process.

Also appearing for the Lovings was Bernard S. Cohen, who quoted Richard Loving as saying, "Tell the Court that I love my wife and it is just unfair that I can't live with her in Virginia." Cohen was asked an obviously strategy-oriented question by Justice Stewart—whether there was any chance that the Virginia legislature might repeal the miscegenation statutes, as Maryland's general assembly had done a month earlier. Said Cohen, "Candidates for state office have told me that they would not sacrifice their political futures by introducing such a bill. They consider it political suicide in Virginia." Cohen went on to say that he was "concerned about a narrow ruling" which would apply to the Loving case but would leave standing a number of related Virginia laws, including one calling for the issuance of a "certificate of racial composition" to those seeking to be married. Justice Black then asked if he would be satisfied with a ruling that "the state cannot prohibit marriage between whites and blacks because of their color." "That would settle our problem," Cohen said.

A central issue in the arguments was whether the Court could strike down the state's entire system of miscegenation laws or whether it would limit itself to the criminal penalties involved in this case. Those penalties applied only to marriages between whites and Negroes—not to marriages between other racial groups. Both Hirschkop and Cohen urged the Court to take the broader view and strike down the whole package of related racially discriminatory legislation. Another Virginia law which declared void any marriage between a white person and a person of any other race was challenged specifically by William M. Marutani, arguing as amicus for the Japanese American Citizens League. He pointed out that there were 1,750 Japanese in Virginia who might be affected by the statute.

In his argument, Virginia's Assistant Attorney General Robert D. McIlwaine III stressed that none of the framers of the Fourteenth Amendment had intended to outlaw statutes against racial intermarriage. The Fourteenth Amendment guarantees of equal protection and due process, relied on here by the Lovings, would never have cleared Congress if the lawmakers had thought those provisions would harm state control over interracial marriages. He contended that states have the power to outlaw marriage between the races just as they have to pass laws against polygamy and incest. Justice Black wanted to know if there could be any reason for the state's antimiscegenation laws other than that "white people are superior to colored people and should not therefore be allowed to marry because it might pollute the white race." Justice Harlan asked how Virginia could "rationalize" her laws in view of the *Brown* school desegregation decision if the historical argument were dropped. And Stewart observed that, putting legislative history aside, the purpose of the Equal Protection Clause was to guarantee that Negro citizens are treated the same as white citizens. McIlwaine argued in reply that Virginia's "strong policy" against interracial marriage was based upon firm scientific evidence. As proof, he waved before the Court a thick volume, *Intermarriage—Interfaith, Interracial, Interethnic* by Dr. Albert I. Gordon, a rabbi who had found that racially mixed marriages have many problems because of social attitudes.[19] McIlwaine cited statements from Gordon's book to the effect that interracial marriages were often contracted by rebellious individuals to express their social hostility. He said that "the progeny are the martyrs" of such unions, which the state had a legitimate interest in preventing. Even if the Fourteenth Amendment is to be considered applicable to mixed marriages, he argued, the states still should retain the power to forbid them because of the "sociological and psychological" evils which attend interracial marriage. This moved the Chief Justice to recall arguments rejected by the Court in the school cases that white children were injured if they attended classes with Negroes. Warren also quoted from a UNESCO committee report to the effect that scientific evidence contradicts racism. The final matter reached by McIlwaine in argument was that of the extent of the state legislation at stake in this case. He argued vigorously that only two sections of the law—one forbidding whites and Negroes to marry and the other an "evasion" statute to cover couples that marry outside the state and then come back to Virginia—were properly before the Court. These two sections, he argued, were the only ones involved in the Virginia Supreme Court of Appeals ruling upholding the case against the Lovings.

The atmosphere into which the Court injected its ruling two months later was considerably different from that of *Brown.* The impassioned oral arguments in *McLaughlin* and *Loving* were familiar and anticlimactic by the mid-1960s; they would have been far more relevant a decade earlier, when the Court would have been "up front" on the issue. By 1964, as the Court noted, Virginia was one of only sixteen states still to have miscegenation statutes, four states having repealed them during the preceding fifteen years. Public opinion was still negative and counter to the liberal views stated by the Lovings' lawyers. Yet the matter was by no means as controversial as it had been, in part because whatever the Court did there would not be a major change in the frequency of interracial marriages. In short, because unpopularity was down to a "safe level," the Court now "could satisfy the equalitarian demands of those who spoke for the conscience of the community."[20]

The Court ruled unanimously that states cannot outlaw marriages between whites and nonwhites. In so doing, Chief Justice Warren used language sufficiently broad and disapproving to leave no doubt that not only Virginia's statute but all similar laws were also voided. Warren began his opinion by describing this case as presenting the constitutional question, never addressed by the Court, whether a statutory scheme to prevent marriages between persons solely on the basis of racial classification violates the Constitution's Equal Protection and Due Process Clauses. Warren noted that the two statutes under which the Lovings had been convicted were part of a comprehensive statutory scheme aimed at prohibiting and punishing interracial marriages. He then knocked down one by one Virginia's arguments in support of the statutes. The state court was no doubt correct, Warren said, in asserting that marriage is a social relation subject to the state's police power. However, the state did not contend that its powers to regulate marriage are not limited by the Fourteenth Amendment. Instead the state had contended that the Equal Protection Clause required only that state penal laws with an interracial element as part of the offense must provide for punishment of members of each race to the same degree. That notion, Warren said, is rejected by the Court. The statutes rest solely on racial distinctions, he continued. And the fact that Virginia only prohibits interracial marriages involving white persons demonstrates that the racial classifications are indeed designed to maintain white supremacy. The Court had consistently denied the constitutionality of measures restricting the rights of citizens on account of race, Warren asserted, because racial classifications violate the central meaning of the equal protection guarantee.

Warren then drew on and adopted an argument which had been put forth in oral argument in *Brown:* based on the Japanese relocation cases, racial classifications were especially suspect—an acceptance and clear statement of the position which the Court had avoided in *Brown.* As if not satisfied with the strength of the equal protection argument, Warren went on to add that the statutes had violated the Due Process Clause as well, because "the freedom to marry has long been recognized as one of the vital personal rights essential to the orderly pursuit of happiness by free men." That freedom, he said, cannot be limited on account of race. Also drawing on his treatment of the history behind the Fourteenth Amendment in the *Brown* case. Warren pointed out, as he had there, that the history was inconclusive. As to the state's arguments that the framers of the amendment did not intend it to make miscegenation laws unconstitutional, Warren said, the Court had rejected the idea that the debates surrounding ratification of the amendment meant that penal laws could contain racial classifications as long as Negro and white were treated equally. He cited the recent *McLaughlin* cohabitation case to buttress the point. In a concurring opinion, Justice Stewart merely noted that he had previously expressed his belief in *McLaughlin* that it was "simply not possible for a state law to be valid under our Constitution which makes the criminality of an act depend upon the race of the actor."

In finally disposing of antimiscegenation statutes, the Court appears to have developed its strategy well. The *Loving* ruling was so unsurprising that it was given only passing attention in the nation's newspapers. While the immediate southern reaction was mixed, the effect was significant. Broad and all-encompassing as it was, the decision both put an end to all antimiscegenation legislation and greatly furthered progress against "suspect classifications" from the legitimacy of children to the assurance of a wife's rights to such benefits as Social Security and workmen's compensation. The Court's strategy in issuing a sweeping decision in this case rather than making it a cautious preliminary first step in its field—as had been customary in other areas—seems wholly justified. The Court had paved the way for this "most sensitive" area by its cases in other desegregation fields. By 1967 the Court had intervened vigorously in cases involving education, transportation, labor unions, public facilities, picketing, voting, and the like. The basic decision regarding miscegenation reached here was appropriately in the sweeping tradition of the basic school decision of 1954, but, with the passage of time and with developing experience, definiteness not present in *Brown* had been dictated.[21]

3

Many facilities in the public sector are aided by private donations and bequests. Such donations, which often go to recreational and educational facilities, are, however, frequently designated for specific projects or limited by specific conditions. Southern donors who lived under "separate but equal" were likely to specify that the facility or fund be limited to use by whites only or the bequest would revert to the donor's estate. One of these arrangements—a "whites only" park held in trust by a city—was challenged as soon as it seemed that *Brown* might be applicable to recreational facilities. *Charlotte Park and Recreation Commission v. Barringer,* although brought under the climate of *Brown,* came within the legal rationale of *Shelley.* Negroes had petitioned to use the golf facilities of a park located on land conveyed to the commission on condition that if any but the white race were allowed to use it, the land would revert in fee simple to the grantor, his heirs, or assignees. The commission then sued for a declaratory judgment. The North Carolina Supreme Court rejected the Negroes' argument that the reverter clause was invalid under the rationale of *Shelley* because enforcement of the discriminatory clause was tantamount to enforcement of a restrictive covenant and thus was state action precluded by the Fourteenth Amendment. The court said that the land would revert not by state action but automatically by the terms of the deed. When the case was appealed to the United States Supreme Court in 1956 the Court refused to review it. There might have been certain circumstances which justified the refusal, the commission having argued that the issues for adjudication were being properly brought in a pending state court case. That a proper remedy was being sought elsewhere is clear from the fact that the owners of the reversionary interest subsequently sold it to the city, which then admitted all races.

The next case in this area involved a discriminatory trust provision governing Girard College, a private educational institution limited to poor, white, male, orphan children and administered by the city of Philadelphia. The benefactor, Stephen Girard, had made specific provision in this will for disposition of his monies if at any time they could not be applied as directed. When Negro male orphans sought and were denied admission to the school, the state of Pennsylvania and the city of Philadelphia joined them in suing the municipal board administering the trust. The plantiffs charged discriminatory state action in contravention of the Fourteenth Amendment. The board argued in its defense that its action was in a "fiduciary" capacity and thus outside the state action concept. The Pennsylvania courts upheld the board's proposition. In late April 1957, however, the United States Supreme Court reversed the Pennsylvania Supreme Court per curiam, holding that the board which operated Girard College was an agency of the state and that therefore even though it was acting as a trustee, its refusal to admit the Negro boys solely because they were Negroes was discrimination by the state forbidden by the Fourteenth Amendment. The case was remanded for appropriate action.

The *Girard College Case* came back to the Court the following year (1958). In an attempt to carry out the provisions of Girard's will after the Court's initial ruling, the trust was conveyed to private trustees who continued the exclusionary admissions policy. The state courts again upheld this arrangement against challenge, saying that no state action was involved. When this state decision was brought to the United States Supreme Court on appeal, the justices dismissed the case. Then treating the appeals papers as a certiorari petition, they also denied certiorari. The appellants had argued in their brief that there was still sufficient state action involved in the running of the school to invoke the Fourteenth Amendment. But the reasons behind both denials seem to have been that the controversy had not been tested against the state's antidiscrimination enactment which seemed applicable to private trustees, and the comparatively very limited effect which any decision involving the unique situation of Girard College might have had on the welfare of the larger minority. At the time, it was feared that the Court's failure to deal with the case might provide a precedent for evasion of school desegregation in the South by conversion to a "private" school system. When action of that sort began, however, the courts were able to deal with it successfully.

Two higher education cases, only one of which came to the Court, were decided on the basis of the first Girard College decision.[22] The one which did reach the Supreme Court involved Sweet Briar Institute, set up decades before in Virginia under the will of a donor who provided funds "for the education of white girls and young women." The college originally brought suit against the commonwealth attorney and against the attorney general of Virginia for a declaratory judgment to interpret the discriminatory provision of the will of its founder. A state court ruled that no controversy existed, that the will was unambiguous and had been well understood for over sixty years, and that to apply the cy pres (deviation) doctrine now after all these years of successful operation would destroy the entire purpose of the will. This state court opinion was appealed, and a federal suit was also instituted. The district court granted a stay of prosecution before testing the constitutionality of the testamentary restriction on grounds that the similar suit in the state court system should be terminated first. In *Sweet Briar Institute v. Button,* the Supreme Court, dictating a prompt disposition, reversed the district court's judgment per curiam and remanded the case for consideration without delay on the merits, although Harlan and Stewart noted that they would have affirmed the district court ruling.

Southern donors also gave restricted gifts to hospitals. When three Negro doctors were denied access to practice in such a private facility in Wilmington, North Carolina, the doctors, guided by NAACP counsel Thurgood Marshall and Jack Greenberg, brought a class action suit in which they claimed that there was sufficient state involvement in the hospital to make their exclusion forbidden state action. In this case, *Eaton v. Board of Managers of James Walker Memorial Hospital,* a federal district court found that the city had a right of reverter in the land and in addition the city named the self-perpetuating board of managers, made contributions, and paid for the care of indigents. Despite these findings, the court said that the charitable hospital corporation was private, with no element of public control over the hospital sufficient to support the lawsuit, which was then dismissed for lack of federal jurisdiction. When the doctors appealed this ruling, the Fourth Circuit, citing the second *Girard College Case,* maintained that a hospital founded by a private benefactor was indeed a private corporation and that the bona fide conveyance of public lands to a private corporation did not make the hospital an agent of the state. This decision was appealed to the Supreme Court, the doctors arguing that they should have been permitted to present the detailed evidence necessary for making a decision on state action at a trial. Only the Chief Justice, Justice Douglas, and Justice Brennan seemed to agree that the doctors should be granted a hearing. A majority of the Court, apparently not yet prepared to take the large step required by a ruling in favor of the doctors, was unwilling to hear the case. If the Court were to find charity to be a public function involving state action, as had been urged, then private institutions of welfare, education, and the like would come under such a ruling. Perhaps a narrower case would be more appealing to the Court. Its ability to select cases certainly allowed the Court to wait for one so that too many as yet not fully examined situations would not be "blanketed in."[23]

The question of park segregation resulting from a discriminatory will provision—the *Charlotte Park* question—and the status of the park facility and its segregation after the appointment of "private" trustees—the *Girard College* question—arose again in *Evans v. Newton.* In the balance was a one-hundred acre park in Macon, Georgia, which had been given in trust many years earlier by Georgia's Senator Bacon for use by white persons only. In 1963 when Negroes were allowed to use the park contrary to the senator's will, some of the park managers went to court to find out how the racial limitation might be enforced. The city officials then turned Baconsfield Park over to "private" trustees who could enforce the all-white testamentary provision. Despite another provision of Bacon's will which indicated the city was supposed to retain perpetual control of the property, the Georgia courts allowed the city to resign its trusteeship. The Macon Negroes who had intervened in that case appealed this action as well as the status of the so-called private park, suddenly making quite important what had been a relatively noncontroversial lawsuit. The Georgia Supreme Court approved the city's resignation, and the challengers, with NAACP counsel, carried the case to the United States Supreme Court. Argument for the Negroes was handled in the Supreme Court by Jack Greenberg of the NAACP Legal Defense Fund.[24] The NAACP's position was that Georgia's legislature had expressly authorized establishment of racially restricted public parks through testamentary charitable trusts by law enacted immediately previous to the senator's bequest; that following creation of such a park and continuous management and ownership by the city and its agents, city officials took all necessary steps to place the park in private hands for the express purpose of continuing operation of the park on a segregated basis; that the Georgia courts were enforcing a will provision directing exclusion of Negroes in preference to a conflicting provision directing perpetual ownership by the city; that the park established by a charitable trust was in all respects a public facility and part of the public life of the community; and that the charitable trust was endowed by the state with judicial administration, tax exemption, perpetual existence, and tort immunity.

Greenberg argued that the statute naturally encouraged if not forced testators to specify segregation and that under the principles announced in the first sit-in cases the testator's personal preference for segregation, if any, must be disregarded. The actions of Macon city and park officials, Greenberg said, were a glaring illustration of state action to enforce segregation, in violation both of *Girard College* and *Shelley* and of the will's stated intent with regard to perpetual retention of control. According to Greenberg, the Georgia courts also had violated the Fourteenth Amendment as interpreted in those cases. Since charitable trusts such as this one were given significant state protection, they must be subjected to special scrutiny before being permitted to make arbitrary exclusions. The trust simply could not be allowed to perpetuate the very type of arbitrary discrimination the Fourteenth Amendment proscribed. The city's official collaboration in preservation of the segregation was crucial, because, Greenberg said, if the city in an attempt to retain the property had resisted the park board's petition that it resign its trust, the Georgia Supreme Court would have been much more likely to choose to follow the will's language with regard to the city's ownership rather than with respect to the racial limitation.

C. Baxter Jones, for Macon, replied that the board of managers of the park had been the agent of Senator Bacon, not the city, whose only tie was that it had appointed the original board and as long as it was a trustee had approved the board's nominations for continuing vacancies. He emphasized the limited scope of the Georgia Supreme Court's decision, which merely accepted the resignation of the city as trustee and appointed new trustees, enforcing no judgment or ruling as related to the intervenors and citing as authority state court approval of such procedure in the *Girard* case. From this he concluded that the Georgia court's decision thus rested on independent state grounds having a fair and substantial basis and that no federal question had been decided nor state law unusually applied. Pointing out that charitable trusts had traditionally been free from government control, he argued that Senator Bacon had selected the beneficiaries of his charity and that no law guaranteed others the right to share in his gift. What the petitioners seemed to be attempting, he said, was to create such rights by citing *Shelley,* asserting them in a state court, and having them denied. Just because some parks are state-owned and state-operated does not mean that charitable trust parks must be considered so also. The same would be true in the case of religious schools, he said; they would be at an end if the Fourteenth Amendment were held to apply to all trusts that perform functions also performed by government. Senator

Bacon's intentions were specific and detailed, and it seemed clear that the racial limitation of the will, not the passive trusteeship of the city, was the important thing to him. If cy pres were to be held applicable, the state courts should so decide, and Baconsfield probably could not continue as a park. Jones was questioned repeatedly by the justices about the park's physical layout. The Chief Justice was particularly interested in the city-built thoroughfare that ran through the park and the whites-only women's teas that were held at the tax-exempt Bacon homestead.

Louis Claiborne, arguing for the United States as amicus on the side of desegregation, stressed the impact of continued discrimination in what, so far as the living were concerned, was a public facility. He also raised the question of whether private successor trustees can operate a segregated park because of the "degree of state involvement"—an approach the Court had taken in the *Burton* case. Claiborne also said, in response to questioning, that the Court's decision in the case could effect the still continuing Girard College litigation.

A newspaper report on the argument was headlined "Court Hints Some Doubt Macon Park is Private." The justices had indicated they saw numerous public features about the so-called private park and had appeared unimpressed by arguments that the park was in the private sector of Macon city life. The headline proved accurate. Instead of reaching petitioners' two basic questions—(1) Can a state petition for new trustees (who would discriminate)? and (2) Has the state become impermissibly involved in the park through state statutes involved in setting up the trust?—or the related question of whether the state could substitute new trustees, the Court dealt with the issue of private trustee operation of a segregated park. In addition to going outside the record for the questions raised, the Court also did so to state that the shift to private trustees had brought no change in municipal concern.

The Court's opinion in the case was written by Justice Douglas, who characterized the case as one involving the reconciliation of two complementary principles, the right of the individual to pick his own associates and the constitutional ban in the Fourteenth Amendment Equal Protection Clause against state-sponsored racial inequality. It could fairly be assumed, Douglas said, that the state court would not have acted as it did if it had not thought that the transfer would accomplish the racial end desired. Had the Georgia courts been of the view that even in private hands the park may not be operated for the public on a segregated basis, the resignation would not have been approved and private trustees appointed. Where the tradition of municipal control had become firmly established, Douglas said, the Court could not take judicial notice that the mere substitution of "private" trustees instantly transferred the park from the public to the private sector. "Under the circumstances of this

case, we cannot but conclude that the public character of this park requires that it be treated as a public institution subject to the command of
the Fourteenth Amendment, regardless of who now has title under state
law." Citing the *Girard College Case* most often—but not citing either *Shelley*
or *Griffin v. Maryland,* the recent and controversial private amusement
park decision—Douglas felt that mere transfer of title did not disentangle
the park from municipal segregation. Accordingly, the decision of the
Georgia Supreme Court was reversed. In a footnote, Douglas noted that,
although it had been argued, the Court did not reach the question
whether the state facilitated the establishment of segregated parks
through the contested state statutes.

Justice White, concurring, would have vacated and remanded for
disposition by the state court, rather than reversed. He relied on the
limited ground that the racial condition in the trust could not be given
effect by the new trustees because it was incurably tainted by the discriminatory state legislation which had validated such a condition. Such a
statute would unconstitutionally depart from a policy of strict neutrality
in matters of private discrimination, White said, because it enlisted the
state's assistance only in aid of racial discrimination and would involve the
state in the private choice of the testator.

The first dissenting opinions, by Justices Harlan and Stewart, held
that the majority decision was more a product of human impulses than of
solid constitutional thinking. The justices wanted the writ dismissed as
improvidently granted, because the large constitutional question was
presented, if at all, with insufficient clarity to justify its adjudication. They
went on to say that the decision could by process of analogy be spun out to
reach privately owned orphanages, libraries, garbage collection companies, detective agencies, private denominationally restricted schools,
and a host of other functions commonly regarded as nongovernmental
though paralleling fields of governmental activity. This would include
many, like Baconsfield, never actually operated by the state but at one
time compelled by state law to discriminate racially or which perhaps had
received some state benefit such as tax exemption. They were concerned
that Douglas's "public function" and "municipal nature" concepts,
coupled with his concept of resultant "nonselectivity" regarding patronage of such a municipal facility, provided an unclear rule for determining
state action and substituted a vague, amorphous, and far-reaching
"catchphrase" approach for the comparatively clear and concrete test of
state action.

Justice Black also dissented, but adopted much the same premise as
had White. Black said that if the Court were to exercise jurisdiction at all
in the case, it should explicitly state that the question of reversion to
Senator Bacon's heirs is controlled by state law and then remand the case

to the Georgia Supreme Court to decide that question. He also believed that the Court could view only the two questions which the state court had decided—the acceptance of the city's resignation as trustee and the appointment of new trustees—and on this basis should dismiss the writ as improvidently granted. In concluding, Black noted that he was not saying that he believed the park could not be operated on a racially discriminatory basis but merely that the Court could not take from the states that which was their due.

All the majority had decided was that the park was irrevocably public not private in character and that it therefore could not be segregated under private trustees. If the real dispute in this case was whether the Court should have made any decision at all, a majority decided that one was warranted since the park had become such an integral part of the city's park facilities. They then concluded that in view of the various complicating circumstances, principally the reversion question, the narrowest possible constitutional decision should be made. The more difficult constitutional questions presented by the case were avoided by the Court's "stretching" as it did. Avoided was any decision based on *Shelley* as to the state court's ability to act in compliance with the city's request for the transfer, that is, the question whether the state court, regardless of its racial neutrality or indifference, could constitutionally act to further the discriminatory intent of the persons who sought the transferral. The Court left alone the new "private" trustees, who had yet not taken any action which could be reviewed, but also avoided any decision regarding the constitutionality of acts of the other principal party, the city. That is, no decision was made on the question whether the city's action in resigning as trustee, while complicated by the fear that the park property might revert, was an unconstitutional endeavor to further segregation. In so doing, the Court avoided condemning the city's action, providing instead an advisory opinion for the city's guidance.

To reach the constitutionality of the action of the other principal, the late Senator Bacon, required dealing with a statutory question, since he had acted according to pertinent state statutes. Although urged by White, this statutory ground was specifically not reached, perhaps because White's position would seem to preclude reversion of the property to Senator Bacon's heirs under state law, the matter raised by Justice Black. By saying nothing about reversion, the majority seemed to leave that up to the state courts, while announcing the constitutional judgment concerning the nature of the park after transferral which would govern such consideration—an enunciation necessary in view of the Court's earlier refusal to hear the *Girard College Case* appeal after a similar transferral.

Reaching for the question it answered allowed the Court to state an expanded state action view, its "public function" doctrine. The vagueness of its decree—its remand for further action—underlines the Court's using the case as a basis for enunciating new doctrine. The Court avoided indicating what matters relating to trusts would be state action, something that would have given the ruling broader applicability. The continuing municipal involvement assumed by the Court, a nonrecurring fact situation, made the Court's ruling limited in its applicability as precedent, but the broad doctrine had been stated. One can thus see *Evans* as an incremental step in the expansion of the state action doctrine as the Court moved toward the critical housing area.

Evans v. Newton became the basis for final disposition of *Girard College*. After the Court's last avoidance of the case, subsequent picketing and violence at Girard had encouraged a new approach to the problem, and the state of Pennsylvania and city of Philadelphia had joined with seven Negro children in bringing a suit in federal court, *Commonwealth of Pennsylvania v. Brown.* In September 1966 a federal district judge ruled on *Evans* grounds that the school could not bar Negroes because to do so was a violation of the state's 1935 Public Accommodations Act forbidding racial discrimination in public places. In November the judge ordered the school to open its gates to Negroes, staying enforcement pending appeal, and to begin preadmission procedures for the seven boys. Subsequently, the Third Circuit reversed this decision on grounds that the question of admission must be decided solely on whether the federal constitutional rights of the seven Negro applicants had been violated. In July 1967 the district judge ruled that the boys' federal constitutional rights were violated by their exclusion solely on grounds of race and broadened his order to include not just the seven who had applied but also all future qualified Negro boys. Execution of this order was again stayed pending appeal, however, and in November 1967 the Third Circuit agreed to review the decision. That court then affirmed the judgment, stating that when the Orphans' Court eliminated the city as trustees and installed its own trustees sworn to uphold the donor's will it was effectively continuing what the Supreme Court had earlier invalidated. The court was certainly significantly involved with current administration of the school through the trustees it appointed. When the case was brought to the Supreme Court again, certiorari was denied, finally bringing the litigation to a close.

Whereas *Evans v. Newton* helped settle the *Girard College* matter, the Macon park matter was not itself settled, and further litigation in the Georgia courts brought the case back to the Supreme Court. On remand, the Georgia Supreme Court had found that Senator Bacon's original purpose could not be carried out and that the trust was terminated and the parkland reverted to Senator Bacon's heirs. There was further remand to the state trial court, where there were arguments on whether the cy pres doctrine—allowing a court to carry a bequest into effect so as to accommodate the testator's will when his exact preference could not be achieved—should be applied. The Negroes who had brought the original suit, joined by the state attorney general, sought to apply the doctrine, claiming that maintaining the area as a park came closest to Bacon's original intent. However the trial court would not go along, and enforced the reverter clause. From that ruling, after an affirmance from the state high court, petitioners again brought the case to the Supreme Court. This time, in *Evans v. Abney,* in 1970 the Court by a five-to-two vote upheld the action of the Georgia court.

Justice Black, who had dissented in the first case, wrote for the Court. Most of his opinion stressed the state's great latitude in determining matters of probate law, to which he added language about the nondiscriminatory result in the case. The latitude given the state courts is seen in his statement that "in ruling as they did the Georgia courts did no more than apply well-settled general principles of Georgia law to determine the meaning and effect of a Georgia will." Those state courts, he said, had determined that Bacon would rather have had the trust fail than have Baconsfield integrated. Claiming there was no state action, Black said "any harshness that may have resulted . . . can be attributed solely to [the Georgia court's] intention to effectuate as nearly as possible the explicit terms of Senator Bacon's will." The Supreme Court had not, he said, dealt with the issue of whether or not Baconsfield should be operated as a park, but only with a more limited question of how, if operated as a park, it had to be operated. Here Georgia trust laws neutral as to race produced the result. Reinforcing his insistence on the state's latitude, Black tried to make clear that other courts in other states could apply cy pres to reach the opposite result.

Black saw "the loss of charitable trusts such as Baconsfield a part of the price we pay for permitting deceased persons to exercise a continuing control over assets owned by them at death," but he also noted that there was no discrimination in the Georgia court's action, in terms of the judges' motivation or in terms of the result: "The termination of the park was a loss shared equally by the white and Negro citizens of Macon since both races would have enjoyed a constitutional right of equal access to the park's facilities had it continued." Justice Douglas and Justice Brennan, both of whom wrote dissenting opinions, disagreed with their colleague on almost every major point. Claiming that the reverter clause in the senator's will did not run to the senator's heirs but to the city, Douglas found the lower court's action doing "as much violence" to what the senator intended as would changing his "all-white" park to an all-Negro one. He thought that a larger share of Bacon's intent could be carried out by desegregating the park than by eliminating its use as a park. "The purpose of the will was to dedicate the land for some municipal use. That is still possible." He also thought that achieving Bacon's basic desire could be "realized only by the repeal of the Fourteenth Amendment."

Brennan stressed the city's involvement in the development of a primitive, undeveloped piece of land into the present park. Such work could not be undone, he noted, so one was not reverting the same land Bacon had given but one in which there had been continuous government involvement. He felt that "no record could present a clearer case of the closing of a public facility for the sole reason that the public authority which owns and maintains it cannot keep it segregated." In a statement the first part of which made a concession used by the majority in the Jackson, Mississippi, pool-closing case the following year, he remarked, "I have no doubt that a public park may constitutionally be closed down because it is too expensive to run or has become superfluous, or for some other reason, strong or weak, or for no reason at all. But under the Equal Protection Clause a State may not close down a public facility solely to avoid its duty to desegregate that facility."

Brennan also disagreed with Black on the state action question. Georgia statutes under which Bacon wrote his will, Brennan said, "expressly authorized and supported the precise kind of discrimination provided for by him." The state could not single out racial discrimination for particular encouragement, as Georgia's statutes under which the will had been written had done. In addition, in accepting the park the public officials were agreeing to leave in private hands the power to revert the property if the city should ever have to desegregate. The facility had been operated as a public facility. On the second point, he stressed that "there is state action whenever a State enters into an arrangement which creates a private right to compel or enforce the reversion of a public facility." Brennan threw in one more state action aspect, drawing on *Shelley*. The city, he said, ultimately had been willing to desegregate; Negroes had wanted to use the park. Therefore, one had willing parties dealing with each other, just as one had a willing buyer and a willing seller in *Shelley*. Here, just as there, a state court interfered with that relation, and *Shelley,* the justice wrote, "stands at least for the proposition that where parties of different races are willing to deal with one another a state court cannot keep them from doing so by enforcing a privately authored racial restriction."

The result in *Evans v. Abney* undid what the Court had seemed to do in *Evans v. Newton*. It was a case of "two steps forward, three steps back," for instead of having a park available on a desegregated basis, no one had the park. It is of little consolation to realize that the Court was consistent in upholding states' leeway in dealing with testamentary matters.[25] The use of law to achieve social change had clearly received a setback. However, in enunciating its ruling in the first *Evans* case, the Court had established an important state action ruling, one to which it did not add in the second opinion, although the dissenters strongly underlined state action considerations which should be taken into account. Perhaps in terms of doctrinal development, the Court had accomplished something even though it had not added to the social revolution for blacks in so doing.

These last cases illustrate the strategy one can call "hitting 'em where they ain't," in which the Court deals with an important doctrinal point in a narrow case with few immediate factual-context ramifications in order to mute unfavorable public and mass-media comment and backlash. The more specific, fact-based, and individual a case is, the less direct precedential value it has. Cases involving wills and testators' intent are appropriate because they are among the most specific in any area of law and are reinforced by the Court's separate treatment of probate law and particular deference to the states in that area. This makes such a case an ideal one for announcing broad doctrines. Cases differ in the breadth of their fact situations. Perhaps the broadest question a court might consider would be of the type (1) "Can a public school system have separate facilities for blacks and whites?" This question is involved in any public school desegregation case, because public schools are more or less the same, or at least have been so treated legally. Whether or not one looks at de jure or de facto segregation, questions involving schools require developing a rule for entire school districts, one thus applicable to all the other school districts in the country. While some segregated schools might remain in a desegregated school district—even one desegregated affirmatively by the school board—the district as a whole would be the basic unit of analysis, and one would be considering what should be done with black children who live in the same district as the whites. One would not likely see a question framed in a school desegregation case, "Can Public School 107, Queens, New York, have separate facilities for blacks and whites?" Even if it were so phrased, it would likely apply "across-the-board" also. This would also be true with segregation within specific schools when school districts bus students from overcrowded white schools to underfilled black ones and keep the white students in separate rooms—a *McLaurin*-type question.

A somewhat smaller fact question than type (1) is type (2) "Can Park X in State Y segregate if it is a private park?" The answer is "Yes" if the park is completely private, but if the park is maintained by public funds, different, and factual, questions arise—the amount of public "character" of the park and the terms of the testator's will. The terms of each will, or at least the state statute under which it was written, tend to be different. A potentially smaller question is of the form (3) "If J marries K, can J be cut off from the will since she is marrying a black?" It is these latter questions, (2) and (3), which are ideal for announcing broad doctrines such as "courts can never enforce racially discriminatory clauses in wills, contracts, or any private conveyances," because of the small extendability of their fact situations.

An example of the latter types of situations prior to *Brown* is *Shelley,* the impact of which extended far beyond real estate. A potential case for the use of the strategy from that period was *Morgan,* because its immediate precedential impact, had the Court used it to invalidate separate-but-equal, would have been not on education but on the much less newsworthy interstate transportation system, with its effect on education coming only later. More recent examples include the *Girard College* and *Evans* park cases, in both of which the state action question was brought up. The *Girard College Case* did increase the reach of the state action doctrine, but the park cases did not, because the Court missed its chance in the second *Evans* case to read adequate state action into what had occurred in Macon. Had it done so, its approach would have applied to numerous nonpark cases even while settling a local controversy that would hardly have had any wide newsworthiness and few direct ramifications. By comparison, in *Brown* a major doctrinal point was made in a case which automatically had broad implications. This suggests that if using cases with a narrow factual basis to enunciate broad doctrine seems an appropriate strategy, one might keep in mind the contrary, or contrapositive, strategy: in dealing with a case with a broad direct factual impact—the sit-ins at lunch counters, for example—one should try to avoid doctrinal pronunciamentos. This is almost "avoid 'em where they are." Certainly the effect, grounded in the Supreme Court's practical eye for what makes newspaper headlines was the same: avoidance of immediate public backlash to the decisions.

Chapter 6

School Desegregation after *Brown*

I N the dozen years after *Brown,* the Supreme Court took little action in the school desegregation area, and did not begin to move firmly and to demand results until the 1968–69 period. However, there were three important southern school desegregation cases in the ten years after *Brown: Cooper v. Aaron,* the Little Rock litigation; *Goss,* on racial transfers; and *Griffin,* the case deriving from the closing of the schools in Prince Edward County. This post-*Brown* decade was also notable for the Supreme Court's treatment of the South's attempts to put the NAACP out of action. After the Civil Rights Act of 1964 was passed, there was important administrative activity concerning school desegregation which was tied to what the courts had done after *Brown II.* While the administrative activity was taking place in 1964 and 1965, school desegregation cases involving both the South and the North were brought to the Supreme Court. Before we look at these developments, we turn to the Court's higher education decisions, first, during the "interim year" between *Brown I* and *Brown II* and, then, in the period after *Brown II.*

1

Immediately after deciding *Brown I,* the Court started to hand down a series of per curiam rulings ordering lower courts to reconsider a variety of cases in light of *Brown,* the authority cited by the Court. During the interim year between *Brown I* and *Brown II,* not a single desegregation case was decided with full opinion. The Court seemed anxious to indicate that the School Cases would apply to segregation in other fields, at the same time wanting the lower courts to indicate what they thought that the impact of *Brown* might be in those areas. On the decision day following *Brown I,* six segregation cases from five different states were disposed of summarily—two in public facilities, one in housing, and three in higher education from Florida, Louisiana, and Texas

The Texas case, *Wichita Falls Junior College District v. Battle,* was reminiscent of the old "constitutional geography" ruling of *Gaines.* A federal

162

court of appeals had upheld a district court ruling that refusal to admit otherwise qualified Negro students to a junior college was unlawful discrimination because attending the school was much less expensive, both in time and money, for those residing in its jurisdiction than was attending like institutions for Negroes in other locations. Because the factual issue as to whether discrimination existed could be resolved on the basis of the policies, practices, usages, and customs described in the case, the appeals court ruled that it was not necessary to determine the constitutionality of the state law requiring such segregation. Asked to review the case, the Supreme Court let the admission order stand by denying Texas a hearing. In the other two higher education cases, the *Tureaud* case involving the junior division of Louisiana State University, from the lower federal courts, and the *Hawkins* litigation involving the law school of the University of Florida, from the Florida Supreme Court, the Court vacated and remanded decisions denying admission to Negroes for reconsideration "in the light of the *School Segregation Cases* and conditions that now prevail."

The Court was to see numerous "repeater" cases like these, including the litigation from Alabama involving Autherine Lucy, with the Florida case showing up several times. "Repeaters" appeared in other areas as well—for example, in public facilities. The *Rice* case involving a Miami golf course in which Negroes were limited to use one day a week had been remanded initially, prior to *Brown,* in light of *Sweatt* and *McLaurin,* and then was denied certiorari. Later, cases involving denial of service in places of public accommodation were to appear at the Supreme Court more than once. In the late 1950s and early 1960s, however, most "repeaters" were lower education cases. The Arlington County, Virginia, *Thompson* litigation appeared once on a jurisdictional question and later on a question of requirements made of school officials after an initial district court contempt finding. The Prince Edward County school case, after its extended appearance as part of the *Brown* litigation, was before the Court several times, including an unused 1958 opportunity for the Court to have made clear that opposition to desegregation was not an acceptable grounds for delay, and came to the Court for rulings on school closings and again in connection with the aftermath of those rulings. The New Orleans *Bush* litigation was also a "repeater"—a multi-repeater if we include litigation testing related provisions of the Louisiana antidesegregation statutes. As this case and the multiple cases from Norfolk, Little Rock, and Delaware suggest, even if a particular case did not repeat, the general litigation which gave rise to it could—and often did—reappear.

As might be expected, enunciation of the "all deliberate speed" doctrine in *Brown II* raised the new question as to whether delay in compliance was justifiable in higher education, as well as whether "all deliberate speed" could be applied in place of the prevailing "personal and present" standard compelling immediate admission to previously all-white institutions. During the first term after *Brown II,* there was great activity regarding these questions. The Court's higher education action initially met with legal delays and violence. In the first case after *Brown II* a federal district court had enjoined officials of the University of Alabama from denying Miss Lucy and other young Negroes the right to enroll there and pursue courses of study, and the injunction had then been suspended. When the case first appeared, the Supreme Court, on the basis of *Sipuel, Sweatt,* and *McLaurin,* vacated the suspension and reinstated the injunction as it had originally been granted. However, shortly after Miss Lucy was admitted to the university, she had to be excluded temporarily because of rioting and violence. An injunction prohibiting the dean from denying her the right to enroll because of race was then affirmed by the circuit court. This time the Supreme Court denied certiorari. Miss Lucy was then expelled by university officials for charging them with misconduct during the trial, and the federal government, remaining aloof, did nothing to help her despite an appeal from certain university officials, thus leaving the University of Alabama segregated—as it was to be until the famous confrontation between the federal government and Governor Wallace seven years later.

These early years saw less complicated cases of Negro admission to formerly all-white universities. One was the federal district court ruling supporting the class action suit by three Negro youths seeking admission to the undergraduate schools of the University of North Carolina on the grounds that the constitutional declaration of *Brown* was by all means applicable to higher education. Here the Supreme Court needed only to affirm the lower court judgment per curiam,[1] but such cases were not the prevailing pattern. The reappearing *Hawkins* and *Tureaud* cases, like the *Lucy* case, were more typical. After the original remand, the *Tureaud* case had been dealt with quickly by the Court of Appeals for the Fifth Circuit, which found no conditions to justify delay and affirmed the district court's injunction without amendments to the original pleading or any new proof. Certain recalcitrants engineered a rehearing order by which the district court was directed to reconsider the case with specific attention to the earlier Supreme Court mandate, since the latter had not reversed but had vacated and remanded with specific directions. On rehearing, the original decision was found to be correct, and the injunction against university officials was reinstated. Apparently satisfied, the Supreme Court denied certiorari.

In the *Hawkins* case, the Florida Supreme Court, recognizing the importance of "conditions that now prevail," had withheld an injunction pending determination of the proper time for Hawkins to be admitted.

Receiving a new application for certiorari in early 1956, the Supreme Court recalled and vacated its previous mandate. In its place the justices entered a new order granting certiorari, vacating the judgment, and remanding the case with these instructions: "As this case involves the admission of a Negro to a graduate professional school, there is no reason for delay. He is entitled to prompt admission under the rules and regulations applicable to other qualified candidates." The Court, which obviously saw no further reason for delay, also denied the board of control's subsequent petition for a rehearing. However, delays continued as the Florida Supreme Court, in the interest of maintaining "peace and order," refused to comply with the Court's directive and told Hawkins he could be admitted as soon as he was prepared to present testimony showing that his admission could be accomplished without doing "great public mischief."

Hawkins's appeal of this ruling was the single higher education case to come before the Court during the 1957 Term. The Supreme Court, perhaps showing some deference to the state courts even after their delays, denied his petition for certiorari, but gave the state a clear picture of its intent. Some bite was added to the denial through the explicit notation that it was made "without prejudice to petitioner's seeking relief in an appropriate United States district court." Absent state court action, the Court's strategy was not to take the case itself but to bury its "advice" in a denial of certiorari and to throw the case into the federal court system. In the federal courts, there would be less sensitivity than in a state court to the argument of "great public mischief" and, should the courts not deliver the judgment so obviously required, the Supreme Court had more direct and politically easier appellate control not vexed by the difficult problems of federalism presented by the Florida Supreme Court's obdurate refusal to comply. This formula was successful, for the following year a federal district court finally awarded Hawkins the immediate admission order he had so long sought.

A single higher education case had come to the Court during the 1956 Term before the final Supreme Court decisions in *Hawkins*. The Sixth Circuit had rejected a five-year "stair-step" desegregation plan for the University of Tennessee on the grounds that racial considerations could not be exploited to remedy problems of overcrowding. The state board appealed, claiming that the case was the first to reach the Court testing the validity of a plan for segregation according to *Brown* and suggesting that the lower courts needed amplification of *Brown*'s principles. The Court denied certiorari,[2] and by doing so signaled to the lower courts that it had had enough of litigation over desegregation of schools and was now throwing the problem back into the laps of the lower courts, who could now, without Supreme Court interference, interpret the ambiguous opinion in *Brown II* as they wished.

2

From *Brown II* to its ruling after holding a special session in the Little Rock case in 1958, the Supreme Court did not hand down any full opinions in the field of lower education. Instead, it disposed of cases with summary actions, mainly certiorari denials but including some per curiam dispositions. With the exceptions of the *Goss* and *Griffin* cases, this basic pattern was to continue after Little Rock until passage of the Civil Rights Act of 1964 changed the context in which the Court operated. Because of resistance to its decisions, after *Brown II* the Court sought to allow time during which the lower federal courts might explore and expand its rulings. These institutions, so much closer to the situations from which problems arose, were allowed considerable leeway in their interpretations of *Brown* doctrine. Only after violence in Little Rock had compelled reaction even on the part of the federal government did the Court at last step in to elaborate on the meaning and message of *Brown*. Although Justice Goldberg was later to remark that by the 1950s, "it was no longer possible for the Court gingerly to enter upon a problem, then to wait for a generation until its handiwork had been tested in experience,"[3] it was precisely this attitude the Court seemed to be taking, if we judge the Court by its actions.

The standard explanation for the Court's obvious reluctance following *Brown* to insist upon "deliberate speed" is that as pragmatists the justices wanted to give the South time to adjust to the desegregation of its school system. But in terms of strategy, the Court had made a basic mistake in announcing the end of the separate-but-equal doctrine in the highly controversial area of elementary school education. The enormous reaction to *Brown*'s legality had "burned" the Court, which then compounded its error. Like a cat reacting to a hot stove by staying away from all stoves, hot or cold, the Court stayed away from the education area except in those few cases—like Little Rock—where it could not possibly avoid taking a firm stand. The net result was to emasculate the "all deliberate speed" language and to indicate that the Court was prepared to look the other way while an entire generation of black students began and graduated from segregated schools after 1954. However, while the effects in education were negative, the Court seemed to learn a different lesson from the same strategic error in *Brown* in areas other than education, where the Court's handling of segregation cases yielded positive strategic results.

After *Brown*, the progress of school desegregation in the next ten years was spotty to negligible. By September 1956, only the District of Columbia had desegregated completely. West Virginia, Maryland, Missouri, Oklahoma, and Kentucky had begun desegregation in more than 50 percent of their public school districts, and Delaware, a border state, had desegregated about one quarter of its districts. In the southern states, about 17 percent of Texas's districts had at least token desegregation, as did a very small fraction in Arkansas and Tennessee. In the remainder of the South, nothing had happened.[4] Resistance continued obdurate for more than a decade after *Brown*.

After *Brown II*, southern federal judges being asked to approve desegregation plans in cases filed primarily by the NAACP faced a difficult situation.[5] The *Brown* decisions had made it possible for Negro parents to seek desegregation, but it was unclear what specific remedies they were to receive. The judges, "accustomed to trying individuals for concrete violations," now in effect had to try the "entire white community . . . for violation of a broad but unspecific constitutional interpretation."[6] As if that were not sufficiently difficult, the executive branch was not providing support. The not unnatural result was that the judge was "inclined to accept at face value state laws plainly designed to prevent enforcement of the Supreme Court decision" and to resolve doubts in favor of school boards, not the Negro plaintiffs.[7] It thus appeared that a community could comply with *Brown* by at most admitting a few Negroes to the previously segregated schools. Supreme Court denials of certiorari permitted the occasional action by some local courts demanding more of school boards but also left standing the predominant token action or non-action. Where no legal action was initiated—true in many areas—the schools were left as segregated as before *Brown I*. Thus did the promise of *Brown* produce limited results, at least in the early years.

The post-*Brown* atmosphere was also conditioned by a significant extrajudicial event that epitomized early resistance to the ruling. On March 12, 1956, 101 United States senators and representatives from the eleven southern states presented to Congress a statement which came to be known as the "Southern Manifesto." In a document, entitled "A Declaration of Constitutional Principles," the southern congressmen criticized the Supreme Court for its 1954 *Brown* ruling in most bitter terms, calling the decision an exercise of "naked power" and a "clear abuse" of judicial authority with "no legal basis." Although the signers did not directly urge violence or illegality in defiance of the ruling, their closing statements in the manifesto made their message quite clear: "We pledge ourselves to use all lawful means to bring about a reversal of this decision which is contrary to the Constitution and to prevent the use of force in its implementation. In this trying period, as we all seek to right this wrong, we appeal to our people not to be provoked by the agitators and troublemakers invading our States and to scrupulously refrain from disorder and lawless acts."[8]

This unprecedented public rebuke of the Court by distinguished members of a coordinate branch of the federal government was probably the single most influential document defying desegregation in the South. It provided important approval of and support for the plan of "Massive Resistance" and made such resistance "socially acceptable" by giving it the blessing of the southern establishment. More important, with the federal government under the Eisenhower administration continuing its notable display of aloofness from *Brown,* intransigence from the South ballasted by the approval of its elected federal representatives could not but debilitate the force of the Supreme Court decision. The Court could not implement *Brown* or any subsequent decision without other agencies forcing a certain amount of compliance. The "Southern Manifesto not only made executive action even less likely but inspired some degree of judicial hesitancy as well, thus seriously hindering any significant extension of *Brown.*

The Court was to do little to monitor the course of school desegregation despite numerous opportunities. However, there was only one such case during the October 1955 Term—*Board of Education of Hillsboro v. Clemons*, from a midwestern, not a southern, state. In 1954 an Ohio school board had attempted to defer desegregation until 1957 when a building program was expected to alleviate a classroom shortage. A zoning plan with a two-part gerrymandered district embracing practically all of the city's colored population had been set up. Objection to the plan was defeated at the trial court level, but the Court of Appeals for the Sixth Circuit reversed the trial court, saying that the plan was brought about as a subterfuge to segregate Negro children who had been admitted to previously all-white schools. The appeals court said such zoning was violative both of state law which forbade segregation and of the Supreme Court decision. The court added that, in the absence of an adequate remedy at law, equitable relief by injunction was essential to protect the children. Immediate admission of those Negro children who had refused to attend segregated schools was required, as was complete desegregation in the city by the next school year regardless of temporarily overcrowded classrooms. The board took the case to the Supreme Court, evidently hoping that the overcrowding might be deemed an acceptable reason for delay, but the Court refused to hear the case. This first disallowance of an attempt at procrastination invoked the federal Constitution in the North, not the South, perhaps foreshadowing the all-pervasive effect which the School Cases were to have on American public education.

The Court also refused to intervene in another northern case in the pre–Little Rock period. The case, from Pennsylvania, involved both alleged racial gerrymandering of school districts and de facto segregation, the root problem in the case. The Department of Public Instruction had presented a new county districting plan to the state Council of Education, which approved the plan despite significant negative sentiment. Subsequently, the governor appeared before the council and, on the advice of his attorney general, warned that he viewed the matter as very serious, arguing that the council should act against even suspicions of segregation in the state's public schools. After this admonition, the council withdrew its approval, apparently feeling that a court would probably rule it unconstitutional. The location of a new junior high school, allegedly placed to create a gerrymandered district, was still in controversy after the Council action, and resulted in a federal court suit, *Sealy v. Department of Public Instruction*. The district court did not rule on the constitutionality of the county plan nor did it require that one free of racial discrimination be presented. The court also held that the location and construction of the proposed junior high school was "unrelated" to the relief the Negro plaintiffs sought because there had not been an adequate showing that the location had been chosen with racial factors in mind. After the Court of Appeals for the Third Circuit affirmed, the plaintiffs asked the Supreme Court for a hearing. They claimed that the district court should have retained jurisdiction of all issues pending full implementation of an integrated public school plan. The Supreme Court declined to enter the case, denying certiorari.

By the 1956 Term the implications of the *Brown* decisions were sufficiently clear to produce a large number of desegregation suits from various parts of the country. A total of eight school desegregation suits, from six different states, this time all but one from the South, were handled by the Court during the term. The Court took affirmative action only in the one northern case—the previously discussed *Girard College* litigation, which was not of the purely public school variety. With all of the southern cases, the Court denied review. Where such action let stand decisions adverse to *Brown*'s intended beneficiaries, the Court passively presided over the dismantling of "all deliberate speed."

1) Turkish students in South Carolina were excluded from white schools. A suit was brought in federal court, but the Court of Appeals for the Fourth Circuit (covering Virginia, West Virginia, Maryland, North and South Carolina) dismissed it. Some of the children had been admitted to white schools by the time their case reached the Court of Appeals, and the court noted that the children might possibly obtain individual administrative relief from the state school boards. *Action by the Supreme Court:* denial of certiorari.[9]

2) The Court of Appeals for the Fifth Circuit, which because it covered Alabama, Georgia, Louisiana, Florida, Mississippi, and Texas was to handle the great bulk of school desegregation cases, was fairly "liberal" on desegregation. In a Texas case, the court did not require the black

plaintiffs to exhaust their state administrative remedies but instead remanded their cases to the district court with instructions to issue an order
requiring a prompt start toward integration "uninfluenced by private and
public opinion as to desirability." *Action by the Supreme Court:* appeal
denied.[10]

3) A suspect North Carolina "pupil placement" plan was challenged
by blacks who alleged that it would not effect bona fide transfers without
regard to race. As it had earlier held in the Turkish students' case, the
Fourth Circuit ruled that the plaintiffs must pursue their state
administrative—although not judicial—remedies, which must be given a
chance to work. *Action by the Supreme Court:* denial of certiorari.[11]

4 and 5) In Virginia, where there was massive public resistance to
desegregation, black school children won a district court injunction banning school board enforcement of racial segregation. The Fourth Circuit
noted that the injunction did not require the school officials to do anything; it simply forbade them to violate the law laid down in *Brown. Action
by the Supreme Court:* denial of certiorari.[12] After efforts by the plaintiffs to
have the school officials declared in contempt were unsuccessful, the case
returned to the Supreme Court in 1958. The district court had ruled that
provisions of the state pupil placement law, held unconstitutional in other
litigation, need not be exhausted before plaintiffs came to federal court,
and had set out for the officials what was required of them: school
desegregation by the start of the next school year. The Fourth Circuit
affirmed. *Action by the Supreme Court:* denial of certiorari.[13]

6) After federal courts in Virginia struck down the pupil placement
laws and the school closing laws, a federal district court required school
officials to comply with a desegregation order. Relying on the pupil
placement statute, the school officials refused to do so. The Court of
Appeals ruled that their violation of the injunctive order resulted from
good faith reliance on the statute and gave the officials until the start of
the next school year to comply with the desegregation order. *Action by the
Supreme Court:* certiorari denied.[14]

7) The Fifth Circuit ruled that a trial court must retain jurisdiction
over a suit even when steps had been taken in compliance with *Brown* so
that the court could exercise supervision over the school board as to the
continuing implementation of *Brown. Action by the Supreme Court:* certiorari denied.[15]

8) Louisiana passed a state constitutional amendment reaffirming
segregation, to which a pupil placement statute was linked. The statute
required that a complicated system of administrative remedies be
exhausted before relief was sought. The Fifth Circuit held that the link-
age of the statute to the amendment made the whole scheme unconstitutional, since the administrative remedies would be futile in light of the

state policy expressed in the constitutional amendment. *Action by the Supreme Court:* denial of certiorari.[16] The case returned to the Supreme Court after the school officials lost an attempt in the Court of Appeals to nullify the previous ruling on the basis that the black plaintiffs had not filed a $1,000 bond. The court held that the technicality did not hurt the defendants inasmuch as they had appealed the case before objecting to the nonfiling of the bond. *Action by the Supreme Court:* certiorari denied.[17]

The first school desegregation case of the 1957 Term, which was to end with the special Little Rock session, came from Tennessee and contained a slightly new feature—an out-of-state agitator attempting to incide disobedience of a court desegregation order. Under a Sixth Circuit order, a federal district court had required Clinton, Tennessee, school authorities to desegregate the county's high school by a certain date.[18] When the desegregated school opened in fall 1956, John Kasper of Washington, D.C., who called himself the executive secretary of the Seaboard White Citizens Council, came to town and began to stir up resistance among the previously resigned townspeople. Before long the protest had reached riot proportions, segregationists from all over the country began gathering in Clinton, and Governor Frank Clement had to send the state police and National Guard to Clinton to restore order. Kasper was arrested and jailed on charges of vagrancy and inciting to riot. When he was released from jail for lack of evidence, he continued to arouse the people to "get" the Negroes despite a restraining order with which he had been served. In a suit brought by the high school principal, in which the United States Department of Justice participated as amicus, the federal district judge who had issued the desegregation order convicted Kasper of contempt of court for violating the injunction against hindering desegregation of the high school and sentenced him to a year in prison. The Sixth Circuit affirmed the conviction on the grounds that the district court, acting under its directive, had jurisdiction of the controversy and proper authority to enforce the desegregation order. The court said Kasper's speeches and organization of a mob in defiance of the court order and Supreme Court decisions were not within the First Amendment's protections, adding that his one year sentence was not cruel and unusual punishment. The Supreme Court declined to review the case.[19]

The next school case, an important one coming from Virginia and the Fourth Circuit, was *Adkins v. School Board of Newport News*, and it indicated a slight tightening of requirements in that jurisdiction. A federal district judge ruled that the Virginia Pupil Placement Law passed in September 1956 was "unconstitutional on its face and must be disregarded." Noting that the law existed in connection with other state statutes providing for school closing and withdrawal of state funds upon departure from a policy of segregation, the district court observed that under the plan, established to defeat *Brown,* the Pupil Placement Board would be "derelict in its duty if it ever permitted admission of a Negro child in a school heretofore reserved for white children, and vice-versa." Nor did the law's administrative remedy, which consumed more than a hundred days, provide a valid reason why there should not be a direct ruling on the statute's validity. Here the district court carefully distinguished the appeals courts ruling upholding North Carolina's comparable statute, because the remedies afforded there did not lead to the complete "blind alley" Virginia's law prescribed. The Fourth Circuit upheld the district court per curiam, saying that the Pupil Placement Law did not deprive the district court of jurisdiction on the exhaustion of remedy theory because the act furnished no adequate remedy and, furthermore, was unconstitutional when considered in connection with other state statutes. Asked to review, the Supreme Court refused.

Also from Virginia was a case from Prince Edward County, which had been part of the original *Brown* litigation. After the original remand of that ruling in 1955, the district court had ordered desegregation from the time that a plan should be readied, thus authorizing delay for making arrangements and recognizing that community opposition might forestall progress. The Fourth Circuit had reversed on the ground that opposition had been explicitly excluded as a proper reason for delay of desegregation.[20] Then in early 1957 the district court, noting that much time and patience would be required to bring about the necessary adjustments on a gradual basis, declined to set any deadline for the start of desegregation. Pointing out that nothing yet had been done despite an order more than a year and a half earlier enjoining racial discrimination in the county's schools, the Court of Appeals then put the district court under its order to require the school authorities to set a definite starting date for desegregation. The appeals court pointed out that this did not mean at once with regard to all grades, if a reasonable start were made with deliberate speed, considering problems of proper administration. The judges also declared that threats that the public schools might be closed if such an order were enforced provided no reason for not proceeding, since a person could not be denied enforcement of constitutional rights merely because of defiant action taken or threatened. When Prince Edward County officials sought review, the Supreme Court denied certiorari.[21]

One other case, involving school desegregation for Harford County, Maryland, was to arise before Little Rock came to the Court. The school board had adopted a plan for gradual desegregation of the schools by which the majority of the elementary schools would be completely desegregated in September 1957, with the remainder to be desegregated in

1958 and 1959. High school desegregation would be similar but more gradual. The plan was amended at the district judge's suggestion to provide for the transfer of qualified students in the high school grades. The judge then approved the plan, excusing its gradualism on the ground that school officials believed the problems accompanying desegregation could best be solved in schools which were not overcrowded and in which teachers were not handicapped by inordinately large classes. The Fourth Circuit approved the district court per curiam, and the Supreme Court denied the case a hearing.[22]

3

In Little Rock, the federal courts, over NAACP objection, had approved a desegregation plan proposed by the city's school board. The very gradual plan was to begin with the senior high schools in fall 1957.[23] The night before the scheduled opening of previously all-white Central High, Arkansas Governor Faubus made an unexpected television address announcing that order would be impossible to restore or maintain if forcible integration were carried out. He then posted the state's National Guard around the school. The next morning, on the advice of the school board, the nine Negro youngsters scheduled to enter the school did not attempt to come and pass through the line of guardsmen. When the school board appealed to the federal district court for advice, the visiting district judge sitting in Little Rock on assignment ordered the desegregation plan into effect "forthwith."[24] The next morning, the nine students peacefully attempted to begin their first day at the high school, but an angry crowd waited to meet them, and the soldiers barred them from entering the school. The district judge then asked United States Attorney General Brownell to order an FBI investigation of the governor's claims that school desegregation in Little Rock would inevitably lead to violence and mob action. When Faubus protested this unwonted intrusion to President Eisenhower, the president took the strongest position he had since *Brown* was announced by saying that it was his duty to uphold the Constitution by every legal means at his command, but apparently he did not sufficiently persuade the governor to desist.[25] A few days later, armed with a four-hundred page FBI report, the judge ordered the federal government to enter the case as amicus curiae and to file a petition for an injunction against Faubus and other state officials to prevent them from interfering with the court's prior desegregation order.[26] The Justice Department complied with the request, thus involving the federal government actively in the solution of the problem.

The district judge pointed out that no acts or threats of violence had occurred earlier and granted a temporary injunction against the governor's use of the state's National Guard.[27] Three days later the guard was removed, and the nine students entered the school for the first time. However, by now the mob had gathered in force and was potentially uncontrollable. After a few hours during which white students staged walkouts and an angry mob milled around the police lines outside the school, the Negro students were withdrawn for their own safety. After President Eisenhower had denounced the "disgraceful occurrences" in Little Rock and had asked those obstructing federal law to cease and desist, the next morning the crowd still barred the black students. The president then federalized ten thousand members of the Arkansas National Guard and for the first time since Reconstruction sent federal troops into the South to protect the rights of Negroes by ordering one thousand paratroopers of the 101st Airborne Division from Fort Campbell, Kentucky, to Little Rock. The following day the nine Negro children reentered the school under federal military protection and stayed there for the rest of the year, as did the soldiers, who were gradually thinned out but never completely removed.

At the end of the school year, the school board asked a different district court judge[28] to suspend operation of the integration plan for two and one-half years because of an "unfavorable community attitude." The board said it had been left standing alone in its respect for the law of the land in the face of federal government apathy and extraordinary state government opposition which included passage of a state constitutional amendment flatly commanding the Arkansas General Assembly to oppose "in every Constitutional manner the Unconstitutional desegregation decisions . . . of the United States Supreme Court," the resultant state laws for pupil assignment, relief from compulsory attendance at racially mixed schools, and establishment of a State Sovereignty Commission. Noting that tensions in the high school were intolerable, the district judge agreed that desegregation should be delayed. The decision, *Cooper v. Aaron,* under the direction of NAACP counsel, was at once appealed to the Supreme Court. Three days later, in a normal instance of not handling appeals which might be viewed as premature, the Court denied the case a hearing in order, as it explained later, that the Court of Appeals for the Eighth Circuit might first consider it. By giving the courts closest to the situation the first opportunity to interpret and appraise the matter, the Court strengthened its strategic position for its later special session. On August 18, 1958, the Eighth Circuit reversed the district court injunction, but withheld enforcement of its order pending a Supreme Court ruling. The Supreme Court, aware of the fast-approaching opening of school and of the extreme resistance to its own rulings, departed from its post-*Brown* pattern of not taking lower education cases and called a special session of the Court for August 28 to hear oral argument.

Five days before the Court convened, the Court received what was, except for the "Southern Manifesto" of two years earlier, perhaps its most sensational rebuke—a series of six resolutions and a committee report adopted by the Conference of Chief Justices of the States criticizing the Court in highly restrained but nevertheless forceful language for a recent tendency to adopt the role of policy maker without proper judicial restraints. The state chief justices never openly suggested that Congress limit the Court's power. However, stating that this was a government of laws and not of men and that the Supreme Court's decisions should be based on the Constitution and not on what temporary majorities might deem desirable, they called upon the Court to exercise self-restraint.

On August 28, 1958, the Court heard oral argument on the school board's application to reinstate the trial court's injunction delaying desegregation. The same day the Court ordered the filing of briefs and set further oral argument for September 11. At the September argument, Richard C. Butler, for the school board,[29] stressed the need for delay in implementing desegregation in Little Rock and said that confusion in Arkansas indicated the need for the Court to state a clearer national policy. *Brown II*'s "deliberate speed" allowed for the flexibility and delay provided by Judge Lemley, Butler said. His basic point was that regardless of the force interfering with desegregation or motivation of those involved, "Where a school board has made a prompt start toward desegregation and has continued throughout to exercise good faith, severe impairment of the educational system both present and prospective because of desegregation entitles the school district to a postponement." Butler argued that with more and more people "going into the extremes," a "reasonable period of calm" was needed for lasting solutions to have a chance because hasty desegregation would increase the danger that "radicals and fanatics" might take over local school boards. He also noted that a state supreme court ruling invalidating the state's statutes would be more fully accepted by the people who "will then have heard from judges that are close to them, close to their own local scene."

Thurgood Marshall countered that Arkansas's laws were "crystalizing" and action was being taken against lawyers so that, if Judge Lemley's two and one-half year delay were granted, there would be no litigation. He said the school board did not intend to do anything to bring about desegregation. He argued that to wait for enforcement of the Constitution is to abandon the Constitution and stressed that personal equities should not be balanced against constitutional rights. The white children who stayed home, refusing to go to school with Negroes, should not be rewarded. To do so would be a "horrible destruction of principles of citizenship," because it would tell them "that the way to get your rights is to violate the law and defy the authorities."[30] Solicitor General Rankin's position for the government as amicus was equally succinct. Rankin argued that law and order throughout the entire country, not simply in Arkansas, was at issue. He claimed that in *Brown II* the Court had rejected the argument that southern school boards were to be left alone to solve their own problems. The element of lawlessness in Little Rock was being watched by policemen throughout the country, "policemen who have to deal every day with people who don't like the law they are trying to administer and enforce." The law could not step aside, he claimed, "at the command of force or violence."

Almost all of the Court's questions, directed primarily to the broad issue of implementing desegregation, were asked of Butler. The relation between the state's action and the school board's position concerned Justices Harlan and Frankfurter. Frankfurter wanted to know whether the board's request for the injunction stemmed from the state's intervention and whether the state's action affected people's opposition to desegregation—something he suggested was the case. He also noted that "the mass of the people" seldom actively support the law but go along with their leaders on new laws to which there is opposition. In responding, Butler tried to play down specifics. He said the school board should not be put in the position of a trucker who is told to drive to his fate over a destroyed bridge; why the bridge was destroyed did not matter. But, responded Frankfurter, "It would not be beyond the powers of a court of equity to require that the bridge be restored." Questions by Justices Black and Brennan were focused on the supremacy of federal law over state law under the United States Constitution. Having obtained Butler's statement that *Brown* was still the law to be followed, Brennan, relying on the Constitution's "supreme law of the land" clause, asked how the Court could allow a delay on the grounds that state officials instead of enforcing consitutional rights had frustrated their enforcement. Butler claimed the school board could not resolve the conflict, but conceded that federal law must prevail. Here he clashed with Chief Justice Warren. Butler started to say, "Mr. Chief Justice, you've been the governor of a great state," but Warren interrupted to say that as governor of California, he had "abided by the decision of the courts." When counsel persisted in saying that weight should be given to Governor Faubus's views, Warren sternly said: "I have never heard such an argument made in a court of justice before, and I have tried many a case through many a year. I never heard a lawyer say that the statement of a governor as to what was legal or illegal should control the action of any court."[31]

Other questions from the justices dealt with the board's present or future actions. Douglas asked about the board's response to an affirmance of the Court of Appeals ruling. It would do little, Butler said, because of pending statutes lessening the board's authority over the schools in favor of state authority. And Frankfurter wanted to know the board's reaction to the suggestion that it seek an injunction against state officials. Those responsible for *Brown* should do it, Butler said—either the "adequately financed and certainly ably staffed" NAACP or the United States Attorney General's office, which, he said, had not yet "grasped" the problem. The specifics of the desegregation plan received little attention, with only Justices Burton and Clark inquiring whether the school board had thought of beginning desegregation in the lower grades rather than at the high school level. The need for clarification in national policy received somewhat more attention. Frankfurter wanted to know why *Brown I* and *Brown II* weren't adequate statements of national policy. Chief Justice Warren asked whether national policy could be clarified if every southern school board postponed desegregation pending clarification and wondered whether clarification would substitute for delay or whether delay was preferred to clarification. Butler responded, "We seek clarification, but we say to make that clarification effective and to keep our public school system intact, we must also have a delay to do it."

The justices' clear emphasis in their questions on matters of implementation, at the heart of strategic considerations, was to be reflected in their decision. Little Rock's public high schools were scheduled to open September 15. On September 12, the Court affirmed the Court of Appeals in a per curiam order effective immediately and to be communicated forthwith to the district court which had granted the stay. On September 29, the Court's full opinion was filed. Here the Court dramatically underlined its unanimity by announcing that the opinion—instead of being signed by only the one justice who drafted it—was signed individually by each judge, in the only time in history this had been done. The forthrightness of the opinion, perhaps "the Court's most searing modern statement in a racial case,"[32] was apparent. After three full terms of refusing to hear appeals in school cases despite significant variations in interpretation of *Brown*, the Court finally said something, in a well-reasoned and forceful statement based firmly on legal precedent.

Dealing with the point raised at argument by Justice Brennan, the Court began by stating that the case raised questions of the highest importance to the maintenance of our federal system of government, since it involved a claim by a governor and state legislature that there was no duty by state officials to obey federal court orders which rested on the Supreme Court's considered interpretation of the United States Constitution. The justices flatly rejected this claim. The Court's judgments in *Brown I* and *II* were described and lengthy quotes from the latter were provided with regard to what could and could not be considered valid reasons for granting delay in implementation. Hostility to desegregation had been specifically excluded, the Court emphasized. The burden had been placed upon state authorities to show necessity for delay, and those authorities were required to make every effort toward realizing the constitutional directive. In other words, the Court's *Brown* directive placed an affirmative duty on the school authorities to go forward in absolute good faith to achieve desegregation of their school districts.

The Court first described the details of the Little Rock controversy, including the school board's work on its desegregation plan and its testimony that a large majority of Little Rock residents, though they might object to the principle behind the plan, thought it in the best interest of all the district's pupils, and the efforts of state authorities in opposition to the school board's efforts. Then the Court emphasized that the local school board and school superintendent, displaying good faith in dealing with the "unfortunate and distressing sequence of events," had made every effort to implement their desegregation plan, had taken various administrative measures to ensure a smooth transition, and had encountered no trouble and made no request for assistance until the governor had intervened and state legislators had taken action. The district court's findings of fact as to conditions at the school and damage to educational progress were accepted but would only be considered in light of the fact, "indisputably revealed by the record," that the conditions were directly traceable to the actions of state officers resisting the directive of *Brown*. That the board members were also agents of the state in terms of the Fourteenth Amendment compelled the Court, although sympathetic with the board's situation, to reject its legal position. Constitutional rights could not be sacrificed to the violence and disorder which followed upon the actions of the governor and legislature, nor could preservation of the public peace be accomplished by denying constitutional rights, something the justices noted had been said in *Buchanan* some forty-one years earlier. Where such difficulties were a product of state action, they could also be brought under control by state action. The constitutional rights of children not to be discriminated against can neither be nullified openly and directly by state legislators or executives or judicial officers nor indirectly by them through evasive schemes, said the Court.

All of this was enough to dispose of the case, the Court noted, but the premise of the governor and legislature that they were not bound by the Court's holding in *Brown* had to be answered. After a review of the long-standing precedent that the federal judiciary is supreme in the exposition of the Constitution, the justices concluded that the Court's interpretation of the Fourteenth Amendment in *Brown* is the supreme law of the land, made binding on the states and all its officers by Article VI of the Constitution. The justices pointed out that while public education is primarily a state responsibility, like all state activity it must be exercised in consonance with federal constitutional requirements. The Constitution created a government dedicated to equal justice under law and the Fourteenth Amendment embodied and emphasized that ideal. Thus state support of segregated schools through any arrangement, management, funds, or property cannot be squared with the amendment's command against state denial of equal protection to any person within its jurisdiction. The judges then drew on language in *Bolling v. Sharpe* to state: "The right of a student not to be segregated on racial grounds in schools so maintained is indeed so fundamental and pervasive that it is embraced in the concept of due process of law." The opinion ended with the reminder that *Brown* had been unanimously decided only after most serious consideration of the issues. As the three new justices now on the Court agree completely with its correctness, "that decision is now unanimously reaffirmed." This reaffirmation was supplemented by Frankfurter's concurring opinion in which he emphasized the illegality and dangerousness of the governor's obstructive activity to the larger concerns of the federal union and the importance and sensitivity of the problem at hand.

The Little Rock case gave the Court an opportunity to write a better opinion than it had done in *Brown I* and *II*. Without some of *Brown*'s broader sociological language or a mention of psychological factors, and strictly on the basis of the Fourteenth Amendment, including its Due Process Clause, the Court declared that racial segregation in the public schools was unconstitutional. The Court also declared that *Brown* had placed an affirmative duty on school boards throughout the land to initiate desegregation of the public schools. By paying an obvious compliment for attempting to act promptly and earnestly, the Court tried to soften the blow necessarily being dealt to the Little Rock School Board as the state agency party to the litigation. By its strong disapproval both of Arkansas officials who had thwarted school board efforts and the comparable officials in other states who had as yet done little or nothing to attempt to comply with *Brown* and by condemning Governor Faubus and others for brazen defiance of Supreme Court decisions, the Court warned others who might be tempted to adopt such tactics that such defiance had never been allowed to exist nor would it be allowed in the future. By promising that the courts would be attuned to ferret out all modes of evasion, the justices answered the governor's threat to close Little Rock's high schools in the face of an adverse decision and tried to head off the development of "private" schools established and supported by public officials.[33]

The Court's solid adherence to the constitutional principles of *Brown* despite all the criticism and outright disobedience which had followed in its wake made the very important point that no one was to expect or hope for a reversal of *Brown* with mere changes in the composition of the Court. The Court had expected desegregation to be a local matter, achieved through local initiative and lower court supervision, but if it were not accomplished at that level the Supreme Court threatened it would not hesitate to step in. The Court had not earlier responded to criticism such as the "Southern Manifesto," perhaps expecting opposition to mellow with successive years. But with continued—and increased—opposition, the Court had realized the necessity to act, particularly with nationwide attention and disapproval directed toward state-perpetrated lawlessness in Arkansas. The renewed criticism of the Court from the states' highest judicial authorities may also have influenced the Court to make a strong declaration unlike its rulings of four years earlier. The speed with which the Court dealt with the situation—the special session of the Court, the prompt per curiam order, the strong opinion which followed, with its serial signing by all the justices—indicates how thoroughly the Court could reinforce its action by a multiplicity of means. Yet Little Rock was a case of outright defiance and confrontation; the more subtle evasions and noncompliance of the Deep South had gone unchecked by the Court.

Further reinforcement came in follow-up Little Rock litigation after *Cooper v. Aaron.*[34] After the crisis, the governor challenged the trial court injunction against himself and the National Guard, the participation of the United States as amicus in the later stages of the litigation, and the power of the president to send federal troops to Little Rock. When he lost all those challenges before the Eighth Circuit, the Supreme Court refused even to hear the case.[35] This time a refusal to hear the case operated to discourage the would-be resisters by not even giving them the satisfaction of a hearing on their challenges. Then, in connection with Faubus's 1958 closing of the Little Rock schools, a federal district court declared unconstitutional the state statute giving the governor the authority to close the schools and to hold an election as to whether or not the schools were to be integrated. The court also invalidated a statute authorizing the governor to withhold funds from a school district in which a school had been ordered closed and to make those funds available to other public or nonprofit private schools attended by the students of the closed school. Making good its warning as to action it would take on schemes developed to avoid desegregation, the Supreme Court affirmed the lower court decision per curiam without a hearing, with only Justice Whittaker indicating he would have heard the case in full.[36] This policy of strength succeeded in Little Rock, where citizens' groups similar to those formed in Virginia organized support for the public schools and recalled the diehard segregationists elected to the school board in 1958. With the situation in Arkansas at least relatively tranquil, the Supreme Court had finally seen the end of litigation from Little Rock.

4

Having dealt with frontal resistance in the Little Rock situation, the Court then had to deal with a more insidious lateral maneuver, the South's effort to limit if not eliminate the NAACP through such mechanisms as licensing laws and laws concerning the proper practice of law. Although ultimately invalidated in the courts, the South's "counter-attack" on the NAACP drew some of the organization's efforts away from school desegregation to the question of survival, incapacitated the organization in some states during the extended litigation, and drained substantial portions of the NAACP's treasury. The states' devices for limiting the NAACP were at least potentially applicable to other groups. Perhaps this is why, in deciding the cases on the anti-NAACP actions, the Supreme Court generally did not explicitly discuss the matter of race and the negative reaction to *Brown* which had obviously led to the southern efforts. The cases, however useful they may be in sustaining a "right of association," thus at times have a ring of unreality. The Court's abstract treatment of the issues also led to less than forceful opinions, quite different from that in the Little Rock case. While generally protective of the NAACP, the Court was not effective in stopping anti-NAACP activity quickly, exercising "the patience but not the eloquence of Job,"[37] and at times returning cases to the lower courts for construction of statutes which at least some of the justices thought were clearly unconstitutional.

The first of the anti-NAACP cases was *NAACP v. Alabama*. It was to come before the Court four times. The state attorney general had filed a suit in state court to enjoin the NAACP from conducting further activities in Alabama and to oust it from the state. Listed as activities in which the association had engaged were the giving of financial and legal assistance to Negro students seeking admission to the state university and the support of the Montgomery bus boycott. The attorney general acted pursuant to a state statute requiring out-of-state corporations, except as exempted, to qualify before doing business in the state by filing their corporate charter, designating a place of business and an agent to receive service of process, and the like. The NAACP, whose first Alabama affiliates had been chartered in 1918, had always considered itself exempt from the statute as a nonprofit membership organization, and had never complied with the qualification requirements. Although Alabama now said the NAACP was liable to criminal prosecution for such infractions, "criminal prosecution and civil action at law afford no adequate relief" for the "irreparable injury to the property and civil rights of the residents and citizens of the State of Alabama" caused by the association's continuing to do business in the state without complying with the qualification statute.

In order to prepare for the hearing in the case, the state moved for the production of a large number of the association's records and papers, including leases, deeds, bank statements, and records containing the names and addresses of all "members" and "agents" of the organization in Alabama, and a state court ordered the NAACP to produce most of these records, including the membership lists. The NAACP then offered to fulfill the formal qualification requirements and submitted the forms prescribed by the statute, although the group still claimed that the statute did not apply. The court then decided that the NAACP had not complied with the order and levied a fine for contempt. After that judgment, the NAACP produced substantially everything the production order required except the membership lists, disclosure of which the group said could not constitutionally be compelled. Because under Alabama law, the contempt judgment foreclosed a hearing on the underlying ouster action and because the state supreme court twice refused to review the contempt judgment, the NAACP appealed the case to the United States Supreme Court, which agreed to decide it.

The NAACP contended that it was constitutionally entitled to resist official inquiry into its membership lists and that on behalf of its members it could assert a right personal to them to be protected from state-compelled disclosure of their affiliation with the association. For its part Alabama contended that the NAACP lacked standing in the Court to assert constitutional rights pertaining to its members. In an opinion by Justice Harlan, the Court declared unanimously that the NAACP could quite properly assert its members' right to withhold information about their connection with the association. He reasoned that to require the members to claim the right themselves would result in disclosure of their affiliation and hence nullification of the right at the very moment of its assertion. Turning to the question of whether the compelled disclosure would infringe upon fundamental freedoms protected by the Fourteenth Amendment's Due Process Clause, Harlan first reviewed cases in which the Court had prevented indirect or even unintended abridgment of rights in order to keep inviolable group association privacy where that privacy was essential for freedom of association itself. Harlan concluded that the state's production order entailed the likelihood of substantial restraint upon the NAACP members' similar right. The NAACP had made an uncontroverted showing that revelation of the identity of its rank and file members had exposed them to economic reprisal, loss of employment, and threats of physical coercion, Harlan said; similar results could be expected here. The state's answer that oppressive effects would be due to private community pressures rather than state action was not sufficient, he continued, because only after governmental action would private action be possible.

The final question of the case, which Harlan answered in the negative, was whether, in seeking to obtain the information, Alabama had demonstrated an interest sufficiently compelling to justify the effect of the disclosure. Harlan noted that the state claimed its exclusive purpose in requesting the membership lists was to determine whether the association was conducting intrastate business in violation of the Alabama foreign corporation registration statute. Harlan then stated that the membership lists did not have a substantial bearing on the purpose, pointing out that the association had admitted its presence and its conduct of activities in the state since 1918, had offfered to comply in all respects with the statute although preserving its contention that the statute did not apply to it, and had complied satisfactorily with all of the production order except for the membership lists. Harlan concluded by overturning the contempt judgment and $100,000 fine and by remanding the case for appropriate proceedings.

As in *Barrows,* the Court had allowed a second party to assert a first party's rights when the latter was unable to do so. The Court also had effectively stopped, at least for a time, a new effort to curtail the expansion and assertion of civil rights that rank-and-file Negroes were undertaking through their associative efforts. The Court also made every effort to base its decision on old and long-accepted doctrines of state action, thus avoiding the appearance of making any special concession for the sake of Negro advocacy. Only the state, which had singled out the association after nearly forty years of activity, could be accused of according any special treatment on the basis of race.

Illustrative of the limitations of the judiciary's enforcement powers and of the difficulties the Court experienced in achieving compliance with its orders in this controversy was the reappearance of the Alabama NAACP before the Court. On remand, when the state claimed that the NAACP had failed in other respects to comply with the court order, the state supreme court had affirmed its previous contempt judgment. This time, under the title *NAACP v. Alabama ex rel. Patterson,* the Court reversed the state supreme court in a per curiam statement containing some harsh words for the lower court's behavior. The prior decision, the Court noted, was based on the fact that the NAACP had fully complied with the state court order except for membership lists. The state itself was bound by its previous position, and the state court was foreclosed from reexamination of its grounds of disposition. "We take it from the record now before us," the per curiam opinion said, "that the Supreme Court of

Alabama evidently was not acquainted with the detailed basis of the proceedings here and the consequent ground for our defined disposition."

The Court returned to the Alabama situation in *NAACP v. Gallion* after dealing with anti-NAACP litigation from Louisiana. In the new Alabama case, the NAACP had brought suit in federal court to enjoin state officials from enforcing a temporary state order restraining the NAACP from doing business in Alabama—obtained on the grounds that it had still not registered as a foreign corporation on the state's terms— and to enjoin the officials' refusal to register it under the relevant statute even after the earlier Supreme Court orders. Claiming it lacked jurisdiction, the district court had dismissed the case. The Court of Appeals for the Fifth Circuit had vacated and remanded this judgment with instructions to permit disposition of the issues in a state court. Weary of the repeated and repeatedly fruitless procedure, the NAACP again petitioned the Supreme Court. The Court now held in a per curiam ruling vacating and remanding the case that the federal court did have jurisdiction over the action. The district court was ordered to proceed with a trial of the issues unless within a reasonable time—a date ten weeks later was specified—the state accorded the NAACP an opportunity to be heard on its motion to dissolve the restraining order and on the merits of the action in which the order had been issued.

That ruling was issued in 1961. The initial Supreme Court decision in this litigation had been in 1958. In 1964, the Court was forced to deal with Alabama's protracted delay once again. The NAACP had finally obtained a hearing below on the merits of the controversy. But the lower state courts had permanently enjoined the NAACP from doing business in the state or from attempting to qualify to do so. The charges ranged from paying and furnishing legal counsel for Autherine Lucy in her attempt to enroll at the University of Alabama to allowing the "illegal" Montgomery bus boycott to be conducted to deprecation of Alabama state courts and officials by levying charges against them during the course of the present litigation. The state supreme court had affirmed on procedural grounds, holding that the form of the NAACP brief did not conform to its rules and saying that it would not even consider the various assignments of error, since it found one among them without merit.

Upon receiving the case this time, the Court endeavored to end the Alabama litigation once and for all, but as Harlan pointed out in the Court's unanimous *NAACP v. Alabama* opinion, not until over five years after the organization had been "temporarily" ousted from the state and had had to make three trips to the Supreme Court. The Supreme Court found the state supreme court's position "wholly unacceptable" as non-federal grounds of decision adequate to bar review of the serious constitutional claims raised, and went on to look at the grounds for permanent ouster. Each of the claims was held to be either insubstantial or without basis for restriction of NAACP members' right to associate in the state. Application of foreign corporation registration laws to the NAACP was described as an attempt to do subtly what could not legally be done openly. The Court reversed the state supreme court judgment and again remanded the case for appropriate proceedings, noting that these should include prompt entry of a decree vacating the permanent injunction in all respects and permitting the NAACP to take all steps necessary to qualify it to do business in the state. Noting that the Court had been asked to write a decree for the state courts, Justice Harlan demurred but indicated that "such a course undoubtedly lies within this Court's power." The Court's deference to usual procedure and to the state courts only thinly veiled the power the Court was willing to use. "Should we unhappily be mistaken in our belief that the Supreme Court of Alabama will promptly implement this disposition," the Court concluded, "leave is given the Association to apply to this Court for further appropriate relief." The Court wanted to make its message this time unquestionably clear. The case did not return to the Court again.

Further indication of the Court's firm position came in a case involving Mississippi's attempt to oust the NAACP from doing business in the state. A lower court had ruled that the state must allow the NAACP, a New York corporation, to do business in Mississippi. The Court declined Governor Johnson's appeal for a hearing and let the lower court decision stand.[38] Shortly before this case, however, the justices had found a way to avoid a related question—that of the liability of the NAACP for actions in which its local chapters had been involved. An injunction and damages had been awarded a Savannah, Georgia, store owner whose neighborhood market in a Negro area had been picketed by local NAACP members engaged in a "selective buying campaign" because the owner had allegedly beat a Negro boy who worked for him. The situation at the small store in the close neighborhood had apparently become somewhat explosive, with several persons suffering violence or threats of violence from the picketers. Because the owner had suffered great economic loss from the picketing, damages had been assessed against both the local NAACP branch and the NAACP headquarters, the New York corporation, alleged to share responsibility for the incidents. On appeal from a local court, the Georgia Supreme Court found the damages awarded not excessive and agreed that the national NAACP organization should be held liable because the local branch, if not its "agent," was at least so closely affiliated with it as to make it share responsibility.

When the case was appealed the Supreme Court granted the case a hearing. The justices then changed their mind and refused to rule,

dismissing the writ as improvidently granted.[39] Douglas, the Chief Justice, Brennan, and Fortas joined in a lengthy dissent to this action. Arguing for reversal of the judgment, they said the First Amendment forbids
the imposition of liability on a national political organization on account
of the misconduct of a local branch without proof that the national
organization specifically authorized or ratified the questioned conduct
performed without its knowledge and by persons beyond its control.
They also insisted that there was no proof provided below that the
national organization knew what those picketing were doing. That the
Court's hesitance to interfere in the case turned on a matter of interpretation of state law was suggested in this dissent. When state policy—here the
law of agency—thwarts an interest to which the federal Constitution
affords special protection, Douglas said, state policy must yield.

The majority's disposition of the case reflected the Court's increasing
hesitance in the mid-1960s to interfere in feuds between the states and the
increasingly powerful Negro organization. When the necessity for overruling the highest state court's interpretation of its own law on a subject
other than race in order to satisfy the complainant arose, the Court seems
to have backed off. The Court's action, or inaction, indicated that although the NAACP would be protected against state efforts to oust it
from or prevent it from conducting its legal business in a state, when its
members resorted to violence or caused the imminent threat of violence
the Court would turn its back.

Among the other states that had tried to restrict NAACP activities
were Arkansas, Louisiana, Florida, and Virginia. Part of Arkansas's efforts to obtain membership lists resulted in *Bates v. Little Rock* when the
Little Rock and North Little Rock NAACP branches, because of their
members' constitutional rights and the anti-NAACP climate in the state,
refused to submit membership lists as required by a 1957 amendment to a
municipal ordinance dealing with occupational license taxes. Bates and
Williams, custodians of the NAACP records, had been tried, convicted,
and fined for violation of the ordinances despite their showing that the
ordinances had resulted in loss of organization membership and that
persons publicly identified as members had been subjected to harrassment and threats of bodily harm. After the state supreme court upheld
the convictions with two justices dissenting, the Supreme Court granted
certiorari and heard argument in the cases. The Court then unanimously
reversed the convictions. Speaking for the Court, Justice Stewart explained that the record demonstrated that compulsory disclosure of the
membership lists would work a significant interference with the members'
freedom of association. Not questioning the government's fundamental
power to tax, Stewart questioned whether there was any relevant correlation between the power to impose occupational license taxes and the

compulsory disclosure and publication of the membership lists, and found no such correlation. Counsel for the city of Little Rock had been unable at oral argument to suggest any activity of these NAACP organizations to which a license tax might attach, Stewart said, and the record below indicated that no tax claim had ever been asserted against either organization. The municipalities had thus failed to demonstrate a justification for the deterrence of free association caused by the compulsory disclosure. It followed, Stewart said, that the organizations could not be punished for refusing to produce information which the municipalities could not constitutionally require. In their brief concurring opinion, Black and Douglas recognized the neat twist which the majority had employed to limit the decision's breadth as much as possible. For them, the essence of the Court's opinion was that the First Amendment freedoms of assembly and association were entitled to no less protection than any other First Amendment rights, applicable to all people under the Constitution, as *NAACP v. Alabama* had held.

Arkansas's attack on the NAACP was not only direct as in *Bates*. The state also used indirect means by seeking the names of the organizations to which schoolteachers in the state belonged. When a state statute required the listing of all organizations to which a teacher belonged in the last five years, there was a challenge which reached the Supreme Court in *Shelton v. Tucker*. Here Justice Stewart spoke only for a narrow five-man majority. He found that the state had an appropriate interest in looking into teachers' qualifications and conceded that the state could ask certain teachers about all their memberships and all teachers about certain memberships. Teachers could also be asked how many organizations they belonged to or the amount of time they spent in organizational activity. However, to compel revelation of every membership is to interfere with the right of association, Stewart said, citing the *Bates* case to support his assertion.

The Court had thus developed a rule applicable to many cases but had avoided a direct ruling on the racial motivation behind the state's attempts. As the late Professor Harry Kalven put it, the Court was "once again able to defeat the Southern tactics without violating etiquette by inquiring into the precise motivation for the statute."[40] In so doing, the Court left itself the task of having to solve many more individual cases concerning such requirements. Justice Frankfurter and Justice Harlan wrote opinions for the four dissenters. Frankfurter felt that the Court was substituting its view of the best way for the state to conduct its inquiry for the one the state had chosen. Harlan, who felt the state's request well within its constitutional powers concerning teacher qualifications, was the only justice to point out explicitly the case's racial aspects. He did this by saying that "in the context of the racial situation in various parts of the country," protection of the constitutional rights affected by the statute demand "the unremitting vigilance of the courts." However, Harlan said, because the statute applied to all teachers, racial discrimination was not involved in the case. Neither Harlan nor Frankfurter were oblivious to the racial aspects of the case, but they showed "greater patience"[41] than the majority, for both would have waited for actual discrimination before invalidating the state's action.

Louisiana's efforts to limit the NAACP were more easily disposed of than those from Alabama and Arkansas. They included a direct challenge to the NAACP as an organization. This came to the Supreme Court in *Louisiana ex rel. Gremillion v. NAACP,* when the state appealed from a temporary injunction won by the NAACP against two state laws. One of the laws forbade any "non-trading" association from doing business in the state if it was affiliated with any similar foreign or out-of-state association which had officers or members of the board of directors who were members of Communist-type organizations listed by the United States Attorney General or cited by the House Un-American Activities Committee. Affidavits disclaiming such affiliations had to be filed annually by such groups, and penalties were provided for failure to file or for false filings. The other law was like that in the Alabama litigation, requiring submission of complete membership lists each year. In an opinion by Justice Douglas affirming issuance of the temporary injunction, the Court held that the first statute violated due process because it "would require the impossible" of the few Louisiana residents or workers, who could not be expected to know the relevant facts about all the officers and directors of the New York corporation. The second statute, Douglas noted, had been passed in 1924 allegedly to curb the Ku Klux Klan but had previously never been enforced against any other organization. He pointed out that when some NAACP affiliates in Louisiana had filed the membership lists in response to the state's suit, their members had been subjected to economic reprisals. Where disclosure leads to such reprisals and hostility, disclosure is not required, Douglas said, following *NAACP v. Alabama.* Although Douglas noted that because the case was at a preliminary stage the Court could not know what facts would later be disclosed at a full hearing, his observations reinforced by the cases he cited clearly indicated to the district court what action it should take. However, the opinion seemed "oddly unsatisfactory" and to lack the "clean logic" of the Court's *Alabama* and *Bates* opinions.[42] This may explain why the authors of those opinions, Justices Harlan and Stewart, only concurred in the result. It was not very long before the Court again assisted in sweeping away Louisiana's anti-NAACP statutes. State law imposed criminal sanctions on parents who accepted anything of value to send a child to a school operated in violation of Louisiana law—that is, an integrated school—or on anyone who gave something of value to the parents for the same purpose, and also penalized the attempt to influence a child, parent, teacher, or school employee to do anything in violation of any law. In *Gremillion v. United States,* the Court affirmed per curiam a lower court ruling invalidating those laws with their definite anti-NAACP implications.

The *Bates* case had not ended even direct state efforts to obtain membership lists. In Florida, such demands occurred in the context of a legislative committee's investigation of Communist activities, and *Gibson v. Florida Legislative Investigation Committee* resulted. Initially, the Florida Supreme Court had ruled that although the NAACP could not be compelled to produce its entire membership list—demanded by the committee—the custodian of the records could be forced to bring them to hearings and to refer to them in answer to questions about particular individuals. The Supreme Court had denied certiorari when the NAACP had asked for a review of that ruling. A legislative committee pursuing the same inquiry then made a much broader request. This resulted in a contempt conviction sustained at the state level. It also produced a badly divided Supreme Court. Not only was the case argued once and then reargued, but when the Court finally ruled, the vote was five-to-four to reverse the contempt conviction, and there were two concurring opinions. Justice Goldberg wrote the opinion of the Court. He emphasized that the NAACP, the subject of the investigation, was, unlike the Communist party, a legislative organization and that no connection between the NAACP and the Communists had been established. In fact, he added, "This very record indicates that the association was and is against communism and has voluntarily taken steps to keep Communists from becoming members." Goldberg stressed the NAACP's unpopularity as one reason it was under investigation, but in reversing the legislature's action he concentrated on the lack of a nexus between the legislature's legitimate aims and its demands on the NAACP for the lists. Although they joined the Court's opinion, both Justice Black and Justice Douglas wrote separate concurring opinions. They emphasized far more heavily than the other justices a "pure" right of association, and Douglas also stressed a right of privacy for those groups which "may not be invaded because of another's perversity." The dissenters, who felt the investigation acceptable, said that the Court had long given approval to government to investigate "Communist subversion," and Justice White, in his separate dissent, pointed out that a favorite Communist activity was to infiltrate other groups.

Virginia's anti-NAACP efforts were centered on the organization's involvement in litigation and were more sophisticated than those we have just seen. Like the Alabama litigation, they took some time to dispose of because of the Court's initial deferential posture toward the state. Virginia was first before the Court in the 1958 Term[43] in *Harrison v. NAACP.* Virginia statutes enacted in 1956 prohibited activity directed to the passage of racial legislation, advocacy of racial integration or segregation, the stirring up of litigation, and the raising or expenditure of funds in connection with racial litigation. A federal district court had invalidated three statutes and on two others requested state construction before making judgment. The state protested this decision, arguing that the state courts should have been given the opportunity to delineate the meaning of all the laws before a federal court could pass upon their constitutionality. In a six-to-three decision, the Court agreed with the state, holding that the challenged statutes left the Virginia courts reasonable room for construction. Such construction might avoid in whole or in part the necessity for federal constitutional adjudication or at least might materially change the nature of the problem. Douglas, the Chief Justice, and Brennan dissented, saying that all the laws were obviously unconstitutional and mere devices and that the Court should not require a procedure which would necessitate delay and expense. The majority's procedural disposition of the case worked hardship on the complainants, and was in effect a concession to the state, perhaps based on the hope that restraint might produce voluntary state cooperation with the inevitable, much as in the early school cases where exhaustion of administrative remedies was required. However, since the Court earlier had made it clear that obvious attempts to harrass the Negro organization through discriminatory legislation would not be tolerated, the basic issue as such was not at stake. The Court exercised some caution by indicating that while the case was on remand pending state determination of the statutes, the federal court should hold it under some arrangement which would protect the rights of the parties.

In addition to suggesting that jurisdiction be retained, the majority justices further indicated that their deference to the state judiciary had limits in *NAACP v. Bennett,* an Arkansas case involving statutes passed in 1958 relating to barratry and to prevention of hindrance of the orderly administration of public schools and institutions of higher learning—in other words, such hindrance as would result from activities directed toward desegregation of educational institutions. Unlike the federal district court in the *Harrison* case, the lower court here, without even looking at the statutes, had referred the case to the state courts for construction of the challenged laws. When the NAACP protested this procedure to the Supreme Court, the majority, over the same three dissents, limited its *Harrison* opinion by ruling that reference to the state courts for construction of the statute should not automatically be made when the validity of a state statute challenged under the United States Constitution was properly before a district court for adjudication. The majority then remanded the case for consideration in light of *Harrison*. The dissenters said that they agreed with the remand but thought, as before, that the district court should be directed to pass on the constitutional issues presented by the case without prior reference to the state courts. The procedure the majority required was cumbersome, but the indication was that federal court should strike state acts where, in the words of *Harrison*, there was no "reasonable room" left for construing them so that they would not obviously be in conflict with the federal constitution. This doctrine lessened the burden on the NAACP when obviously discriminatory laws were involved. On the other hand, it required the state to act very cleverly indeed if it wished to enact such legislation. It also vested considerably more discretion in the federal district courts than a first reading of *Harrison* might have indicated, and the two decisions together had a generally favorable effect on the Negroes' legal organization.

These procedural rulings, important as they were, were hardly the end of Virginia's activity. Like other states, Virginia had a statute regulating the legal profession in the state and prohibiting activities adjudged as improper solicitation of legal business. Under this prohibition, a successful state court action was brought against the activities of the NAACP and its Legal Defense Fund, its affiliates, and legal staff operating in the state. The NAACP then appealed to the United States Supreme Court in *NAACP v. Button*. The problem the justices faced was that Virginia had invoked a wholly legitimate and even high-principled statute to accomplish an unlawful end. In another split opinion, a majority of the Court, speaking through Justice Brennan, upheld the organization's activities as modes of expression and association protected by the First and Fourteenth Amendments against Virginia's argument that the NAACP engaged in improper solicitation of legal business. In the context of the NAACP's objectives, the majority said, litigation was a form of political expression protected by the First Amendment. The state had failed to advance any substantial regulatory interest, in the form of substantive evils flowing from the organization's activities, which could justify the broad prohibitions imposed. For example, there had been no evidence that the NAACP had interfered in the conduct of litigation. Furthermore, Justice Brennan said, a broad statute like the one before the Court could easily be used selectively against unpopular causes. Thus, he ruled, the state statute as construed by the Virginia Supreme Court to cover the NAACP's activities was unconstitutional, violating the Fourteenth Amendment by unduly inhibiting protected freedoms of expression and association. Although he joined the majority, Douglas also wrote a separate concurrence, emphasizing his view that the law obviously had been applied to "get" the NAACP. Justice White concurred in part and dissented in part. Whereas he agreed that the statute was unconstitutional as construed, he believed that a narrowly drawn regulatory statute should be within the power of the state. Harlan, Clark, and Stewart dissented in favor of the state regulatory power over the legal profession, noting that even regulation of free expression was sometimes permissible. The warning to the various NAACP branches to use care and not coercion in their practices must have brought at least a little satisfaction to Virginia, which had narrowly missed winning its case.

Of all the anti-NAACP cases, *Button* is perhaps the one in which the Court most obviously faced difficulties in deciding whether or not to recognize explicitly the state's motivation in developing its regulation. Yale law professor Charles Black said the Court "play[ed] Hamlet with only oblique reference to the Prince of Denmark" in the case because the majority did not deal openly with the case's racial implications or underscore "the substantial national political interest which was being infringed." He argued that it would have been better for the Court to say directly that the NAACP's work was aimed at protecting "vital nationally created rights" through federal and state litigation and that "no state had any business interfering in a process crucially concerned with the implementation of national rights." This, Black says, would have been to talk about "what was really at stake."[44] Harry Kalven suggested that for the Supreme Court to decide cases without reference to the environment which gave them birth may result in a "parody of legal wisdom" or a decision incomplete in solving the problem. He argued that because Justice Brennan did "not seem to have had the courage of his First Amendment convictions" his opinion left the inference that the state by focusing its regulation more carefully could stop the NAACP from recruiting cases vigorously. Yet Kalven also noted that had the Court explicitly recognized the South's motivation, it would have risked "giving constitutional litigation the appearance of civil war and of giving us a parody of legal neutrality."[45] This meant that Justice Douglas was accurate in his views as to Virginia's racial motivation but for the Court to have adopted his opinion would have been strategically unwise.

5

When the September 1958 school term opened, violent and other overt attempts at official state-level resistance had subsided but had not disappeared. School desegregation statistics indicated that considerable progress had been made in the biracial school districts of Oklahoma and that a small number of additional districts in Missouri had desegregated, bringing the total compliance figure for both states to almost 90 percent. Progress comparable to the previous year was made in Kentucky, bringing 70 percent of that state's biracial school districts into the classification of having made a start toward desegregation. A slight beginning was made in Virginia and in North Carolina. But efforts toward compliance had stopped in Arkansas and Tennessee. Efforts were not resumed in Delaware and Texas, and the remaining six southern states still had done nothing at all statistically relevant in response to *Brown*.[46]

After the *Cooper* case, there was another lapse of several years before the Supreme Court handed down full opinions on school desegregation. *Cooper* was thus an exception—dictated by its circumstances—to the Court's backing off from its position in *Brown*. Numerous cases in the aftermath of *Cooper* were disposed of with summary action. This suggested to litigants and their counsel that the Court strongly preferred adjudication of school problems to take place at the lower levels of the court system. The result was that the volume of school litigation coming to the Supreme Court thus dropped off, being surpassed in the 1959 and 1960 Terms by jury selection and criminal procedure cases and replaced as time went on by the public accommodations area. But in 1963 and 1964 the Court finally took direct action on schools and also took indirect action in a closely related and important public facilities case in which the Court's impatience with the snail's pace of desegregation was evident. Shortly afterward, as a result of the passage of the 1964 Civil Rights Act, the executive branch of the government became far more actively involved in school desegregation, yet the Court's reticence had an effect on what could be accomplished administratively. After initial administrative action, activity resumed in the courts, and the Supreme Court had to deal in 1964 and 1965 with a number of cases from both the South and the North.

In short, 1964 was a watershed in terms of judicial action with respect to school desegregation. For one thing, it marked ten years from the announcement of *Brown I*. For another, it was the time of decision in the *Griffin* litigation involving the closing of the schools in Prince Edward County, one of the areas involved in *Brown*. Before we turn to that decision and the one immediately preceding it involving racial transfers in Knoxville, we need to look at the types of cases brought to the Court in the post-*Cooper*, pre-*Goss* (Knoxville) and *Griffin* period, roughly 1958 through 1964. Through these cases, we can see the issues which the Court chose not to decide either by refusing review in the exercise of the "informed discretion" (what has been called "informed arbitrariness") which allows it to accept the cases it wants and reject the others without providing an explanation, or by deciding cases in a summary fashion which also provides little public guidance.

Delaware Desegregation Plans. After the *Gebhart* case, decided along with *Brown*, the Delaware Board of Education had ordered local school boards to submit desegregation plans. Waiting out the state board, the local boards had done nothing. Then, to the state board's dismay and indignation, a federal judge ordered the board to submit a statewide plan within sixty days. The board tried to make the issue educational administration, but the Third Circuit affirmed,[47] and the Supreme Court denied certiorari. The board then submitted a grade-a-year desegregation plan like one approved for Nashville, Tennessee, which the district court approved over the parents' protest, saying that any thought of total and immediate desegregation in the state was "out of the question." However, the Third Circuit found that circumstances differed between Delaware and Nashville, refused to apply standards for the latter to Delaware, and ordered submission of a desegregation plan for all grades for Negro children who wished it. Asking the Supreme Court for a stay and for review of the case, the board argued that the Court of Appeals should not be able to use a differing evaluation of present and future local circumstances to invalidate a gradual desegregation plan formulated "in good faith" and approved by a district court.[48] The Supreme Court, apparently unpersuaded, refused the stay and denied certiorari. Although there was some subsequent litigation in the lower federal courts to make practice more closely approximate statewide policy, this was the last school litigation from Delaware the Court was to be asked to hear.

Alabama Pupil Placement Laws.   In a case brought by the Reverend Fred Shuttlesworth rather than by children seeking admission to desegregated schools, a federal district court upheld Alabama's pupil placement laws on the grounds that they provided the legal machinery for the orderly administration of the schools in a constitutional manner so as to admit students on the basis of merit rather than race or color. Although the law's author had stated that the law's purpose was to reinforce rather than eliminate segregation, the district court, following the normal practice of not looking at motivation, said it must presume that the law would be administered in a constitutional manner but warned that if it was not the court would not hesitate to strike it down. On appeal, in a per curiam decision the Supreme Court affirmed the judgment upon the district court's limited grounds.[49] The Court's action here may have resulted from the fact that while Alabama's attitude toward desegregation was clear—the state legislature had passed a *Brown* nullification resolution— the massive resistance which later characterized the state's stance had not yet set in, and Alabama Negroes had yet to bring pressure to bear. Facing extreme resistance in Arkansas and Virginia, the Court might have hoped to avoid it in Alabama if the state were allowed to proceed in good faith. Certainly the state would have in mind both the precedent of Little Rock and the Court's action only a few months before negating the state's order against the NAACP as examples of action the Court was willing to take.

North Carolina Pupil Placement Laws.   In 1959, with Justice Douglas on record for granting certiorari, the Court left undisturbed a Fourth Circuit ruling that a school board could continue a pattern of segregated schools which had resulted from the practice of assignment by race, since school children were provided with administrative procedures by which they might individually seek reassignment.[50] This left in place a requirement—of individual appearance before the board to request assignment to a specific school before resort to a federal court—which was less stringent than the Fifth Circuit's standard by which, without requesting admission to a particular school, students could request that a discriminatory policy be enjoined. Another adverse ruling came in 1959 in an appeal by Negro students deterred by unfriendly school officials with whom they had to have assignment interviews. The Fourth Circuit denied their request to bypass the administrative procedure, requiring them to exhaust state administrative remedies before resort to the federal courts.[51] The NAACP claimed that because so much time had already elapsed since *Brown* with so little accomplished, the courts could no longer presume that school officials would respond in good faith to transfer requests; endless review was required to accomplish anything under the laws, the group argued. Perhaps because a little progress had been made in the state in 1957, the Court may have thought it best to allow the Fourth Circuit to do what it could without interference, and certiorari was denied. Although North Carolina did not resort to massive resistance like Virginia's, the irony was that initial token desegregation did not bring greater long-term results than massive resistance, and, in fact, more was accomplished quickly in Virginia than in North Carolina.

Louisiana Statutes. The New Orleans litigation was among the most complicated of the school cases. It was in and out of the courts as the legislature in almost continuous session resisted the rulings of federal District Judge J. Skelly Wright. In cases in which he designated the federal government as amicus, Wright invalidated statutes which provided for integration solely by order of the legislature and which empowered the governor to assume the duties of the school boards or to close the schools altogether as well as to withhold supplies and funds from desegregated schools.[52] Acting affirmatively to condemn the legislative action, the Supreme Court sustained Judge Wright per curiam.[53] In a non–New Orleans case, the Court issued another per curiam affirmance to sustain the ruling of a three-judge court which had declared invalid as a violation of the Equal Protection Clause a statute allowing a school board to close down the public schools and to arrange for a system of private schools through leases and tuition grants.[54] The Supreme Court, despite its agreement with the lower court's position, did not speak out directly on the question of tuition grants, important in the later Prince Edward County case.

South Carolina Class Action. Desegregation had been nonexistent in

Clarendon County, South Carolina, which had given rise to the 1954 *Briggs* case. Around 1960 some Negro residents representing students seeking assignments to a number of different schools attempted to institute a class suit to spur action. The federal district court, following Fourth Circuit practice, refused to hear the case as a class suit. However, the Court of Appeals reversed, ordering the district court to hear the suit and thus indicating that its policy of marking time in hopes that school officials would face up to the inevitable was no longer in force. After the Supreme Court denied certiorari,[55] preserving their victory, the Negro parties failed to follow through.

Virginia School Transfer Provisions. A transfer plan provided that for elementary school pupils, if original assignment according to residential zoning resulted in a student's being placed in a school in which he would be in a racial minority, the student could transfer. At the high school level, whites could go where they wished but Negroes wishing to go to the white high school had to meet residence criteria and pass tests. A federal district court upheld the elementary school provisions, but invalidated the high school plan, saying that attendance at the city's high schools should be based solely on the student's choice or preference. The Fourth Circuit affirmed that part of the district court's ruling, but at the same time invalidated the racial minority transfer plan, holding that although the plan might seem valid on its face and might seem to apply to all regardless of race, its purpose and effect were to retard integration and retain segregation of the races.[56] The Supreme Court denied review to this ruling, a forerunner of many later "freedom of choice" decisions.

Desegregation Speed in Alabama. In early summer 1963 a federal district court had refused either to issue an immediate order requiring the submission of a desegregation plan for Mobile County, Alabama, or to issue an injunction against further operation of segregated schools there. The judge instead had set a trial date in the fall for presentation of a plan for the 1964–65 school year. The Fifth Circuit found school board administrative problems not the fault of the plaintiffs, who had been trying for nearly a year to get school authorities to desegregate the schools. The appeals court said the district court should have granted a temporary injunction. Ruling as well that the officials had no acceptable reason for further delay, the judges ordered that by August 1, 1963, the board must submit a plan involving at least the first grade then and at least one grade per year thereafter. Although the question of timing of a plan is an important one, the Supreme Court's refusal to hear the case[57] may have been based on a desire to reserve its attention for cases involving more substantive aspects of desegregation, particularly where the lower courts were producing some forward movement.

Another Alabama case involved six Negro children who had been granted a transfer to a white high school. In a suit brought by a white student, a federal court had enjoined the transfer the day before school was to start. The Fifth Circuit vacated the order prohibiting the transfer and itself ordered no interference with the school board's desegregation plan until the appeal could be decided on the merits. The Supreme Court refused to hear this case,[58] a predictable action both because acceptance of the case would only have delayed the desegregation process and because the appellate court's ruling meant that voluntary progress under the school board's direction should not be hampered while final decision was being made on the desegregation plan, a positive ruling from the high court's perspective.

Desegregation in Atlanta. The summary decisions described above were reached without oral argument. In one case, however, summary action by the Court came only after oral argument was heard. In the fall of 1961, Atlanta under court order had put into effect a graduated transfer plan involving a pupil placement statute in conjunction with a grade-a-year plan. Because the initial assignment system, by which all Negroes were sent to Negro schools and all whites to white schools, remained unchanged, the plan resulted in the transfer of only selected Negro students to white schools at the rate of one grade per year from the top down, with the plan not reaching the first grade until 1970. In *Calhoun v. Latimer,* the district court and the Fifth Circuit approved the plan. Atlanta Negro parents, with NAACP counsel, then carried their appeal to the Supreme Court, supported by the federal government as amicus. The NAACP attacked the whole idea of maintaining racially separate school systems with desegregation only by transfer and urged that *Brown* required boards to reorganize schools into unitary nonracial systems. The question of acceleration of the grade-a-year plan seemed primary. However, the NAACP also argued for application of *Brown* to assignment of school personnel and teachers, saying that a school with an all-Negro or all-white staff was labeled an all-Negro or all-white school just as effectively as if there were a sign on the door. The Court was not to rule on this question in this case, but it would soon leave undisturbed favorable lower court action on the matter.[59]

At argument, the Atlanta school board indicated that since 1961 it had voluntarily undertaken to proceed beyond mere administration of the pupil placement statute. Candidly conceding the illegality of some past devices which it had hoped would help make desegregation acceptable to the public, the board insisted that it was presently taking further steps to hasten the process. Confusion thus arose as to exactly what changes had been made—changes which would have to be understood before the Court could rule on its validity. This led to the Court's per curiam order vacating and remanding the case in view of a new school board plan, with the district court to hold "a proper evidentiary hearing" on the new developments. The justices, however, said that the time for deliberateness was over and urged speed in the case in line with directives such as that in *Watson,* the Memphis parks case of the same year. While this statement seemed to be movement away from "all deliberate speed," its placement in a vacate-and-remand order substantially reduced its visibility or, what amounts to the same thing, conveyed the message that the Court itself deliberately wanted to decrease the force of the statement by placing it in a per curiam order.

These cases present a pattern in which the Supreme Court with very limited exceptions turned aside cases or, when it accepted them, ruled in summary fashion. Perhaps the members of the Court underestimated the cumulative retarding effect of individual rulings. They may have felt they could affect only a small number of school districts in which individual suits were then being brought because, in an area of litigation arising under the Constitution, factual variations are constitutionally significant, giving only limited precedential value to opinions in individual cases. This could have created the situation noted by Griswold in another context, where "language used in one case [would have] to be qualified or explained away when a different case arose with slightly different facts."[60] While a single all-encompassing solution could not be developed overnight, largely because the Court could deal with only those cases coming to it, the justices certainly impeded the progress of desegregation by failing even to begin to develop doctrine with respect to implementation—for example, some partial rules for particular categories of situations.[61] The Court's actual course of action left doctrine to be stated solely through the inference-drawing of those watching the Court's summary dispositions and refusals to review, and resulted in increased use of tactics for delay followed by increased litigation as people sought to know what was on the Court's mind.

6

Transfer and pupil placement plans in Tennessee gave rise to much litigation, particularly in the urban areas of Knoxville, Memphis, and Nashville—some of it still continuing in the 1970s. Three terms after the matter was brought to the justices' attention, they agreed to hear argument concerning minority race transfers. The question first had come to the Court in connection with Nashville's desegregation plan, which called for integrating a grade a year, beginning with the first grade, and for "minority race transfer," by which students assigned to schools in which their race was a minority might transfer to one in which their race predominated. Upholding the transfer provision, the district court said that the nondiscriminatory right to transfer, though racially based, did not appear to violate the Constitution. The plan was also upheld by the Sixth Circuit, which observed that as long as the child was free to attend an integrated school he would not be deprived of his constitutional rights if his parents chose to send him to a school which only one race attended—at least as long as there was no indication of limitation or coercion regarding the freedom to choose. The Negro parents appealed to the Supreme Court for a hearing, arguing both that the plan as a whole should be speeded up and that the minority transfer provision should be struck down because it perpetuated rather than limited racial discrimination, but the Court denied certiorari.[62] Although the lower court's judgment as to the integration plan's time element seems to have been unquestioned, there were three votes—those of Warren, Douglas, and Brennan—to hear the case and deal with the recognition of race as an absolute ground for the tranfer of students between schools.

When Tennessee's pupil placement law later received differing treatment in two federal district courts, the Supreme Court also denied review shortly before accepting the Knoxville litigation. In a Memphis case, the pupil placement statute was held to furnish an adequate plan for nondiscriminatory operation of the city school system, but another district court held that the law had nothing to do with desegregation and provided at best a most time-consuming and cumbersome procedure for transfers. When the Memphis decision was appealed, the Sixth Circuit, finding the law of some administrative purpose but not serviceable as a plan to convert a biracial school system into a nonracial one, reversed the district court. The judges called tokenism the board's action in admitting only thirteen Negro children to white schools by fall 1961. The appeals court also refused to uphold the Tennessee statute as a plan for desegregation or to require exhaustion of remedies under the plan before resort to the courts. With the support of the Memphis Citizens' Council as amicus curiae, the school board carried the case to the Supreme Court, arguing that in earlier suits in some other circuits such tokenism had been found acceptable and asking for clarification or explanation of the 1958 *Shuttlesworth* decision involving the upholding of a similar Alabama statute. As noted, the Court would not hear the case.[63]

The *Goss* case from Knoxville, which the Court did accept, involved transfer provisions like those upheld in the Nashville case. Federal judges had approved minority race transfer provisions for the school systems in both Davidson County and Knoxville, Tennessee. The position of the Negro children before the Supreme Court, argued by NAACP counsel Jack Greenberg, was that provisions whereby students could transfer only from schools in which their race was a minority to schools in which their race was a majority were unconstitutional because race was the sole criterion for transfer.[64] Under the overall desegregation plans—also challenged as invalid—school districts were to be rezoned without reference to race. However, the transfer provisions were claimed to perpetuate rather than alleviate the preexisting racially segregated school systems. Greenberg said he saw *Brown* as meaning "there shall be no racial distinction whatsoever in the school system" but not compulsory intermixing. Greenberg also argued that no child should be permitted to transfer because of a racial desire. He agreed that exceptions had to be made for anyone emotionally or educationally disturbed, but said that the plan seemed to assume that such a situation existed.

K. Harlan Dodson, Jr., speaking for the Davidson County Board of Education, complained at the outset that the Court must consider the issues in a vacuum because no student in the majority had asked for a transfer to get out of the school to which he had been assigned, so no one had been denied a transfer, which might have been granted because of overcrowding. Knoxville Board of Education counsel S. Frank Fowler pointed out that although no majority requests had been made in his system, he said he thought they would be granted, since desegregation in the city had been a quietly conducted process. Jack Petree, for the Memphis Board of Education as amicus, raised one new point. He argued that the economically affluent would not be touched in any event because they would move to suburbia. The economically poorer, on the other hand, would be forced to swallow their constitutional rights if the provisions were removed because of the emotional and educational difficulties they would face by suddenly being made a minority group.

The United States also appeared as amicus. The government's participation reflected continuing national policy, said Assistant Attorney General Burke Marshall, and its interest stemmed from the fact that these were the first school desegregation cases the Court had taken for argument since *Cooper*[65] and that these transfer provisions, operating explicitly on grounds of race, were not unique. Arkansas, Alabama, North Carolina, Louisiana, and Florida all had similar statutes, Marshall noted, and similar plans had been introduced in other cities in more states. Marshall said he read *Brown II* as ordering school boards to create desegregated school systems operated according to the Constitution. *Brown* should absolutely control transitional plans because of this affirmative duty to move, he argued.

Both the school board attorneys and Burke Marshall were questioned heavily, the school board lawyers being almost continuously interrupted by questions and statements from the bench. Most of the questions dealt with the closely related issues of whether the school board plan encouraged segregation and whether it actually involved discrimination, a point on which Marshall was pressed particularly hard. The justices also showed an interest in the meaning of *Brown* for school board action, and there were some questions as to why the school board retained the school desegregation plan it had adopted.

During the school board lawyers' presentation, Justice Goldberg pointed out that the school board, not the parents, defined conditions involving racial criteria for transfer requests. Justice White asked why if the board agreed that segregation by operation of the law could no longer be part of the public education system it had invited parents to think in those terms. He also asked if any white students had transferred back. The Chief Justice brought out the point that the school board was in effect writing into its rules the segregation policies of the people, making no provision for those who were not segregation-minded, and he later ventured the opinion that the school board was encouraging segregation. During Marshall's appearance, after commenting that both sides were treated equally so that he wondered where the discrimination against Negroes was, Justice Stewart pressed Marshall to repond to the argument that transfers were not the fault of the school board but were sought through the voluntary wish and affirmative desire of parents and child. Marshall answered that it would be different if everyone could secure such "voluntary" transfers, even to attend an integrated school. Goldberg had followed up Stewart's first question by remarking that constitutional discrimination existed under the transfer plan with respect to both sides, since neither was free to choose integration but rather was frozen in the majority school, and Harlan now stated that it was as if the state had passed a law saying that those who believed in segregation could transfer, while those who did not could not. Continuing his colloquy with Marshall, Stewart drew on the desegregation-integration distinction and said that *Brown* had to do with keeping people out, that it didn't say anything about compelling a biracial student body. Marshall replied that that was not what he was talking about, but Stewart insisted nevertheless that no one was kept out under these plans, that personal wishes were met, not government action taken. After Marshall reiterated that school board action was state action, Justice Black switched the discussion back to the meaning of *Brown*, asking about counsel's statement that "there must be movement toward integration," which implied an end to "all deliberate speed." "That was not *ad infinitum*," Marshall replied. When Black asked if responsible officials were liable to broader order and decree where no move was made in the direction of desegregation, Marshall agreed, as he did when the Chief Justice asked if it was his position that the overall plan resulted in a built-in system of segregation. Stewart, who asked about the stairstep plan being used in the city, also wanted to know how far the city was from nearby Clinton, which had experienced great disturbance over school desegregation; counsel asserted that the board couldn't just throw away the plan. The plan, he noted, had been adopted under the same district judge who had ruled in the Clinton case. Justice Goldberg also pressed counsel as to why the city retained the plans if they were no longer useful, but counsel kept saying that individual choice was important and was allowed under the plans.

When the Supreme Court handed down its decision in an opinion written by Justice Clark, the justices unanimously reversed the judgments below. At the start, Clark pointed out that certiorari had been limited to the question of whether these Negro school children seeking desegregation of their public school systems had been deprived of their rights under the Fourteenth Amendment by means of the transfer provisions. The Court found that they had been so deprived. Because the plans were based solely on racial factors which inevitably led toward segregation of students by race, they ran counter to the admonition of *Brown II*. The recognition of race as an absolute criterion for granting transfers which operate only in the direction of the transferee's majority race is no less unconstitutional than its use for original admission or subsequent assignment to public schools, Clark concluded. The ruling, although quite clear, had a relatively narrow scope—one-way transfers. Thus the Court had made the scope of the ruling fit with its low-profile position adopted through nonacceptance of most cases. The same strategy was to be true with *Griffin,* the next case, which was narrow in being restricted to partial school closings, although there was broad language about speed and the power of the lower court to take appropriate action.

7

The Knoxville case had been relatively straightforward, even if several years had elapsed between the time the issue first was brought to the Supreme Court and the time the justices issued an opinion in the *Goss* litigation. The Prince Edward County litigation involved much more. In other areas of the country, schools remained segregated but at least they remained open. Here they were closed, leaving Negro children without an education for several years. The action was taken as part of a plan of "Massive Resistance," with the full force of the state behind it although ultimately only one county was involved. There had been a federal district court which had resisted implementation of school desegregation before *Cooper* and continued to do so later. There were difficult constitutional questions posed by such devices as state tuition grants used in all-white private schools. Perhaps most important was the symbolic aspect, not merely because black children were out of school and "Massive Resistance" was at stake but more so because Prince Edward County had been one of the five areas directly involved in *Brown v. Board of Education*. Ten years after *Brown,* nothing had happened in one those cases, a fact which must have brought home forcefully the slow pace of desegregation to the justices of the Supreme Court.

Virginia school closing litigation began after Governor Almond of Virginia—who as attorney general had argued the *Davis* case for the state in the Supreme Court—closed schools in three counties when he was faced with court orders for 1958 desegregation. A group of white parents in Norfolk County concerned about the proper education of their children brought suit challenging the state's school closing law. In January 1958 a three-judge federal district court, anticipating the ultimate *Griffin* ruling, held the law unconstitutional, reasoning that having accepted the responsibility of maintaining and operating public schools Virginia could not close one or more schools solely because children of different races had been assigned to them and at the same time keep the state's other public schools open on a segregated basis.[66] The state routinely took the case to the Supreme Court, but the Court never had to rule on the appeal. When the state court also held the laws unconstitutional in a suit the state had brought,[67] official resistance apparently collapsed, and the case in the Supreme Court was never prosecuted, leading to its dismissal pursuant to the Court's Rule 14.[68] Such a dismissal, which is essentially automatic, is to be distinguished from various rules as to standing and justiciability, used by the judges to dispose of certain issues; they are not precise, and in fact are somewhat "accordionlike" in character. Yet even without Rule 14, it is doubtful that the Court would have ruled on the case, because the justices certainly were in agreement with the force of the decision. The only aspect which might have caused concern to them was the indication that if a state closed *all* its public schools perhaps a state school closing law might be constitutional, an inference which the Court could have avoided had it written its own decision.

Even after "Massive Resistance" collapsed, Prince Edward County continued to cause trouble, partly because of judicial foot-dragging by the lower court. After the Fourth Circuit had ordered the district court to require county school officials to set a starting date for desegregation, the district judge set 1965 as the date, stating that overly hasty action would be much less conductive to law enforcement than would carefully considered delay. The Fourth Circuit found this unreasonable and directed the judge to order qualified Negro students admitted to the white high school for the following year—in September 1959. Perhaps because the decision again showed that public opposition was not acceptable as a basis for delaying desegregation and perhaps because the justices were optimistic that resistance in this last Virginia county might diminish over the summer months, the Supreme Court denied review.[69] If it turned out that the Court was wrong, the case would be the responsibility of the Fourth

Circuit, which had achieved success recently in the rest of the state. Another example of a Fourth Circuit ruling denied review was another Norfolk case. After enjoining enforcement of the Virginia school closing law, a federal district judge also enjoined enforcement of a Norfolk ordinance and resolution cutting off funding and ordered the Norfolk school board to comply with prior decrees, requiring desegregation. His order was affirmed by the Fourth Circuit, and the Supreme Court promptly denied review,[70] the problem of Norfolk being considered settled beyond question.

After the earlier litigation concerning the start of desegregation, in 1959 Prince Edward County schools had been closed according to a local option provision rather than have the county submit to court-ordered integration.[71] In the 1959–60 school year a private segregated school for white students had been set up. The school was first supported with private funds but subsequently state and county tuition grants permitted its comfortable continuation. Negro parents went four years without schools for their children, but then with outside help they too opened a private school for the 1963–64 school year. They also pursued litigation directed at the education situation in the county and finally obtained a ruling from the Supreme Court. In this litigation, *Griffin v. County School Board of Prince Edward County,* the federal district court enjoined state support to whites-only schools operated by the Prince Edward School Foundation. The court also held that public schools could not remain closed while the schools were open in other counties. This ruling had been vacated by the Fourth Circuit, which had instructed the lower court to abstain pending the finality of state court action in separate litigation. The Virginia Supreme Court then ruled that the state's constitution did not compel either reopening of the schools or providing money to run them. Negro petitioners had appealed the Fourth Circuit order. On September 30, 1963, Justice Brennan stayed the Court of Appeals ruling pending a filing of a certiorari petition. On January 6, 1964, the Court granted certiorari and did so in a way that called particular attention to the case and indicated judicial impatience with the slow progress of desegregation. Instead of being handed down with a mass of other orders, the certiorari grant was announced separately in a two-page ruling. The Court stated that despite numerous district court and Court of Appeals rulings, "the mandate issued at the time of the *Brown* case has never been implemented." Furthermore, the judges said, "in view of the long delay in the case since our decision in the *Brown* case and the importance of the questions presented," the case was to be heard on the merits without waiting for final Court of Appeals action—action the justices noted they had taken in some other major cases including President Truman's seizure of the steel mills.[72]

At oral argument,[73] attorney J. Segar Gravatt for the county and state Assistant Attorney General McIlwaine said the Court lacked the power to order the schools reopened. Neither governmental unit had violated the rights of anyone and no one had a federal constitutional right to attend a public school, they said, arguing that there was nothing to require Prince Edward County to maintain schools. Other political subdivisions in the state, operating under the state's local option arrangement, did not have public schools but rather sent children elsewhere, they pointed out. Both maintained that the local option-tuition grant program of the state was an effort "to enlarge the opportunities" of the students as to where they would go to school. Gravatt said that the county's new school, open to Negroes—in fact, open to all students—had been set up for them the previous fall through the activities of the Justice Department and state and county officials. NAACP general counsel Robert Carter argued basically that the "local option" system could not be used to permit a county to abandon public education in order to evade a court desegregation order even if counties were not required by state law to run public school systems. Early in his argument, Carter made a psychological point when he reminded the Court that because of the various time delays in the litigation a third set of students was presently involved in the case. An entire generation of Negro children—the ones Robert Kennedy called "the generation without an education"—had not been allowed or permitted to enjoy the constitutional right which the Court had said was theirs in 1954. The methods the county used were, as Carter put it, a "more genteel attempt to evade the Constitution" than the methods which had been adopted in Arkansas, but results were similar, and the Little Rock situation was thus relevant, Carter argued, because the Court had there declared it would not tolerate evasions of school desegregation orders. Supporting Carter's position was Solicitor General Cox, amicus curiae for the United States.[74] His appearance, which indicated executive involvement in school desegregation, was an important aspect of this case. Cox said the Prince Edward County situation discriminated against both white and Negro students since any student living there was denied the right to public education granted all others in the state. Cox urged that the courts judge the case in terms of the total situation, putting aside arguments that the state does not discriminate because of the local option provision and the county does not because all residents are treated equally.

The justices' numerous questions—principally about depriving Negro children of their constitutional rights, and including questions about the public status of the new school for Negroes—were almost completely aimed at Virginia counsel, and the Chief Justice played a central role, making little pretense of hiding his feelings. Justice Stewart interrupted Gravatt with the remark that it seemed that the plan completely deprived people of the opportunity to an integrated public school in the county, something everyone else in the United States was entitled to under the Constitution. Gravatt replied that the county was trying to give everyone a chance to extend his liberties but that the Negroes there had refused to take advantage of the opportunities offered them. Then Chief Justice Warren posed a series of questions about the new school: "You were operating a public school when you did that, weren't you?" he asked. "We were contributing to . . ." Gravatt began to say. "No, you were operating," the Chief Justice interrupted. "We don't operate these schools, sir." "That is a public school, isn't it?" "Yes, in terms of the Fourteenth Amendment." "It is an integrated school, isn't it?" "Yes." "Then haven't you abandoned your position of not having an integrated public school?" "Yes." Warren's questioning produced not a legal but a psychological point: why continue with this at the least "unusual" school system when the obvious reason for it had already been internally contradicted? Black then entered the melee: "Does Virginia have a right to follow its program for the purpose of avoiding desegregation?" Gravatt replied that he avoided saying it the way Black had; it was not done to avoid integration but in an effort to expand liberties. "That's evasive. Getting away from lawyer's language, that's correct, isn't it?" "Yes." When Gravatt turned to the argument that the Virginia plan gave students greater freedom of choice, the Chief Justice again broke in. "May I ask about those little colored children who have been without education? Have they had freedom?" "They've had liberties," said Gravatt. "No, have they had freedom?" "Yes, sir." "Freedom to go through life without an education," the Chief Justice retorted.

When the Court rendered its decision about four months later, ten years had passed since the *Brown* declaration. As might be expected, the opinion by Justice Black managed to get in a few pointed words about the pace of "deliberate speed" although it was not an issue in the case. However, the opinion was narrow in its handling of principal issues raised by the case: 1) the constitutionality of private tuition grants and tax credits which amounted to use of public funds to pay for private school tuition and 2) the Fourteenth Amendment validity of a state's total abandonment of all or part of its system of public education. Noting that there had been entirely too much deliberation and not enough speed in enforcing the constitutional rights enunciated in *Brown* and that the time for mere "deliberate speed" had run out, the Court upheld the district court's 1961 injunction against paying tuition grants and giving tax credits while public schools in the county remained closed because those grants and tax credits had been essential parts of the county's program to deprive petitioners of the advantages of a public school education enjoyed by children in every other part of Virginia. Black said the county's school closing was quite obviously intended to ensure that white and colored children in Prince

Edward County would not uder any circumstances go to the same school. The Court specifically noted its agreement with the district court that petitioners had been denied equal protection of the laws when these schools closed while those in all other counties remained open, particularly where the county was simultaneously contributing to the support of the private segregated white schools which replaced the public schools. Emphasizing its awareness of the many years which had been lost in litigation, the Court remanded the case to the district court with directions that it enter a decree which would guarantee that the petitioners get the kind of education given in the state's public schools. The lower court was specifically authorized to require school officials to exercise their power to levy taxes to raise funds to reopen, operate, and maintain without racial discrimination a public school system in Prince Edward County like that operated in the rest of Virginia. The last holding—that the federal court was empowered to order reopening of public schools in the county—was too much for Justices Clark and Harlan, but they joined in the rest of the Court's opinion to provide unanimity on the limited condemnation of school closing and private tuition grants to avoid school desegregation.

Reviewing the Supreme Court's 1963 Term, Philip Kurland called the Prince Edward case "one of the many factual situations that compels the Court to resort to unbecoming and unfortunate methods for assuring that its will is done."[75] He suggested that what the Court considered to be the Equal Protection Clause violation was not clear, and argued that the Court should have indicated whether the discrimination was at the state level—closing schools in one county while leaving them open elsewhere—or at the county level—tuition grants and tax exemptions by county officials. Had the discrimination been found to be statewide, he wrote, the state would normally have been given the choice of closing all the schools or opening them in Prince Edward County—a choice the Court did not allow. Whether or not one agrees with Kurland's legal argument, the Court's opinion was limited in the sense that it did not go so far as to declare unconstitutional the use of public funds to pay grants for private school tuition and left unanswered the broad question of whether a state constitutionally could abandon totally its system of public education. Clearly the Court wished to avoid an across-the-board ruling on the former issue where related but as yet unanswered questions, including the constitutionality of using public funds to aid private parochial schools, might be affected. The peculiar circumstances of tuition and tax concessions in Prince Edward County, so obviously intended to avoid school desegregation, made a limited ruling not only possible but also adequate for later application to similar ruses concerning racially segregated education.

As to the abandonment issue, it was wholly unnecessary for the Court to go further than to say that under these conditions closing public schools and then contributing to the support of private segregated schools was contrary to equal protection. The majority of the public, no matter what their feelings about segregation, was likely not to find acceptable extended school closing where the only replacement was by wholly private effort. Thus it was not necessary for the Court to encroach further on state prerogatives to achieve the desired result. By giving the lower federal court specific authorization to reopen the public schools, the majority had added great strength to the force of its decision and virtually ensured the end of this or any similar attempt to stifle desegregation. In fact, the district court promptly issued the order directed, and the county supervisors levied the necessary taxes to reopen the schools in the fall.

Even though it reopened the schools, the county did not easily give up segregation. The county allowed Negroes to attend the public schools but still offered the tuition grant program to white parents who wished their children to continue attendance at the all-white "private" schools. The Negro parents sought an injunction against the private tuition grants, arguing that the program still amounted to publicly supported segregated education. Unsuccessful in federal district court, they appealed to the Fourth Circuit, which found the tuition program unconstitutional and ordered the district court to enjoin the grants to private schools so long as they excluded Negroes. Because formal action in the case could not be completed before the September opening date, the court sought an informal agreement with state and county officials not to make the payments in advance of the normal September issuing date. The county response was a hastily called board of supervisors meeting the night of August 4, 1964, a telephone roundup of white parents, and the swift approval of 1,217 tuition grant applications—a "midnight transfer" of more than $180,000 of county money to white parents resisting school desegregation—all before the courts could do a thing. The six county supervisors who had transferred the county funds were cited for civil contempt for their actions, which they never attempted to defend on grounds of propriety. Instead they insisted that the contempt citation rested on an overexpansive view of the power of federal courts. In June 1966, the Fourth Circuit's five judges unanimously stated that the supervisors' conduct had been improper, but the judges split three-to-two over the use of the contempt power.[76] The majority, calling the midnight maneuver a flagrant attempt to evade the effect of a possible adverse decision, ruled that the six were personally liable to replenish the county treasury with the money they had sought to place beyond court control. The minority agreed with the majority's finding that the supervisors' conduct was "contemptible," but said they could not agree that it was "contemptuous" and thus legally punishable. The case was then appealed to the Supreme Court. However, although Justices Black and Stewart indicated they would have heard the case, the Court declined to enter this controversy again, thus allowing the Fourth Circuit's decision to stand.[77]

Eight months later, by mid-July of 1967, the Prince Edward County dispute was buried. The money owed was repaid—most of it by recovery from parents to whom the grants had been paid, by public contribution, and by loan raised by the supervisors—and the contempt citation was lifted, although the case was left on the court's docket with an outside chance that some other development could come. Although mostly segregated education was still the pattern, with the majority of white students in private schools and Negroes in the public schools, public money could no longer be appropriated for the former. At this late date and for the time being, just about all that could be done by the courts had been done.

8

In dealing with the question of school desegregation in *Brown,* the Supreme Court was pretty much on its own, with no support from Congress and little from the executive branch, although President Eisenhower's Solicitor General finally took a position against *Plessy* during oral argument. What followed the Court's action was criticism from the southern wing of Congress and inaction on the part of the congressional majority, although the first voting rights bill since Reconstruction was passed in 1957 and was somewhat strengthened in 1960. President Eisenhower's support for *Brown* was lukewarm, as we have noted, and his action during the Little Rock crisis, while seemingly decisive, was taken only with the greatest reluctance and not with reference to the merits of the dispute but only to the need to enforce court orders in general. Nor were his administration's resources committed to the removal of desegregation. The Department of Justice and United States Attorneys were not to intervene in school desegregation matters unless the courts requested them to do so.[78]

The Supreme Court's hesitancy in *Brown II* has been justified as a recognition of the anticipated lack of support from the executive branch and from Congress or as at least allowing the latter two time to catch up. That is, the Court's strategy is said to follow from its being alone. On the other hand, the administration's non-action may have reinforced the ineffectiveness of the Court's strategy. While the Court's initial actions might have been firmer had it known it could count on executive support, there is some question of the sort of lesson it "learned" from what Eisenhower's waffling produced. It seemed consistently to retreat and to "read the returns" as always showing that whatever you did would be

resisted rather than seeing that firm initial action might overcome some of
that resistance. In any event, the Court's wish-washy position in *Brown II*
certainly allowed the administration the luxury of the position it took.
Certainly, the Court's failure to spell out actual requirements provoked
considerable resistance when an agency requiring change later demanded action by the school districts, as happened when the Office of
Education began to move on the HEW guidelines in 1965. And it also
meant that administrators had to do the whole job for themselves when
they finally got started.

With the Kennedy administration in office, there was an important
change in posture from what the Eisenhower administration had not
done. The president did far less than he had promised during the
campaign—for example, concerning housing discrimination—and while
Justice Department efforts to enforce civil rights were often far from
energetic,[79] the difference in posture was visible. It resulted in part from
pressure by Representative Adam Clayton Powell (D-N. Y.) to get legislation enacted which could cut off funds to states not complying with *Brown*
and in part from the fact that blacks, who had not been part of
Eisenhower's constituency, were definitely part of the Democratic constituency which had narrowly elected Kennedy. Whatever the reasons, the
result was that the judiciary had some executive branch assistance and was
no longer playing a solo part in the desegregation drama; one saw a
developing interaction between executive and judiciary. The judiciary
could be more sure of executive branch assistance to follow up rulings,
and, more important, there now was executive branch involvement in the
early stages of some desegregation controversies. This meant that to some
extent the executive branch helped set the Court's agenda, either by
pressing cases which ultimately came to the Court—and which could be
less easily turned away with a coordinate branch of the government
playing a part in the litigation—or by affecting the posture of "normal"
school desegregation cases which would have come to the Court in any
event.

Once Congress passed the Civil Rights Act of 1964 and the Department of Health, Education and Welfare developed its desegregation
guidelines, one had both legislative and executive branches sharing the
stage with the Court. We shall see that what the courts had done before
1964 affected what the executive branch was able to do administratively
and that such administrative action in turn affected subsequent litigation.
But first we should look at the litigation which developed from the prime
early example of a desegregation controversy in which, unlike the Little
Rock situation where the federal government was caught largely by sur
prise, the federal government was involved from an early stage. That
example, which came from higher education rather than lower educa-

tion, was, of course, the attempt by James Meredith to gain admission to the University of Mississippi. Here the Justice Department had entered the Meredith suit for admission to Ole Miss as soon as it became clear that Governor Ross Barnett would stand in opposition to the enforcement of federal law.

Meredith v. Fair involved the original question of Meredith's admission to the university. The district court at first said no racial discrimination had been proved and dismissed the suit, but the Fifth Circuit reversed and ordered Meredith enrolled. Desperate legal manuevering filled the summer of 1962. A single Fifth Circuit judge stayed the enrollment order four times, each time only to have the original circuit panel, and finally Justice Black acting as Circuit Justice, remove the stay orders. The state governor, legislature, and judiciary worked together to convict Meredith of an unrelated and trumped up criminal charge which, under a law fashioned for the occasion, forbade his entry into the university. The Justice Department then aided in another legal battle which resulted in the Fifth Circuit's invalidation of the legislature's bill and of Meredith's conviction as well as of the local court's injunction forbidding his enrollment, with the governor and others enjoined from interfering with Meredith's entrance into the school. When they did so anyhow, they were charged with contempt of court and convicted.[80] Only after all this maneuvering in the courts and personal attempts at persuasion on the part of President Kennedy with Governor Barnett was Meredith finally escorted to the campus by federal marshals and Deputy Attorney General Katzenbach. It was then that the rioting and ugliness seen around the world broke out.[81]

When the Supreme Court entered the picture in the *Meredith* case, the violence had gone beneath the surface and the situation was largely controlled and under careful surveillance; what remained was a mopping up of legal maneuverings, pursued to the very end probably out of some sense of bitter pride and political necessity. Just one week after rioting had raged on the Mississippi campus, the Court denied a hearing to the state's appeal of the Fifth Circuit admission order. Four months later, the same treatment was given to a suit challenging the Fifth Circuit's decision that allowed the United States to enter the suit below as amicus, to institute proceedings ancillary to the cause of the first suit, and to enforce relevant federal court orders.[82] The Court's role in the drama had been completely passive, as it left untouched matters obviously long settled.

The *Meredith* case was important, but during the Kennedy administration there were few major school desegregation initiatives. This was partly a result of problems of what the federal statutes allowed the government to do, and partly a matter of will. The administration supported the NAACP in its court efforts, as we have seen from Burke Marshall's amicus appearance in *Goss*. But it was with the Johnson administration that activity became greater. Before he died, President Kennedy had proposed major civil rights legislation. His assassination provided much of the impetus for the passage of that bill as the Civil Rights Act of 1964. Most attention during the fight to pass the legislation was focused on the public accommodations provisions, but of particular importance for school desegregation was Title VI, which allowed the cutting-off of funds to units of government practicing discrimination. When the act was passed, except for "impact" grants for educating children of armed services personnel, relatively little federal money was going to most southern school districts. Then the passage in 1965 of the Elementary and Secondary Education Act (ESEA) brought massive allotments and the possibility of a real "carrot" to bring about desegregation: if you want the money, desegregate, was the message. Title VI of the 1964 act thus became crucial in the field of education, and it became the basis of federal administrative intervention in the desegregation process.

The sponsors of Title VI had tied the provision to court rulings because they did not want conflict between administrators enforcing the fund cutoff provision and the federal judges who had been dealing with school desegregation since *Brown II*. The Supreme Court's lack of forceful follow-up action after *Brown* may thus have made it easier to obtain acceptance for Title VI than if the Court had forged ahead. However, while enforcement could increase if and when the courts moved ahead, the absence of Supreme Court rulings on major aspects of desegregation meant the executive branch had little to use in trying to hold school districts to higher standards than those of the local federal district judge. Strengthening existing court orders and developing new legal doctrine in the area of desegregation was possible, and Titles IV and IX of the Civil Rights Act authorized such litigation, but the necessary Justice Department resources for such a task were not readily forthcoming, reinforcing the importance of existing judicial rules.

HEW officials administering Title VI were willing to accept court orders as indicia of desegregation.[83] Like the congressmen who had enacted the provision, they did not want to pit their judgment concerning desegregation remedies against that of federal judges familiar with the details of cases and the locale from which they came. Were a proposed desegregation plan to be rejected by a judge and then imposed by an administrator, the situation would be even more difficult. However, the effect of administrative acceptance of court-ordered desegregation plans had a "multiplier effect." Accepting a plan required by a judge in one district made it extremely difficult to require more of other districts. Some of those plans were quite weak, allowing "a substantial group of the most important districts of the South . . . to continue receiving Federal aid while stretching the process of token integration over the period of a decade."[84] Because such plans provided a lowest common denominator, they made it difficult if not impossible for the administrators to force other districts to abolish segregation immediately. The weakness of court-ordered plans also led a number of school districts, previously resistant to moving on desegregation, to go to court where they could find a sympathetic judge, often not difficult.[85] This further reinforced the minimum to which administrators could hold other districts. When these districts submitted desegregation plans incorporating elements accepted elsewhere by the courts, how was one to reject such plans, particularly when they were voluntary?

If administrative guidelines were to be based on court decisions, the criteria of those decisions had to be utilized. Here again the Supreme Court's refusal to hear cases had a major, if unintended, effect. Decisions of the courts of appeals and the district courts had to be used. But because of the differences between courts of appeals and within each circuit, the question became how to determine what the decisions meant and which of the many decisions to use. The Office of Education, not equipped with a ready-made staff of legal experts, turned to law professors. It was they who developed the standards to be used in the South, but their lawyerlike language caused confusion for southern school officials when it was not sufficiently clear.

Implementation of the administrative guidelines—the HEW Guidelines—was neither prompt nor smooth. In addition to considerable delay, there was difficulty in tieing the guideline developers into existing departmental structure or settling important differences with other parts of the executive branch. As Orfield noted in his definive study of the process, "Passage of the act was only the beginning of a lengthy internal struggle for a vigorous enforcement policy."[86] "Months were to pass," he adds, "before the administrative requirements for Title VI enforcement were understood and before the lines of responsibility were clarified."[87] Matters were made worse because the enforcement task had been given to an agency which had strong ties to local schoolmen and which was not accustomed to imposing national law differing from local ways of doing things. Even when the standards were developed, the Office of Education was not adequately staffed to enforce them. Its officials did not adequately understand the effort which would be necessary—either the type of effort or its magnitude. Furthermore, the enforcement postures of the various agencies involved in desegregation differed considerably. HEW was cautious; Defense was active; Justice was middle-of-the-road; the Civil Rights Commission was aggressive. The agencies could accomplish much when they worked together, but these divergences in posture made it unlikely they would do so. In addition to interagency disagreement, there was also intraagency division in HEW—for example, between the law professor-consultants and the more entrenched field relations staff and between higher officials in HEW and the Office of Education itself. There was more than one enforcement staff, and there was a wide range in the degree of activity exhibited by the department. With all this intersecting activity, it is surprising that much was accomplished. And certainly more could have been done. When some districts were prodded into agreeing to relatively firm compliance plans, the action was not then used to drag other districts along, perhaps because determination to cut off aid was lacking. Recalcitrant districts thus found they could wait before having to do anything.

Despite all the resistance and the conflict within the bureaucracy, the guidelines, which required all grades be opened to Negroes by fall 1967, did bring about change.[88] Where total resistance to desegregation had existed, the first year under the provisions of Title VI wiped out most of it, and movement continued beyond that first year, particularly where totally segregated districts had existed. The number of black students moving into previously all-white schools under the guidelines was not great; most schools were still segregated. But, just as *Brown I* had been a psychological victory, the guidelines placed the federal executive branch clearly on the side of desegregation and provided an important blow against those school officials who had felt they could continue doing substantially nothing. However, the effect of the guidelines, though great where resistance was strongest, was not as great where even token progress had been made prior to 1964. In part because the courts had been concerned about the start of desegregation, not with performance standards, greatest attention was devoted to the recalcitrance of the Deep South, not the partial movement in other parts of the South.

One of the reasons the guidelines may not have accomplished what they might have done is that instead of using Title VI's fund cutoff provision, the Justice Department used the slower and less productive method of bringing lawsuits against districts not living up to their desegregation plans. Yet this method did result in some accomplishments. Freed from having to deal with many cases by the new administrative action, the courts were able to deal with new issues such as the meaning and operation of "freedom of choice" plans. Moreover, when the guideline enforcement effort slowed down, going to court provided a way to beef it up. Just as desegregation efforts had moved from the courts to administrative action related to the court's rulings, so they moved back to the courts. And because of some serious difficulties in the guideline enforcement effort—such as the debacle involved in withholding funds from the Chicago school system—further court action was almost necessary before anything more could be done administratively. Yet the judicial action turned out not to be sufficient by itself. It did not guarantee further administrative activity perhaps because when Supreme Court victories were won in 1968 and 1969 the Nixon administration rather than the early Johnson administration was the one which had to carry out the enforcement. In other words, civil rights groups had gone back to court to get improvements in the guidelines but the administrators generally wouldn't go along, or at least would not incorporate some of the new victories in the administrative standards. One thus had the irony of the Court taking forceful action only at a time when those willing to follow through administratively were leaving the scene or had already left.

Where does the Supreme Court fit into this administrative story? We must recognize that, in the absence of both the Civil Rights Act and the financial inputs of the Elementary and Secondary Education Act, earlier Supreme Court firmness and particularity on school desegregation might not have produced as substantial results. Yet had the administrators been able to start earlier, the courts also could have moved sooner to issues not handled in the guidelines, as they did when the HEW Guidelines were developed. In short, firmer initial Supreme Court action might have accelerated the whole process. Given the ultimate reliance on court decisions as the test of what was required by the administrative officials, both because of the "legislative history" of Title VI and the lack of any other standard, the Supreme Court missed an opportunity to have greater influence. Of course, had court decisions been stronger, Title VI might not have been tied to them, but the Court could have given the other two branches something more with which to work. While there may have been some warrant for the fear that once it began to regulate, the Court would have had to become a "super school board" immersed in detail, whatever the reality the Court's post-*Brown* hands-off strategy allowed most southern judges to avoid following *Brown*'s thrust. The Court would have produced far more desegregation with either an initial flat "forthwith" order strengthening the hand of local school officials and the federal district judges or some other "message" conveying more to those who were watching.

A particular area in which the Court missed an opportunity was faculty desegregation. Had faculties been desegregated, the entire school desegregation process probably would have moved faster. White teachers in black schools would have ended the idea of "all-Negro equals inferior," and blacks might have been more willing to enter previously all-white schools if at least a few black teachers were there. Instead, the Court appears to have taken the same position that Office of Education officials later did, feeling that to force the issue would increase resistance by state and local school officials.[99] Yet without guidance from the Court, local pressures tended to take over—in other problem areas as well as this one—reinforced by the general workings of the federal judicial system in which it was difficult to get into federal court to invalidate state laws and in which federal judges were unwilling to question or test the motives of state officials. The result was often unconscionable delay in either starting or carrying out the implementation of desegregation and a further "stretch-out" once the process of compliance was finally begun. As our examples have shown, the Court often seemed willing to tolerate it, even though there may have been good reason to leave particular decisions alone. Only in 1968 and 1969 was the Court to adopt a different and more forceful posture. Yet, before we can examine what happened then, we need to look at cases which were brought to the Court in the mid-1960s, at the time the administrative activity described here was taking place. We should not leave the impression that no judicial action was taking place, for there was some—both in the South and, increasingly, in the North.

9

Although the focus of action shifted to HEW in 1964 and 1965, action in the courts was not at a standstill. During this period, a number of decisions on school desegregation, including federal funding of schools and the pace of desegregation, were forthcoming from the courts, and school litigation from the North also appeared. The Supreme Court continued to decide many cases by denying review or by giving only per curiam rulings. Before it reached the question of federal funding for schoolchildren, the Court had had an opportunity to deal with federal funding of hospitals. Negro doctors and patients who had been discriminated against by a North Carolina private hospital, a recipient of federal Hill-Burton Act funds, had sought a federal court declaratory judgment that the Hill-Burton Act clause which allowed use of federal funds to construct segregated hospitals was unconstitutional. The district court, looking at day-to-day control, had found that hospitals were not agents of the state, that tax exemptions and state licensing were not state action, and that government contributions did not constitute governmental control.[90] The government permitted segregation but did not require it, the court ruled. The following year the Fourth Circuit reversed this decision on the basis of the recently decided *Burton* public accommodations case. The Hill-Burton clause allowing exceptions to its nondiscrimination provision was declared unconstitutional on the grounds that the hospital's receipt of Hill-Burton funds indicated a pattern of state and federal involvement. When the state chose to direct Hill-Burton money to private hospitals to avoid desegregation, those hospitals became agents of the state subject to Fourteenth Amendment prohibitions. Both the hospital and the state asked the Supreme Court for a hearing, and the United States submitted an amicus brief favoring the appeals court's decision. The Supreme Court refused review,[91] surely lending strength to the Fourth Circuit's ruling but doing so through the least active role possible. Its action was particularly noteworthy because a federal statute had been invalidated.

Questions about segregation in local schools receiving federal funds were raised for the first time in two school cases denied review in the 1964–65 period. Before passage of ESEA, some Louisiana school districts were receiving federal "impact" financial assistance because of enrollment of children of service personnel from nearby military bases. Seeking to affect racially discriminatory practices, the United States brought a federal court suit to bar racial segregation of the "federal" children on the basis of the districts' previous assurances that they would treat children of service personnel "on the same terms, in accordance with the laws of the state" as they treated local children. Also raised in the suits were questions whether the United States could use judicial proceedings to obtain specific performance of the assurances and whether, independent of them, the government could sue on behalf of its personnel. Unsuccessful in the Fifth Circuit, the United States sought review by the Supreme Court, Solicitor General Cox emphasizing the adverse rulings' potential for casting doubt upon promissory assurances exacted as conditions of other federal grants, particularly terminal ones like those for the construction of various facilities. Applicability of rulings on these issues to other areas such as federal assistance to home builders could also be foreseen. The Court declined to hear either case.[92] Perhaps the Court wished to stay out of this area of federal assistance until Congress acted, particularly as the denial of review did not bar the federal government from attempting to use nonjudicial means to enforce nonsegregation assurances.

Two other school cases during this mid-decade period did not involve funding but had particularly racist overtones. In one, a group of white students in Georgia brought suit challenging *Brown* on grounds that it had been based upon false testimony. They argued that the state should not be forbidden by the Fourteenth Amendment from classifying its school-children on the basis of racial characteristics having educational significance—that is, differing educational aptitudes—even though such classification might result in continued separation in the schools by race. The students lost in the lower courts, and Georgia requested a Supreme Court hearing, supported by amicus briefs submitted by Virginia, North Carolina, Mississippi, Arkansas, Louisiana, Alabama, and South Carolina. The Court refused to grant the petition.[93] In the other case, Mississippi school officials, arguing that "education" and not "mixing" was the paramount consideration and that as school officials they could best determine how to achieve this goal, tried to assert that innate differences in aptitude between the races provided a reasonable basis for classifying and assigning children by race. The Fifth Circuit ruled that this could not justify continued school segregation, and the Supreme Court let the ruling stand.[94]

A possible change in the Court's tone could be seen in two cases involving the speed of desegregation. In the per curiam order in each case was the curt announcement that "delays in desegregation of school systems are no longer tolerable." The first order, in *Bradley v. School Board of Richmond,* covered a consolidation of two Virginia suits. School desegregation plans had been approved by the district court without hearing despite plaintiffs' charge that faculty members were allocated on a racial basis under the plans. The Supreme Court, saying that "delays in desegregating school systems are no longer tolerable," unanimously vacated and remanded the ruling to the district courts for full evidentiary hearings. The second, *Rogers v. Paul,* involved a class action suit seeking to bring about and to speed up pupil and faculty desegregation of the Fort Smith, Arkansas, high schools, based both on *Brown* and "extent of curriculum" grounds. The Court's brief and unsigned order, described as "pending immediate desegregation" of the schools, commanded the immediate transfer of the Negro petitioner to an all-white high school and suggested that others similarly situated might transfer as well. While there was no dissent on the merits, Justices Clark, Harlan, White, and Fortas dissented from the summary disposition, indicating they would have set the case for argument and full consideration. In these two per curiam orders the Court discarded its rule of "all deliberate speed" and indicated that school cases representing still unreviewed modes of retarding desegregation were subject to peremptory disposition. However clear the abandonment of "with all deliberate speed" may now seem, the decisions were not to have the effect of getting school boards to move. The low visibility of the brief per curiam orders had much to do with this. If the Court was trying to convey that "all deliberate speed" was on its way out, one may question whether decisions of this sort were the way to accomplish it; certainly those who did not wish to move quickly appeared not to have heard the word. If this was the absolute end of "with all deliberate speed," as some scholars claim, *Alexander v. Holmes County* four years later would not have been necessary.

Although northern school cases were to be of substantial importance for the Court in the 1970s, some cases appeared as early as the mid-1960s. Some of these cases involved a problem supposedly restricted to the North—de facto segregation—while others were from the North but involved the same issues to be found in southern litigation, for which those rulings obviously had relevance. On the question of de facto segregation, the Court refused a hearing to cases which had gone in opposite directions below. In a case from New Rochelle, New York, a federal district judge, affirmed by the Second Circuit, had held the "neighborhood school" policy of the school board unconstitutional because it resulted in the school in the predominantly Negro residential area having a black enrollment of 94 percent. The district judge attributed this to the board's deliberate drawing of school zone lines. He reasoned that there was no legal or moral distinction between segregation established by the formality of a dual system of education, as in *Brown,* and that created by gerrymandering districts and transferring students, and he concluded that the Constitution imposed upon the board a duty to end segregation. The Court denied review in 1961.[95] In Gary, Indiana, Negro pupils had argued that the Fourteenth Amendment required a school board to take steps consistent with sound and rational educational administration to remedy racial imbalance where the board was administering a compulsory public school system in which virtually all Negro students were confined to totally or predominantly Negro schools. The school board was alleged to violate the requirement of equal educational opportunity mandated by the Fourteenth Amendment by acquiescing in the existence of segregation or a racially imbalanced school system. The federal district judge refused to accept the pupils' contention that the school board maintained a constitutionally prohibited segregated school system. Blaming the segregation on housing rather than conscious school board policy, he declared that racial balance in the public schools was not constitutionally mandated. The Court of Appeals for the Seventh Circuit affirmed this judgment, holding that nothing in the Constitution required that a school system honestly developed on the neighborhood school plan must be destroyed or abandoned because the resulting effect was one of racial imbalance. The conflict in holdings between the Seventh Circuit (Gary) and the earlier Second Circuit (New Rochelle) rulings was used as the basis for asking the Supreme Court to review the case. The Court's refusal to deal with the issue in 1964 led to the removal of a provision specifically prohibiting de facto segregation from the Civil Rights Act's Title VI.[96]

Another case based largely on de facto issues came from Kansas City, Kansas, when a group of Negro parents assisted by "Inc. Fund" counsel contended that the school board, contrary to the directive of *Brown* and the mandate of the Fourteenth Amendment, had engaged in policies and activities which had increased and entrenched rather than alleviated racial segregation in the school system—for example, dividing an elementary school district for junior high school assignment purposes in such a way that the majority of pupils were channeled into a school in which their race was predominant. The parents contended that not the school board's public pronouncements but their acts should determine the question of intent and good faith. The district court ruled that the board had acted in good faith by drawing the line on the basis of population studies indicating predictable pupil loads and the number of pupils that each of the junior high schools could accommodate. The Tenth Circuit affirmed, holding that although the Fourteenth Amendment prohibited segregation it did not command integration of the races in the public schools. Negro children had no constitutional right to have white children in school with them, the judges said. Repeating its New Rochelle and Gary posture, the Supreme Court in 1965 denied the parents a hearing, but this time Justice Douglas indicated he would have granted certiorari.[97]

Despite statements by the Court itself that conflicts between the lower appellate courts and "the importance of the question" are principal reasons for granting review, the Court does not always grant review where intercircuit conflicts exist, even when the issue is important—as de facto segregation certainly was and is. These three northern school segregation cases make this clear. They also reinforce the idea that the Court takes cases it feels like taking—on the basis of the direction the justices want to go and their view of the Court's overall constitutional strategy. As the New Rochelle, Gary, and Kansas City cases, which would have brought *Brown* bluntly home to the North, suggest, when accepting cases might endanger the political viability of the Court or of its strategy in a particular area, the review will be refused.

The first of the cases from the North which was not strictly speaking a "northern case," *McNeese v. Board of Education,* involved questions of exhaustion of remedies and was decided by the Court in 1962 with full opinion. Negro students had claimed that the school they were required to attend was zoned to be exclusively Negro and that white students who had been moved there because of overcrowding in a nearby white school were segregated within the building by means of separate entrances and classrooms. The lower federal court had granted the school officials' motion to dismiss, and the Court of Appeals had affirmed. The Negro students then appealed to the Supreme Court. That they had not first sought relief under a state law providing a remedy should not be a reason for ruling against them, they said, because the remedy was not available in practice. The Supreme Court speaking through Justice Douglas ruled that plaintiffs' federal case should proceed to a hearing, as it was by no means clear that Illinois law provided an administrative remedy sufficient to preclude prior resort to a federal court to protect federal rights. Other provisions of state law seemed to make the federal rights asserted subject to such tenuous protection that prior resort to a state court was certainly not necessary, said Douglas. Only Harlan disagreed, saying local authorities should hear the claims first. This case was the first full opinion case since *Cooper* and the Court's first explicit statement on exhaustion of remedies, more than five years after the issue had been raised in the Court in cases from the Fourth and Fifth Circuits. The ruling potentially affected many districts, but it came too late to assist in prompt implementation of *Brown*.

Three other northern cases in the 1964–65 period were relevant to the southern situation. They dealt with specific remedies taken to eliminate desegregation. As with most of the purely southern cases, the Court decided to hear none of them. In the first, the state courts had held that the New York City Board of Education might use racial considerations in fixing the boundaries of a new junior high school scheduled to be constructed in Brooklyn, which the board had done in such a way that no transfers had to be made within existing districts to achieve a viable racial balance. The court construed *Brown II* not to compel affirmative integration by such practices as busing or to allow use of a quota system but expressly to authorize school boards to take race into consideration in delineating school zones. The case thus presented in its simplest form the question of whether a school board could take race into account in determining educational policy. The Court declined to hear the case,[98] perhaps because a decision impinged on the larger de facto segregation problem the Court was avoiding.

Two other cases raised the question of the constitutionality of the so-called Princeton Plan for pairing predominantly white and Negro schools to achieve a better racial balance in each. One contested pairing in Malverne, Long Island, elementary schools had been ordered by New York Commissioner of Education James E. Allen, Jr., after a fact-finding committee had found the racial imbalance in the Malverne area to be a classic case of de facto segregation caused by racial neighborhood patterns and not by discriminatory acts of local officials. Although the committee had found no gerrymandering, overcrowding, or disparity in the quality of the school facilities or instruction, it declared that racial imbalance, no matter what its cause, created social, psychological, and educational problems that local school officials must correct. Three white parents challenged the commissioner's action, contending they were deprived of equal protection of laws or liberty without due process of law by the exclusion of their children from the neighborhood schools and by their transfer to more distant schools solely to achieve a racial mixture. The New York Court of Appeals ruled that the commissioner's directive, being neither arbitrary nor illegal, was not subject to judicial review.

In asking the Supreme Court for a hearing, the parents warned that unless the Court was prepared to countenance the compulsory ethnic dispersion of Jews, Catholics, and others on a quota basis the pairing plan should be declared unconstitutional. The Court declined to hear the case.[99] In so doing, it left standing decisions like the earlier New Rochelle ruling supporting affirmative action to correct racial imbalance in a case in which not direct legal segregation but housing patterns had resulted in school segregation. When a second New York case involving a challenge to a school pairing was similarly refused a hearing,[100] a strong indication was given that federal courts would not disturb action taken under the Princeton Plan. In fact, the commissioner of education came out of these cases with a strengthened hand and virtually unlimited discretion in dealing with school desegregation. Through inaction, the Court was thus both able once again to avoid having to rule frontally on the matter of de facto segregation and to leave undisturbed a situation in which those seeking the ends which it seemed to espouse operated from a position of strength. It thus gained time for formulation of comprehensive and persuasive arguments by those dedicated to affirmative abolition of de facto segregation. The busing issue had not been involved here; hence the possibility of a later test on that question remained. The cases also indicate that the Court was willing to show deference to state officials not only when they might be thought to work out basic means of compliance with *Brown* if left alone but also when they already were moving on their own in advance of the Court's doctrine.

These cases in the somewhat more than a decade since *Brown I,* reinforced by Title VI and the HEW Guidelines, set the stage for the Court's end-of-1960s action on school desegregation. Yet the Court had been concerned with other race relations policy areas in addition to education. Besides miscegenation and gifts of land, at which we have already looked, there was activity in housing, voting, and access to public facilities, transportation, and places of public accommodations—areas to which we now turn.

Chapter 7

Housing and Voting Rights: Sustaining the Statutes

D URING the late 1950s and early 1960s, while devoting substantial attention to the plight of the black minority, the Court was also trying to cope with other controversial areas of the law. These other areas provided the strategic environment in which the Court decided its race relations cases. Before we turn to examine the Court's treatment of housing and voting rights cases, a brief examination will help us understand more fully what the Supreme Court did—or did not do—after *Brown II*.

Perhaps the most prominent mid-1950s battleground was that of internal security, to which the Warren Court turned after *Brown*. In *Pennsylvania v. Nelson* (1956), the Court invalidated a state law that had been applied to a person accused of subversion of the national government; the justices held that federal internal security laws preempted the field. Then, in the *Slochower* case, the Court held that New York could not dismiss a professor who had invoked the Fifth Amendment before a Senate investigating committee. The House Un-American Activities Committee found its contempt power circumscribed in the *Watkins* case, in which the Court held that the committee had asked questions not pertinent to its investigation. Chief Justice Warren coupled the Court's decision with criticism of the committee, of the ambiguity of the resolution by which it was established, and of the House of Representatives for not having supervised the committee's work. The Court also limited the reach of the Smith Act's provisions concerning conspiracy to overthrow the government by force and violence. Mere abstract advocacy of overthrow not accompanied by specific incitation to violence could not constitutionally be prohibited, the Court said in *Yates v. United States*. The Court next ruled, in *Jencks v. United States*, that, as a condition of proceeding with a criminal prosecution in which FBI agents would testify, the government must make available to the defense the written reports of the FBI agents who would testify. The cumulative effect of these decisions, coming as they did immediately after southern hatred of the Court for the *Brown* decision had developed, led to a number of serious efforts in Congress to reduce the Court's jurisdiction.[1]

Although these efforts to contain the Court did not become law, they were not lost on the Court. The "Southern Manifesto" had not produced retreat, and the criticism by the state chief justices had not led to dilution of the force of the Court's Little Rock decision, but the latter criticism— based in large measure on these internal security decisions—and the congressional attempts led the Court to "back off" from the full force of some of its rulings. Thus in the 1959 *Barenblatt* decision the Court found that there was no First Amendment "right of silence," and ruled that a person could be held in contempt of Congress if he failed to answer pertinent questions. The same year the Court held that an employee could be dismissed for failure to answer questions about Communist affiliations if the discharge was couched in terms of "doubtful trust and reliability" of the employee.[2] Also in 1959 the Court held that states could enforce their own state internal security laws and carry out investigations of subversives.[3] A Supreme Court taking this defensive action was not likely to engage in bold initiatives in the desegregation area. However, after the turmoil over internal security had died down in the 1960s, the Court was able to resume its work in the race relations field more easily. The Court was able also to edge back to the liberal side in the internal security area, qualifying and hedging its 1958–59 decisional pattern.[4] But other civil liberties problems had come to compete for the Court's attention. These included free speech questions, reapportionment, school prayer, and criminal procedure.

Obscenity provides a bridge between the late 1950s and the late 1960s. The Court's key case was *Roth v. United States* (1957). In a decision which seemed to reflect strategy much more than legality, the Court on the one hand ruled that obscenity was not protected as free speech but on the other hand so defined obscenity that it was difficult to obtain convictions.[5] Later, other elements were added: to be obscene something had to be "utterly without redeeming social importance," but one could judge material aimed at a particular group in terms of that group's standards, material aimed at children could be judged by different and less strict standards than those used for adults, and the way material was advertised was held to constitute part of the definition of whether or not it was obscene.[6] Another major area of free speech law opened up by the Court concerned libel, particularly suits brought by public officials against their critics. The Court's major ruling in this area, in 1964, was *New York Times v. Sullivan,* which involved a libel suit brought by the Police Commissioner of Montgomery, Alabama, over an advertisement protesting police brutality against those trying to achieve their civil rights. Sullivan, who had not been mentioned by name in the ad, won a judgment of $500,000 in the Alabama courts against the Reverend Ralph David Abernathy, whose group had placed the ad, and the *Times.* In deciding in favor of Abernathy and the *Times,* the Supreme Court declined to decide the case on the easily available narrow grounds that an impersonal attack could not be used to show personal libel, and said that public officials could not collect for libel unless they could show that the allegedly libelous statement was made with "malice"—that is, when it was known to be false or it was made "with reckless disregard of whether or not it was false." The new standard, a sharp departure from the common law of libel, helped protect the rights of those directing commentary at public officials.

In 1960, the Court had invalidated a particularly blatant attempt to disfranchise black voters. The Alabama legislature had redrawn the boundaries of the city of Tuskegee in such a way as to exclude all but a few black residents. The day after the bill was enacted, the local newspapers made much of the "joke" that the blacks had suddenly "moved out of town." Although the statute was neutral on its face—merely revising the city's borders—the Court sensed a particularly frontal and basic challenge to desegregation, and the Court, in *Gomillion v. Lightfoot,* overturned the legislature's action. Two years later, the Court began its active thrust into the "political thicket" of reapportionment by ruling in *Baker v. Carr* that reapportionment claims could indeed be heard by the courts. Despite Justice Frankfurter's doomsday dissent in *Baker,* in which he claimed that the Court was going to ruin its future over this issue, the Court, in rulings Chief Justice Warren was later to say were the most important of his career on the Court, went on to require "one man-one vote" reapportionment for congressional districts (*Wesberry v. Sanders*) and districts in both houses of state legislatures (*Reynolds v. Sims*).[7] The Court's rulings elicited substantial reaction, most notably the unsuccessful attempt by Senator Dirksen (R-Ill.) to amend the Constitution to allow one house of each state legislature to be apportioned on the basis of factors other than population. However, reapportionment took place with relative ease, and the attacks abated as those dependent on underpopulated districts were reapportioned out of office or were joined by legislators from the many new urban and suburban districts.[8] Thus Frankfurter's dire prophecies failed to materialize, the Court probably felt confirmed in its liberal attitudes, and Frankfurter's dissent may have had the ironic effect of encouraging the Warren Court to stick to its guns. The Court was not likely to pull back as it had done in the late 1950s in internal security.

The reapportionment cases were also important for their possible relation to the area of race relations. The justices might have been concerned only to assert simply as a matter of principle that each person was entitled to the franchise equally without regard to where he or she lived.

However, by providing districts of equal size so that urban blacks could elect legislators of their own race the Court may have used these cases to help blacks work "on their own" for certain goals. In this view, the cases were a supplement to the Court's other rulings providing and guaranteeing blacks' access to the franchise. If people were able to utilize the ballot rather than the law as a primary tool, the Court would have been relieved of considerable work load at the same time the thrust of its desegregation decisions was reinforced.

After reapportionment, the Court chose an issue—prayer in the public schools—which was to produce massive noncompliance[9] and another attempt to amend the Constitution to overrule the Court. The justices first declared unconstitutional New York's state-composed compulsory prayer in *Engel v. Vitale,* provoking one congressman to say, "They've put the Reds in the schools; now they've taken God out." A year later, in *Abington School District v. Schempp,* compulsory Bible-reading and recitation of the Lord's Prayer in public schools were invalidated. Noncompliance with the Supreme Court was greatest in the South, perhaps because school prayer was used heavily there but also probably as a result of earlier resistance to the Court's school desegregation rulings, which now undoubtedly was reinforced. Certainly the school prayer controversy did nothing to help the Court's legitimacy in the South or to assist with post-*Brown* desegregation compliance.

Apart from its desegregation rulings, the Warren Court is perhaps best known for its "criminal procedure revolution." In the 1960s, although continuing to use the doctrine of "selective incorporation"—that only portions of the Bill of Rights were intended to be included or incorporated in the Fourteenth Amendment as prohibitions against the states—the justices read into the Due Process Clause almost all of the relevant sections of the Bill of Rights. The "revolution" started in 1961 when the Court ruled in *Mapp v. Ohio* that improperly seized material could not be introduced is state criminal trials. Two years later the Court ruled in the famous *Gideon* case that indigents accused of felonies and major misdemeanors were entitled to have an attorney appointed to represent them in court. These two decisions were followed by the *Escobedo* and *Miranda* cases, which provoked the ire of the law enforcement community and its congressional supporters.[10]

Escobedo involved the Chicago Police Department's refusal to let Danny Escobedo and his attorney see each other during a station house interrogation, at which the police obtained a confession. The Supreme Court's decision invalidating the confession can be read as dealing only with the right of access to one's own attorney, but broad language used by the justices raised fears that all defendants had a right to have an appointed lawyer represent them during interrogation. That latter issue was resolved by the Supreme Court in the *Miranda* ruling in which the Court held that no confession obtained during an in-custody interrogation was valid unless the person being questioned had been properly informed of his rights. Because few persons realized at the time that relatively few convictions depended on confessions or that persons warned of their rights would continue to answer policemen's questions, the reaction to the ruling was vehement and negative. The Court did not back off in the face of this massive criticism nor did it stop extending Bill of Rights protections to defendants in the states[11] or imposing new limits in the area of search-and-seizure.[12] In fact, while Congress was passing the Omnibus Crime Control and Safe Streets Act of 1968 as part of its reaction to the Court, the Court announced its decision in *Duncan v. Louisiana* extending the right of jury trial to the states.

The Court did hand down a number of decisions favoring the law enforcement position, for example, in *Terry v. Ohio* upholding a limited "stop-and-frisk" by police of those acting suspiciously even when probable cause for an arrest did not exist,[13] but those decisions were generally ignored in the outpouring of negative rhetoric. Fahlund has argued that at least some of the Court's pro–law enforcement decisions were "consciously formulated" to calm the Court's critics. He notes a close relation between percentages of both the Court's decisions and the justices' votes not favoring the defendant, on the one hand, and the levels of opposition to the Court, on the other.[14] The Court's response to critcism of its law enforcement rulings is even clearer, Fahlund says, in the decisions as to whether to grant retroactive application to the new constitutional rules, where the justices' interest in the effects on law enforcement was quite evident both from their questions at oral argument[15] and from frequent references in their opinions. The Court responded to its critics by limiting the effect of its earlier rulings so that a general "jail delivery" would not occur,[16] although the result was doctrinal inconsistency which can be explained only as a "political response by the Court to its hostile publics" allowing the Court to build up public confidence which might allow greater judicial activity at a later date.[17]

The Warren Court may have become better known today for its criminal procedure work than for its landmark race relations decisions, in part because the criminal procedure rulings came later. Yet the two were related—in more than the sense that the race relations rulings provided the strategic environment for the criminal procedure cases. The Court's feelings about law enforcement may have been formed in part by what it had seen of the open use of southern law enforcement to aid segregation and to repress demonstrations. More importantly, it appears that the Court was motivated by the desire to help blacks achieve equality. Thus, holding back from dealing with the criminal procedure area may have been unavoidable because of the disproportionately greater involvement of blacks in the criminal justice system and the prejudice to which they were and are subjected in that system. Rules developed for all defendants would certainly benefit blacks. Thus we see the possibility, stronger than with respect to reapportionment, that the Court used its rulings across a broad front in the aid of attaining the dominant goal of equality.

2

Outside of school desegregation, housing and voting rights are two of the most important areas of race relations, both because of the basic importance of the rights and because of their intimate relationship to education and to the efforts of minorities to achieve equal rights. Not only is voting the most basic right of citizenship, but, as we have noted, it provides a way for minorities to seek redress of grievances and work toward equality through the electoral process without the Court's help. Housing and school desegregation are closely related, as the question of de facto segregation resulting from housing patterns makes clear. While the Court was reluctant to deal with that subject, it might have ruled on the discriminatory acts which assisted in producing the patterns. Yet although a number of cases involving such crucial matters as public housing and urban renewal were proffered to the Court for decision, the Court did little about housing until 1967 and 1968. The Court simply did not avail itself of early opportunities to try to bring about school desegregation through forceful action against housing discrimination.

In addition to their basic substantive importance, housing and voting rights are important for another reason, the basis on which the Court decided cases in the two areas. In many areas of race relations such as education and public accommodations, the Supreme Court was faced with constitutional questions which were difficult to avoid—although not completely unavoidable, as we shall see in public accommodations—because there was little federal statutory law. The interpretation of that law would have been the Court's preference, particularly with its post-1937 habit of deference to the congressional will, as we have seen with respect to transportation. In the absence of a statute, there was no way the Court could have shifted from a request to answer the question, "Is this discriminatory action a violation of the Fourteenth Amendment?" to the far easier question, "Did Congress have the power to deal with this discriminatory activity?" Yet unlike other areas, the Court's actions with respect to housing and voting rights turned on congressional enactments. The Court initially did not have a statute on which to rely in deciding housing cases, but by the end of the Warren Court it ultimately used both new (1968) and old (1866) statutes in deciding its key case in the area, thus making its prime business reinforcement of congressional activity. Reliance on and reinforcement of newly passed statutes was even clearer in the area of voting rights. The white primary cases had been decided on direct constitutional grounds, but activity after the mid-1950s revolved around the Voting Rights Acts of 1957 and 1960, one part of the Civil Rights Act of 1964, and the Voting Rights Act of 1965, the major piece of legislation on the subject. The questions under the early 1957 and 1960 statutes were ones of interpretation; the questions under the major 1965 enactment were those of both interpretation and constitutionality.

In the housing area *Shelley* in 1948 and its follow-up cases in 1950 were the last the Supreme Court was to hear and decide for quite some time. Perhaps because of the inaction of both the other branches of government even after the Court's strong statement on enforcement of restrictive covenants, it was not until the mid-1960s that the Court accepted and decided a housing case. Not many such cases were presented to the Court, perhaps in recognition of the Court's avoidance of that area but perhaps more the result of the Court's preoccupation with other areas such as education and voting. New issues such as public housing and state fair housing laws were presented, giving the Court an opportunity to get involved, despite its obvious disinclination to do so.

The first public housing case involved the Public Housing Administration (PHA), a part of the Federal Housing Administration. The PHA did not require local projects to have "open occupancy" rules. Where segregated housing was made compulsory by local groups involved in PHA-supported projects, attempts were sometimes made to require the federal agency to withdraw its funding. The PHA contended that because of its location in the District of Columbia such suits were procedurally impossible, since jurisdiction could not be obtained against the local housing authorities who should be joined in any such suit against the PHA in the District's courts. Perhaps through a tactical error, the PHA submitted defenses on the merits in one segregation suit in a local authority's district in Georgia, and the Fifth Circuit held that it had thereby submitted itself to jurisdiction, regardless of subsequently submitted venue arguments. The district court then held that the plaintiff did not apply properly for housing and thus lacked standing to raise the constitutional issues. Despite its earlier holding in a bus case that it was not necessary to test personally and undergo arrest for a law which clearly denied a right in order to bring suit to assert the right in general, the Fifth Circuit affirmed, in *Cohen v. Public Housing Authority,* but was more forthright in indicating the real reason behind its ruling. The judges stated in effect that in their opinion the real constitutional issue here should not be pressed, because "actual segregation is essential to the success of a program of public housing in Savannah."

In his petition asking the Supreme Court to review this first housing case to reach the Supreme Court since *Brown II,* NAACP counsel Thurgood Marshall argued that contrary to the lower courts' rulings the plaintiff had standing to sue to require the PHA to adopt a policy of racial equity in housing projects, even though she had failed to prove formal application to and exclusion from a particular project—an application she contended would have been futile. Marshall further argued that the due process requirements of the Fifth and Fourteenth Amendments imposed a constitutional duty on the PHA to refrain from approving and aiding racially segregated public housing. On the contrary, the PHA was supposed to require availability on a nondiscriminatory basis. For the PHA, Solicitor General J. Lee Rankin, arguing against certiorari, said that both courts below had found that the petitioner had never attempted to apply for admission to any of the projects and that she thus had no standing to sue. This position was seconded by the Housing Authority of Savannah, Georgia, locally involved in the case. In denying certiorari in 1959, the Supreme Court seemed to be acquiescing in the Fifth Circuit's strategic considerations. Perhaps because of its experience with the *Shelley* case a decade earlier, during which the FHA—the PHA parent agency—had rescinded its recommendation of the use of restrictive covenants in housing, subsequently making further progress, the Court felt that for the time being matters would be better left to the discretion of the federal agency which controlled the standards of the local authorities it funded.

Less than a year later a similar case involving some FHA federal funds, *Barnes v. City of Gadsden,* came to the Court, and Negro complainants again failed in an attempt to stop a housing program which would perpetuate racial segregation. Here the challenge was to the validity of urban redevelopment plans which, it was alleged, were expressly designed to effectuate residential racial segregation. Relief was sought to prevent private redevelopers from discriminating between purchasers on the basis of race. The Fifth Circuit held that there was no threat of immediate injury to the complainants, and dismissed the case over Judge Rives's dissent that the court should make a declaration that redevelopers in the renewal area might not discriminate. The Supreme Court refused to review this ruling, thus leaving the litigants without recourse until after the renewal project was completed, when suit might be brought to prove discrimination by redevelopers.

Two more housing cases were denied a hearing by the Court later in the same term. The *Levitt* case, the first, involved a New Jersey fair housing statute. Levitt the builder had challenged the jurisdiction of the state Division Against Discrimination, which had ruled that Levitt's refusal to sell to a Negro violated the state antidiscrimination law covering FHA-insured housing. The state court upheld the constitutionality of the law, as did the New Jersey Supreme Court. The latter said that appellants had shown no actual injury because of the requirement and ruled that publicly assisted housing was a "reasonable" classification especially in view of a pressing need for adequate housing for minority groups. Levitt asked the Supreme Court to review the case on appeal, challenging the constitutionality of the state law, but the division argued that congressional failure to adopt antidiscrimination provisions in enacting the various FHA laws did not equal a congressional policy forbidding states to do so. The Supreme Court did not rule on the question, dismissing the case per curiam "for want of a substantial federal question," with only Justice Black indicating that the Court should have taken the case to give it a full hearing. The implication of the dismissal was that if the state courts construing such a law upheld it, this was the final word on it at least for the time being.

The term's other case, *Bernstein v. Real Estate Commission,* concerned a real estate broker, not a developer, but also involved a state fair housing law which prohibited misrepresentation by real estate brokers. The law was enforced by the state Real Estate Commission by means of the state's licensing authority. Bernstein, the broker, and his associate apparently specialized in sales of residential properties to Negroes in formerly all-white areas. His license had been suspended as a result of "block-busting," particularly the posting of a "sold" sign on property not in fact sold, with the alleged intent of soliciting sale of property in the area on the ground of loss of value due to the entry into the neighborhood of persons of another race. The commission had held that his practices were intended to promote panic and instability in the vicinity of the falsely posted "sold" sign for the purpose of exploiting and capitalizing on existing prejudices to obtain as many listings as possible and depreciate property values. Appealing the suspensions in the state courts, the brokers had contended that the complaints upon which the commission had acted constituted unlawful conspiracy against the civil rights of themselves and their customers in that in substance the complaints were intended to prevent Negroes from purchasing and occupying homes of their own selection, in violation of constitutional guarantees. The brokers, showing considerable *chutzpah,* thus attempted to capitalize on the rights of Negroes to whom they hoped to sell the property, at the expense of the white owners from whom they were virtually extorting property. A municipal court, declaring that the Real Estate Commission was not concerned with "block-busting" but with dishonest practices, affirmed the commission's findings and conclusions, and the Maryland Court of Appeals affirmed that ruling, maintaining that it would not further consider the brokers' discrimination charges because the question was not specifically before it. The brokers tried to appeal their case, but the Supreme Court agreed with

Maryland's position by dismissing "for want of a substantial federal question," as it had done in *Levitt*. Although the Supreme Court's support had been at best indirect, state court enforcement of fair practices statutes could thereafter be expected to continue undisturbed by the federal judiciary.

The problem of state court invalidation of state fair housing laws or denial of enforcement still remained, however, and arose in a case the following term to which the Court was also to deny a hearing in 1962. Washington's law prohibited discrimination based on race or national origin in publicly assisted housing, but the Washington Supreme Court had held that the statute contravened the Fourteenth Amendment's Equal Protection Clause by unreasonably discriminating against owners of publicly assisted housing in favor of owners who did not obtain public loans to build their homes. Concurring judges argued that the state constitution guaranteed the right to voluntary sale, while the dissent cited *Levitt's* holding that publicly assisted housing was a reasonable category under the state's police power. The Supreme Court refused to grant certiorari,[18] but Chief Justice Warren and Justice Stewart dissented, saying they would have vacated the judgment and remanded to determine if the lower court's ruling was based on adequate nonfederal grounds. Their comment points to the possibility of nonfederal considerations which could have gone into the decision, but the result was at least temporarily negative with respect to the open housing cause.

Another case from the North which the Court also turned aside, *Progress Development Corporation v. Deerfield Park District,* illustrated the legal complexity in the housing area. In 1959 the Progress Development Corporation, a Chicago group which had been seeking land in the suburbs for integrated housing for middle-class groups, bought land in Deerfield for construction of a subdivision of fifty-one homes ranging in price from $30,000 to $40,000. Considerable progress had been made on construction of two model homes when it became known locally that the developers intended to sell nearly one-quarter of the homes to Negro families. Opposition became vocal, and the city building commissioner, charging violations of the building codes, halted construction on the homes. The Deerfield Park Board met and agreed to condemn the land for six park sites, with the acquisition then being approved by more than two-to-one at a board-called referendum which produced a record voting turnout. The corporation then sued the city, charging deprivation of its right to hold and convey property. The trial record indicated plainly that the public protest had been racial in nature, but it was also evident that the park board had previously unsuccessfully sought approval of bond issues for more parks in the area. In addition, testimony showed that acquisition of the sites had been recommended before the corporation had acquired any land in the area, that a park was definitely needed there, and that these were the only available sites in that section of the park district where vacant land could be obtained for park purposes. Although the acquisition had not been approved prior to disclosure of the corporation's intentions to sell homes to Negroes, no evidence was presented proving conspiracy to discriminate on the part of any member of the park board, nor was any collusion between the city officials and the park district shown.

The corporation lost its case in the state courts, although the state supreme court had remanded it to the trial court for a decision whether the taking of the land was necessary and for a public purpose and on whether it was done to prevent the sale of homes to Negroes, thus interfering with equal protection and the right to do business. At this point, the corporation took the case to the Supreme Court, charging that the park board and the city had applied the eminent domain law in a racially discriminatory fashion. The Court denied review, probably being reinforced in its decision by the ambiguities of the case, by the necessity of judging motives, and by the fact that the state remand left the case without a final judgment below.

From a long-term perspective, this refusal meant that the Court had not heard any housing cases since 1953. Following the 1962 Term no cases involving racial discrimination in housing were brought before the Court until 1965, but when a case arose then the Court was again to deny certiorari. *Barnes v. Sind* involved a complicated contract default suit which resulted when developers of an all-white housing project in Maryland tried to avoid a contracted sale when they discovered that the would-be purchaser was a Negro. The Negro agreed to accept an "equivalent" but in his opinion less desirable house in another part of the development. When the developers refused to comply with this settlement agreement, Barnes brought a federal court action for specific performance of the contract and for damages caused by the delay, which resulted in award of a quitclaim deed and $1,500 in damages. He then appealed, claiming that the deed was deficient in not requiring inclusion of a special warranty as called for in the original agreement and as was customary in Maryland. Such a warranty would enable him to sue the defendants if subsequently he should sustain damages by reason of their failure to obtain joinder by the wife of one of the sellers in bar of her dower rights in the land. The Court of Appeals refused this request, commenting that it was doubtful the wife of the seller had any dower interest in the land and that in any event this should have been tested earlier. Despite a strong dissenting opinion, the judges further ruled that Barnes was not entitled to specific performance of the purchase terms because apparently he was not prepared to pay the full purchase price without deduction for any claimed defect in the property; the judges thus limited him to his damages for breach of contract.

In his brief asking the United States Supreme Court to review the case, counsel for Barnes argued that whereas in *Shelley* racial discrimination had been judicially assisted by the lower courts through a grant of specific performance, here the same was accomplished through refusal of specific performance. The situation was even worse here, counsel insisted, because in this case it was done by a federal rather than a state court. On the other side, counsel for respondents argued that Barnes had erred irrevocably in his failure to make Sind's wife also a party—thus limiting his possibilities of settlement under Maryland law—and in his failure to make a real contract and to be prepared to pay the full purchase price of the original house. The Court might have been thought to be more receptive to housing cases in 1965 than it had been earlier. It was, after all, three years after President Kennedy's executive order directing federal agencies to take action to prevent discrimination in the sale or rental of "residential property and related facilities" owned by or aided and assisted by the federal government.[19] However, the Court, perhaps feeling that this case was not the one to use to reenter the housing field, would have no more of it than of the earlier ones.

In 1967, the Court also turned away a case, *Green Street Association v. Daley,* involving urban renewal and the important question of federal agencies' primary responsibility to hear initial complaints in such matters. The case centered on a so-called conservation project in Chicago involving the bulldozing of about six hundred dwelling units to make way for parking lots, new streets, a pedestrian arcade, and other assets for a regional shopping center. The condemned dwellings, in an area into which blacks had begun moving in 1950, were 85 percent owned or occupied by blacks. They contended that housing segregation would be officially maintained by the project, that this project and others like it inevitably—and sometimes deliberately—destroyed housing occupied by minority groups, and that the persons displaced by such projects were relocated according to race. At the heart of the complaint was the allegation that the project was really a scheme to create a "no-Negro buffer zone" to make the shopping area more attractive to white patrons. The Green Street Association, a nonprofit neighborhood group, and 127 Negro residents of the area then sought an injunction. After a district court order that the suit be dismissed, in January 1967 the Seventh Circuit affirmed on grounds that such challenges to the taking of private property could be properly weighed in state court condemnation proceedings and that the 1964 Civil Rights Act did not give the residents and the association the right to sue the federal government to halt the program. The petitioners then asked the Supreme Court to hear the case, requesting that such urban renewal projects that perpetuate racially segregated housing be outlawed. They asserted that four-fifths of the homes and apartments to be demolished had been classified as "standard"—in other words, they were not slums. They further asserted that the city planned to relocate residents in the area "according to race, the policy and practice which the city of Chicago has in fact adhered to in prior urban renewal projects." Thus, they argued, those projects built with federal aid and approval were in violation of Title VI of the 1964 Civil Rights Act barring discrimination in federally assisted programs. The city of Chicago, urging the Court not to grant review, denied the allegation that segregation would be "officially maintained" by the project and argued that the Central Englewood project was a small part of a large urban renewal plan for the South Side which could not be judged discriminatory because the area was predominantly non-Negro when the project was originally planned. The city's position on the relocation plan was that it merely "recognizes the existence of racial concentration in existing housing patterns" and that as far as the official role in relocation was concerned "the city does not and cannot require displacees to relocate in any particular location—they are free to relocate wherever they please." The city also argued that the 127 Negroes who joined in the suit had failed to show they would suffer damages. In addition, the Justice Department suggested to the Court that it should stay out of the case on the theory that the complaint should have been directed to the Department of Housing and Urban Development (HUD), the responsible federal agency.

The Court did indeed not take the case, but it moved with considerable speed to hand down its ruling. The various petitions in the case had been filed and were ready for the Court's attention May 27, and just two days later, May 29, the Court issued its notice that the case would not be heard, Justice Douglas going on record to grant certiorari. The prompt action strongly demonstrated both the Court's sensitivity to the petitioners' plea when demolition of their homes had already begun and its awareness of the seriousness of the charges made. Its speed in making certain it would not cause further delay in the misdirected appeal, perhaps the most the Court thought it could do for the petitioners, also indicated the Court's feeling following the advice of the Justice Department that deference to existing law required application to the appropriate federal agency before resort to action by the Court.

3

The first housing case since 1953 to receive full hearing and opinion by the Court was *Reitman v Mulkey*, which came to the Supreme Court more than a dozen years after *Brown* and immediately before the Court

had begun actively to reenter the school desegregation area. California
had adopted significant fair housing legislation, the Unruh Civil Rights
Act of 1959 prohibiting racial discrimination by business concerns, including real estate dealers, and the Rumsford Fair Housing Act of 1963
forbidding racial discrimination in the sale or rental of private dwellings
containing more than four units and in the disposal of publicly financed
single-family homes. Immediately upon passage of the latter act, a bitter
campaign to repeal the legislation was initiated in the state, spearheaded
by the California Real Estate Association. The November 1964 election
included a measure entitled "Proposition 14" which provided that
"neither the state nor any subdivision or agency thereof shall deny, limit
or abridge, directly or indirectly, the right of any person, who is willing or
desires to sell, lease orrent any part or all of his real property, to decline to
sell, lease or rent such property to any person or persons as he, in his
absolute discretion, chooses." While it did not speak of them directly, the
amendment had the effect of repealing both the Unruh and Rumsford
acts—but it did far more. When Proposition 14 was approved by the
voters, two-to-one, a suit was filed by Mr. and Mrs. Lincoln W. Mulkey, a
Negro couple from Santa Ana, against Neil Reitman and other Orange
County apartment owners and managers. Charging that rental of available apartments had been denied to them solely because they were Negroes, the Mulkeys challenged the constitutionality of the new provision.
The trial court ruled for the apartment owners and managers, thus
arguably posing a *Shelley*-type issue about the state's "neutrality" when it
had turned aside a claim based on the earlier fair housing legislation.
When the Mulkeys appealed to the California Supreme Court in May
1966 those justices ruled, five-to-two, that Proposition 14 was unconstitutional because it violated the United States Constitution's Fourteenth
Amendment. The Court declared that it was now "beyond dispute that
the Fourteenth Amendment, through the equal protection clause, secures, without discrimination on account of color, race [or] religion, 'the
right to acquire and possess property of every kind.' "

This time the landlords appealed to the United States Supreme Court,
contending that the California ruling would mean that once a state had
passed a law for nondiscriminatory sale and rental of housing, it could
never withdraw to a "neutral" position in order to allow individual preference to operate freely. Lawyers for the Negro tenants and would-be
tenants argued that the state constitutional amendment placed the state
on the side of racial discrimination by going beyond merely repealing
antibias laws to disabling all branches and levels of state and local government from moving in any way against racial bias in housing. Neither side
contended that adoption of the amendment by initiative procedure made
it any different from an act of the legislature for the purposes of Court

review. Although the Court had never held that a state has a constitutional duty to prevent private individuals from discriminating, the Supreme Court decided to review the case.

Perhaps the Supreme Court could have left the case alone by declining to grant certiorari. This was particularly true where the facts of the California situation were so much a part of the case. However, the fact that the California court had found support for its conclusions in United States Supreme Court decisions made such an option difficult because refusal to hear the case in that context would have given firmer support to the California court's rulings than if the state court had relied more heavily or entirely on state law.

Argument before the Supreme Court in the *Reitman* case was begun by Samuel O. Pruitt, Jr., representing the real estate interests.[20] Pruitt defended Proposition 14, which he said merely reestablished the long-standing common law rule governing private property and its disposition, restoring to the property owner freedom to sell or rent his property "according to his conscience." He argued that if the California decision on fair housing were upheld all states could pass fair housing laws that could not subsequently be repealed. To Herman F. Selvin, representing the Negroes, Proposition 14, which he insisted was discriminatory state action, made "a constitutional right out of racial discrimination." Selvin emphasized the fact that the constitutional amendment precluded the legislature—the ordinary lawmaking body—from dealing further with racial discrimination in housing and the fact that it also restricted the state courts from exercising their powers. Solicitor General Marshall appeared as amicus supporting the California Supreme Court's ruling. In his brief he had stressed the peculiarities of Proposition 14, pointing out that it went beyond mere repeal and asserted an affirmative right to discriminate. He also had noted that the enactment of the measure as a constitutional amendment insulated the right of individuals to discriminate from the normal legislative processes. He had also attempted to allay fears that such a ruling might discourage other state legislatures from enacting fair housing legislation because any attempt to repeal them later would be unconstitutional.

At oral argument Marshall contended that California's voters had acted unconstitutionally in approving an amendment broad enough to outlaw local efforts to ease racial discrimination in housing, which he thought among the most promising developments in the drive for non-discrimination. He contended that Proposition 14 as a constitutional amendment was state action contrary to the Fourteenth Amendment because the state had "put its thumb on the scales" in favor of racial discrimination. Marshall's position that the strong wording of Proposition 14 would have the effect of encouraging discrimination was reinforced by the argument of A. L. Wirin, counsel for the Los Angeles chapter of the American Civil Liberties Union, sponsor of the challenge. Wirin conceded that a referendum merely repealing the legislature's fair housing laws would not have been unconstitutional, but argued that the use of the initiative procedure—which can be repealed only by another vote of the people—frustrated the normal operation of the legislature and removed the state from the neutral position it must maintain regarding race. Marshall went beyond even this argument to suggest that all statewide popular ballots are unconstitutional when they act to the detriment of a minority race. Minority groups can get legislation passed for their benefit in legislatures, he said, but "everybody knows minority groups do not have the strength to win a popular statewide vote." The losers in the Proposition 14 vote were "the underprivileged people of California," he said, and "you don't win a statewide vote without lots of hard cash."

The justices asked many questions of all four attorneys. The questions had several principal foci. One was the effect of the proposition, particularly in relation to the Rumsford-Unruh legislation, and its effect on the courts—including its relation to federal civil rights statutes. Another was the ramifications of the Fourteenth Amendment, including the matter of requirements that amendment imposed on states and the effect of the method used in California. The meaning of the state court's ruling provided another focus.

The most frequent question concerned whether Proposition 14 repealed the Unruh and Rumsford legislation or did more than that. This question was asked by Justices White, Fortas, Brennan—more than once—and, less directly, by Justice Black, who asked whether the people could have Rumsford but not a repealer. Brennan, Douglas, and Stewart all wanted to know whether the constitutional question would have been the same if Unruh and Rumsford had never been enacted—that is, whether in those circumstances Proposition 14 would still be affirmative action violating the Fourteenth Amendment. White asked whether the proposition created a constitutional right to discriminate and wanted to know how the justices were to know that the proposition's purpose was to permit the people to do what the state could not do. Chief Justice Warren wanted to know if there were any other statutes circumventing the Fourteenth Amendment or cases sustaining statutes saying the people can discriminate. Black followed up by asking about the *Civil Rights Cases*. When Pruitt replied, "Those cases say states can do nothing," Warren rejoined, "I agree, but here we have more."

Fortas, whose concern throughout was whether court jurisdiction would be affected by the proposition, asked if it involved a constitutional right or if it was merely a direction to the courts. He also asked Marshall if a state could tell courts not to entertain housing discrimination cases.

Marshall: "Well, that's this case." Fortas: "I was sort of thinking that was this case." White asked what would happen when a person under a restrictive covenant change his mind—would the proposition give the courts power to enforce the agreement of whether it would bar the agreement? Continuing, he asked whether the courts were foreclosed from enforcing or not enforcing the agreement. Justice Stewart had early asked Pruitt whether Proposition 14 applied to public accommodations, which would have raised the problem of federal preemption because of the 1964 Civil Rights Act. In a question not unlike Stewart's, Chief Justice Warren asked whether the proposition would prevent state cooperation with the federal government and whether the courts could enforce federal rights with the proposition present in the state constitution.

Although they did not come to the case from the same position,[21] Justices Black and Douglas asked Pruitt whether, although the proposition did not either forbid or coerce, California had enacted a policy that Negroes could not rent. Pruitt responded by saying that the state had enacted freedom of regulation. Could California authorize private discrimination, asked Justice White—not racial discrimination, just private discrimination? When he received an affirmative reply, he asked whether Pruitt had to take that position. Discrimination was part of the cost of freedom, Pruitt replied.

Black, who later asked if the state could withdraw from an area, pressed Selvin on the question of whether the Fourteenth Amendment required enactment of antidiscrimination laws. When Selvin said it did not, Black persisted, "Then what's wrong with this policy?" When Selvin said it was because policy had been made a constitutional right, Black continued by asking whether the Fourteenth Amendment prohibited a state from staying out of the area. Harlan, in asking Wirin why California had entered the housing scene in 1959, inquired whether the state had been compelled to do so by the Fourteenth Amendment. (No.)

Stewart later was interested in whether it made any difference what instrumentality violated the Fourteenth Amendment, and, along the same lines, Black later asked whether only the method was being attacked. Marshall replied, no, the substantive encouragement was at issue, but Black indicated that he felt the method was being attacked impliedly. Fortas questioned whether putting a provision in the state constitution was state action because it was beyond the reach of the ordinary legislative processes, and White asked whether the withdrawal of power to prevent racial discrimination included withdrawing the people's power to do so.

The fact that the state court's opinion had been less than clear obviously frustrated the justices, whose attention to the lower court's rationale produced their most explicit strategic questions as they searched for a basis on which to affirm the lower court. White asked soon after argument began about the meaning of that opinion, and Brennan asked whether the lower court would have said the same thing if Unruh-Rumsford had been part of the California Constitution. Brennan also asked Wirin how the California court had construed the people's action in enacting Proposition 14. After White asked whether the California court explained how Proposition 14 encouraged discrimination, Brennan inquired directly what the United States Supreme Court was to do if the justices could not tell what the California Supreme Court had decided. As Brennan remarked, "We have had this trouble with your court before. . . . Just two years ago we had to send a case back because we didn't know what they said." Exemplifying the strategy-related questions were those by Brennan as to whether the United States Supreme Court was held to the California court's interpretation of the proposition, by White as to whether Proposition 14 was open for a new interpretation by the federal high court, and by White's earlier inquiry as to whether the Supreme Court should affirm on the basis of the opinion below or on other grounds.

Having accepted the case, the Supreme Court could have affirmed without opinion. Not only would that have given even greater weight to the California court's interpretation of the Supreme Court's cases than denying review but it might have "seemed like an abject confession of the Court's inability to justify its conclusion."[22] Having decided to hear argument, the justices were committed to a full opinion ruling, one in which they might have tackled the "affirmative action" equal protection issue head-on. But they did not do that. At the very end of May, after political activity against the reinstated Rumsford Fair Housing Law had gathered strength and a repealer had passed the state senate, the Supreme Court announced its decision in *Reitman v. Mulkey,* ruling five-to-four that adoption of Proposition 14 amounted to racial bias by the state. Justice White wrote for the majority; there was a concurring opinion by Justice Douglas; and Justice Harlan wrote for four dissenting justices.

In speaking for the Court, Justice White did not set out a clear statement of what the Fourteenth Amendment required, but instead relied primarily on the California Supreme Court's decision. He noted at the outset that the California court quite properly undertook to examine the constitutionality of the contested amendment in terms of its "immediate objective," its "ultimate impact," and its "historical context and conditions existing prior to its enactment"—judgments frequently undertaken by the Supreme Court itself. White stated that the Supreme Court understood the California court had not taken the position that a constitutional violation derived from the mere repeal of Unruh and Rumsford. He also said that court had not read either the Supreme Court's cases or the Fourteenth Amendment as establishing an automatic constitutional barrier to the repeal of an existing law prohibiting racial discrimination in housing, nor did it rule that a state may never put in statutory form an existing policy of neutrality with respect to private discrimination. It had in fact rejected the notion that the state was required to have a statute prohibiting racial discrimination in housing. Instead, White said, the state tribunal, dealing with the amendment as though it expressly authorized and constitutionalized the private right to discriminate, had held that the purpose and intent of this particular amendment was to authorize private racial discrimination in the housing market, to repeal acts forbidding such discrimination, to forestall future state action that might circumscribe this right, and to create a constitutional right to discriminate in the sale and leasing of private property on racial grounds—which would admittedly be unavailable under the Fourteenth Amendment should state action be involved. The state court thus concluded, said White, that the amendment encouraged—and significantly involved the state in— private racial discrimination contrary to the Fourteenth Amendment. White said that the California court could very reasonably have concluded that the amendment's announcement of the constitutional right of any person to decline to sell or lease his real property to anyone would and did have wider impact than a mere repeal of existing statutes. It would embody in the state's basic charter, immune from legislative, executive, or judicial regulation at any level of state government, the right to discriminate—including the right to discriminate on racial grounds—so that those practicing racial discrimination could now invoke express constitutional authority free from any official censure or interference. White than added that the Supreme Court had never attempted the "impossible task" of formulating an infallible test for determining whether the state "in any of its manifestations" had become significantly involved in private discrimination. White quoted from the 1961 *Burton* case the idea that only by sifting facts and weighing the circumstances on a case-by-case basis could a "non-obvious involvement of the state be attributed its true significance" and emphasized that the California court, armed with the knowledge of the facts and circumstances concerning the passage and potential impact of the amendment, had engaged in that process and made acceptable conclusions.

Although Justice Douglas joined the majority, he held an even broader view of the kinds of state action the Fourteenth Amendment could reach. He drew an analogy between what Proposition 14 sanctioned and what the earlier invalidated restrictive covenants had sought to accomplish. Proposition 14, he said, allowed California's citizens to let private groups do what the state government could not have done. Douglas also wrote that state-licensed real estate brokers in effect exercised a zoning function. When their refusal to place Negroes in white neighborhoods took place "in an environment where the whole weight of the system is on the side of discrimination," the licenses they held meant that their discrimination was forbidden state action.

Justice Harlan obviously disliked the majority's use of the California court's opinion and differed as well with his colleagues on the Fourteenth Amendment's requirements. Harlan said the majority's conclusion was reached only by relying on the state court's conclusion and asserting in effect that the provision's requirement of passive official neutrality was camouflage. He said he viewed that California ruling as resting entirely on a conception of the compulsion of the Fourteenth Amendment. As state court interpretation of federal constitutional law, Harlan asserted, it should carry no weight in the United States Supreme Court—unlike a state court's findings of fact which should be given great weight. Proposition 14, Harlan argued, had merely moved the state back to a neutral position on housing; that it was done in the form of a popularly approved initiative should add to, not detract from, its constitutional validity. Proposition 14, adopted through the most democratic of processes, was neutral on its face—simply permissive of private decision-making rather than coercive—and required no affirmative governmental enforcement of any sort. Basically, Harlan's constitutional argument was that the Fourteenth Amendment did not undertake to control purely personal prejudices or to require the states to pass laws to prevent such private discrimination, though it of course did not disable them from so doing. It merely forbade a state to use its authority to foster discrimination based on such factors as race. Harlan felt that no state enactment should be struck down on the basis of the amendment without persuasive evidence of an invidious affirmative purpose or effect of actively fostering discrimination. Furthermore, Harlan found the concept of state action which focused on "encouragement" of private discrimination, on which the Court had relied, a "slippery and unfortunate criterion by which to measure the constitutionality of a statute simply permissive in purpose and effect, and inoffensive on its face." He noted that the Court's decision had far-reaching possibilities: laws that do nothing more than passively permit private discrimination could be said to tinge all private discrimination with the taint of unconstitutional state "encouragement." He found the Court's decision in this case "not only constitutionally unsound, but in its practical potentialities short-sighted." In conclusion, he commented that it was legislatures rather than courts which should delineate the difficult lines which must be drawn in this area.

The Court's decision, which critics have said is unsatisfactory because it "contributed little to the development of a doctrinal explanation of the commands of the Fourteenth Amendment,"[23] was influenced by Justice White's efforts to limit the opinion's reach to the specific California facts, seen in his emphasis that the new California law was one particularly difficult to review because of the unusual process from which it had resulted. The opinion's limited nature was reinforced by White's approval of the California court's conclusion that a state is not required by the Fourteenth Amendment to have fair housing legislation—a point reinforced by Harlan's statement that the provisions of Proposition 14 did not require an affirmative action of any sort.

White's opinion taken together with Harlan's make the case difficult for anyone on either side of the open housing controversy to use. A part of the unsatisfactory result came from the lack of clarity of the California opinion and from its reliance on the United States Supreme Court. By relying in turn on the state court through selective "nibbling here and there for quotations and half-quotations," the latter produced the situation suggested by Karst and Horowitz in which "an editorial cartoonist might caricature two robed judges, each pointing at the other. The caption would read, 'He did it.' "[24] The United States Supreme Court's reliance on the state court also meant that there would be serious future problems if a court in another state were to uphold instead of overturn a provision like Proposition 14—problems created by the Court's failure to take the responsibility for developing national constitutional law by making a more direct and independent statement as to what the Fourteenth Amendment required. Yet for all these criticisms, short-run strategic considerations may have dictated the result. Short of no decision at all, the Court may have done the most which could have been expected, given the complexity of the problem and its newness to the Court. The Court's opinion, particularly because of its explicit deference to the state court, gave far greater legitimacy to the California court's ruling than would have resulted from either a denial of review or a summary affirmance. And, although the Court did not confront the key state-action question directly—just as it had refused to do in the sit-in cases prior to passage of the Civil Rights Act of 1964—the Court certainly did not hide the issue. Although there are difficulties in doing so, the opinion can be read for more than a ruling applying only to California, and the result in the case certainly added a notable increment to the law of equal protection.[25]

4

The Supreme Court's most important housing case came before the justices in 1968 at the time Congress was considering fair housing legislation and was decided in the same term with *Green,* the Court's first major step toward requiring affirmative school desegregation action. The year 1968 was thus to be a crucial year for race relations decisions. In the public accommodations area, the Court had appeared to wait for Congress to act so that the justices could avoid deciding major Fourteenth Amendment issues. However, in the housing area the Court did not use current legislative activity as an excuse to avoid ruling on the constitutionality of the old, post–Civil War statute invoked by those claiming discrimination. It should be noted, however, that in housing the Court was not being asked to decide a constitutional question *in vacuo*—in the absence of a statute—as had been the case concerning public accommodations. Here were both existing legislation and proposed legislation perhaps prompted in part by judicial inaction. The latter legislation was referred to in oral argument, and by the time the Court handed down its decision in *Jones v. Mayer,* the law had been passed. Thus, with Congress clearly "moving," the Court's action in this case can be seen as an important example of reinforcing Congress as well as of "taking a lead" from the action in which the legislative branch was engaged.

Jones v. Mayer was brought by a couple—a black man and his white wife—who wanted to buy a house in the St. Louis suburban subdivision of Paddock Woods and were refused because of race. Their lawyer found an old neglected 1866 statute (42 U.S.C. 1982) passed to implement the Thirteenth Amendment, and they sued the developer, citing that statute. The district court dismissed the case and the Court of Appeals for the Eighth Circuit affirmed, reviewing a wide variety of grounds for reversal but refusing to adopt them without Supreme Court direction. With the case in this posture, the Supreme Court accepted it for a full hearing.

At oral argument, Samuel Liberman of St. Louis, for the Joneses, wanted the justices to look at the statute's legislative history.[26] Those who wrote the law, he said, knew that slavery could be imposed by discriminatory acts of individuals as well as by state governments. Noting that there had not been much interpretation of the statute, he called attention to dicta in *Hurd v. Hodge,* the District of Columbia case accompanying *Shelley,* but said the state action requirement mentioned there concerning Section 1982 had been eliminated by the Supreme Court's language in *United States v. Guest,* in which the Court had sustained indictments against purely private individuals for interfering with the civil rights of blacks.[27] Because the statute, although first enacted under the Thirteenth Amendment, had been reenacted in identical terms under the Fourteenth, Liberman also tried to show state action through regulations the community had to comply with—rules which made the developer build streets, sidewalks, water and sewerage systems, and the like, and which, he said, gave the developer a quasi-state function.

On the other side, Israel Treiman also relied on statutory interpretation and tried to distinguish the Court's decision in *Marsh v. Alabama,* the "company town" case, finding more applicable a New York case in which Jehovah's Witnesses were said to have no right to distribute pamphlets in an apartment house in a development similar to Paddock Woods.[28] Attorney General Ramsey Clark, who argued for the government as amicus, called discrimination in the sale of housing the country's most harmful form of discrimination and asserted that the Fourteenth Amendment bars state involvement in housing segregation. He said that *Shelley* had applied to only a few but the present case would affect far more. He found the parks and pools in Jones's case similar to those in *Evans v. Newton,* and he drew most heavily on the *Marsh* case, claiming that "regardless of ownership, the public interest cannot be yielded." He said that the developer clearly performed governmental functions. Under Missouri law, he noted, the subdivision would qualify as a city of the fourth class. If Jehovah's Witnesses could be allowed to distribute literature in a company town, Clark said, certainly a person should be allowed to live in a community like Paddock Woods without regard to race. Clark also called to the Court's attention what it was probably already aware of—that Congress was considering a bill. Several other amici urged a wide variety of grounds in support of petitioners. Included were the Ninth, Thirteenth, and Fourteenth Amendments. Their key argument was that no state action need be shown because 42 U.S.C. 1982 had been passed under the Thirteenth Amendment which barred the vestiges of slavery absolutely, without a requirement of state action.

These basic presentations gave rise to many questions directed to all three counsel. Relatively few had to do with a straight Fourteenth Amendment argument. However, there were many questions about the background of the 1866 law, some clearly strategic questions on the relation between the law and the bill before Congress, and a wide variety of questions on the characteristics of the subdivision. Questions on this latter point were brief but important. For example, Justice Fortas asked Liberman whether the land was zoned for the benefit of the developer, and Justice Harlan wanted to know whether this was because of the subdivision's size. There were questions about how many families there were in the subdivision (Marshall), about the presence of industry (Stewart), and as to whether public recreation facilities had been carved out of the community (Warren). Stewart's questions about the presence of federal or state mortgage loans—which the developer had avoided—were followed up by Fortas, who tried to ascertain whether mortgages operated at the level of the individual. Brennan also asked whether the developer had authority to make assessments, and Warren, clearly getting close to the state action issue, wanted to know whether the developer's duties were intended to relieve the state of similar duties. Later, Warren asked Treiman, the developer's attorney, who owned or furnished the water supply, the sewer system, and the fire services. Marshall's and Stewart's questions about the presence of families and industry were clearly related to the relevance of the *Marsh* case, and Stewart remarked that because it had no industry, the subdivision was not like the town involved in *Marsh*. Also with respect to *Marsh,* Marshall pressed Treiman as to whether Paddock Woods would qualify as a fourth-class city. When Treiman conceded that the community if incorporated could not exclude Negroes and Catholics because a Fourteenth Amendment violation would be involved, Marshall wanted to know what the difference was: "What does a city of the fourth class have that Paddock Woods does not have?" Treiman said, "It is a political subdivision of the state," but that was far from the end of the exchange. Marshall kept pressing Treiman on the difference between this case and *Marsh* and the ability of an individual to know the difference between public and private streets in the community, and both he and Warren asked firmly whether the right to distribute pamphlets was entitled to greater protection than the right to live in a community. Indicative of Justice Black's position on this issue was his comment that the Court had stated in *Marsh* that private property was treated as public unless operated as private.

A point on which much of the opinion, but not the argument, turned was raised by Harlan: whether the 1866 act was applicable to individual houses. When Liberman said, "That question is not before the Court at this time," Harlan replied, "I know, but what is your answer?" Liberman: "Yes, in my opinion." Similarly, Warren asked what there was in the language of the Thirteenth Amendment's sponsors to indicate it was not aimed at individual conduct. Stewart wanted to know whether the law had originally been enacted under the Thirteenth Amendment and, if it were valid under the Thirteenth, whether one needed to bother with state action, and Black had several questions about whether the 1866 statute had depended on the existence of state laws, particularly the Black Codes, so that the federal law changed with state law and was inapplicable in a state with no discriminatory statute.

The Court's strategic situation—that is, Congress's consideration of a new statute concurrent with oral argument—produced both questions and comments from the justices. When Marshall asked Treiman whether there was any law permitting developers to discriminate, Treiman responded, yes, until Congress passed the law before it. Marshall then observed that "this Court can do it"—that is, dispose of the situation. When Black followed Marshall by asking whether Congress could outlaw discrimination in the sale of housing, Treiman retreated, saying, "I'd rather not answer that question." Referring directly to his own *Marsh* opinion, Black observed, "I have said Congress has the power." Earlier, Clark had been asked whether the bill before Congress was as broad as the 1866 statute and whether it would be available to Jones. It depends, said Clark, but damages would not be, but Clark said in response to a question from Justice White that the new bill would not cancel the 1866 law, although Clark assumed that the old law would not be enforced. White also wanted to know whether the old law could be used to reach the exceptions written into the new statute.

The opinion for the Court in *Jones v. Mayer* in favor of the Joneses was written by Justice Stewart, whose concerns at oral argument had clearly been settled. He began by noting that the case did not involve a comprehensive fair housing statute—as 42 U.S.C. 1982 certainly was not such a statute. Stewart then detailed the differences between Section 1982 and the 1968 Civil Rights Act—passed since oral argument. The new statute dealt with discrimination on the basis of religion and national origin as well as race; Section 1982 dealt only with race. Section 1982 did not deal with discrimination in services or facilities in connection with sale or rental, nor with discrimination in financing although such matters might be covered by Section 1981, dealing with contracts. The new act also provided for federal administrative agencies to help private parties and for the attorney general to initiate civil actions when a pattern or practice of discrimination exists. Not mentioned by Stewart but worth noting is the fact that the 1968 statute exempted direct sales and rentals; Section 1982, which did not, was thus broader in that regard. Stewart concluded, "It would be a serious mistake to suppose that 1982 in any way diminishes the significance of the law recently enacted by Congress."

Revealing the Court's desire to move incrementally, Stewart then discussed *Hurd v. Hodge,* the case in which the Court had last looked at Section 1982. That case had been in the context of government-aided discrimination through the federal courts, not "purely private" discrimination. Looking directly at the statute, Stewart found that on its face it prohibited all discrimination against Negroes in property sale or rental; "all" included private owners, not just public officials. Stewart's look at legislative history persuaded him "that Congress meant exactly what it said." Nor had further examination of later legislative history, particularly surrounding the 1870 act which followed the passage of the Fourteenth Amendment, revealed any alteration in Section 1982. Non-use of Section 1982 also had not negatively affected its force, Stewart said, quoting from the government's statements at oral argument. Having looked at the statute's purpose, Stewart turned to the central question of the Congress's power to pass the act. He found that the power clearly existed: "If Congress has power under the Thirteenth Amendment to eradicate conditions that prevent Negroes from buying and renting property because of their race and color, then no federal statute calculated to achieve that objective can be thought to exceed the constitutional power of Congress simply because it reaches beyond state action to regulate the conduct of private individuals." In extremely positive language, he ended by saying, "At the very least, the freedom that Congress is empowered to secure under the Thirteenth Amendment includes the freedom to buy whatever a white man can buy, the right to live wherever a white man can live. If Congress cannot say that being a free man means at least this much, then the Thirteenth Amendment made a promise that the Nation cannot keep."

Douglas concurred, but only to add some explication to the Court's opinion. Justices Harlan and White dissented, with Harlan writing for both. Most of Harlan's opinion was devoted to statutory interpretation, but its real thrust, shown in his first sentence, was strategic: "The decision in this case appears to me to be most ill-considered and ill-advised." Arguing that the Court's own precedents ran counter to the Court's construction of the statute, Harlan found that construction to be "almost surely wrong, and at the least . . . open to serious doubt." He was led to that conclusion by extended statutory interpretation reinforced by a "less tangible" consideration—that those who wrote the statute shared an "individualistic ethic . . . which emphasized personal freedom and embodied a distaste for governmental interference." Harlan's strategic concerns, reinforced by what he saw as the Court's misguided reading of the old statute, led him further to say that the writ of certiorari should have been dismissed as improvidently granted because the political process had operated to produce the passage of the 1968 Open Housing Act, thus clearly diminishing the "public importance" of the case. Although he felt that usually cases once accepted should be decided, "mature reflection" had led him to the opposite conclusion here. He drew on the Court's action in the *Rice* cemetery case to buttress this view, saying that the difficulties of *Jones v. Mayer* were certainly at least as great as the ones in that earlier case. Had the petition for certiorari been filed a few months later, with the act already passed and in effect or nearly so, the Court would probably not have granted review, he said, pointing out all that would be available to petitioner within a few months.

Shortly after the Court's ruling, Justice Stewart was to answer Harlan in the pages of the *Wall Street Journal* by pointing out the problems which would have been created had the Court ruled in any other way. The *Journal* had claimed in an editorial that by going well beyond Congress's recent statute the Supreme Court had come close to being an "alternate legislature." That led Stewart to write a letter to the editor, in which he noted that "the Supreme Court held (1) that this law means what it says, and (2) that Congress had Constitutional power to pass it. You say this made the Court a 'legislature.'" He then asked, "What would the Court have been if it had held (1) that the law does not mean what it says, or (2) that Congress did not have the power to pass it? I add only that Congress, having enacted 42 U.S.C. 1082, remains free to amend it at any time."[29]

Perhaps the Court could have used devices other than that of deciding the case directly on the merits, including Harlan's proposed certiorari dismissal, a mootness argument advanced by respondents, the technical claim that no remedy had been provided, or a per curiam affirmance of the Court of Appeals. The Court, however, drew sustenance from what Congress had done and took more direct action. Here the Court had not ventured into uncharted waters without political support, and, instead of offering a constitutional opinion unrelated to the application of a particular statute, in fact had affirmed the work of an earlier Congress. The Court of Appeals ruling had posed a wide range of questions, none of which could go unanswered, just as the California court's use of United States Supreme Court opinions in *Reitman v. Mulkey* could not be ignored. In affirming Congress's right to act in this area, one other broad strategic matter may have been in the backs of the justices' minds. The Court had been faced with a number of de facto segregation education cases which had generally been turned away.[30] Affirmation of open housing policy might help eliminate de facto segregation without the Court's having to rule against the latter directly. This explanation involves attributing goals not on the record to the Court, but it is not unlike the Court's possible use of reapportionment to increase the political power of blacks.

Jones v. Mayer has been called perhaps "the most far-reaching race relations case since the Civil War."[31] By treating discrimination as a badge of slavery instead of becoming entangled in the state action question which had so plagued the Court in the sit-in cases or even in the only somewhat less complex issue of the effect of discrimination on interstate commerce, the Court potentially made enactment of antidiscrimination legislation easier because the constitutional basis was less limited. It is certainly true that had *Jones* been decided before *Brown,* some of the problems created in desegregation doctrine by reliance on the Fourteenth Amendment would have been eliminated, and the right to an integrated education would have been obvious, for school segregation was definitely one of the badges of slavery. Yet we can only speculate here for, as is obvious, *Jones* came at the end of the Court's work, not the beginning; it was *Brown,* not *Jones,* which was decided first.

Although the Court was to go on to rule, in *Sullivan v. Little Hunting Park,* that damages—and not merely declaratory relief—could be recovered under Section 1982, that decision was anticlimactic. *Jones v. Mayer* had been the Warren Court's major housing case—and one of its most important rulings in its entire output of race relations decisions. While the Court had been slow to come to the housing area, leaving the Vinson Court's *Shelley* and *Barrows* rulings as the landmarks while it regularly denied review and devoted its attention to other matters, the Court had ended its housing action, begun only a year before with *Reitman v. Mulkey,* on an extremely upbeat note, at the same time resuscitating a century-old statute and making so clear that Congress's new act complemented it that the Court was not faced with a constitutional challenge to the latter.

5

Few voting rights cases came to the Warren Court in its first few years, when it was immersed in questions of education, public facilities, and transportation. In one voting rights case, the Court merely denied review after a lower court had invalidated the requirement that the designation "Negro" be placed after the name of a Negro candidate on a ballot.[32] More important was the *Lassiter* case, a challenge to the use of literacy tests. Here the Court, although it could have disposed of the case on the basis of discriminatory application of the tests, a question which had been raised in the case, held that the tests were not per se unconstitutional. This ruling, broad because the Court reached the constitutionality question, left it open to hold them invalid as applied, and the Court provided the plaintiff an opportunity to obtain relief on the basis of the statute's application.

Activity on voting rights began to build up in the 1959 Term as a result of cases generated by the 1957 Civil Rights Act. The law, which had created the United States Commission on Civil Rights and a new Civil Rights Division within the Department of Justice, allowed the Department of Justice to bring civil suits on behalf of Negroes denied the right to vote in federal elections. Four cases involving the 1957 act and the 1960 act, which strengthened it, were decided in the 1959 Term of Court. They resulted in unquestionable Court support for congressional power to enact the legislation. In the *Raines* and *Thomas* cases brought by the federal government against voting registrars under the 1957 act, the Supreme Court's brief action reversed one district court and affirmed another so that voting officials in Georgia were enjoined from depriving certain persons of voting rights because of their race or color, and a voting registrar in Louisiana was enjoined from challenging—on a racially discriminatory basis—the right of certain Negro citizens to remain on the registration rolls as qualified voters. In *United States v. Alabama,* registrars had resigned, and the Justice Department brought suit against the state. The suit was rejected by both the trial court and the Court of Appeals, but the 1960 act allowed such suits, thus permitting the Supreme Court to hold per curiam that the federal government had the power to bring such cases. When this case later reappeared as a challenge to a Court of Appeals ruling that a district court could affirmatively order registration of Negro voters found to have been denied registration because of their race and color, the Supreme Court affirmed per curiam, citing the earlier *Thomas* ruling.

An important case from this term, *Hannah v. Larche,* assisted the United States Civil Rights Commission. The commission had developed procedural rules which provided that the identity of those bringing complaints to the commission need not be disclosed and that those persons questioned by the commission were not to cross-examine other witnesses. Various voting registrars called before the commission in Louisiana challenged the rules, and obtained an injunction against the commission's holding hearings. When the commission asked for direct review of the district court's rulings the Supreme Court granted a request to advance the case. In an unusual move, the Court heard oral argument on the question of jurisdiction on the appeal and on the accompanying certiorari petition, which had been filed before the Court of Appeals for the Fifth Circuit ruled in the case, and on the merits as well. Granting both the appeal request and the certiorari petition, the justices upheld the commission, ruling that the commission had the authority to issue the contested rules and that the rules did not violate due process.

The Court's vote was seven-to-two, with Frankfurter concurring separately, and Black and Douglas dissenting. The Chief Justice himself wrote for the Court, sustaining the agency on the grounds that the rules were not unlike those in any government investigation. He stressed that the commission's function was "purely investigative and fact-finding"; the commission did not determine either criminal or civil liability, issue orders, or impose legal sanctions. When government agencies make binding determinations, Warren said that it was "imperative" procedures "traditionally . . . associated with the judicial process" be used, but use of "the full panoply of judicial procedures" was not necessary when only fact-finding investigations were being undertaken. If such investigations had to be conducted as "trial-like proceedings," Warren said, they would be "completely disrupted," with collateral issues diverting the agency and makings its proceedings "interminable."

Except for his initial recitation of facts, Chief Justice Warren's opinion, a treatise on administrative investigations, was devoid of any indication of the case's context—the fear of blacks that they would be subject to retaliation and intimidation if they made their complaints in public. In his separate opinion supporting the commission, Justice Frankfurter adverted to this situation in saying, "We would be shutting our eyes to actualities to be unmindful of the fact that it would dissuade sources of vitally relevant information from making that information known to the Commission" if sources had to be revealed and if cross-examination were allowed. Douglas and Black called most attention to the racial context of the case. They did not feel that due process should be altered simply because the majority wished to protect those complaining about deprivation of voting rights. "Important as these civil rights are, it will not do to sacrifice other civil rights in order to protect them," they wrote, arguing that the commission and the Court majority were taking short cuts to sustain unconstitutional procedures. They likened the commission's proceedings to those legislative committee sessions at which, knowing the Fifth Amendment would be invoked, the committee called persons before it to testify in order to "pillory" the witnesses, and further noted that such a hearing would prejudice any later trial which might result. For them, the Civil Rights Commission was conducting a trial on the question of whether the registrars had committed a federal offense, so that a grand jury, indictment, and trial was the only appropriate way to proceed.

The following term, the Court further reinforced the federal government's voting rights activities. A Negro college student helping register voters in Mississippi had been struck by a registrar while assisting a Negro man and woman to register, and when he reported the incident to the sheriff was charged with breach of the peace. The federal government tried to enjoin his prosecution. Recognizing the intent of the county's actions, the Court of Appeals for the Fifth Circuit held that the 1957 Civil Rights Act authorized a government suit to enjoin a state criminal trial the purpose of which was to intimidate potential Negro voters. Asked to review the case, the Supreme Court denied certiorari.[33] Later that same term, the Court put an end to a case which had been four years in the court.[34] A Mississippi registration official had resisted the Justice Department's efforts, based on Title III of the 1960 Civil Rights Act, to get registration records. The Court of Appeals upheld the federal government, and the Supreme Court denied certiorari. In so doing, it reinforced both the government's claim, upheld by the Fifth Circuit, that it was merely making an investigation to find out whether there had been discrimination. If investigation could not proceed, the government clearly would not be able to act at all.

In the 1964 Term, two cases involving the voting provisions of the 1964 Civil Rights Act came before the Court from Mississippi and Louisiana. Here, in opinions written by Justice Black based on the Fourteenth and Fifteenth Amendments, the Court gave affirmative support to the government's attempt, through the attorney general, to sue a state and its officials over state laws prescribing literacy tests which federal officials alleged were discriminatory.[35] Black further criticized one of the tests as giving registrars "a virtually uncontrolled discretion as to who should vote and who should not." Although Black clearly stressed the Fifteenth Amendment, using the Fourteenth only with respect to the issue of registrars' discretion, Justice Harlan wrote a concurring opinion to say he thought only the Fifteenth could properly be used.

The Court's key decision in the voting rights area, *South Carolina v. Katzenbach*, involved direct challenge to the 1965 Voting Rights Act. This first omnibus voting rights law provided that where 50 percent of the population in a jurisdiction (county) had not registered or had not voted, literacy tests and other "devices" were to be suspended for a period of five years from the last shown discrimination and that no further changes in election laws were to be made without prior approval by the attorney general or the federal district court in the District of Columbia, thus taking the cases away from southern federal judges. Furthermore, under the act, federal registrars could be sent into the affected jurisdictions. The "trigger provision" had been so artfully drawn that, for all practical purposes, only the southern states or portions thereof had been covered. South Carolina then brought a case in the Supreme Court's original jurisdiction challenging the new law's constitutionality. Indicating its awareness of the legislation's importance, the Court agreed to hear the case under this procedure, and invited any state to file petitions to participate in oral argument as amicus curiae. As a result, six southern states appeared in opposition to the act, and two northern states joined the attorney general in supporting it. After the eight hours of argument, Chief Justice Warren thanked all participants for their cooperation in helping "to accelerate the case for an early judgment."

The themes generally advanced in argument[36] were, on the one side, a plea for old-fashioned states rights and criticism of trial by legislation. On the other side, there was a lengthy discourse on the necessity for effective enforcement of Fifteenth Amendment rights. Underlying all argument was disagreement over whether the "triggering" and enforcement provisions of the act constituted legislation "appropriate" to enforcement of the Fifteenth Amendment. The six southern states argued that the act was not "appropriate," that it granted the right to vote to citizens unqualified under state law, violated the principle of equality of statehood, contravened the Fifth Amendment, and, furthermore, was not reasonably designed to enforce the Fifteenth Amendment— in fact constituting a legislative trial. The United States argued that Congress had comprehensive authority to protect and enforce Fifteenth Amendment rights free of racial discrimination implemented by state literacy tests and that the provisions of the act relating to suspension of tests and devices used as "engines of discrimination" was a proper exercise of congressional power.

First to appear was David W. Robinson for South Carolina. Robinson disclaimed any challenge to the purpose of the act or its broad remedial provisions, and said his complaint lay with the "automatic freezing" of state literacy tests, for which certain sections of the act provided, and with the criminal sanctions imposed by other sections. Robinson asserted that the act was invalid because it deprived South Carolina and her citizens of basic rights secured by other provisions of the Constitution and therefore lay beyond powers granted by the Fifteenth Amendment. The Constitution does not give the power to fix qualifications for voting nor the power to suspend reasonable state restrictions on voting. Robinson also argued that if South Carolina's illiterates, representing 20 percent of the population, were excluded from voting tallies, the state would touch the national average. Although the light vote brought the state within the act, he argued, a state cannot force its citizens to vote. Studies show, he said, that many Negroes are non-voters, both in the South and the North.

Virginia Assistant Attorney General R. D. McIlwaine III also appeared, arguing the basic position that power to alter, amend, or suspend voter education qualification tests was not conferred by the Fifteenth Amendment. Louisiana Attorney General Jack Gremillion, who argued that Congress was never meant to have the power to invalidate state laws or voter registration, asserted that the census on which figures for application of the act were based were erroneous. Among other ineligibles, he argued, fifty thousand felons "roaming around" Louisiana had not been properly accounted for, and three hundred thousand illiterates were similarly improperly reflected. In actuality, he asserted, Louisiana's voting turnout was in excess of 70 percent. Furthermore, he stated, in thirty-one parishes Louisiana had been registering voters under court orders.

Francis J. Mizell, Jr., Governor Wallace's personal counsel, appeared for Alabama. He argued that the act denied access to the courts and constituted an unlawful delegation of judicial power to the United States Attorney General. Alabama Attorney General Richmond Flowers, continuing for the state, declared that although he deplored the violence at Selma—the catalyst for the new civil rights law—passage of the act had been precipitous. Alabama's literacy test was fair and simple, he argued, and involved only an inquiry into whether the prospective registrant is literate; it did not require tests of interpretation of difficult constitutional passages. For Mississippi, Attorney General Joe Patterson argued that a state also needs protections against discrimination, and Charles Clark, Special Assistant Attorney General, asserted that the act constituted a bill of attainder. The state of Mississippi, Clark said, is being punished without a trial or, more specifically, has been subjected to a legislative trial.

Last to appear in opposition to the act was E. Freeman Leverett, Georgia Deputy Assistant Attorney General. He directed his argument to the arbitrariness of the triggering provision and the enforcement provision of the test-freezing section of the act. He argued that there was no rational connection between voting turnout and discrimination. Georgia is within the act, he pointed out, while Florida, Texas, and Arkansas, with a lower percentage of registered voters but with no literacy tests, are not. Thus, he said, no state action brings the act into play, only the apathy of the voters. Since Congress could not directly supersede state qualifications for voting, they should not be allowed to do so indirectly. Leverett also asserted that Section 2 of the Fifteenth Amendment not only did not authorize the act in dispute but prohibited it. Congressional proscription of "any" discrimination could not be upheld under that section. The key to Section 2 is that the legislation must be "appropriate," he said. This word "cuts down" the meaning of the word "legislation"; it limits legislation to the scope of Section 1 of the amendment, which goes only to state action. The burden of proof imposed by the act is exceedingly difficult, he added. Leverett contended that if the principal provision concerning freezing of tests falls, the enforcement provision must also fall, but must go anyway because no state law can depend upon the assent of the federal government. In conclusion, he suggested that to invest the District Court for the District of Columbia with the authority to render opinions which could later be challenged was, in effect, an effort to invest it with authority to render advisory opinions. Admitting that discrimination had occurred in Georgia, he did not think this prevented the state from claiming the protection of the Constitution. "Congress cannot invoke, to appease a mob, an unconstitutional act to a constitutional end," he said.

Attorney General Katzenbach appeared for the federal government. He argued that Section 2 of the Fifteenth Amendment gave an express power to enforce Section 1 and that the Voting Rights Act was an appropriate, fair, and reasonable means of achieving enforcement. Three elements underlie the legislation, he said: literacy tests have been widely used as engines of discrimination; despite prior legislation, Congress, taking relevant facts into account, concluded that the scheme of county-by-county investigation was too slow; and an urgent need exists for immediate compliance with the Fifteenth Amendment. Section 4 of the act was meant to strike at forms of tests capable of abuse and so used. It would be wrong to think of this case as involving a matter of fairness, he said, maintaining that the tests have not been applied at all to whites. While the states argued much in their briefs about the value of an intelligent electorate, even a South Carolina illiterate can vote if he has three hundred dollars. The common thread in these cases, Katzenbach said, is the actual abuse, inherent possibility of abuse, and evidence of abuse of rights through literacy tests. The candid inception of the southern literacy test lay in a desire to discriminate. The Fifteenth Amendment speaks to the states as well as to the federal government, and "Congress waited too long to enforce the Fifteenth Amendment." As for Mr. Leverett's charge of "mob" pressure on the Congress, Katzenbach maintained that the law was a response to a crisis engendered by public loss of confidence in the political institutions of the nation to deal with Negro disfranchisement. "Public sentiment was outraged."

Also supporting the statute was Levin H. Campbell, Assistant Attorney General of Massachusetts,[37] who asserted that the act was concerned only with those literacy tests that were engines of discrimination. He was followed by former Solicitor General Archibald Cox, as Special Assistant Attorney General of Massachusetts. Cox's argument consisted of five propositions: 1) The act is concerned with suspension only in circumstances where its use carried undue damage of discrimination in applications resulting in a denial of the right to vote. Literacy tests might bear harder on Negroes than whites because the former have a higher rate of illiteracy or because the test is administered unfairly. The unfairness is the matter in question here. 2) Authority given to Congress carries with it the power to forbid states to foster future violations. Whenever a power had been given to Congress, Congress may exercise it. 3) Congress may act selectively, and is not bound to deal with every aspect of a problem. 4) The act's dominant test applies everywhere; its application is uniform; a state that has not discriminated and yet falls within the trigger need only come to court to be vindicated. 5) The propriety of the legislation was established by *Louisiana v. United States,* a case not truly distinguishable, which asserts congressional power to deal prospectively with a violation. An equity court deals with the danger of violation, not punishment.

There was considerable questioning by the justices, particularly of Katzenbach and others appearing on behalf of the act. Certain types of questions were asked persistently. One set dealt with Congress's power generally to deal with practices affecting voting. Thus Justice White asked whether Congress could suspend a discriminatory state law. No, said Virginia's attorney, even with a direct Fifteenth Amendment violation. Black followed up, "Suppose there were no doubt that enforcement of the Fifteenth Amendment was impossible unless tests were suspended or abolished. Still no law?" He kept pressing as to where counsel found the basis of his position, and then asked, "What does Section 2 of the Fifteenth Amendment do?" Black persisted with Mississippi's counsel, "If something impedes that right [to vote], are you saying that Congress can't act?"[38] Justice White brought up the related matter of whether the Court rather than Congress could act and also asked whether Congress had said that tests would be suspended until the states were no longer using them for discrimination and whether it was being asserted that court orders were the appropriate device to deal with voting discrimination.

Whether Congress could abolish literacy tests specifically came up repeatedly. When Robinson said, "If Congress decides that literacy tests are bad, they should have abolished them," Black pressed the matter of Congress's power to do so. When Katzenbach appeared, Black asked, "Are you conceding that Congress has no power to permanently outlaw such practices?" Despite a partial evasion—"I think that would raise difficult questions"—Katzenbach said "Yes." However, the attorney general said "I think so" when Douglas asked him, "Assuming discrimination, could Congress abolish literacy tests?"—anticipating Congress's action in the 1970 Voting Rights Act, which the Court was to sustain. On the matter of literacy tests per se as against their use as "engines of discrimination," Justice Stewart argued that the statute led to registration of illiterates; he asked specifically about Congress's abolishing Wyoming's literacy test. When Justice Fortas intervened to say that the first question was whether the purpose of the act was within Congress's Fifteenth Amendment power, Cox responded by saying that courts had an obligation to defer to Congress's judgment about the relationship: "Congress, after all, knows more about voting than anyone." That issue of the rationality of Congress's action was present throughout the questioning, as was the question of whether the Court had to deal with the matter of Congress's rationality. As Black posed it, "What difference does rationality make if Congress has the right to pass the law? . . . Why can't Congress do away with any test if it thinks it necessary?" The justices also tried to see whether Congress could have used alternative methods or had sufficient information on which to base its acts. Stewart claimed, "The Act is not the only or even the best way" and suggested re-registration of everyone after discrimination as a specific alternative, but the other justices seemed less concerned with this point.

Congress had not named specific states in the act but had all but done so. In fact, at one point Justice Brennan commented, "The function of the state selection was to catch the states that were in fact caught." White asked Katzenbach whether it would have made any difference if the states had been named. And he asked further, "Didn't Congress effectively name the states by including a date?" Harlan also asked, "Could they have picked Alabama alone?" Later Brennan wanted to be sure that Katzenbach was saying "that if the states were named there would still be no constitutional problem." The states' assertion that Congress had passed a bill of attainder led Fortas and White to point out that the act provided a remedy by allowing the states to go to the District of Columbia and argue that voting tests had not been used discriminatorily and White to ask counsel how this affected his argument of unequal treatment. Black also took exception to the bill of attainder argument: "I can't see a bill of attainder. It is not a punishment to be required to obey the Constitution, is it?" He received the weak response that it was when a class was singled out.

Also at issue were the inferences Congress could draw from low votes. For example, Stewart had trouble understanding the connection between literacy tests, connected with registration, and the vote. Katzenbach, who said that the relevant test was the vote, asserted that getting accurate registration figures was difficult, so voting figures had to be used by

Congress, something it could reasonably do. Justice Clark asked whether Congress had considered using primaries in the one-party states, receiving the answer, "They considered it, but in '64 there was a good hot presidential race." White then posed the problem of a high vote in a primary where there was competition and a low vote in the general election and also asked about the inference to be drawn from the connection between a low vote coupled with a "device" such as a literacy test. He wanted to know why no inference was drawn from a low vote in the absence of a test. "Why is it rational to cover only discrimination from certain tests?"

The question of Congress's rationality was strategic in the sense that the Court was looking for a proper legal basis for validating the statute. However, there were other strategic questions—for example, whether the statute's provisions were separable so that the remainder would be saved if parts were found improper. And the justices kept asking whether certain provisions of the act, or certain issues, needed to be ruled on at the present time. Thus Black more than once asked whether the Court needed to pass on the sections imposing criminal sanctions, which South Carolina had challenged. Here Katzenbach would not let the Court off easily. Trying to keep the justices "in bounds," closing off available escape routes, he said that the test suspension and enforcement sections were so interrelated that it would be hard to decide one without the other. When Katzenbach raised the matter of the state's failure to give an equal educational opportunity to Negroes, thus producing functional illiteracy used to disfranchise Negro citizens, Stewart interjected that the question of that relationship was not before the Court. When Brennan followed up by asking, "Does this educational point bear on the appropriateness?" Katzenbach said it was a congressional consideration "but we don't need to reach it in this case."[39]

Only seven weeks later, the Court handed down its decision, by the Chief Justice for a virtually unanimous Court. Great care was taken to answer all the arguments which had been raised, and the many questions raised at oral argument were dealt with, but the force of the Court's persuasion was immediately made clear. The Court held that the provisions of the 1965 Voting Rights Act pertaining to the suspension of eligibility tests or devices, review of proposed alterations of voting qualifications and procedures, appointment of federal voting examiners, examination of applicants for registration, challenges to eligibility listings, termination of listing procedures, and enforcement proceedings in criminal contempt cases were "appropriate means" for carrying out Congress's constitutional responsibilities under the Fifteenth Amendment and were consonant with all other provisions of the Constitution. Reflecting Justice Black's questions, the sections providing for criminal sanctions, which South Carolina had also sought to challenge, were ruled not before the Court on the grounds that since no person as yet had been subjected to or even threatened with them the attack on them was premature. Warren reviewed the Fifteenth Amendment, the act's predecessors, and the legislative history of the act itself, including the facts of discrimination practiced in the southern states and the slow, slow progress which had been achieved in the area through the case-by-case litigation method of dealing with the problem. Emphasizing Congress's conviction that sterner measures were needed to satisfy the demands of the Fifteenth Amendment, he observed that the act as a whole "reflects Congress' firm intention to rid the country of racial discrimination in voting." In answering the question of whether Congress had exercised its powers under the amendment in an appropriate manner, Warren stated, first, the amendment allowed Congress the use of any rational means to effectuate the constitutional prohibition of racial discrimination in voting, superseding contrary exertions of state power, and, second, the Court had upheld this power as far back as the 1880 case of *Ex parte Virginia*. The specific remedies and their application are not outside the purview of Congress, the Chief Justice stated, and are legitimate responses to a recognized problem, as is confinement of remedies to a small number of states and political subdivisions.

Warren also dealt in detail with the various points raised by South Carolina and supporting amici. The bill of attainder argument was dismissed immediately on the ground that this and the principle of separation of powers were protections for individual persons and private groups, those particularly vulnerable to nonjudicial determinations of guilt—not for the states, which are not persons within the context of Fifth Amendment due process. The doctrine of the equality of states applies only to the terms upon which states are admitted to the Union, not to remedies for local evils which have subsequently appeared. The formula provided is relevant to the problem being dealt with, theoretically and practically, and where other sections treat other circumstances differently this is appropriate since other problems prevail. Suspension of literacy tests was upheld on the ground that earlier decisions, although upholding the constitutionality of such tests, had also noted that the tests could be unconstitutionally employed. Congress had reasoned that states which had been letting white illiterates vote for years could not sincerely complain about dilution of their electorates through registration of Negro illiterates and had rejected the alternative of requiring complete registration of all voters as too harsh on many whites.

The Court also held that Congress could appropriately limit litigation to the federal district court in the District of Columbia pursuant to the Article III power to "ordain and establish" inferior federal tribunals. The burden of proof on the states automatically brought under the act was found not to be impossible, particularly since the relevant facts concerning the conduct of voting officials were peculiarly within the knowledge of the states and political subdivisions in which they were operative. Alabama's contention that the provision forbidding review of the findings which triggered the act's application was unconstitutional was also rejected, on the basis of various examples in which statistical determinations by the Census Bureau and routine analysis of state statutes by the Justice Department were similarly allowed. A state can always go into court, it was reminded, if the formula is improperly applied. The provision requiring review of subsequent state voting legislation by the district court or the Justice Department was upheld on the theory that exceptional conditions could justify legislative measures not otherwise appropriate. Congress had seen attempts to subvert federal voting legislation in the past, and expecting the same in response to this new law had responded in a permissible manner. Georgia's contention that the district court was authorized to issue advisory opinions was also rejected with the comment that a state wishing to make use of a recent amendment to its voting laws has a concrete and immediate controversy with the federal government.

Wrapping up discussion of other sections of the act, the Court upheld appointment of federal examiners as an appropriate response to voting registration problems, remarking that this provision was closely related to earlier remedies previously authorized. The Court rejected Georgia's claim that the attorney general was free to use his power under the act in an arbitrary fashion, noting that another section not before the Court set adequate standards to guide his discretion and that the special termination procedures furnished provided indirect judicial review for the political subdivisions affected. And in the closing the Court, through Chief Justice Warren, made this statement: "Hopefully, millions of nonwhite Americans will now be able to participate for the first time on an equal basis in the government under which they live." The Court's social convictions about the revolution in which they were participating could not have been made more explicit.

Justice Black wrote a separate opinion dissenting in part because he could not accept the constitutionality of Section 5, the enforcement provisions. Proceedings under that section would, he said, be a far cry from traditional constitutional notions of what constitutes "a case or controversy." That states were required to submit their polices to the federal government for prior approval ran counter to his concept of the federal system. Other parts of the Constitution are offended, he maintained, where the government is given the power to veto state laws.

The next voting rights decision to be handed down, coming immediately after the Voting Rights Act case, was also crucial. The year before, in *Harman v. Forssenius,* the Court had struck down Virginia's poll tax requirement to the extent that it affected federal elections. In *Harper v. Virginia State Board of Elections,* the Court at last invalidated the requirement by a state of the payment of a poll tax as a prerequisite to voting in state and local elections. While the poll tax requirement created problems by no means exclusively racial in impact, but rather problems affecting the lower economic class in general, the lower economic class in states which had a poll tax requirement were generally predominantly Negro, making the actual impact of the requirement essentially racial.

Oral argument in the case[40] had to do largely with the general proposition that poll tax requirements necessarily discriminate against poorer citizens, that personal wealth has nothing to do with one's qualifications as a voter, and that such laws violated both due process and equal protection under the Fourteenth Amendment. The reality of the racial incidence of the resultant discrimination was a matter which loomed large in the minds of both counsel and the Court. It was pointed out early in the argument that according to the 1960 census, 28 percent of all Virginia families had incomes of less than three thousand dollars, and 54 percent of all Negro families fell into that low earnings bracket. United States Solicitor General Thurgood Marshall, appearing as amicus, was even more specific. "With the 1965 Voting Rights Act in force," he warned, "the poll tax is the last weapon of the states to bar Negroes from voting." He stressed the urgency of striking the tax because of its effect on Negro voting in the South, pointing out that many thousands of people in Mississippi and Alabama—which had similar voting restrictions—who were eligible to vote for the first time under the 1965 act did not pay a poll tax. "If the poll tax is held constitutional, they can't vote."

Robert L. Segar, arguing for the Negroes, also pointed out that it was a well-known fact that Negroes were significantly less better off than white people from an economic standpoint and remarked that it was not hard to see therefore how an "economic weapon" was chosen to bar Negroes from voting. Said Black, "I suppose if a state could show that it had no motive to discriminate against Negroes, the poll tax would be all right?" "No," replied Segar. "This is not our only argument. A poll tax imposes an economic hardship on people who can't afford it. And the people who can't afford the poll tax are usually Negroes." When Harlan asked him if there was any evidence to show that the application of the poll tax discriminated against Negroes, Segar replied that it did not discriminate against them as applied, but did so directly. George D. Gibson, counsel for Virginia, defended the poll tax as rational, serviceable, and nondiscriminatory, arguing that the states have unlimited and unequivocal power to set voter qualifications, except as guided by the Fifteenth, Nineteenth, and Twenty-fourth Amendments. Answering a question from Fortas, he said that a state could bar Negroes from voting in the absence of the Fifteenth Amendment, and later insisted that "whatever may be the case in other states, Virginia's poll tax does not discriminate on the basis of race." Fortas asked, "Suppose it were proven that the purpose and effect of the poll tax were to deny the right to vote on the basis of race?" "If the effect of the poll tax was to discriminate on the basis of race, your Honor would have a case under the Fifteenth Amendment." The "basic aim" of the tax, Gibson said, "was to eliminate illiterates. But even if the Legislature had 'impure motives,' the poll tax could be upheld. Evidence of impure legislative motive is not the test."

The Court's decision, which in effect suggested that the Fifteenth, Nineteenth, and Twenty-fourth Amendments might be mere surplusage, was handed down a month later. It was written by Justice Douglas for a six-to-three majority. A citizen's right to vote, Douglas said, is protected by the Fourteenth Amendment. A state making the affluence of the voter or payment of any fee "an electoral standard" violates the Equal Protection Clause of that amendment. Voter qualifications have no relation to wealth nor to paying or not paying a poll or any other tax, Douglas asserted, and lines that are drawn by money are as disfavored as those drawn by race. Since wealth, like race, creed, or color, is not germane to one's ability to participate intelligently in the electoral process, the requirement of a fee as a condition for obtaining the ballot causes an "invidious" discrimination that runs afoul of the Equal Protection Clause. We have never been confined to historic notions of equality in determining what lines are constitutionally discriminatory, Douglas explained; the Equal Protection Clause is not shackled to the political theory of a particular era, any more than due process is restricted to a fixed catalogue of what was at a given time deemed to be the limits of fundamental rights.

Justice Black, dissenting, said that the majority was giving the Equal Protection Clause a meaning it never had merely to accord with current egalitarian notions. There is no assertion that race is involved in the poll tax Virginia sought to impose, he insisted, and the Court in this decision is using a natural law-due process formula that is bad constitutional law. Moreover, the Court was overturning a unanimous decision not yet thirty years old.[41] Harlan and Stewart also dissented, arguing that there was both historical and judicial reason for supporting the imposition of a poll tax.

The significance of the majority opinion was its endorsement of the position that curbs on the right to vote must be uprooted once and for all, whether their incidence be racial or economic in character. To reinforce its ruling, the Court held, in a one-line per curiam ruling, that imposition of a poll tax by Texas as a condition of voting in state and local elections violated Fourteenth Amendment due process requirements, on the basis of *Harper*.[42] Further reinforcement came in *Campbell v. Hamer*, albeit more indirectly. The case was brought as a class action by those denied the right to vote because, while registered pursuant to a federal court order, they had failed to pay poll taxes during the two previous years and because they had not registered within the state law's time frame involving a deadline two months prior to the court order. By the time the Fifth Circuit got the cases, in which injunctions against the elections were sought, the elections had occurred, but the Court of Appeals nonetheless held that the elections should have been enjoined, and remanded the case with instructions to set aside the elections. An appeal of this decision by the county of this decision was turned aside, the Court denying certiorari.

Reinforcement was to be the order of the day throughout the following perod, particularly with respect to coverage of the 1965 act. Once the act was sustained, the question often became whether specific state actions were subject to the approval of the attorney general and then to the testing of them in the District Court for the District of Columbia. In the first such case, state voting officials had refused to place the names of those certified by federal voting examiners under the act on their voting lists, claiming that they were not subject to application of the act. The federal government had then sued to enjoin this refusal and the state's failure to provide assistance to voters who, because of illiteracy or other handicap, might need assistance as required by state law. A three-judge federal court had granted the injunction. The Supreme Court, receiving the case directly on appeal, affirmed per curiam without a hearing, although Justices Black and White would have heard argument.[43] The effect of the order was that Louisiana was conclusively subject to the provisions of the act and that lower courts were to be allowed discretion with respect to specific orders.

One of the cases illustrating this reinforcement questioned whether changes in election laws were within the coverage of the prior-approval provision of the 1965 act. Involved were changes in write-in provisions, new qualifications for independent candidates, a change of the school superintendent from an elected to an appointed basis, and a change in the county board from election by district to at-large elections. The Court held all such changes within the scope of the act, and further held that individuals could bring suits to obtain declaratory judgments that such provisions were within the scope of the preenforcement approval requirement. At another time, when a state changed many of its polling places, the Court held such changes also covered.[44]

The voting rights cases, in which the key decisions came in 1965 and 1966, sustained the most basic right of citizenship, both in terms of Congress's action in the Voting Rights Act of 1965 and in terms of the Constitution itself with respect to the poll tax requirement. As in the housing area, where the Court's crucial ruling came a couple of years later, the effect was to sustain and reinforce what Congress had done. Yet in dealing with areas of race relations other than education during the 1960s the Supreme Court had not been restricting itself to areas where the Congress had already acted. The most notable of these was the area of public accommodations, involving the question of whether a private proprietor could refuse service on the basis of race and then call upon public officials to enforce his racially based refusal. That question was ultimately resolved by Congress in the Civil Rights Act of 1964, but not before the Court had been faced with many cases from the sit-ins. Although the Court was able to use the Civil Rights Act to remove the constitutional problem—never answered—from consideration, the pattern of cases before that ruling was quite different from any we have seen thus far, and it is therefore important for us to turn to an examination of the cases in transportation and public facilities which preceded and led into the public accommodations cases, then to an examination of the latter, and finally to cases involving general protest by blacks claiming violation of their rights. The latter cases are closely related to voting, as many of the protests and demonstrations of the 1960s were over denial of voting rights on the basis of race before Congress had acted in 1965 and the Court had sustained its work.

Chapter **8**

The Civil Rights Movement: Public Accommodations and Protest

Closely associated with voting is protest. Before attention turned to the Vietnam war, the activities of the civil rights movement in the 1960s were focused on voting rights. Deprivation of rights in this area produced marches and demonstrations. However, the areas in which new modes of public protest first arose were transportation and public accommodations—characterized by sit-ins and, in transportation, by "freedom rides." Public accommodations attracted more attention than transportation because of the symbolic importance of a person's being able to eat a meal where he or she wanted, because of the resistance of private proprietors to having to serve persons of another color, and because of the fact that the subject was the core of the Civil Rights Act of 1964. The public accommodations cases provide a stark contrast with the school desegregation area and allow us to see the many strategies the justices can use when they do not wish to engage in a straightforward attack on a problem. In those cases, the Court, drawing on the law of public facilities, on the "state action" doctrine, and on rules of criminal law and procedure, did not reach the basic constitutional issue thrust upon it—of the right of a proprietor to refuse service because of a person's race—or deal directly with the right to protest, in spite of the fact that nonviolent protesters were protected from conviction.

Once the Court handed down its decisive ruling on public accommodations in which it upheld Congress's handiwork, the Court dealt more directly with protest, much of which in the post-1964 period came from voting rights activities. At first directed toward protesting particular alleged wrongs and discriminatory practices, in other instances the protest was of a very general nature—for example, protest of discrimination against Negroes by the officials, citizenry, customs and practices of some town or city. The methods of civil rights demonstrators became widespread and were popularized as Gandhian in origin and religious—moralistic—in motivation. "Civil disobedience" became the cause, cry,

265

and tool of the civil rights movement—in effect having a "life of its own" apart from the discrimination being protested. Particularly significant was the Court's treatment of marches and demonstrations, especially those directed at or occurring near courthouses and jails, to which the judges' own resistance developed quickly. Also important was the Court's treatment of technical problems of law employed to protect protesters from unfair treatment at the hands of the law itself, particularly the question of removal of their cases from state courts to federal courts.

1

Brown had not explicitly overruled *Plessy* in the transportation area, but the demise of separate but equal was not long in coming there, and the Court was eventually to finish off what it had begun in the *Morgan* and *Henderson* cases. But before that came to pass, considerable resistance to full desegregation occurred, particularly with respect to local bus service and with respect to the facilities—restaurants in particular—used in connection with bus travel. Thus transportation became an object of protest by Negroes seeking to assert their rights, and was highlighted by the Montgomery bus boycott which brought the Reverend Martin Luther King, Jr., to the attention of the nation. Not many transportation cases came to the Supreme Court, which used commerce-related grounds to dispose of some of the early ones, but the cases were important because the first public accommodations cases involved transportation-related facilities.

Brown, of course, had cast doubt upon the continued validity of the *Plessy* doctrine. About six months after *Brown II*, the Interstate Commerce Commission, citing *Brown I*, completely reversed its earlier decisions and declared that the separate but equal doctrine would no longer be considered a valid application of the statute.[1] Changed social conditions called for the formulation of a new public policy which would serve to "preserve the self-respect and dignity of citizenship of a common country," said the commission. Yet it was to take more than this statement to bring change, and much additional litigation was necessary. One of the most effective ways to insure nondiscrimination might have been to threaten discriminators with damage suits. However, as southern juries generally were not sympathetic with the Negroes' complaints, attempts were made to bring such suits before northern juries. This was done by naming as defendant the parent company rather than the subsidiary which perpetrated the discrimination.

One parent company which defeated such a suit was based in California. A Negro passenger who had bought a through ticket on a journey into the South later brought suit to recover damages from the company on grounds that his civil rights had been violated when he was segregated from white passengers on a southern connecting carrier which was a subsidiary of the parent company. In *Spears v. Transcontinental Bus System,* a California federal district court, affirmed by the Court of Appeals, held that the parent company was not liable for damages merely because it had sold the bus ticket to someone later discriminated against. In the absence of any showing that the parent company had direct operating control of any kind over the rules, regulations, or policies of the subsidiary company, it was ruled, the parent company was also not liable on the ground that the action of the subsidiary was equal to the action of the parent. When the Supreme Court was asked to review this case, it refused. Subsequently, the lower courts continued to require suit to be brought against the offending line, often at the place where the wrong occurred. This and the varying degrees of relationship between parent and subsidiary companies made suits like *Spears* very difficult to maintain.

In the first term after *Brown,* the Court was also asked to hear a case involving bus segregation in Columbia, South Carolina. A federal district court dismissed the complaint without trial, holding that *Plessy* was still the law, but the Fourth Circuit ruled that the plaintiff was entitled to have her suit tried, because state laws requiring segregation of white and Negro passengers in intrastate transportation violated the Fourteenth Amendment. Where an intrastate bus driver acted like a policeman pursuant to state law, the appeals court held, there was sufficient action under color of state law to support a claim against the carrier itself for a violation of the Civil Rights Act. In asking for a reversal of this decision, the company stressed that there was great need for a Supreme Court decision in view of the Court's "notable hesitancy, if not determination" not to strike down *Plessy* definitively, in view of "greatly conflicting" circuit court decisions in the lateral application of *Brown,* and by reason of the "real problem" of the states in controlling social racial strife. On the other side, NAACP counsel urged affirmance, stressing that *Plessy* was out and *Henderson* was in. The Court seemed to indicate extreme impatience that such claims of constitutionality should seriously be raised at this late date. Citing only a case in which an appellant had been awarded damages because his opponent had made an appeal "based on frivolous grounds and causing delay," the Court dismissed the appeal per curiam.[2] Although the circumstances of the case below—the suit had still not been heard at the trial court level— indicated that the dismissal was probably on grounds that the appeal was premature, the Court's action was at first widely interpreted as a repudiation of *Plessy,* and a number of southern bus companies began to announce desegregation of their bus lines. Thus because of its ambiguity and unusual choice of citation for an ordinarily routine dismissal the Court perhaps accomplished somewhat more than it had expected to result from the order.

In December 1955 the great Montgomery bus boycott protesting the "back of the bus" seating policy began. It proceeded with astonishing success, carrying over into 1956 and resulting in the first clear statement by the Supreme Court that the right not to be discriminated against because of race in public transportation was a federal right capable of protection. Mrs. Browder, a Montgomery Negro woman who had been arrested for refusing to move to the rear of a bus when ordered to do so by a driver, brought suit with three others in federal court to challenge the constitutionality of state and local laws requiring segregation in transportation facilities. Two months after the Supreme Court's action in the Columbia, South Carolina, case, a three-judge district court, holding the state and local ordinances enforcing bus segregation constituted a denial of rights under the Equal Protection and Due Process Clauses, issued an injunction prohibiting Montgomery's Mayor Gayle and other officials from enforcing them. The court also ruled that *Plessy* was no longer valid because it had been impliedly though not explicitly overruled. Five months later, in *Gayle v. Browder,* the Supreme Court affirmed per curiam, citing *Brown* and two post-*Brown* public facilities cases. By this grouping of citations, the Court indicated clearly that the constitutional prohibition against enforced segregation found in *Brown* was to be extended to transportation not through the federal commerce clause which could not be relied upon here, but through an individual's constitutional rights. However, this comparatively noncommittal manner of deciding the case might have meant that a number of the justices were reluctant to divide the force of their desegregation effort, even though transportation would have been a relatively less controversial area in which to act. And we find that *Gayle* did not close off even direct local segregation.

After this brief sally, the Court resumed its reticence in this area. In so doing, it allowed a method of evasion to stand. After a local challenge of an ordinance requiring racial segregation on buses, Tallahassee adopted a new ordinance which made it a crime to occupy any seat or standing space other than that which the bus driver might assign for the sake of proper weight distribution in the bus, the health and safety of the passengers, and general peace and order. The effect of the ordinance was to put seating at the discretion of the driver, who let Negro sections of the buses be nonsegregated but kept white sections segregated. Challenging the ordinance in the state courts in *Speed v. City of Tallahassee,* Negro complainants contended it was a mere subterfuge to avoid the dictates of the *Gayle* ruling. After having been convicted of a misdemeanor for disobeying a driver and having the conviction affirmed by a state circuit court "without reaching a racial question," the complainants brought their case to the Supreme Court. There they contended that the ordinance was unconstitutional both on its face and as applied. They argued that the ordinance's vague and indefinite standards and their conviction for orderly refusal to return to segregated seats arbitrarily assigned to them by the driver were violative of due process and that, furthermore, the ordinance also violated the Fourteenth Amendment because it was applied so as to segregate because of race or color. City authorities contended that the ordinance was a reasonable exercise of the state police power and pointed out that no facts of racial motivation in the assignment of seats had been presented or admitted by the driver. When the city also claimed that the Court was without jurisdiction because the circuit court's judgment was not final, not having been reviewed by two higher state courts, petitioners responded that review was available below only with respect to procedural or jurisdictional questions, not with respect to the denials of their constitutional claims which had occurred in this case.

Despite these arguments, the Supreme Court denied a hearing to the case. The denial seems to have been based on the procedural matters raised by the city,[3] but by allowing such an obvious subterfuge to stand, it left a potentially great crack in the newly constructed wall against racial segregation in local transit[4] and temporarily decreased the strength of the Court's stand against such segregation. Furthermore, the denial of review violated the strategy of taking some cases after a major ruling to "bat down" opposition before it became too great, particularly where the rulings below had been adverse. However, the loophole was later closed by the Fifth Circuit when it ruled that state action was present in state prosecution of persons violating the discriminatory regulations of private intrastate carriers.[5]

The *Speed* certiorari denial had been adverse to Negroes' civil rights. In another case, a decision favorable to the assertion of civil rights was also turned aside. When Negro complainants in New Orleans obtained an injunction against enforcement of all Louisiana laws requiring segregation on buses, street cars, railways, or trolley buses in the city, the Fifth Circuit, citing *Gayle* as a holding, affirmed and declared all such state laws unconstitutional. The Court further ruled that, contrary to the city's contentions, it was not necessary for complainants to be arrested for violating the laws before they could test them. Still not providing a definitive statement which might eliminate hopes of segregating local transit, the Supreme Court denied certiorari.[6] Then, shortly thereafter, the Court took affirmative action through a per curiam ruling. A Negro had boarded a bus in Memphis and had taken a seat in the front. He had been ordered both by the bus driver and by police officers to go to the rear, get off, or be arrested. He left the bus peacefully, but later instituted an action challenging the validity of the state statute requiring such segregated seating arrangements. In *Evers v. Dwyer*, in a holding with clear implications for subsequent cases involving the assertion of civil rights, the Supreme Court said that this incident, notwithstanding that the complainant had boarded the bus for the purpose of instituting the action, presented an "actual controversy" concerning the validity of the state law, entitling him to bring a class action seeking a declaration as to his claimed constitutional right to travel on buses without being segregated. Reaching the merits, the Court outlawed Memphis's continued enforcement of bus segregation.

That the Court meant the area to be closed, even though it had avoided explicit statements, may also be seen in *Bailey v. Patterson*, a case involving Freedom Riders in Jackson, Mississippi, who had filed a class action in federal district court to enjoin enforcement of Mississippi's travel segregation statutes. The injunction they sought was against all methods of enforcement, including breach-of-peace prosecutions in connection with the travel statute. The three-judge district court which was convened abstained from ruling on the statutes until the Mississippi Supreme Court had interpreted them, even though it had done so years before. This caused the travelers, with amicus support from the Justice Department, to take a direct appeal to the Supreme Court, which then vacated the three-judge court's ruling and remanded the case to the regular district court where the suit originated. In its brief per curiam opinion, the Court said, "We have settled beyond question that no state may require racial segregation of interstate or intrastate transportation facilities. The question is no longer open; it is foreclosed as a litigable issue." Because "the constitutional issue is essentially fictitious," no three-judge court was required in the case, which could thus not be brought up on direct appeal, although the Supreme Court did have jurisdiction to determine the authority of the court below and to make an appropriate corrective order. By its remand to a single-judge district court with a direction for expeditious disposition of appellants' claim of right to unsegregated transportation service, the Court seems to have closed the chapter of public transportation discrimination, even though it left unanswered the question as to whether injunctive relief against state court prosecutions was precluded by the statute providing for injunctions "in aid of [the court's] jurisdiction."

Louis Lusky, commenting on the case, has noted that in using the frivolity argument the Court broke new ground without either briefs or full argument on the question, adopting "novel legal principles" involving a shift from the rule that a three-judge court is improper when plaintiff's argument is frivolous to a rule that three-judge courts are inappropriate when the defendant's argument is frivolous.[7] In the context of this case, the latter position might seem to aid the Negro plaintiffs, who would not have to suffer delay while a three-judge court was convened. However, there was a corresponding disadvantage because appeals from the single-judge court could not get to the Supreme Court directly but only through the Court of Appeals. Lusky also suggests that plaintiffs would have a new threshold problem: whether to ask for a single-judge court because the statute was obviously invalid or for a three-judge court because the law was only arguably invalid, greatly extending appeals from decisions on that jurisdictional point.

From the Court's perspective, rather than the plaintiff's, there may have been good reason for what the Court did. Because appeals from three-judge courts go directly to the Supreme Court, they lengthen the Court's docket,[8] but the Court may find it harder to turn them away because, unlike cases coming from the courts of appeals, they have not already had one review and, as well, supposedly fall within the Court's mandatory jurisdiction. The *Bailey v. Patterson* "resolution" of the technical issues may thus be seen as part of the Court's docket-management tactics. As Lusky said closer to the time—and out of irritation: "Until some better explanation comes along, it seems reasonable to view the case as an index of the great need of a frightfully busy Court to channel cases of this type through the courts of appeals."[9]

2

Most of the cases involving challenges to segregation of public facilities—including courthouses, parks, swimming pools, and golf courses—came after *Brown* and were completed by 1963; later public facilities cases were more centrally concerned with protest methods than with desegregation. Initially used by the Court to show the intended applicability of *Brown* "across the board," the area later was used to show the Court's impatience with the slow pace of desegregation. Prior to *Brown*, the Court had had a few public facilities cases. They did not point in a single direction, although, coming after the higher education cases, they had begun to cast doubt on the equality of separateness. One case, *Winkler v. Maryland,* involved the strictly segregated tennis courts operated by the city of Baltimore's Board of Recreation and Parks. After giving notice to the board and requesting that the segregation policy be changed, and after obtaining a permit to play, an interracial group showed up and began to play. When a large crowd gathered to watch, police asked the players to disperse and then arrested them for "conspiring to disturb the peace." When the players tried to bring their resulting convictions to the Supreme Court, the state pointed to the fact of the crowd and the police assertion that trouble was feared as reasons why the convictions were valid. Although the Court's First Amendment free speech doctrine had been that the police have a duty to protect those exercising their First Amendment rights rather than arrest them because an angry crowd starts trouble, the Court denied certiorari, thus letting the convictions stand. The Court also denied certiorari in another Maryland case, *Boyer v. Garrett,* involving racial segregation in athletic activities in public parks and playgrounds. Here the lower court had noted that separation was the normal treatment of the races in Maryland, that the city park commissions had the power to make rules for preserving order in the city's parks, and that separateness was justified to avoid racial conflict. Certiorari denial was based on the petition's not having been timely filed, suggesting that the Court may have used the time technicality to avoid the issue.

At about the same time, *Rice v. Arnold,* an NAACP case involving a lower court decision upholding Miami city officials' permitting use of city golf courses by Negroes on only one specific day each week, reached the Court. In an argument which was to appear in several other cases, Miami claimed that the loss of revenue resulting from integration of the golf courses would force the city to close them to everyone. The Supreme Court vacated the lower court ruling, remanding for reconsideration in the light of the recently decided *Sweatt* and *McLaurin* cases. In so doing, the Court quietly hinted that the new concept of equality embodied in those decisions might be extended to other areas. This, however, was not to be the end of the Supreme Court's contact with the *Rice* case. Ruling that *Sweatt* and *McLaurin* were not controlling in the area of recreation, the Florida Supreme Court again affirmed the Miami restrictions, this time including among the grounds for affirmance certain procedural matters indicating that Rice had adequate means under state laws by which to test the "reasonableness" of the one day per week rule. This time, although Justices Black and Douglas would have granted certiorari, the Supreme Court declined to hear the case, giving as its reason that there were adequate nonfederal grounds for the decisions below which precluded the Court's intervention. One other pre-*Brown* recreation case involved a lower court decision favorable to Negroes. Lower federal courts had ordered that Negroes be admitted to one of Kansas City, Missouri's, all-white swimming pools. The district court had utilized "separate but equal," and the Court of Appeals, accepting the district court's statements about physical differences between this pool and that provided for Negroes, had based its ruling on the *McLaurin* ground that since Negroes were admitted to the park in which the pool was located and all the other park facilities, they should be admitted to the pool as well. Here, as with *Rice* and *Boyer v. Garrett,* the Supreme Court denied certiorari.[10]

Two of the immediate post–*Brown I* cases were from the public facilities area. The first, from Louisville, Kentucky, was an NAACP-directed case which involved equality of separate recreational facilities afforded Negroes and whites by the city and exclusion of Negroes from an amphitheater located in a "white only" city park. Only the latter issue was presented in *Muir v. Louisville Theatrical Park Association,* the appeal by the Negroes to the Supreme Court. The high court's action was to vacate the judgment and remand the case for further consideration in light of *Brown* and "conditions that now prevail." Subsequently, the matter was settled when the theatrical association voted to offer tickets to the general public. The second case, from Houston, Texas, concerned the exclusion of Negroes from the city's municipal golf courses. The Court of Appeals for the Fifth Circuit had held that the golf courses were facilities separate and apart from the municipal parks in which they were located and that failure to allow Negroes to use the golf courses located only in white parks was discrimination against them which could not stand even under the rule of separate but equal. Here, the Supreme Court simply denied the city's request for a hearing.[11]

After *Brown II,* the Court took more positive, although summary, action in the public facilities area. In the *Dawson* case from Baltimore, after the Miami *Rice* decision but before *Brown,* a federal district court had rendered judgment adverse to the Negro complainants, perhaps seeing a sufficient legal and practical distinction between the *Rice* situation of part-time discrimination on a city golf course and the perhaps more "sensitive" situation of segregation of public beach and bathhouse facilities raised in *Dawson.* The district court again ruled against the Negroes after *Brown,* saying that the Supreme Court's decision did not apply to other fields, where "separate but equal" still applied. The Fourth Circuit then reversed, holding that the *Brown* doctrine applied across the board and without undue delay. The appeals court reasoned that if the police power could not be invoked to sustain racial discrimination in the schools, where attendance was compulsory and racial friction might be apprehended from the enforced commingling of the races, it could not be sustained with public beach and bathhouse facilities, the use of which was entirely optional.

On appeal, Maryland explained that the *Brown* decisions had given rise to concerted efforts to expand the decisions into fields not reasonably comprehended within their terms, causing uncertainty and indecision on the part of state officials. Maryland complained that the officials were caught between emotional and psychological pressures from the people whose lives had been lived under "separate but equal" and an earnest desire to see that the constitutional guarantees of all were protected. Because of the opposite directions in which the district court and Court of

Appeals had headed, Maryland pleaded with the Court to elucidate the issue as to whether the school decisions were broader in scope than they were in language. The state's argument was basically that in *Brown* the Court had been careful not to overrule the separate but equal doctrine, but merely to subtract from it, and then only in public education. Segregation there had been found "not reasonably related to any proper governmental objective," but here there was a very proper governmental objective—avoidance of possible race conflicts—to be served. It was especially important to serve this objective, it was argued, if acceptance of non-discrimination in those fields where constitutional guarantees did require abandonment of separate but equal were to be assisted. Noting that emotion in Maryland and the southern states concerning intermixing of races in bathing facilities was higher than any other field of human relations except possibly miscegenation, the state asked also that if the *Brown* doctrine were extended here, it be done directly, not by inference, but at the same time be allowed to come slowly, as in *Brown II*. NAACP counsel urged for Dawson that the appeal be dismissed and the Court of Appeals decision allowed to stand, or, in the alternative, that the opinion be affirmed. Racial segregation could not be held to deny due process and equal protection when practiced in public schools, counsel argued, and not in public recreation.

Despite these statements—and despite the fact that it took affirmative action rather than merely dismissing the appeal—the Supreme Court proceeded cautiously, affirming without comment. It seems clear that the Court might not have adopted the appeals court's argument had the justices written their own opinion. However, in view of the Court's manipulation of previous cases it seems most likely that the Court wished its steps in this area to be viewed as incremental. This conclusion is strengthened by the fact that after the *Dawson* decision the Court ruled similarly in the *Holmes* case involving municipal golf facilities, there extending *Brown* by vacating an adverse lower court decision per curiam. Thereafter, principally in lower federal courts, with an occasional bolstering from the Supreme Court, came a gradual broadening of the field of publicly owned facilities under the *Dawson* purview—from beaches and golf courses to city and state parks, swimming pools, libraries, theaters, hospitals, and courtrooms. The Supreme Court's relative reticence made evident that it wished this broadening of applicability to seem a natural and obvious process rather than a matter giving cause for great concern.[12] Had the Court wanted it to be otherwise, it could have issued a clear, direct statement.

After *Dawson* and *Holmes*, the Court generally reverted to the practice of not accepting public facilities cases. Up to this point, those cases had been straightforward: did *Brown* apply to parks and the like? Hereafter, while such cases, for example, involving courthouses, still arose, the cases often were more complicated because they involved methods of evasion which might have seemed facially valid. Here the Court turned aside cases in which lower courts had expanded Negroes' rights, although it later gave greater strength to such rulings by citing some of them to support other decisions.

Brought to the Court in the 1956 Term, *Department of Conservation and Development v. Tate* dealt with one of the principal tactics employed to avoid desegregation—private leasing of publicly owned facilities in the hope of disengaging state action from the discrimination. Involved in the case were certain portions of a state park from which private lessees were excluding Negro patrons. After the appeals court's *Dawson* opinion but before the Supreme Court had ruled, a federal district court, upon hearing certain Negroes' complaint, granted a permanent injunction restraining the department, their lessees, agents, and successors in office from denying any persons of the Negro race, by reason of their race and color, the right to use and enjoy the facilities of the park, on the basis of Fourteenth Amendment equal protection rights. In a case such as this, the court ruled, the normal lessor-lessee relationship must give way to the constitutional rights of the citizenry as a whole. Not only did the court extend the Supreme Court's prohibition of discrimination to privately leased portions of publicly owned facilities but it went further. The court stated that it was not passing upon the right of the department to sell or lease such facilities "in absolute good faith" by giving due notice of its intentions in such a manner that all interested parties, regardless of race, might avail themselves of the equal opportunity afforded to submit bids. However, it warned such a proposed sale or lease should contain specific provisions as to all terms and conditions, and any attempt to "negotiate" a sale or lease so as to continue discrimination would be completely scrutinized by the court. The power to sell or lease, the court declared, must not include the power to discriminate. This decision was subsequently affirmed by the Fourth Circuit, and was brought to the Supreme Court where it was denied a hearing. That this denial of review was meant to be supportive of the lower court can be seen in the Supreme Court's later citation of *Tate* and of another case rejecting the implication of the dicta of *Tate* itself that circumvention could occur through a purportedly bona fide sale.[13] This not only indicated further agreement with the *Tate* language but also can be seen as evidence that the Court wished desegregation of privately leased public facilities to appear as a logical incremental step from its own earlier pronouncements.

During the same term as *Tate,* the Court also faced an attempt to limit this category of forbidden state action to the performance of "governmental" functions. Involved in the case were a municipal beach and swimming pool operated on a segregated basis, which the city of St. Petersburg, Florida, threatened to close when Negroes attempted to use them. When suit was brought to enjoin the segregation of the facilities, the city claimed it was managing them in a "proprietary" capacity and that thus they were not within the protection of the Fourteenth Amendment's prohibition against discriminatory state action. A federal district court, however, held that the Fourteenth Amendment prohibited racial discrimination by the city in any capacity, including its "proprietary capacity" as a municipal corporation, with the possible exception of actions in a fiduciary capacity. Affirming, the Fifth Circuit pointed out that financial loss could not be invoked to justify illegal operation. Judge Rives said that while closing the pool would be unfortunate, there was "no ground for abridging the rights of the appellees to its use without discrimination on the ground of race so long as it is operated." When the city took the case, *City of St. Petersburg v. Alsup*, to the Supreme Court, the Court denied certiorari. Here as with the *Tate* case, the Court subsequently cited the ruling, lending an aura of approval to it.[14]

In the 1958 Term, the Court continued its avoidance of difficult public facilities issues. For example, the Court merely affirmed per curiam a fairly routine ruling by the Fifth Circuit, based on *Holmes,* that the Louisiana law and New Orleans ordinance requiring segregation in city parks were unconstitutional.[15] No difficult or subtle questions of state action were involved in the case. In another case, *Dawley v. City of Norfolk,* however, there was a very different kind of public facility in which racial segregation was being practiced. Here the question was whether racial discrimination could be practiced in a city courthouse by the use of discriminatory signs designating the various separate facilities within the building—from the courtroom to the men's room. Both the federal district and appeals courts had ruled that the matter was one within the jurisdiction of the judges of the state courts housed in the building and that interference on the part of a federal court was not required. The Supreme Court passed up the opportunity to agree or disagree with this judgment by denying certiorari. While one can see such an outcome as deference to the federal judges close to the situation, the case contains the additional controlling fact of deference to state judges, particularly important because after *Brown II* the matter of jurisdiction between the state and lower federal courts had been especially sensitive.

3

Several more public facilities cases were to arise in the early 1960s, and in one of them, a case from Memphis involving desegregation of that city's parks announced just a week before the *Goss* racial transfer school plan from Knoxville, the Court indicated its increasing impatience with the snail's pace of school desegregation during the eight years since it had been ordered. Before it reached that case, the Court had again to deal with methods used by municipalities to evade desegregation of such facilities as golf courses and then had to look again at courtroom desegregation. The Court started with *Hampton v. City of Jacksonville*, a follow-up to *Tate* and *Alsup*.

Faced with the prospect of legal action which would have forced desegregation of its public golf course facilities, Jacksonville, Florida, had chosen to sell the property to private individuals, conditional upon continued use of the property for a golf course for twenty-one years, with automatic reversion to the city if this contractual obligation was breached. Attracting no offer as high as the appraised value of the land apparently because of the use restriction, the city had suffered at least a paper loss in the transaction. The sale was challenged by certain Negro citizens of Jacksonville. A state circuit court held in 1959 that, although carried out for the public, operation of recreational facilities was not a governmental function which a city was compelled to perform. The city was therefore free to dispose of the facilities at less than the property's appraised value, in the absence of a showing of illegality, fraud, or abuse of authority in making the sale. When federal suit was brought, the district court refused in mid-1961 to enjoin either the sale or racial discrimination by the new private owners, holding that the reverter clause was insufficient to show "state action" in the control of the facilities' operation. Almost a year later, however, the Fifth Circuit, reasoning that the use clause could be compared to a restrictive covenant like that in *Shelley*, reversed. Over a vigorous dissent, the judges held that the reverter provision in the use clause gave the city such "complete present control" of the land that the new purchasers were "state agents" within the purview of the Fourteenth Amendment.[16] Coming after the Supreme Court's citation of the earlier *Tate* public facilities case, the Fifth Circuit's finding was not a great departure from precedent, but can be seen as the next logical step in a dynamic line of judicial decision-making. The Supreme Court, asked to review, declined, perhaps because the Court of Appeals had taken a somewhat larger step than the Court itself wanted to take at that time. The justices may not have objected to the lower court's making the ruling for it,[17] a strategy of using lower court decisions to guide and develop the Court's incrementalism used again in other areas.

After this initial certiorari denial, the Court quickly began to decide public facilities cases with opinion and to reach issues not directly dealt with for several years. Thus, in *Johnson v. Virginia*, the Court finally declared unconstitutional as a violation of equal protection the old practice of segregated seating in southern courtrooms. The justices held affirmatively that courtrooms were public facilities which the states could not segregate. The issue, which the lower federal courts had generally sought to avoid because of the underlying issue of federalism, was not a new one. As the decision did not occur until 1963, nine years after *Brown* and eight after *Dawson* and *Holmes,* and was announced in a per curiam order, it was most incremental and was in line with the Court's overall strategy in extending Fourteenth Amendment due process and equal protection rights to those from whom they had been previously withheld. Only a month later, there was a per curiam invocation of the new doctrine in a reversal of a Louisiana contempt citation of a Negro who had refused to obey a state court's order to move to the colored section of a segregated courtroom.[18]

Then came two park segregation decisions, just as long in coming as had been the courthouse cases. The first was *Wright v. Georgia,* in which the Court reversed breach of peace convictions of several Negro youths who had been playing basketball in a white park in Georgia and had refused to disperse on order by a policeman. The policeman's action had been defended on grounds that he had feared trouble might have started if the Negroes were allowed to remain in the park, even though the record demonstrated that no trouble was imminent when the orders and arrests were made. The Court handled this defense neatly by ruling that the policeman's command was in fact an unconstitutional attempt to enforce racial segregation in a municipal park. The fact that others might have breached the peace if the Negro boys had been allowed to remain in the park did not justify punishment of constitutionally right conduct in which the boys had been engaged. The ruling reflected and implemented much of the Court's reasoning with respect to unconstitutional state action from the sit-in cases decided during the same term, but the Court could have reached its decision without any such reliance because of the long and definite post-*Brown* history which the area possessed. That the Court viewed the case separately from the sit-in cases is indicated by its unanimity in *Wright,* which contrasts widely with the justices' variety of opinions on the sit-ins. In fact, *Wright* may have been used to bolster the sit-in cases rather than vice-versa. In any event, the finding in *Wright* was necessary to uphold the Court's rulings about desegregation in public parks. Otherwise, police could have used pretexts of possible disorders to undercut the Court's basic doctrine.

The second case was more important because it showed the Court's great impatience with the slow post-1954 pace of desegregation. *Watson v. City of Memphis* involved a suit by certain Negroes, twice defeated in lower federal courts, seeking immediate and complete desegregation of all facilities controlled by the Memphis City Park Commission. Representing the Negroes were NAACP Legal Defense Fund lawyers. The United

States submitted a brief as amicus on the side of anti-gradualism. At stake was the effect of *Brown*'s "all deliberate speed" directive on other areas in which desegregation was ordered. Arguing for petitioner Watson was Mrs. Constance Baker Motley of the NAACP.[19] Her position encompassed three points: 1) the Memphis Negroes' right to use of the city's parks should have been immediately enforced as a "personal and present" right; 2) *Brown II* did not apply to public recreation; and 3) if *Brown II* were to apply to complex problems of desegregating, it still would not apply here, because there was no demonstration of any complex physical problem with which the city officials had to deal. Justice Stewart commented immediately that these were three alternative arguments getting less and less extreme, thus indicating his awareness that in view of the Court's relative inactivity and restraint in the area to date counsel was uncertain how far the Court could be persuaded to go in her direction and wished to be prepared for the range of possibilities.

Mrs. Motley argued that prior to *Brown,* Fourteenth Amendment rights had always been called "personal and present constitutional rights" and had been immediately enforced—as in the higher education cases. After *Brown,* she contended, the per curiam affirmance in *Dawson* indicated that *Brown II* was not to apply to public facilities. She also argued that apart from precedents there were strong policy considerations why *Brown II* should be limited rather than expanded. The deliberate speed doctrine, widely interpreted as substituting a doctrine of gradualism for the separate but equal doctrine, had been reinforced by the weight of litigation—which had been on the question of how fast the school boards have to go and which had resulted in the admission of very few Negroes to the schools. Extension of the doctrine from schools to parks would mean gradualism in every area in enforcing Negroes' constitutional rights. On a practical level, Mrs. Motley contended that if twenty thousand white children moved to Memphis, the local authorities would take care of the problem, so why was it not possible here? Gradualism has produced more, not less, confusion, she said, because Negroes have not been advised when parks are desegregated; they can only tell by whether or not a policeman chases them out once they have entered.

Arguing for the city, Thomas R. Prewitt claimed that Memphis had devised a ten-year program for desegregation, was fulfilling and even accelerating it, and should be allowed to do so gradually in order to make the necessary accommodations for this transition in their large and fine system of public recreational facilities. He said also that since the district court had not yet been able to rule on the plan because the appeal had been immediately entered no particular plan was before the Court. Thus the only question was whether any delay at all was permissible with respect to the park and playground system as contrasted with the school system, not whether *Brown II* should have been ruled applicable to a public facilities case at the outset.

The justices indicated that since both questions had been considered by the Court of Appeals, the Supreme Court also could deal with them. Their questions focused on practical circumstances and the relief requested. As to the latter, Justice Stewart asked Mrs. Motley if what she sought was a ruling that there was no room for delay of any kind any place for any reason with respect to park and playground systems—and hence that there should be no gradualism at all in this area. Concerning circumstances, the justices wanted to know, for example, why it was more complicated or took longer to desegregate parks and recreational facilities than schools, particularly in view of Prewitt's concession that the same children were involved and that the school and parks were operated from the same building. When Chief Justice Warren, interested in whether schools and recreation were different, pointed out that the children had to go to school but did not have to go to the playgrounds, Prewitt emphasized the point by saying that participation on the playgrounds is voluntary and that the city did not want to discourage it. The Chief Justice commented that Memphis was continuing a community feeling that there should be segregation, not a justifiable reason under *Brown,* although Prewitt said delay had been granted because of the number of supervisors needed.

The status of the plan developed by local authorities was explored also. Stewart wanted to know whether any plan, either approved or disapproved by anyone, was before the Court. Whether any desegregation had taken place under the gradual plan supposedly adopted by the city was the subject of inquiry also. After Mrs. Motley responded that although about two-fifths of the neighborhood parks were available to Negroes but that various city stadiums, a museum, swimming pools, community centers, a golf course, and various other facilities were still unavailable to them, the justices pressed Prewitt as to whether the program was being put into effect. Warren asked why, if the city were really trying to remedy the segregated situation and give people their rights, some newly opened parks had nevertheless remained segregated. Warren reminded Prewitt that he had admitted that "the people of Memphis" were not in favor of park integration. Answers to persistent questions by Justice White—as to why so many more supervisors were said to be needed for an orderly transition—and Goldberg made it evident that only one playground, in a neighborhood now virtually all Negro, was definitely desegregated by the city and that the next two planned for desegregation were in similarly changed neighborhoods. In closing, the Court asked for statistics on the racial makeup of the city and on the number of Negro children "integrated" into the city's public schools and requested that a copy of the proposed ten-year park desegregation plan be made available to it.

When the Supreme Court handed down its opinion, it was unanimous and was charged with impatience. As the Court had first used the area of public facilities to extend *Brown* across the board, it now chose a public facilities case to declare strongly its displeasure at the rate at which desegregation in all areas had been progressing since *Brown*. Reversing the district and appeals courts' decisions, the Court ordered the immediate desegregation of all facilities controlled by the Memphis Park Commission. Characterizing its decision as one taken directly from precedent, the Court held, first, that the passage of time and the numerous desegregation decisions since *Brown* had obviously tempered the present import of policy considerations behind "with all deliberate speed." In holding gradualism not applicable to public recreational facilities, the Court cited examples of "the repeated and numerous decisions" giving notice that these racial practices were illegal, in none of which "was the possibility of delay in effecting desegregation even considered." The Court thus showed its displeasure with the generally slow pace of school desegregation everywhere in the nine years since *Brown* and served notice on all school officials that more speed was in order. The Court also held that desegregation of parks did not present the same kinds of difficulties involved in school desegregation, where attendance was compulsory, the adequacy of teachers and facilities crucial, and questions of geographic assignment often of major significance. Further delay could not be upheld unless it was demonstrated that constitutionally cognizable circumstances warranted such a delay, the justices said. Finding further that the city's reasons for continued delay were not substantial and that the evidence did not indicate that violence would result from prompt desegregation, the Court held that desegregation must ensue, emphasizing that constitutional rights could not be denied because of hostility to their assertion or exercise. In *Watson* the Court was saying that the near-decade of procrastination was to be brought to a halt and desegregation was to be faced up to at last. Because of the legal and practical connection between public schools and recreational facilities, the case offered an attractive opportunity to do so. The situation was made even more strategically appropriate for the Court's ruling by the participation of the federal government, which the Court may have wanted to enlist in implementing the constitutional declaration it had rendered nearly a decade earlier in what amounted to a federal vacuum.

The urgency that the Court had begun to show in *Watson* was reflected also in a New Orleans parks case, *City of New Orleans v. Barthe*. The case involved all city-owned and city-operated parks, playgrounds, community centers, and all recreational cultural facilities and activities administered by the city recreation board. Negro residents of New Orleans had brought suit against the city and others to force desegregation of city parks and other recreational facilities. They secured from a three-judge federal district court a ruling requiring forthwith desegregation of the facilities, including all programs directed, supervised, or maintained by the recreational department. In granting the preliminary injunction, the district court noted that the challenged segregation policy resulted from the Louisiana Anti-Mixing Statute as well as from long-standing custom. The court pointed out that the city had nineteen Negro and one hundred white playgrounds, the former by no means equal to the latter, and ruled that to the extent the city had relied on the anti-mixing statute, it had relied on a law unconstitutional on its face. Citing *Watson,* the court said segregation of such public facilities can no longer be tolerated or observed, whether brought about by ordinance, policy, or custom. The judges said that they could have taken the position that a three-judge court should not even decide the case because there was so little substance to the constitutional question the city raised in alleging its right to maintain such segregated facilities, but they said they were nevertheless deciding the case in the interest of expediting justice. The city carried the case to the Supreme Court, where it argued in its brief both that the state statute had not yet been passed upon by state courts and that it was valid under the police powers of the state for the purpose of protecting the public health, morals, and the peace and good order. The city denied that its action was caused by race. Comparing the statute to the power to license doctors, the city argued that the separation of the races required by it was only incidental to the greater burden of protecting life, health, and property, which it was intended to meet. Furthermore, arguing that the Supreme Court did have jurisdiction in the case, the city contended that no injunction should have been granted, for the city officials were high class men. No showing had been made that they would disobey the lower court's judgment or that conditions existed that required the urgency of injunctive processes to secure compliance with the court's mandate.

NAACP counsel moved that the Court either dismiss the appeal or affirm the judgment below. However, counsel argued also that the Court in fact lacked jurisdiction of the appeal because a three-judge court—not required where prior decisions make frivolous any claim that a state statute involved is not unconstitutional—had not been necessary for disposition of the case below. What the Court should do, counsel urged, was to take certiorari jurisdiction of the case and render judgment on the merits. Counsel contended that none of the city's claims were novel, all having previously been rejected by the Court expressly and by implication as far back as *Buchanan.* No showing of clear abuse of discretion on the part of the lower court in granting the injunction had been made; merely asserting that the appellants are "high class men" was not enough to avoid injunctive relief.

Rather than scheduling the case for argument, the Court, making its decision per curiam on the basis of the briefs, granted the NAACP's motion to dismiss the appeal. The Court treated the appeal papers as a certiorari petition before judgment—done also in the Prince Edward County school case just six weeks earlier—"in view of the long delay in the case since . . . *Brown* . . . and the importance of the questions presented." Granting certiorari, the Court affirmed the judgment of the district court, citing a 1961 Term public accommodations case and *Watson.* Black, Harlan, and White noted that in their opinion the case was not appealable to the Court of Appeals. The Supreme Court, they argued, should have dismissed the appeal to allow the Court of Appeals to decide whether the appeal of the case was properly pending before it. In support of this position, they cited *Bailey v. Patterson,* the 1961 Term transportation case in which a three-judge court had been ruled unnecessary because the question of whether the segregation defended was constitutional was "no longer open; it is foreclosed as a litigable issue."

No matter which of the dispositions had been implemented, the implication was that the importance of the right asserted warranted no further delay in finally disposing of the case and that the challenged legislation under which the city defended its segregation policies was beyond question unconstitutional. The difference in the two courses of disposition, in effect, was that the majority's, with the unusual procedural short-circuiting of the appellate process, was more rapid and direct. Like the three-judge court which had virtually apologized for rendering a decision in the case, the Court majority seemed to wish to make its position on the substantive matter unquestionably clear. The very fact that the city could argue as it had would seem to warrant this disposition. The Court usually cuts through its own procedures to help weed out cases, but here it was done so that the Court could achieve a particular result or at least achieve it much faster than might otherwise have occurred. The Supreme Court's action in granting certiorari saved the plaintiffs from having to return to court to obtain the relief they were seeking. Particularly where the lower court action was favorable and a remand would produce no further amplification, this seemed the best tactic.

The Court's subsequent mopping-up in the public facilities area required little action. *Hamilton v. Alabama,* which came a year after the *Johnson* courthouse case, was a mixture of public facilities and criminal procedure. A young black woman had been held in contempt by the Alabama Supreme Court for refusing to comply with the segregated seating arrangements in the courtroom and for refusing to answer a lawful question in the courtroom when called by her first name. When she appealed her conviction to the Supreme Court, she won a summary decision on only the question of courthouse segregation, not on the "first-name" matter, of principal interest to her. Citing *Johnson*, in a per curiam decision the Court reversed the state court judgment, thus stating that it was no longer open to question that a state may not constitutionally require segregation of public facilities. Here lawyers' tendency to present multiple issues and alternative grounds for decision and to argue every possible basis for winning a case was a disadvantage from complainant's perspective, although it allowed the Court to avoid the new question. Justice Black concurred but cited as controlling the 1959 Term *Thompson* public accommodations case to indicate he found no evidence to support the conviction; he apparently wished to view the grounds for reversal as more procedural than substantive. Finally, Clark, Harlan, and White noted that they would have denied certiorari, thus avoiding the case altogether.

Another public facilities case coming a few years later dealt with a Mississippi beach front built largely with federal "rivers and harbors" funds—a twenty-four-mile-long strip of sand pumped up from the Mississippi Sound under the auspices of the Army Corps of Engineers. Involved in the suit were twenty-nine Negroes who sought to use the beach and were expelled and arrested allegedly to enforce private property rights of beach-front land owners. The convictions, grounded on a state court holding that title to the land was indeed private, were appealed from the Mississippi Supreme Court for review by the United States Supreme Court under NAACP Legal Defense Fund guidance. The state asked the Court to delay any action until a related suit in Mississippi federal court brought by the Justice Department to enforce its construction contract that called for "public" use of the property should be decided. Calling the Biloxi beach "one of the largest man-made beaches in the world," the NAACP moved for outright reversal of the 1963 convictions. In *Mason v. City of Biloxi,* the Court chose the latter course of action and through a per curiam order reversed the convictions. While the constitutional issue was thus settled, use of the brief method of disposition allowed the Court to avoid having to deal frontally with the question of federal development of the beach. The related Justice Department suit was left pending before federal District Judge Harold Cox. Only one justice, Harlan, indicated that he would have heard argument in the case.

4

For an extended period, particularly after *Brown,* the Court avoided cases in the school desegregation area. A definite contrast is provided in the field of public accommodations, where the Court accepted many cases and decided the vast majority on the merits. However, the Court regularly avoided a broad ruling like *Brown* in the latter area, so that those protesting denial of service in restaurants and elsewhere found their convictions reversed without the Court reaching the issue they wanted reached. As Jack Greenberg has remarked, "The sit-in decisions were characterized by wholesale granting of certiorari and by studious avoidance of the broad constitutional issues underlying the details of particular cases. The ad hoc character of the decisions, however, did not interfere with consistent results. In case after case a majority of the Court consistently upheld the protestors."[20] From 1957 through 1967, the Court granted review in 61 of 81 cases (75.3 percent) involving sit-in demonstrations and related issues. In all but four of the 61 (93.4 percent), the Court decided the cases in favor of the demonstrators or the sit-in movement.[21] This made the pattern of decision like that before, rather than after, *Brown,* as the Court in the 1927–54 period had "refused to declare that segregation in schools violated the 14th Amendment, while at the same time rejecting as unequal every instance of segregation brought before it."[22] The protesters' rate of success before the Supreme Court is even more startling if we recognize that, contrary to the pattern in other areas of civil rights, where lawyers tried to choose which cases would go to the Court, in part to avoid bringing very many "losers" and thus hurting the civil rights movement,[23] lawyers bringing sit-in cases to the Court were not particularly selective in their choice of cases. Not "preplanned," many sit-in cases arose almost spontaneously when someone was arrested for sitting-in, and the civil rights lawyers, who did not have a prearranged litigation strategy, had to develop one as they went along.

Grossman, who suggests that "the key decision was the one to grant review" because almost all the cases granted review were decided favorably to the demonstrators, infers from this fact that "the policy of at least four Justices—and probably more—was one of granting review in virtually every case in which a favorable decision for the demonstrators could be secured."[24] This did not mean unanimity—in fact, there was considerable disagreement within the Court, not limited by the Court's narrow grounds. Moreover, those grounds helped produce disagreement as some of the justices thought their brethren should have gone farther.

The pattern of the Court's rulings was clearly incremental, easy for the Court because of the large number of cases. And approving Congress's handiwork, as the Court did with respect to the 1964 Civil Rights Act, was a more gradual move than having to rule directly on basic constitutional issues posed by the protesters. However, incremental movement or not, the Court seemed to be stretching so hard at times to avoid the constitutional question that it looked like an india-rubber man. Moreover, the use

of procedural defects to reverse the convictions did not legitimize the
sit-in behavior itself—something the judges probably wanted to avoid—
but it also did not "effectively discard the tradition of segregation in public
accommodations,"[25] which the justices clearly did want to eliminate.

Although there were a few public accommodations cases before the
1959 Term of Court, the first important cases arose then; they included
the *Thompson* case from Louisville, important for the standard that a
conviction could not be supported in the absence of evidence. The years
of 1960 and 1961 saw *Boynton v. Virginia,* involving a restaurant in a bus
terminal, which served to tie transportation and public accommodations
together, and *Burton v. Wilmington Parking Authority,* involving a restaurant in a parking garage, important for its enlargement of the "state
action" concept. Then came a long series of more typical sit-in cases,
entailing refusals of service to blacks in privately owned restaurants. After
the *Garner* case, the 1962 and 1963 Terms saw considerable oral argument of such cases—seven, including *Peterson* and *Lombard,* in the 1962
Term, and five in the 1963 Term, which included *Bell v. Maryland,* two
cases from Columbia, South Carolina, and the reargued amusement park
case of *Griffin v. Maryland*, initially argued in the 1962 Term. All these
cases came prior to the Civil Rights Act of 1964. Passage of that statute was
followed quickly by argument of and decision in the two cases challenging
the act's validity, *Heart of Atlanta Motel v. United States* and *Katzenbach v.
McClung,* and by the Court's disposition of the pre-act convictions still
pending, in *Hamm v. City of Rock Hill.*

The first important public accommodations case did not arise until the
1959 Term. Two earlier cases, however, merit attention. Once was a
pre-*Brown* case from the District of Columbia, the other a certiorari denial
of a post-*Brown* Fifth Circuit ruling. In the former, *District of Columbia v.
Thompson Co.,* the Supreme Court upheld the enforcement of statutes
pertaining to the District which made it a crime to refuse a person service
in a restaurant on account of race or color. The restaurant company
argued that the failure of the executive branch to enforce these laws over
the years—that is, their non-use over a long period—must have resulted
in their modification or even repeal. Ruling against the company, the
Court said that hardship might exist if criminal laws had been "so long in
disuse as to be no longer known to exist" and then were enforced against
innocent parties, but that would not invalidate the laws. Congress's power
to pass a law prohibiting discrimination against Negroes by restaurant
owners and managers, the Court said, was like states' police power to pass
similar legislation. No mention was made in the decision of the Commerce
Clause powers, which Congress used later to enact broader legislation

The second case was *Derrington v. Plummer.* Here the Fifth Circuit
ruled that discrimination in a privately leased restaurant housed in a

Harris County, Texas, public courthouse was state action in violation of equal protection. The court found that one portion of a building planned, built, and maintained by the county with public funds and used for a public function could not be considered to be diverted to purely private use. The state could not escape from its commitment to provide restaurant facilities equally for all citizens by leasing the restaurant, the Fifth Circuit said. However, probably hoping to mollify opposition to its decision by trying to set up a clear distinction as to what did and what did not bring state action to bear in such a case, the judges suggested that if the government had any otherwise useless surplus property, a lessee of that kind of property might exercise the prerogative of a wholly private proprietor as long as there was no purpose of discrimination or joinder in the enterprise or express reservation of control by the governmental unit. When asked to review the decision, the Supreme Court declined the invitation.

The immediate effect of the *Plummer* decision was to link the areas of publicly owned public facilities and privately owned public accommodations so that any racial discrimination in any portion of a going public concern, even that perpetrated by a private lessee, would be state action forbidden by the Fourteenth Amendment. This ruling and the *Tate* decision on leasing public facilities together meant that in public facilities and public accommodations the lower federal courts had ruled that private lessees of public property might not discriminate because of race and that the Supreme Court had let the decisions stand.

In the 1959 Term, when the majority of race cases came from an area other than education for the first time since *Brown*—probably an indication of the broadening spectrum of civil rights cases—the Court decided a case which resulted in a ruling the Court subsequently used to deal with cases arising from sit-ins or other demands for service. In *Thompson v. City of Louisville,* the incident leading to the Negro petitioner's arrest seemed rather innocent. Thompson had gone into a cafe he ordinarily frequented and had had a sandwich and beverage while waiting for a city bus. He was standing in the middle of the floor tapping his foot to the music when two policemen came in. Observing Thompson for a time, the police arrested him for loitering although no complaint had been made either by the manager, who knew Thompson, or by anyone else present. When Thompson argued against the arrest for loitering, the police charged him with disorderly conduct. He was subsequently convicted and fined for both offenses in city police court. Unable to appeal within the state, Thompson took his case directly to the Supreme Court, contending that he was merely "shufflin' " and that the arrests and prosecution were reprisals for having employed counsel and for having demanded a judicial hearing to defend himself against prior and allegedly baseless police charges. Under Kentucky law, he explained, convictions bar suits for malicious prosecution and even false imprisonment, the effect which the latest baseless arrest and conviction were intended to have.

The Supreme Court agreed to hear "Shufflin' Sam's" case, and through its decision established crucial precedent for the subsequent rash of southern sit-in arrests. Justice Black's opinion reversing the convictions for a unanimous Court noted that the question before the Court was whether the charges were so totally devoid of evidentiary support as to render the convictions unconstitutional under the Due Process Clause of the Fourteenth Amendment. Decision of this question, Black continued, turned not on the sufficiency of evidence but on whether the conviction rested on any evidence at all. The evidence presented failed to prove all three elements of the loitering charge under Kentucky law, the Court said, as it was obvious that the petitioner was welcome in the cafe according to the manager, was not without means of support, and was not boisterous. As for the disorderly conduct charge, the only evidence presented there was the single statement of one of the policemen that the petitioner was "very argumentative." "Thus we find no evidence whatever in the record to support these convictions," Black said. He thereby established the principle that when an arresting officer charged that the mere presence of a particular person in a restaurant was a violation of some statute, the charge obviously was a gross misapplication of the law and thus a denial of due process.

5

The connection between transportation and public accommodations was perhaps no more clearly shown than in *Boynton v. Virginia,* decided in the 1960 Term. The circumstances of the case were simple and were on the whole typical of later sit-in cases—as was the Court's approach in deciding it. Boynton, a Negro law student, bought a Trailways bus ticket from Washington, D.C., to Montgomery, Alabama, and boarded the bus. When the vehicle reached Richmond, Virginia, the driver pulled up at the Richmond Trailways Bus Terminal and announced to his passengers that there would be a forty-minute stopover. Boynton got off the bus and went inside to get something to eat. Disregarding the racial division in the restaurant in the terminal, he sat down in the white section and attempted to order a sandwich and tea. First a waitress and then the assistant manager of the restaurant requested and instructed him to move from the white portion to the colored portion of the room. When he refused on grounds that he was an interstate bus passenger, they called a police officer and had Boynton arrested. He was tried, convicted, and fined for having "unlawfully" remained on the terminal restaurant premises after having been forbidden to do so by the assistant manager, the person in charge of the premises at the time. Boynton maintained in the Virginia courts that he had a federal right as an interstate passenger to be served without discrimination by this restaurant used by Trailways for the accommodation of its interstate passengers, that thus he had been on the restaurant premises "lawfully" rather than "unlawfully" as charged, and that he had remained there not "without authority of law" but under its protection. He argued that the application of the Virginia trespass law to him was a violation of the Interstate Commerce Act and the Equal Protection, Due Process, and Commerce Clauses of the United States Constitution. Despite these arguments, the Virginia courts, through the state supreme court, upheld his conviction.

The petition for certiorari which Boynton presented to the Supreme Court was confined to the constitutional issues of whether his conviction was invalid as a burden on commerce forbidden by the Constitution and whether the conviction violated the Due Process and Equal Protection Clauses of the Fourteenth Amendment. It did not mention the essentially statutory question involving the Interstate Commerce Act. However, at argument Thurgood Marshall barely mentioned the constitutional issue, preferring to call the arrest a violation of the act, not an undue "burden" in interstate commerce. By his emphasis, Marshall thus provided the Court with a way to avoid the constitutional questions entirely. Relying on *Morgan,* he contended also that any restaurant set up for the purpose of serving food to passengers is, like the bus, engaged in interstate commerce. *Boynton* had looked like a deceptively easy sit-in case until it became apparent that the lack of one fact in the trial record might force the Court to an otherwise avoidable constitutional question. It had been established at trial that the restaurant operated under a lease from Trailways Bus Terminal, Inc., but nothing had been introduced to show who owned the terminal corporation. The Court was technically confined to the trial record in disposing of the issue. If the Court could not consider the restauranteur as anything but a private businessman, then, having granted certiorari and heard the case, it had little choice but to meet head-on the controversial state action questions underlying the sit-in movement, which it had tried so carefully to avoid thus far.

At oral argument,[26] counsel for Virginia admitted that if the bus company operated the restaurant it could not refuse service to Negroes. He argued, however, that the bus company had no control over the restaurant and that as a private business it could discriminate as it chose. Even if the bus company did own the terminal, which counsel said the Court couldn't consider since the information had not been before the lower courts, the restaurant still had the right to discriminate unless it was totally controlled by the terminal. Solicitor General Archibald Cox, in a position typical for him because in sit-in cases he tended to argue in favor of those sitting-in but on relatively narrow grounds,[27] produced documents showing that the bus line did own the terminal and could be connected with the restaurant. Despite the Solicitor General's material, the absence in the trial record of such evidence seriously bothered the justices, who clearly had no desire to tackle the underlying constitutional issue of the case—whether the state's action in making an arrest to support a private businessman's desire to discriminate was a violation of the Fourteenth Amendment. Justice Stewart pointed out that if the Court ruled that any restaurant could not discriminate against passengers in interstate commerce, it would affect the tiny lunchrooms attached to gas stations at which buses sometimes stopped as well as the large city bus terminals. When Marshall indicated that there were not many of the former left, Stewart retorted that he had stopped at one the previous weekend.

In deciding the *Boynton* case, the Court was faced with several alternatives. To hold that the trespass arrest and conviction springing from the terminal restaurant's refusal of service to Boynton was an undue burden on interstate commerce, one option, would have required that one of two things be established: that the restaurant was indeed an integral part of that interstate transportation or that Boynton's status as an interstate passenger protected him from enforcement against him of any private discrimination by any state authority. To establish the first, it would be necessary to implement exactly the same kind of reasoning and holding which were required for a statutory ruling, thus making the latter still more attractive. To establish the second point, it would be necessary to make an extremely broad ruling applicable to virtually all private places of business at which an interstate traveler might stop; yet in 1960 the constitutional or statutory support for such a holding would have been difficult if not impossible to find. Alternatively, in the constitutional sphere the Court could have found that the arrest and conviction, springing from an exclusion based on race, violated Boynton's Fourteenth Amendment rights. This, too, would have required establishment of some completely new precedent like that on the underlying issue of whether any official enforcement of a private businessman's racial discrimination could be prohibited as state action in violation of the Fourteenth Amendment, at least where the party involved could claim status as an interstate traveler. Such a holding would be similar to a state action ruling relating to enforcement of restrictive covenants but its application would be much broader. Because there was evidence that the restaurant's assistant manager had specifically objected to Boynton's presence, the *Thompson* precedent was of no use—it prohibited the Court from looking at the "sufficiency" of evidence. In any event, the racial basis of the desire to exclude was the only ground upon which the evidence might be found insufficient.

The decision illustrated that the Court would cut through procedural restraints when it was strategically helpful to do so. Although hindered by lack of information about the terminal's ownership, the Court "reached through" this impasse to decide the general issue related to it in order to avoid another, much broader, issue which the Court was already assiduously trying to avoid deciding. Announcing the Court's decision and illustrating the "search for the narrow ground and avoidance of general pronouncement . . . [which] typified the jurisprudence of protest decisions in years to come,"[28] Justice Black stated that while the Court ordinarily limited its review to the questions presented in the petition for certiorari, the case would be best decided not on the constitutional questions but on the Interstate Commerce Act contention raised in the Virginia courts. Because discrimination based on color was at the core of all three questions presented by the case, the Court thought it appropriate to proceed at once to the statutory issue. Fitting the case where precedent was available, the justices found *Boynton* a logical extension of *Mitchell* and *Henderson* that should buses in transit decide to supply dining service, they could not discriminate within this service under the applicable Interstate Commerce Act provisions, nor could restaurants owned, operated, or controlled by bus companies. Conceding that the record did not show active operation or control of the terminal or restaurant by the bus company, the Court found the act's protections against discriminatory transportation services not so narrow as to exclude facilities not owned, controlled, or operated but nevertheless comprising an integral part of transportation. Thus if the bus carrier volunteered to make terminal and restaurant facilities available to interstate passengers as a regular part of its transportation, and the terminal and restaurant acquiesced and cooperated in this undertaking, then the latter must perform these services without the discrimination prohibited by the act. The justices found that the lease agreement signed between the bus terminal and restaurant companies indicated that no matter who might have technical title or immediate control of various activities within the building, the facility as a whole had as its principal and regular purpose filling the needs of bus company passengers. Passengers had a right to expect that voluntarily provided transportation food service—essential to interstate bus passengers—would be rendered without discrimination. Thus Boynton did indeed have a federal right to remain in the white portion of the restaurant and was there "under authority of law."

In an obvious concession to Justice Stewart's tiny service station lunchrooms, Black went on to say that the Court was not deciding that every time a bus stopped at a wholly independent roadside restaurant the act required that restaurant service be supplied in harmony with its provisions. However, where, as in this case—decided on its facts— circumstances showed that the terminal and restaurant operated as an integral part of the bus carrier's transportation service for interstate passengers, an interstate passenger need not inquire into title or contractual documents in order to determine whether he has a right to service without discrimination.

Justices Whittaker and Clark dissented along the lines of objections made at oral argument, first, on grounds that the question of a violation of the Interstate Commerce Act had not properly been before the Court, and, second, on grounds that even if the Court had been able properly to decide the case on the act, the facts did not warrant the decision because of the missing evidence as to ownership or control and because they were not prepared to go so far as to say that regular "use" by the carrier made the restaurant a facility "operated or controlled" by it within the meaning of the act.

Narrow though it was in relation to the broad questions on which the Court could have made a pronouncement, *Boynton* had important effects. The following September, the Interstate Commerce Commission altered its regulations and prohibited interstate buses from either providing or utilizing segregated facilities. The ruling also was used in later judicial decisions. In *Thomas v. Mississippi* the Court was faced with a Mississippi Supreme Court decision affirming the conviction and sentence of a Negro "freedom rider" for disorderly conduct when he refused to obey a police officer's command to move from a "white" waiting room in an interstate bus terminal. Here, citing *Boynton,* the Court reversed the lower court judgment per curiam. Similar dispositions occurred in *Callender v. Florida*—reversing convictions under a state unlawful assembly statute based on attempts by three "freedom riders" to integrate segregated facilities at an interstate bus terminal—and in *Abernathy v. Alabama.* The latter case involved demonstrations protesting discrimination in public accommodations connected with interstate travel facilities. A group of "freedom riders" claiming protected activity had appealed their state trial court breach of peace convictions, but the Court of Appeals of Alabama had affirmed on grounds that under the circumstances of great public excitement and the temper of the crowd the defendants must have known that their conduct was calculated to incite breach of peace in violation of state statutes. The Supreme Court's per curiam reversal of the state courts, citing the Motor Carrier Act's service-discrimination ban and *Boynton,* made the decision simple and incremental.

6

The Court's next important public accommodations case, also some-what tied to transportation, was *Burton v. Wilmington Parking Authority*. One day in August 1958 Burton, a Negro, parked his car in a public parking building in Wilmington, Delaware. He then proceeded to the Eagle Coffee Shoppe, a restaurant located within the building, and sought service. Refused service solely on the basis of his race or color, he filed suit against the restaurant and the parking authority charging that such refusal abridged his rights under the Equal Protection Clause of the Fourteenth Amendment. The state courts denied both his Fourteenth Amendment claim and his further argument that the refusal violated a state public accommodations law relating to inns. The judges said that the restaurant was not an inn within the meaning of the state statute, that it was covered by another statute governing restauranteurs' discretion re-garding customers, and that Eagle in refusing Burton was acting in a purely private capacity under its lease. Burton brought the case to the Supreme Court on appeal, claiming that an unconstitutional construction of the state statute had led to the denial of his Fourteenth Amendment claim. The Court agreed at once to give Burton a hearing, postponing consideration of the question of jurisdiction.

Louis L. Redding, counsel for Burton, argued in his brief that the state court had become involved in state action repugnant to the Fourteenth Amendment when it had construed a state statute, which on its face imposed no racial test, to authorize racial discrimination in a state-owned public facility. Redding charged that the court had assumed facts outside the record of the case, had failed to recognize the interelationship of a public lessor of a state-owned public facility with its lessee, and had improperly absolved the lessor of the duty to accord equal protection of the laws. Where *Shelley* forbade judicial enforcement of racially dis-criminatory pacts, Redding said, the court here both construed and enforced an otherwise nonracial statute in a discriminatory way.

To establish the public nature of the restaurant, Redding noted the money invested in and now received from the facility by the state. He reasoned that if it is public property, it cannot be used to maintain racial discrimination; if the situation were one of private funds in the custody of public trustees, then it cannot be done either, according to the *Girard College Case*. Having total control—that is, ownership of the fee—the authority should have found a lessee who would have agreed to operate the restaurant consistently with its constitutional duty. Redding closed by remarking that discrimination could not be practiced in the parking portion of the building, so why could it be in the restaurant? In his reply brief, Redding said that the invalidity of the statute had been asserted from the outset as the basic claim to be reviewed on appeal. That position was not diminished by a recognition that conflicting decisions on the important constitutional question of whether government property can be employed discriminatorily afforded a sound alternative basis for the Supreme Court's consideration on certiorari.

Solicitor General Rankin as amicus submitted a brief arguing that if a state cannot participate in the administration of a private trust which draws racial discrimination, as in *Girard College,* then it follows that it cannot lease its own property for a use which would involve denial of access on the basis of race. Rankin also pointed out that previous lower court rulings all involved facilities which although operated by non-governmental lessees were open to the public generally, like Eagle.

Counsel for Eagle urged the Court not to take jurisdiction of the appeal because to do so would require deciding the legality of the statute. Counsel argued that this had no bearing on the primary question— whether the lessee is a state agency—and required solving a very difficult problem—whether the judicial enforcement doctrine of *Shelley* encompasses a court's acceptance of a pleading by way of defense. Counsel further claimed that it was "in the public interest" that the Wilmington Parking Authority be able to obtain the largest amount of money from leasing this extra space—an objective which could be accomplished only if there is no federal interference with operation of the business by the private entrepreneur in any manner it sees fit. The only real question with regard to the state statute was whether the restaurant had violated federal law, counsel asserted. If so, then the law's constitutionality or the justifiability of the restaurant's acts under it are irrelevant, for it must yield to the federal law. They would also be irrelevant if the restaurant had not violated federal law and had a common law right to discriminate, bringing the focus back to the *Shelley* question. Eagle's counsel also argued against a straight Fourteenth Amendment ruling on certiorari because the Court had provided no general definition in prior cases, in which it had made variant decisions depending on the facts of the particular case—by evaluating the degree of control held by the state, by estimating the amount of state financial assistance, and by determining the relationship of the activity to public purposes. He also noted that the Court had denied certiorari to many similar cases. Eagle should get immunization from the Fourteenth Amendment because it was a "special" lessee performing a service which presumably the public agency couldn't perform for itself and furnishing the additional money needed for the larger facility to exist, he said, claiming that "despite the momentary injustice of racial discrimination," this would "result in the long run in a greater measure of equal protection of the laws."

Wilmington Parking Authority counsel moved to dismiss or affirm on grounds that no substantial question was presented because the Delaware Supreme Court's decision did not depend upon a determination of the validity of a state statute but rather on a determination that Eagle Coffee Shoppe, Inc., was not an agency of the state of Delaware. Counsel argued directly that Eagle was not a parking authority agent but a private business. Neither the amount of public monies involved nor the fact that the authority was making money from the arrangement made for state action, he claimed. Although the leasing itself was vital to the functioning of the parking facility, the activity of the restaurant itself, which just happened to be the highest bidder, was not. The restaurant was thus not "integrally related" to the parking authority's function; therefore it was not bound by the constitutional requirement of non-discrimination. There was also, he said, no intention to use the lease as a subterfuge.

Burton was a peculiar case in several respects. The record was rather unclear, and questions the Court asked of both sides met with responses such as "I don't know" or "It doesn't appear from the facts as I understand them." The facts were relatively complex inasmuch as different interpretations could be placed upon the "public" character of the state-owned parking facility and upon the spread of this character to the restaurant in question. Was it partly a question of how the restaurant appeared to the public? Its proximity to the garage? Its lease with the city? Its ownership? Was there direct access from the garage to the restaurant? Perhaps the very nature of the facts suggested to the Court that this was a relatively "safe" case in which to make an important doctrinal pronouncement in the public facilities area.

The Court's opinion was written by Justice Clark, who had dissented in *Boynton*. One justice concurred and three dissented. The Court avoided the difficulties a statutory ruling on the state law would have presented and decided the constitutional issue. Treating the appeal papers as a certiorari petition, the Court held the exclusion of Burton from the restaurant, under the circumstances shown, to be discriminatory state action in violation of the Equal Protection Clause. Clark's conclusion was that the Eagle Coffee Shoppe, together with other leased portions of the building, constituted a physically and financially integral and, in fact, an indispensable part of the state's plan to operate its project as a self-sustaining unit. He reasoned to this conclusion by noting that the restaurant was in property not intended to be surplus but money-making and that numerous benefits, ranging from certain tax exemptions on the one hand to additional demand and considerable rental revenue on the other, were mutually enjoyed through the arrangement by both the restaurant and the public parking garage, despite the fact that the authority had no original intent to place a restaurant in the building and its presence there was only a happenstance resulting from the bidding for use of unused portions of the total facility.

Noting also that Eagle had affirmatively alleged that for it to serve Negroes would injure its business, Clark pointed out that profits earned by racial discrimination not only contributed to but were indispensable elements in the financial success of a governmental agency, something the judges found particularly offensive. Adding up all the factors contributing to the building's public nature, he concluded that there was present that degree of state participation and involvement in discriminatory action the Fourteenth Amendment was designed to condemn. The mere fact of a lease—in which the state had declined, though it possessed the power, to require the lessee to discharge the responsibilities of the Fourteenth Amendment as a consequence of state participation—did not absolve the lessee from discharging those responsibilities while it reaped the benefits of the state participation. By its inaction, Clark said, seconding the chancery court below, the authority, and through it the state, had not only made themselves party to the refusal of service but also had elected to place the power, property, and prestige of the state behind the admitted discrimination. When a state leases public property in the manner and for the purpose shown to have been the case here, then the lessee must comply with the proscriptions of the Fourteenth Amendment as though they were written into the lease itself. Clark noted the impossibility of fashioning set formulae by which every state leasing arrangement could be tested, but declared that, contrary to the respondents' prophecy of nearly universal application of the Court's ruling, the holding was as limited as the specifically defined limits of the Court's inquiry into the particular situation.

The principal concern of all those writing separate opinions was the majority's "headstrong" behavior in reaching a constitutional question before it was "unavoidable." Stewart, concurring, thought that the lower court judgment must be reversed by a much more direct route. The restaurant had relied upon a state statute permitting a restaurant proprietor to refuse to serve those whom he thought would be offensive to the major part of his customers. The state supreme court apparently had construed the statute to authorize discrimination based exclusively on color. Thus the authoritatively construed statute was clearly unconstitutional, Stewart said. Harlan and Whittaker, dissenting together, were greatly concerned about where the majority had left the concept of "state action." They would have requested the state supreme court to clarify its construction of the statute, which they found highly ambiguous. If it were found that the court had indeed construed it as Stewart argued, the case could then be disposed of accordingly and the much broader questions the majority had reached avoided. Only if it were found that the court had meant only that Eagle was free to serve only those whom it pleased would the "state action" question be unavoidably presented, they maintained, and only then should this be decided. Frankfurter, concerned with judicial restraint, objected that the majority took no position regarding the statutory meaning but instead went immediately to the constitutional questions. He agreed with Harlan that because the state court's opinion lent itself to several views the proper course would be to send the matter back for clarification, only later if necessary reaching the serious questions which the majority had prematurely considered.

Of all the justices, only Stewart seemed positive that a ruling involving state action could be avoided. The dissenters indicated a belief that the question would ultimately have to be faced, but sought to secure at least a delay so that some other alternative might come to the surface. The only alternative indicated by the dissenters to a finding that Eagle was involved in state action because of its particular relationship to the public facility—a ruling broad in relation to Stewart's position—was a finding that police enforcement of the trespass statute was state action violating equal protection because of the racial basis on which the statute was invoked. However, this finding, broader still, was the one the Court assiduously wished to avoid, because of its complications in view of the common law right of the private individual to discriminate. If, on the other hand, the case had been decided as Stewart had suggested, *Burton* would have provided no precedent at all. It would have been distinctive only for its narrowness in the face of a much broader issue. As it was, the ultimate effect of the *Burton* decision was to bring a significant portion of what had formerly been considered public accommodations matters directly into the area of public facilities. By doing so, the Court appears to have sought to extend important constitutional protections to long-oppressed black minorities in a manner which would effect more immediate and widespread results than had—say—the School Cases and which would also further expansion of the *Shelley* doctrine to preclude judicial enforcement of any charge in which the claim of "discrimination" might be raised. Use of government ownership and involvement as the decisive criteria provided the means of avoiding extension of *Shelley.* Converting the appeal to a request for certiorari, suggested in the briefs, a not uncommon Supreme Court practice, avoided further delay in the case and in deciding the important questions it raised.

Because of the case's factual "mix," the doctrine resulting from it could only be interpreted in light of the peculiar complex of facts of the case. Hence in a latter case the option would be open to say that either a) the doctrine is of general applicability or b) the doctrine only applies to situations like *Burton*—which could be interpreted to say that the doctrine was unique. The possibility of such contrary options might have commended this particular case to some justices as a vehicle for a broad pronouncement. Interestingly enough, in subsequent litigation interpretation (a) tended to prevail for a strange reason: any attempt to limit *Burton* to its facts failed because no one could figure out exactly what the facts were. The amorphous, ambiguous, and gap-laden set of facts in *Burton* led busy lawyers to take the Court's opinion at its word and to despair of any attempt to relate the opinion to the facts. Hence, the *Burton* case has assumed a very large importance indeed in the doctrinal dialectics of the desegregation decisions.

7

Following *Burton* in 1961 was *Garner v. Louisiana,* bridging the gap between *Thompson* and the highly controversial sit-in cases of subsequent years. A number of Negro students in Baton Rouge had sought non-segregated food service at local department or drugstore lunch counters, and upon having been refused remained seated quietly until arrested and taken away by police. They were convicted of disturbing the peace. Denied relief through the Louisiana Supreme Court, they carried their appeal to the United States Supreme Court. In arguments typical of those to be made in most of the sit-in cases, they contended that 1) their convictions were based upon no evidence of guilt and thus deprived them of due process as defined in *Thompson,* 2) they were convicted under a state statute the provisions of which, as applied to their acts, were so vague, indefinite, and uncertain as to offend due process, 3) the decisions below conflicted with the guarantee of freedom of expression, and 4) the decisions also conflicted with the Supreme Court's prior decisions condemning racially discriminatory administration of state criminal laws, in contravention of the Fourteenth Amendment's Equal Protection Clause. With regard to the last point, petitioners contended that the participation of the police and judiciary to enforce a state custom of segregation resulted in the use of "state action" plainly violative of the Fourteenth Amendment. Even if these cases do contain a relevant component of "private action," petitioners argued, that action is substantially infected with state power and thereby remains state action for the purposes of the Fourteenth Amendment. These arguments, like those in later cases, sought to tie the states to private discrimination through arrests or through licensing of businesses. The last point in the briefs was an effort to get the Supreme Court to say that discrimination in public accommodations violated the Fourteenth Amendment even if state involvement was only indirect. Such a statement could then have been used with Congress and at the state and local level to obtain nondiscrimination statutes.

The Solicitor General, as he was to do in all the sit-in cases of the early 1960s, filed an amicus brief supporting the demonstrators. However, the government's support was largely symbolic because the grounds urged for reversal were narrow. As Solicitor General Cox stated in *Garner:* "The United States is . . . deeply concerned when many of its citizens are arrested and convicted of crime without due process of law, and in a manner which denies them equal protection of the laws. . . . [But] it is unnecessary to reach the constitutional problems common to the so-called sit-ins generally. . . . The government believes that it may be able to assist the Court by focusing upon issues which are dispositive without involving broader and largely uncharted questions concerning the meaning of state action."[29]

Warren's opinion for the Court in *Garner* indicated that the Court found it unnecessary to reach the broader constitutional questions presented.[30] The convictions were reversed, the Chief Justice explained, because they were so totally devoid of evidentiary support as to be violative of due process, as in *Thompson.* The records contained no evidence to support a finding that petitioners disturbed the peace either by outwardly boisterous conduct or by passive conduct likely to cause public disturbance, leaving only the arresting officers' opinions that petitioners should not sit peacefully in a place where custom decreed they should not sit. Nor was there any indication in the record that the trial judge took judicial notice of racial segregation in the South as a basis for his decision, as state law permitted him to do, Warren said, although such judicial notice could not substitute for a trial, and petitioners had to have an opportunity to challenge it. Warren's comments were designed to avoid an important aspect of the factual situation: the possibility of violence stemming from the mere presence in the same restaurant of both whites and blacks. Even if the real question were whether or not a private property owner and proprietor of a private establishment had the right to serve only those whom he chooses and to refuse to serve others for whatever reason he may determine—a question not presented—these convictions still would not stand, Warren said. Although Louisiana alleged the evidence proved elements of certain other crimes, he concluded that the court must rest its opinion on whether the evidence supported a finding that the petitioners' acts caused the disturbance of the peace for which they were convicted.

Concurring in the judgment, Frankfurter agreed that "mere presence" had not been made a crime by the statute. Douglas concurred but on wholly constitutional grounds, saying that racial tension might have justified the convictions under state law but no state could constitutionally enforce a policy of segregation in restaurant facilities. Harlan also con-

curred in the judgment but on grounds that the conduct involved was a
form of expression constitutionally protected or that the state statute
under which petitioners had been convicted was unconstitutionally vague
and uncertain. Harlan went to great lengths to argue that the *Thompson*
doctrine did not fit these cases, calling it a case involving a situation which
was unique in the annals of the Court and warning that unless it was
applied with the utmost circumspection, it was bound to lead the Court
into treacherous territory.

With other sit-in cases facing it, the majority was probably concerned
with establishing a standard or doctrine sidestepping the larger constitutional questions. However unique some justices might call it, *Thompson*
seemed to provide just such a formula, which Kalven has called "su-
premely neutral and [applying] a rule that has nothing to do with the race
issues as such."[31] Yet *Thompson* allowed the justices to deal with their
feeling that common to all sit-in cases was the idea that the mere presence
of a Negro in a white restaurant constituted a punishable violation of
some local law or custom. Certainly in *Garner* the Court was helped by the
fact that breach-of-peace rather than trespass charges had been brought.
Had the latter been pressed—true in some later sit-in cases—the constitutional question would have been forced because "the peaceful staying on
the property of another without his consent would be adequate evidence
of a criminal trespass under a properly drawn statute."[32]

The majority's ruling also indicates that an opinion by the Court can
be seen as both broad and narrow at the same time, depending on one's
perspective.[33] Use of the *Thompson* lack of evidence ground meant that the
opinion was narrower than if the Court had dealt frontally with the
question of permission to take action to redress racial grievances
generally—the position which the Court wished to avoid because it might
give license for greater disruption later. This case and others stemming
from sit-ins are narrow because they do not discuss the cause of the
demonstration. Instead they deal only with the particular question posed
in the case. Yet that makes them more broadly applicable later because
they could be extended to more types of protest situations undertaken for
a wide variety of "causes." If instead of saying that the conviction of a
demonstrator must be set aside when there is a lack of evidence, the
opinions had instead said, "No demonstrator for the civil rights of blacks
could be convicted without evidence" or "There must be a much higher
level of evidence against demonstrators for civil rights of blacks to convict
them," it would be narrow because not extendable to other demonstrations—no matter how broad a protection it might seem to the Negroes
and their cause at the time. The breadth of the Court's opinion is thus
affected by the degree to which racial reality is explicitly recognized by the
Court.

Kalven later remarked that *Garner* "had obviously put a considerable strain on legal doctrine and gave promise of future cases which would be even more troublesome to handle."[34] The division of opinion among the justices and the great difficulty the sit-in convictions presented for the Court were also reflected in the fact that similar cases docketed later in the 1961 and 1962 Terms were held by the Court for over two years before decision, and even then resulted in a series of split opinions. In the meantime, a case-by-case method similar to that suggested by Harlan was employed in other litigation involving sit-ins granted a hearing in the 1962 Term. Two of the next three cases involved actions not brought after arrest for sitting-in but brought in civil suits by those not served. *Turner v. City of Memphis* involved a Negro man who had been refused nonsegregated service in a Memphis Municipal Airport restaurant operated by Dobbs House, Inc. He sought an injunction against such discrimination on Fourteenth Amendment grounds and alleged that Dobbs had acted under color of state law. Dobbs and the city asserted the restaurant was a private enterprise to which the amendment did not apply. Then, turning around, they invoked Tennessee statutes which authorized the state Department of Conservation to issue necessary rules and regulations for hotel and restaurant safety and sanitation, making violations of such regulations a misdemeanor. The department's Division of Hotel and Restaurant Inspection had promulgated a regulation providing that restaurants catering to both white and Negro patrons should be arranged so that each race was segregated. Because the lease agreement between Dobbs and the city provided that the leased premises could be used only for lawful purposes, the city maintained that unless and until the regulation was declared unconstitutional it would have to object to desegregation of the restaurant as violative of state law and the lease. Dobbs House, similarly, argued that desegregation of the restaurant would subject it to forefeiture of the lease.

When Turner moved for summary judgment before a single district judge, the appellees successfully opposed the motion in favor of a requirement that a three-judge court must be convened to hear the questions regarding the constitutionality of the statutes and regulation. Turner appealed from this ruling, both to the Sixth Circuit and directly to the Supreme Court. The latter postponed consideration of jurisdiction to a hearing on the merits, and, after argument, handed down its judgment per curiam. The Court treated Turner's jurisdictional statement as a petition for certiorari, granted it, and vacated and remanded to the district court. The Court found the convening of a three-judge court unnecessary for disposition of the case because, as Dobbs had conceded, the restaurant was subject to the strictures of the Fourteenth Amendment under the *Burton* rule. The statutes and regulation could have furnished a

defense to the action only insofar as they expressed an affirmative state
policy fostering segregation in publicly operated facilities, a contention
foreclosed by previous opinions. No issue remained to be resolved on the
merits, and thus no reason existed why the case should not be disposed of
as expeditiously as possible without awaiting decision on the appeal of the
Sixth Circuit.

The next case, *Taylor v. Louisiana,* was more in the *Thompson* and
Boynton traditions. Here the Court reversed per curiam Louisiana convictions of six Negro petitioners for offenses against state breach-of-the-
peace statutes. The incidents leading to the convictions had taken place
when the Negroes, four of whom were interstate bus passengers, had
attempted to sit in the white waiting room of a bus depot. The Court
reasoned that since the only evidence to support the charges was that they
were violating a custom that segregated people in waiting rooms according to race, a practice not allowed by federal law in interstate transportation facilities, then the convictions could not stand. The Court's brief
opinion pointed out that the record showed the Negroes had been quiet,
orderly, and polite and that the trial court had said that their mere
presence in the white waiting room was enough to make them punishable
under the statute. Only Harlan took exception to this peremptory handling of the case and said he would have granted certiorari and set the case
down for argument. Frankfurter, whose health would soon force him to
leave the Court, took no part in the case.

Another post-*Garner* case, *Williams v. Hot Shoppes, Inc.,* involved an
Alexandria, Virginia, restaurant that had refused service to a Negro
resident of Washington, D.C., on the basis of a Virginia law requiring
restaurants either to segregate their facilities or to exclude Negro patrons.
Williams, the Negro, contended that the restaurant manager had denied
him service solely because he was a Negro and because the manager
believed that according to state law he was required to do so. Thus, he
argued, the refusal to serve was state action of the sort prohibited by the
Fourteenth Amendment and Civil Rights Act of 1875 and subsequent
laws. The federal district and appeals courts in the District of Columbia
held that the 1875 act did not apply because its relevant sections had been
declared unconstitutional long ago. On questions of more recent law—for
example, whether the refusal to serve had to be interpreted as state
action—the appeals court, with two judges dissenting, ruled it should
refrain from a decision on the merits until Virginia courts had interpreted
the state law. Williams then took his case to the Supreme Court, contending that the 1875 act had valid application in the present day to state action
throughout the United States. On this basis, he argued, the Virginia
restaurant was covered by the terms "inns and other places" of public
accommodation contained in that act and that thus his exclusion because

of the allegedly invalid state statute stated a claim for a civil penalty and full costs under the act. The respondent resturant raised both a technical argument, saying that Williams's petition was not timely presented, and a substantive one, claiming that the 1875 act was not applicable and that the restaurant was private not public. With only Justice Douglas dissenting and thus underlining the case's substantive importance, the Court decided to refuse the case a hearing. There may have been several reasons behind the Court's refusal. The existence of a technicality as to the timeliness of the petition certainly provided nonsubstantive justification for denial. Substantively, the facilities were more "private" than those in the other sit-in cases so far presented. The incident involved only a single individual, not a large-scale "sit-in," and, further, did not involve an arrest for refusal to leave but an individual's civil suit for violation of his individual constitutional rights for refusal to be served. The case further involved a federal law of ancient and questionable status and a state law which had yet to be interpreted for modern times by the state courts. Both the latter inevitably involved the right of the private entrepreneur to choose and refuse his patronage, and to have decided this case in Williams's favor would have required the Court to go considerably further in the area of public accommodations than it wished, unlike cases involving arrests and convictions based solely on color or some state law or custom distinguishing between colors, which could readily be overturned on grounds that the law, although legal on its face, was discriminatorily applied.

8

During the 1962 Term, the Court's attention in the area of race relations was devoted primarily to public accommodations, where a majority of cases were decided per curiam. Having accepted a great many cases, the Court could not possibly handle each with full opinion—nor did it need to do so when facts were somewhat similar. Instead, the Court had to engage in a variety of docket-management techniques, including not only these summary dispositions but also grouping of cases. In early November, the Court heard argument in seven cases, one of which, *Wright v. Georgia,* was a public facilities case involving parks, and another of which, *Griffin v. Maryland,* was not decided until after reargument a year later. The remaining five cases dealt with the question of what constituted state action for purposes of establishing an Equal Protection Clause violation with respect to sit-ins. In *Peterson v. City of Greenville,* the accused had been arrested after remaining seated at the lunch counter of a Greenville department store, notwithstanding the manager's announcement, made in the presence of police, that the counter was being closed and that everyone was to leave the area. The manager testified later that he would have acted as he did independently of the existence of a local ordinance requiring separation of the races in restaurants. In *Gober v. Birmingham,* trespass convictions had occurred for violation of a city ordinance requiring segregated facilities in public eating places. Connected with the same incident was *Shuttlesworth v. Birmingham,* covering the conviction of two Negro ministers for aiding and abetting a violation of that ordinance. In *Avent v. North Carolina,* a group of Negro and white students had been convicted of unlawful entry and trespass for entering the luncheonette of a privately owned variety department store in Durham, which had a city ordinance requiring restaurant segregation. They had refused to leave the lunch counter at the order of the manager. Finally in *Lombard v. Louisiana,* convictions had occurred for violation of a statute requiring persons to leave business premises after being so ordered by the person in charge of the business. The Negroes had remained seated at the refreshment counter of a department store after having been ordered to leave. In this New Orleans situation, there was no statute or ordinance requiring restaurant segregation, but there had been public statements by the mayor and chief of police that sit-ins were not in the public interest and that those involved would be prosecuted.

In oral argument in *Avent,* the first case argued,[35] Jack Greenberg told the Court that the broad question need not be reached. He stressed instead the issue of whether there was a Fourteenth Amendment violation from state use of its police power to enforce segregation stemming from community custom generated by state law. He mentioned both the Durham ordinance and North Carolina segregation statutes covering a wide range of situations. Opposing counsel, Assistant Attorney General Ralph Moody, said a property owner can exclude anyone for whatever reason, although he conceded that unconstitutional discrimination would exist if the state by law required refusal of service to Negroes. The trespass statute, he stressed, was neutral, and state enforcement was only to protect a property owner's rights. State statutes were either being eliminated or not being enforced. By arguing that state action was not involved, Moody seemed to be trying to force the basic issue, to "hem in" the Court so it would have to reach the matter it had not yet reached.

The arguments made by these men were generally like those made by the attorneys in the other cases. In the Birmingham cases, Mrs. Constance Baker Motley, for the NAACP, said that Birmingham's segregation ordinance was part of a "massive" segregation policy. There was, she said, no evidence that a store employee had called the police: the manager had told those sitting-in that he would violate the law by serving them. She argued that the only evidence on the record to support convictions of the ministers was that a minister had asked for sit-in volunteers, promising to get them out of jail if arrested. Another minister had done no more than drive some of those sitting-in to a meeting at which the protest was discussed. Neither, she said, urged violation of any valid ordinance, and she argued that the only way to uphold their convictions was to hold a sit-in protesting against state-enforced segregation to be a violation of the ordinance itself. Watts Davis, Birmingham city attorney, argued that the city ordinance could have no effect on the store owners. He conceded, however, that he did not have a particularly strong case against the ministers. He said in the *Gober* case that the "state action" issue was not properly before the Court, because Alabama procedure required that it be raised affirmatively as a defense in special pleadings. This caused Black to say that the trespasser "bore the burden of proving the proprietor's motivation," not, he thought, a good rule of law. In rebuttal, Mrs. Motley said no procedural irregularities existed in the case, because the state court had considered the issue.

In the Louisiana case, John Nelson, for the protesters, said that the custom of segregation, induced by the state, and the local officials' statements left little choice to restaurant owners about discriminating. The state was not, he said, refereeing a battle between neutrals, for the idea that the state was neutral here was a fantasy. As the Louisiana court had excluded evidence concerning possible cooperation between store manager and police, Nelson wanted the Supreme Court to give directives on remand "so we can try this case" by defining the limits of peaceful protest. For New Orleans, Attorney General Jack P. F. Gremillion said that the officials' statements were to preserve law and order, not segregation, because the sit-ins would have led to riots. "The state," he said, "faces a dilemma. If we don't maintain law and order when these situations arise, the federal government sends in the marshals and in some cases even troops. If we do maintain law and order, we are brought before this Court for violating someone's constitutional rights." Solicitor General Archibald Cox also presented argument. Assuming for purposes of argument that a property owner could select customers on the basis of color, he said that what was involved in these cases was prior state action violating equal protection of the laws. These convictions could not be "color blind" if decisions to segregate might have been affected by the existing statutes. Cox thought the Court need not go beyond holding that the state would have to prove that discrimination was based on the proprietor's own choice; the presumptions arising from the ordinances had not been overcome here.

The justices' questions in the cases were of several types. They wanted to know whether they were faced with the same broad constitutional question posed earlier. Chief Justice Warren asked Mrs. Motley whether her case wasn't *Garner* all over again, and Black asked Greenberg whether the question did not always revert "to whether the store has the right to select its customers on a basis of color." What constituted state action was another focus of questioning. Justice Brennan, for example, asked Jack Greenberg whether "mere arrest and conviction" constituted such action, and Douglas asked Cox whether jailing someone for sitting-in was state action. The focus on state action led Black to ask Greenberg whether discrimination in New York or Montana would be different from that in the South. The relationship between custom and an explicit state requirement was also explored. Here Justice Black asked whether segregation laws deprived the owner of a right to choose his customers. When Justice White indicated he thought that one could say proprietors discriminate because they wanted to, Greenberg reiterated that "a community choice that has been imposed upon the man" was operative, not private choice. In related questioning, Justice Black asked Mrs. Motley whether the store owners would be violating a city law if they served Negroes. She agreed. He suggested to counsel for Birmingham that perhaps the law hadn't been enforced largely because it was being obeyed, adding "I personally do not see how in this case anyone can say that the merchant decided for himself that he would not sell." Black was also concerned about whether the store owners knew about the ordinance—although he clearly thought they all would have had to know—and about its invalidity. On this latter point, he wanted to know how the people in Birmingham "could be presumed to know that this Court's rulings had invalidated the ordinance when almost every public official in the deep South has been telling them that this Court's ruling in *Brown* . . . was unconstitutional."

A further extension of the relation of custom and law came in questions about the effect of repealing all segregation statutes. Thus Black asked Jack Greenberg whether the custom of segregation would end if the laws were taken off the books. "I think it would go far toward attenuating the custom," Greenberg said, expressing a position not always adopted by his colleagues. Justice Stewart asked Cox if the latter's argument would be swept away by statutory repeal. Black asked Louisiana Attorney General Gremillion whether customary practice would be the same as statute law, and Justice Goldberg asked "if custom could not be more a persuasive influence than an ordinance." Douglas also asked an evasive Cox whether segregation could be perpetuated through private choice.

There were, of course, questions specific to each case. Thus, in *Avent* there were questions about what was a business affected with a public interest and about whether keeping a Negro already in a store from part of the store was different from not letting him in at all. In *Lombard*, Gremillion was asked about the state court's refusal to admit evidence and about the mayor's statement. In *Gober*, one justice wanted to know whether the store where the arrests had occurred had changed its policy;

another wanted to know the basis of the conviction—trespass after warning, not merely for shopping in the store, a distinction Douglas thought was "semantics." Goldberg said he thought it important for the state to show that the owner, rather than the state, ordered the people off the premises. In *Shuttlesworth,* the question was whether the ministers had urged violation of the statute.

The Court's problem in deciding these cases was a mixture of environment, doctrine, and strategy. By the time the 1960 sit-in cases got to the Court, the atmosphere had changed from that in which they had initially occurred. The Court was faced with deciding peaceful sit-in cases in the context of an escalation of tactics and a change in focus to "political" protest and to lunch-counter protest. The risks that decisions on other than narrow grounds would be misread increased. Although there was some effort to have the Court deal with broad constitutional questions relating to sit-ins, the option most frequently presented to—and explored by—the Court was the particularistic one of finding state action in the situations of these cases, not likely to result in a clear, direct rule but strategically useful because a prematurely developed rule might encompass many situations later to arise for consideration by the judges.[36] Yet the law seemed to require a rule of some generality.[37] The problem, in short, was to rule against racial discrimination in a legally acceptable way. Certainly using state action, whether narrowly or broadly defined, to decide the cases was almost impossible to avoid, because of lawyers'—and the Court's—preoccupation with the subject since the *Civil Rights Cases* of sixty years before. Because of the Court's ruling there, reinforced ever since, that private action could not be reached under the Constitution, to decide in favor of the Negroes on broad grounds would have forced the Court to dispose of those old cases, just as disposition of *Plessy* had been a problem in *Brown.*

Explicit state action in the form of current laws or policy statements by the executive would provide the easiest—as well as the narrowest—"out" for the Court. However, it was not the only possibility, particularly when lawyers were suggesting that the choices by the restaurants' proprietors were indeed "free choices" and "private decisions." However, acceptance of such assertions did not necessarily mean that the Court would have to rule on the "ultimate" constitutional question posed by the sit-in. The justices had the option of finding that past law produced the situation of segregation in sufficient degree to constitute state action, although under this approach differences in state legal patterns would leave different results from one state to another. So would reliance on the custom of the area, which would also force the Court to determine what constituted custom and leave the implication that the private choice of the proprietor would be immune from the law where no custom could be found. Yet leaving private choice beyond the reach of constitutional regulation was not a fully neutral response, because people might tend to think nonregulation was the "right" solution and might become more resistant to positive action from the other branches of government. On the other hand, to include under the rubric of state action choices we normally consider to be private would plunge the Court into large new areas of litigation of extreme difficulty—including much northern school desegregation, making such a plunge unwise from the point of view of docket-management because many private actions previously settled elsewhere would be brought to the Court.

The other option apparently not discussed by the lawyers or the justices was use of the standard of expectation of service by the general public, suggested by Lewis as one that would carry force "for the layman and the lawyer and in a way that will have application across the land" yet which would not reach too far. If a place customarily served all whites without exception, it would be considered a place of public accommodation required to serve all regardless of color, because it is in these situations, Lewis argues, that "discrimination is particularly humiliating to the Negro." On the other hand, if an enterprise were private so that even whites did not expect to be admitted without some "arbitrary" criterion being applied, then the place would not be covered.[38]

The Court took narrow ground in ruling in favor of the Negroes in all five cases by finding state action violating the Equal Protection Clause. By finding that state action in a city ordinance or state law requiring segregation in restaurants—except in *Lombard,* where it was found in the public officials' statements—the Court established a new rule for disposing of sit-in cases. The convictions in *Peterson* were reversed, Chief Justice Warren said, because the manager's decision to exclude, despite his statement of independent action, was made in view of, or in the context of, the local ordinance—a conclusion which forced Justice Harlan to dissent. In *Lombard,* the Chief Justice reasoned that the public statement had "at least as much coercive effect as an ordinance" and that the statements had not been directed merely to preserving the peace. Here Harlan would have vacated and remanded for examination of evidence indicating collaboration between police and the store. In *Gober,* with Harlan again dissenting, the trespass convictions were reversed per curiam, with the Court citing *Peterson.* In *Shuttlesworth,* the related Birmingham case, Warren set aside the aiding-and-abetting convictions on the grounds that since the *Gober* convictions were gone, no crime existed which could have been abetted. Harlan thought a vacate-and-remand ruling was called for, as it was unclear that the ordinance's involvement had been considered below. In *Avent,* where Harlan was still in dissent, the Court issued a per curiam ruling that the state supreme court had erroneously assumed that no city ordinance requiring segregation existed at the time the state court had reviewed the convictions and vacated and remanded the case for further consideration.

Three weeks after the *Peterson* set of cases was decided came four similar judgments, all per curiam. The first, *Randolph v. Virginia,* was handled in the same way as *Avent.* The case involved a Negro who, with a much larger group of demonstrators, had been convicted of trespass for remaining on the premises of a Richmond, Virginia, department store after being ordered to leave and after being refused service in the all-white restaurant maintained within the store—a refusal coming from the store owner's duly authorized agent. Once again, relevant city ordinances requiring segregation in such places of public accommodation were not properly considered in the case; therefore the Court vacated the judgment below and remanded the case for reconsideration in light of *Peterson,* with Harlan noting his partial dissent. Handled in precisely the same fashion were *Henry v. Virginia* and *Thompson v. Virginia,* decided by identical per curiam orders.

The last sit-in case during the 1962 Term was *Wood v. Virginia,* involving convictions for trespass of black youths resulting from an incident at a drugstore lunch counter in Lynchburg, Virginia. Appealing to the Supreme Court, the Negroes maintained that the arrests and convictions were made pursuant to state custom and policy which in effect had the power of law. They contended that a marked jury selection list had been implemented for their trial and complained that the courtroom had been segregated and that they had been harrassed by the trial judge. Glossing over these other claims, the Court granted certiorari in this case, vacated the judgment below, and remanded the case for consideration in light of *Peterson.* As in all these cases, Harlan noted his separate partial dissent, as explained by his opinion in *Peterson* and *Avent.*

As this Term ended, a series of nine sit-in cases, all but *Lombard* directed by NAACP counsel, had been rapidly diposed of in a manner made to appear quite incremental because of the brevity of opinions and because of the systematic identification of some ordinance, regulation, official statement, or inflexible custom which brought an element of impermissible state action to bear on the discrimination perpetrated in an otherwise private establishment. Such simple grounds for reversal would be less available for the cases in the following terms. Thus the rule established by *Peterson,* and implemented with such consistency during this 1962 Term, was to have but brief application outside this grouping of cases. As the states and local jurisdictions rescinded their laws directly dictating segregation, protection of the right to service without discrimination in places of public accommodation became a more difficult matter for the judiciary. Yet this disposition of the cases allowed the Court to borrow time for itself and for the nation. By reading the action of private managers as state action, the Court may have made it impossible for some managers to enforce some choices that were in fact private. However, this result was only temporary, and the right of managers to make their own choices was not yet foreclosed because the Court had not reached that issue. Whichever way the Court would ultimately decide—to leave private choice to discriminate unfettered or to require that blacks be served—the *Peterson* set of rulings might have helped achieve greater acceptance for it. Were the Court to arrive at the latter answer, the intervening time would have been used by the protesters "to educate whites in the justice of their claim and in the importance they attach to it."[39]

The sit-in cases of the 1962 Term thus represented a distinct tactic by the Supreme Court—avoidance of constitutional issues coupled with a result-oriented message that the Court would ferret out any and all possible factual ways of reversing sit-in convictions in the South. The message communicated was clear, and the strategic result was indeed to discourage private restaurant discrimination. Unfortunately, the overall strategy would have been far more creative and innovative had it been used in place of the explosive *Brown* case in 1954, where a relentless series of reversals of all plans by boards of education claiming that separate facilities were in fact "equal" could have blunted resistance to school desegregation and avoided, perhaps, the fifteen-year period of inaction after *Brown* when an entire generation of schoolchildren attended schools that were virtually totally segregated while the Supreme Court refused to listen to cases alleging that *Brown* was being covertly subverted.

Grossman has noted that in the public accommodations area "major decisions were frequently followed by gaps,"[40] and both *Garner* and the *Peterson* set of rulings were followed by the Court's denial of certiorari petitions. One case in which the Court took that action despite an interesting factual twist was *Sullivan v. Nesmith,* involving a group of whites who had been arrested when eating peaceably with Negroes in a Montgomery, Alabama, restaurant.[41] They brought suit charging false imprisonment, malicious prosecution, and violation of civil rights against the city police commissioner and other officers who had arrested and charged them with disorderly conduct in violation of a recently enacted city ordinance. The persons involved in the arrests were a white professor and his wife and a group of Negro and white students from an Illinois college on a field trip in Montgomery to study the use of the nonviolent techniques as a method of sociological change in relation to the Montgomery bus boycott. The group had met in the morning with the Negro Montgomery Improvement Association to discuss the boycott and tactics used in it, then had broken for lunch together in the private dining room of a Negro cafe in a Negro area. The dining room was not visible from the street to passersby, but someone observing the group entering the cafe had placed an anonymous call to police that an integrated group had gone in to the establishment. Apparently others soon became aware of the group's presence inside also, for by the time police arrived a crowd had gathered outside the cafe and was evidently watching to see what was going to happen. The police then arrested the Illinois group and took them away from the restaurant, after which the instant suit ensued.

The federal district court denied charges that the group had been dealt with unjustly, but the Fifth Circuit reversed this judgment and remanded the case to the lower court on the basis of *Thompson,* holding that the defense of justification—because of the crowd that had gathered—or of mistake of law or fact—concerning the ordinance and what constituted a violation of it—were not available to the police in the circumstances of this case. The appeals court indicated that as in *Thompson* the convictions were so devoid of evidentiary support as to be violative of the constitutional rights of the individuals involved, and when the Supreme Court was asked by Montgomery officials to review this decision, it refused to do so.

9

In the 1963 Term, the Court heard another batch of sit-in cases. Five were argued together. Four, handled by NAACP counsel, had been docketed the previous term, and a fifth, *Griffin v. Maryland,* which had been argued with the previous term's cases, was reargued at the same time. In *Bell v. Maryland* a group of students had been convicted of violating a Maryland criminal trespass law for their participation in a sit-in protest demonstration at a Baltimore restaurant which refused to serve Negroes. In *Barr v. Columbia* a Negro group was convicted of trespass and breach of peace for sitting and waiting for service at the lunch counter in a pharmacy which had a policy of permitting only whites to sit and eat. In *Bouie v. Columbia* there were convictions for trespass under a South Carolina statute prohibiting entry on the lands of another after notice had been given not to enter. A Negro group had refused to leave a booth in the luncheonette department of a drugstore despite requests to do so. In *Robinson v. Florida* Negro defendants had been convicted of a misdemeanor for remaining or attempting to remain in a main department store restaurant after being requested to depart.

Although the facts in each of these cases varied slightly, the issues and arguments they raised were essentially identical. In the *Bell* arguments,[42] NAACP attorney Jack Greenberg stressed from the outset that the choice of the proprietor to have certain persons ejected in situations such as these was not an authentically private decision but was influenced by the customs of the community. He contended that this choice of the community was in turn to some significant extent influenced by the historical pattern of state laws directed toward sustaining a segregated society. The state denied equal protection of the laws, he concluded, when it ranked above the values of the Fourteenth Amendment the claim of the proprietor, licensed by the state for the purpose of being open to the public, of the right to exclude some persons from his establishment solely on grounds of race. Greenberg said that the state had an affirmative responsibility to protect Negro citizens. Although the particular form this protection takes is another question, it certainly should not be arrest and conviction for crime. In his rebuttal, Greenberg insisted that the issue at hand was not the question of whether the proprietor had a right to select his customers or, if not, the question of what in the Constitution deprived him of that right, but instead was the question of whether the proprietor could invoke the full machinery of the state police, the prosecutor, the courts, and so forth to impose criminal sanctions on the Negro citizens who sought service in places of public accommodation open to all except Negroes. "The only proposition we are hearing today is that these criminal convictions cannot stand" because state enforcement of a businessman's racial prejudice cannot coexist with *Shelley v. Kraemer,* Greenberg said. In fact, because these were criminal cases, involving prejudices acted out in the public area, they were stronger than *Shelley.* No weakening of the genuine rights of privacy is implied, Greenberg said. "We are not talking about homes, churches, car pools and so forth. We are talking about places of public accommodation."

The essence of Greenberg's legal position, therefore, was that a state would violate the Fourteenth Amendment if it used enforcement machinery in aid of a private policy of discrimination. Interestingly, the reverse of this proposition was emphatically denied in "affirmative action," "benign discrimination," and school busing cases in the early 1970s. In those cases, the Supreme Court moved toward accepting the proposition that state or federal action to remedy prior conditions of state-countenanced racial discrimination was constitutional even if officials were directed to make decisions explicitly based on race, such as explicit minority-group or female preferences. The Constitution, as these future cases were to show, is not at all "color-blind" if (a) a remedy rather than an original policy is involved and (b) the remedy relates to a previous violation of the Constitution. However, in the 1963 Term, these future qualifications and difficulties relating to remedies and state enforcement actions were only hazily, if at all, in the background; the immediate issue was overt southern enforcement of obviously discriminatory private decisions and policies.

Loring E. Hawes, Assistant Attorney General of Maryland, argued that *Bell* was different from the other cases because there was a warning given by the manager; the police were as neutral as possible; there was no arrest; and no one was taken into custody. Petitioners had been served on previous occasions in restaurants in the same general area, negating any community custom of segregation and demonstrating that the segregation was purely the choice of the private owner. State licensing and health statutes applied equally to all facilities serving the public—and the health statutes to private homes as well. Furthermore, the state trespass statute was not directed against sit-ins for segregated facilities or anything of this sort, but sought merely to enable the private property owner to forbid trespassers on his property. Even after exhaustive study of the Fourteenth Amendment in *Brown* the Court had been unable to determine the amendment's purpose with any certainty, Hawes said, claiming that Negro rights were certainly not the only thing. When Goldberg pressed him for trying to play the matter down, Hawes responded that the Thirteenth, Fourteenth, and Fifteenth Amendments had not yet been completely expanded outside the requirement of proof that the state was really involved in the alleged denial of rights. He certainly didn't see how that could be found in this case, he said. He also said that the state of Maryland could not be held responsible for this conviction, since the officers of the state if anything discouraged the owner and since there was no evidence of any forewarning or collusion. Maryland Assistant Attorney General Russell Reno also argued for the state that the real issue—whether Negroes have a constitutional right to be on the premises—should not be avoided by attempting application of the "void for vagueness" doctrine urged by the United States. He conceded, however, that the Maryland court had not been specific on the "crossing-over" aspect of the trespass, which he said was covered by the statute.

In *Barr,* Matthew Perry suggested some aspects of state involvement in discrimination. He noted that the Negroes were advised that demonstrations would not be tolerated, the store owners were told that the Negroes were headed in their direction, and the police were already at the stores when the sitters-in arrived. The police told the owners, he said, how the demonstrators should be asked to leave. The authorities' warning that demonstrations were not acceptable indicated the city's initiative in maintaining segregation. Mrs. Motley, arguing *Bouie,* stressed that a statute was not necessary to show where state action discrimination resulted from custom generated by long-standing policy of the state. In reply, city attorney David Robinson II said that a decision by the state to discriminate has not occurred after a private individual has made the decision. The state's involvement was neutral with respect to the trespass laws, he said. He saw no difference here from the situation in which the owner asked any unwanted customer to leave. He said the alternative to use of the trespass law would be "chaos" or self-help by the owner. He distinguished *Shelley* on the grounds the state there had the only effective means of contract enforcement; here self-help provided another avenue. John Sholenberger, also arguing for the city, said the Court could not consider the government's vagueness argument because it had not been raised by the Negroes.

In *Robinson* Alfred I. Hopkins, for the Negroes, said that the decision of the managers to exclude Negroes stemmed from community custom, which for state action purposes he saw as no different from formal segregation. He noted that extensive state regulation of restaurants included ethical practices as well as health measures and indicated state involvement in segregation. For Florida, Assistant Attorney General Georgieff argued relatively broad rather than narrow grounds. He distinguished custom from state action. He said the courts cannot impose sanctions on all the people if they don't want to associate with Negroes; the courts can impose sanctions only on the state. He also distinguished *Shelley*, with its willing buyer and willing seller, from the sit-in situation. Because police who observe a crime must make an arrest, their activity was, he said, neutral. On the licensing point, he noted that both cars and homes were licensed, the latter at least as much as restaurants, yet they were still seen as private. To use the licensing aspect to achieve state action would lead to "no end" of regulation through that route. He asked the Court not to use the federal government's narrow ground to decide the case. If the Court found state action, it should "have at it," as long as it was aware that people might have to wear pistols to defend private property.

The Justice Department was again a participant. Originally, the department had taken what was becoming its standard unaggressive position—that the cases could be decided on narrow grounds—which contributed to the Court's less-than-constitutional grounds resolution of most of the cases in this area. Solicitor General Cox had indicated that he would be prepared to make a full statement if the justices disagreed with his earlier narrow claim. The Court, over the dissents of Black, Clark, Harlan, and White, then requested the department to express the government's views on the constitutional issues; the dissenters' objection was that the Court should not request an additional brief where the department had chosen not to take a position. But the maneuvering was not yet over. After the order for fuller briefing, the Kennedy administration saw that a positive constitutional ruling certainly would not help its effort to get its interstate-commerce-clause-based bill through Congress and that such a bill would extend protections to more Negro citizens and would be easier to enforce than a Supreme Court decision, particularly one under the Fourteenth Amendment. The department thus tried to reverse field and to get the Court to delay a decision on the sit-in cases until after

Congress acted. However, Cox was without success in this attempt, either with the Court directly or indirectly through the Attorney General of Maryland, whom he wanted to persuade to petition the Court to remand *Bell* to the Maryland courts. Apparently the attorney general would have supported the proposal, but the Chief Justice of Maryland wanted the Court to decide the cases on the merits. At that point, Cox did submit a brief, arguing that a state was responsible for discrimination if long-standing custom is commanded or supported by state law.[43]

At oral argument, Ralph Spritzer, speaking for the government, avoided the constitutional issue. He took a narrow position which helped "tilt" the Court, contending that the demonstrators in these cases had not been given adequate warning about the illegality of their conduct. He also reminded the Court of the tradition of deciding cases on narrow grounds and called the justices' attention to action pending in Congress. The narrowness of his argument is shown by his claim that in the South Carolina and Maryland cases refusal to leave after warning was not encompassed by provisions about entry after warning. He also stressed that criminal cases were involved, requiring a strict reading of prohibitory statutes, particularly where protest—and thus First Amendment freedoms—was implicated. Though his specific argument was somewhat different in the Florida case, it was similarly concerned with narrow problems of notice to those sitting in.

Questioning by the justices was far-ranging. In *Bell,* Justice Goldberg wanted to know what Greenberg would say about discrimination with respect to houses (the right of privacy would be dominant), private clubs (unless a sham), and buying or selling cooperatives (it would depend upon how public or private). Chief Justice Warren wanted to know of Hawes if the petitioners did not have a right to be on the property until told to get off. (Yes, but they had no right to push past the barricade after the hostess and manager had told them they couldn't be seated, saying, "We haven't integrated as yet.") Were they prohibited from being on the property under the statute? (Yes, the crime had taken place when they pushed past the hostess and went and sat down—the "cross-over.") Goldberg's questions in *Bouie* presaged the broad position he was to take in the opinions in these cases. After asking Mrs. Motley if anything was segregated in South Carolina, he went on to ask if she would say that even if all state laws concerning segregation were wiped out, the exclusion here would still be unconstitutional. (Yes, the effect of the state's previous policy would still be there.) After asking, "How long would the state have to purge itself?" the justice asked Mrs. Motley if she meant the state affirmatively would have to pass a statute which gave the right to proceed against discrimination. He also wanted to know about the application to northern states and the extent of the statutes there. In her reply Mrs. Motley observed that such a statute had recently been passed in Maryland—thereby providing the Court with the grounds it ultimately used to dispose of that case—although she argued that such action had been too recent to say the old state policy would not still influence owners of such facilities and that since the incident in the *Bell* case had preceded enactment of the statute the latter was not involved here. Stewart commented that Mrs. Motley's rule would require a psychoanalyst to determine state and private attitudes. Mrs. Motley was asked by Justice Brennan whether a store owner should be kept from claiming he made a "private" choice, in view of all the enactments concerning segregation. She said yes. On the other side, Robinson was asked about the role of custom in the state and about the state's insistence on segregation. He said that the state was now making progress, including desegregation of its state universities. In *Robinson* the justices also asked how one could determine the state's custom.

In *Griffin v. Maryland,* the fifth case, a group of Negroes attempting to enter the private Glen Echo Amusement Park near Washington, D.C., had been ordered to leave the park by an employee who also happened to be a deputy sheriff. Upon their refusal to leave and their attempt to protest their exclusion as based solely on race, the members of the group were arrested and subsequently convicted on charges of criminal trespass. As has been noted, the case had been argued during the previous term but had not been decided, instead being restored to the docket. At initial argument,[44] Joseph Rauh had made a very broad argument—broader than those in the sit-in cases argued at the same time—saying not only that *Shelley* required reversal of the convictions but that the Court should reconsider and overrule the *Civil Rights Cases.* Rauh claimed that this case, with its fusion of private and public power, was an even stronger one than *Shelley,* because the state helped arrest the Negro at the private facilities rather than simply convicting him when someone else brought him to court. He thought that amusement parks and restaurants holding themselves open to the public should be considered "the state" for Fourteenth Amendment purposes. He recognized that his argument about the *Civil Rights Cases* need not be reached, but suggested for the Court to do so would establish a rule to dispose of the many cases coming before the Court. He thought such a ruling would impose a positive duty upon proprietors to serve, regardless of race, and thus avoid getting the state to refrain from interfering. He wanted not just the right to sit in for his clients, but also the right to be served. Among the questions asked Rauh at this round of argument were whether self-help would be encouraged if the Court accepted the broad argument and whether the Court would be resurrecting the old federal public accommodations statute if it overruled the *Civil Rights Cases.* Arguing Maryland's position, Assistant Attorney General Robert Murphy, in addition to saying he did not think that licensing converted the park into a public facility, said that the deputy sheriff was under the park's, not the state's, control with his salary being paid by a detective agency. This prompted Chief Justice Warren to remark that to have someone with a badge order a person to leave a place seemed quite significant.

Rauh's basic position at reargument was much like his earlier one. He asserted that the policeman-employee, and thus the authority under which the exclusion was effected, was public and not private and that therefore state action contrary to the Fourteenth Amendment lay behind and rendered invalid the state trespass convictions. Rauh admitted that a private right to discrimination does exist but emphasized that a state cannot support it. He added that the state could not create or recognize a private right of discrimination either, but observed that the Court probably would not reach that point. Counsel insisted that his was a simple case, and went on to explain the applicability of *Shelley*. He discussed the confusion of public and private authority involved in the case, and then noted that *Burton* and *Lombard* also provided authority for his position. The state cannot license a man to serve the public and then make it possible for him to serve whites only, Rauh declared. Summing up, Rauh said that self-help was nonexistent. "State enforcement of private discrimination has kept segregation alive in America today." As for the home, he said, the Second and Fourth Amendments would protect private rights there, as under English common law.

Perhaps because they had heard the case once before and also because of the reach of Rauh's broad argument, the justices questioned him heavily. They wanted to know whether the Court would have to overrule the *Civil Rights Cases* and whether Rauh was placing no reliance on the Thirteenth Amendment. Goldberg commented that counsel should have leaned a little on that amendment, as it contained no state action requirement. After a Stewart question as to why an owner could not open to all the public but Negroes, Goldberg said that not the Court but the Constitution had made it clear that race is an unreasonable distinction. Harlan objected, saying that it sounded as if the justice had meant irrespective of state action. Rauh was also asked about private discrimination in a home. The question was posed, "On what constitutional provision rests the argument that there is no private right of discrimination in a place of public accommodation? What about a church?" The justices also asked whether anyone had a right to enter private property and to sue if refused admittance on the basis of race. Rauh noted that the case involved not a church or a home but the biggest place of public accommodation in the Washington metropolitan area. Assuming a right of self-help to enforce private rights, the justices asked whether Rauh's argument forbade private owners a judicial remedy if self-help was unable to enforce their private rights or if they were injured when attempting to do so. In a related question Justice Black asked about the effect of the assault against the group on the use of the trespass law. (It could not be a defense.) Commenting on the many statutes forbidding such racial discrimination, Stewart asked, "Doesn't this seem redundant under your . . . argument?" (They are methods of implementing the Fourteenth Amendment's prohibition.)

Several alternatives were visible to the justices at the time of their decision. The first, should they reach the constitutional question, was an extension of the *Shelley* state action doctrine that they had been avoiding. The second was a position that state inaction in enforcing a constitutional right amounted to state action in support of infringement of that right. Finally, there was the position that private discrimination in public places could not be reached, at least not through the Fourteenth Amendment. Each of these alternatives appeared nearly equally unsatisfactory. The justices knew that political settlement was in the offing, making further alternatives available from outside the judicial realm. From the beginning of the Kennedy administration in 1961, a new sense of executive initiative and leadership had become apparent in the field of civil rights. In the last weeks of the 1962 Term, during the docketing of these cases, this new executive leadership had urged upon Congress the most sweeping civil rights legislation in history. After President Kennedy's death, President Johnson had resumed the initiative after the cases were argued. The new civil rights legislation had been passed by the House February 10, had been awarded the first cloture vote ever on a civil rights bill in the Senate June 10, and had been passed with certain revisions in that chamber June 19, three days before the Court handed down these opinions. Just ten days after the decisions, July 2, the House adopted the Senate version and the president signed the bill into law. Because it was based largely on the Commerce Clause, this law meant to the Court that it might never have to face the constitutional question which the public accommodations cases had so persistently presented. Furthermore, numerous states and municipalities already were, and most assuredly would be in the future, considering similar legislation within their own borders. Obviously, Maryland, which was involved in this litigation, already had done so.

The most striking aspect of the decisions in these cases was the great division of opinion which they so obviously provoked within the Court regarding the difficult constitutional issues presented. So great was that division that nearly every justice—seven of the nine—wrote an opinion. In the prevailing opinion in *Bell*, a core of three justices—Brennan, Clark, and Stewart—avoided decision of the basic issue, ruling instead that the case should be remanded to the Maryland Court of Appeals because of the passage of a state public accommodations statute after the convictions.

The meaning and effect of that statute on the case were primarily for that court, the justices held in reversing the convictions and remanding the case. It was not clear whether the Maryland general savings clause would save these convictions after the enactment of state and local public accommodations laws. That, it was ruled, should initially be determined by the Maryland Court of Appeals. Brennan went to some length to explain that it seemed clear from past state court decisions that under Maryland common law the supervening enactment of the public accommodations statutes, abolishing the crime for which the petitioners were convicted, would cause the Maryland Court of Appeals now to reverse and order the indictments dismissed.

Douglas, concurring, argued that the underlying constitutional question should have been decided at this critical hour and that it was an inexcusable default on the part of the Court not to have done so in the face of continued *apartheid* in what was supposedly a modern, democratic nation. In the second part of his opinion, in which he was joined by Goldberg, he went on to argue that the Fourteenth Amendment forbade racial discrimination in public accommodations. He concluded that he would have reversed the judgment below outright and directed dismissal of indictments. Goldberg, also concurring, then explained for himself and the Chief Justice that although he joined in the Brennan opinion, he disagreed profoundly with the dissenters' conclusions on the underlying constitutional issues. It was the intention of the Fourteenth Amendment's framers, he argued, that it should outlaw discrimination in public accommodations, and along the lines of *Burton* he proposed a holding that state inaction in enforcement was tantamount to state action.[45] Although both Goldberg and Warren agreed with the majority that the constitutional issue should not be reached, they felt compelled to say, since the matter had been broached so strongly by the dissenters, that their conclusion on the constitutional issue was quite a different one, in the same direction as that of Douglas.

The dissent written by Black, and joined in by Harlan and White, agreed with Douglas that the constitutional issue ought to have been decided, not avoided. It is unfair to civil rights demonstrators and to property owners alike, wrote Black, as well as against the public interest not to decide this question now. As Professor Kalven put it, Black thought it "unfair, uncandid, and imprudent to lull the public and the protest movement into a false sense of constitutional security."[46] Where Douglas reached a positive conclusion on the Fourteenth Amendment question, Black could not have been more negative, arguing that the Fourteenth Amendment left private property owners free to choose which customers they would serve in accordance with their own personal prejudices and that although Congress and state legislatures might have the power to

ordain otherwise, the Fourteenth Amendment by itself had no application to private discrimination, only to action which could be attributed to
the state. Because Black's opinion was written during the congressional
debate on the Civil Rights Act, his comments on action by Congress could
easily have been intended to communicate that the Court would look
favorably on a new statute.[47]

The Court was even more split in the *Barr* case than it had been in *Bell.*
Writing for the majority, Justice Black explained that since the *Barr*
defendants had been polite, quiet, and peaceful in their demonstration
from the time of entry to departure, and since the only showing to justify
the arrests and prosecution was the suggestion that their mere presence at
the pharmacy lunch counter might possibly tend to move onlookers to
violence, the convictions under the breach of peace charges had to be
reversed and the case remanded, on *Thompson* grounds that there was no
evidence to support them under the state's own law. Breach of peace was
not the only ground under which the *Barr* defendants had been prosecuted, however, and with regard to the remaining charges, under a
criminal trespass statute, the justices expressed considerable variance of
opinion. For the majority, a per curiam reversal and remand was
adequate to dispose of the convictions. The statute which the defendants
supposedly violated was found to be so vague that it denied due process.
As in *Bell,* Douglas would have reached the constitutional question and
reversed, ordering dismissal of indictments. Goldberg and the Chief
Justice also cited their separate opinion in *Bell.* Black, Harlan, and White
dissented as in *Bell.* They said that their review of the evidence in this case
with regard to the criminal trespass charges convinced them that the
arresting officers here had done nothing to justify a holding that they
were acting for the state in an unconstitutional way. As before, they
believed that this was the only ground upon which the decision should
turn.

In *Bouie,* the majority opinion, again by Brennan, cut an even finer
distinction regarding the state trespass statute under which the Negro
defendants had been convicted. Brennan explained that the statute in
question prohibited entry on the lands of another after notice not to
enter, but that in applying its 1961 construction of the statute to the case,
the South Carolina Supreme Court had read the statute as prohibiting the
act of remaining on the premises after being asked to leave. This, concluded Brennan for the majority, amounted to a denial of due process to
the *Bouie* defendants, for it deprived them of fair warning at the time of
their conduct that their act was rendered criminal by the statute; the
convictions were therefore reversed.[48] Once again, Goldberg and the
Chief Justice, though joining with the majority, pointed to their *Bell* views
on the constitutional question, as did Douglas, Black, and Harlan. White

dissented, declaring, as in *Bell,* that no city ordinance, official utterance, or state law of any kind was involved in this case. As for the majority's disposition on the vagueness ground, they said it seemed quite obvious and similarly should have been readily apparent to the defendants that they would violate the statute by staying after being asked to leave, too.

In the *Robinson* case, a wholly different ground again provided the basis for reversal and remand. The majority opinion was by Justice Black. In this case, he explained, the trespass convictions had to be reversed on the ground that through its board of health regulations, which required separate facilities for each race whether employed or served in places of public accommodation, the state of Florida had become involved to such a significant extent in bringing about restaurant segregation that the defendants' convictions for refusal to leave the restaurant premises upon the management's request had to be considered to reflect that state policy and thus were violative of the Fourteenth Amendment. Douglas would have reversed as in *Bell,* and Harlan, dissenting, said he considered himself bound by *Peterson* and was thus acquiescing in the judgment.

The opinion in the *Griffin* case was written by the Chief Justice. He utilized still different grounds for settlement. In setting aside the convictions, Warren reasoned that Negroes had been denied the equal protection of the laws secured by the Fourteenth Amendment when ordered to leave and then arrested for trespass, despite the fact that there was no disturbance or violence, by someone deputized as a sheriff and employed by the park and thus under contract to protect and enforce the racial segregation policy of the management. The park employee's status as a county officer contributed an element of impermissible state action to the exclusion from the private facility, although on orders of private management. Once again Douglas, concurring, noted that he would reverse as in *Bell.* Clark noted his concurrence on the understanding that the Court merely held that the state was here a joint participant in the challenged activity before any charges were made regarding the defendants. Harlan, dissenting, disagreed, saying that the state's involvement was no different from what it would have been if the arrests had been made by a regular policeman dispatched from police headquarters.

The greatest dispute involved in these cases was not for whom to decide—that is, whether to affirm or reverse—although certainly this was important, but whether through the cases to reach the overriding constitutional question as to whether the activities of the sit-ins and demonstrators were constitutionally protected. There were four justices— Douglas, Black, Harlan, and White—who believed the constitutional question should be decided now, but, they disagreed on the direction to take. Conversely, there were five justices—Brennan, Clark, Stewart, Goldberg, and Warren—who thought the constitutional issue should be avoided now. As to the direction of a constitutional decision, should it be made, three—Douglas, Goldberg, and Warren—would have held that the Fourteenth Amendment did protect such activities, although two of the three wished to avoid the issue now. Three other justices—Harlan, Black, and White—all of whom were convinced the matter should be decided now, would have decided the issue in the negative. Finally there were three justices—Brennan, Clark, and Stewart—who not only believed the issue should be avoided now, but also preferred to withhold any comment whatsoever on their ultimate views. Because no decision was made on the constitutional question of the private right to discriminate within otherwise public accommodations, there was no available statutory ground, and there were basically only two constitutional grounds available for disposition of cases. The choice of grounds was also a matter of controversy. The choice fell, generally, between the Fourteenth Amendment equal protection grounds and the requirement of due process. Those preferring settlement of the constitutional question were of course prone to an equal protection basis for settlement, while due process was viewed by the other side as a tried and true means of avoiding this same constitutional question entirely.

The Court's critics during this period cried most loudly that the Court acted like a legislature. However, there was no better strategy than to avoid decision of a matter splitting its own ranks by relying on the fact that the legislature was acting. The Court's internal division may be a sufficient explanation of its failure to decide the basic constitutional questions involved in these sit-in situations, but there is no question that knowledge that Congress was doing something gave all the justices some reason to postpone again dealing with the issue, particularly in cases in which some of the Court's members would have decided in favor of a freedom for the restaurant owner to discriminate. The Court had to dispose of these cases in some manner because they had already been long delayed and because personal rights of many individuals hung in the balance. Since the acts for which these defendants had been prosecuted would in the future be rights federally protected, the individuals should be exonerated by whatever means possible. In each of these cases, precedent dictated a slightly different tack, but once the decision to exonerate in the simplest fashion had been made, the holdings themselves were matters purely academic.

Douglas, probably motivated as much by concern that the states might retaliate by overturning the Court on remand as by concern for his view of constitutional purity, felt it necessary to speak out further. Part of his speaking out was highly emotional, shown in his use of the word *apartheid*, which did not contribute to rational decision of the underlying questions in the case. If, as Douglas felt, the decision weakened the law's prestige, the nation seemed not to have noticed. People quickly turned their attention to the passage of the Civil Rights Act, which they acclaimed even though its basic standard was narrower than that Justice Goldberg had proposed. Whether Goldberg's or Douglas's constitutional standard would have solved broader social problems is not at all clear. Paulsen argues that racial unrest in the North would still have occurred in 1964, because the controversy there went far beyond access to public accommodations, deriving as it did from "a combination of lack of jobs, inadequate housing, poor education, poverty, and human frustration."[49] Nor, with respect to public accommodations itself, would a Douglas-based ruling have prevented lunch counter and restaurant owners from resort to self-help, as Lester Maddox was to do at his Pickrick Restaurant, or from attempting to discourage black customers through poor service or poor food. A broad decision undoubtedly would have helped change the atmosphere but would not by itself have eliminated all resistance. As Paulsen put it, "The walls of segregation are not so feeble that they will fall to a sounding of Gideon's trumpet."[50]

Douglas was not the only justice concerned about the law's position. Black, Harlan, and White were concerned with the purity of the Court's role in the life of the nation and the dimension of violence they saw in this new political activity. Yet Black's opinion, whatever advantages it may have had in terms of congruence with the Constitution's literal language and precedent, would also not have resolved the social problem which gave rise to the sit-ins, nor would it have provided public tranquility. The civil rights movement would not have been easily turned aside by his negative conclusion, and indeed more rather than less unrest might have resulted. To have accepted Justice Black's position on the sit-ins at a time when the Civil Rights Act was almost passed would also have been a serious if not disastrous strategic mistake because, although Congress was proposing to use a different constitutional basis for its statute than that at issue in these cases, work on the new statute would have been badly undercut.

Immediately after the *Bell* set of decisions, four more sit-in cases awaiting Court action received summary treatment. In the first, *Williams v. North Carolina,* in a per curiam order the Court granted certiorari, vacated judgments below, and remanded the case to the state supreme court for consideration in light of *Robinson v. Florida.* The case involved a Negro convicted for refusing to leave the soda fountain of a privately owned retail drugstore in Monroe, North Carolina. After having been forbidden to remain there, having been repeatedly warned to leave by two of the store's managers, he had left and reentered the store. Douglas noted separately that he would have reversed outright as in *Bell,* and Black, Harlan, and White similarly noted their dissent. The following three cases, all under NAACP guidance, were handled in similar fashion. The first, *Mitchell v. City of Charleston,* involved twenty-four black high school students convicted of trespass and of opposing and interfering with police in discharge of official duties for refusing to leave the lunch counter of a Charleston, South Carolina, general merchandise store upon request of the manager and the chief of police. The South Carolina Supreme Court had affirmed the trespass convictions but reversed on the second charge since the students had merely displayed "inaction" rather than active interference. The United States Supreme Court, granting certiorari and rendering judgment per curiam, reversed the remaining convictions with a citation of *Bouie.* Douglas agreed with the reversal, but said he would have done so on the basis of his opinion in *Bell.* Again, the three dissenters still dissented.

The second case, *Fox v. North Carolina,* represented the trespass convictions of a group of Negroes prosecuted for their refusal to leave the lunch counter area of a general merchandise store in Raleigh, North Carolina. The lunch counter had been clearly set apart from the rest of the store as a food service area, and was known to be restricted to white persons. It had been objected in the courts below that the Negroes were merely testing the store's policy, that they had no desire or expectation of service, and that they had violated a local trespass statute by remaining in the area after the store manager told them to remove themselves from it. Citing *Robinson,* as in the other North Carolina case, the Supreme Court vacated the judgments and remanded the case for renewed consideration. Douglas would have reversed outright, and Black, Harlan, and White again voiced dissent.

The final case of this series, *Drews v. Maryland,* involved a group of Negroes and whites convicted of disorderly conduct and disturbance of the peace after their refusal to leave an all-white amusement park in Baltimore County, Maryland, upon order of the guard. Apparently, a crowd gathered when the group refused to leave the park, emotions ran high, and violence was feared imminent by park officials, who called county police officers to eject the demonstrators. The record was unclear as to whether the park guard had the power to make arrests, but it did seem to indicate that it was after his order to leave, dictated by his employer's discrimination policy, that the disturbance began and crowds gathered. In any event, the Court ordered the conviction judgments below vacated and the case remanded, so that the Maryland Court of Appeals might consider the charges again, this time in light of *Griffin* and *Bell.* As before, Douglas would have reversed outright as in *Bell,* and the three justices would have dissented.

The Maryland Court of Appeals, seemingly taking final retaliation against the Supreme Court, reaffirmed the *Bell* convictions returned to it on remand, ruling that the state general savings clause did apply to these convictions and that they were not abated under Maryland common law despite subsequent passage of state and local public accommodations statutes. The same court similarly reinstated and reaffirmed its original judgments in *Drews,* distinguishing the Supreme Court's *Bell* ruling by saying that the state public accommodations statute did not cover amusement parks, and distinguishing *Griffin* on the ground that the only county police officers shown involved in the incident by the record were those who had come to the park to remove the demonstrators after park officials had reason to believe serious violence might erupt because of the demonstrators' presence. *Bell* was not appealed again to the Supreme Court, but *Drews* was. When the Court was asked to review the reaffirmance, the dissenters apparently tightened ranks and led the Court to avoid further action. The appeal was dismissed "for want of jurisdiction," and, treating the appeal papers as a petition for certiorari, the Court similarly denied that form of review. Only the Chief Justice and Douglas, whose views on the constitutional issue had been made clear in *Bell,* indicated their dissent from the denial of certiorari. Goldberg, whose views had also been made clear but who was about to leave the Court to become United Nations ambassador, made no separate statement. Once the state court had settled the matter of state law involved, there was no jurisdiction on appeal, and to hear the case on certiorari entailed constitutional considerations which no four justices were willing to undertake even though the lower court had taken advantage of their split in the *Bell* litigation and even though allowing such a decision to stand was particularly dangerous as an indication of what the Court wanted to achieve.

10

The Congress and the president had attached much importance to the 1964 Civil Rights Act. Just over three months after the law's enactment, the Court granted hearing to two cases challenging the public accommodations section of the act, thus assisting those—including the other branches of the national government—who wanted a prompt answer to their questions as to the law's validity. While such cases involving challenges to major new federal statutes would have been hard to ignore, the Court by its action indicated its awareness of the legislation's significance. One case, *Heart of Atlanta Motel v. United States,* involved a motel in Atlanta found to have violated Title II of the act; in the other, *Katzenbach v. McClung,* the United States Attorney General was appealing from an injunction against enforcement of the act won by a relatively small Birmingham restaurant in a suit filed within two hours of the president's signing of the act.[51]

At oral argument in the *Heart of Atlanta* case, Moreton Rolleston, Jr., attorney and part owner of the Atlanta motel, described the fundamental issue of the case as the question of whether the Congress had the right to take from a private business the owner's choice of running his firm and choosing his customers as he wished.[52] Although his attack was directed primarily against application of Title II to hotels ("You could find against the restaurant and for the motel but not vice versa.") Rolleston attacked Title II of the act broadly. He suggested five separate grounds on which the Court could declare it unconstitutional: 1) The *Civil Rights Cases* were still the "law of the land," and when the Court had said there, "No one will contend that the power to pass [the Civil Rights Act of 1875] was contained in the Constitution before the adoption of the last three Amendments," it was certainly aware that the commerce clause was in the Constitution. 2) "Neither the Fourteenth Amendment nor the Constitution prohibits racial discrimination by an individual." The wrongful act of an individual, unsupported by any such authority, is simply a private wrong, he said, and cited Justice Black's *Bell* dissent. "You . . . said in substance that the Constitution, including the Fourteenth Amendment, did not prohibit an individual from practicing racial discrimination unsupported by any state action." "In and of itself it did not," clarified Black. "That is this case exactly," came the response. 3) The Civil Rights Act of 1964 was an unlawful extension of the power of Congress under the Commerce Clause. The framers of the Constitution intended to cover commerce as known in business fields, such as transportation and movement of articles of agriculture or products of industry. Rolleston distinguished the extensions of the commerce power recognized in antitrust law, wage and hour legislation, and labor statutes because each set up some standards by which the courts could determine if the particular business involved was engaged in interstate commerce. The present law made every business subject to federal law, he said. Commerce has got to stop somewhere, he insisted. "If you don't accept that fundamental, I'm lost." Unless this Court says that commerce ends with personal liberty, then there is no end to it, he asserted. Goldberg inquired whether Rolleston were asking the Court to overrule *Wickard v. Filburn,* in which a farmer's withdrawal of wheat from the market was held to affect interstate commerce so that Congress could regulate the withdrawal.[53] In response, Rolleston said that "if you buy that theory," then Congress could cover every activity, every facet of life. He added that if this Court will let Congress do anything it wants to under the commerce clause, then there is no reason for the Supreme Court, whose function is to adjust and maintain the balance of powers between the various governments in this country. 4) The act violates the Fifth Amendment. 5) The act violates the Thirteenth Amendment. Rolleston asserted that involuntary servitude embraced compulsory service by one to another in commercial transactions.

Rolleston also contended that even if the act was intended to relieve the burden put upon interstate commerce by racial discrimination, it had not done so because there was no such burden. When Rolleston attempted to point up the lack of need for accommodations for Negro interstate travelers by telling the Court that in the two months that court order had opened his motel to Negroes, he had had thus far only three requests from Negroes for rooms, Goldberg quipped, "Have you been irreparably damaged by being compelled to admit them?" Concluding, Rolleston said that he got the impression from the government that Congress had passed the Civil Rights Act to help the businesses of thousands of whites in the South. If this is so, he said, "Please don't do us any more favors."

Solicitor General Archibald Cox called the Civil Rights Act "the most important legislation enacted in recent decades," and "one of the half dozen most important laws . . . enacted in the last century." "Happily," he continued, "the difficulty of the constitutional issues is not equal to their importance." Cox viewed Title II as resting upon the powers delegated to Congress to regulate commerce among the several states and upon the power to enact laws that were necessary and proper to effectuate the commerce power. The title's constitutionality, he explained, was sustained by "principles that are so familiar because they have been applied over and over again, applied indeed throughout our entire history. . . . We do not seek the extension of any existing principles here. *A fortiori*, we invoke no new doctrine." Cox put the government's position regarding the statute in the form of a syllogism. The major premise was the familiar rule that Congress under the Commerce Clause and the Necessary and Proper Clause had power to regulate local activities with such a close and substantial relation to commerce that their regulation may be deemed appropriate or useful to foster or promote such commerce or to relieve it of burdens and obstructions. The minor premise was that Congress had ample basis upon which to find that racial discrimination does in fact constitute a source of burden or obstruction to interstate commerce. Ergo, the prohibition of racial discrimination is a legitimate exercise of the commerce power.

Racial discrimination was, indeed, a "national commercial problem," Cox said, and the importance of any individual establishment and its link to commerce must be judged not as an isolated phenomenon but as part of a complex and interrelated national problem. He called attention to the impact of racial disputes and civil unrest upon the flow of investment and the loss of retail sales. If retail stores cannot sell, they in turn will not buy from wholesalers, who in turn must necessarily reduce their out-of-state purchases. Similarly, an American Legion convention with as many as fifty thousand persons had been shifted from New Orleans because nonsegregated facilities could not be assured. Cox thus sought to secure

Negro civil rights by defining them in terms of white rights to make a profit, just as the Court had done in *Shelley*. However, when asked by Justice Goldberg, "Isn't there a moral problem, also?" Cox responded that while the statute was indeed addressed to a grave commercial problem, Congress in addressing itself to that problem was also keeping faith with the promise of the Continental Congress that all men are created equal. "The failure to keep that promise lay heavy on the conscience of the entire nation, North as well as South, East as well as West."

Cox suggested that the motel owner's Thirteenth Amendment argument "would turn the world upside down." Even Alice at the end of her long journey through the looking glass, he said, would be surprised to hear that restaurants and other places of public accommodation are being held in involuntary servitude and that the Anglo-American common law for centuries has subjected to slavery innkeepers, hackmen, carriers, wharfingers, ferrymen, and all kinds of other people holding themselves out to serve the public. Cox also said that the *Civil Rights Cases* had not involved the Commerce Clause and that Congress had sought by the 1875 Civil Rights Act to eliminate discrimination in many areas that at the time were clearly local activities not affecting interstate commerce, perhaps using the Fourteenth Amendment so that the statute would reach many things that did not affect commerce.

The broad questions argued in *Heart of Atlanta* concerning Title II's application to motels and hotels were considerably narrowed in the *Katzenbach v. McClung* argument over the validity of the title's provision affecting restaurants. Both lawyers caused problems for the Court when each argued a narrow position. On the merits, the argument came down to one question: Did Congress exceed its powers when it barred discrimination by a restaurant whose only connection with interstate commerce was the serving of food that had moved in interstate commerce? Cox began by seeking the Court's disapproval, on jurisdictional grounds, of the lower court's grant of an injunction against enforcement of the act in an action brought by a restaurant that, Cox asserted, was neither threatened with imminent enforcement of the act nor with irreparable injury and thus had "no occasion for picking a quarrel with us." Nearly every member of the Court questioned Cox about this jurisdictional "side-step." Cox explained that, although he would welcome a broad ruling on the validity of Title II, he was disturbed by the jurisdictional question. Cox assured the justices he was not seeking a disposition solely on the jurisdictional grounds, but would be satisfied in this respect by a statement from the Court disapproving the district court's procedure. He made three arguments against allowing such suits: 1) Courts should not unnecessarily resolve constitutional questions. 2) Determination of what cases to litigate is an important part of the administration of law and justice that devolves upon the government. 3) Allowing such suits presents a real danger of unnecessary interference with the normal processes of law enforcement.

On the merits, Cox invoked the same legal principles he had asserted as the foundation for the validity of the ban on discrimination in hotels and motels. Discrimination in restaurants that either serve or offer to serve interstate travelers, or serve food that has moved in interstate commerce, he contended, does have a real effect upon interstate commerce. Once again, Cox pointed to the effect upon such commerce of demonstrations by Negroes against discrimination in public eating places. He also pointed to the reduction in the number of potential customers caused by the discouragement of Negro patronage, which in turn reduced the quantity of goods purchased through interstate channels. Cox also argued that prior decisions required neither proof nor legislative findings where the constitutionality of legislation turned upon whether conditions existed that might lead the legislative body to conclude that the challenged measure was a means reasonably adopted to a permissible object.

Robert McDavid Smith appeared for the Birmingham restaurant. He at once limited the issues he would argue before the Court by saying, "We don't contend that Congress doesn't have broad powers to regulate local activities that have a close and substantial connection with interstate commerce" nor the right to bar discrimination in some places of public accommodation. However, the act had brought within its terms restaurants that had no demonstrated connection with interstate commerce. Smith stated that it was not his purpose to make arguments based on the Fifth, Ninth, Tenth, or Thirteenth Amendments or to urge the inapplicability of the act to any restaurant other than the one which he represented. "We only say that the precedents relied on by the government are not authority for applying the Act to this restaurant." The narrowness of Smith's approach to the case provides ample explanation for the unanticipated narrowness of the approach the Solicitor General had employed. Smith's position was that Title II's food-served test was unconstitutional, there being no congressional determination that racial discrimination affects interstate commerce nor in the act any language such as the Taft-Hartley Act provision requiring the labor practice condemned to be in interstate commerce. Coverage under the food criteria was not even keyed to the current operations of a restaurant, but rested solely on the past activity of such an establishment, for example, its serving of food that "has moved" in interstate commerce—such as a North Carolina restaurant covered because a Virginia ham remained in its storehouse even if it never imported one single Virginia ham after the act's enactment. Smith summed up his argument by pointing up the difference between using the commerce power to regulate the use of goods, as previous legislation had done, and using the power to regulate conduct totally unrelated to the government of goods in commerce, which he felt the 1964 Civil Rights Act attempted to do.

Questions from the justices in these two cases were concentrated in relatively few areas. It was clear that they wanted to sort out the relation between Commerce Clause and Fourteenth Amendment arguments. After Harlan had noted, "The government is not relying on the Fourteenth Amendment in this case," Black queried, "Suppose Congress had expressly relied on the Fourteenth Amendment. Could this Court decide that the statute is unconstitutional on the ground advanced by the litigant that it exceeded the power of Congress under the Commerce Clause?" Harlan then repeated, "Here it is perfectly clear that the government is relying on the Commerce Clause. This discussion may be interesting but it is not germane." Later, Justice Goldberg, who was also concerned with the constitutionality of state public accommodations laws, expressed concern over the Solicitor General's reliance on the Commerce Clause to the exclusion of the Fourteenth Amendment. "Does this mean that the government loses the day in this Court if the Court decides that your position on the Commerce Clause is not to be sustained?" Cox, who found the alternative unlikely, said that the government would be hard put to prove facts establishing state action in this case unless one were prepared to say that a state's mere failure to put a stop to discrimination in itself constitutes state action—precisely the point which had been causing difficulty for the justices in the sit-in cases. Goldberg, persisting, asked whether even in the absence of the Thirteenth, Fourteenth, and Fifteenth Amendments Congress could have adopted an equal accommodations law for the slaves. Harlan suggested that since the problem of racial discrimination was specifically dealt with through the Civil War amendments and that those amendments limited federal power to discrimination based on state action, it could be argued that strictly local action by private individuals could not be reached by Congress even under the Commerce Clause. Cox replied that he did not believe that the grant of additional power through the Fourteenth Amendment could be construed as a curtailment of the existing power under the Commerce Clause. Harlan answered, "It's very difficult to read these debates without reaching a conclusion that the dominant purpose of Congress was to deal with racial discrimination." Related to this line of questioning were some questions about past cases. Justice White asked Rolleston, "Didn't the Court put the Commerce Clause expressly aside in the *Civil Rights Cases*?" Rolleston did not know. Saying counsel had not touched upon them, Black drew counsel's attention to a long line of commerce cases starting with *Gibbons v. Ogden*. In reply, Rolleston invoked *United States v. Yellow*

Cab. He said that if the transportation by taxicab of out-of-state residents or travelers from a railroad station or an airport to a motel is not part of interstate commerce, as the Court there held, how can anyone logically urge that the hotel or motel to which they are transported is involved with interstate commerce?

The justices also wanted to know whether Congress had exercised its power validly in outlawing discrimination in restaurants that serve or offer to serve interstate travelers. Goldberg asked such a question, and Harlan, who with the Chief Justice pressed counsel to devote his time to the question, expressed the judgment that though property rights are protected by the Constitution, such rights are subject to an exercise of state police power and valid exercise of Congress's commerce power. For him, the question was "whether this attempt to affect private property rights through the exercise of federal power under the Commerce Clause is a valid exercise of that power." The reach of Cox's argument was pursued in hypothetical questions. Could Congress make it unlawful for a man to beat his wife if he smoked cigarettes from another state? Or, as Stewart put it, could Congress "make it a federal offense for a man to beat his wife with a baseball bat imported from another state?" (Yes, under an earlier case,[54] although the government need not go that far here.) The justices also dealt with the question of whether Congress had to make findings to support its action, and Justice Black declared in *Katzenbach v. McClung,* "I don't agree that Congress has to make any findings" in order to impose a ban on discrimination. The issue for Black was whether a restaurant that discriminates on account of color can be held liable solely because it serves food that has moved in interstate commerce. Harlan, who had asked whether Congress could preclude the Court from determining whether the activities regulated do in fact affect commerce, noted that he thought it a "very persuasive argument" that, in the absence of a clear congressional determination that there was such a connection between the discrimination and food shipped in interstate commerce, Congress nevertheless failed to provide any procedure by which a restaurant so situated could have it determined that its operation did not affect interstate commerce. When Stewart remarked, "A restaurant could then get out from under the statute by careful purchasing of only local goods," Cox agreed. Stewart also asked Smith whether a court could make a determination under the Civil Rights Act as to whether or not the firm involved is in fact engaged in interstate commerce. Black returned to the issue to ask, "If Congress said the Act applied only to restaurants 50 percent of whose customers were interstate customers, would that be constitutional?" ("Yes, Your Honor.")

On the matter of whether discrimination imposed a burden on commerce, Black asked Rolleston what it could be called other than a burden upon commerce when the facts showed that hundreds of people could not find a place to stay during their interstate journeys. In *Katzenbach v. McClung,* Justice Goldberg inquired if since a person has to eat, it necessarily follows that there is a reduction in the amount of foodstuffs shipped in interstate commerce. Cox: Even if it did not reduce the flow of interstate commerce, it would distort it. Stewart suggested that the statute was in fact an effort by Congress to remove the cause of civil rights demonstrations that had so demonstrable an effect upon interstate commerce.

In the second week of December 1964—less than six months after enactment of the 1964 Civil Rights Act—the Court announced its unanimous approval of the basic public accommodations sections of the far-reaching statute. Writing for the Court, Justice Clark engaged in a systematic review of the arguments made in the cases. In *Heart of Atlanta Motel,* he first set aside the *Civil Rights Cases* of 1883 as without precedential value because the statute there had not been based on the Commerce Clause. He thought that Justice John Marshall's commerce test from *Gibbons v. Ogden* should be applied here—whether the activity sought to be regulated is "commerce which concerns more States than one" and has a real and substantial relation to the national interest. It was long ago settled, he said, that movement of persons through several states was included in commerce, there being no difference whether the movement is commercial or not. Turning to the legislative history of the Civil Rights Act of 1964, Clark found much evidence that the discrimination banned by the act placed a real qualitative and quantitative burden on interstate commerce, thus passing the *Gibbons* test. While Congress had also legislated on moral grounds, Clark said, that did not render its statutes any less valid. The overwhelming evidence is of a disruptive effect of racial discrimination on commercial intercourse—an effect which gave Congress the power to enact appropriate legislation. That the motel might be local in character also did not matter, Clark said, again drawing on the Court's past opinions, if interstate commerce felt the pinch from the local squeeze.

The motel's Fifth Amendment argument was set aside also. Clark observed that attacks on similar legislation in thirty-two states had not been successful. Even if there were economic loss from the legislation—a loss he doubted would occur—the legislation would still be valid. And there was, he said, certainly "no merit" in an "involuntary servitude" argument, as the common law innkeeper rule requiring that all be served had long predated the Thirteenth Amendment. In conclusion, he found Congress's action to be within the Commerce Clause power as it had been interpreted by the Court for 140 years. While one could argue that Congress could have pursued other methods to eliminate the effect of racial discrimination on interstate commerce, that was a policy matter for Congress, not the courts. All that the Constitution requires is that the means chosen be reasonably adapted to the end permitted, and Congress's choice cannot be said to be not so adapted.

In the *McClung* case, Clark dealt first with the argument that the case should be dismissed because the act authorized only preventive relief and no threat of enforcement had been made. However, he said, since the injunction initially requested was made on the basis of the act's unconstitutionality as applied to a restaurant and since it was important that a decision on the act's constitutionality be announced as quickly as possible, the Court would deal with the constitutional question. Indicating how awkward it would have been to have avoided the broad issue in *McClung* when the Court had reached the statute's merits in *Heart of Atlanta,* Clark noted that portions of *Heart of Atlanta Motel* answered many of the questions raised in *McClung.* This showed that the docket-management device of "pairing" cases seems to have had some effect in assuring that the Court would reach the merits. Clark went on to conclude that the food-served test portion of the act was constitutional. Congress had had ample basis upon which to conclude that the legislation would deal with the evil it desired to remove. Congress had made its decisions on the basis of an impressive array of testimony that discrimination in restaurants had a direct and highly restrictive effect upon interstate travel by Negroes and had placed a burden on interstate commerce by affecting the flow of merchandise generally. Aware of discrimination throughout the country, Congress could have focused on the connection between the individual restaurant and interstate commerce. Nor was case-by-case determination needed; its absence in other legislation such as the Fair Labor Standards Act had been upheld earlier and was appropriate here as part of the regulatory scheme Congress had established.

There were three concurring opinions covering both cases. Justice Black wanted to emphasize two points. One was that it would be ironic to use a due process argument to strip Congress of power to protect Negroes from discrimination when due process plays so important a part in the Fourteenth Amendment, the purpose of which was to protect Negroes. The other was that there was no need to consider the act's constitutionality under the Fourteenth Amendment because of its validity under the Commerce Clause. Douglas, on the other hand, argued that a Fourteenth Amendment basis for the decision would have a much more settling effect on the problem, making unnecessary litigation over whether a particular restaurant or inn was within the commerce definitions of the act or whether a particular customer was an interstate traveler. The act would thus apply to all customers in all the places enumerated in the act, thus putting "an end to all obstructionist strategies and finally clos[ing] one door on a bitter chapter in American history." Goldberg wanted to make clear he felt that Congress clearly had authority to enact such legislation under both the Commerce Clause and the enabling clause (Section 5) of the Fourteenth Amendment—an argument similar to that first argued by Justice Harlan, dissenting in the *Civil Rights Cases* of 1883, that Section 5 does not require "state action" if Congress enacts legislation based upon provisions of the Fourteenth Amendment such as the Equal Protection Clause.

Apart from the Commerce Clause basis of the decision, the new feature of these cases and the legislation involved in them was whether or not the Fourteenth Amendment implications of such legislation should be considered or discussed. The majority wished to avoid all consideration of the Fourteenth Amendment's applicability to the new public accommodations law. Six justices were willing to admit, as Douglas emphasized, that the act was not founded on the Commerce Clause to the exclusion of the Fourteenth Amendment's enforcement clause, but one justice, Black, was adamant that the latter should not be considered. Two justices were quite willing to base the decision on this broadest possible plane, openly concerned as they were with the moral aspects of the evils the act sought to end. But the majority's desire to avoid such a broad decision, anticipated by the government's hesitancy to argue broadly before the Court, clearly was based on the implications for "state action" entailed in recognition of the Fourteenth Amendment. State action in these circumstances would have included, as the Douglas concurrence specifically recognized, enforcement—by the state judiciary under trespass and similar laws—of racial discrimination as practiced by individuals. It was this aspect of discrimination in public accommodations, its perpetration by private individuals in their privately owned places of business, which had so concerned and split the Court in its previous, pre–1964 Civil Rights Act, public accommodations rulings. If the logic behind an application of the *Shelley* doctrine to public accommodations were broadly extended, why would it not similarly be prohibited state action for a court to uphold any expression of private discrimination—say, by a private club, or by an individual hosting an "open house" in his own home? The interstate commerce definitions provided by Congress in the 1964 act avoided any such difficulties and offered both a clear basis for prohibition of private discrimination, with broadly public impact, and a clear definition with consequent due process implications, of when, where, and how such discrimination was prohibited. Thus, while seeming to concede that the Congress had relied in part on its power to legislate under the Fourteenth Amendment, the majority chose to avoid any broad ruling on the constitutionality of the act, which was, after all, the broadest of its kind in history, and which unquestionably had been upheld under one basic constitutional provision. If at some future time the validity of the act's application to some questionably interstate commerce-affecting facility should be raised, or if Congress should decide to legislate more broadly in the accommodations area, then the Court could of course take up any such matter when so confronted with it in argument. For the time being, however, the act as applied to inns and restaurants in interstate commerce had been upheld, in a manner least offensive to those who would most oppose it.

11

Concomitant with the question of the 1964 act's constitutionality was the question of its retroactivity with regard to abatement of pending public accommodations cases involving state trespass convictions obtained before enactment but based on the attempted exercise of rights now guaranteed by the new legislation. The Court answered this question on the same day it rendered its two decisions upholding the act. Here, however, the justices were without the unanimity they had shown on the question of the act's constitutionality. The matter of abatement raised very different problems, as the argument before the Court showed. Two cases, consolidated for argument one week after the *Heart of Atlanta* and *McClung* cases were argued, brought the abatement question to the Court. One case, *Lupper v. Arkansas,* involved trespass convictions of a group of young Negroes who had sought service in a Little Rock department store's mezzanine tearoom and had been arrested and prosecuted upon their refusal to leave. The other case, *Hamm v. City of Rock Hill,* involved conviction for trespass for participation in a sit-in at the lunch counter of a McCrory's chain store in 1960. In both cases, immunity from prosecution was claimed under the Civil Rights Act of 1964. Since the act specifically declared protected the type of conduct for which appellants were being prosecuted, they said the convictions, pending when the act was passed and still pending, should be abated, as was the intent of Congress.

Appearing for the appellants was Jack Greenberg.[55] Saying that the incident here was quite like the scores of cases brought to this Court already and the perhaps three thousand now pending in state courts, Greenberg argued "fair warning" and "vagueness" grounds against the arrest and conviction of Hamm, and maintained that Congress had the power to say by definition that use of the trespass statute in those situations did constitute state action for the purposes of Section 1 of the Fourteenth Amendment. His primary argument was that the case fell within Brennan's *Bell v. Maryland* abatement rule. "If this were a federal conviction, the Civil Rights Act of 1964 would supplant it." Pointing out that the South Carolina law in addition contained an abatement provision,

Greenberg argued, "Federal law being supreme, and Congress having exercised paramount authority under the Commerce Clause and the Fourteenth Amendment, both of which authorized the national government to displace state authority, the federal statute is to be read as abating the state conviction on these facts were they to occur tomorrow," he said. Greenberg said the abatement argument applied with singular appropriateness to the cases at bar in that they involved some of the very persons who had acted at the risk of their liberty to arouse the conscience of the nation to pass the very legislation which they now claimed protected them and their actions. He also argued that the state statute applied only to an order to leave the whole premises, not just part of an establishment, and that Hamm had been denied due process because it was never shown that he had been ordered to leave the whole premises and then refused and because neither the prosecutor nor the trial judge specified the law under which he was charged, one of which had been declared unconstitutional.

For the state, South Carolina Attorney General Daniel R. McLeod argued that appropriate facts were not on the record to show that the McCrory store was covered under the act for the purposes of this case and that Congress's intent was that where prosecution was to be abated, it was so specified, not done here. The only recourse for refusal of service is a suit for injunctive relief, he said; refusal to leave is not an appropriate defense to a prosecution for trespass.

The justices' questions at argument fell into several categories. For one thing, they wanted to know the type of case involved.[56] When Douglas asked in what category these cases were, he was told merely sit-ins like this one, not including cases involving parades or picketing or voting rights or street demonstrations. When Black asked if it included disorderly conduct conviction cases, Greenberg replied that it involved only breach of peace and trespass for sitting at a counter, demanding food service, and the like. Brennan asked if there were a distinction between the two categories, and Greenberg replied that since *Garner* almost all were trespass cases. For another, the justices showed increasing concern about the peacefulness of protest activities. Brennan asked if counsel would apply the same analysis to a conviction for disorderly conduct as to a conviction for violation of a trespass statute, and Stewart asked if someone could be convicted for disorderly conduct if the evidence supported it. (Yes.) Goldberg emphasized, "You don't assert that you can get your rights established by law by improper reasons?" Definitely not, replied Greenberg. Stewart asked if most of the cases dated back to the spring of 1960 sit-ins, and Brennan asked if all were outstanding. Greenberg explained that some individuals were being held awaiting trial, but that almost all cases involved convictions that had been stayed at various levels or which had been stayed and were in process now.

As to the legal basis of the cases, Stewart asked whether the Fourteenth Amendment alone could be relied on—whether the Civil Rights Act was needed at all in these cases. Then Goldberg asked why counsel was arguing the broader point in a case in which the Fourteenth Amendment wouldn't apply but commerce would, and also asked if this case should be considered covered under the commerce power where the trial had been held before passage of the act. Finally, in a question clearly related to strategy, Goldberg asked whether the case should be remanded with a request for focus on this problem or whether it was a question of such importance that the Supreme Court should decide on the available record and without reference to the Civil Rights Act. When Greenberg replied that for the sake of Negro travelers the Civil Rights Act should apply and be applied as soon as possible, Harlan seemed piqued: "We still have a federal system, don't we?" Goldberg commented that counsel might argue that great disturbances would ensue if many were punished for their past acts. Black quizzed Greenberg until he admitted that the basic point involved was whether from the act and its history it could be shown that the legislation really does bar certain prosecutions. Then Black together with Brennan pressed counsel as to whether he would argue that Congress was constitutionally compelled to reserve for abatement explicitly, if it is reserved. Counsel replied, "I don't think I have to argue that." Harlan later also asked whether the question of retroactivity had ever arisen during the legislative debate, and Greenberg said it had not.

When the decisions were delivered, completing the triumvirate of December 14 civil rights rulings, the opinion was again by Clark with concurrence by Douglas and Goldberg, but this time there were four separate dissents. Ordering the convictions vacated and the charges dismissed, Clark ruled that still-pending state trespass convictions were abated by passage of the 1964 act, since nonforcible attempts to gain admittance or to remain inside establishments covered by the act were immune from prosecution; the act had now been specifically noted as a defense; and its availability was not limited solely to those pursuing statutory remedies. If the convictions were federal, they would clearly abate, Clark said, and the fact that they were initiated by the state is "a distinction without a difference." Enacting so drastic a change as the substitution of a right for a crime, Congress under the Supremacy Clause could not have intended the act to operate in the limited sense South Carolina advocated. "The principle of abatement is so firmly imbedded in our jurisprudence as to be a necessary and proper part of every statute working as a repealer of criminal legislation," he claimed. Then, revealing the strategic problem, Clark said that if the Court did not hold that Congress did not exercise its power in the act to abate such prosecutions, "we would then have to pass on the constitutional question of whether the

Fourteenth Amendment, without the benefit of the Civil Rights Act, operates of its own force to bar criminal trespass convictions, where, as here, they are used to enforce a pattern of racial discrimination." Clark went on cautiously, "Since this point is not free from doubt and since as we have found Congress has ample power to extend the statute to pending convictions we avoid that question by favoring an interpretation of the statute which renders a constitutional decision unnecessary." In short, now that Congress has exercised its constitutional power in this area and declared that the public policy of the country is to prohibit discrimination in places of public accommodation, there is no public interest to be served by the further prosecution of persons like Hamm and Lupper.

Concurring together, Douglas and Goldberg, because of their broader view of the 1964 Civil Rights Act, found the issue of this case much simpler than did those adhering to the Clark position. For them, Congress in passing the act had not merely sought to remove burdens from interstate commerce but had sought also to protect and enforce the Fourteenth Amendment right to be free in places of public accommodation from discriminatory treatment based on race. This view of the act led simply and directly to the position that Congress could appropriately conclude that all state interference with the exercise of that Fourteenth Amendment right should come to a halt upon passage of the act, that the state should not be permitted to insist upon punishing someone whose only crime was assertion of such right—albeit prior to the present legislation's enactment—and that the Court should not in any event put its stamp of approval on such state prosecutions, whenever they arose.

The four dissenting opinions were strongly worded. Black declared that the Federal Savings Statute should apply in such situations and that there were no grounds for abatement, Congress having said nothing about it and perhaps not even having the power to do so. Harlan and White seemed to agree that Congress had neither the power nor the intent to accomplish the majority's result. Harlan said that the doctrine of abatement could not be applied across different sovereignties by use of the Supremacy Clause unless explicitly intended by Congress and that even then the application would be unprecedented. White's dissent showed concern for judicial legitimizing of "massive disobedience to the law, so often attended by violence." He said the majority was here imputing "to the silence of Congress an unusual and unprecedented step which at the very least poses constitutional problems of some import." Stewart, writing the only "gentle" dissent, did not go as far as to find Congress without power or intent or to urge affirmance of the judgments but said that because Congress had not been shown to have provided that such nonfinal state convictions were to be abated, he would vacate the judgments and remand the cases to the state courts for reconsideration in light of the supervening federal legislation. Stewart claimed reliance on the *Bell* decision, saying that the Court there declared that a state's abatement policy was for the state to determine.

The situation of Hamm and others whose fate resided in the outcome of this decision was, as Greenberg had so passionately observed, quite similar to the situation of the disappointed parties in the highly disputed *Rice* cemetery case of the year intervening between *Brown I* and *Brown II*. The majority seemed anxious to avoid a repeat performance of that incident, particularly one involving far more people, though one of the *Rice* dissenters, Justice Black, disagreed that Congress had provided that option in this instance. If the majority had taken the other option which must have seemed open to it—remanding such cases to state courts for determination of state abatement policy in the first instance—undoubtedly a large number of these demonstration cases would have been brought back to the Court in the near future. Through its decision the Court was able decisively to take advantage of the congressional enactment to eliminate hundreds of sit-in cases from present and future dockets. This made the *Hamm* decision a stroke of strategic genius, in which federal governmental consensus was used to short-cut final settlement of a problem threatening disruption of the nation. The Court foresaw the difficulties of extreme disobedience to the law pointed out by Justice White, but the justices had already begun to speak to this problem and would do so more decisively in the future as it became necessary.

As was common practice, in the wake of *Hamm* the Court swept away nonfinal convictions in a number of already-docketed similar sit-in cases. In *Blow v. North Carolina,* the justices vacated judgments of the North Carolina Supreme Court affirming the convictions of Negro demonstrators for violating a statue making it a crime to enter upon the lands of another without a license after being forbidden to do so, and remanded for dismissal of indictments. Since the restaurant and adjoining motel, under the same management, were on the same interstate highway, were advertised extensively, and served and offered to serve interstate travelers, the Court said they were places of public accommodation under the 1964 act, and the convictions were abated by passage of the act as in *Hamm.* Similarly, *McKinnie v. Tennessee,* a Tennessee Supreme Court decision which had affirmed convictions for conspiring to injure the trade of a white cafeteria owner of Negro college students who had congregated in the small vestibule of the cafeteria when refused admission, thus physically blocking entrance and exit of patrons, received a per curiam reversal. In a third case, *Walker v. Georgia,* the Court reversed, also per curiam, a Georgia Supreme Court decision sustaining the trespass conviction of a white person who had entered a restaurant with Negroes and refused to leave when ordered to do so by the manager, again on the basis of *Hamm.* In all of these cases, it should be noted, Black, Harlan, and White said they would affirm as in *Hamm,* while Stewart said he would vacate and remand for reconsideration as suggested there. In *Parrot v. City of Tallahassee,* the Court cited *Robinson v. Florida* in its per curiam reversal order of a Leon County, Florida, Circuit Court decision affirming the convictions of two white students for trespass for refusing to comply with requests by the owner and the police that they leave the premises of a restaurant they had attempted to enter in the company of Negro students.

During the 1965 Term of the Court, four cases provided the swan song for public accommodations disputants. Not one case received a hearing. As far as the Court was concerned, the matter was closed, and any broadening of application under the act was a subject for the lower courts to deal with. The Court was not foreclosed from entering the field again at some future date to affirm what those lower courts had done, but for the time being, it was not considering these cases. The first case to be turned down by the Court during the term resulted from the much-publicized Lester Maddox Pickrick Restaurant incident. When three Negro ministerial students had attempted to integrate his restaurant, Maddox, who with his fellow businessman, the operator of the Heart of Atlanta Motel, had filed the first suits challenging the constitutionality of the 1964 act, had literally chased them out of his restaurant with pistol in hand, backed up by segregationist supporters wielding the ax handles for which Maddox was to become famed. The resulting suit, in which a federal district court had upheld the power of Congress and enjoined Maddox from such interference with potential customers, had become a contempt proceeding after *Heart of Atlanta* when Maddox still refused to allow Negroes in the Pickrick. Found guilty of contempt and ordered to pay a fine of two hundred dollars for each day he continued to disobey the injunction, he appealed to the Supreme Court, but the justices dismissed *Maddox v. Willis* for want of jurisdiction. For men like Lester Maddox, who ultimately decided to close up and sell his restaurant rather than serve Negroes, the 1964 act was a bitter pill to swallow. Time was needed to allay such emotions, and the Court allowed the lower courts to handle the act's application slowly without further entering the fray.

The next case, *Cuevas v. Sdrales,* involved an attempt to extend coverage of the act and was handled in similar fashion. It resulted from an action for an injunction and damages brought by a Negro against a Utah tavern owner for his refusal to serve. A federal district court and the Court of Appeals held that beer was not food within the meaning of the 1964 act and that since no food was sold at the tavern, the establishment did not come within the definition of a place of public accommodation within the meaning of the act. The Supreme Court refused to hear the case. Perhaps desegregating taverns was more controversial than desegregating restaurants, and perhaps the justices would have preferred more time before having to rule on the question of coverage. However, although the Court was later to read the act's coverage provisions liberally,[57] the Court did not provide a good "signal" in the first such case by leaving undisturbed lower court judges' action in reading the act narrowly.

The next two cases involved matters more technical than substantive and thus were somewhat different. The first, *Lance v. Plummer,* had arisen from a suit in which Plummer and seven other Negroes won an injunction forbidding interference with compliance with Title II against twenty-one individuals and corporations who were owners, managers, or operators of certain restaurants and motels in St. Augustine, Florida, and against several members of the Ku Klux Klan. Lance, a white policeman not a party to the original injunction, was stationed in one of the restaurants. He supposedly was protecting the Negroes who came there but in fact apparently acted to harrass Plummer and others, using foul language and following them in his car after they left. When Plummer then sought to have Lance held in civil contempt, the district court read its order as enjoining not only those named but also any other persons to whom notice or knowledge of the order might come. Indicating its extreme displeasure with the deputy sheriff's performance, the judge ordered him to give up his badge and cease his functions as a peace officer until the court was satisfied that he was no longer engaging in any of the acts the injunction prohibited. When the Fifth Circuit approved the district court's order, Lance's attorneys carried the case to the Supreme Court, challenging as a denial of due process not only the district judge's order against Lance but also the whole summary contempt proceeding. Acting with traditional deference to the lower federal courts in matters of this nature, the Supreme Court declined to hear the case. While the Court's avoidance of this case perhaps should not be read to endorse judicial removal of state officers with whose policies the courts disagreed, the district judge's assumption of "unprecedented and highly dangerous" power to remove a state officer was, nevertheless, too much for Black and Harlan, who noted their dissent from the Court's denial of certiorari.

The final case in this term was, appropriately, one in which a broad legal victory had been won below by Jack Greenberg and the NAACP Legal Defense Fund. Tolg, a white graduate student and teaching assistant at Miami University (Ohio), had been arrested and convicted under a trespass statute for his participation in a 1965 sit-in with a mixed group at a segregated restaurant in Atlanta. Convicted on the charge in federal district court despite his assertions along the constitutional lines avoided in *Bell* that his arrest and prosecution under the statute were a denial of rights, he continued his appeal within the federal court system while in prison. The Fifth Circuit, which did not hear the appeal until after *Hamm,* reversed, with instructions to the court below to grant the writ of habeas corpus and to order Tolg's release under the indictment. According to representatives of the state, who sought Supreme Court review of the reversal, the Fifth Circuit's decision seemed 1) to interpret the 1964 act as conferring a blanket immunity from prosecution under criminal trespass laws upon persons seeking service in places of public accommodation, regardless of the nature of their activities, and 2) to interpret the *Hamm* abatement principles as rendering void even those convictions which had become final prior to the act's effective date, provided only that the sentence had not been completely served, thus making such convictions susceptible to collateral attack and allowing a retroactive intrusion into state criminal law. Greenberg's argument spoke right to the Court's sore point: the case contained no conflicts to warrant review by the Court, for the demonstrators were peaceful, quiet, and orderly, and made no moves except in self-defense. The Court had before it the *Rachel* removal case which it would decide one week later, and in which Tolg was also a party. Predictably in this matter of applying a new standard so recently formulated, it let the Fifth Circuit's decision stand without comment. As it had after *Brown* and after so many crucial cases, the Court chose to allow its new standard for abatement in public accommodations to work itself out in the lower federal courts. Again, it should be noted, once these last pre-act cases were disposed of, the issue would not arise again. As Grossman has noted, the Court took almost every case which came before it after the 1964 act was passed, either to reinforce the *Hamm* decision or "to clear up some tangential issues relative to sit-in demonstrations not previously decided."[58]

The Court's activity in this area was truly amazing, not only for its contrast with what the Court had thus far not done in enforcing school desegregation but also for the unusual way the justices disposed of a large volume of cases. As has been noted, of the eighty-one cases the Court took in this area between 1957 and 1967, three-fourths were decided in favor of the demonstrators, but only four of these sixty-one (6.6 percent) involved broad constitutional rulings.[59] Virtually every other case was decided on subsidiary, although not necessarily unimportant, grounds, making this an area where "perhaps it could be said that never had the Supreme Court used so many cases to make so little law."[60] One reason for the Court's limited dispositions and incremental decision-making was a problem in formulating the law. As Greenberg has suggested, "In part, cases may have gone off so narrowly because general propositions concerning the right to demonstrate cannot be stated as simply as general propositions governing the right to desegregated education."[61] But more was involved because the Court would normally not decide so many minor criminal cases with limited issues. One must see the technical grounds used to decide these cases in their race relations context. Because those sitting-in were seeking to achieve the goal of racial equality propounded by the Supreme Court itself in *Brown,* the justices undoubtedly wanted them protected from prosecutions as they tried to make their views known. As Greenberg put it, "The Court has long recognized the 'chilling' effect of pending criminal prosecutions on speech. One might analogously describe the Court's repeated reversals of protest demonstration convictions as having a 'thawing' effect."[62] This view of the Court's action is reinforced when we realize that the Court tended to take cases more frequently when several or many people were involved than when only one was involved. If from two to fifty persons were indicted, the Court seldom refused to take the case, and never refused when more than fifty persons were involved. This meant that the Court was taking the cases with greater social consequences, as well as showing greater sensitivity to the heightened possibility of due process violations when large numbers of protesters were dealt with en masse by the criminal justice system.[63] However, the Court did begin to have increasing trouble in deciding in favor of the protesters where mass demonstrations were involved instead of sit-ins by a relatively small number of people. In a sense, if the right to protest were to become "thawed" too far, the Court would have to face a different set of problems from those encountered with respect to peaceful sit-ins. For this reason, while overturning convictions through the variety of means we have seen so that under most circumstances the states could not punish the demonstrators, the Court avoided stripping the states of their basic power to control disorders. But the Court did not give full constitutional validation to the protesters' position. Thus, as Grossman concludes, "the Court satisfied neither side completely, nor alienated either side totally."[64]

12

Beginning with the first sit-in cases and extending beyond the Court's central actions in that area in 1964 were cases involving more general protest. In this area, as in the sit-in cases, the Court chose at first to avoid an explicit statement on the question of actually or at least arguably disruptive behavior in tense situations. Its first major ruling upheld peaceful political protest on broad grounds relating to the First Amendment freedom to petition for redress of grievances. Only subsequently did the Court move on, albeit perhaps impatiently, to deal with situations involving protests in more complicated "times, places, and circumstances." In the first general protest case, *Edwards v. South Caroli-*

na, the Court reversed state supreme court convictions for breach of peace of a group of Negro high school and college students who had peacefully assembled at the site of state government in South Carolina's capital and there peacefully expressed to the citizens and officials of the state their grievances about rights prohibited to Negroes. In reasoning similar to that in the *Thompson* and *Garner* public accommodations cases, the Court said that in arresting, convicting, and punishing the students under the circumstances disclosed by the record—that is, peaceful behavior punished under highly generalized charges and questionable application of breach of peace laws—the state had infringed upon the students' rights of free speech, free assembly, and freedom to petition for a redress of grievances in violation of First and Fourteenth Amendment rights. Clark, dissenting, said that in his view the manner in which the students had exercised those rights was by no means the passive demonstration described by the majority's opinion but was, as the city manager of Columbia had testified, a dangerous situation building up and creating an actual interference with traffic and imminently threatening disturbance of the peace of the community. Clark acknowledged the priceless character of the First Amendment freedoms, but warned that they provided no absolute immunity from action necessary to protect society. Notably, in this first case involving civil disobedience, demonstrators were warned thereby of the limitations of their license.

The other case during the same term was from the same state and involved similar circumstances. *Fields v. South Carolina* involved a large group of Negro students who had marched through the downtown of racially tense Orangeburg to demonstrate their dissatisfaction with racial segregation and second-class citizenship accorded them in the city and the state. When they ignored police officers' requests to disperse, they had been arrested for breach of the peace and had been convicted, with the convictions being sustained through the state supreme court. The convictions were on the ground that the students' behavior caused fear and tended to incite a riot or other disorderly conduct or serious trouble. The students contended that the charges were groundless and that their behavior was constitutionally protected. Rendering judgment in the case per curiam, the Supreme Court vacated the state supreme court conviction and remanded the case for consideration in light of *Edwards.* The *Fields* case returned to the Court because, on remand, the state supreme court reaffirmed the convictions, refusing to accept dictation from the federal government that it could not punish activities of civil rights demonstrators. The Supreme Court, emphasizing the firmness of its position, now affirmatively reversed the convictions per curiam, overriding the state court.

Shuttlesworth v. City of Birmingham was handled in a manner clearly indicating the fine line of distinction against which the justices weighed civil disobedience incidents. In this controversy, the well-known civil rights advocate the Reverend Mr. Fred Shuttlesworth had been convicted of interfering with a police officer in the discharge of his duty. The minister attempted to block the path of the Birmingham police chief while the latter was taking a group of "freedom riders," nonviolent public protesters, into protective custody in the city police headquarters. The Alabama Supreme Court upheld the conviction, despite Shuttlesworth's contention that the police chief was not performing a legal duty. When Shuttlesworth petitioned the United States Supreme Court, the conviction was reversed per curiam, a type of disposition used frequently by the Court in this area. The implication of the cases cited was that conviction for attempting to block an official but illegal act was a violation of due process and that the ruling below did not rest on adequate nonfederal grounds to deprive the Court of jurisdiction. The next case, like *Fields,* had returned to the Court after the South Carolina Supreme Court had reinstated breach of peace convictions despite a Supreme Court vacate-and-remand disposition. In *Henry v. City of Rock Hill,* the Court now reversed the convictions per curiam, explaining that here, where the Negroes had been arrested for "loud and boisterous singing" during a demonstration which they held and which had caused crowds to gather, tensions to develop, and so forth, the petitioners had been engaged as in *Edwards* and *Fields* in "peaceful expression of unpopular views" and convicted of an offense so generalized as to be "not susceptible of exact definition"—in fact, on evidence which showed only that their views necessitated police protection. Once again, the high state court was rebuffed with a show of the strength of the Court's position regarding demonstrators.

Just one month after its much-heralded public accommodations decisions of the 1964 Term, the Court took the opportunity to announce some future guidelines for both civil rights demonstrators and public officials charged with regulation of the traffic and maintenance of the order which the demonstrators might threaten. The case was *Cox v. Louisiana,* and involved convictions of several persons who had participated in a demonstration protesting the arrest of certain civil rights leaders in Baton Rouge. Cox had led a group of about two thousand students in a protest against segregation and discrimination in the city and state and against the arrest of certain fellow students who were at the time undergoing trial. On the day of the trials, the group had assembled peaceably at the state capitol building in Baton Rouge, then had marched to a position directly across the street from the courthouse in which the trials were being conducted, where they sang, prayed, and listened to a speech by Cox. The police arrested certain of the demonstrators, including Cox. They were subsequently convicted of disturbing the peace, obstructing the public passageways, and picketing near a courthouse contrary to state law. The demonstrators protested their arrest and prosecution on free speech, assembly, and due process grounds, and from adverse judgments in the Louisiana state courts won review before the Supreme Court. In the Supreme Court, the first opinion in the case, by Justice Goldberg, handled the convictions under breach of peace and obstruction of public passageways. The facts in the case, Goldberg said, were strikingly similar to those present in the *Edwards* and *Fields* cases; similarly, by the breach of peace convictions, Louisiana had infringed upon the demonstrators' rights of free speech and assembly. Furthermore, the Louisiana statute involved, as authoritatively interpreted by the state supreme court, was unconstitutionally broad in scope. The Court also found constitutionally defective the Louisiana statute that on its face forbade all street assembly and parades but in practice was shown to have been applied at the unfettered discretion of local officials.

At the conclusion of his statements giving the Court's holdings regarding the convictions under both statutes, Goldberg, reflecting the tone of the Court's rulings in this area that protest must be peaceful or the Court would not protect it, went on to issue a kind of warning for street demonstrators which this case seemed to invite. Rights of free speech and assembly, he said, do not mean that everyone with beliefs or opinions to express may address a group at any public place and at any time. Governmental authorities have the duty and responsibility to keep the streets open and available for movement, and a group of demonstrators could not insist upon the right to cordon off a street or an entrance to a public or private building and allow no one to pass who did not agree to listen to their exhortations.

Cox's conviction under a Louisiana statute punishing picketing near a courthouse with the intent of obstructing justice or influencing judicial officers led to a second opinion, again by Goldberg. The highest public officials of the state, in the presence of the sheriff and mayor of Baton Rouge, had in effect told the demonstrators that they could meet across the street from the courthouse, 101 feet from the steps. The Court found that Cox and other demonstrators had been misled by the public officials and that due process did not permit their conviction under the statute after such an impression had been given. The Court found the fact—that the demonstration had been conducted with police permission across the street from the courthouse—the equivalent of advice that a demonstration held at that place would not be one "near" the courthouse within the terms of the statute. However, the Court found the statute sufficiently narrow and specific to reject the claim that it unconstitutionally infringed upon freedom of speech and assembly, and in so doing upheld the right of states to limit courthouse picketing. Although the laws under which the officials operated had a valid basis, the Court made clear that they could not be used in a discriminatory manner to stifle political opposition or public protest at the will of the incumbent officialdom.

Goldberg's second opinion also ended with a caveat. Nothing we have said here, he warned, should be interpreted as sanctioning riotous conduct in any form or demonstrations, however peaceful their conduct or commendable their motives, which conflict with properly drawn statutes and ordinances designed to promote law and order, protect the community against disorder, regulate traffic, safeguard legitimate interests in private and public property, or protect the administration of justice and other essential governmental functions. Then, speaking to public officials, he pointed out that there was an equally plain requirement for laws and regulations to be drawn so as to give citizens fair warning as to what is illegal and for regulation of conduct that involves freedom of speech and assembly not to be so broad in scope as to stifle the First Amendment freedoms which need breathing space to survive.

With respect to the opinions, no justice dissented from reversal of the breach of peace convictions, two dissented from reversal under the obstruction statute, and four dissented regarding the courthouse picketing ban. Black concurred in the first Goldberg opinion, but said he would declare both the statutes involved unconstitutional as too broad and vague. Together with Clark, he found the obstruction ordinance unconstitutional on Fourteenth Amendment equal protection grounds, too, since it specifically exempted picketing and assembly by labor unions protesting unfair treatment of union members. White and Harlan, though concurring in the reversal of breach of peace convictions with citation of *Edwards,* dissented from reversal under the obstruction statute, disagreeing that the statute was unconstitutional either on its face or as applied. Finally, all four of these justices protested reversal under the courthouse picketing ban, Black explaining that they believed the state had power to protect those in the courthouse from intimidation of this nature and that they disagreed that permission had been given to the demonstrators as the majority viewed it. In reversing these convictions the Court enunciated a general position regarding the guidelines which both demonstrators and public officials should follow in dealing with the new phenomenon of political expression spreading rapidly through the country. Unlike the sit-in cases, where the Court had found for the demonstrators without reaching the constitutional issue, here the Court also found for the demonstrators—on comparable grounds—and also reached the constitutional issue and a result which disfavored the protesters.

A case which provides a comparison with *Cox* is *McLaurin v. City of Greenville,* in which the petitioner had been convicted in city court of disturbing the peace for his protest outside the local courthouse of a verdict of disorderly conduct against two Negro girls immediately after their trial had been completed. During the trial, which was conducted in a room crowded with onlookers and tense in atmosphere, McLaurin, protesting that the courtroom was segregated, had refused to take a seat as directed by an officer inside, and when he left the room was refused reentry because it was already filled beyond capacity. As soon as he learned that the guilty verdict had been delivered against the girls, he began to exhort a Negro crowd outside the building, shouting and otherwise expressing his views as to the injustice perpetrated within, until officers on the scene began to fear that a breach of peace, perhaps even a riot, was imminent. One of the officers, a Negro, apparently had spoken to McLaurin suggesting he move on or modify his behavior, and when the latter refused, he was arrested by that officer. White officers also present testified that they had also feared a possible riot and were about to arrest McLaurin when the Negro policeman did so. McLaurin challenged the statute under which he was charged as being so vague and indefinite as to permit punishment of the exercise of one's right to free speech. The state courts, through the Mississippi Supreme Court, disagreed, and found that the evidence presented amply supported the conviction. *Cox* and *Wright v. Georgia* were distinguished on their facts. The Supreme Court refused to review, although the Chief Justice, Douglas, and Brennan went on record for certiorari.

The field of civil disobedience provided the largest number and two of the most controversial cases to be considered in the civil rights area during the 1965 Term. The first case to be decided involved once again criminal prosecution of Birmingham's civil rights activist, the Reverend Fred L. Shuttlesworth. This time he was engaged with other city Negroes in a selective buying campaign to protest racial discrimination in various Birmingham stores. When he and a group of persons were standing outside a local department store, a police officer asked the group to disperse, saying that they were obstructing the sidewalk. The others apparently moved on, but Shuttlesworth refused to go, asking the officer what law could possibly be offended by his standing in front of a department store window. He was then arrested and subsequently convicted of violations of city ordinances prohibiting loitering on a street or sidewalk so as to obstruct free passage and refusing or failing to comply with a lawful order of such officer. Losing his appeal in Alabama courts, Shuttlesworth sought review in the Supreme Court, which agreed to hear his case. He obtained a unanimous reversal, but four justices noted separate concurrence as to the grounds for reversal. Writing for the majority, Stewart reversed one of the convictions because it was based on an unconstitutional construction of a statute made two years earlier, a construction far too broad and vague for due process. Another conviction was also reversed because of an absence of evidence that Shuttlesworth was guilty of violating the ordinance under the narrow constitutional construction given the otherwise overbroad language by the Alabama Supreme Court. Douglas, concurring, emphasized that out of the original group only Shuttlesworth remained after the order to move on, hardly the basis for "obstructing" the sidewalk. Brennan's concurrence rested specifically on the state court's narrow construction of the second ordinance. Fortas and the Chief Justice thought it necessary to make clear that the defendant could not be convicted on the facts in this case even after the ordinance involved in the first count should be properly construed, for he had not been obstructing free passage. Thus, although there was unanimity in result, early seeds of disagreement in point of view were clearly visible, and narrow grounds were used to reach the result.

In *Brown v. Louisiana,* five young Negro men from the environs of Clinton, Louisiana, challenged their convictions under a state breach of the peace statute for their refusal to leave the adult reading or service room of an all-white regional branch library. Custom challenged by the local CORE chapter dictated that the branch library was an all-white sanctuary and that the red bookmobile served whites only, the blue one Negroes only. One Saturday morning the five Negroes entered the library reading room and one of them requested a book from the librarian. Finding it was not in the branch library but could be ordered from the regional library, she told him he could be notified to pick it up at the bookmobile when it came—he was later so notified—or that it could be mailed to him. After settling this business, the five remained in the library, the one sitting at a reading table and the others standing around quietly. There were no other patrons in the library during this period, which amounted to ten to fifteen minutes at most. The librarians asked the Negroes to leave the library, but before they ever had a chance to call the police, the sheriff and his deputies arrived and again asked the five to leave. When they refused, they were arrested for "not leaving a public building when asked to do so by an officer," a state breach of the peace offense. The sheriff, explaining why he had come so promptly without being called, testified at the trial that he had been informed that the CORE members planned a "sit-in" at the library that morning.

When the case came to the Supreme Court for review, the Court was badly split in reversing the conviction. Three justices—Fortas, the Chief Justice, and Douglas—held that, in staging a peaceful and orderly protest against the library's unconstitutionally segregated operation, the Negroes were lawfully exercising their constitutional rights to freedom of speech and assembly and petition for redress of grievances and that thus they could not constitutionally be punished for breach of the peace. Mixing narrow and somewhat broader grounds, they found no evidence to support the convictions under the *Garner* rule, and citing *Edwards,* declared that the statute could not be applied constitutionally to punish these actions in these circumstances. Next followed a concurrence by Brennan, largely on *Cox I* considerations—that the statute contained such a broad definition of breach of the peace that it could be applied to constitutionally protected activities and should thus be declared invalid without deciding whether defendants' conduct was within the scope of constitutional protection. White's concurrence was similarly based. Because the defendants' brief stay in the library was not significantly different from normal use of the facility, he felt there was no evidence of violation under the statute, so the defendants must have been asked to leave solely because of their race and thus their convictions denied them equal protection. Finally, there was a single, impassioned dissent by Black, joined by Clark, Harlan, and Stewart, which emphasized more than anything else a fear that the license being granted to sit-ins by the majority was too broad and permeated with dire future implications. Of all buildings in which peace, order, and quiet are necessary, it is the library in which such an environment is absolutely essential, Black wrote. No racial discrimination had been practiced in this case; the Negro patron had been served, his book ordered and his legitimate business in the library presumably done. There was no rule restricting the state's power to enforce the breach of peace provision of the statute to maintain peace and order in public libraries so essential to their very function. The Court, Black said, had simply substituted its judgment for that of the Louisiana courts as to what conduct satisfied the requirements of the state statute. If the Court lends its stamp of approval to this sit-in, what is to stop demonstrations—which might not be so "peaceful"—in libraries not empty? No demonstration inside such a facility, by its very nature disruptive, should ever be allowed. "The holding in this case today," Black concluded, "makes it even more necessary than ever that we stop and look more closely at where we are going."[65]

What perhaps distinguished *Brown v. Louisiana* from other protest cases and perhaps helped dictate the Court's strategy was that public facilities discrimination cases were becoming a thing of the past. The Court's position on the subject had been made unmistakably clear in cases like *Wright* and *Watson,* the 1964 Civil Rights Act had included a section (Title III) on the subject—which made the position of Congress more explicit and authorized suit by the attorney general upon complaint by aggrieved individuals—and in general the law—judicial and legislative—was clear. The opinions by the majority justices in this case, at least those by Fortas and White, emphasized above all the peacefulness of these petitioners' conduct and the reality of the racial discrimination involved. The language of the majority can hardly be viewed as enunciating any sweeping approval of library demonstrations. Notice was thereby served on states and localities that their discriminatory practices could validly be challenged by methods like these, but the strength of the dissenters' opinion served to qualify and limit the majority's action.

With the first case of the 1966 Term in this area, the Court upheld convictions of civil rights demonstrators for the first time in the 1960s. *Adderly v. Florida* involved Negro students from Florida A & M University who had marched from the school to a Tallahassee jail in September 1963 to protest the arrests the previous day of fellow students attempting to integrate local public theaters and to protest state local segregation policies generally, including segregation of the jail itself. They arrived at the jail singing freedom songs and clapping, and were asked by a deputy sheriff, evidently surprised by their arrival, to move back so as not to block the jail entrance. Still singing and clapping, they moved back to a position on the jail service driveway and an adjacent grassy area. When the sheriff arrived he told the demonstrators that they were trespassing upon jail property and must leave or face arrest. Ten minutes later he warned them again. When not all the group left, the sheriff placed the 107 remaining on jail premises under arrest. The 32 in *Adderly* were subsequently convicted in a joint trial on a charge of "trespass with a malicious and mischievous intent" on county jail premises under a state statute providing for general malicious trespass. Having appealed without success in the state courts, they asked the Supreme Court for review. There the demonstrators argued as they had from the beginning that their cases were controlled by and must be reversed according to *Edwards* and *Cox,* for their convictions denied them rights of free speech, assembly, petition, due process, and equal protection and that the Florida trespass statute under which they were charged was void for vagueness. They contended also that the doctrine of abatement announced in *Hamm* should apply to them, that "petty criminal statutes" should not be available for use to violate minorities' constitutional rights, and that, finally, *Garner* and *Thompson* should apply because their convictions were based on a total lack of relevant evidence and therefore denied due process. The state appeared to argue with little expectation that it might win the case, Florida's counsel seeming to be unfamiliar with the circumstances. He said that the demonstrators were blocking the service entrance to the jail, that the sheriff as its legal custodian had the right to demand that they leave the premises so that the normal functions of the property might be resumed, and that there had been functional concerns rather than racial discrimination involved in his objection to their presence.

Black and four other justices made up a narrow majority upholding the convictions. The crucial vote in swinging this decision was that of

Justice White, who had concurred in the *Brown* library case because the demonstrators' stay in the library was no different from normal use of the facility. Here he felt such justification was obviously lacking. The majority's opinion was broad in being clear and complete: all the petitioners' grounds were rejected. Of crucial importance to the majority was a distinction made between a public building such as a jail, built for security purposes, and state capitol grounds, traditionally open to the public, as in *Edwards*. Here, Black said, the demonstrators had entered the jail grounds through a driveway used only for jail purposes, they had made no warning nor received any permission from the sheriff, and the statute under which they were prosecuted was by no means vague but rather aimed at conduct of one limited kind, giving ample notice, and the trial court had carefully charged the jury as to its meaning. The sheriff, as jail custodian, had the power, Black said, to direct that this large crowd of people get off the grounds. There was no evidence he had exercised this power in discriminatory fashion, and the state, no less than a private property owner, has power to preserve the property under its control for the use to which it is lawfully dedicated.

The petitioners' argument that they had a constitutional right to stay on the property over the jail custodian's objections was based, Black felt, on the assumption that the people who want to propagandize protests or views have a constitutional right to do so whenever, however, and wherever they please. This proposition, vigorously rejected in the *Cox* cases upon which petitioners rely, was again rejected. The Constitution does not forbid a state to control the use of its own property for its own lawful nondiscriminatory purpose. The invocation of the *Hamm* doctrine of abatement was dismissed on grounds that a public jail, not a place of public accommodation, was involved and that a trespass on jail grounds could be prosecuted regardless of the fact that it was the means of protesting segregation in establishments covered by the 1964 Civil Rights Act. Finally, a review of the facts of the case as described by both sides to the dispute was said to show an abundance of facts to support the jury's verdict of guilty. At stake in this decision, as the majority saw it, was the same prospect that had so worried the dissenters in the *Brown* public library case of the previous term: if this demonstration, although quiet, was allowed in this public building to which quiet and order were essential, would the allowance seem to license future demonstrations, not so quiet and orderly, in similar public buildings? Here, the building was a public jail, and the prospect a precedent which would seem to leave authorities powerless to deal with invasions of jail premises.

In dissent, Justice Douglas, joined by the Chief Justice, Brennan, and Fortas, deplored the grave consequences which could be expected to ensue from this allowance by the Court of the use of a trespass law to bludgeon those who peacefully exercised a First Amendment right to protest to government against one of the most grievous of all modern oppressions being inflicted by some of our states on certain minority citizens. When a county jail housed political prisoners or those whom many think are unjustly held, Douglas said, it became an obvious center for protest. Holding a rather different view of the facts from Black, Douglas claimed the sheriff was well aware of the demonstrators' purpose to protest the arrest of fellow students for trying to integrate public theaters; there was no violence nor threat of violence and no attempt to effect a jailbreak or to storm the jail or even to enter the building; the group had moved back as instructed; the normal routine of the jailhouse was not upset; and the students had never located themselves so as to block the jail entrance—in fact, both the sheriff and the deputy sheriff had been able to drive up the driveway to parking places near the entranceway without obstruction. We do violence to the First Amendment, Douglas said, when we permit this "petition for redress of grievances" to be turned into a trespass action only because of the sheriff's fiat; the consequence is the placement of awesome power in the hands of public officials to decide whose ideas may be expressed and who shall be denied a place to air their claims and petition their government.

As in the earlier demonstration cases, the force of the opinions as a whole—embodying both majority and minority viewpoints—was a thoughtful and prudent notice that civil rights demonstrators, armed with and protected by strong new federal laws asserting their rights to equal citizenship, should turn first to the courts for adjudication of those rights before trying to exercise unfettered rights to demonstrate in protest against alleged denials. Their frustration at continued denial of their rights by certain states and localities was explicitly recognized, but the danger to all states and the whole governmental system was recognized as well. Strategically, the issue here was the delicate balancing of freedom of expression and public order. The disagreement was over the use of this case to delineate the balance and over the language to be used. Thus the question was whether the Court should have waited for a case in which the jail was stormed or similar violence had actually disrupted the function of some public building under the guise of First Amendment protection before expounding such limitation.

The difficulty of the question of balance before the Court cannot be overestimated, nor can the fact of increasingly violent public protest during this period be overlooked. As the Court had taken upon itself some years earlier to serve notice to the states that Negroes' constitutional rights could not be trampled upon, it inevitably felt the duty in light of present realities to serve notice upon the demonstrators that their rights did not license them to commit violence against public law, peace, and order. The question was when and how this was to be done, and in this case in 1966 an impatient majority chose to do it at last openly in the first case to come before it involving a demonstration at a public jail. From the perspective of the penalties imposed, about which the justices had shown concern during oral argument, this may also have been an appropriate case to serve notice on the demonstrators as to the limits to their conduct. The maximum prison sentence under the statute was three months, the maximum fine one hundred dollars—not inordinately great as compared with the greater constitutional questions the majority viewed as controlling.

In the last case to come before the Court during the 1966 Term, the Court went further along the lines begun in *Adderly*. Involved in *Walker v. City of Birmingham* were demonstrations conducted in 1963 in that troubled Alabama city after the issuance of a temporary injunction against 139 individuals and two organizations enjoining, among other things, participating in or encouraging mass meetings or mass street parades without a permit as required by Birmingham ordinance. The marchers had not formally sought a parade permit, having been told informally they would not get one. The city, notwithstanding, obtained an injunction against the march, the injunction tracking the language of a city ordinance which vested virtually unlimited discretion in officials to determine who could march. In requesting the injunction, city officials had said that the previous week's sit-ins, mass demonstrations, parades, trespasses, unlawful picketing, and so forth had violated numerous state statutes and city ordinances, were calculated to provoke breaches of the peace, threatened the safety, peace, and tranquility of the city, and placed an undue burden and strain upon the manpower of the city police department. The day after city officials won their injunction, five of the eight petitioners in this case held a press conference at which they declared their intent to disobey the injunction because "in all good conscience we cannot obey unjust laws, neither can we obey unjust use of the courts," and because the injunction was "raw tyranny under the guise of maintaining law and order." The next day, Good Friday, a crowd of demonstrators marched as originally planned, and on Easter Sunday, they began a "walk to jail," but violence occurred, in which onlookers had participated and rocks had been thrown, hurting a newsman and damaging a police motorcycle. Subsequently, city officials brought suit against the eight petitioners here for contempt of court for violating the injunction by leading the demonstrations. All were Negro ministers, including the Reverend Martin Luther King, Jr., Wyatt T. Walker, Fred L. Shuttlesworth, and Ralph Abernathy.

The ministers argued that the injunction and the Birmingham parade ordinance were unconstitutionally vague, overburdening and restraining free speech, and that the ordinance was arbitrarily and discriminatorily administered. The state circuit court refused to consider these contentions, because there had been no application for a parade permit, nor had there been a motion to dissolve the injunction. Thus, the only issues before the court were whether the local judge had had jurisdiction to issue the injunction and whether thereafter the petitioners had knowingly violated it. Answering both questions in the affirmative, the court fined each of the ministers fifty dollars and sentenced each to five days in jail. The Alabama Supreme Court upheld this judgment, again emphasizing that no effort had been made to dissolve or comply with the injunction before defying it. In the United States Supreme Court, the city of Birmingham argued that the case should be governed by the rule established by the Court in 1922 that an individual cannot test the validity of a court order by disobeying it and then challenging the order when he is prosecuted for contempt. For Dr. King and the other ministers, NAACP counsel argued that an exception to this rule should be made when the court order and the statute upon which it was based were both patently unconstitutional and were being used to stifle freedom of expression and assembly, as was contended to be the case here.

In handing down its five-to-four decision affirming the convictions, the Court refused to depart from the rule governing the proper course for a person legally restrained by what he regarded as an unjust court order. Writing for the majority, Justice Stewart explained that even though substantial constitutional questions could be raised in view of the generality of language in the parade ordinance and the vagueness of the temporary injunction, the fact that the petitioners had not attempted to have the injunction dissolved or modified by a court, or to secure the permit required under the ordinance, instead having deliberately violated it with the expectation of going to jail, meant that they were not entitled to have these constitutional issues considered and were properly convicted of contempt. One may sympathize with the impatient commitment of these petitioners to their cause, Stewart wrote, but respect for judicial process is a small price to pay for the civilizing hand of law, which alone can give abiding meaning to constitutional freedom.

The Chief Justice, joined by Brennan and Fortas, wrote the first dissenting opinion. He would have reversed the convictions on First Amendment grounds, citing *Cox* and *Edwards* and the well-known attitudes of Birmingham officials toward Dr. King and civil rights workers in general. Douglas's dissent, joined in by the other three dissenters, emphasized petitioners' attempts to get parade permits before the injunction was issued and likened court enforcement of the unconstitutional ordinance through the injunction to the situation in *Shelley*. Also joined by his three brethren, Brennan dissented, commenting on the weapon for infringing freedoms which the majority opinion had let loose; the state courts could now punish as contempt what they could not otherwise punish at all.

In this case, as in *Adderly,* the punishment had been relatively small—five days in jail and a fifty dollar fine each. Here, too, it may have been an important factor for the Court in determining how to decide the case. This was reinforced by the comment of one of those directly affected, the Reverend Mr. Shuttlesworth, the day after the ruling. "When you consider all that the Birmingham movement accomplished in advancing civil rights," he said, "I'm glad to pay the very small price of five days in jail."[66] From this point of view, the Supreme Court had to uphold the rule of law involved in sustaining the sentences against him and the others, and in terms of his commitment, it was but a small price to pay.

As if to reinforce the point it had made in *Walker v. City of Birmingham,* the Court subsequently reversed criminal convictions stemming from the same incident and based on the ordinance which the city had implanted in the injunction. The Reverend Mr. Shuttlesworth had been arrested for marching without a permit. The Court, using a variety of grounds, invalidated the conviction. The vote was unanimous, although Justice Marshall did not participate; Justice Black concurred without opinion; and Justice Harlan wrote a concurring opinion. The Court first said that an ordinance giving authority to someone to issue or withhold a permit, without clear standards, was unconstitutional on its face. But the Court went further by saying that the limiting construction put on the ordinance by the state courts was not enough to save the ordinance if it were improperly administered—and then found that it was administered in terms of the ordinance's broad language, not the limiting construction.

All of this—and broad language about First Amendment rights to protest—was not unusual, and followed from past cases, including *Cox v. New Hampshire.* What was surprising was Justice Stewart's language indicating that "a person faced with such an unconstitutional licensing law may ignore it and engage with impunity in the exercise of the right of free expression for which the law purports to require a license." Perhaps the strength of the language stemmed from the fact that a prior restraint was involved, but it was not language one would have expected after the "lesson" the Court had "taught" to the ministers in the earlier case about not obeying an injunction. The Court may have been trying to make up for *Walker.*

Justice Harlan was obviously more troubled by the situation, saying, "The difficult question this case presents is whether the Fourteenth Amendment ever bars a State from punishing a citizen for marching without a permit which could have been procured if all available remedies had been pursued." But even he recognized the "severe impact" of the "slow-moving procedures" which someone seeking a permit would have to go through, particularly by comparison with the quick procedures the Court had demanded in the area of movie censorship.[67] In any case, what had been difficult for the Court several years before now was apparently easy, even though the violence surrounding the problem of obtaining civil rights for blacks had not abated—and had become even worse in the "long hot summers"—and the Court was willing to speak straightforwardly.

The cases involving some violence were handled somewhat differently from the others. In *Diamond v. Louisiana,* the petitioner, not a student but a civil rights activist, had been charged with and convicted of having encouraged Southern University students to hold unruly, unauthorized demonstrations on campus to protest various campus policies, to march through the university buildings while classes were being conducted, and to boycott and leave classes in a manner intended to disturb the public. The trial court ruled that his hortatory speeches were sufficient for conviction, and the state supreme court refused to hear an appeal on grounds that the trial had unquestionably been fair. Diamond sought to bring his case to the Supreme Court for review on grounds that he had not been properly prosecuted under the Louisiana law and that the statute itself was unconstitutionally vague. When Diamond's petition, prepared by NAACP counsel, had first been considered by the Supreme Court, certiorari had been granted and the case set for argument. After argument, however, the Court issued a per curiam opinion without comment, dismissing the writ of certiorari as improvidently granted. Its reasons for so doing cannot be known precisely, but it is most likely that the Court found an adequate basis for the convictions under Louisiana law. Commenting on this case later, NAACP Legal Defense Fund head Jack Greenberg noted that during oral argument, Justice Black had asked one question of counsel, "whether or not it was the contention of counsel that while this particular defendant really had not acted properly, he was being prosecuted improperly." Greenberg said that counsel had conceded that the defendant had not been acting properly, but argued that he felt the prosecution was technically deficient.[68] This put the justices in the position in which they would have had to affirm for the first time a state court conviction arising from a civil rights incident. In view of the many groundless convictions which had come before them for review in recent years, they wished to avoid doing so, and also wished to avoid serving as a "court of errors" with respect to state procedure, necessary to reverse on the grounds the prosecution was procedurally dubious. They wanted neither to approve the form of the prosecution below nor to appear to give approval to what this particular defendant had done, and thus used the only means by which avoidance was now possible.

Dismissal of the *Diamond* case may also have fitted the Court's strategy of asserting that civil rights activity conducted in an orderly and peaceful, nonviolent manner was to be unhesitatingly protected under the federal Constitution and laws, but that when it became violent and seriously disruptive, or became merely an excuse for violent behavior on its face violative of public order and law, it would fall outside the realm of constitutional immunity. This was the earliest indication of this reservation on the part of the Court, one which anticipated changing public opinion with regard to demonstrations which became violent. As Grossman has noted, "It is instructive . . . that the only case in which there was good evidence of violence by a demonstrator, *Diamond* v. *Louisiana,* was dismissed by the Court."[69]

In *Ford v. Tennessee,* difficulties similar to those of the *Diamond* case were presented. Here a group of Negro youths had been convicted in state courts of disturbing a religious assembly at a church youth rally in Memphis, in violation of a state statute protecting citizens in their worship services. A local white church had leased a public amphitheater in the city for purposes of holding a religious youth rally. When Negro youths showed up in an allegedly obviously planned demonstration, they were asked to leave. When they refused, they were offered seats and asked to sit down so that the assembly might continue undisturbed. Instead the group moved through the aisles and rows of seats causing "great disturbance," and were subsequently arrested and removed. With NAACP counsel, they petitioned the Supreme Court to hear their case, arguing that since the auditorium was a public facility they could not be excluded, that there was no evidence of guilt violative of the statute against them since it outlawed only noisy, profane, rude, indecent, or similar acts and that the convictions amounted to state enforcement of segregation. The state contended that the law reached any willful disturbance of a religious assembly, the facts showing a well-planned scheme to create an incident. Four months after dismissing *Diamond,* the Supreme Court declined to review the case, Douglas alone noting that he would have granted a hearing, perhaps because the group had originally been told to leave what was in fact a public facility and because the white group had as obviously wanted to exclude the Negroes as the latter had allegedly wanted to disturb the whites. In addition to the problems raised by the disturbance, the lease issue created a complication. If the auditorium was leased only to white groups, the Court would have had a fairly standard public facilities case, although one made more complicated by the intentional disruption. But if all private groups could lease the facility and exclude those not part of their group—that is, have a private meeting in a public facility—the issue would be quite different, and the disruption would be even harder to defend.[70]

In a related northern case, *Baer v. New York,* a CORE member had attempted unsuccessfully to gain entrance to the Syracuse, New York, police station, saying that he wished to see the chief of police. The station had been closed to all but those persons who had specific business within because of anticipated racial demonstrations at the time. When Baer, the CORE member, was told that he could not see the police chief, he refused to leave the steps outside the building. He was thereupon arrested and subsequently convicted for violation of a city ordinance making it unlawful to loiter in or around a public building or to obstruct stairways thereof so as to prevent free access by members of the public and, also, for violation of a New York statute making it unlawful, with intent to provoke a breach of the peace, to act in such manner as to disturb, annoy, interfere with, obstruct, or be offensive to others. He challenged the statutes in the courts below as void for vagueness and said his conviction violated his constitutional rights of assembly, petition, and free speech, but he failed in all appeals. When he then asked the Supreme Court to review his case, bringing it up on appeal, he was refused a hearing. The Court rendered a per curiam order dismissing the appeal for want of a substantial federal question. Only Justice Douglas said that he would have noted probable jurisdiction. The tenseness of circumstance so often mentioned by various justices in cases of this type was apparently felt to be present here, and thus no substantial federal question was presented but merely a matter of "necessary state action reasonably designed for the protection of society" such as Clark had discussed in his dissent in the first civil disobedience case decided, *Edwards v. South Carolina.*

13

A procedural issue of considerable importance in relation to protest was that of the removal of cases from state courts to federal courts. Faced with prosecution in the state courts for actions stemming from protest activity, those persons involved felt they could either have the prosecutions dismissed in federal court or at least have a fair trial there. In their efforts, they relied on a federal statute providing for removal of certain cases from state to federal courts. Initially, the Court denied review in a northern demonstration-disruption case posing the issue, but the justices shortly thereafter grappled with the problem in a fully argued case. Behind the avoided case were incidents involving nearly fifty persons prosecuted for various acts designed to disrupt highway and subway traffic to the New York World's Fair in order to publicize grievances over "denial of equal protection of the laws to Negroes in the city, state and nation with reference to housing, education, employment, police action, and other areas of local and national life too numerous to mention." The charges against the group ranged from assault, disorderly conduct, and resisting an officer to loitering at a school building, inducing truancy, and obstructing railway cars. The defendants sought removal of their cases to a federal court on the ground that their acts were made "under color of authority" derived from various laws and constitutional provisions guaranteeing equal rights and freedom of speech. The district and appeals courts denied removal on the basis that any person claiming the benefit of the removal statute must point to some law that directs or encourages him to act in a certain manner, not just to a generalized constitutional provision or an equally general statute that may impose some liability on persons interfering with him. These persons were found not acting under any such laws, and thus not entitled to removal to federal court.

When the demonstrators in this case, *Galamison v. New York,* asked the Supreme Court to give them a hearing, they were denied it. In the first place, the Court would not lightly reach out to take a case away from a state court untried and hand it to a federal court which had earlier refused to accept the claimed right to removal. In the second place, the activities involved here were of questionable immunity, as they would have to be balanced and tested against laws providing for the public health and safety and against certain criminal behavior. From the facts of the case, it seems likely that at least some of the activities would have failed such a test, and it is therefore not surprising that the Court declined to hear the case even though it involved interpretation of a federal statute. During the next term, armed with appeals in cases from those on both sides of the question, the Court would review this matter thoroughly.

In declining to take on this case, the Court may also have been making a broader policy judgment. The protesters' acts of civil disobedience were totally unrelated to the ends they sought. Tieing up traffic has little to do with the goal of equal protection for blacks. In sharp contrast are the sit-in cases in which the refusal to leave a particular lunch counter was related to desegregating that same lunch counter. The latter or "related" civil disobedience cases, although of course posing problems of the defiance of the law, at least seemed to be finite and containable from the viewpoint of the legal system as a whole. But the former "unrelated" type if countenanced by the courts would threaten disruption of the entire society. If people could, for example, block highway traffic in order to publicize any goal they desired, society would pay the cost not only in terms of inconvenience to motorists but perhaps the loss of lives when ambulances and fire engines could not get through. Since it would have been unlikely in the extreme that the Supreme Court, or any court, would have countenanced this "unrelated" type of civil disobedience, the Court's refusal to hear the case was probably the best tactic it could have used, given the Court's sympathy with the goals the protesters espoused if not with their methods.

Shortly before deciding the removal issue, the Court passed up another case in which a civil rights worker had been prosecuted for vagrancy because of her participation in voter registration activities in Mississippi. Unsuccessful in obtaining removal of her trial to federal court on grounds she could not get a fair trial in state court, she appealed to the Supreme Court. There the state said she had failed even to attempt to exhaust state judicial remedies. Her NAACP counsel argued that her case should be heard along with the removal cases recently accepted for hearing, in order to have a grouping of similar suits and assure full canvas of the issues. The Supreme Court denied certiorari, apparently finding the two cases it would hear later to be more appropriate and adequate for resolution of the issues in question.[71]

It was in two cases decided in the last days of the 1965 Term that the Court explored congressional statutes providing for removal of criminal cases from state courts to federal courts under some circumstances. One of the cases, *Georgia v. Rachel,* involved twenty persons arrested early in 1963 when they sought to obtain service at a number of privately owned restaurants open to the general public in Atlanta, Georgia. They were indicted under a state statute making it a misdemeanor to refuse to leave the premises of another when requested to do so by the owner or person in charge of the establishment. They alleged that they were arrested to perpetuate customs concerning racial discrimination in places of public accommodation and that they could not enforce their federal constitutional and statutory rights in the state courts because the state by statute, custom, usage, and practice supported racial discrimination. They claimed also they were being prosecuted for acts done under color of authority derived from the federal Constitution and laws and for acts consistent with the Constitution and such federal laws. In the other case, *City of Greenwood v. Peacock,* twenty-nine persons engaged in civil rights activity during 1964 in Leflore County, Mississippi, were prosecuted on various criminal charges. Some were charged with obstructing the public streets while engaged in attempting to encourage Negro voter registration. In addition to contending their inability to enforce their rights in state courts, they claimed that their acts were done under color of federal authority and challenged the state law as unconstitutionally vague and as unconstitutionally applied to them as part of a policy of state and city racial discrimination. Others persons arrested denied they had engaged in conduct prohibited by valid laws, claiming their arrests and prosecutions were intended to harrass them as well as to deter them from exercising a protected right to protest racial discrimination and segregation. All sought removal of their cases to federal court.

In *Rachel,* the district court in Georgia had remanded to the state court, whereupon defendants appealed to the Court of Appeals for the

Fifth Circuit. Before the appeals court could rule, Congress passed the Civil Rights Act of 1964, and *Hamm* was decided. Thereupon, the Court of Appeals reversed the district court's remand. The situation in *Peacock* was somewhat more complicated, as it involved two cases, one brought to the Supreme Court by the city.[72] The Fifth Circuit had reversed and remanded to the district court for a hearing on defendants' allegations, although simultaneously rejecting claims under 28 U.S.C. 1443(2) because it was available only to federal officials or those under color of federal law. The city contested the court's interpretation of 1443(1) in allowing the removal hearing, whereas the defendants contested the limitation imposed by the Court of Appeals on 1443(2).

At one point during oral argument, Justice Fortas remarked on "the delightful à la carte menu" that lawyers for those seeking removal had presented. That "à la carte menu," expanded by the positions of counsel in opposition, was indeed varied. From the viewpoint of counsel for these demonstrators, the element of violence was implicity recognized, and the most limited ruling was asked for, one more limited than that urged by the government. Should not those legitimately asserting constitutional rights be somehow safeguarded within the process for punishing abuse of such rights on both sides? Should not the legitimacy of an alleged assertion of a federal right be adjudged in the first instance by a federal court? In *Rachel*, from the state's viewpoint, the element of violence loomed most important: What was the scope of the demonstrators' privilege? Should not the state be allowed to determine when that scope was exceeded? In *Peacock,* Mississippi's position was basically the same as that of Georgia's *Rachel* position: Congress has left the prerogative to the states in the first instance, relying on the discretion of their courts.

Argument in *Georgia* v. *Rachel* was begun by Assistant Solicitor General George K. McPherson. He contended that the appeals court had had no jurisdiction to consider the appeal because notice of appeal of the district court's remand order was filed six days beyond the ten-day time limit required by the Federal Rules of Criminal Procedure. He further said that the petition for removal had failed to allege sufficient facts or valid grounds for removing the state prosecution to the federal court and that the Fifth Circuit had erred in directing the district court to look for only one criterion in the hearing and to dismiss the state court prosecution if that single element was found—that the defendants were arrested and removed from the establishment because of racial discrimination. The Fifth Circuit should be overruled, McPherson concluded, the district court's remand order to the local court sustained, and the cases sent back.

Georgia Assistant Solicitor General J. Robert Sparks, who continued the argument, dealt primarily with statutory questions. If the Court did not agree that the circuit court lacked jurisdiction, the case involved an extremely complex problem construing the Reconstruction Congress Civil Rights Removal Statute. Sparks argued that earlier Supreme Court rulings on the statute, including *Strauder* and *Rives,* had indicated that the discrimination necessary to establish removal had to be set out in a state statute which prevents the exercise of a constitutional right, is unconstitutional, or denied a defendant in state court an equal right. For other alleged discrimination, defendants had to defend themselves in the state courts, reserving their federal rights and bringing their claims to the Supreme Court on certiorari. Instead of showing such prerequisites, Sparks said, the defendants in these cases have asked for removal on a mere statement of conclusions—the facts of the case, the statement that Georgia by statute, custom, usage, and practice supports and maintains a policy of racial discrimination, and the presumption that they cannot enforce their rights in state courts, before a trial has even occurred. They do not even challenge the constitutionality of the trespass statute or the constitutionality of its application. Continuing, Sparks said respondents say defendants being prosecuted for exercise of the right to equal public accommodation granted by the 1964 act may remove to federal district court whether the statute involved violates these rights on its face or as applied; they argue that persons prosecuted in the exercise of 1964 act rights are "insulated from the prosecutive process." If the Court should adopt this, Sparks warned, it would create a virtual no-man's-land in law enforcement in cases arising under the act. He pointed out that the construction of the removal right which the respondents requested had been specifically rejected by Congress in writing the 1964 act, Title IX of which did make reviewable in higher federal courts the action of federal district courts in remanding a civil rights case to state courts.

For the respondents, Anthony G. Amsterdam argued that the construction of the civil rights removal statute was most important in his case, different from *Peacock.* He said that while he would like to see the claims in both allowed, the latter might well be decided in favor of remand to the state court, but not *Rachel.* Because of the general deterrent effect of a prosecution, the very pendency of a state court prosecution for a federally protected right is a denial of that right and of the ability to enforce that right, Amsterdam said. This justifies a jurisdiction which allows the question of whether the prosecution shall go on to be tried initially in federal, not state court, but which does not insulate persons who engage in that conduct from prosecution. If a case were remanded to the state courts and later appealed to federal court, a federal district judge sitting alone would have to decide the same issue again. The merit of his narrow position, he pointed out, is that in no case is the state court deprived of power to proceed except in cases that should not be there in the first place; the matter being tried in federal court is simply whether or not federal protection does void the prosecution of the case. Later, he argued that Congress had really established what was in effect a conclusive presumption that in all cases where a person is arrested in the course of civil rights activity, he shall be tried by a federal district court, a much broader position.

Representing Greenwood, Hardy L. Lott argued in *Peacock* that the Fifth Circuit's ruling amounted to a holding that the mere institution of a prosecution by the policemen for an improper motive, to deny the exercise of civil rights, was sufficient ground for removal. Stewart asked, "Isn't it possible to read the statute that way?" Lott replied that the Supreme Court had ruled in seven straight cases that under the statute one has to demonstrate denial or inability to enforce in the state courts due to a state statute, as reasonably read or as interpreted by the highest court of the state, or to a state constitutional provision, and that the acts of state officers in advance of the trial were not sufficient because the presumption is that the state court will correct any such error. To affirm the Fifth Circuit's position, Lott concluded, you would have to overrule all of those cases and in effect be amending the congressional statute to sustain that opinion. An amendment to this effect was attempted in Congress in the 1964 act, Lott reminded the Court, but it failed. Two of the Peacock lawyers advocated it there. If the *Peacock* rule were adopted, Lott continued, almost any defendant could remove his case from police court to federal court by alleging he was associated with some civil rights group and in civil rights work and was arrested for something on an improper motive. Furthermore, under the *Peacock* rule, you would have one or possibly two trials in federal court—a lengthy matter—on any allegation, the first to examine—even before the court knew whether it had jurisdiction—the motive of whoever brought the charge. Then if the motive was determined to be bad, removal jurisdiction would be established and a trial on the merits would be necessary in federal court to see if the defendant was guilty or not, because he still could be. This statement drew an objection from Justice Fortas, who said that he did not read the Fifth Circuit decision that way.

Benjamin E. Smith opened argument for the *Peacock* defendants. He said that what they were looking for and could not get in Mississippi state courts was a fair trial, because Peacock was working to get Negroes registered to vote—anathema to local segregationists. This is what Congress was thinking of in 1866 when it passed this Civil Rights Removal Bill, Smith said. Louis F. Claiborne, Assistant to the Solicitor General, appeared for the United States as amicus. He explained that the government saw the statute as stating four distinct grounds for removal. The government relied on the denial of rights clause, he said, as being applicable where the institution of prosecution or a formal court proceeding is itself so grave a denial that no matter when acquittal results it will be too little too late. The government also relied on a color of federal authority ground, which Claiborne invoked as applying only to activity specified in federal laws in terms providing for equal rights. Furthermore, Claiborne said, the defendant should be entitled to removal so long as his petition alleges a case which on its face would require dismissal or acquittal if his allegations are true—which should be determined by a trial jury, not a judge initially, and thus the removal remedy was designed by Congress as a matter or precaution. Fortas asked Claiborne if he felt he was closer to Mr. Amsterdam than to Mr. Smith. Except that Mr. Amsterdam never sees a trial in federal court, and that is what removal is all about, Claiborne replied.

Of the positions assumed by the lawyers, that of counsel for Peacock was the most extreme, calling for the broadest construction of the right to remove. Whenever a petitioner claims that racial bias of some kind will prevent him from receiving a fair trial in a particular state or local court system, he should be entitled to a hearing in federal court. The position of the government was somewhere between the narrow stance taken by Amsterdam in *Rachel* and the extreme stance taken by Smith. Whenever, in a very particularized petition, a defendant alleges his prosecution has resulted from a truly legitimate federally protected civil rights activity, he should be entitled to a hearing in federal court, and if still necessary to a trial before a federal jury. This rule would apply to the whole country, no matter what the particular jurisdiction, and would be a matter within the discretion of the lower federal courts.

The questions asked of the lawyers—particularly of Smith and Claiborne—clustered into several basic sets. Whether state or federal courts should try the issues in the cases was one. White asked Sparks if an actual trial of whether the federal public accommodations privilege had been exceeded should take place in a state court. Yes, replied Sparks; otherwise federal district courts would be trying municipal court cases on matters such as disorderly conduct. Clark then asked how defendants would proceed if they wanted to claim defense under *Hamm* and *Lupper*. Sparks explained that if no evidence of violence was prosecuted by the state, a mere hearing would suffice to dismiss; if there was a question whether federal privilege had been violated, a jury trial could occur; if there was a question as to what was violated, a trial before the court would be appropriate. Fortas challenged Amsterdam's assertion that a federal court would initially try whether or not the state prosecution should continue, saying that this assumed a conjecture that the state courts would act less fairly and less quickly than would a federal court. White asked if, under counsel's interpretation, the federal court had to determine whether a federal right is being prosecuted and then, if alleged, whether the proprietor's rights were violated—all to be done by a federal judge alone, not by jury. When White pointed out that the alternative to Amsterdam's position was to have the whole trial in federal court, so that the federal defense could be presented to the jury along with the facts, Amsterdam said this was the government's *Peacock* position, adding he would be delighted to have such an expansive reading of the statute, "but we haven't asked that much here." When White suggested that such a reading would apply only to cases like this one, Amsterdam indicated it could apply beyond sit-ins to demonstration cases generally. White also asked whether there would ever be a criminal trial in a federal court or whether the case would either be dismissed or remanded for state trial. Would you have what amounts to federal habeas corpus before trial, he wanted to know. He then asked if the federal protection defense could be raised again on remand to a state court (yes) and if there could be more than one removal petition (not ordinarily).

There were also questions as to when removal should be required, the type of hearing in federal court, and the grounds for removal. Justice Fortas asked Smith whether he would limit removal to civil rights situations. (No.) Would he apply it to the trial of, say, a white civil rights worker? (Yes.) To any case involving persons of the opposite race? (Yes.) Then Fortas remarked, "Your position makes the charge rather irrelevant. You are concerned only with whether a fair trial can be had on the basis of the administration of justice in that particular state court jurisdiction, not the question whether violence or violation of law are involved." (Right.) Then Black wanted to know whether this should apply to white labor unionists.[73] ("I don't think it can, as it seems to have been passed and to now be applicable only for the protection of colored people.") That is putting a gloss on the statute, remarked Douglas, because it speaks in terms of any person denied equal protection. Fortas said he found the Fifth Circuit to be saying that the Supreme Court decisions articulated in terms of the absence of any state statute or state constitutional provision did not apply because here the difficulty stemmed from application of a state statute so as to deprive the accused of his equal civil rights, an effort to interfere with the rights of free assembly, free speech, or whatever. He asked Lott whether he felt that amounted to an inquiry into the motive of the prosecution. Douglas asked whether the statute did not speak in terms of protection of constitutional, inherent rights, like the free exercise of religion as in the Jehovah's Witnesses cases. (No.) But isn't the mere fact of arrest and prosecution a constitutional deprivation? Yes, but Congress has not given you removal jurisdiction in such a case. That is the question in this case? Yes, Congress has left it to the advisory power of the state court, and if they don't do it, ultimately to this Court.

The interrelationship between these questions over the scope of removal and the procedures to be utilized also showed up in some questions. White asked Claiborne how he would handle a case in which an otherwise valid state law was discriminatorily applied. The Chief Justice inquired about the procedure to use for the two here charged with operating motor vehicles in an improper manner. Also raised was the question, asked by Stewart, of whether those seeking removal were relying on the language or the general history and purpose of the Removal Act. After asking Smith about the application of the act to rape, murder, and arson cases (It would not apply, he said), Stewart pressed again as to the language on which he relied. Are you relying at all on Section 2 of 1443? Well, said Smith, two voting rights acts to encourage Negro registration had been passed, officials like Attorney General Katzenbach were urging civil rights groups to get people registered, and this is what Peacock was doing, so he should have some protection coming. Stewart also asked Claiborne about rape, murder, and burglary. Claiborne said that such a defendant could not remove unless the case involved, say, murder in self-defense arising out of exercise of rights, not just on an unfair trial expectation.

The justices' insistent questions about the range of cases covered by removal was the best evidence in these cases of their concern with strategy, and was reinforced by their other questions as to the number of cases pending and as to whether any cases stemming from the more recent violent ghetto riots were being brought up on removal. Thus Black asked whether efforts had been made to remove to federal courts in any post-Watts cases. Amsterdam replied that he thought not. In the New York riot cases? Yes, though the *Galamison* opinion effectively barred this in the Second Circuit. That the lawyers were aware of this concern of the Court is shown in Smith's comment that if he had started to tell the Court that removal was going to cover due process of law claims, a furor would arise over how widespread the effect of the Removal Act was. "It could be interpreted that way," he said, "but I just don't think in all practicability it would do any case any good." In *Rachel*, Harlan asked how many other cases the district judge had before him on removal (81), and White pressed counsel as to how many cases were pending decision of the two cases (103 in Georgia alone). He also wanted to know why any were still pending, now that *Hamm* had clearly demonstrated the Court's position on the relevant federal law. Some cases went beyond *Hamm-Lupper* in involving violence by the demonstrators—vandalism in restaurants— counsel replied. White persisted, wanting to know why cases protected by the 1964 act and *Hamm* were even still filed, why they had not been dismissed long ago. Here Sparks explained that they had been on appeal since before *Hamm* and that none of the lower courts had jurisdiction to dismiss them until their mandate was returned. Brennan then wondered if the Court could, then, just dispose of some of these cases and handle

them that way, on confession of error and so forth. Injecting state prerogative and pride, Sparks emphasized that Georgia wanted them back in
the state courts for proper disposition.

The justices were also concerned about a possible barrage of lower
federal court cases if a broad construction were made of the statute. This
concern was shown by questions by Black and the Chief Justice as to
whether the law would apply to all the states. Black also asked whether
anyone alleging facts enough to bring them under the statute, whether
true or not, would get removal. When told yes, Black commented that it
sounded as if any case, criminal or civil, in which a colored person were
involved could require that a federal judge pass on whether prejudice was
involved. Counsel said this risk should not bar a correct decision in this
case, because a clear decision on the scope of the removal statute should
end mistakes of law. White here helped out counsel by suggesting he was
speaking only of cases in which the conduct for which a defendant is being
prosecuted in a state court is itself permitted expressly by federal law.
Exactly, counsel said, we're not reaching to cases where the claim is made
that a defendant won't get a fair trial. One final strategic matter arose at
the end of the questioning of Claiborne: Should the Court go for a broad
rule or a narrow decision of these cases? How should it frame a decree?
White asked a question of pure strategy, "We should not treat this case in
the abstract and set down some ground rule to remain?" No, Claiborne
emphasized, the particular terms of the remand are most important.

Inevitably, the Court was to answer its own questions. At the very close
of the 1965 Term, in *Georgia v. Rachel* came the opinion for the Court by
Justice Stewart. At the beginning of the opinion, in a footnote, was a
compliment to one of the lawyers. Stewart cited an article by Amsterdam,[74]
calling it a "remarkably original and comprehensive discussion of the
issues presented in this case and in *City of Greenwood v. Peacock.*" Stewart
held that removal could be had under the Civil Rights Removal Statute,
1443(1), upon allegation that the prosecutions stemmed exclusively from
the respondents' refusal to leave places of public accommodation covered
by the 1964 Civil Rights Act when they were asked to leave solely for racial
reasons. The 1443(1) language concerning "a right under any law providing for . . . equal civil rights," said Stewart, means any law providing for
specific civil rights stated in terms of racial equality. Thus, broad First
Amendment and due process contentions do not support a removal claim
under the statute, but the 1964 act does in that it confers specific rights of
racial equality. As construed in *Hamm,* the 1964 act's Section 203 prohibited even prosecution based on refusal to leave such premises when the
request to leave was made for racial reasons. If the latter was true, then the
mere pendency of the prosecutions would enable the federal court to

make a firm prediction that the defendants would be denied their rights
in the state courts, since the burden of having to defend the prosecutions
would itself constitute a denial of right conferred by the 1964 act. Such a
basis for prediction is the equivalent of a state statute authorizing the
predicted denial—a requirement established by the leading cases interpreting 1443 (1). If the district court finds in this case that the defendants
were ordered to leave facilities covered by the act solely for racial reasons,
then they have a clear right to removal under 1443(1) and to dismissal of
the proceedings. Accordingly, an order was entered affirming the Fifth
Circuit judgment ordering a hearing in district court. Then came a
concurrence by Douglas, in which he was joined by the Chief Justice and
by Brennan and Fortas. Douglas emphasized that the Fifth Circuit had
ruled correctly that if the repressive acts were done "for racial reasons"
then the district court should order dismissal of the indictments without
further proceedings. Underlying the Court's deep concern with the problem of violence in civil rights activities, Douglas added that if the service
were denied because of disorderly conduct or other unlawful acts, then
the federal court would not grant removal.

Immediately after *Rachel* came the Court's opinion in *City of Greenwood
v. Peacock,* again written by Justice Stewart. Here an order was entered
reversing the Fifth Circuit's judgment ordering a district court hearing.
Section 1443(2), Stewart said, confers the privilege of removal only upon
federal officers or agents and those authorized to act with or for them in
affirmatively executing duties under any federal law providing for equal
civil rights. Section 1443(1) does not apply here as it did in *Rachel* because the federal rights invoked—First Amendment rights of free
expression—include some that clearly cannot qualify as rights under laws
providing for "equal civil rights," and that "to obstruct a public street,
contribute to the delinquency of a minor, drive an automobile without a
license, or bite a policeman" are actions not immunized from state prosecution by any federal law. Therefore, distinguishing this case from
Rachel and putting it in line with older cases, Stewart concluded that it is
not enough under 1443(1) to allege that federal equal civil rights have
been illegally denied by state administrative officials in advance of trial,
that the charges are false, or that a fair trial in a state court would not be
possible. If these claims are true and not vindicated by the state courts,
Stewart emphasized, many remedies are available, the most obvious of
which is vindication on direct review by this Court. Other remedies, such
as injunction, vacation of convictions, federal habeas corpus, damage suits
against state officers, and even prison terms for those who conspire to
deprive others of the free exercise of their rights, might be found in the
lower federal courts. Past opinions of the Court construing this removal

statute properly held that the provisions of 1443(1) do not operate to work a wholesale dislocation of the historical relationship between the state and federal courts in the administration of criminal law.

If the "strained" interpretation of 1443(1) urged by the petitioners here were to prevail, Stewart said, there would be a phenomenal increase in the number of criminal removal cases as well as in the time and expense involved for all. He declared that whether the long-standing relationship of the state and the federal courts has been such a failure that it should not be revolutionized, whether this will do anything toward promoting increased responsibility of the state courts in the area of federal civil rights, and whether this would be promoted by denying them any power at all to exercise that responsibility are grave questions not for this Court but for Congress, which could provide for broader removal. Stewart was saying that the federal courts cannot be expected to carry forever the whole burden of protecting rights. The states must realize that the time for sincere compliance with federally dictated equal civil rights and for stoppage of discrimination against those attempting to exercise such rights is long overdue, but the states are to be given this further chance to "deliver." They must, in effect, meet the challenge offered by Congress and the Court to act with responsibility, or Congress—because the problem seems so complex and fundamental as to be best suited to legislative solution—might have again to reconsider the removal doctrine.

Then came Douglas's opinion, again joined by Warren, Brennan, and Fortas; here the *Rachel* concurrence had become a dissent. Douglas argued that the 1964 version of the 1866 Civil Rights Act and the 1965 Voting Rights Act make clear that if the defendants' allegations here are true, the state prosecutions constitute a denial of "a right under any law providing for the equal civil rights of citizens." Douglas agreed that in providing for appeal of remand orders in civil rights removal cases, Congress meant for the Court to reconsider the doctrine of *Rives* and *Kentucky v. Powers,* but felt that those cases should not be followed so as to limit removal to instances in which the inability to enforce equal civil rights springs from a state statute or constitutional provision compelling the forbidden discrimination. The dissenters felt confident that federal district judges would not lightly assume that state courts would shirk their responsibilities and that the federal judges would thus remand cases unless there was clear and convincing evidence that the allegations of inability to enforce equal civil rights were true—thus respecting the legitimate interests of federalism which *Rives* sought to protect. The numerous other federal remedies pointed to by the majority, Douglas said, were all enacted about this same time, further demonstrating Congress's concern to protect from state court denial the equal civil rights of United States citizens. These defendants' civil rights may, of course, ultimately be vindiated if they persevere, live long enough, and have the patience and the funds to carry their cases for some years through the state courts to this Court. But it was precisely that burden that Congress undertook to take off the backs of this persecuted minority and all who espouse the cause of their equality.

As these results show, the *Peacock* case provides an example of the situation when the same strategic questions asked by the justices do not lead to the same result. Justices Stewart, White, and Douglas had all asked whether Congress had covered the situation before the Court and had wanted to know whether the statute could be read so that mere arrest, rather than a state statute or constitutional provision, could be considered an interference with constitutional rights sufficient to justify removal from state to federal courts. But Stewart and White ended up agreeing that the statute could not be so construed, and Douglas ended up in dissent.

The decisions together seemed on the surface to provide grounds for denial of removal if the state merely contested a petitioner's allegations regarding the indictment or if the state were able to include in the indictment charges other than trespass or breach of peace. They also seemed on the surface to distinguish between public accommodations and voting rights activities, definitely applying the statute to activities in the realm of public accommodations under the 1964 act, potentially leaving advocates of voting rights and other nonpublic accommodations causes—that is, nondiscrimination in employment—to suffer prosecution more than those involved in public accommodations cases. The time and expense the *Peacock* majority feared would result from federal removal cases would now be incurred by these individuals who would have to take their cases through the entire course of the state courts and seek alternative remedies, probably in the federal court system. The expense would hardly be greater than if removal and trial in federal court on the removal were to occur first. In the latter situation, if one's case were remanded to the state courts, it would simply be a matter of federal expense first and then state expense, rather than the reverse, and if one prevailed in federal court the expenses would be considerably reduced.

The judges had an increasing desire to avoid having to determine whether the particular activity of a group of demonstrators fell within or outside the protection of the Constitution, especially after the state courts had already so judged. They clearly had been trying to find some definitely unconstitutional state statute or statutory application which disallowed the prosecution of the demonstrators, although such a judgment sometimes required an awareness of the lack or presence of violence or real disturbance on the part of the demonstrators. The Court's action in denying the removal right to the *Peacock* defendants was consistent with this position. Among violations of conduct for which persons could be prosecuted were some traditionally within the state's right and duty to prosecute, such as contributing to the delinquency of a minor. The burden was on the demonstrators themselves to keep their conduct within specifically constitutionally protected rights, although responsibility to recognize fairly the demonstrators' newly delineated constitutional rights was placed on the state courts. The Supreme Court itself was still the end of the line of appeal if this responsibility were not undertaken.

Unlike specific individual instances in which the Supreme Court had attempted to avoid friction-causing interaction between the federal courts and the state judiciary, *Rachel* and *Peacock* were intended to avoid intimate, day-to-day friction between federal and state judiciaries.[75] The *Rachel-Peacock* rulings also provide an example of the relation between the substance of a ruling and docket-management and of the multiple ends which can be served by a single case. By construing the right of removal narrowly, the Court not only avoided friction with the states but also avoided a barrage of federal court cases which might reach the Supreme Court faster than they would if they had to work their way up through the state court system and which could perhaps be turned away only with greater difficulty.

As was traditional, in the wake of *Rachel* and *Peacock* came the summary disposition of a number of pending similar cases. First was *Baines v. City of Danville,* which involved convictions for violating an injunction and temporary restraining order proscribing participation in mob violence, rioting, and incitement to such conduct in summer 1963 demonstrations. The 105 Negroes charged sought removal of their cases to federal court, saying they could not expect a full and fair trial in Danville, that they had been engaged in conduct protected by the First Amendment, and that the injunction which they were charged with having violated was unconstitutional on its face or as applied. The local federal district court had remanded the cases to the state courts, and the Fourth Circuit, agreeing with this judgment, had dismissed further appeals. Before final entry of the appeals court opinion the Civil Rights Act of 1964 became effective. The appeals court granted a rehearing, but after lengthy review of the legislative and judicial history of the removal statute held over a lengthy dissent by two of its members that these cases were not removable on any of the grounds advanced. The Supreme Court, asked to review, held the case until after *Rachel* and *Peacock,* and then decided it summarily on the basis of the latter, granting certiorari and affirming the judgments per curiam. The Chief Justice, Douglas, Brennan, and Fortas dissented, saying they would reverse as in *Peacock.*

Wallace v. Virginia involved behavior of a very different sort. The petitioner was a Negro Harvard Law School student on a summer clerkship with a Richmond, Virginia, law firm which had represented Negroes in a number of school and other cases with racial significance. He had been sent to Prince Edward County in connection with the firm's representation of some arrested civil rights demonstrators. He had sought to visit a client in the courthouse, been intercepted by a deputy sheriff and other officers, and after a scuffle, had been locked up. After paying a fine for resisting arrest, he was charged with seven additional counts, one of which was a felony count for assaulting the deputy sheriff. Alleging that the charges had been increased when it was discovered that he was associated with the Negro civil rights law firm, he sought removal on grounds he had been accosted by the officers on account on his race, that he had only resisted an effort to interfere with his conduct of lawful business, that he had been exercising constitutional rights in aid of those of his employer's clients, that the prosecution against him was part of a community plan to frustrate the civil rights movement, and that local prejudice in Prince Edward County made improbable his securing a fair trial there. The local federal district court had remanded his case to the state court, and the Fourth Circuit had agreed that it was not removable, with two judges dissenting as in *Baines*. Once again, the charges against Wallace were in the nature of matters traditionally within state court discretion, and the responsibility to act fairly was left upon the state by the Supreme Court. Citing *Peacock*, the Court again granted certiorari and affirmed the circuit court's judgment per curiam.

In *Anderson v. City of Chester*, not from a southern state but from Pennsylvania, the Court simply let stand the denial of removal of pending state criminal cases involving civil rights demonstrators where the Third Circuit had held, after Pennsylvania's argument that the prosecutions were for riotous conduct beyond the range of federally protected First Amendment rights, that no evidence had been presented to sustain the allegations or the expectation of discrimination in the state courts. Only Douglas and Fortas dissented from the denial of certiorari. The question of a conflict in the circuits as to the breadth of the removal right, raised below, had been settled as far as the majority was concerned.

Forman v. City of Montgomery, handled in similar fashion, involved 167 persons, some Negro and some white, being prosecuted for activities engaged in as part of a civil rights demonstration in Montgomery, in which through sit-downs on the streets and sidewalks they had allegedly blocked vehicular and pedestrian traffic. The demonstrators sought removal to federal court alleging that their acts had been done pursuant to the First, Thirteenth, Fourteenth, and Fifteenth Amendments, as well as federal voting legislation and the 1964 Civil Rights Act, and that they could not enforce their rights in the Alabama courts because Negroes were systematically excluded from service as jurors and because the judges and juries of the state were openly and notoriously biased against them and their cause. The local federal district court, denying the petition, emphasized the obstruction of the streets and sidewalks and opined that although judicial processes were available for protecting constitutional rights, disorderly conduct was not constitutionally protected. The Fifth Circuit affirmed per curiam, and the Supreme Court, when asked to review, denied the case a hearing, with only Douglas noting that he would have heard the case. For the time being, the matter of the scope of the right to removal had been settled, along lines in which the legitimacy of the conduct engaged in, although on the surface indirectly, was of crucial importance.

In *Hawkins v. North Carolina,* a Negro dentist in Charlotte, North Carolina, had been arrested while engaged in a voter registration campaign and subsequently indicted for unlawfully interfering with a special voter registration commission and for unlawfully and fraudulently procuring the registration of certain persons not qualified to vote under state law. Claiming that he had merely rendered requested assistance, that the state's purpose was to harrass him, and that he could not obtain a fair trial in the state courts, he sought to remove his case to federal court. After losing in the federal district court, he lost again in the Fourth Circuit, which ruled summarily that his case was clearly not removable under *Rachel,* on the ground that his allegations as to what had happened in the incident were in contradiction with the allegation of the indictment. One of the circuit judges, concurring, said that removal could not be had because *Peacock* had specifically distinguished voting rights from public accommodations as far as removability was concerned. The Supreme Court denied certiorari, with the Chief Justice, Douglas and Fortas indicating they would have granted the petition. Reopening of the *Rachel-Peacock* controversies this soon after those rulings was apparently more than the Court majority (including Brennan, who had joined these three there) wanted.

In the Supreme Court's treatment of protests by both blacks and whites aimed at achieving racial equality we have seen considerable hesitancy to validate the means used in attempts to publicize grievances and achieve that equality. That hesistancy can be seen under the surface of the Court's treatment of the public accommodations cases, where the Court was also troubled by a most vexing constitutional problem as it tried at least implicitly to balance rights of private entrepreneurs with the rights of other citizens to nondiscriminatory service in places open to the public. It could be seen far more obviously in the doctrine developed as to both the substantive and procedural aspects of general protest, particularly where any violence was involved or the means used seemed to the justices to be inappropriate or unreasonable, and in the divisions within the Court prompted by such cases. Yet one should be careful about doubting the Court's overriding commitment to racial equality; had such a commitment not been present, even the results of the sit-in and other protest cases would have gone heavily against the blacks. And, anyone who had any doubts about what the Supreme Court under the leadership of Chief Justice Earl Warren would do in other substantive areas had to wait only a short time after the protest and removal cases to see the full force of the Court's action. That came in the housing area, in the cases of *Reitman v. Mulkey* and *Jones v. Mayer,* already discussed, and in the school desegregation cases of the late 1960s which followed shortly. If the South had been led to believe by the Court's actions through 1964 that it would not be forthright with those states and districts which had tried to delay as long as possible complying with the doctrine of *Brown* and had not heard—or had ignored—the message of cases like the Memphis *Watson* parks case and *Griffin v. County School Board of Prince Edward County,* the years 1968 and 1969 were to disabuse them of the idea that the Court would remain inactive. Those years saw the Warren Court cut down the last of the major foot-dragging mechanisms, "freedom-of-choice," and saw the Court in its first major ruling under its new Chief Justice, Warren Earl Burger, finally put to rest the "all deliberate speed" doctrine of *Brown II.*

Chapter 9

"Freedom-of-Choice" and the End of "Deliberate Speed"

Aᶠᵗᵉʳ the Supreme Court's 1964 ruling in the Prince Edward County school litigation its attention had turned to other areas of segregation and discrimination such as protest, voting, and housing. One of the reasons for the Court's change in direction was that the federal executive branch had entered into the desegregation area with the development of the HEW Desegregation Guidelines. As the guidelines became established, some new school desegregation activity developed in the lower courts because of the guidelines' basis in judicially developed standards. The lower federal courts in the South began to accept the guidelines, thus tying litigation and administration more closely together. And in the second half of the 1960s, school desegregation cases with considerable potential impact began working their way up to the Supreme Court, engaging the Court's attention once again more than a dozen years after *Brown I*. That the Court's inaction in the school desegregation area had begun to produce considerable criticism is evident. Clearly the Court had not put an end to the delay it had in effect encouraged in *Brown II*. But the criticism in the late 1960s cut deeper than the Court's earlier opinions.

The most forcefully stated negative view of the Court's work was that of NAACP attorney Lewis Steel in a 1968 article entitled "Nine Men in Black Who Think White."[1] Steel grudgingly gave the Court some limited credit: the Warren Court had "eliminated from the law books some of [the Supreme Court's] more atrocious decisions." However, "never has it indicated that it is committed to a society based upon principles of absolute equality." The "symbols of racism," not the "ingrained practices" of white supremacy, had been eliminated. Steel contended the latter were either condoned or overlooked by the Court. What was worse, the Court's decisions had led people, particularly "a confused, miseducated and prejudiced white public," to believe that blacks had been given full rights. What particularly bothered Steel was that the Court had catered to public opinion and in *Brown* had really done little more than codify a reevaluation of race relations taking place in other American institutions. It was not only the late nineteenth-century *Plessy* Court which had been affected by the temper of the times. Steel felt this had regularly been the case: "Since the Civil War, [the Court] has allowed itself to be swayed by the prejudices and mores of whites and, more recently, by their fears that equality for Negroes would adversely affect them." This he contrasted with the Court's actions in other policy areas, where the Court had "to a much greater extent, acted without regard for popular opinion." Steel thought the Court was still in "the shadow of the 19th century," and argued, "In recent years, a cautious Supreme Court has waltzed in time to the music of the white majority—one step forward, one step backward and sidestep, sidestep."[2]

1

Although the Supreme Court's ruling in *Brown II* was based on the assumption that the primary enforcement of school desegregation would rest in the district courts, the leading role was actually taken by the United States Courts of Appeals. Foremost in this regard because it encompassed most of the Deep South was the Court of Appeals for the Fifth Circuit. That court began the legal action which preceded the Supreme Court's finally moving away from the position criticized by Steel. Central to that action were the Fifth Circuit's rulings in the *Singleton* and *Jefferson* cases, which served to "bind together" judicial and administrative rulings and to bring state policy into line with national policy as well as to make new policy. In the first *Singleton* case, involving the Jackson, Mississippi, schools, Judge John Minor Wisdom—who was to write all the doctrine in these cases—said that the Fifth Circuit would give great weight to the HEW Desegregation Guidelines in deciding school desegregation cases. Stating that all three branches of government had a common objective, he ruled that judicial requirements should not be less burdensome than the HEW Guidelines, thus preventing school districts from obtaining refuge from the guidelines in weak judicial orders. In a footnote, Judge Wisdom attacked Judge Parker's dictum in the *Briggs* case that *Brown* had required only desegregation, not integration. In the second *Singleton* case (*Singleton II*), Wisdom went further to hold that the *Briggs* dictum could not bar the right of a Negro child to transfer to a white school.

The *Jefferson* case involved seven Louisiana and Alabama school systems. Here a three-judge panel of the Fifth Circuit, with Judge Wisdom again writing, ordered the school systems to desegregate classrooms, facilities, and staffs by the 1967–68 school year. Although he restricted himself to de jure segregation, Judge Wisdom used unusually strong language in holding that school officials had to take "affirmative action" to reorganize their schools into "unitary, nonracial systems." As he put it, "The only adequate redress for a previously overt system-wide policy of segregation directed against Negroes as a collective entity is a system-wide policy of integration."[3] Just as he had in *Singleton*, the judge found favor in the HEW Guidelines, saying they provided "the best system available for uniform application and the best aid to the courts," which the judge said were not the best place to bring about prompt and uniform desegregation because judges "do not have sufficient competence—they are not educators or school administrators—to know the right questions, much less the right answers" to ask school officials about desegregation plans presented to the courts. Wisdom also found the guidelines "strongly similar to the standards the Supreme Court and this court have established." District courts should make few exceptions to the guidelines, Wisdom declared, with any exceptions tailored to fit the Fifth Circuit's holding rather than to defeat it or HEW's intent. Again the judge held that court desegregation standards should be no lower than HEW standards.[4] When the Fifth Circuit heard the *Jefferson* case en banc, it strengthened this aspect of Judge Wisdom's ruling. In *Jefferson II*, the full court, in an eight-to-four vote, adopted the majority opinion of Judge Wisdom's original panel and made only minor modifications in the panel's decree. The judges ruled that school officials had an "affirmative duty" to bring about integrated school systems "in which there are no Negro schools and no white schools—just schools." However, the court seemed to go beyond *Jefferson I* by mandating the HEW Guidelines for circuit-wide use and as well by telling the district courts to give great weight to future guidelines. The Fifth Circuit also indicated that more might be required in the future in its comment that freedom-of-choice was but one of the tools available at that stage to convert dual school systems into unitary ones. The objective, which was to be overriding, was "educational opportunities on equal terms to all." If a plan involving freedom-of-choice were ineffective, "longer on promises than performance," the officials should try other tools. The judges noted that "freedom-of-choice" was not a "sacred talisman," but only a means to an end required by the Constitution.

Judge Gewin, dissenting, called the opinion and decree "an abrupt and unauthorized departure from the mainstream of judicial thought," and Judge Griffin Bell thought the opinion adopted "seriously erodes the doctrine of separation of powers" and that "much of its language . . . adds confusion and unrest to the already troubled area of school desegregation." He thought also that "overtones of compulsory integration and school racial balances . . . can only chill the efforts of school administrators to complete the task of eliminating dual school systems in the South."

Even the full court's ruling was not enough to quiet matters. First, Louisiana and Alabama requested the court to recall or delay its order for total school integration in the six southern states, a request immediately denied without comment. Then the six Louisiana school districts went to the Supreme Court for a stay of execution with respect to the Fifth Circuit's immediate integration order pending their appeal to the Court for a hearing. State officials argued that prompt enforcement would cause administrative chaos, further contending that the order was unconstitutional because it imposed an affirmative duty on school districts to do away with segregation and that the circuit court's reliance on the HEW Desegregation Guidelines violated the principle of separation of powers. The Department of Justice in response argued that desegregation would be delayed another full year if the Court agreed to the stay, since routine handling would require months. The Supreme Court's 1954 desegregation decision has already been avoided too long in the Deep South, the Justice Department declared, and the time has run out on delays in school desegregation. The request, referred by Justice Black to the whole Court, was refused, removing the last judicial barrier to forthwith enforcement of the Fifth Circuit's order. Through its refusal to interfere with the order, the Court indicated its approval of this historic school integration decision—approval subsequently reinforced by the Court's denial of certiorari in the case. Forceful action had been taken, and the Court had shown that not even a summary affirmance was needed because of the clear nature of the result years after *Brown I*.

At the same time appeals were being undertaken in the *Jefferson* case, another sweeping decision was being rendered and challenged in another suit involving Alabama public schools. In *Wallace v. Lee*, a three-judge federal court in Montgomery had ordered the Alabama State Board of Education to begin desegregation of all public schools in the state by the fall of 1967. The court's ruling was the first since 1954 to place an entire state rather than an individual school district under a single injunction to end racial discrimination. Based on the conclusion that, through their control and influence over local school boards, state school authorities had flouted every effort to make the Fourteenth Amendment a meaningful reality to Alabama's schoolchildren, the federal court injunction ordered Governor Lurleen B. Wallace and ten other state officials to take "affirmative action to disestablish all state-enforcement or encouraged public segregation and to eliminate the effects of past . . . discrimination."[5] The state was ordered to abandon a school construction program that had produced inferior educational opportunities for Negroes in

Alabama and told to adopt the freedom-of-choice system for every student
in the state beginning in the fall of 1967. The understanding was that if
this did not accomplish significant desegregation other methods would be
used. And the court directed the state to have local schools initiate remedial programs for Negroes to overcome the effects of prior discrimination. State vocational schools, most colleges, and all public elementary and
secondary schools were covered. Furthermore, a state law providing
tuition grants to students attending private schools was declared unconstitutional, on grounds it was intended to promote and finance a private
school system for white students not wishing to attend integrated schools.
The court emphasized it was not deciding the validity of the HEW
Guidelines, under heavy attack in the state. However, as a practical
matter, the court's decision at the time superseded the HEW Guidelines,
which before *Jefferson* had not applied to any schools already under court
order to desegregate.

Ever since *Jefferson,* Governor Wallace and her husband had been
promising to fight the desegregation order by every available "legal"
means. If necessary, said Governor Wallace, she would ask her state
legislature to give her personal control over the public schools so that she
could defy the federal courts. In April, the Wallaces had called a meeting
with three other Deep South governors—McKeithen of Louisiana,
Johnson of Mississippi, and Maddox of Georgia—to try to convince them
that they should go as far as Alabama in opposing the Fifth Circuit's
desegregation orders. They had been unsuccessful. The other governors
had agreed to condemn the court action, but said they would not defy it
openly. Even as the meeting was taking place, the Supreme Court had
refused to delay enforcement of *Jefferson.* This left the Wallaces in a
rather difficult position, for indications were that their own local school
officials were willing to abide by the orders if allowed to do so. All the
governor could do was attempt to convince her people that such court
orders threatened everything they held sacred. She then initiated a speaking campaign to convince Alabamians they did not want compliance,
telling them that the order would force white children to go to all-Negro
schools and Negro students to white schools; that it would require the
closing of every Negro college, junior college, trade school, and every
all-Negro secondary and elementary school in the state; that it would
mean the court would determine the assignment of pupils and the granting of certificates to teachers; and that the order had been rendered in
malice and animosity.

Three weeks after the ruling in the case, the state requested and was
denied a stay of enforcement of the federal court's statewide school
desegregation order pending an appeal to the United States Supreme
Court. Five weeks later, Justice Black received Alabama's request for a

stay and referred the matter to the entire Supreme Court, which then denied it without comment. Except for explicit affirmance of the lower court's decree—to come slightly later in the year—the matter could be considered largely settled. The lower courts, which had decreed that the time for delay was over, were deemed most capable of solving the local problems. During the following term, the Supreme Court went further in this Alabama case by affirming, in a two-line per curiam order, the lower court's statewide desegregation decree and a follow-up decree ordering another Alabama county school board to comply with it.

After the *Wallace* cases, and before getting to "freedom-of-choice," the Court had to dispose of two more cases. One, *Dowell v. Board of Education of Oklahoma City,* was traditional in that it was applicable primarily to a single school system. Involved was a federal district court order requiring very specific procedures to be undertaken by the Oklahoma City school board in a broad court-conceived plan of school desegregation. The school board had challenged the district court's order in the federal Court of Appeals. The Tenth Circuit ruled that the broad plan was appropriate, approving the plan in almost every respect. The judges held that the lower court's entry of the plan after receipt of a study of the city school system by a panel of court-appointed experts was not in error, in view of the school board's own refusal to take prompt, substantial, and affirmative action to eliminate unconstitutional racially discriminatory practices. The plan which the Tenth Circuit approved was a very broad and specific one, based on an in-depth study by experts. It ordered the combining of specified schools, a majority to minority transfer policy as space permit ted (the opposite direction of previous such plans), and the desegregation of all faculty personnel so that by 1970 the ratio in each school was equivalent to the ratio of the races employed in the entire system. The lower court's use of experts to devise a school desegregation plan was a significant innovation. When asked to hear the case, the Supreme Court denied certiorari. The Court also took such action in a less traditional case, a follow-up to the question of desegregated education for military children. The *Bossier Parish* case was a class action brought by the parents of Negro children of Air Force base personnel at Barksdale Air Force Base, Louisiana, who sought relief from the local school board's refusal to permit their children to attend integrated public schools. The district court granted an injunction ordering the school authorities to submit a desegregation plan. Hearing an appeal by the authorities, the Fifth Circuit affirmed the lower court's injunction. The judges pointed out that the board had received and accepted federal funds for the maintenance and operation of their schools after passage of the Civil Rights Act of 1964 and had made assurances to the federal government that the children of base personnel at Barksdale would be admitted to school on the same terms as resident children. The court thus concluded that these parents were entitled to bring a class action representing all Negroes residing in that parish to enforce their constitutional right to desegregated education. The school board had argued that the base was not "within the jurisdiction" in terms of the Fourteenth Amendment, but the Fifth Circuit clearly rejected that argument because of the board's own actions and agreements with regard to the base.

2

"Freedom-of-choice" plans had been the principal device adopted by southern school boards faced with the provisions of Title VI and HEW's Guidelines. In large school districts, the plan sometimes started with every student being assigned to a particular school, either the one to which he had been going or the one nearest home. The student was then allowed a "free transfer" to another school. In small school districts—for example, those with only two schools, one previously all-white and the other all-black—every student would indicate where he would attend school. The usual effect was that a certain percentage of black students, perhaps 15 to 20 percent would choose to transfer to the "white school," while no whites would transfer to the black school, leaving 80 to 85 percent of the blacks in a segregated situation. Three cases involving the freedom-of-choice plans arrived at the Supreme Court in the late 1960s from three different federal circuits: in the Fourth, New Kent County, Virginia, where there was a white school at one end of the county and a school for blacks at the other; in the Eighth, Gould, Arkansas, where the school campuses were only eight to ten blocks apart; and in the Sixth, Jackson, Tennessee, a much larger school system with a "free transfer" plan. In the Virginia and Tennessee cases, freedom-of-choice had been imposed by the lower courts; in the Arkansas case, the lower courts had approved such a plan in part because of Department of Health, Education and Welfare approval, providing an example of judges "taking their lead" from administrative action. The three cases were argued together in April 1968, with the Solicitor General also making a presentation covering all three cases.[6] Because of the importance of these cases at the "end of the road" from *Brown v. Board of Education,* oral argument and the justices' questions are especially important and therefore warrant detailed examination. Fourteen years had passed since *Brown.* The attorneys for the school districts successfully resisting desegregation could see the end of minimal, token desegregation action, and began to dig in their heels. Although they did not refuse to comply—as had some of the Southern amici in *Brown II*—they claimed that their clients had done as much as they could and that public education would be destroyed if more were demanded. They coupled their defense with a form of counterattack, stressing their belief that the Negroes wanted their own schools. As a result, the justices' questions were particularly searching.

In *Green,* the first case to be argued, Samuel Tucker, for the blacks, stressed the fact that as a result of the New Kent County school board's refusal to obey *Brown,* "three years ago no child of either race had been brought into contact with persons of the other race as part of his normal, daily public school experience." He contended that the school board "had no intention of complying [with *Brown*] unless required" to do so. He saw the issue in the case as whether the school board had a "constitutional duty immediately to assign children to each of the public schools so that children of all races will attend schools indiscriminately." Tucker in effect was asking the Court to have the school board override an individual student's free choice of schools and take race explicitly into account in making assignments of students to schools.

In New Kent County, Tucker said, freedom-of-choice was "merely an impermissible expedient to evade the [board's] constitutional duty." The board had deliberately selected "the only available alternative, cumbersome though it may be, by which segregation might continue." Overnight, Tucker said, the board could simply assign all children in the western half of the county to one school and all in the eastern half to the other school; alternatively, one school could be made an elementary school and the other the high school. Tucker said that where there is residential segregation, school boards use zones and assign students to attend schools in the zone, thus forcing school segregation; where there is no residential segregation, the school board pleads it should not force children to go to school with children of the other race. "Force is seen as normal government regulation when it is used to retain segregation but school boards seem to make it sound horrible when used to put children of both races into school together." Calling attention to the fact that HEW could only require such speed as judicial opinions seem to require, he asked for a firm ruling. "These kinds of struggles are going to continue as long as school boards and federal judges can read judicial dicta and make semantic arguments contending that public authorities are not required to use the more or the most expeditious means of accomplishing total, rather than token, desegregation." The dictum which bothered him most, and which he thought had to be "laid to rest," was Judge Parker's dictum that *Brown* did not require integration, only desegregation. Noting that this was "unfortunately . . . still law as far as the Fourth Circuit is concerned," he added that the right to a choice by the child or his parents, "so blindly assumed, has been accorded an overriding constitutional dimension."[7]

Frederick T. Gray, for the school board, said that one had to go directly to *Brown* itself to determine what the Supreme Court had meant.

The question was, he said, "Does *Brown* compel integration?" He answered his own question in the negative, noting that the petitioners were confusing *Brown* with the "recently decided" *Jefferson* case. Gray said that the question of compulsory integration "wasn't even here" in *Brown,* and quoted Thurgood Marshall, "All we are asking for is to take off state-imposed segregation." Even if Judge Parker's statement had been dictum when first stated, "it did not remain dictum very long," having been adopted by court after court. *Brown* had said that one must "take down the fence" keeping students apart. Here, not liking the choices which parents and students had made, the petitioners were asking the Court to put back the fence, thus depriving people of equal protection.[8] Gray also stressed the role of the Negro school as a community center, indicating that "they" don't want to lose that school.

Most of the questions asked of Gray had to do with why freedom-of-choice was adopted and why choices were made under the plan, including the matter of community pressure and the history of the community.[9] After asking whether the county had had freedom-of-choice before 1965, Justice Marshall asked whether Gray was now saying that the 1965 plan was adopted without regard to race or color. Marshall continued, "Was it brought about because of the *Brown* decision or not?" (Unquestionably.) "So race was involved in it?" A frustrated Gray said, "Race *had* to be involved in it." Marshall: "Was it adopted with any purpose than to perpetuate as much segregation as you could? . . . The plan was conceived in an atmosphere of race?" By a school board "with a sworn duty to preserve public education and to better public education," was the reply.

Interested in what motivated the parents' decisions, Justice White asked, "What would you say if the state said, 'Put out the free choice form' and then at the bottom line was 'Why do you choose this school?' and the parents put down, 'I prefer to go to a white school,' and the Negroes put down, 'I prefer to go to a Negro school,' and transfers were allowed on that basis?" White followed this with questions as to whether freedom-of-choice plans allowed parents to make their choice based on race or allowed them to consider racial differences between the schools. Would it be permissible, he continued, for *all* the parents to get together and decide that the white children would go to one school and the Negro children to another? Yes, Gray answered, under the plan and under the Constitution.

The Chief Justice was more concerned with the related matter of community pressures and history which might affect choices. He asked, "Didn't we say in *Brown* that we couldn't let the feelings of the community delay this 'deliberate speed' we spoke of?" Gray responded by asking who could complain of a denial of equal protection of the laws. Warren answered, "If I was a Negro in Kent County, I would." The Chief Justice also asked whether in judging the freedom-of-choice approach, the Court could take into account "what has happened in that county for 100 years before . . . segregation in all things, buses and trains and everything else," and whether a large Negro percentage of the population meant greater resistance to desegregation. In response to Gray's comment that by signing the choice form, one could go to either school, Warren said, "But the social and cultural influences, and the prejudices that have existed for a century there are themselves written into that [approach]." Later, after asking whether a white child had ever been admitted to the colored school (No), Warren asked, "Isn't the net result that while they took down the fence, they put booby traps in the place of it, so there won't be any white children go to a Negro school? . . . Isn't the experience of three years . . . some indication that it was designed for the purpose of having a booby trap there for them, that they didn't dare to go over?" Gray: "If the free choice of an American is a booby trap, then this plan has booby traps."

Earlier, Marshall had asked about specific pressure: "Assuming a Negro parent wants to send his child to the . . . previous white school and his employer said, 'I suggest you not do it,' would that be freedom-of-choice?" Gray agreed it would not, but in response to Marshall's follow-up said that it had not happened here. Marshall also dealt with pressures on the white parent: "Isn't it true that what you're really saying is that if a white parent wants to send his child to the Negro school, he has a perfect right to make that choice and send that child to that school and take his chances with his neighbors and his employer?"

The result-oriented nature of the inquiry was clear. As Warren put it in his last question to Gray during the latter's initial presentation, "Is it accomplishing the purpose of *Brown* or its progeny when there hasn't been a single white child go to that school that is entirely Negro? Is that accomplishing any purpose for *Brown*?" Gray said in response, the purpose of *Brown*—the striking down of compulsory segregation—was "totally and completely accomplished."

In *Monroe*, the Jackson, Tennessee, case, James Nabrit III argued that "the courts should require school boards to begin affirmative steps to thoroughly dismantle the dual system and bring about a system which is no longer segregated." He thought the result called for was clear: "It is not enough merely for the boards to stop their illegal and unconstitutional practices, but that in addition, the school authorities have to take steps designed to actually reform the dual system of schools they've built up, to integrate them, if you will. We urge that the remedy must be designed to cure the evil, and the evil is the racially segregated school system that the authorities have put together." Put differently, the real issue was whether "real reform" or only "nominal and token compliance" would be demanded by the courts. Here, the lower courts had agreed with the school board that its only obligation was to stop assigning students on the basis of race—which it had done, having been fined one thousand dollars for its earlier discrimination in handling applications—and to assume neutrality. It didn't matter to those courts, said Nabrit, what happens; it doesn't matter if the schools remain largely segregated as before. The trial judge had thought that his task was not to maximize integration, not to find out why the school board's plan retained much segregation, but to find a nonracial explanation for the plan. He was required to approve any arrangements which did not have a clear abuse of discretion, that weren't obviously phony. If the judge looked at what is the most reasonable way for eliminating segregation, Nabrit said, we would get substantially different results. For him, "The policy of neutrality is not good enough to undo what they've done. . . . Where they were engaged in vigorous efforts to maintain segregation, they must engage in equally vigorous efforts to dismantle the dual school system they created," so that "segregation is not just being carried on under another guise."

Russell Rice argued the case for the Jackson officials. His basic constitutional position was that he had never read *Brown* as a command for "racial mixing as such," but only as requiring stopping segregation on the basis of race and choosing some other factor. He argued that the "free transfer" plan was permissible under the Court's prior rulings. Rice's argument was peppered with remarks about Jackson. He stressed that "we're not a racist town; we're not fighting the problem," but conceded that the town had been slow in getting started on desegregation, and said, "We do extremely well in our community, in view of the uncontrolled forces that are now loose in this country."[10] He said also that rigidity in an assignment plan would produce resegregation within three years by causing the whites to move and claimed that an integrated education was no freedom whatever and would be educationally harmful to some children "who absolutely [need] the right to stay out of an integrated education." Rice ran into many questions. Asking about the location of school zone lines,[11] Justice Warren wondered why there were all Negroes and no whites at one school: "Could it be that the lines have anything to do with it? Why were they drawn like that, an irregular line going clear across the city?" (We were trying to find natural boundaries, Rice said.) Then Justice White asked, "What have natural boundaries got to do with educational considerations?" Warren also queried whether the record contained anything as to the "fairness" of the plan as utilized, and followed this question by asking, "Is there anything to indicate whether it has functioned equitably in the past? Is there anything to indicate that this was an attempt to do the equitable thing or whether there was discrimination on the part of the board?" Noting that a line had been drawn for the high schools, Marshall wanted to know why the same line could not have been used for the junior high schools. "Just on the question of energy, wouldn't it have been easier to do that than all this other involved business?" When Rice said he had no pride of authorship in the particular lines, Marshall responded, "Would you be willing to put that line there now and say that everybody on this side goes to the one junior high school and everybody on the other side goes to one of the other two?" Rice responded, "I'm not agreeable to doing it because I don't think it's constitutionally required."

As to result, Justice White, citing *Goss* on the point that no official transfer plan could stand that had racial segregation as its "inevitable consequence," said, "I suppose that would apply to so-called unrestricted transfer plans." Yes, Gray said, if that were the inevitable result. Well, asked White, "How non-inevitable in Jackson?" Related was White's earlier question as to whether "it was predictable that there would be this pattern of school attendance" under freedom-of-choice and later questions from Marshall and Fortas. Marshall's questioning of Rice was extended:

"But the transfer plan was so that people who had a desire to attend a school of one racial group could do so?"
"For any reason."
"And you realize that this was allowing for the individuals on their own to use their racial prejudices to determine which school they would go to?"
"I don't know that I realize that at all, your honor."
"Didn't you realize that there was some white people living next door to their Negro high school that wouldn't go there?"
"I had no idea."
"What do you think happened that there's none there?"
"They don't wish to go there."[12]

Fortas was dubious as to whether an all-white community would have had free transfer. He asked, "In other places where they have all-white communities are free transfer plans very common? Would you find them at all?" And he wondered aloud whether it was a "common experience to have a free transfer plan where the child has for whatever reasons his parents think a good one, the absolute right to transfer to any school he wants." Perhaps not as absolute as this case, Rice replied. Also related to the operation of the plans were questions about the availability of bus service. Upon being told there was no school bus service, Warren elicited the fact that the Negroes would have to walk, use their own autos, or take city buses—involving a downtown transfer—to get to far-away schools.

The pattern of presentation and questioning in the *Raney* case, involving the Gould, Arkansas, district, with its two schools eight to ten blocks apart, was different from that in the two previous cases. Jack Greenberg, for the black petitioners, said that the case involved "an issue of remedy, that is, what a school district must do to come into conformity with the requirements of this Court" in *Brown,* not only after having maintained segregation for generations but after having maintained it for a decade after *Brown.* He claimed that the free-choice plan was adopted ten years after *Brown* with both the intent and effect of maintaining an all-Negro school and admitting a "small and stable proportion" of Negroes to the previously all-white school. He reinforced this claim with citations from the school district's brief and by noting that "the superintendent refers to the white school as 'our' school but the Negro school is 'the Negro school.' " There was also a salary differential between white and Negro teachers. "They felt they could get the Negro teachers cheaper and they didn't see any reason why they shouldn't." And the Negro school was "decidedly inferior" and "indeed unaccredited," he added. Greenberg wanted the Court to "announce that there is a positive duty on the part of school systems to disestablish pre-existing segregated systems. He said that it is not enough merely to announce something which is called 'freedom-of-choice.' " Furthermore, "The option which produces the greatest departure from the pre-existing system should be used rather than the one which produces the least, especially where the option which produces the least was adopted with that expectation in mind." Perhaps freedom-of-choice might be necessary in some communities, particularly where residential segregation was rigid, but that would not be a problem, Greenberg said, because "there has to be the traditional flexibility of a court of equity and the general principles . . . are not terribly difficult."

In questioning Greenberg, Justice Black was seriously troubled by the compulsion aspect of alternatives to "freedom-of-choice": "Why would it not violate a man's right to enjoy the equal protection of the laws contrary to the Fourteenth Amendment to compel him to go to a school that he was against going to, and leave others free?" Greenberg said that no one had questioned as a denial of a constitutional right the typical earlier assignment of an individual to a specific school. As Black did not later dissent from the Court's ruling and led the Court to "desegregation now" a year later, it is unclear whether he was persuaded by Greenberg's answers to his questions or whether he was simply testing counsel. Justice White asked if it were permissible to draw school zones "based on racial considerations" in eliminating segregation. It is necessary to unscramble a racially segregated situation, said Greenberg, referring to the children's game, "Don't Think of an Elephant"; all they do, he said, is think of elephants. "You can't integrate the school system but don't think about race."

Later, in rebuttal, Greenberg said the cases "come down to several propositions," of which the "most prominent" was "whether or not a school system has disestablished segregation when it continues to remain in existence the all-Negro school which is the symbol of the segregated system in circumstances when quite reasonable steps can be taken to end that situation." He then ended with a ringing statement: "When this Court expounds that Constitution, it states a proposition and a principle which as a practical matter at any given moment may not be actually attainable but something that we at least want to work towards and that proposition, as I see *Brown,* is that this shall be one country rather than two and that we should not acquiesce in various schemes and devices to frustrate the principle of the *Brown* decision, which I think is perhaps the greatest thing ever to have come out of this Court in the history of this nation."

Robert V. Light, for the Gould School Board, started his presentation by noting that Greenberg had changed his views since writing *Race Relations and American Law* in 1959, in which he had said there was no constitutional objection to a nonracial standard in education which produced no Negroes in certain schools. "I endorse . . . and embrace that principle entirely," said Light.[13] Light focused attention on improvements in the school district since the trial, including the closing of the teacher's salary gap and the replacement of the old Negro high school. The school board had acted in "perfect good faith" in adopting freedom-of-choice and in "undertaking to secure the rights of every child." Not only was there no intimidation against the Negroes, but the board went out and encouraged them to send children to the white school. On a paternalistic note, he added, "There's not a member of the school board that doesn't have Negro people living on their property." He noted that Gould had a cotton-oriented economy. Light's legal argument had two major aspects, one relating to *Brown,* the other to freedom-of-choice. There was "no intimation" in *Brown* "that the Constitution compelled the intermingling of the races by any sort of predetermined mixture." After *Brown,* all the Courts of Appeals which handled substantial school desegregation litigation were, he said, unanimous in reading *Brown* as Judge Parker had. His adversaries' alternatives, "suggested for purely racial reasons, to achieve a purely racial result," did not square with the Court's insistence on neutrality with respect to race. Only *Jefferson* broke with the above-mentioned pattern. "That decision is just *wrong,*" he said; it required the Fifth Circuit to overrule "some fifty of its own constitutional decisions on that point." Light said that the Civil Rights Act of 1964 used by Judge Wisdom did not require "affirmative manipulation" of students. Officials' legal duty was "what was already their legal duty under the Fourteenth Amendment as construed by *Brown.*" Even if Congress's intent in the 1964 act was unclear, Light argued, it was cleared up by a 1966 amendment to the Elementary and Secondary Education Act which did not require transportation of students or teachers "to overcome racial imbalance."

With respect to freedom-of-choice, Light first said that assigning students to zones was the predominant way of determining school attendance in this country, but freedom-of-choice was next.[14] He said that free choice had been the long-standing pattern for college attendance for the nation's entire history, and had been used ever since *Sweatt* and *McLaurin* in those states which had had segregation at the college level. College-level free choice, he stressed, had produced an attendance pattern similar to that in this case, because the vast majority of "these people . . . want to attend school with members of their own race." Anticipating the problem posed by later HEW suits aimed at segregated colleges, Light said that if the Court were to adopt the rule the petitioners wanted, "What will happen to all of those all-Negro colleges" and to the vast majority of Negro college students at predominantly- or all-Negro schools?

Turning to the effect of alternative attendance arrangements on the local schools, Light said making one school an elementary school and the other a high school would result in the former having 157 white students and 247 Negro students and the latter having 157 white students and 301 Negroes. Backing his position with citations from the United States Commission on Civil Rights, he said, "The white students would not continue to attend those schools. . . . They would flee just as inevitably as they have fled from the public schools of Washington, D.C., and go to private schools, go stay with relatives in some other school district, but they leave." Light said he was unable to characterize the reason, except to say that what had gone on for one hundred years in the community could not be ignored: "Whether that history's right or wrong, whether it's moral or Christian, it's gone on; it's a fact we have to deal with, and that has produced two groups of people with such cultural differences in that community that when the predominant culture becomes that of the Negro people in the community, the white people flee from it; it's not acceptable to them."

Questions asked of Light mostly dealt with the distribution of children and the reasons for using freedom-of-choice over other alternatives. Marshall wanted to know if there were any white students in the Field Elementary School and if not why not. When told no white had exercised his right to go there, Marshall asked, "What could be the reason for that?"—a question he himself almost answered by asking further: "Could it possibly be that the white parents don't want to send their children to a school that paid $45,000 to build the educational part of the school and $82,000 for the gymnasium? Could it be that they'd rather go to a nice school than a nice gymnasium?" When Light commented that the Negro facility, which was more than merely a gym, was better than some white schools Marshall twitted him, "Then the white people have a law suit?" Not to be put down so easily, Light responded, No, because they have a free right to go to either school.

As to the reasons for freedom-of-choice, Marshall pressed Light, "You didn't get it until you were up against the wall. You could have taken the two schools together and combined them physically . . . could have made one an elementary, one a high school." Marshall also suggested that Field Elementary, built in 1954, could have been placed on the white campus (no further space, Light said), or the school board could have had one large elementary school and one large high school "without much trouble." Light conceded it was a possibility. Drawing a line midway between the two school complexes was another option mentioned by Marshall, who said, "You could have drawn [the line] right down the middle of the county and detoured the penitentiary [Laughter], and said everybody on this side goes to this one, everybody on the other side goes to the other one." Then, in one of several jabs he took at Light, "Once you did that, you could consider both of them as *your* school." Pursuing the same point somewhat later Chief Justice Warren, in what was more a statement than a question, asked whether the school board wasn't "merely bowing to the imperatives of community feeling rather than . . . bow-[ing] to the law," so that, "if permitted to go on, it will go on indefinitely that all of the white students will go to one school, or practically all, and practically all the Negroes to another, and the desegregation decisions get frustrated entirely."

Marshall engaged with Light in two extended dialogues which were attempts, polite but quite pointed, to expose the South's resistance. As the NAACP's counsel in *Brown* and the only Negro on the Court, Marshall was perhaps the most appropriate justice to pursue the matter. His personal involvement and "representativeness" of Negroes were obvious to all concerned. He began by asking how many private schools there were in Gould. None, came the reply. "Then we don't have to worry about that problem, do we?" When Light responded that there were no private schools in Prince Edward County until recent years, Marshall came back with, "I understand that's over with now, too . . . because they weren't private. You don't think that your county would try to do what Prince Edward County did (No, Sir) when this Court found that was wrong. You wouldn't *think* of doing that." Marshall then turned to the future: "How long do you think it would take for your county to reach the point where they wouldn't mind the white children attending a school that was two-to-one Negro? How long before your county got around to that point?" Here, disclaiming clairvoyance, Light said, "It would largely coincide with the length of time it took the Negro people to decide they didn't want to

keep their own school and use it as a community center and attend school
with members of their own race." Marshall quickly turned to exceptions to
Light's generalization. "You aren't speaking for all the Negroes, are you?"
In saying what, Light asked. "In saying they want to be by themselves in
their own little school where they're so happy?" Then, "How many Negroes do you know in that county, personally?" When Light suggested his
contact was professional, Marshall pressed, "You're speaking for *all* of
them." "I'm not speaking *for* them, but *of* them," said Light.[15] "You say
that Negroes in Gould love to be by themselves in their own school
building. You really mean *some,* don't you?" Light responded, "You've
taken some liberties with what I've said."

During rebuttal, Marshall was at Light again, this time more by way of
statement: "Do you have any residential segregation in Gould? The answer is No. . . . The white and colored children play together, they
sometimes eat together and the only time they're segregated is in school
and in church. Is that an accurate statement? . . . You've never seen
white and colored kids playing together in that county? [Light said he
wasn't in Gould often.] Well, have you seen white and colored kids playing
together in Little Rock . . . in the streets and everyplace where they live?
I'm trying to get where you've got all this hostility. . . . You said they'd be
hostile to each other. Where did they get the hostility: from the church or
the school?"

There was one more presentation in the cases, that of Louis Claiborne
for the federal government. Claiborne kept stressing that freedom-of-
choice was affirmative action by the states to retain segregation and that in
these cases "normal, old-fashioned geographic zoning would achieve
either a substantial measure or complete desegregation." While the persistence of segregation so many years after *Brown* called for a remedy,
Claiborne said he was not asking for "busing or any other extraordinary
measures," merely for an "old-fashioned, traditional system of neighborhood schools," which would have been used "except for the effort to
escape the racial integration that would follow" from it. Noting that,
despite respondents' suggestion, there is no constitutional right for children to choose their own schools, Claiborne said, "*Brown* did not condemn
the old system of assigning children to a school in the best interests of the
district as a whole." The present cases involved not merely "abdicating
responsibility" but the "taking [of] affirmative steps; they're going very
far out of their way to create, to make possible a resegregation or a
perpetuation of segregation within these school districts. They're not
merely letting the assignments fall where they would be under geographic
zoning. . . . They have taken quite extraordinary measures to avoid the
natural result."

It was this use of free choice as an "artificial device to delay, to retard, even to defeat desegregation" that the government condemned. Claiborne went on to call freedom-of-choice "educational nonsense," "a purely haphazard system" which ignored the educational point of view, a method which "imposes a special financial burden" because of long-distance bus routes and "an administrative nightmare" if it worked as it were supposed to, both because of all the forms and letters one would have to "send out, receive, tabulate, [and] count,"[16] and because "results are unpredictable" and one couldn't plan school buildings "on any intelligent basis." The point was, he said, that free choice wasn't supposed to work, for if it did, it would be self-defeating. All the Negroes would transfer to the previously white school, which would then have overcrowding problems, causing compulsory assignments. The device, he said, was "calculated on the theory that the whites will all choose to attend the white schools and that very few Negroes will overcome the burden and have the courage to take the adventure into a school where they have been shunned, where they don't expect to be welcomed." Saying that freedom-of-choice plans were a "transparent device to enable white students . . . to . . . continue segregation . . . in a way the state itself cannot," Claiborne claimed "the state appears at least to be applauding, to be encouraging, to be at least sanctioning and approving a choice made on the basis of race." The state had thus hardened racial attitudes, "which it is the whole purpose of desegregated education to relax," as well as compounded the injury of Negro children. While the government was not arguing here that the state had an "affirmative obligation to take special measures to achieve racial balance . . . the state must at least avoid resorting to extraordinary measures which can only be in their purpose and effect to retard desegregation." Claiborne also pointedly addressed himself to the school board argument that whites would move out of the district: "The more school districts are subjected to the same constitutional standard, the less place there is to flee to; the more tuition and so-called private schools are stricken down, the less attractive the alternative of private schooling becomes, and it works perhaps a little bit like a public accommodation law, if everybody has to desegregate and there's no place else to go, pretty soon people stay where they once were."

Questions directed to Claiborne concerned primarily the type of test to be used in measuring various methods for desegregating. First, Justice White asked, "What if old-fashioned neighborhood zoning produced no integration at all, left segregation where it was?" That would be a quite different case, presenting different problems, Claiborne said, and the school board might have an affirmative duty at least not to choose the alternative producing the least change. Posing another hypothetical question, Justice Fortas, noting that free choice had put 20 percent of the Negroes in the previously all-white school, asked whether Claiborne would still be dissatisfied with 20 percent of the Negroes in the white school and 20 percent of the whites in the Negro school. We're not playing a game of statistics, the lawyer said, an answer too flip for the justice: "We're not playing games; it's deadly serious." Fortas, continuing, asked whether the test of a result were to be a "statistical test" or if not, good faith. Fortas also stated Claiborne's position: "You're saying that the standard of compliance with *Brown* in a previously segregated school district should be whether of the alternatives reasonably available, that alternative was adopted which would result in the maximum desegregation." Claiborne backed away, saying one need not go that far because free choice was so "obviously . . . cumbersome, out-of-the-way, transparent." Since some alternative methods were alleged by respondents to produce movement out of the school districts, Justice White then asked whether Claiborne was assuming that such movement would not occur or whether he was saying it was irrelevant. Claiborne, evading, said that "frightening prospect," always put forward, tended to argue against any desegregation. "I understand that," White said, "but you say that as a matter of fact, you dispute it." (No basis to do that here.) "If you accepted it, would you say it's irrelevant?" (Yes.) Finally, Justice Brennan, relatively silent throughout the cases, asked what was the most obviously strategic question: What should the Court do? Should the Court say not only that freedom-of-choice was not a viable alternative but go beyond that and require that a geographic zoning plan be adopted? "What do we do" after condemning freedom-of-choice, "remand and tell the district court the board has to come up with some more satisfactory alternative?" "Would it be appropriate," he wanted to know, "for this Court to say, 'These two it appears on this record would be satisfactory as a remedy, but you go ahead, district court, and choose between them,' limiting the district court to a choice between the two?" His questions made clear he thought it "singularly inappropriate" for the Court to prescribe plans.

When the Court handed down its rulings, less than two months later, Justice Brennan's opinions for a unanimous Court were short and to the point. He took less than twenty-five pages to deal with all three cases. Brennan's emphasis was on the ultimate goal of "disestablishing" or "dismantling" dual school systems and doing it effectively, and he stressed the difference between the tasks immediately after *Brown II* and those at this much later date, particularly where a school board had done nothing in the interim. Immediately after *Brown II,* one had to make "an initial break in a long-established pattern," and to find a place in previously white schools "for those Negro children courageous enough to break with tradition," he said, citing the Little Rock case. However, one should not confuse the "immediate goal," which was only a "first step," with the "ultimate end," which "was and is" a "unitary, nonracial system of public education." While *Brown II* showed "awareness that complex and multi-faceted problems would arise which would require time and flexibility for a successful resolution," the burden even then was on the school boards to show the need for additional time to comply with the ruling, and the school officials "were nevertheless clearly charged with the affirmative duty to take whatever steps might be necessary to convert to a unitary system in which racial discrimination would be eliminated root and branch." That burden had not changed, the justice said: "The burden on a school board today is to come forward with a plan that promises realistically to work, and promises realistically to work *now*."

While Brennan did not hold that freedom-of-choice plans had no place in desegregation, it was clear that the Court was now interested in results. This was particularly true where, as in these cases, the school districts had waited ten years after *Brown* to begin desegregation. Such "deliberate perpetuation" had compounded the harm of a segregated school system and made an ineffective desegregation plan "intolerable." "Freedom-of-choice," while not impermissible, was not to be "an end in itself." Where other ways of desegregating—ways which promised "speedier and more effective conversion to a unitary, nonracial school system"—existed, freedom-of-choice was not acceptable. It was not acceptable here, where it had burdened the Negro children and parents, and instead of furthering desegregation had brought about "minimal disruption of the old pattern" and retained "the comfortable security of the old, established discriminatory pattern," particularly where the school officials had not managed to justify their program in terms of particular local needs.

Brennan also had some words for the district courts. He chided the district court in *Raney* for having dismissed the parents' complaint, noting that the Court in *Brown II* had intended that lower courts retain jurisdiction until dual systems were in fact "disestablished." Not only must the school board "establish that its proposed plan promises meaningful and immediate progress toward disestablishing state-imposed segregation," but the district court must weigh such a claim both in terms of the local factual situation and "in light of any alternatives which may be shown as feasible and more promising in their effectiveness." The court could approve a plan where the school board was found to be acting in good faith—found, not merely that the board asserted it was so acting—and where the board's plan had "real prospects" for working. Even then, Brennan said, "whatever plan is adopted will require evaluation in practice; the court should retain jurisdiction until it is clear that state-imposed segregation has been completely removed."

The word "integration" had not been used by Brennan; throughout he used less emotive words like "dismantling." By the frequency with which it had begun to call for speed and to show its impatience with foot-dragging, the Court provided continuity with the past and showed that it did not think that what it was doing was particularly surprising. The complete unanimity and the dispatch and terseness with which the Court handled the cases served to reinforce this message—if the message were ever to get across to those affected. The Deep South seemed to react with shock, but the rulings were really incremental, being built on earlier statements about the need for speed, starting with the *Watson* parks case and including the low-visibility *Bradley* (Richmond) ruling. Yet they can also be seen as the beginning of judicial "affirmative action"—as the Civil Rights Act of 1964 and the resultant HEW Guidelines were the major initial actions on the part of the legislative and executive branches.

The freedom-of-choice cases showed that a new pattern in the Supreme Court's treatment of lower education cases was developing. For quite some time after *Brown II* many cases went all the way to the Supreme Court only to be denied a hearing. Now, however, fewer cases were being brought up. Perhaps this situation resulted in part from the Court's insistent demand for results. The *Green* trilogy was an obvious reminder of the Court's position stated as early as *Cooper* and reiterated in the *Watson* parks case and *Griffin,* among others. Perhaps it also came in large measure from the forcefulness of the Fifth Circuit's *Jefferson* rulings. To the extent it was from the latter, the Court's "docket-management" had paid off: the lower court with greatest responsibility for school desegregation had pushed hard, had reached decisions more advanced than those which the Supreme Court confronted directly might have decided, and the judges had made clear they meant business. While school officials might have been inclined to appeal all cases to the top, the Fifth Circuit's actions seemed to depress such activity. This left the high court with the task of reinforcing the lower courts in the occasional case now appealed, a far simpler task than reaching decisions like *Jefferson* without initial action by those lower courts or trying to provide backbone for those courts had they not shown it themselves. The Fifth Circuit's own docket-management—consolidation of cases for hearing and decision—further reduced the number of cases for the Supreme Court even when they were appealed. Yet *Green* created problems for the Fifth Circuit. Its *Jefferson* rule had seemed clear enough; yet less than a year after it mandated uniform HEW Guidelines in all federal district courts in the Fifth Circuit, the Supreme Court displaced the Court of Appeals' work by adopting new doctrine in *Green* which went beyond the guidelines.

One case decided in the spirit of the *Green* trilogy, although not directly involving freedom-of-choice, allowed the Supreme Court to reinforce the discretion of southern federal judges, at least when they headed in the direction the Court intended. Judge Frank Johnson, who had been monitoring school desegregation in Montgomery once it finally began in 1964, had issued a broad order in 1968 in another effort to speed up the desegregation process. That order had involved matters of constructing new schools so that their location would not perpetuate segregation, adoption of nondiscriminatory bus routes, and detailed steps to eliminate a community impression that one high school and two new elementary schools were primarily for white use. Those elements in the order were not challenged. However, Judge Johnson had also provided for faculty desegregation, stipulating that the ratio of white to Negro faculty should be "substantially the same" in each school in the system, indicating numbers for schools of different sizes. The Court of Appeals panel which first heard the case affirmed Johnson's order only after modifying it because the numbers requirements were thought to be too rigid. Rehearing en banc was denied by an evenly divided twelve judges. It was in this posture that the Supreme Court received the case, *United States v. Montgomery Board of Education,* on certiorari.

After argument, the Court, speaking through Justice Black, unanimously affirmed Judge Johnson's original order. Black used his opinion to indicate, first, why *Brown II* had not left matters solely in the hands of the school districts but had involved the local federal courts as well. He then traced the history of the current case, noting Montgomery's reluctance to begin compliance with *Brown.* Referring to the earlier Alabama cases, he said, "The state government and its school officials attempted in every way possible to continue the dual system of racially segregated schools in defiance of our repeated unanimous holdings that such a system violated the United States Constitution." He said that up to May 1964 "Montgomery County . . . had operated . . . as though our *Brown* cases had never been decided." This sort of situation, he said, "imperatively" required the "coercive assistance of courts." He then took the opportunity to praise both the judge—by name, an unusual act for the Court—and the school board, the latter for showing "a growing recognition . . . of its responsibility," with the judge making "a constant effort . . . to expedite the process of moving as rapidly as practical toward the goal of a wholly unitary system of schools, not divided by race as to either students or faculty." Given that the school board was trying to gain time and the judge was constantly trying to push the board, what the judge had done was not inflexible, as his past rulings, which he had "left open for experimentation," had shown. Thus his order, not inflexible as claimed by the Court of Appeals, "was adopted in the spirit of this Court's opinion in *Green,*" with the appeals court's modifications detracting from the order's force and from the judge's "capacity to expedite, by means of specific commands, the day when a completely unified, unitary, nondiscriminatory school system becomes a reality instead of a hope."

One could read Justice Black's opinion narrowly, setting it firmly in the context of a flexible judge and a responsive school board operating in frequent interaction with each other, and say that it meant little outside of Montgomery. However, the fact that the Court issued a full opinion, rather than a short per curiam affirmance, suggests that the Court was doing all it could both to reinforce a certain type of judicial discretion and judicial authority—shown in the parts of *Brown II* Black chose for elaboration—and to stress the fact that full and prompt compliance was the order of the day. What is also significant is that the case gave the Court an opportunity to confront the "numbers issue" in race relations—the question of whether specific, or at least fairly specific, ratios could be used as an "affirmative action" device to remedy past racial discrimination. Quotas had always posed problems for the liberals backing desegregation because such devices had often been used against them in the past in matters such as admission to private colleges or to graduate school. Hence using quotas in a positive way was not easy. The unanimity in the Court's ruling was perhaps achieved more because the judges saw the case as one of reinforcing a lower court judge in a desegregation case than because they saw themselves issuing a definitive ruling on quotas, but the case is nonetheless extremely important for that reason as well.

3

After *Green*, the problem became one of obtaining compliance from the many districts in which freedom-of-choice plans had not produced action. The United States and private litigants kept going to southern federal courts to obtain desegregation orders in line with *Green-Raney-Monroe*. The lower courts began to recognize that more action was required, but, as before, they differed as to how much they demanded. The action of some courts, however, was to produce an end to "all deliberate speed." Some school districts used the damage from Hurricane Camille as an additional excuse for not being able to bring about immediate compliance with *Brown*. The more important hurricane from the perspective of judges unwilling to accept the natural disaster as another ground for delay was the one which led to the Supreme Court's action, fifteen years after *Brown I* and fourteen years after *Brown II*, to end the *Brown II* formula which had led to delay. Perhaps the hurricane had started to blow with *Green*, but it was to come with full force to the recalcitrant school districts in late 1969 in one of the first actions taken by the Court with the new Chief Justice, Warren Burger, in charge.

Final action on "all deliberate speed" began with a set of consolidated cases decided by the Fifth Circuit and remanded to the lower courts under the name of *Adams v. Mathews*. The Court of Appeals then required elimination of all-Negro schools as a vestige of a dual school system; freedom-of-choice was outlawed if all-Negro schools remained. However, even some district judges who recognized that *Green* standards had not been met were unwilling to throw out freedom-of-choice.[17] When after the *Adams v. Mathews* remand the district court in Mississippi again approved freedom-of-choice, the United States, beginning the *Alexander v. Holmes County* case, went back to the Fifth Circuit, asking for desegregation orders to be effective in September 1969. The Court of Appeals ordered the district court to formulate plans to disestablish dual districts, with implementation to occur by the requested September 1 date. The Department of Health, Education and Welfare filed plans on August 11, which it said were administratively and educationally sound. However, despite this action and the "Desegregation Policy Statement" issued by HEW Secretary Finch and the attorney general the previous July 3—in which they had said that school districts must complete desegregation "at the earliest practicable date" on the basis of a plan which "promises realistically to work now," with the terminal date for full compliance generally being the 1969–70 school year[18]—eight days later Finch asked for an extension to December 1 for filing after more study. Finch's letter was reinforced by a Department of Justice motion to the same effect. The Court of Appeals then asked the district court to hold a hearing on the request. After holding that hearing, the district court recommended that the secretary's requested delay be granted. When HEW's request was also granted by the Fifth Circuit, the NAACP carried the case to the Supreme Court. Although using strong language about the delaying process and the difficulties caused by "deliberate speed," Justice Black in an in-chambers opinion denied a petition for vacation of the Court of Appeals' modification of its earlier order.[19] A petition for certiorari was then filed. On October 9, 1969, the Court granted that petition and denied a cross-petition.

In their brief, petitioners stressed that the time for implementing *Brown* had run out: "This is the only rule of law which will effectively disestablish the dual school systems: 15 years is enough to solve administrative problems. This is the only rule of law which will effectively deal with the problem of evasion: 15 years is enough to tolerate defiance of the Constitution." Petitioners also attacked the government's seeking delay, because that action "has intensified the very resistance it professes to seek to overcome." Any recognition of excuses for delay, by either the executive or the judiciary, would generate only further excuses and more demands for concessions, they said, also arguing that desegregation should occur now. They felt that any problems remaining could be worked out during the desegregation process.

In response, the school districts raised a host of questions involving freedom-of-choice, "forced integration," the survival of all-black schools after removal of forced segregation, conflicts between rulings of the Fifth Circuit and those of other circuits, and the conflict of the Fifth Circuit's rulings with those of the Supreme Court. The school districts argued, *inter alia,* that 1) a petition for rehearing en banc was still pending before the Fifth Circuit, so the matter was not final; 2) the desegregation plans had not been subject to a hearing; 3) under the circuit's accelerated schedule, a study of plans by HEW and work with the school boards by HEW had not been posible; 4) the lower courts' findings of fact should not be disturbed; and 5) the Fifth Circuit had pulled the rug out from under "thousands of devoted educators" in the area covered by the circuit by adding requirements not in keeping with *Brown I* and *II* and the *Green-Raney-Monroe* set of cases. Coming after *Jefferson II, Green* had "affirmatively declined to hold that the Fourteenth Amendment requires compulsory integration in public schools," the school districts argued. *Jefferson,* said to have overruled eight Fifth Circuit cases decided over several years and to have announced "a dramatic and revolutionary writ contrary to the constitutional principles" of the Supreme Court and other circuits, was the principal cause of the "present chaos and confusion" and had led to deterioration of the schools.

Fronting for its own Department of Health, Education and Welfare and opposing the NAACP for the first time in contemporary desegregation litigation, the United States had opposed granting the certiorari petition and now opposed putting the original HEW orders into effect. While agreeing that "deliberate speed" was not appropriate, HEW said it needed time. In addition, HEW pointed out that after the September start of school one could not go back to the beginning of the year. The National Education Association also filed an amicus brief, taking the position that the delay granted by the Fifth Circuit was not justifiable in terms of either administrative inconvenience or warnings of "chaos or confusion." One needed to look, they said, at the effects of delay in human terms. Additional children were obtaining their education in racial isolation and were suffering continuing psychological damage of the sort referred to in *Brown I.* Furthermore, delay would weaken the position of those already complying even in the face of community opposition. Claiming that *Jefferson* had had little effect in equalizing facilities, the NEA said that "the only practical procedure for the elimination of the qualitative differences in black and white schools is complete integration."

Oral argument in *Alexander* was lengthy,[20] and, as the Court grappled with the issue of bringing an end to "all deliberate speed," it was punctuated by considerable questioning of counsel for the NAACP and counsel for the government but not of Mississippi's counsel; it was also characterized by particularly forceful rhetoric reflecting the parties' awareness of the case's importance as a potential watershed in the battle over desegregation. NAACP counsel Jack Greenberg began by suggesting that the cases involved the issue of timing of desegregation and the procedures for accomplishing it. The question was how much longer Negro children must wait "to realize their constitutional right to attend desegregated school systems required by this Court nearly 15 years ago." The Court's statement as to timing had to be "unequivocal," he said; certain procedures were required because the law had been disobeyed and the courts below had not required obedience. Greenberg claimed that Mississippi's resistance to the Fourteenth Amendment had been "second to none," and he noted that desegregation had not been accomplished at the University of Mississippi until more than ten years after *Sweatt v. Painter,* and then "only after what can be called resistance with the quality of rebellion and that at the cost of life." Similarly, he pointed out, shortly after the *Evers* desegregation case was filed, Medgar Evers was shot and killed, which he said raised serious questions about whether freedom-of-choice could be a reality in Mississippi, as the school districts claimed. The worst part of the matter, said Greenberg, was the behavior of the federal district judges, who had consistently used their discretionary authority in such a way as to delay matters and both exploited "ambiguities, real ambiguities, and fancied ambiguities in the decisions of this Court and the Court of Appeals" and had refused to follow the "plain intendment" of those courts, even upholding freedom-of-choice plans on the "totally unsupported finding that freedom-of-choice might work in the future."[21] The result had been to preserve a status quo of "segregation or minimal, token desegregation."

Greenberg, who said the desegregation plans were "as careful and detailed as one might hope for," attacked HEW for failing to substantiate its request for delay and for being "completely open-ended" as to when compliance with new plans would have to occur. Greenberg reminded the justices that the Court of Appeals had thought in terms of eight days (August 23–September 1) and that an educational expert had confirmed the adequacy of such a period. Greenberg interpreted the government's statement that the school board should bear the burden in an expedited review for any delay beyond the Christmas recess or mid-semester as an indication of support for "litigation forever,"[22] which he found "most distressing." Greenberg asked the Supreme Court to do two things: 1) to issue a statement that "petitioners are entitled to have their constitutional rights vindicated now, without postponement for any reason," something he said was not very new as the Court had already done this "not entirely explicitly but fairly explicitly," and 2) more important, to institute procedures to make such a declaration effective, including putting the HEW plans into effect immediately.

Greenberg was obviously troubled by how much the Court should say on timing. He clearly agreed with Justice Black's in-chambers opinion that "the time is now." Although he recognized that time would be necessary to call children to classrooms, notify bus drivers, and the like, he thought that no more than the eight-day period indicated in the plans was necessary "and probably less." His basic concern was that the school districts would exploit any judicial statement seeming to authorize even limited delay. Yet on balance he thought a fixed deadline "vastly preferable to reiteration of principles about desegregation as soon as possible which will result in further litigation." He argued against accepting administrative reasons for delay because they elevated the importance of disruption and threats of disruption, and "anyone . . . who believes that his resistance will stimulate an administrative issue which will leave resolution in the courts is given an incentive to make or threaten trouble." He argued that a way had to be developed to diminish litigation, because "the ingenuity of lawyers and judges knows no limit when the incentive is sufficient." Because allowing segregation to be the status quo pendente lite had meant "a premium on litigating *ad infinitum,*" the Court should make integration the rule, something Greenberg felt a "simple enough" resolution in this case.

Greenberg drew on the argument of the NEA—"which knows a thing or two about education"—to support his position that there was no reason why desegregation couldn't occur immediately, even though it would interrupt the school year. Indeed, he said, "there is some considerable educational gain to be achieved by showing the children that the laws cannot be flouted with approval." As he also stated it, "Any pretense of legality should be stripped from those continuing to segregate; they should not be able to parade respectably under the cloak of complying with the so-called 'deliberate speed' doctrine. It should be indubitably clear that they are law violators, and I think in this county lawfulness counts for something." Mississippi schoolchildren, Greenberg claimed, "have not learned that the Constitution is to be protected, defended, cherished, and lived." The order he sought from the Court, he said, was necessary "not merely because another fortnight of a dual school system is intolerable but rather because another fortnight of unwarranted displacement of the Constitution is intolerable."

Louis Oberdorfer made a brief appearance for the Lawyers' Committee for Civil Rights Under Law to indicate the group's concern that actions of the lower courts and of the federal government "might tend to cause an unraveling of the atmosphere of respect which has been developed over these recent hard years." Arguing against attempting to set desegregation guidelines for the first day of school because it served as an invitation to those who would try to interfere, he thought reorganization of the schools could be better accomplished during the school year, because the students and teachers would be in school, the courts would be in daily business, and the Supreme Court would be in session.

The Justice Department's position was presented by Jerris Leonard, head of the Civil Rights Division, who wanted the Court of Appeals delay order affirmed. He urged the Court "not to be too caught up in the frustration that counsel have portrayed to the Court" and instead stressed an optimistic point of view because substantial breakthroughs had taken place. While he conceded that it was a long way to the end of the road, he argued that *Green,* only eighteen months old, not *Brown,* should be the base line from which to measure progress. Substantial progress had occurred since the latter decision, he said. Leonard stressed the need for properly drawn plans and asked the Court to give weight to the professional judgment of the people at HEW, who needed more time if the plans were to be more refined and complete so that, for example, bus drivers would know where to pick up the schoolchildren. Without such plans, he claimed, one would return to the situation in which the district judge and lawyers for the parties would "be sitting across from each other with the school district map, drawing lines and sticking pins and drawing some more lines." In support of his position, Leonard stressed concern for the children involved: "Many hundreds of thousands of the children that we're talking about are children of very tender age. Many of these little people are six and seven and eight and nine years old. What you do with them can have an effect on their total future life." "We're trying to improve the education of the Negro children; we know we will improve the education of the white children by desegregation anyway, but," Leonard said, "let's try to do it with some order."

Mississippi Attorney General A. F. Summer began his state's presentation. In his brief statement, he claimed that the record did not show the noncompliance with the law and disobedience which petitioners claimed it showed, and he stressed his opinion that a single rule for both de facto and de jure segregation should apply. "We feel we no longer have de jure segregated schools but de facto just as those in other parts of the nation." Using statistics from northern cities, he asked whether Mississippi could be asked to take affirmative action while cities like Chicago and St. Louis could be "exempt" from petitioners' constitutional principle.

Former American Bar Association President John Satterfield presented most of Mississippi's case. He attacked the lack of a record, statements about Mississippi's noncompliance, and petitioner's prayer for relief. He argued that the Court of Appeals had ruled without record, evidence, or briefing as to the merits, but only briefing as to timing, and that the Court of Appeals, despite its statements to the contrary, had "wholly failed" to accept the district court findings. On noncompliance,

Satterfield said the record contained evidence that many of the districts had complied with the requirements both of older cases and of *Green* as well, so that in most of the districts "the vestiges of a dual school system have been removed." Satterfield called petitioner's prayer for relief "amazing" and claimed it asked that there be no hearing by the district court, that plans—already withdrawn—be instituted without a hearing by any court under any circumstances and that state and local officials not be allowed to participate in development of the plans. Furthermore, he argued, what petitioners wanted required overruling and modifying of "*Brown I, Brown II, Cooper, Green, Raney* and all the other cases decided by this Court." Although the districts he represented had complied with the district court's and Fifth Circuit's requirements up to 1966 that freedom-of-choice plans were proper, he said, the Court was now being asked for compulsory assignment, which may end up "on racial grounds" alone even if called something else. Such a ruling, Satterfield said, would conflict directly with the Sixth Circuit's *Goss* decision—which he said conflicted with *Jefferson*—and there would also be conflicts with other circuits as well. Satterfield also had something to say about timing. He suggested that petitioners' "now" meant " 'Yesterday,' 'have already worked,' or tomorrow morning at 7:15, Eastern Daylight Savings Time." Instead, he claimed, " 'Promises realistically to work now' necessarily refers to the realism with which it may be reasonably expected to work and not that it has theretofore done so." He said he recognized that somewhat greater speed was required than in the past, and that deliberate speed "is no longer the call of the day," but that did not mean that desegregation could be required without hearings and orderly procedures or without plans.

Many questions were asked of Greenberg. The first of them related to the way in which objections could be made to the desegregation plans. White asked him whether the Court of Appeals order had contemplated filing of objections, hearing, and appellate review within the eight-day August 23–September 1 period. Chief Justice Burger followed up this question by asking whether the order could be interpreted as being put into effect pending the filing of objections and review. Burger then asked, "Would it have been within the power of the Court of Appeals to let that plan be carried out pending any further proceedings?" (Greenberg: "Oh certainly, Mr. Chief Justice, and that has occurred on other occasions.") Later Justice White said to Satterfield that he did not understand that the items to which Satterfield was objecting would be foreclosed "from objection and ultimate review by this Court if necessary." As if supporting Greenberg's earlier contention, Satterfield replied that objection would be foreclosed as a practical matter: "While there might be a later appeal, it would be water down the drain." The justices were concerned also about the effect of midyear changes on children. After asking whether many children would have to change schools and teachers, White asked whether their going to a different school with a different teacher would pose any difficulty with respect to their completing their work. Greenberg said it would, but thought no more than where other interruptions—for example, from a teachers' strike—had occurred.

The differences between the positions of the Justice Department and the petitioners were explored. Chief Justice Burger, for example, noting it was "swiftly approaching" November 1, suggested to Greenberg that the difference between the two "really comes down to something like sixty days, more or less." When Greenberg said there were lots of differences, particularly in the government's willingness to "litigate forever" during the maintenance of segregation, Burger responded, "I didn't read his brief that way," with which Justice Harlan agreed. In fact, Burger said he read the government's statement "as contemplating and certainly permitting doing just what you had suggested earlier, namely implementing . . . and then litigating against the background of that implementation. I had thought that you and the Department of Justice were on collision course here, coming very close together." Greenberg replied that he would be very pleased if they would agree to implementation pendente lite, but he felt there was still disagreement as to timing.

Also much at issue was the kind of order Greenberg wanted and the question whether the Court was being asked to appraise or evaluate the plans. Justice Harlan's concern was whether petitioner's argument meant different rules for each section of the country, "or does your proposition go to all school cases no matter what part of the country?" Oberdorfer was also pursued concerning the order, Harlan asking what date Oberdorfer suggested. "We haven't been in the crucible of detail," he responded. Then Black asked, Are you in agreement with Greenberg that "the thing to say is that the dual system is over and that it is to go into effect *today* and it's not reason for delay . . . that things will not be perfect the first day, the thing to do is to go at it *now*?" When Oberdorfer said, "without knowing what 'now' is," Black responded, "when we issue an order," adding, after a slight pause, "if we do"—which produced much laughter. Black then asked whether there was reason to wait on future arguments about "deliberate speed," and Douglas threw in, "except that you would like to have us act with all deliberate speed." (Again laughter, and Oberdorfer replied, "Faster than that, your honor.") Justice Black also pressed Leonard on the need for HEW plans, wanting to know if they did more than delay and ending his interrogation with the remark, "Too many plans, not enough action." White asked whether the government's plans after the Court of Appeals' delay were different from the original plans and whether the government's witnesses disagreed with the original plans. The Chief Justice, trying to assure himself that the case would not delay plans further than the December 1 date granted by the Court of Appeals, asked whether revised plans would be submitted on that schedule. Yes, they would be and things would go ahead, Leonard responded. Leonard's plea "not to do something precipitous like the *pendente lite* idea" was promptly met with Black's question, "Would anything be precipitous in this field now with all the years that have gone by?" Continuing his pursuit, Black asked, "Are you arguing for perpetuation of the term 'with all deliberate speed'?" After Leonard said that was not the law and was "by the boards," Marshall tried to get him to recognize that the Court had already talked of a need for speed, directing his attention to *Cooper*. When Leonard said Little Rock was a different situation, Marshall called attention to each justice having signed his name to the opinion, "which is very seldom done," and then asking, "Wasn't that a slight warning?"

The Court's response to all the argument and questioning in *Alexander* was handed down only six days after argument in a brief but pointed two-page per curiam ruling which served further to underscore the Court's impatience and to remind people that, despite Jerris Leonard's claim that it was "only 18 months since *Green,*" the end of "all deliberate speed" was not a new idea in 1969. Saying that the issue in the case was "of paramount importance," the Court ruled that requests for delays in desegregation should have been denied and held that "continued operation of segregated schools under a standard of allowing 'all deliberate speed' for desegregation is no longer constitutionally permissible." All school districts had to abandon dual school systems "at once" and to operate "now and hereafter" unitary systems. Fully accepting petitioners' main contention—that desegregation pendente lite should be the rule—the Supreme Court gave the Court of Appeals authority to make determinations and enter orders with receiving further submissions or hearing more argument. The district court was to make no changes in those orders without a ruling from the Court of Appeals, which was to "retain jurisdiction to insure prompt and faithful compliance with its order."

Nothing could have been more definitive. More than fifteen years after *Brown I* and more than fourteen years after *Brown II*, immediate action "at once," not deliberate speed, was without question the order of the day. Nevertheless, it took a while for the idea to sink in, even in the Fifth Circuit, which had been so forward-looking earlier. *Alexander* was handed down during the third round in the *Singleton* litigation. The Fifth Circuit judges apparently "could not believe that the Supreme Court intended for them to issue orders that required the relocation of hundreds of thousands of school children in the middle of an on-going school year"[23] and allowed a two-step process for desegregation in that case. When that case was appealed to the Supreme Court in *Carter v. West*

Feliciana Parish School Board, the justices used a per curiam ruling, as they had in *Alexander,* to reverse the Court of Appeals. However, Justices Harlan and White, in a separate statement, spelled out what they thought *Alexander* meant. They suggested that when freedom-of-choice had not produced results, the burden in school desegregation cases shifted to the school board, with immediate relief available to the complainants; they thought that in those circumstances eight weeks was the maximum allowable time to bring about desegregation. Their statement in turn prompted Justices Black, Douglas, Brennan, and Marshall to append another statement in which they said that Harlan and White were retreating from *Alexander.* Chief Justice Burger and Justice White also wrote separately, saying they thought it unsound to reverse the Court of Appeals summarily. Two months later, in the *Northcross* case from Memphis, the Court issued another per curiam ruling directed to the Sixth Circuit. Here the justices held that the appeals court had been in error in holding *Alexander* not applicable and had improperly reversed the trial court's finding that a dual school system was still being operated. This time the Chief Justice concurred only in the result, feeling that the absence of two justices— Marshall did not participate and Fortas had left the Court—made it unwise to decide the case without at least expedited oral argument. He also indicated his impatience to spell out more clearly what was "stated, albeit perhaps too cryptically" in *Alexander* and to deal with alteration of school district zones and with busing in the context of remedies for segregated schools. It was also after these rulings, the standard follow-up to any major ruling—such as *Alexander* was, despite its quietness—that the Court was to move on to matters like school busing and interdistrict remedies, both in the South and the North. What *Alexander,* reinforced by *Carter,* had done was to give practical force to the doctrinal shift—the requirement that something affirmative be done—first seen in *Green.* It was only then that "massive integration" of the South could begin. The "revolution" which at times had seemed to operate with only a slow evolutionary pace, had finally come to fruition.[24]

4

After *Alexander* and *Carter,* one could take the position that much had been accomplished, even though it had taken considerable time. Doctrinally, in the substantive areas of education, public accommodations, public facilities, voting, and housing, the Court had done much even though in some instances the Court's important actions came after rather than before congressional action. Although Congress and the executive branch finally caught up with the Supreme Court, school segregation had

begun to end in much of the South after the mid-1960s, and the Court
had reinforced the work of its coordinate branches of government.

Twenty years after *Brown,* there was considerable desegregation of the
schools. Many of the last holdouts had fallen into line after either *Green* or
Alexander and *Carter.* In fact, desegregation had proceeded further in the
South than in the North, producing complaints from the South about
unequal treatment. HEW figures for 1972 showed that in the eleven
southern states, 46.3 percent of black elementary and secondary school
pupils—up from 40.3 percent in 1970—now attended schools that had
been majority white, whereas in thirty-two northern and western states
only 28.3 percent of blacks were in such schools in 1972, up only slightly
from 27.6 percent in two years. Similarly, only 8.7 percent of black pupils
were in formerly all-black schools in the South, whereas 10.9 percent of
black students in the North and West were in such schools. While such
statistics could be adduced to indicate the Court's success, at the same time
there were also negative signs. There were some places where virtually
nothing had happened after 1954,[25] particularly where districts had been
willing to give up federal funding, and in late 1973 a new suit alleging
systematic discrimination against blacks resulting in large numbers of
poor, all-black schools was filed in Topeka, the locus of the *Brown* litigation.[26] New methods apparently had been developed to relegate black
students to less desirable situations in school or to eliminate them from
schools altogether—the "pushout." Moreover, private school enrollment
had risen substantially, making the HEW statistics less significant because
of the fact that the private schools—especially in the South—remained
segregated. And in higher education, the Legal Defense Fund had initiated complex litigation against HEW in which the lower court ruled, in
what promised to be only the initial stages of the suit, that HEW had failed
to enforce compliance with Title VI of the 1964 Civil Rights Act and
ordered ten states to produce comprehensive plans for desegregating
their colleges and universities.[27] After the Nixon administration's not-so-
"benign neglect" and nonenforcement with respect to school desegregation and its rewriting of desegregation rules to make eligible a number of
large cities whose funds had earlier been cut off, it was no wonder that in
January 1975 the United States Commission on Civil Rights issued a
report which castigated HEW's Office of Civil Rights and other federal
agencies for failure to enforce existing laws and regulations.

Changing views of the Court's work seemed to supplement the administration's changed posture. Some persons who earlier had been supportive of the Court's action now felt the Court had gone as far as it should go.
For example, in 1970 Alexander Bickel argued that dismantling school
segregation had not created integrated schools, particularly in the North.
Black leaders there were trying to decentralize schools, "accepting their

racial character and attempting to bring them under community control,"[28] and were no longer pressing for integration, which was in any event nearly impossible to achieve. While Bickel was answered promptly,[29] his statement was representative of a considerable—and increasing—body of thinking.

A principal reason for executive inaction was that there was little pressure to do anything. Not only had some academic observers like Bickel changed their minds but public opinion about busing was negative, and "liberal" legislators from the suburbs had changed their positions. As desegregation had become a national, not a regional, issue, attitudes had shifted, and were fueled by questions about the effectiveness of education raised by findings that education plays little part in obtaining jobs and that racial mixing has little effect in improving the educational level.[30] That such findings were regularly and seriously questioned by other experts was almost immaterial; the findings fit the national mood and further reinforced it. The change in attitude could be seen most obviously in the ease with which antibusing legislation regularly passed the Congress, particularly the House of Representatives. This legislation produced little actual legal damage because it invariably included a provision allowing the courts to set aside the law or to interpret it in line with past Supreme Court rulings, but its symbolic effect was great. At a minimum, it showed clearly that one could not expect legislative support for school desegregation like the earlier congressional commitment to rights in the areas of public accommodations, voting, and housing. Thus, although the legal principle of desegregation was well established, as the nation's bicentennial came and passed one did not find substantial support in either the legislative or executive branches for further forward movement in dealing with desegregation where formal barriers had been set up or for developing and enforcing the necessary remedies for discrimination imposed over many long years.

More reexamination of the Court's race relations actions occurred on the twentieth anniversary of *Brown I.* Coming as they did at a time of growing new crises in school desegregation, many of the comments were not sanguine. Perhaps the best answer as to where we stood was provided by headlines like "20 Years of School Integration Won Much, But Much is Undone," or titles like "The Sound of One Hand Clapping," subtitled, "20 Years After Brown: Negro Progress and Black Rage."[31] Certainly the blacks' economic situation coupled with the failure of the promise of *Brown* and the inability of methods of nonviolent resistance to "overcome" discriminatory treatment had led to a hardening of position and increased anger. As former Solicitor General Cox summed it up:

Although accomplishment is all about us, there are stark reminders of the difficulty of translating law into practice. In Topeka, Kansas, home of the Brown family, gerrymandered school districts still preserve racial segregation. In Boston the School Committee has stalled, delayed and evaded legal obligations, and Boston's racists have almost won their fight to gut the State's racial imbalance law. There are Topekas and Bostons across the country. The gap between our professed ideals and the law has been closed, but there is now a wide gap between the law on the one hand and the realities of life on the other.[32]

As those who had participated in *Brown* or its aftermath looked back from the vantage point of 1974, they produced a wide range of views, running from positive responses to mixed evaluations to the position that *Brown* had become irrelevant to blacks' needs. One of the most positive evaluations came from former Justice Arthur Goldberg. He felt that *Brown* "had a profound impact as a constitutional signpost pointing toward the elimination of all kinds of legal barriers based on race" and that the case gave an indication that the Supreme Court would take a different, more positive approach to the constitutional issues coming before it in which fictions would be set aside to look at the patent realities underlying the rhetoric before the Court.[33] Certainly the decision served to increase the public awareness of the issue of civil rights.[34] Former NAACP attorney, now federal district judge, Constance Baker Motley, felt that *Brown* had "visibly" changed the national status of blacks, and that it served as "a second Emancipation Proclamation" by freeing blacks from inferiority feelings.[35] And Harvard law professor Derrick Bell said that *Brown* did "much of what it was intended to do" in terms of racially based dual school systems in the South, where it was intended to operate.[36] Perhaps the best summary statement, capturing the hope stimulated by the decision but also embodying recognition of goals not met, is also Bell's: "The Supreme Court's decision in *Brown v. Board of Education* was less a promise than an opportunity."[37] The Court had withdrawn approval of segregated schools, but did not guarantee school systems fully integrated on the basis of race.

The mixed nature of *Brown*'s effect, seen in Bell's statement, was also clear in the evaluation made by the United States Commission on Civil Rights. Where Bell had said that *Brown* had accomplished much, the commission instead emphasized "a conflicting picture of success and failure" which did not meet expectations of those who saw *Brown* as a "turning point in the racial life of the Nation."[38] The commission also talked of the "mixed feelings" many had about the decision "in spite of the progress which has been achieved" and noted the "small comfort" which those presently victimized by segregation could take from knowing that they might achieve parity in education with their neighbors over a space of several more generations, or from seeing progress when "significantly more benefits" had been achieved by others.[39] Part of the problem in the 1970s, noted by both Bell and the United States Commission on Civil Rights, was what we might call a shift in focus which had occurred as attempts were made to implement *Brown*. Bell argued that desegregation was seen as the most appropriate, if not the only, remedy for the constitutional evil of racially segregated schools. The strength and scope of resistance to desegregation was so great, he claimed, that compliance with *Brown* was measured in terms of the admission of black schoolchildren to previously all-white schools or the degree to which black and white children were "interspersed" in the same school. The result was that *Brown's* ultimate goal—equal educational opportunity—dropped out of sight.[40] Coming at the problem from a slightly different perspective, the United States Commission on Civil Rights noted that if equal educational opportunity were the goal to be achieved through desegregation, then many people, even some supportive of *Brown*, felt that desegregation had to be justified by improved educational attainment of school children in desegregated schools, particularly as reflected in test scores. Such feelings had displaced the issue from desegregation's "legal and moral grounds" to scientific research, although the commission insisted that the issue remained governed by the Constitution, not results.[41]

The passage of twenty years has also meant that many people who grew up in the crucible of desegregation in the 1950s and even the 1960s, for whom *Brown* was a living presence—even though not an implemented reality—are now older, with their children knowing of the case only as history which took place before they were born. As Ruby Martin argues, most blacks less than twenty-five years old "have no historical background, appreciation or understanding" of *Brown;* in a position not far from that of Lewis Steel noted earlier, she said that many believe that the case was initiated not by blacks but by whites attempting to keep their control over blacks.[42] Regardless of the force of this belief, other observers argue that, particularly for blacks in the central cities of our large metropolitan areas—rather than in rural areas in the South—the *Brown* ruling has "little practical relevance,"[43] particularly where the Supreme Court has now refused to allow inter-district desegregation remedies unless it can be shown that suburban school districts also discriminated, and has also refused to interfere with use of the property tax as the basis for school financing despite the fact that it produces substantial variation in the amount of money available for educational funding.[44] The psychological significance of *Brown* as a symbol has long since begun to wear away, so that, Motley argues, it now requires a "new rationale" cast in terms of segregation being bad "because the only way blacks can get an equal education is to go where the money is."[45] Perhaps more important with respect to *Brown's* relevance is that, perhaps out of desperation, blacks in central cities have shifted their focus to obtaining political and economic power, something seen as more important in terms of controling their fate than is school busing. The efforts to extend *Brown* to the large urban areas of the nation without altering its thrust to take into account the changed circumstances in which its application is asked, means, Bell has said, that its impact has been weakened because barriers to desegregation are "for all practical purposes . . . virtually insurmountable."[46]

The desegregation controversy still exists, burning brightly in communities, large and small; judicial action is still taken, as judges throughout the country try to deal with affirmative action programs and new questions posed about segregation both de jure and de facto; but the national emotive force has gone out of the activity. Thus, we stand looking backward at recent history. The story of the Court's strategies regarding the development of a legal principle is virtually complete.

THE WIDE VARIETY OF STRATEGIES employed by the Court during the fifteen years from *Brown I* through *Alexander v. Holmes County* gives rise to some general observations about those strategies. The Court was certainly engaged in politics, if engaging in politics means dealing with important political issues and attempting to achieve large societal results. It seems clear that the justices were not simply confining their work to the adjudication of the competing equities of the particular adversary parties before the Court in any given case. That is hardly surprising, for the Court which sits at the apex of the national court system, and, indeed, of the system created by all the courts in this nation's federal governmental structure, has become increasingly a "constitutional court." Yet what we find is that in the exercise of its strategies the Court seemed more effective the more it acted like a conventional court and the less it painted in broad-brush strokes which its opponents might claim were those of a legislative body. That is, the Court generally was most effective when it confined itself to the issues presented in a case, rendered "exact justice" to the parties, issued full reasoned opinions, and the like. There were, however, strategies not judicially conventional but which nevertheless seemed appropriate—like "salami-slicing" incremental movement and the "hit 'em where they ain't" approach of the gifts-of-land cases. Such strategies, which we think were most effective, or the suggested alternatives we think would have been more effective for the Court, are ways of turning a revolution into an evolution, of turning a large dispute into a series of smaller disputes by judicial management. As such, they are appropriate to a Court faced with constitutional problems having a large social impact. Having made these general observations, we now turn to a review of strategies the Court used as it worked toward its goal of desegregation.

Selecting Cases. A considerable amount of the Court's strategy revolved around the selection of cases, although that selectivity varied considerably between areas. The Court took almost all the cases in some areas—for example, public accommodations—but it also took almost none in others, such as lower education after *Brown II* or voting rights after the *Smith v. Allwright* white primary case. The choice of cases within policy areas particularly occupied the Court's attention. Such single-case selectivity allowed the Court to weed out cases with peripheral issues and to choose narrower cases over broader ones. This strategy, which also provided a fuller record and more background for later cases, made it easier to handle the more difficult later cases if the right first case had been chosen. Thus after avoiding protest cases which had elements of disruption the Court upheld peaceful protest, and only then went on to deal with more difficult situations.

Much of the Court's selectivity was related to the grounds raised in a case. Presumably, if a constitutional question was baldly or frontally presented, the Court could only have accepted it knowing that the constitutional question would have to be decided. Yet even here the Court had choice. In many cases, alternative grounds of decision were available because lawyers presented a large "à la carte menu." This made it possible for the Court to accept many public accommodations cases, even knowing—at least after the first few—that the broad constitutional question of the right to discriminate was going to be presented and to resolve them short of the basic constitutional question. However, there were times when having accepted a case perhaps thinking there was a limited nonconstitutional escape at least potentially available, the Court found after briefs and oral argument that it was not so. However, the Court, particularly in the public accommodations area, demonstrated how it could avoid deciding issues although it did not delay deciding cases. Such action was facilitated when one party argued procedural matters while the other concentrated on substantive issues. This was true both because procedure provides an escape from substantive issues and because for the Court to go outside the record to decide a case on procedural grounds is considered more acceptable, or at least less unacceptable, than for it to do so with respect to doctrinal matters. The Court's ability to shift a case brought on appeal to the certiorari category, then to grant review limited to only certain questions, expanded its options even further.

The largely judge-made nature of the rules on such matters as standing and justiciability, used in the relatively expansive reading of standing in such cases as *Barrows v. Jackson,* the suit for damages for sale to a Negro in violation of a restrictive covenant, *Evers v. Dwyer,* a Negro boarding a bus to initiate a suit, and the anti-NAACP cases, in which an organization was allowed to assert its members' rights, also provided the Court with much strategic flexibility in controlling the arguments made to it by controlling who brought cases to the Court. The Court also used its residual control of amicus participation at the brief-submitting stage and full control over amicus participation at oral argument to assist in controlling the grounds presented to it by controlling who argued cases. Such choice is important because the positions raised by lawyers, although often diverse, can constrain the Court if the positions do come close together. In fact, lawyers have effectively removed important aspects of a case from the judges' realm of decision by agreeing on them, as they did with respect to the negative effect of shifting children from school to school as facilities shifted between equal and being unequal. However, the justices sometimes appreciated being constrained, and used lawyers' arguments as an excuse for not reaching certain broader questions they might have otherwise preferred to avoid. The onus of making a decision was removed if the parties were relatively close together, as Chief Justice Burger thought they were in *Alexander v. Holmes County.*

When the justices wished to avoid the problem of lawyers' forcing the Court to a particular position they used another strategic move: the grouping of cases for hearing and decision. Although this had a drawback—it made the use of procedural escapes less available because the Court's disposition of several cases on technical grounds at the same time would have raised far more questions than its doing so with a single case—the grouping of cases provided the Court with both a more fully amplified set of facts and a more complete range of strategic options. Although not used often because of the Court's basic tendency to hear only single cases, such grouping assured the justices that the cases being argued were not unique and allowed the Court to draw particular attention to the broad policy implication of the issue being litigated. As to the former point, the implementation order in *Brown* might have been quite different had the Court heard that case alone because of Kansas counsel's position that the consequences of desegregation would not be serious— clearly not the situation in the Deep South. Another use of the coupling of cases was evident with *Heart of Atlanta Motel v. United States* and *Katzenbach v. McClung* on Title II of the Civil Rights Act of 1964. With the two decided together, an easy case—*Heart of Atlanta*—paved the way for resolution of a harder one—*McClung.*

The selection of individual cases and the grouping of cases did not always provide the Court with what it wanted. Certiorari petitions contained far less than the later briefs; oral argument revealed still more unanticipated ramifications. This sometimes led the justices to go outside the boundaries established by the parties' arguments. However, only rarely did the Court go outside the record, because dissenters quickly met such action with the claim it was improper. Except for the more-than-century-old *Dred Scott* decision, none of the cases cited by Murphy in which the Court went outside the record were race relations cases.[47] In the first *Evans* park case, the Court seemed to go outside the record for certain facts in order to avoid a broader question, but the Court was not really going beyond the parties, who had added to the record in their argument. A similar situation occurred in the *Boynton* case, in which the statutory issue, not raised in the certiorari petition, was argued by Thurgood Marshall. However, the fact that the matter of the bus terminal's ownership was not formally before the Court gave the justices much trouble, an indication of their preference for staying within the "four corners" of the record. Of course, the grouping of cases can substantially expand the record—as was evident at the outset in *Brown I*.

The effects of selectivity before a major ruling may be different from selectivity later in a line of cases. When the Court was not pushed hard to decide a particular issue, turning away cases was not costly for it. However, after basic doctrine had been set forth the Court had to change its task to that of reinforcing its position. Granting or not granting review at that point thus had potentially many more implications. Turning away cases served as one form of reinforcement because granting certiorari soon after a major ruling could leave the impression that the principal issue had not been settled. However, where the Court's initial statement had been ambiguous or was met with evasion or resistance, the Court was almost required to take cases to clarify the law or to strike down opposition before it increased. A strategy to be posited from these observations is for the Court to take at least a few cases where lower court rulings at least sustained the Court's position or were neutral.

Deference and Delay. Closely related to selectivity, because it served to reduce the number of cases coming to the Supreme Court as well as the number decided on the merits, was the Court's strategy of showing deference to lower court judges. This deference could be seen in the Court's allowing state judges to work out matters like segregation of courthouses for themselves and included following lower courts' findings of facts, adopting their constructions of statutes—although the Court was not willing to have lower federal courts automatically extend such deference and therefore produce delay—and following state courts' reasoning where possible. The Supreme Court's greater deference to state than to federal judges could be seen in the justices' tendency to be more specific in telling federal courts how to take care of unanswered matters. With state courts, the justices, following what they thought were sound principles of federalism, left the choice of procedure for performing required tasks more to state judges. When deference simply meant that the issue appeared later, all that was gained was delay, because "repeater" cases interfered with lowering the docket level.

Even when deference did not produce action consonant with the Supreme Court's goals, "going the extra mile" with the state judges often seemed required to avert either defiance of the Supreme Court's rulings or day-to-day friction between federal and state judiciaries, for example, over the question of removal of civil rights cases to the federal courts. The *Georgia v. Rachel* and *City of Greenwood v. Peacock* rulings on that subject show that the Court was able to serve multiple ends through a single ruling: by construing the right of removal narrowly, the Court not only avoided friction with the states but also assisted in docket-management by avoiding a barrage of federal court cases. Yet whether the Court's forbearance was productive in its race relations cases is not at all clear. In the area of school desegregation, leaving matters in the hands of the lower courts did not produce compliance, particularly beyond the Border States and the rim of the South. The costs of forbearance were also evident in the remand of the *Bell* sit-in case, where convictions were upheld. That case tells us that if the Court wants something done, even strong suggestions or hints about the outcome are not always enough; direct follow-up action must occur when lower courts are hard of hearing.

The justices' deference to their federal brethren, great at the beginning even when those courts did not move very fast—for example, when the Supreme Court early accepted the Fourth Circuit's exhaustion of remedies doctrine—evaporated as time went by, and the Supreme Court moved quite quickly even when it had to reverse lower federal courts to get them to respond to the increased tempo to which the Supreme Court had been pointing. Where the lower courts handed down strong decisions, the Court was less likely to intervene. Although this meant that some decisions were handed down which were more advanced than what the Supreme Court would have announced directly, deference here allowed the lower courts to move the law ahead more or less incrementally and in effect to do the Supreme Court's work by creating a base on which the Supreme Court itself could build or which it could approve rather than having to break new ground by itself. For example, in the area of de facto segregation, which the Court seemed particularly anxious to avoid, the effective rule was that lower courts could move ahead if they wanted to, but the Court would not prod those courts which would not upset segregation of this variety.

The Court's desire to draw on the actions of others was particularly noticeable with respect to congressional activity, utilized as soon as it was available—for example, in the voting rights area in which federal government authority provided under the 1957 and 1960 Civil Rights Acts was promptly reinforced. The Court's staying away from broad constitutional questions in the 1963 Term sit-in cases can be explained in terms of the concurrent congressional consideration of public accommodations laws, an interpretation reinforced by the swiftness with which the Court upheld those laws, cutting through procedural escapes urged by both parties in *Katzenbach v. McClung* and applying the doctrine of abatement to pre-act sit-in prosecutions in *Hamm v. City of Rock Hill*.

Executive aloofness after *Brown* created substantial strategic problems for the Court because it deprived the justices of action toward which to be deferential. The executive branch's continued lack of support may help explain why the Supreme Court generally stayed away from the lower education area after *Brown II,* at least until some affirmative help was available during the Kennedy administration. In housing, FHA unwillingness to act can similarly explain the Court's avoidance of early cases. When the executive branch did appear in support of a civil rights claim, the Court attempted to enlist its further support through its decisions in that direction, as in the *Watson* Memphis parks case.

While deference was at times productive and seemed advantageous, delay was an important result of the Court's reacting to its strategic environment. The Court seemed to delay reaching whole areas of race relations law—cemeteries, mixed marriages, gifts of land—and as well to delay reaching issues within other areas and to delay decisions in individual cases. The latter was a temporary, relatively short-term matter in most instances, whereas the former was far more serious. Some delay was certainly necessary, however. Not all issues could be dealt with the instant they first appeared. The Court's own rules also required that some cases be dismissed no matter how much the justices might have wanted to hear them. The Court's general rules as to how it should operate as a court—its rules on standing and justiciability and the *Ashwander* rules counseling restraint in not deciding issues "in advance of necessity"—also had the same effect. However, delay also had some virtue, as, for instance, when it served to permit several cases to arise before one of them was accepted for review. This enabled issues to mature before the Court had to deal with them. The Court's allowing some time to pass gave greater force to a decision; when the Court did not "jump in with both feet" at the time an issue was first raised, the public became aware that the matter being dealt with was of more significance because it had manifested itself a number of times. Likewise, the Court's delay for a more nearly unanimous vote to resolve dissension within the Court may also have been helpful. The Court found that waiting could produce a less hostile atmosphere for the reception of its opinion—something most obvious with the miscegenation ruling, which did not come until at least ten years after the issue was initially raised.

However, delay was often dysfunctional. For example, the use of a particular ground for deciding a case in order to avoid ones perceived as more complicated made getting back to the latter grounds increasingly difficult. This was true both with the Fifteenth Amendment in the voting cases and the constitutional questions in the transportation cases. When, having opened up an issue, the Court seemed unwilling to get in further, perhaps because the justices were unclear where the course of litigation would take them, the result was often to leave untouched decisions adverse to the intended beneficiaries of the initial ruling. This created more damage than if the Court had left the area untouched initially both because it seemed to give greater legitimacy to the negative rulings and to show the Court's unwillingness to follow up on its initial commitments—thus encouraging disobedience of its will.

Incremental Action. Many of the Court's strategies centered on how to dispose of a case. Whatever the means used, the Court generally moved incrementally, whether through marginal adjustments in doctrine in those cases decided with opinion or through other mechanisms such as summary judgments or refusals to review. One might not unnaturally tend to think of incrementalism as building upward or forward. There is, however, no necessary straight-line forward progression. Incrementalism includes movement both forward and back. Once it has started down a certain road, the Supreme Court has not always moved inexorably forward toward a stipulated goal. There has been wavering, perhaps necessary to hold the Court together, an indication of the relationship between internal and external strategies. For example, while the Court was generally protective of the NAACP when the South started belaboring the organization, there was wavering when the Court allowed cases to go back to the lower courts for construction of statutes which appeared unconstitutional, at least to some justices. There was also some serious retrogression, as in the older white primary cases, when the Court upheld the discriminatory action of the Texas Democratic party in *Grovey v. Townsend,* and in the second Macon park case affirming Georgia court enforcement of the reverter clause in Senator Bacon's will, as well as the Court's acceptance of a separate, poor law school in Oklahoma after seeming to order "admission now" in the *Sipuel* litigation.

Yet despite these examples most of the Court's movement could be construed as progress. In fact, the problem was more often that the Court did not move far enough forward, not that it did not move forward—as, for example, in not using *Morgan* and *Henderson* to deal with *Plessy* in the transportation field. Even when the Court had not decided a case in a particular area for a long time, when it moved forward the Court did not always take a large step forward, although the long time since the earlier rulings probably had increased the possibility for larger change. But there were major "breakthroughs" which seemed to be more than merely incremental. *Brown* was seen as one by many people, although we must remember it did not produce a direct overruling of *Plessy.* The "freedom-of-choice" cases and *Alexander,* with their demands for affirmative public action and for immediacy, can also be seen as major "jumps," although they certainly built on action which had been taking place both in the lower courts and in the legislative and executive branches. Perhaps the reason the Court did not engage in more nonincremental moves is that the justices were aware of the negative reaction to such decision-making. Certainly the shock at the reaction to *Brown*—and to decisions in other areas such as internal security—may have scared the justices off from the forceful follow-up which seemed necessary. *Cooper v. Aaron* was, of course, an exception. After the reapportionment rulings and Frankfurter's departure from the Court, the justices began to move away from incremental decisions toward stronger constitutional rulings, at least in some fields, but less so in the race relations policy area.

Summary Disposition. Summary disposition was one major technique used to dispose of cases, a strategy with mutiple uses usually dictated by the strategic environment. Thus when lower courts looked for guidance in a murky area, a summary decision by the Supreme Court seemed to be a "cop-out," a procrastinating device. As Justice Brennan recently remarked, such action "offers only the most obscure guidance," in which the judges "have deliberately and effectively obscured the rationale underlying the decision. It comes as no surprise that judicial attempts to follow our lead conscientiously have often ended in hopeless confusion."[48] However, when lower courts "needled" the Supreme Court by sending up cases for the Court to reconsider, summary actions—particularly affirmances—were the best "off-putting" strategy to discourage such lower court action. Summary disposition may have been necessary in any event once the Court accepted a large number of cases in a particular policy area. Certainly not all cases could have been given full signed opinions, and many may not have needed such treatment if the issues raised were clear and had previously been dealt with by the Court. Yet once the Court saw fit to take the case, some action was necessary, and summary disposition was a good way out. This was particularly true when a change in factual or legal circumstances had occurred after the lower court decision but prior to review or final determination by the Supreme Court. This tactic was reinforced by the consideration of comity if state action was involved.[49]

The Court at times created strategic problems for itself when it sent a case back to the lower court for final action. Lower courts defied the Supreme Court or evaded the Court's clear intention underlying remand by reaffirming convictions or otherwise arriving at the same position by some other doctrinal means or by the use of procedure. Sometimes this occurred because in trying to determine the law, the Court paid inadequate attention to the case's formal disposition, important not only with respect to summary actions but also for cases decided with opinion.[50] When cases involving evasion or defiance came back to the Court as "repeaters," as happened not infrequently after initial summary dispositions but at other times as well, the Court was faced with the difficult alternatives of adding to its case load or allowing defiance, even if through the low-visibility mechanism of denying review. If the Court allowed such "repeater" cases to stand untouched, it damaged its image and the thrust of its policy. However, where the Court had initally vacated and remanded a case to show deference to the lower courts, its direct action when the case showed up again was criticized less than if the justices had intervened the first time they had the case.

Yet one must recognize that where the will to resist was great, almost any Supreme Court action would have resulted in repeater cases; for example, it was in large measure the persistence of those unwilling to comply that produced the extended *NAACP v. Alabama* litigation. The reappearance of that case was not for the Court's lack of trying to get the state to move from its adamant position. However, when initial rulings were ambiguous or weak, the Court perhaps could be blamed for poor strategy, at least in docket-management terms. Yet, even here, "repeaters" provided one of the most important ways for the Court to know what is going on—for example, that school desegregation was not going to be settled easily at the district court level.

Summary dispositions did provide a useful reinforcement tool for the Court, fitting somewhere along a continuum from denial of review to full-opinion treatment. In this connection, per curiam rulings had a way of serving to reinforce earlier doctrine by suggesting that the Court thought the matter clear and that the topic should be closed. *Alexander v. Holmes County* is one such example of this use of the device. However, per curiams announcing doctrine attracted less attention than signed opinions, were less strong than full opinion rulings, and provided less of a basis for future action. As a recent national commission stated, "A dismissal or summary affirmance with bare recitation of result and without citation cannot be considered the equivalent of plenary disposition for purposes of providing an adequate body of precedents on recurring issues of national law."[51] As Justice Rehnquist recently remarked, summary affirmances "are not of the same precedent value as would be an opinion of this Court reaching the question on the merits."[52] Even if the Court does mean a summary action to be less than a full opinion ruling, it must still be prepared to accept the responsibility for even a per curiam decision when the media report that "the Supreme Court decided that . . ." and most people focus on what the Court did—on its result. In addition, if the Court was serious about getting its message across—for example, about the need to increase the pace of desegregation—transmitting messages in such lower visibility decisions was not the most effective strategy even if those decisions reinforced earlier action. Reinforcement could be better achieved through alternative methods such as strong language in the Court's opinions or the sweeping away of any "pains or penalties" imposed on those availing themselves of Court-declared rights—as with damage suits after the Court had said in *Shelley* that restrictive covenants could not be enforced by the courts. Speed in reaching a decision and special ways to give particular prominence to a case were other methods of reinforcement. A range of devices was used in a single case to bring about enforcement, but only in truly extraordinary situations such as Little Rock because the Court could not afford to use all its weapons all the time or it would have exhausted itself and its good will.

Broader Options. Summary decisions by the Court can be said to be narrow dispositions of cases. There are, of course, a variety of broader options available, although there are a number of different meanings for breadth and narrowness with respect to the Court's rulings. There have been a variety of reasons why the Court has issued broader or narrower rulings. One is that a broader opinion—at least one less tightly written—attracts more votes. Yet if by broader we mean "more encompassing doctrine," precisely the opposite may apply: a narrower ruling could attract more votes. Deciding a case on broader grounds meant that more precedents were available to the Court. Similarly, by not focusing its rulings on race, the Court had far more upon which it could draw. Furthermore, a case decided on broad grounds, particularly if not restricted to race, would be more broadly applicable to other situations, as with the anti-NAACP rulings, applicable to many organizations, or the demonstration cases. Similarly, the "Shufflin' Sam" Thompson case, although narrow in relation to what parties were seeking in the public accommodations area, produced the widely used "lack of evidence" test. By using "neutral principles" or grounds which were less race-specific, the Court obtained greater acceptance for its decisions. Broad rulings were also useful—and perhaps necessary—for docket-management purposes. The abatement ruling in *Hamm* can be seen as an alternative to having remanded the cases for consideration of the question of coverage under the 1964 Civil Rights Act and as a way of avoiding rulings—then or in the future—on the basic constitutional question avoided by the Court for so long. In the anti-NAACP cases, the Court may have realized that if it were not going to deal with matters directly, and if the executive branch were not going to provide much help in enforcing the Court's past rules, it had to facilitate "private attorneys general" in their efforts, at least by removing obstacles in their path.

Narrow rulings were used as a delaying tactic and were related to docket-management in clearing away the underbrush before or as prep-

aration for an unmistakeable direct attack on a particular practice. More
fundamentally, they were issued to avoid broad repercussions. After the
earlier resistance to the broad ruling in *Brown I,* the Court turned to
narrower rulings in the public accommodations area until Congress
acted. Or a narrow ruling was found necessary to fit in with the Court's
overall "profile" in the policy area. The scope of rulings was made to fit
with the position achieved by accepting only a few cases for review, as in
the lower education area after *Brown.* Thus the *Goss* ruling, one of the first
handed down on methods of desegregation, was basically limited to the
question of one-way transfers. Even *Griffin,* while ending the central
aspect of one of the singularly most noncompliant school districts in the
country, was narrow in being restricted to partial school closings.

The Court's Language. When the Court moved away from summary
dispositions and handed down decisions with opinions, whether signed or
per curiam, the Court's language—or rhetoric—came to be of particular
importance. Here it is crucial to remember that, as Rohde points out, "It is
in the majority opinion, rather than in the decision coalition, that the
Supreme Court makes policy" and, more important, "The major role of
the Supreme Court in the American political system is not merely to
guard against errors by lower courts, but to articulate general constitutional and legal principles."[53] Rhetoric has been important not only for
developing the substance of policy but for docket-management as well.
The narrower the grounds the Court used in reaching a result, the more
likely other cases were to come to the Court; the fewer the issues resolved
out of those presented in a given case, the more likely there was to be
further litigation. If a case was settled "on its facts," it had little if any
precedential value, meaning that other cases with different fact
situations—that is, virtually all others—would be brought to the Court to
be screened out. If a statute was interpreted instead of a constitutional
issue reached, the latter would still be present, and a ruling on it was quite
likely to be sought before people would be satisfied that the highest court
in the land had done its full duty. Thus how the Court wrote was clearly
relevant for the administrative task of docket-management. If the Court
used its opinions in aid of managing its docket, it needed broader rather
than narrower grounds. The intentional or unintentional clarity or ambiguity of the Court's language was also important. Ambiguity meant that
people had difficulty applying the case to the situations facing them, and
the ruling resulted in a "stretch-out" of compliance. More litigation resulted also, although that was perhaps not to the Court's disadvantage if it
wanted to monitor and control an area of policy. The problems are,
however, made clear in Jack Greenberg's remark, at oral argument in
Alexander, about white school officials using not only the "fancied ambiguities" but also the plan ambiguities in the Court's opinions to resist

desegregation. Those who resisted obeying would in any event imagine there were ambiguities in what was clear to everyone else, and then obviously exploit any real ambiguities the Court's opinions contained.

In choosing the rhetoric to use, the Court continuously had to be aware of its multiple audiences and their expectations that they hear law from the Court—that the Court not act "legislatively" or sound as if it were doing so. This meant the Court had to carry on its important educational tasks quietly rather than "at the top of its voice." Whereas the Court had to act within the constraints imposed by people's expectations, it still had considerable freedom. The justices could talk directly to particular audiences and to their interests, as they may have been doing in addressing white sellers of property in the housing convenant cases. State officials were pacified through language about the state's police powers and states' rights. Certain words rather than others were used. Instead of "integration," one talked of disestablishing dual school systems. All such language indicates again the deference the Court showed to its audiences. However, the Court was able to be firm, as in the Little Rock case, which contained strong warnings to state officials not to disobey *Brown,* or in *Lane v. Wilson,* which warned against "sophisticated as well as unsophisticated" methods of disenfranchisement. Warnings could also be directed at those seeking their civil rights, as Justice Goldberg did in the demonstration cases in telling the demonstrators about the limits of acceptable conduct.

Of particular importance in the race relations cases was the inclusion of historical arguments and material from the social sciences. Use of the latter was generally not a wise strategy, because of the lack of acceptance of social science evidence—at least at an explicit level—in this country and the feeling that the Court ought to be "talking law," not relying on what Senator Fulbright once called the "socialistic sciences." The use of history by the justices was more problematic. In its favor is the idea that while the United States is in many respects a nontraditional—or antitraditional— nation, its people respect continuity with the past and at least like to see the past invoked as justification for what they are now doing so that action does not seem too "radical." On the other hand, history written for use in litigation—"law-office history"—has seemed to be "forced," even to some of those who helped prepare it, and a prostitution of history's intended purposes. People get distressed when the Court seems to want to turn to history and then does not utilize it, as in *Brown.* There may not have been "abuse" of history in *Brown,* as it is not clear what the Fourteenth Amendment's framers meant to do, if indeed one can ever make such a determination. However, if a justice stretched history to fit his own preconceived goals, as Miller has argued Goldberg did in *Bell,* then history—and presumably the Court—got a bad name. This was particularly true when historical material was used in such a way that it did not add to a justice's opinion, and the more so when the historical record was plain and the historical argument was central to the justice's argument. And because "history . . . belongs to the public memory," ensuing arguments over it, unlike those over a narrow legal point, are not merely of interest to lawyers and scholars. Thus, Miller asserts, history's "use and misuse affects the political values of the nation."[54]

The Court's use of history was not matched by its explicit attention to race. The racial element of many of the cases, despite its centrality in fact, was often played down by the Court. The justices did this very early, ignoring *Cumming*'s racial discrimination elements and claiming, over Justice Harlan's dissent in *Plessy,* that separateness was only inferiority if the Negro wanted to see it that way. The Court also avoided the race issue in the public accommodations cases, in the protest cases, in the anti-NAACP cases, and elsewhere as well. It did so even when explicitly racial language was before the Court.[55] To be sure, there were times when the Court did poke beneath the surface, despite its general disinclination to examine motives. The justices wanted to know what had led to the resistance in Little Rock, and commented on it directly in their opinion. In *Griffin,* there was questioning as to the real reason for the plan for separate schools. Justice Marshall pressed counsel hard in the freedom-of-choice cases as to the racial basis of the free-choice plans, despite the individualistic rhetoric in which they had been wrapped. And, of course, in *Brown* itself, the "pivotal point" in the area of race relations, the subject was faced directly and openly. There would be disadvantages if the Court were to talk openly about race. Not only would the scope of the Court's opinions be limited to other racially related situations, but the racial fears of the racially fearful would be heightened. Although that might happen anyway—that is, indirection might have produced the same result—we cannot be sure. Yet not talking of race clearly has drawbacks, particularly if the Supreme Court is to act at least somewhat as a court. Failure to be "open" about the subject exposed the Court to the criticism that it was engaging in "legalistic reasoning" that showed its "distaste" for the whole subject of race relations.[56] More important, if we are already, in the language of the Kerner Commission, two nations—not merely in attitudes, but in terms of citizenship[57]—we probably cannot achieve racial peace without recognition of what is at stake; here the Court's role in spelling out the racial problem is crucial. Were the Court to speak more openly of the racial basis of the cases before it, instead of heightening tension the Court might lessen "rather than mirroring or exacerbating the nation's moral overstrain."[58]

Examination of the United States Supreme Court's handling of a particular area of policy over a period of more than two decades has allowed us to identify and to call attention to the types of strategies which the Court may use—and which we think it did use in dealing with race relations from *Brown* through *Alexander*. To what extent the Court's strategy-related behavior seen in this area of central constitutional significance would be repeated in other areas—obscenity, church-state relations, criminal procedure, interstate commerce, regulation by administrative agencies—is unclear. The same Supreme Court which behaved strategically with respect to constitutional litigation might act differently in other issue areas, for example, with respect to traditional matters such as taxes, patents, and admiralty law. Although in some lines of nonconstitutional Supreme Court decision-making such as employee injury (FELA) cases, one might find a result-orientation and the use of strategy,[59] in most business fields, the Court, adopting a perspective quite different from the set of attitudes with which it views constitutional litigation, has essentially been an "umpire" between the courts of appeals rather than an expounder of the Constitution and has tended for the most part to behave like any other appellate court, disposing of ordinary litigation rather routinely. Such traditional behavior with respect to nonconstitutional cases has formed an important element of the background for the Court's work in the constitutional area and indeed, some say, has imparted a more balanced perspective than if the Court dealt only with constitutional issues—which have become an increasing proportion of the Court's work in the second half of the twentieth century. Yet even if we are in error as to the differences between constitutional and nonconstitutional litigation— which in fact at times intersect—the study of the development of the Court's strategy on a constitutional issue such as desegregation extending over a definable time period can still help illuminate the general behavior of the Supreme Court. This volume should indicate the range of strategies available to the Court and what it is capable of doing, even though the Court might tend to exercise that capability most fully only with respect to constitutional issue-areas such as desegregation.

Notes
Table of Cases Cited
Indes

Notes

Preface

1. We fully agree with S. Sidney Ulmer: "Concern over the Supreme Court's myth is . . . totally out of place among the principles that should guide the scholarly enterprise."— "Bricolage and Assorted Thoughts on Working in the Papers of Supreme Court Justices," *Journal of Politics* 35 (May 1973): 301. Recently one of the justices himself joined the effort to dispel a number of myths about the Court—concerning the judges' "vacations," their workload, law clerks' influence, and five-to-four decisions. See Lewis F. Powell, Jr., "Myths and Misconceptions about the Supreme Court," *American Bar Association Journal* 61 (November 1975): 1344–47.
2. For treatment of that subject, see Daniel Berman, *It Is So Ordered* (New York: W. W. Norton, 1966) or Richard Kluger, *Simple Justice: The History of* Brown v. Board of Education *and Black America's Struggle for Equality* (New York: Knopf, 1976). See also Clement Vose, *Caucasians Only: The Supreme Court, the NAACP, and the Restrictive Covenant Cases* (Berkeley: University of California Press, 1959).
3. Jonathan Casper, *Lawyers before the Warren Court: Civil Liberties and Civil Rights, 1957–66* (Urbana: University of Illinois Press, 1972).
4. Hans Linde, "Judges, Critics, and the Realist Tradition," *Yale Law Journal* 82 (December 1972): 230.
5. Ibid., p. 232.
6. Walter F. Murphy, *Elements of Judicial Strategy* (Chicago: University of Chicago Press, 1964), p. 4.
7. David W. Rohde, "Policy Goals and Opinion Coalitions in the Supreme Court," *Midwest Journal of Political Science* 16 (May 1972): 208–24. See also David W. Rohde and Harold J. Spaeth, *Supreme Court Decision Making* (San Francisco: W. H. Freeman, 1976).
8. Martin Shapiro, *Law and Politics in the Supreme Court* (New York: Free Press, 1964), reviewed by Anthony A. D'Amato, *California Law Review* 53 (1965): 713–19; Arthur S. Miller, "On the Need for 'Impact Analysis' of Supreme Court Decisions," *Georgetown Law Journal* 53 (1965): 365–401.
9. Jack Greenberg, "The Supreme Court, Civil Rights, and Civil Dissonance," *Yale Law Journal* 77 (1968): 1520–44. Although his approach is somewhat different, also relevant is the study by Joel B. Grossman, "A Model for Judicial Policy Analysis: The Supreme Court and the Sit-In Cases," *Frontiers of Judicial Research,* ed. Joel B. Grossman and Joseph Tanenhaus (New York: John Wiley, 1969), pp. 405–60. Some early and important generalizations regarding strategic options in a nonjudicial context can be found in Roger Fisher, "Slicing Up the Cuban Problem," *New Republic,* June 15, 1963, pp. 13–15. See also Roger Fisher, *International Conflict for Beginners* (New York: Harper and Row, 1969).
10. On the former, see Frederick Wirt, *The Politics of Southern Equality* (Chicago: Aldine, 1970) and Robert Crain et al., *The Politics of School Desegregation* (Garden City: Doubleday 1969); on impact, see Stephen L. Wasby, *The Impact of the United States Supreme Court: Some Perspectives* (Homewood, Ill.: Dorsey Press, 1970) and Theodore Becker and

429

Malcolm Feeley, eds., *The Impact of Supreme Court Decisions: Empirical Studies,* 2d ed. (New York: Oxford University Press, 1973).

11. For an excellent collection of materials, see Joel B. Grossman and Mary H. Grossman, eds., *Law and Change in Modern America* (Pacific Palisades, Calif.: Goodyear Publishing Co., 1971).

12. For the best overview of research on the Supreme Court, see Walter F. Murphy and Joseph Tanenhaus, *The Study of Public Law* (New York: Random House, 1972). Samples of the judicial behavior literature can be found in two collections edited by Glendon Schubert: *Judicial Behavior: A Reader in Theory and Research* (Chicago: Rand McNally, 1964) and *Judicial Decision-Making* (New York: Free Press, 1963). Another collection of materials, illustrative of a variety of approaches, is Thomas Jahnige and Sheldon Goldman, eds., *The Federal Judicial System* (New York: Holt, Rinehart, and Winston, 1968).

13. Arthur Larson, "The New Law of Race Relations," *Wisconsin Law Review* 1969: 471.

14. See Charles A. Miller, "Constitutional Law and the Rhetoric of Race," *Perspectives in American History,* ed. Donald Fleming and Bernard Bailyn (Cambridge: Harvard University Press, 1971), 5: 197–98.

15. Quoted by J. Woodford Howard, "The Fluidity of Judicial Choice," *American Political Science Review* 62 (March 1968): 53.

16. See Berman, *It Is So Ordered;* Kluger, *Simple Justice;* and Albert P. Blaustein and Clarence Clyde Ferguson, Jr., *Desegregation and the Law: The Meaning and Effect of the School Segregation Cases* (New Brunswick, N.J.: Rutgers University Press, 1957).

17. There are a number of volumes providing extended historical treatment. These include Loren Miller, *The Petitioners: The Story of the Supreme Court of the United States and the Negro* (Cleveland: World Publishing Co., 1966); Benjamin Muse, *Ten Years of Prelude: The Story of Integration Since the Supreme Court's 1954 Decision* (New York: Viking Press, 1964); and Reed Sarratt, *The Ordeal of Desegregation: The First Decade* (New York: Harper and Row, 1966).

18. "To define the more general social ends sought through law, the ranking of such values, and the functional . . . relations of law to other social institutions often requires that we look for trends or patterns that are not openly declared. Important dimensions of social existence become visible and to some extent measurable only when we look at the sequence and the context of events—when we look at events in time, that is, historically."—James Willard Hurst, "Legal Elements in United States History," *Perspectives in American History,* ed. Donald Fleming and Bernard Bailyn, 5: 38.

19. For a fuller exploration of the functions and problems in the use of oral argument as a data base, see Stephen L. Wasby, Anthony A. D'Amato, and Rosemary Metrailer, "Oral Argument in the Supreme Court: Its Functions and Use as a Data Base" (Paper presented to meetings of the Southern Speech Association, Tallahassee, Florida, April 1975) and "The Functions of Oral Argument in the U.S. Supreme Court," *Quarterly Journal of Speech* 62 (December 1976), pp. 410–22.

20. Both quoted in Commission on Revision of the Federal Court Appellate System, *Structure and Internal Procedures: Recommendations for Change* (Washington, D.C. 1975), pp. 104–5.

21. Lewis F. Powell, Jr., "The Level of Supreme Court Advocacy" (Speech to Fifth Circuit Judicial Conference, May 27, 1974), p. 4.

22. Arthur S. Miller and Jerome A. Barron, "The Supreme Court, The Adversary System, and the Flow of Information to the Justices: A Preliminary Inquiry," *Virginia Law Review* 61 (1975): 1208.

23. Albert M. Sacks, "Foreword: The Supreme Court, 1953 Term," *Harvard Law Review* 68 (November 1954): 98.

24. Charles Rembar, "Introduction," *Obscenity: The Complete Oral Arguments Before the Su-*

preme Court in the Major Obscenity Cases, ed. Leon Friedman (New York: Chelsea House, 1970), p. xviii.

25. Milton Dickens and Ruth E. Schwartz, "Oral Argument Before the Supreme Court: Marshall v. Davis in the School Segregation Cases," *Quarterly Journal of Speech* 57 (February 1971): 32–42.
26. Leon Friedman, "Introduction," *Argument: The Oral Argument Before the Supreme Court in Brown v. Board of Education of Topeka, 1952–55* (New York: Chelsea House, 1969), p. vii.
27. Dickens and Schwartz, "Oral Argument Before the Supreme Court," p. 41.
28. Stephen L. Wasby, *Continuity and Change: From the Warren Court to the Burger Court* (Pacific Palisades, Calif.: Goodyear Publishing Co., 1976).

Chapter 1. Introduction: The Supreme Court and Strategy

1. Roscoe Pound, *Justice According to Law* (New Haven: Yale University Press, 1951), p. 30.
2. Graham Allison has suggested this applies to most organizations: "In policy making. . . . the issue looking *down* is options: how to preserve my leeway until time clarifies uncertainties. The issue looking sideways is commitment: how to get others committed to my coalition. The issue loking *upwards* is confidence: how to give the boss confidence in doing what must be done."—"Conceptual Models and the Cuban Missile Crisis," *American Political Science Review* 63 (September 1969): 711.
3. Walter F. Murphy, *Elements of Judicial Strategy* (Chicago: University of Chicago Press, 1964), pp. 187–88.
4. Ibid., p. 193.
5. See Anthony A. D'Amato and Robert O'Neil, *The Judiciary and Vietnam* (New York: St. Martin's Press, 1972).
6. See, for example, Martin Shapiro, "Stability and Change in Judicial Decision-Making: Incrementalism or Stare Decisis?" *Law in Transition Quarterly,* 2 (Summer 1965): 155.
7. Murphy, *Elements of Judicial Strategy,* pp. 203–4.
8. S. Sidney Ulmer, "Parabolic Support for Civil Liberties: The Longitudinal Behavior of Hugo Lafayette Black, 1937–1971," *Florida State University Law Review* 1 (Winter 1973): 149.
9. G. Gregory Fahlund, "Retroactivity and the Warren Court: The Strategy of a Revolution," *Journal of Politics* 35 (August 1973): 570–93. Barth has noted, "Judges were concerned with problems of implementation and compliance long before impact analysis became an important subject of judicial studies."—Thomas Barth, "Perception and Acceptance of Supreme Court Decisions at the State and Local Level," *Journal of Public Law* 17 (1968): 309. For a more recent example of judicial awareness of the potential effect of Supreme Court rulings, see Justice Powell's opinion in the property tax school financing case, San Antonio School District v. Rodriguez, 411 U.S. 1 at 57*n* (1973).
10. 409 U.S. xxxv at xvi (1972).
11. See for example, S. Sidney Ulmer, "Earl Warren and the *Brown* Decision," *Journal of Politics* 33 (August 1971): 697, drawing on Justice Burton's papers.
12. David Manwaring, "The Flag-Salute Case," in *The Third Branch of Government: 8 Cases in Constitutional Politics,* ed. C. Herman Pritchett and Alan Westin (New York: Harcourt, Brace and World, 1963), pp. 27–28.
13. Allison, "Conceptual Models and the Cuban Missile Crisis," p. 708. Allison urges us to consider what he calls Organizational Process and Bureaucratic Politics Models in looking at what organizations do and not to restrict ourselves to the Rational Policy Model. The last named focuses on conscious strategy, which Allison says is "sometimes

operative," but he adds that it is most often the case that "the game is begun by the necessity that something be done, either in response to a *deadline* . . . or an event."—Graham Allison and Morton H. Halperin, "Bureaucratic Politics: A Paradigm and Some Policy Implications," *Theory and Policy in International Relations,* ed. Richard H. Ullman and Raymond Tanter (Princeton, N.J.: Princeton University Press, 1972), p. 50. In these situations, "existing organizational routines" become the "effective options open to government leaders confronted with any problems."—Allison, "Conceptual Models and the Cuban Missile Crisis," p. 699. The most complete explication of Graham Allison's argument is to be found in his *Essence of Decision: Explaining the Cuban Missile Crisis* (Boston: Little, Brown, 1971).

14. Murphy, *Elements of Judicial Strategy,* pp. 9–10.
15. Jeanne Hahn, "The NAACP Legal Defense and Educational Fund: Its Judicial Strategy and Tactics," in Stephen L. Wasby, *American Government and Politics* (New York: Charles Scribner's Sons, 1973) p. 393n.
16. Murphy, *Elements of Judicial Strategy,* p. 31.
17. Ibid., p. 5.
18. Ibid., p. 4.
19. In responding to threats, the Court formed the minimum-winning coalition only 23 percent of the time, most frequently (26 percent of the time) being unanimous. By contrast, in nonthreat situations, the Court formed minimum-winning opinion coalitions 40 percent of the time. David W. Rohde, "Policy Goals and Opinion Coalitions in the Supreme Court," *Midwest Journal of Political Science* 16 (May 1972): 218–19. By combining five- and six-member coalitions, 63 percent of the coalitions were minimum-winning in nonthreat situations, with only 43 percent being of that size in threat situations.
20. 409 U.S. liv. The case was Walling v. Bello Corp., 316 U.S. 624 (1942). See also Alexander M. Bickel, ed., *The Unpublished Opinions of Mr. Justice Brandeis* (Cambridge: Harvard University Press, 1957).
21. For a more extended presentation of this discussion, see Stephen L. Wasby, *Continuity and Change: From the Warren Court to the Burger Court* (Pacific Palisades, Calif.: Goodyear Publishing Co., 1976), pp. 33–40.
22. Farr v. Pitchess, 409 U.S. 1243 (1973), *citing* Maryland v. Baltimore Radio Show, 338 U.S. 912 at 919 (1950).
23. "Retired Chief Justice Warren Attacks, Chief Justice Burger Defends Freund Study Group's Composition and Proposal," *American Bar Association Journal* 59 (July 1973): 728.
24. Fred M. Vinson, "Work of the Federal Courts," *Courts, Judges, and Politics,* ed. Walter F. Murphy and C. Herman Pritchett (New York: Random House, 1961), pp. 55–56.
25. Jones v. Mayer, 392 U.S. 409 at 478–79 (1968).
26. "Retired Chief Justice Warren Attacks," p. 728.
27. Glendon Schubert, *Quantitative Analysis of Judicial Behavior* (Glencoe, Ill.: Free Press, 1959), pp. 55–67. Schubert suggests that this derives from the Court's need as part of its supervisory power over the lower federal courts to explain to them what the law is.
28. Analysis by Stephen L. Wasby of data coded by David Gruenenfelder, Southern Illinois University at Carbondale.
29. Schubert, *Quantitative Analysis of Judicial Behavior,* p. 66. See also the statement that "justices grant certiorari primarily to reverse decisions below" in J. Woodford Howard, "Litigation Flow in Three United States Courts of Appeals," *Law & Society Review* 8 (Fall 1973): 47.
30. Eugene Gressman, "The National Court of Appeals: A Dissent," *American Bar Association Journal* 59 (March 1973): 257.
31. See Stephen L. Wasby, *The Impact of the United States Supreme Court: Some Perspectives*

(Homewood, Ill.: Dorsey Press, 1970), p. 247.

32. Dissenting, Paris Adult Theater I v. Slaton, 413 U.S. 49 at 83 (1973). See also Albert M. Sacks, "Foreword: The Supreme Court, 1953 Term," *Harvard Law Review* 68 (November 1954): 99.

33. Sacks, in "Foreword," has pointed out that "many unsigned opinions are indistinguishable in form and content from others whose author is identified" (p. 99).

34. Charles A. Miller, "Constitutional Law and the Rhetoric of Race," *Perspectives in American History,* ed. Donald Fleming and Bernard Bailyn (Cambridge: Harvard University Press, 1971), 5: 197.

35. Charles A. Miller, *The Supreme Court and the Uses of History* (Cambridge: Harvard University Press, Belknap Press, 1969), pp. 9, 11–12.

36. Our thanks to Jerry Larson for the comment which led to this idea.

37. See Henry Hart, "The Supreme Court, 1958 Term. Foreword: The Time Chart of the Justices," *Harvard Law Review* 73 (November 1959): 96; Martin Shapiro, *The Supreme Court and the Administrative Agencies* (New York: Free Press, 1968), p. 43.

38. See Allison and Halperin, "Bureaucratic Politics," p. 53.

39. Fred Graham, *The Self-Inflicted Wound* (New York: Macmillan, 1970), p. 171.

40. Charles A. Miller, *The Supreme Court and the Uses of History,* p. 170.

41. Charles A. Miller, "Constitutional Law and the Rhetoric of Race," p. 200.

42. Charles L. Black, Jr., *Structure and Relationship in Constitutional Law* (Baton Rouge: Louisiana State University Press, 1969), p. 13.

43. Ibid., p. 30.

44. Ibid., p. 25.

45. See particularly Younger v. Harris, 401 U.S. 37 (1971).

46. See the suggestions by the dissenters, Screws v. United States, 325 U.S. 91 (1945).

Chapter 2: Before *Brown*

1. For a discussion of the origin and development of "equal protection," see Robert Harris, *The Quest for Equality: The Constitution, Congress, and the Supreme Court* (Baton Rouge: Louisiana State University Press, 1960).

2. See Charles A. Miller, "Constitutional Law and the Rhetoric of Race," *Perspectives in American History,* ed. Donald Fleming and Bernard Bailyn (Cambridge: Harvard University Press, 1971), 5: 172–73. In 1970, Louisiana finally passed a law allowing a person with 1/32 Negro blood to call himself white.

3. Hall v. DeCuir, 95 U.S. 485 (1878).

4. Bearing out Harlan's prediction and indicating that Justice Brown's language of "voluntary consent" would not be followed was the ruling in Berea College v. Kentucky, 211 U.S. 45 (1906), sustaining a statute prohibiting blacks and whites from commingling, even where—as at the college—they were doing so voluntarily.

5. The economic argument used by the school officials was similar to that made by Jackson, Mississippi, municipal officials in closing their swimming pools in the late 1960s, after a federal court had ordered desegregation of the pools. To be sure, they closed *all* the pools rather than only those for blacks, but the economic necessity argument was accepted by the Supreme Court, in Palmer v. Thompson, 403 U.S. 217 (1971). Thurgood Marshall, in dissent, angrily argued that the Court was setting the clock back *seventeen* years (to *Brown v. Board of Education);* perhaps, in view of *Cumming,* he should have said *seventy-two* years.

6. Respectively, United States v. Reese, 92 U.S. 214 (1875); United States v. Cruikshank, 92 U.S. 542 (1875); and Ex parte Yarbrough, 110 U.S. 651 (1883).

7. The opinion was originally assigned to Frankfurter but was reassigned to Reed after a note from Jackson to Chief Justice Stone pointing out that "Mr. Justice Frankfurter

unites in a rare degree factors which unhappily excite prejudice. In the first place, he is a Jew. In the second place, he is from New England, the seat of the abolition movement. In the third place, he had not been thought of as a person particularily sympathetic with the Democratic party in the past." On the other hand, Reed was Protestant, from Kentucky, and a former Democratic office holder. See Alpheus Thomas Mason, *Harlan Fiske Stone: Pillar of the Law* (New York: Viking Press, 1956), pp. 614–15. See also the discussion of the "public relations" aspect of opinion assignment, in David W. Rohde, "Policy Goals, Strategic Choice and Majority Opinion Assignments in the U.S. Supreme Court," *Midwest Journal of Political Science* 16 (November 1972): 657.

8. Rice v. Elmore, 165 F. 2d 387 (4th Cir. 1947), *cert. denied,* 333 U.S. 875 (1948). The Court also denied certiorari with respect to a successful attack on literacy and character tests, Wright v. Mitchell, 154 F.2d 924 (5th Cir. 1946), *cert. denied,* 329 U.S. 733 (1946), and a case involving an elaborate procedure for exhaustion of state remedies, Peay v. Cox, 190 F.2d 123 (5th Cir. 1951), *cert. denied,* 342 U.S. 896 (1951). Another case was dismissed for lack of a substantial federal question, Franklin v. Harper, 205 Ga. 779, 55 S.E.2d 221 (1949), *appeal dismissed,* 339 U.S. 896 (1950). In one instance, a successful challenge to Alabama's "understand and explain" provision, Schnell v. Davis, 81 F. Supp. 872 (S.D. Ala. 1949), was affirmed per curiam, 336 U.S. 933 (1949).

9. Grady v. Garland, 89 F.2d 817 (D.C. Cir. 1937), *cert. denied,* 302 U.S. 694 (1937); Mays v. Burgess, 147 F.2d 869 (D.C. Cir. 1945), *cert. denied,* 325 U.S. 868 (1945), *rehearing denied,* 324 U.S. 896 (1945).

10. Hansberry v. Lee, 372 Ill. 369, 24 N.E.2d 37 (1940), *rev'd,* 311 U.S. 32 (1940).

11. Clement Vose, *Caucasians Only: The Supreme Court, The NAACP, and the Restrictive Covenant Cases* (Berkeley: University of California Press, 1959) tells the story.

12. Trustees of Monroe Church of Christ v. Perkins, 147 Ohio St. 537, 72 N.W.2d 79 (1947), Amer v. Superior Court of California, unreported, and Yin Kim v. Superior Court of California, unreported, *cert. denied,* 334 U.S. 813 (1947).

13. Oral argument from 16 L.W. 3219–24, by permission, and in part from Vose, *Caucasians Only,* pp. 200–205.

14. He also used an old California case holding unconstitutional enforcement of a covenant against renting to a "Chinaman." Gandolfo v. Hartman, 49 F. 181 (1892).

15. One might note the similarity between these questions and the matter of Georgia's provisions allowing the transfer of land in a will with racial restrictions, pointed to by the dissenters in Evans v. Abney, 396 U.S. 435 (1970), the second Macon park case, to be discussed later.

16. The concession is interesting, because the Supreme Court has now distinguished between race and poverty, even when the claim is made that the latter is simply a cover for the former. Thus special votes on "open housing" referenda, when such votes are not required for other issues, have been invalidated, Hunter v. Erickson, 393 U.S. 385 (1969), but referenda on low-income housing have been upheld, James v. Valtierra, 402 U.S. 137 (1971).

17. See Louis Henkin, "*Shelley v. Kraemer:* Notes for a Revised Opinion," *University of Pennsylvania Law Review* 110 (February 1962): 477.

18. Ibid., p. 474.

19. Weiss v. Leaon, 359 Mo. 1054, 225 S.W.2d 127 (1949); Correll v. Earley, 205 Okla. 366, 237 P.2d 1017 (1951); Roberts v. Curtis, 93 F.Supp 604 (D.D.C. 1950); Phillips v. Naff, 332 Mich. 389, 52 N.W.2d 158 (1952); Saunders v. Phillips, 191 Md. 707, 62 A.2d 602 (1948), *cert. denied,* 336 U.S. 967 (1949); Barrows v. Jackson, 112 Cal. App. 2d 534, 247 P.2d 99 (1952).

20. Oral argument from mimeographed transcript, Library of the Supreme Court, October 1952 Term, No. 517.

21. Oral argument from 14 L.W. 3339–43 (1946).
22. Oral argument from 18 L.W. 3277–79 (1950).
23. Railroad Company v. Brown, 84 U.S. 445 (1873).
24. Oral argument from 18 L.W. 3279–81 (1950).

Chapter 3. The School Cases: The First Two Rounds

1. Gunnar Myrdal, *An American Dilemma: The Negro Problem and American Democracy* (New York: Harper, 1944).
2. On these points, see Phineas Indritz, "Implications of *Brown*," *The Continuing Challenge: The Past and the Future of Brown v. Board of Education* (Evanston, Ill.: Integrated Education Associates, 1975), pp. 1–2.
3. See Jeanne Hahn, "The NAACP Legal Defense and Educational Fund: Its Judicial Strategy and Tactics," in Stephen L. Wasby, *American Government and Politics* (New York: Charles Scribner's Sons, 1973), pp. 387–99, especially p. 393. Hahn points out that such pressure not only made the NAACP bring cases where they would have preferred not to do so, for example, where there was heavy black population, but also made the group's development of strategy difficult.
4. Anthony Lewis, "The Supreme Court and Its Critics," *Minnesota Law Review* 65 (January 1961): 307.
5. Hirabayashi v. United States, 320 U.S. 81 (1943); Korematsu v. United States, 323 U.S. 214 (1945).
6. See Arthur Larson, "The New Law of Race Relations," *Wisconsin Law Review* 1969: 506; Arthur Kinoy, "The Constitutional Right of Negro Freedom," *Rutgers Law Review* 21 (Spring 1967): 387–441.
7. Fear that the Covenant would be used as a basis for civil rights legislation in this country was one of the important reasons why it was not ratified by the Senate, as well as a cause for the Bricker Amendment limiting the executive's authority to enter into executive agreements without the consent of Congress. We are indebted to Randall Nelson for reminding us of this context.
8. Furman v. Georgia, 408 U.S. 238 at 375 (1972).
9. There was no segregation in the three-grade junior high schools or the other three-grade senior high schools of the state.
10. Justice Burton recorded that the vote to note probable jurisdiction was seven to "note" and one (Jackson) to "hold," with no vote recorded for Chief Justice Vinson—S. Sidney Ulmer, "Earl Warren and the *Brown* Decision," *Journal of Politics* 33 (August 1971): 690n. This account differs from that of Daniel Berman, *It Is So Ordered* (New York: W. W. Norton, 1966). Berman says that only four votes were cast for accepting *Brown* and *Briggs* (p. 47).
11. S. Sidney Ulmer, "Parabolic Support for Civil Liberties: The Longitudinal Behavior of Hugo Lafayette Black, 1937–1971," *Florida State University Law Review* 1 (Winter 1973): 137.
12. Ulmer, "Earl Warren and the *Brown* Decision," p. 691.
13. Albert M. Sacks, "Foreword: The Supreme Court, 1953 Term," *Harvard Law Review* 68 (November 1954): 97.
14. Our material on oral argument was initially taken from the transcripts, Library of the Supreme Court. The transcripts have now been printed, in *Argument: The Oral Argument Before the Supreme Court in* Brown v. Board of Education of Topeka; *1952–55*, ed. Leon Friedman (New York: Chelsea House, 1969).
15. Justice Frankfurter also commented on the differences between the Kansas and Delaware cases because similar findings of fact were treated quite differently.
16. The classic case is the man who accused his neighbor of borrowing his teakettle and

then cracking it. The neighbor's defense: "I did not borrow the teakettle. And it was cracked when I borrowed it."

17. Carter also attempted to show that *Gong Lum* was irrelevant where the constitutionality of the system is under attack and where inequality in fact exists, because in that case there was no showing that the child's educational opportunity had been diminished from having to attend the Negro school and the Court had assumed that equality in fact existed. The power of the states to make racial distinctions in their school systems also had not been at issue, he said.

18. At first somewhat confused as to whether he was arguing that the statute was permissive, Hayes clarified himself by saying that there was not even any authorization for the schools to be run in a segregated manner.

19. For Redding's reminiscences about the Delaware litigation, see Louis L. Redding, "Delaware's Contribution to *Brown*," *The Continuing Challenge*, pp. 25–29.

20. Nabrit also had to say, as he began his part of the presentation, "It would appear necessary that petitioners make clear the position which they take."

21. Milton Dickens and Ruth E. Schwartz, "Oral Argument Before the Supreme Court: Marshall v. Davis in the School Segregation Cases," *Quarterly Journal of Speech* 57 (February 1971): 36.

22. Frankfurter said the chancellor's opinion was particularly competent and that "it was an unusual opinion, as opinions go."

23. Kotch v. Pilot Commissioners, 330 U.S. 552 (1947).

24 The source of our information is Justice Burton's docket book, as discussed by Ulmer, "Earl Warren and the *Brown* Decision," pp. 691–92.

25. Ulmer, "Parabolic Support for Civil Liberties," p. 138.

26. Berman apparently thought Minton on the other side. See *It Is So Ordered*, p. 114.

27. Ulmer, "Earl Warren and the *Brown* Decision," p. 697. On the basis of Burton's comments, either Frankfurter, Reed, or Jackson was a member of the majority then.

28. Ulmer, "Parabolic Support for Civil Liberties," p. 138.

29. Oral argument from mimeographed transcripts, Library of the Supreme Court, and from 22 L.W. 3157–63 (1953).

30. Davis responded by noting that eight of the ratifying states had reestablished school segregation shortly after ratifying the Fourteenth Amendment.

31. Douglas had noted that he was unable to ascertain whether the government had actually taken a position on the merits of the constitutional controversy. For further discussion, see Berman, *It is So Ordered*, pp. 83–85, and Anthony Lewis, *Portrait of a Decade* (New York: Random House, 1964), pp. 23–25.

32. There is a story that lawyers arguing a case before the Court hired a lip-reader to find out what the justices were whispering to each other; after one had leaned over and said something to a colleague, the lip-reader was asked what had been said. He reported that the justice had said he wished Frankfurter would shut up so the lawyer could get on with his argument. See Berman, *It Is So Ordered*, p. 68n.

33. This was not to be the last of the open exchanges between Warren and Frankfurter. In 1962, after Frankfurter "ad libbed" in reading a dissent, Warren castigated him: "That was not the dissenting opinion that was filed. That was a lecture. It was a closing argument by the prosecutor to the jury. It is properly made perhaps in the conference room. As I understand it, the purpose of reporting an opinion in the Court is to inform the public and not for the purpose of degrading this Court."—Quoted in James F. Simon, *In His Own Image: The Supreme Court In Richard Nixon's America* (New York: David McKay 1973), p. 64.

34. Korman admitted that public statements by some board members indicated they were convinced that the time for integration had come. He assured the Court that the board members were nevertheless all in favor of having him represent them.

35. Frankfurter later observed that it was easier to read an intent not to compel segregation into the statute than to figure out the content of the 1866 debates over it.
36. To attack racial classifications as invalid, one had to depart from a factual record of lack of equality, he said. Marshall's argument attacking the validity of separate but equal met intense questioning; he faced fifty-three questions in about forty to forty-five minutes. Dickens and Schwartz, "Oral Argument Before the Supreme Court," p. 37.
37. Because he was arguing against desegregation, Moore wanted to avoid the question. "It really distressed me to face that question," he said.
38. "Interview with Earl Warren," Public Broadcasting System, December 11, 1972. Warren also admitted to some ignorance as to why the case had not been decided after the first round of argument.
39. Ulmer, "Earl Warren and the *Brown* Decision," pp. 692–93.
40. Berman, *It Is So Ordered,* p. 114.
41. Ulmer, "Earl Warren and the *Brown* Decision," pp. 694–95.
42. Ibid.
43. See S. Sidney Ulmer, "Bricolage and Assorted Thoughts on Working in the Papers of Supreme Court Justices," *Journal of Politics* 35 (May 1973): 306–8.
44. Ulmer, "Earl Warren and the *Brown* Decision," p. 695.
45. Ibid., p. 697n.
46. Ibid., p. 698.
47. Ibid., p. 699.
48. Berman, *It Is So Ordered,* p. 114. The holdouts were the ones who did not participate in the luncheons with the other justices during consideration of the case. They were also the ones who had asked the most questions, if to the always-voluble Frankfurter and Jackson we add Reed. By contrast, there had been few questions from the "majority" side, except possibly from Black, with almost none from Warren. See Ulmer, "Earl Warren and the *Brown* Decision," p. 698n.
49. Berman, *It Is So Ordered,* p. 114.
50. S. Sidney Ulmer to Stephen L. Wasby, August 9, 1973. We are indebted to Professor Ulmer for sharing his views with us.
51. Phineas Indritz, "Implications of *Brown*," pp. 1–2.
52. Kinoy, "The Constitutional Right of Negro Freedom," p. 425.
53. Frank T. Read, "Judicial Evolution of the Law of School Integration Since *Brown v. Board of Education*," *Law and Contemporary Problems* 39 (Winter 1975):7.
54. Jack Greenberg, "The Supreme Court, Civil Rights, and Civil Dissonance," *Yale Law Journal* 77 (July 1968): 1522. See also the comment of another of the lawyers in the case, who said that *Brown* "completely recast" the psychological dimensions of American race relations, at the same time leaving unchanged the "pre-existing pattern of white superiority and black subordination."—Robert L. Carter, "The Supreme Court and Desegregation," *The Warren Court: A Critical Analysis,* ed. Richard Sayler et al. (New York: Chelsea House, 1969), p. 56.
55. Arthur J. Goldberg, *Equal Justice: The Warren Era of the Supreme Court* (Evanston, Ill.: Northwestern University Press, 1971), p. 6.
56. Michael Lewis, "The Negro Protest in Urban America," *Protest, Reform, and Revolt: A Reader in Social Movements,* ed. Joseph Gusfield (New York: John Wiley, 1970), p. 177.
57. See Greenberg, "The Supreme Court," p. 1522. He says that enforcement was "their least important aspect" for that period.
58. On the newspapers, see Gerald A. Weihs, "Editorial Reaction to *Brown v. Board of Education* as It Reflects on the Court's Strategy" (MS., Northwestern University Law School, 1970). For a general discussion of the decision's impact, see Stephen L. Wasby, *The Impact of the United States Supreme Court* (Homewood, Ill.: Dorsey Press, 1970), pp.

169–85, especially pp. 175 ff.

59. Reed Sarratt, *The Ordeal of Desegregation: The First Decade* (New York: Harper and Row, 1966), p. 2.

60. See the hypotheses at Wasby, *The Impact of the United States Supreme Court,* pp. 253–54, 264.

61. Ulmer, "Bricolage and Assorted Thoughts on Working in the Papers of Supreme Court Justices," p. 291.

62. Paul Rosen, *The Supreme Court and Social Science* (Urbana: University of Illinois Press, 1972), p. x.

63. Herbert Wechsler, "Toward Neutral Principles of Constitutional Law," *Harvard Law Review* 72 (May 1959): 32.

64. Philip Kurland, "Toward a Political Supreme Court," *University of Chicago Law Review* 37 (Fall 1969): 45.

65. Derrick A. Bell, Jr., "Waiting on the Promise of Brown," *Law and Contemporary Problems* 39 (Spring 1975): 345.

66. Dissenting, in Dick v. New York Life Insurance Co., 359 U.S. 437 at 458–59 (1959).

67. Paul A. Freund, "Why We Need the National Court of Appeals," *American Bar Association Journal* 59 (March 1973): 248.

68. See Stephen L. Wasby, *Small Town Police and the Supreme Court: Hearing the Word* (Lexington, Mass.: Lexington Books, 1976).

69. Charles S. Hyneman, *The Supreme Court on Trial* (New York: Atherton Press, 1963), pp. 210–11.

70. Television interview, May 17, 1974.

71. Goldberg, *Equal Justice,* p. 25.

72. The basic work on opinion leaders is Elihu Katz and Paul Lazarsfeld, *Personal Influence* (Glencoe, Ill.: Free Press, 1955).

73. On low levels of knowledge about the Court, see particularly Kenneth M. Dolbeare, "The Public Views the Supreme Court," *Law, Politics, and the Federal Courts,* ed. Herbert Jacob (Boston: Little, Brown, 1967), pp. 194–212, and Walter F. Murphy and Joseph Tanenhaus, "Public Opinion and the United States Supreme Court: Mapping Some Prerequisites for Court Legitimation of Regime Change," *Frontiers of Judicial Research,* ed. Joel Grossman and Joseph Tanenhaus (New York: John Wiley, 1969), pp. 273–303.

74. Walter F. Murphy, *Elements of Judicial Strategy* (Chicago: University of Chicago Press, 1964), p. 128.

75. J. Woodford Howard, "The Fluidity of Judicial Choice," *American Political Science Review* 62 (March 1968): 49–50.

76. Stephen L. Wasby, "The Pure and the Prurient: The Supreme Court, Obscenity, and Oregon Policy," *The Supreme Court as Policy-Maker: Three Studies on the Impact of Judicial Decisions,* ed. David Everson (Carbondale: Southern Illinois University Public Affairs Research Bureau, 1968), pp. 82–116.

77. A particularly negative view is expressed by James F. Simon: "The chief justice's opinions often sounded more like civics lectures or Sunday sermons than learned expostulations on the law. There were few precious quarries of legal insight to be mined by meticulous scholars."—*In His Own Image,* p. 64.

78. Sacks, "Foreword: The Supreme Court, 1953 Term," p. 98. See also Kenneth Clark's observation that the opinion was "eloquent, simple, and direct."

79. "The less clear and direct the policy communication from the Supreme Court the more likely are resisting circuit judges to 'misunderstand' it and continue along their path."—Martin Shapiro, *The Supreme Court and the Administrative Agencies* (New York: Free Press, 1968), p. 177.

80. See Ulmer's comment that the attack on the Warren Court did not stem merely from its

results but was a "response to the Court's lessening adherence to *stare decisis.*" "Bricolage and Assorted Thoughts on Working in the Papers of Supreme Court Justices," p. 292.

81. Ernest Kaiser, "The Federal Government and the Negro, 1865–1955," *Science and Society* 20 (Winter 1956): 52.

82. Wechsler, "Toward Neutral Principles of Constitutional Law," pp. 11, 19, 32, 50. Relying on the Thirteenth Amendment would have placed the decision "squarely . . . on the ground that segregated education had demonstrably over a long period resulted in inferior education for Negroes, and that this in itself was an unconstitutional deprivation."—Larson, "The New Law of Race Relations," pp. 507–9.

83. Hans Linde, "Judges, Critics, and the Realist Tradition," *Yale Law Journal* 82 (December 1972): 229.

84. See Arthur S. Miller and Ronald F. Howell, "The Myth of Neutrality in Constitutional Adjudication," *University of Chicago Law Review* 27 (Summer 1960): 664. For further discussion of the "neutral principles" issue, see Jan G. Deutsch, "Neutrality, Legitimacy, and the Supreme Court: Some Intersections Between Law and Political Science," *Stanford Law Review* 20 (January 1968): 169–261. Sometimes a case can be extremely significant for the result it reaches even if it is totally lacking principle. An example is the Pentagon Papers case, New York Times v. United States, 403 U.S. 713 (1971), which produced nine separate opinions and no majority opinion.

85. Arthur S. Miller and Ronald F. Howell, "The Myth of Neutrality in Constitutional Adjudication," p. 662.

86. See Martin Shapiro, *Law and Politics in the Supreme Court* (New York: Free Press, 1964), p. 31.

87. Lewis M. Steel, "Nine Men in Black Who Think White," *New York Times Magazine,* October 13, 1968, pp. 57, 112.

88. Linde, "Judges, Critics, and the Realist Tradition," p. 233.

89. Ibid., p. 234: "A President who had nothing to say about *Brown* could not well have remained silent about the federal District."

90. See Keyes v. Denver School District, 413 U.S. 189 (1973). It has been suggested that the opinion by Judge Wisdom of the Court of Appeals for the Fifth Circuit making the de jure-de facto distinction clearer and firmer caused much of the problem of different treatment between the North and South. The case was United States v. Jefferson County Board of Education, 372 F.2d 836 (5th Cir. 1966). Read, "Judicial Evolution of the Law of School Integration," p. 24n.

91. Briggs v. Elliott, 132 F.Supp. 776 at 777 (E.D.S.C. 1955). More recently, President Nixon's first Secretary of Health, Education and Welfare, Robert Finch, argued that the Supreme Court had outlawed only deliberate discrimination on the basis of race, not segregation per se: "If you look at the Supreme Court decision, segregation, in fact, is not prohibited by law," he said. "What is prohibited is deliberate discrimination."

92. The dictum by Parker was not put to death in the Fifth Circuit, which handled the bulk of the Southern school desegregation cases, until 1965.

93. Charles L. Black, Jr., *The People and the Court: Judicial Review in a Democracy* (Englewood Cliffs, N.J.: Prentice-Hall, 1960), p. 139.

94. Kurland, "Toward a Political Supreme Court," p. 29.

95. Black, *The People and the Court,* p. 139.

96. See Murphy, *Elements of Judicial Strategy,* p. 66; Ulmer, "Earl Warren and the *Brown* Decision," p. 702.

97. Charles S. Hyneman, *The Supreme Court on Trial* (New York: Atherton Press, 1963), p. 213.

98. See Linde, "Judges, Critics, and the Realist Tradition," pp. 243–44. Examples would be the Steel Seizure and Pentagon Papers cases.

99. "A justice who is willing to make all the modifications suggested by his colleagues is liable to find he has fathered an amorphous mass of doughy sentences rather than a strong statement of law"—Murphy, *Elements of Judicial Strategy*, p. 24.

100. L. Brent Bozell, *The Warren Revolution* (New Rochelle, N.Y.: Arlington House, 1966), p. 54. See also the attack by historian Alfred Kelly, who helped the NAACP respond to the Court's question as to the meaning of the Fourteenth Amendment. He says that in asking about the intentions of the Fourteenth Amendment's writers, the Court was asking questions of the past that the past cannot answer. Kelly distinguishes between "historians' history" and "law-office history"; the latter is put together by the opposing sides in an adversary legal situation to buttress their claims. Because the latter "is almost completely irresolvable, even by the Supreme Court of the United States, into anything resembling historical truth," it should not used by the Court.—Alfred H. Kelly, "Clio and the Court: An Illicit Love Affair," *The Supreme Court Review 1965*, ed. Philip Kurland (Chicago: University of Chicago Press, 1965), p. 156. Kelly, also claiming that "The truth of history does not flow from its usefulness" (p. 157), says it should not be rewritten to serve the Court's ends.

101. Alexander M. Bickel, "The Original Understanding and the Segregation Decision," *Harvard Law Review* 69 (November 1955): 64–65. See also Alexander M. Bickel, *Politics and the Warren Court* (New York: Harper and Row, 1965), Appendix, esp. pp. 256–61. Bickel was Frankfurter's law clerk during the period under consideration.

102. Edmond Cahn, "Jurisprudence," *New York University Law Review* 30 (January 1955): 157–58.

103. "Sociology has always played a part in the decision-making process, although frequently it comes in wearing a mask. Sometimes the mask is public policy or the interests of justice, sometimes judicial notice or common knowledge, sometimes legislative or constitutional facts."—John Minor Wisdom, "Random Remarks on the Role of Social Sciences in the Judicial Decision-Making Process in School Desegregation Cases," *Law and Contemporary Problems* 39 (Winter 1975): 137.

104. Godfrey Hodgson, "Do Schools Make a Difference," *Atlantic* 231 (March 1973): 37. Or, as Linde, "Judges, Critics, and the Realist Tradition," puts it, "When a holding is rightly a principled interpretation of the Constitution, it is not strengthened by masquerading as a constitutionally irrebutable finding of fact" (p. 243). Charles L. Black, Jr., has asserted that the charge that the *Brown* ruling was "sociological" was a "canard" if it meant "that anything like principled reliance was placed on the formally 'scientific' authorities, which are relegated to a footnote and treated as merely corroboratory of common sense."—"The Lawfulness of the Segregation Decisions," *Yale Law Journal* 69 (January 1960): 421 at 430*n*. But in response to Black, it may be pointed out that the Court often makes some of its most important points in footnotes which have subsequently become famous among students of constitutional law. Moreover, the Court appears to have relied upon the sociological data to provide a main plank in its argument that separate facilities in 1954 were unequal even if they were equal in the days of *Plessy*.

105. See particularly Stell v. Savannah-Chatham County Board of Education and Lawrence Roberts, 220 F.Supp. 667 (S.D. Ga. 1963), *rev'd*, 333 F.2d 55 (5th Cir. 1964), and Evers v. Jackson Municipal Separate School District, 232 F. Supp. 241 (S.D. Miss. 1964), *rev'd*, 357 F.2d 653 (5th Cir. 1966).

106. Henry Levin, "Education, Life Chances, and the Courts: The Role of Social Science Evidence," *Law and Contemporary Problems* 39 (Spring 1975): 239.

107. For a broader discussion of the role of "harmfulness" in school desegregation decrees, see Owen M. Fiss, "The Jurisprudence of Busing," *Law and Contemporary Problems* 39 (Winter 1975): 194–216. Fiss discussed the harm to be determined, the costs of the remedies to be imposed, and the relationship between them, and points out increasing

questioning about the harm of segregation, particularly where it does not stem from racial assignment to particular schools, as well as about the relationship between that harm and remedies like busing.

108. The data actually cited by the Court was later examined exhaustively by many social scientists who concluded that it suffered from bias and poor experimental procedures and was not replicable.

109. Sacks, "Foreword: The Supreme Court, 1953 Term," p. 98.

110. Ibid.

111. Constance Baker Motley has suggested that the Court may not have accepted the NAACP's argument based on *Sweatt* because there had been no dual system of graduate schools in the South as there was in lower education, so "admission" in the graduate school context did not mean the same thing it meant in lower education.— "Twenty Years Later . . . ," *The Continuing Challenge,* pp. 11–15.

Chapter 4. The Implementation Round and *Brown II*

1. In addition to the transcripts, oral arguments can be found in *Argument: The Oral Argument Before the Supreme Court in* Brown v. Board of Education of Topeka, *1952–55,* ed. Leon Friedman (New York: Chelsea House, 1969) and at 23 L.W. 3253–60 (1953). In *Argument,* the third round consumes two hundred pages, while the first round takes up one hundred and sixty pages and the second round occupies only about one hundred and fifty pages.

2. Steiner v. Simmons, 111 A.2d 574 (Del. 1954).

3. John W. Davis was too ill to appear in oral argument, although he had assisted on the briefs.

4. Constance Baker Motley has recently commented that the Court asked the NAACP to file another brief "solely on the class action aspect of these cases," with the NAACP attorneys being somewhat surprised by the request.—"Twenty Years Later . . . ," *The Continuing Challenge: The Past and the Future of* Brown v. Board of Education (Evanston. Ill.: Integrated Education Associates, 1975).

5. S. Sidney Ulmer, "Earl Warren and the *Brown* Decision," *Journal of Politics* 33 (August 1971): 698.

6. S. Sidney Ulmer, "Courts as Small and Not So Small Groups" (New York: General Learning Press, 1971), p. 24. The remainder of this paragraph relies on this source.

7. S. Sidney Ulmer, "Parabolic Support for Civil Liberties: The Longitudinal Behavior of Hugo Lafayette Black, 1937–1971," *Florida State University Law Review* 1 (Winter 1973): 139.

8. S. Sidney Ulmer, "Bricolage and Assorted Thoughts on Working in the Papers of Supreme Court Justices," *Journal of Politics* 35 (May 1973): 305n.

9. Ulmer, "Courts as Small and Not So Small Groups," p. 25.

10. Joseph B. Robison, "Speeding Reforms," *The Continuing Challenge,* p. 35.

11. Constance Baker Motley has said that the NAACP attorneys were aware in 1954 "that there were severe limits to the judicial process," and that their hope was "simply that the court would not formally substitute the philosophy of gradualism for the discarded doctrine of separate but equal."—"Twenty Years Later . . . ," p. 15. Thus the NAACP not only did not gain the position for which Marshall argued, but the worst fears of the organization were realized.

12. Robert L. Carter, "The Warren Court and Desegregation," *Michigan Law Review* 67 (December 1968): 243.

13. In his television interview in December 1972 Chief Justice Warren said that one justice had suggested that it would be nice if implementation came by the centennial of the Fourteenth Amendment; that would have been 1968.

14. Carter, "The Warren Court and Desegregation," p. 243.
15. Jack Greenberg, "The Supreme Court, Civil Rights, and Civil Dissonance," *Yale Law Journal* 77 (July 1968): 1524.
16. See also the comments by Malcolm X: " 'That was one of the greatest magical feats ever performed in America,' I'd tell them. 'Do you mean to tell me that nine Supreme Court Judges, who are past masters of legal phraseology, couldn't have worked their decision to make it stick as *law*? No! It was trickery and magic that told Negroes they were desegregated—Hooray! Hooray!—and at the same time it told whites, 'Here are your loopholes!' "—*The Autobiography of Malcolm X* (New York: Grove Press, 1966), pp. 242–43.
17. Murray Edelman, *The Symbolic Uses of Politics* (Urbana: University of Illinois Press, 1967) and *Politics as Symbolic Action: Mass Arousal and Quiescence* (Chicago: Markham, 1971).
18. The idea that law is self-executing is part of the "myth of rights." See Stuart A. Scheingold, *The Politics of Rights: Lawyers, Public Policy, and Political Change* (New Haven: Yale University Press, 1974).
19. The phrase was attributed by *Law Week* to Virginia's Archibald Robertson, but he used "with all reasonable speed." Frankfurter, who had used the phrase a number of times before, used it in his January 1954 memo to his colleagues. Others, including Warren, attribute the phrase to Justice Holmes, in Virginia v. West Virginia, 222 U.S. 17 (1911).
20. Robert L. Carter and Thurgood Marshall, "The Meaning and Significance of the Supreme Court Decree," *Journal of Negro Education* 29 (Summer 1955): 397–404.
21. Alexander M. Bickel, *The Least Dangerous Branch* (Indianapolis: Bobbs-Merrill, 1962), pp. 252, 254.
22. Matthew Holden, Jr., *The Politics of the Black "Nation"* (New York: Chandler, 1973), p. 139.
23. Daniel J. Gifford, "Communication of Legal Standards, Policy Development and Effective Conduct Regulation," *Cornell Law Review* 56 (February 1971): 443.
24. Gary Orfield, *The Reconstruction of Southern Education: The Schools and the 1964 Civil Rights Act* (New York: John Wiley, 1969), p. 108.
25. Kenneth Clark, "The Social Scientists, The *Brown* Decision, and Contemporary Confusion," *Argument*, ed. Leon Friedman, p. xxxvii.
26. Ibid., pp. xxxiii, xxxvii.
27. Gifford, "Communication of Legal Standards," p. 443.
28. William M. Evan, "Law as an Instrument of Social Change," *Applied Sociology*, ed. Alvin Gouldner and S.M. Miller (New York: Free Press, 1965), pp. 285–91. See Holden, *The Politics of the Black "Nation,"* p. 182, for another formulation, in which he suggests that rules are most easily administered where, *inter alia*, "the compliance action by an official is relatively clear, the official is relatively immune to sanctions by those who should prefer him not to comply, and those who prefer him not to comply cannot prevent compliance by removing themselves from the process—except at the risk of losing important benefits." He finds enforcement more difficult in education than with respect to voting rights because not only is the action to be taken by the black student or parent not simple but "it is not clear when administrative officials are trying to comply and when they are 'filibustering,' the officials are open to sanctions by white students and/or parents who prefer nonchange, and the option of moving out of the school area or district means that a dip in segregation is followed by 'resegregation.' "
29. J. W. Peltason, *Fifty-Eight Lonely Men: Southern Federal Judges and School Desegregation* (Urbana: University of Illinois Press, 1971 [1961]), p. 245.
30. Ibid., p. 246.
31. Melvin M. Tumin et al., *Desegregation: Resistance and Readiness* (Princeton, N.J.: Princeton University Press, 1958), p. 165.

32. Clark, "The Social Scientists," p. xxxviii.
33. Chief Justice Warren, saying the Court didn't expect that compliance would be immediate, has indicated, "The best we could look for was a progression of action."—Interview, Public Broadcasting Service, December 11, 1972.
34. Clark, "The Social Scientists," p. xxxiii.
35. Gifford, "Communication of Legal Standards," p. 443.
36. Arthur J. Goldberg, *Equal Justice: The Warren Era of the Supreme Court* (Evanston, Ill.: Northwestern University Press, 1971), p. 60.
37. Hans Linde, "Judges, Critics, and the Realist Tradition," *Yale Law Journal* 82 (December 1972): 239.
38. Walter F. Murphy, *Elements of Judicial Strategy* (Chicago: University of Chicago Press, 1964), pp. 125, 172.
39. Carter, "The Warren Court and Desegregation," p. 246. See also Clark, "The Social Scientists," p. xxvii.
40. Murphy, *Elements of Judicial Strategy*, p. 175.
41. Ibid., p. 175. Even when he is unsure about this environment, a justice "still might decide to pursue a 'damn the torpedoes' strategy and forge ahead," if "he judges that the immediate importance of the decision of the policy announcement is so immense that even martyrdom would be an acceptable price."
42. James F. Simon, *In His Own Image: The Supreme Court in Richard Nixon's America* (New York: David McKay, 1973), p. 69.
43. See Robert G. Dixon, Jr., *Democratic Representation: Reapportionment in Law and Politics* (New York: Oxford University Press, 1968).
44. Later, in Virginia, when schools were closed as a result of "Massive Resistance," white parents were among those most active in seeking the reopening of the schools.

Chapter 5. Issues Avoided: Cemeteries, Miscegenation, Gifts of Land

1. In his petition for rehearing, counsel for Mrs. Rice gave some indication of what had transpired during the original oral argument.
2. This might not have happened, however, even if Harlan had voted for certiorari. Frankfurter at times refused to vote on the merits in some cases, particularly those involving the Federal Employer Liability Act (FELA), even after four of his colleagues had voted to grant the writ—behavior later criticized by Harlan himself. It is thus possible that even had Harlan voted to take the rehearing, the Court might have again tied four-four with Frankfurter not participating, taking Mrs. Rice no further than she had been after the case was first heard.
3. Gunnar Myrdal, *An American Dilemma: The Negro Problem and American Democracy* (New York: Harper, 1944), p. 60.
4. Jack Greenberg, *Race Relations and American Law* (New York: Columbia University Press, 1959), p. 344.
5. Monks v. Lee, 48 Cal. App.2d 603, 120 P.2d 167 (1941), *appeal dismissed*, 317 U.S. 590 (1942).
6. City of Birmingham v. Monk, 87 F.Supp. 538 (N.D. Ala. 1949), 185 F.2d 859 (5th Cir. 1950), *cert. denied*, 341 U.S. 940 (1951).
7. See Robert J. Sickels, *Race, Marriage, and the Law* (Albuquerque: University of New Mexico Press, 1972), p. 3. The result was thus the same as in Pace v. Alabama, 106 U.S. 583 (1883), decided directly by the Court under a similar statute.
8. Walter F. Murphy, *Elements of Judicial Strategy* (Chicago: University of Chicago Press, 1964), p. 193.
9. Herbert Wechsler, "Toward Neutral Principles of Constitutional Law," *Harvard Law Review* 72 (May 1959): 34.

10. Alexander M. Bickel's attempt to justify the action in terms of an expansive view of the Court's discretion—*The Least Dangerous Branch* (Indianapolis: Bobbs-Merrill, 1962), p. 174—met with unusually sharp criticism. See Gerald Gunther, "The Subtle Vices of the 'Passive Virtues'—A Comment on Principle and Expedience in Judicial Review," *Columbia Law Review* 64 (January 1964): 11–12.

11. Murphy, *Elements of Judicial Strategy*, p. 103. In following that advice, the Court was operating contrary to the stricture later stated by Justice Goldberg: "There is no justification for the Court to avoid deciding a citizen's substantial claim of constitutional right on the basis that it may injure itself if it decides that case and vindicates those rights."—Arthur J. Goldberg, *Equal Justice: The Warren Era of the Supreme Court* (Evanston, Ill.: Northwestern University Press, 1971), p. 60.

12. Oral argument from 33. L.W. 3137–38 (1964).

13. This bracketing also occurred on the matter of whether the Court had to overrule *Pace v. Alabama*. Coleman agreed with Justice Stewart that he was asking for overruling of part of *Pace*, but said its reasoning had been undermined by more recent antisegregation decisions, including one invalidating a Louisiana law against interracial boxing.

14. Immediately before deciding *McLaughlin*, the Court decided an election case with some partial relevance. In *Virginia State Board of Elections v. Hamm* and *Tancil v. Wools*, involving racial designations on various forms—poll tax, residence certificates, registration lists—the lower court had upheld as a valid requirement for statistical purposes a statute requiring racial designation in divorce decrees, although voter-related designations were invalidated—230 F.Supp. 156 (E.D.Va. 1964). The Supreme Court affirmed per curiam, 379 U.S. 19 (1964).

15. We think there will be a closer correlation between the questions a justice asks and the position he later takes if he is writing a separate (concurring or dissenting) opinion than if he has taken on the institutional task of writing for the Court. Particularly in point here is the opinion of Stewart, who had been criticial of miscegenation laws during argument, and who attacked them directly in his concurring opinion.

16. Sickels, *Race, Marriage, and the Law*, pp. 102–3.

17. Although it had referred to scientific writings in the lower courts, the ACLU did not mention them in its appeal to the Supreme Court.

18. Oral argument from *Washington Star*, April 10, 1967; *New York Times*, April 11, 1967, p. 16; *Washington Post*, April 11, 1967, p. 4A.

19. In addition to Rabbi Gordon's work, Button also quoted a physiology professor (from *Science*) and William Shockley (from a *Time* article). The ACLU, we should note, also introduced scientific evidence, particularly a letter from anthropologists to the *New York Times* and an article in *Saturday Review*. See Sickels, *Race, Marriage, and the Law*, pp. 105–7.

20. Sickels, *Race, Marriage, and the Law*, pp. 63, 31.

21. Compare Sickel's statement, *Race, Marriage, and the Law*, p. 7: "A broad new rule is demanded; the courts act cautiously for fear of provoking an ugly public response; in the debate between reformers and conservatives that ensues, an increasingly realistic assessment of the limited role of law emerges and reduces the interest of all parties in the outcome of the legal struggle; meanwhile considerations of legal and moral consistency make a decision unavoidable in the long run; when it comes, the decision is neither feared nor carried out at the levels originally anticipated."

22. The other was *Coffee v. Rice University*, where an exclusionary provision had been placed in the institution's charter by its original benefactor. A Texas district court allowed the university to admit Negro students despite the provision on the ground that the earlier restriction rendered impracticable the main purpose of the original benefactor—to further "first class" education. A state appeals court rejected an attempt by alumni, students, and donors to the university to test that earlier ruling,

saying they were part of the general public without any special interest in the university's action and held their case nonjusticiable. 387 S.W.2d 132 (Ct. Civ. App. Texas 1965).

23. Not until four years later, after the *Burton* public facilities ruling, did the doctors receive relief from the Fourth Circuit—Eaton v. Grubbs, 329 F.2d 710 (4th Cir. 1964).

24. Oral argument from *Washington Post,* November 11, 1965, p. A21, cols. 1–2.

25. Shortly after *Evans,* the Court upheld Louisiana's right to refuse to allow illegitimates to recover from the estate of their father who died without a will—Labine v. Vincent, 401 U.S. 532 (1971).

Chapter 6. School Desegregation after *Brown*

1. Board of Trustees v. Frazier, 136 F.Supp. 589 (N.D.N.C. 1955), *aff'd,* 350 U.S. 979 (1956).

2. Booker v. Tennessee Board of Education, 240 F.2d 689 (6th Cir. 1957), *cert. denied,* 353 U.S. 965 (1957).

3. Arthur J. Goldberg, *Equal Justice: The Warren Era of the Supreme Court* (Evanston, Ill.: Northwestern University Press, 1971), p. 5.

4. For statistics, see United States Commission on Civil Rights, *With Liberty and Justice for All* [abridgment of Commission report for 1959] (Washington, D.C.: Government Printing Office, 1959), pp. 119, 123.

5. The story has been told in greatest detail in J. W. Peltason, *Fifty-Eight Lonely Men: Southern Federal Judges and School Desegregation* (Urbana: University of Illinois Press, 1971 [1961]). See also Kenneth Vines, "Federal District Judges and Race Relations Cases in the South," *Journal of Politics* 26 (May 1964): 337–57. On a more recent situation, see Michael W. Giles and Thomas G. Walker, "Judicial Policy-Making and Southern School Segregation," *Journal of Politics* 37 (November 1975): 917–36, using 1970 data.

6. Gary Orfield, *The Reconstruction of Southern Education: The Schools and the 1964 Civil Rights Act* (New York: John Wiley, 1969), p. 16.

7. Ibid., p. 18.

8. *Congressional Record,* March 12, 1956, pp. 4460, 4515–16.

9. Hood v. Board of Trustees, 232 F.2d 626 (4th Cir. 1956), *cert. denied,* 352 U.S. 870 (1956).

10. Jackson v. Rawdon, 135 F. Supp. 936 (N.D. Texas 1955), 235 F.2d 93 (5th Cir. 1956), Rawdon v. Jackson, *appeal denied,* 352 U.S. 925 (1956).

11. Carson v. Warlick, 238 F.2d 724 (4th Cir. 1956), *cert. denied,* 353 U.S. 910 (1957).

12. Thompson v. County School Board of Arlington County, 144 F. Supp. 239 (E.D. Va. 1956), County School Board v. Thompson, 240 F.2d 59 (4th Cir. 1956), *cert. denied,* 353 U.S. 911 (1957).

13. 159 F. Supp. 567 (E.D. Va. 1957), 252 F.2d 929 (4th Cir. 1958), *cert. denied,* 356 U.S. 958 (1958).

14. School Board of Charlottesville v. Allen, 1 R.R.L.R. 886 (E.D. Va. 1956), 240 F.2d 59 (4th Cir. 1956), *cert. denied,* 353 U.S. 910 (1957).

15. Wichita Falls School District v. Avery, 353 U.S. 938 (1957), *denying certiorari* to 241 F.2d 230 (5th Cir. 1957).

16. Bush v. Orleans Parish School Board, 138 F.Supp. 337 (E.D. La. 1956), Orleans Parish School Board v. Bush, 242 F.2d 156 (5th Cir. 1957), *cert. denied,* 354 U.S. 921 (1957).

17. 163 F.Supp. 701 (E.D. La. 1958), 242 F.2d 253 (5th Cir. 1958), *cert. denied,* 356 U.S. 969 (1958).

18. McSwain v. County School Board, 138 F.Supp. 571 (E.D. Tenn. 1956). The Court of

Appeals order was 214 F.2d 131 (6th Cir. 1954), *reversing* 104 F.Supp. 861 (E.D. Tenn. 1952).

19. Kasper v. Brittain, 245 F.2d 92 (6th Cir. 1957), *cert. denied,* 355 U.S. 834 (1957).

20. County School Board of Prince Edward County v. Allen, 149 F.Supp. 431 (E.D. Va. 1957), 249 F.2d 462 (4th Cir. 1957).

21. 164 F.Supp. 786 (E.D. Va. 1958), 266 F.2d 507 (4th Cir. 1959), *cert. denied,* 355 U.S. 953 (1958).

22. Moore v. Board of Education of Harford County, 152 F.Supp. 114 (D.Md. 1957), *aff'd sub nom.* Slade v. Board of Education of Harford County, 252 F.2d 291 (4th Cir. 1958), *cert. denied,* 357 U.S. 906 (1958).

23. Aaron v. Cooper, 143 F.Supp. 855 (E.D. Ark. 1956), later *aff'd,* 243 F.2d 361 (8th Cir. 1956).

24. 2 R.R.L.R. 934 (E.D. Ark. 1957). Initial approval for the desegregation plan had been given by Judge John Miller, from Arkansas's other judicial district, there being no resident district judge in Little Rock at the time. Because Miller disliked presiding over the school desegregation controversy, he had it transferred to the docket of Judge Roland Davies, federal judge for the District of North Dakota, then sitting in Little Rock on assignment. Peltason, *Fifty-Eight Lonely Men,* p. 152. For complete accounts of what transpired at Little Rock, see Peltason, *Fifty-Eight Lonely Men,* pp. 161–78, and Anthony Lewis, *Portrait of a Decade* (New York: Random House, 1964), ch. 4 et passim.

25. Governor Faubus and President Eisenhower met at Newport on September 14, 1957.

26. 2 R.R.L.R. 941 (1957).

27. 156 F. Supp. 220 (E.D. Ark. 1957).

28. Judge Harry J. Lemley, who usually sat in eastern Arkansas.

29. Oral argument from 27 L.W. 3065–68 (1958), and Anthony Lewis, *Portrait of a Decade,* pp. 57–58.

30. He also said, "I don't worry about the Negro kids' future. They have been struggling with democracy long enough; they know about it."

31. Anthony Lewis, "Supreme Law of the Land Still Rests in High Court," *Portland Oregonian,* July 14, 1974, p. F3.

32. Charles A. Miller, "Constitutional Law and the Rhetoric of Race," *Perspectives in American History,* ed. Donald Fleming and Bernard Bailyn (Cambridge: Harvard University Press, 1971), 5: 199.

33. Walter F. Murphy, *Elements of Judicial Strategy* (Chicago: University of Chicago Press, 1964), p. 106. He adds, "As important as the tone of the statement were citations to two decisions by courts of appeals which held unconstitutional state attempts to continue segregation by leasing state property to private corporations."

34. After the Supreme Court ruling, the case reappeared in the Eighth Circuit, where the court ruled that Negro students were entitled to an injunction restraining board members and the school superintendent from leasing the public schools to private firms without approval of the district court. Aaron v. Cooper, 261 F.2d 97 (8th Cir. 1958). Later, the district court issued an order in accord with that mandate. 169 F.Supp. 325 (E.D. Ark. 1959).

35. Faubus v. United States, 254 F.2d 797 (8th Cir. 1959), an appeal from Aaron v. Cooper, 156 F. Supp. 220 (E.D. Ark. 1957), *cert. denied,* 358 U.S. 829 (1958).

36. Aaron v. McKinley, 173 F. Supp. 944 (E.D. Ark. 1959), *aff'd sub nom.* Faubus v. Aaron, 361 U.S. 197 (1959).

37. Charles A. Miller, "Constitutional Law and the Rhetoric of Race," p. 199.

38. Johnson v. NAACP, 385 U.S. 820 (1966), *denying review* to NAACP v. Thompson 357 F.2d 831 (5th Cir. 1966).

39. NAACP v. Overstreet, 221 Ga. 16, 142 S.E. 2d 816 (1965), 384 U.S. 118 (1966).

40. Harry Kalven, Jr., *The Negro and the First Amendment* (Chicago: University of Chicago

Press, 1965), p. 101.
41. Ibid., pp. 102–3.
42. Ibid., p. 98.
43. That term the only three race relations cases involved anti-NAACP matters.
44. Charles L. Black, Jr., *Structure and Relationship in Constitutional Law* (Baton Rouge: Louisiana State University Press, 1969), pp. 47, 48.
45. Kalven, *The Negro and the First Amendment,* pp. 85–86.
46. For statistics, see United States Commission on Civil Rights, *With Liberty and Justice for All,* pp. 119, 123.
47. Buchanan v. Evans, 152 F. Supp. 886 (D. Del. 1957), 256 F. 2d 686 (3rd Cir. 1958), *cert. denied,* 358 U.S. 836 (1958).
48. Ennis v. Evans, 172 F. Supp. 508 (D. Del. 1959); 281 F.2d 385 (3rd Cir. 1960), *stay denied,* 364 U.S. 802 (1961), *cert. denied,* 364 U.S. 933 (1961).
49. Shuttlesworth v. Birmingham Board of Education, 162 F. Supp. 372, 384 (N.D. Ala. 1957), *aff'd,* 358 U.S. 101 (1958).
50. Covington v. Edwards, 165 F. Supp. 957 (M.D.N.C. 1958), 264 F.2d 180 (4th Cir. 1959), *cert. denied,* 361 U.S. 840 (1959).
51. Holt v. Raleigh City Board of Education, 164 F. Supp. 853 (E.D.N.C. 1958), 265 F.2d 95 (4th Cir. 1959), *cert. denied,* 361 U.S. 818 (1959).
52. Williams v. Davis, 187 F. Supp. 42 (E.D. La. 1960); Bush v. Orleans Parish School Board, 188 F. Supp. 916 (E.D. La. 1960), Bush v. Orleans Parish School Board, 190 F. Supp. 861 (E.D. La. 1960). Another was his striking down of "interposition" statements suspending *Brown* in Louisiana as usurpation of state powers, in a suit brought by the federal government—United States v. Louisiana, 188 F. Supp. 916 (E.D. La. 1960).
53. Orleans Parish School Board v. Bush, 365 U.S. 569 (1960), and City of New Orleans v. Bush, 366 U.S. 212 (1960). Earlier, motions for a stay were denied in a per curiam opinion, Williams v. Davis, 364 U.S. 500 (1960). The complexity of the New Orleans litigation is illustrated by the list of reported decisions in *Bush v. Orleans Parish School Board,* as provided by Read, "Judicial Evolution of the Law of School Integration Since *Brown v. Board of Education," Law and Contemporary Problems* 39 (Winter 1975): 14–15*n*—138 F. Supp. 336 (E.D. La. 1956) (three-judge court), *motion for leave to file petition for writ of mandamus denied,* 351 U.S. 948 (1956); 138 F. Supp. 337 (E.D. La. 1956), *aff'd,* 242 F.2d 156 (5th Cir. 1957), *cert. denied,* 354 U.S. 921 (1957); 252 F.2d 253 (5th Cir. 1958), *cert. denied,* 356 U.S. 969 (1958); 163 F. Supp. 701 (E.D. La. 1958), *aff'd,* 268 F.2d 78 (5th Cir. 1959); 187 F. Supp. 42 (E.D. La. 1960) (three-judge court), *motion for stay denied,* 364 U.S. 500 (1960), *aff'd,* 365 U.S. 569 (1961); 190 F. Supp. 861 (E.D. La. 1960) (three-judge court), *aff'd,* 366 U.S. 212 (1961); 191 F. Supp. 871 (E.D. La. 1961) (three-judge court), *aff'd sub nom.* Denny v. Bush, 367 U.S. 908 (1961); 194 F. Supp. 182 (E.D. La. 1961), (three-judge court), *aff'd sub nom.* Tugwell v. Bush, 367 U.S. 907 (1961), *aff'd sub nom.* Gremillion v. United States, 368 U.S. 11 (1961); 204 F. Supp. 568 (E.D. La. 1962), 205 F. Supp. 893 (E.D. La. 1962), *aff'd in part and rev'd in part,* 308 F.2d 491 (5th Cir. 1962). Read points out that the Supreme Court never issued a full written opinion during the course of the litigation (p. 15*n*).
54. St. Helena Parish School Board v. Hall, 197 F. Supp. 649 (E.D. La. 1961), *aff'd,* 368 U.S. 515 (1961).
55. Board of Trustees v. Brunson, *cert. denied,* 373 U.S. 933. Below: 311 F.2d 107 (4th Cir. 1962).
56. School Board of Charlottesville v. Dillard, 203 F. Supp. 225 (W.D. Va. 1961), 308 F.2d 920 (4th Cir. 1962), *cert. denied,* 374 U.S. 827 (1963).
57. Davis v. Board of School Commissioners of Mobile County, 219 F. Supp. 542 (S.D. Ala. 1963), 322 F.2d 356 (5th Cir. 1963), *cert. denied,* 375 U.S. 894 (1963).
58. Gibson v. Harris, 322 F.2d 780 (5th Cir. 1963), *cert. denied,* 376 U.S. 908 (1964).

59. In *Board of Public Instruction of Duval County,* a district judge had held that no determinations based upon race or color could be employed in the operation of the public school system, and that *Brown* was misread or misapplied when it was construed simply to confer upon Negro students the right to be considered for admission to a "white" school. Accordingly, he granted an injunction enjoining the school officials from assigning teachers, principals, and personnel to schools on the basis of race, either their own or that of the students in the various schools. The Fifth Circuit, affirming this decision, in a broad application of the rights accrued under *Brown,* 326 F.2d 616 (5th Cir. 1964), noted that *Brown* and *Cooper* compelled the entry of the injunction by the district court, even without a showing of injury to the plaintiffs, who were minor Negro students in that school system asserting the rights of Negro teachers and other school personnel. The Supreme Court did not review the decision, 377 U.S. 924 (1964).
60. Erwin N. Griswold, "Search and Seizure—A Dilemma of the Supreme Court" (1974 Roscoe Pound Lectures, University of Nebraska, March 18 and 19, 1974; mimeographed).
61. Ibid., p. 24. The argument is well stated for the administrative area by Kenneth Davis, *Discretionary Justice* (Urbana: University of Illinois Press, 1972). Davis says that when an agency does not feel ready to announce a broad rule, it can—and should—announce less formal generalizations perhaps covering hypothetical situations.
62. Kelley v. Board of Education of Nashville, 139 F. Supp. 518 (M.D. Tenn. 1956), 270 F.2d 209 (6th Cir. 1959), *cert. denied,* 361 U.S. 924 (1959).
63. Northcross v. Board of Education of Memphis, 302 F.2d 818 (6th Cir. 1962), *cert. denied,* Board of Education v. Northcross, 370 U.S. 944 (1962).
64. Oral argument from mimeographed transcript, Library of the Supreme Court, October 1962 Term, No. 217.
65. Counsel apparently forgot *Calhoun v. Latimer,* argued to the Court but decided without full opinion.
66. James v. Almond, 170 F. Supp. 331 (E.D. Va. 1959).
67. Harrison v. Day, 106 S.E.2d 636 (Va. 1959).
68. Almond v. James, 359 U.S. 1006 (1959).
69. County School Board of Prince Edward County v. Allen, 164 F. Supp. 786 (E.D. Va. 1958), 266 F.2d 507 (4th Cir. 1959), *cert. denied,* 360 U.S. 923 (1959).
70. Duckworth v. James, 170 F. Supp. 324 (E.D. Va. 1959), 267 F.2d 224 (4th Cir. 1959), *cert. denied,* 361 U.S. 835 (1959). The prior decree was Beckett v. School Board, 2 R.R.L.R. 337 (E.D. Va. 1957).
71. For an account of the school closings, see Bob Smith, *They Closed Their Schools: Prince Edward County, Virginia, 1951–1964* (Chapel Hill: University of North Carolina Press, 1965). Other accounts of the earlier Massive Resistance are Robbins L. Gates, *The Making of Massive Resistance: Virginia's Politics of Public School Desegregation, 1954–1956* (Chapel Hill: University of North Carolina Press, 1962 and 1964), and Benjamin Muse, *Virginia's Massive Resistance* (Bloomington: Indiana University Press, 1961).
72. Youngstown Sheet and Tube Co. v. Sawyer, 343 U.S. 579 (1952).
73. The only oral argument originally available was from the *Washington Post,* March 31, 1964, p. 2.
74. The government had tried to intervene as a party but was denied by the trial court.
75. Philip Kurland, "The Supreme Court 1963 Term—Foreword: Equal in Origin and Equal in Title to the Legislative and Executive Branches of Government," *Harvard Law Review* 78 (November 1964): 158.
76. Prince Edward County Board of Supervisors v. Griffin, 363 F.2d 206 (4th Cir. 1966).
77. 385 U.S. 960 (1966).
78. See John T. Elliff, "Aspects of Federal Civil Rights Enforcement: The Justice Department and the FBI, 1939–1964," *Perspectives in American History,* ed. Donald Fleming

and Bernard Bailyn, particularly pp. 641–49.

79. Victor Navasky says Robert Kennedy "put the doers in the Hoffa-chasing business and the thinkers in the rights-protecting business."—*Kennedy Justice* (New York: Atheneum, 1971), p. 408.

80. On certification from the Fifth Circuit of the question of Governor Barnett's right to trial by jury in a criminal contempt case, the Supreme Court, over dissents by Justices Black and Goldberg, answered that in general he was not entitled to a jury, but added that punishment without a jury in criminal contempt cases could not be more than could be assessed in petty offense cases (thus probably no more than forty-five to sixty days in jail) if no jury were used. United States v. Barnett, 376 U.S. 681 (1964). See Sheldon Tefft, *"United States v. Barnett:* 'Twas a Famous Victory,' " *Supreme Court Review 1964,* ed. Philip Kurland (Chicago: University of Chicago Press, 1964), pp. 123–36.

81. Navasky, *Kennedy Justice,* presents an interesting account, pp. 159–242, in which blame is placed on the administration for not moving more firmly at an earlier date.

82. Mississippi v. Meredith, 372 U.S. 916 (1963).

83. The following treatment of guideline development and enforcement is based on Orfield's definitive account.

84. Orfield, *The Reconstruction of Southern Education,* p. 72.

85. There was "a rush of 20 Louisiana districts into sympathetic district courts," forcing the Legal Defense and Education Fund (the "Inc. Fund") to appeal such orders to get them up to the higher HEW standards. However, the Inc. Fund, not clearly understanding what was involved in administrative policy, at first "generally supported standards consonant with the court decisions" instead of fighting for still higher ones.—Orfield, *The Reconstruction of Southern Education,* pp. 129, 125.

86. Ibid., p. 48.

87. Ibid., p. 61.

88. The United States Commission on Civil Rights was later to observe, "Despite cautious use of the enforcement mechanism, HEW had made more progress toward desegregation than had been achieved through litigation in the 10 years following *Brown. Twenty Years After Brown: Equality of Educational Opportunity* (Washington, D.C.: Government Printing Office, 1974), p. 17.

89. Title VI's legislative history, interpreted by some to mean that employment patterns could not be a criterion for cutting off funds, did complicate the administrative position.

90. Simkins v. Moses Cone Memorial Hospital, 211 F. Supp. 628 (N.D.N.C. 1962).

91. Moses Cone Memorial Hospital v. Simkins, 323 F. 2d 959 (4th Cir. 1963), *cert. denied,* 376 U.S. 938 (1964).

92. United States v. Madison County Board of Education, 219 F. Supp. 60 (N.D. Ala. 1963), 326 F.2d 257 (5th Cir. 1964), *cert. denied,* 379 U.S. 929 (1964); United States v. Bossier Parish School Board, 220 F. Supp. 243 (W.D.La. 1963), 336 F.2d 197 (5th Cir. 1964), *cert. denied,* 379 U.S. 1000 (1964).

93. Stell v. Savannah-Chatham County Board of Education and Lawrence Roberts, 220 F. Supp. 667 (S.D. Ga. 1963), 318 F.2d 425 (5th Cir. 1963), and 333 F.2d 55 (5th Cir. 1964), *cert. denied,* Roberts v. Stell, 379 U.S. 933 (1964). Subsequently, the district court held a hearing with respect to the school integration plan, so that the important factor would not be race but the best possible educational benefits for all the children, 255 F. Supp. 83 (S.D. Ga. 1965), subsequently enjoining the county board from maintaining a school system with any distinction based on race, although distinctions based on age, mental qualification, intelligence, and the like were to be maintained, 255 F. Supp. 88 (S.D. Ga. 1965).

94. Jackson Municipal School District v. Evers, 357 F.2d 653 (5th Cir. 1966), *cert. denied,*

384 U.S. 961 (1966).

95. Taylor v. Board of Education of New Rochelle, 191 F. Supp. 181 (S.D.N.Y. 1961), *aff'd,* 294 F.2d 36 (2nd Cir. 1961), *cert. denied,* Board of Education v. Taylor, 368 U.S. 940 (1961).

96. Bell v. School Board of Gary, 213 F. Supp. 819 (N.D. Ind. 1963), 324 F.2d 209 (7th Cir. 1963), *cert. denied,* 377 U.S. 924 (1964). Without guidance from the Court, even the bill's sponsors were apparently unwilling to act. See Orfield, *The Reconstruction of Southern Education,* p. 43.

97. Downs v. Board of Education of Kansas City, 336 F.2d 988 (10th Cir. 1964), *cert. denied,* 380 U.S. 914 (1965).

98. Balaban v. Rubin, 379 U.S. 881 (1964), *denying cert.* to 14 N.Y.2d 193, 199 N.F.2d 375 (1964).

99. Vetere v. Allen, 382 U.S. 825 (1965), *denying cert.* to 15 N.Y.2d 259, 206 N.F.2d 174 (1965).

100. Addabbo v. Donovan, 382 U.S. 905 (1965), *denying cert.* to 16 N.Y.2d 619, 209 N.F.2d 112 (1965).

Chapter 7. Housing and Voting Rights: Sustaining the Statutes

1. The story is best told in Walter F. Murphy, *Congress and the Court* (Chicago: University of Chicago Press, 1964).

2. Lerner v. Casey/Beilan v. Board of Education, 357 U.S. 468 (1958).

3. Uphaus v. Wyman, 360 U.S. 72 (1959).

4. See, *inter alia,* Elfbrandt v. Russell, 384 U.S. 11 (1966), striking down an Arizona statute embodying a positive loyalty oath coupled with prosecution for remaining a member of certain organizations, and Keyishian v. Board of Regents, 385 U.S. 489 (1967), invalidating the New York Feinberg Act because it made "treasonable" or "seditious" utterances grounds for dismissal from one's job.

5. Material was obscene if it appealed to "prurient interest" when it was judged in terms of the dominant theme of the work taken as a whole, judged by contemporary community standards and the average person in the community.

6. Respectively, Memoirs v. Massachusetts, 383 U.S. 413 (1966); Mishkin v. New York, 383 U.S. 562 (1966); Ginsberg v. New York, 390 U.S. 629 (1968); Ginzburg v. United States, 383 U.S. 463 (1966).

7. It has been suggested that *Reynolds* "not only illustrated the chief justice's break with his political past, but with his judicial past as well." In *Brown I* and *II,* Warren may have counseled restraint and "in 1964 he dutifully enunciated arguments against the Court's taking action," but at the later time "his impatience with the arguments was apparent, even in recitation."—James F. Simon, *In His Own Image: The Supreme Court in Richard Nixon's America* (New York: David McKay, 1973), pp. 67, 68.

8. For a full account, see Robert G. Dixon, Jr., *Democratic Representation: Reapportionment in Law and Politics* (New York: Oxford University Press, 1968).

9. See Robert Birkby, "The Supreme Court and the Bible Belt," *Midwest Journal of Political Science* 10 (August 1966): 304–19, and H. Frank Way, "Survey Research on Judicial Decisions: The Prayer and Bible Reading Cases," *Western Political Quarterly* 21 (June 1968): 189–205. A recent study is that by Kenneth M. Dolbeare and Phillip Hammond, *The School Prayer Decisions: From Court Policy to Local Practice* (Chicago: University of Chicago Press, 1971).

10. That reaction was reinforced both by the Court's failure to say that untainted confessions could be introduced and by the application of the decision to *trials* started after the date of the *Miranda* rulings, not to *interrogations* after that day. See Johnson v. New Jersey, 394 U.S. 719 (1966).

11. Extension of the privilege against self-incrimination, Malloy v. Hogan, 378 U.S. 1 (1964) and of the right to confront witnesses, Pointer v. Texas, 380 U.S. 400 (1966), had occurred before *Miranda*. Extension of the double-jeopardy rule, Benton v. Maryland, 395 U.S. 784 (1968), came afterwards.

12. E.g., Chimel v. California, 395 U.S. 752 (1969), limiting searches subsequent to a valid arrest to the area "under the control" of the person arrested.

13. See also Warden v. Hayden, 387 U.S. 294 (1967), discarding the "mere evidence" rule in searches, and Berger v. New York, 388 U.S. 41 (1967), where the Court struck down New York's wiretapping statute as too broad, but established standards for allowing electronic surveillance subject to a warrant.

14. G. Gregory Fahlund, "Retroactivity and the Warren Court: The Strategy of a Revolution," *Journal of Politics* 35 (August 1973): 570–71, 571n.

15. In the case on the retroactivity of the rule excluding improperly seized evidence from trial, "the Court had solicited from the National District Attorneys' Association, amicus curiae, statistics of the large number of New York prisoners who would have been able to seek retrial under a retroactive application" of the rule.—Fahlund, "Retroactivity and the Warren Court," p. 590.

16. Compared to the 72 percent rate favorable to the defendant at which the Court decided all 179 criminal procedure decisions from 1962 to 1968, it decided only 40 percent of the 15 retroactivity cases in that direction.—Fahlund, "Retroactivity and the Warren Court," p. 573.

17. Ibid., pp. 572–73, 592.

18. Jones and Washington State Board of Discrimination v. O'Meara, 58 Wash. 2d 793,265 P.2d 1 (1961), *cert. denied*, 369 U.S. 839 (1962).

19. Executive Order No. 11063, 27 F.R. 11527 (1962).

20. Oral argument from 35 L.W. 3337–40 (1967). Excerpts appeared in the *New York Times*, March 21, 1967, p. 20, and March 22, 1967, p. 24.

21. The difference between Black and Douglas created problems for Wirin when, in answering a Douglas question about the meaning of *Shelley*, Wirin suggested that there the courts had taken affirmative action but that strict neutrality by the state was acceptable. When Douglas commented, "I'm trying to help you," Wirin replied, "I know you are, Mr. Justice Douglas, but I'm trying to convince Mr. Justice Black, and I think this is the first time I'm having trouble."

22. Kenneth L. Karst and Harold W. Horowitz, *"Reitman v. Mulkey:* A Telephase of Substantive Equal Protection," *The Supreme Court Review 1967.* ed. Philip Kurland (Chicago: University of Chicago Press, 1967), p. 76.

23. Ibid., p. 40.

24. Ibid., p. 45.

25. Ibidl, p. 57. Karst and Horowitz observe, "Two generations of legal realists have accustomed us to finding our law first in what courts do rather than in what they say. What the Court did in *Reitman v. Mulkey* was to make another important contribution to the growing law of 'substantive equal protection.' "

26. Oral argument from 36 L.W. 3385–87 (1968).

27. The indictments had been under 18 U.S.C. 241 (conspiracy to deprive someone of civil rights), for the murder of Lemuel Penn on the highways of Georgia as he traveled through the state. While only private individuals were involved, the Court majority found state involvement because part of the plan of harrassment had been false reports made to law enforcement officials in order to get them to arrest blacks. However, six justices—three of the six-man majority and the three dissenters—had indicated they were willing to include purely private conspiracies within the reach of the statute. In the companion case, United States v. Price, 385 U.S. 787 (1968), involving the murders of three civil rights workers at Philadelphia, Mississippi, the

Court sustained indictments under both 18 U.S.C. 241 and 18 U.S.C. 242 (the "color of law" provision), but both law enforcement officials (sheriffs and deputy sheriffs) and private citizens—working with each other—had been involved there.

28. Watchtower Bible and Tract Society v. Metropolitan Life Insurance Company, 297 N.Y. 339, 79 N.E.2d 433 (1948).

29. "Letters to the Editor: Justice Stewart Dissents," *Wall Street Journal,* July 3, 1968. The editorial was "The Alternate Legislature," *Wall Street Journal,* June 20, 1968.

30. In addition to the cases from Gary, Indiana, and Kansas City, Kansas, there had been a Southern case, Chandler v. Savannah Board of Education, 313 F.2d 636 (5th Cir. 1963), *cert. denied,* 375 U.S. 835 (1963), and one from Cincinnati, Deal v. Cincinnati Board of Education, 369 F.2d 55 (6th Cir. 1966), *cert. denied,* 389 U.S. 847 (1967).

31. Arthur Larson, "The New Law of Race Relations," *Wisconsin Law Review* 1969: 471.

32. Key v. McDonald, 125 F.Supp. 775 (W.D. Okla. 1954), 224 F.2d 608 (10th Cir. 1965), *cert. denied,* 350 U.S. 895 (1955). On this point, see also Anderson v. Martin, 206 F. Supp. 700 (E.D. La. 1962), 375 U.S. 399 (1963), invalidating a Louisiana statute involving designation of race on nomination papers and ballots, and the rulings on Virginia's statute requiring designation of persons by race on poll tax, residence certificate, and registration lists and on assessment forms, Virginia State Board of Elections v. Hamm and Tancil v. Wools, 379 U.S. 19 (1964).

33. Wood v. United States, 377 U.S. 850 (1963), *denying cert.* to 295 F.2d 772 (5th Cir. 1962).

34. Lewis v. Kennedy, 377 U.S. 932 (1964), *denying cert.* to Kennedy v. Lewis, 325 F.2d 210 (5th Cir. 1963).

35. United States v. Mississippi, 380 U.S. 128 (1965), and Louisiana v. United States, 380 U.S. 145 (1965). Below, respectively: 229 F. Supp. 925 (S.D. Miss. 1964) and 225 F. Supp. 353 (E.D. La. 1964).

36. Oral argument at 34 L.W. 3249–53.

37. Massachusetts's brief had been joined by eighteen states, including five with literacy tests.

38. Here Mississippi's counsel raised the issue of Congress's barring Communists from union office, which the Court had held was attainder.United States v. Brown, 381 U.S. 437 (1965). "If this was attainder," he argued, "the Congress couldn't act under the Fifteenth Amendment as they have here." This argument did not, however, deter Black from his feeling that the 1965 Voting Rights Act was not attainder.

39. The issue was later raised in Gaston County v. United States, 395 U.S. 295 (1969), where the Supreme Court clearly rejected the state's argument that it was illiteracy, not racial discrimination, which was leading to lower voting rates.

40. Oral argument from 34 L.W. 3261–63.

41. Breedlove v. Suttles, 302 U.S. 277 (1937).

42. Texas v. United States, 384 U.S. 155 (1966). Below: 252 F. Supp. 234 (W.D. Texas 1960).

43. Louisiana v. United States, 386 U.S. 270 (1967). Below: 265 F. Supp. 703 (E.D. La. 1966).

44. Allen v. State Board of Elections, 393 U.S. 544 (1969).

Chapter 8. The Civil Rights Movement: Public Accommodations and Protest

1. NAACP v. St. Louis-San Francisco Ry. Co., 297 ICC 335 (1955).

2. South Carolina Electric & Gas Co. v. Flemming, 128 F.Supp. 469 (E.D.S.C. 1955), 224 F.2d 752 (4th Cir. 1955), 351 U.S. 901 (1956). The case cited was Slaker v. O'Connor, 278 U.S. 188 (1929).

3. Three years later, the Court denied certiorari in a Tallahassee sit-in case in which the

same procedural problem had arisen, reinforcing this interpretation of the *Speed* denial.—Steele v. City of Tallahassee, 365 U.S. 834 (1961).

4. Shortly thereafter, when its segregation ordinances were challenged, Birmingham, Alabama, adopted a similar ordinance, and a challenge to it was unsuccessful.—Cherry v. Morgan, *dismissed as moot,* 3 R.R.L.R. 1236 (N.D. Ala. 1958).

5. Boman v. Birmingham Transit Co., 280 F.2d 531 (5th Cir. 1960).

6. Morrison v. Davis, 252 F.2d 102 (5th Cir. 1958), *cert. denied,* 357 U.S. 944 (1958).

7. Louis Lusky, "Racial Discrimination and the Federal Law: A Problem in Nullification," *Southern Justice,* ed. Leon Friedman (Cleveland: World Publishing Co., 1967), p. 272. Originally at *Columbia Law Review* 63 (November 1963): 1163–91.

8. Chief Justice Burger's arguments for eliminating direct appeal from those courts and for eliminating the courts themselves are part of this concern.

9. Lusky, "Racial Discrimination," p. 276. His objection is that this limitation in its jurisdiction is "unpredictable."

10. Kansas City v. Williams, 104 F. Supp. 848 (W.D. Mo. 1952), 205 F.2d 47 (8th Cir. 1953), *cert. denied,* 346 U.S. 826 (1953).

11. Holcombe v. Beal, 103 F. Supp. 218 (S.D. Texas 1950), 193 F.2d 384 (5th Cir. 1951), *cert. denied,* 347 U.S. 974 (1954).

12. Martin Shapiro suggests that while these post-*Brown* public facilities decisions might appear to present "an incremental pattern," this appearance is only a result of "the discrete and serial form that litigation necessarily takes," with the justices having already decided to desegregate all public facilities. However, his suggestion that the justices had a "desire to keep their cards close to the vest until each was played" indicates a conscious strategy was involved, whatever the constraints of serial litigation, which, of course, is always the case in any issue-area. See "Stability and Change in Judicial Decision-Making: Incrementalism or Stare Decisis?" *Law in Transition Quarterly* 2 (Summer 1965): 145–46.

13. The citation of *Tate* was in Burton v. Wilmington Parking Authority, 365 U.S. 715 (1961). The latter case was Hampton v. City of Jacksonville, 304 F.2d 320 (5th Cir. 1962).

14. Compare Palmer v. Thompson, 403 U.S. 217 (1971), where Jackson, Mississippi, did close its pools in the face of an approaching desegregation order, citing economic problems. Here the city was upheld explicitly by the Court.

15. New Orleans Park Improvement Association v. Detiege, 252 F.2d 122 (5th Cir. 1958), *aff'd,* 385 U.S. 54 (1958).

16. The Court of Appeals ruling was put to further use by the Court of Appeals itself in Hammond v. University of Tampa, 344 F.2d 951 (5th Cir. 1965) where, because the university had been established on land leased from the city and used a surplus city building, the judges found sufficient state involvement in the school to constitute state action under the Fourteenth Amendment.

17. Some indirect approval was given when it was later cited approvingly in a discussion of the state action concept in one of the sit-in cases by Douglas, concurring, in Lombard v. Louisiana, 373 U.S. 267 (1963).

18. George v. Clemons, 373 U.S. 241 (1963), unreported below.

19. Oral argument from mimeographed transcript, Library of the Supreme Court, October 1962 Term, No. 424.

20. Jack Greenberg, "The Supreme Court, Civil Rights, and Civil Dissonance," Yale Law Journal 77 (1968): 1532.

21. Joel B. Grossman, "A Model for Judicial Policy Analysis: The Supreme Court and the Sit In Cases," *Frontiers of Judicial Research,* ed. Joel B. Grossman and Joseph Tanenhaus (New York: John Wiley, 1969), p. 439. The rate of acceptance of petitions was higher at the end of the period. Sixteen of the twenty rejected petitions came in the first half, but

of the last forty-one cases, the Court declined review to only four. Cases coming from the state courts were more likely to be heard. Over four-fifths of those cases—54 of 65, or 83.1 percent—were accepted, while only half—eight of sixteen—of the cases from the federal courts were accepted. Ibid., p. 438.

22. Ibid., p. 442.
23. Jonathan Casper, *Lawyers before the Warren Court: Civil Liberties and Civil Rights, 1957–66* (Urbana: University of Illinois Press, 1972), p. 149.
24. Grossman, "A Model for Judicial Policy Analysis," p. 438.
25. Ibid., p. 439.
26. From an article by James E. Clayton, *Washington Post,* October 13, 1960, p. D7, cols. 1–3.
27. Casper, *Lawyers before the Warren Court,* p. 147. Whether this position stemmed from a lawyerly feeling that the Court should avoid broad questions, whether he was trying to protect the Court from attack, or whether he was concerned, at least later, with the development of the Civil Rights Act of 1964, is unclear. However, "Some of the lawyers tended to resent [his] position," particularly "when a lawyer was bent upon having the Court decide the broad issue." Said one lawyer: "I'm not satisfied with the outcome of *any* of the sit-in cases . . . because here I blame Cox. I believe that the principle that a policeman can't go into Woolworth's counter and arrest a man there trying to get a hamburger should have been established, but Cox wouldn't take it—he tried to argue each case on some technical grounds. . . . [One of Cox's amicus briefs] was one of the most pusillanimous documents I have ever read, in the sense that he didn't come to grips with any of [the issues]."—Casper, *Lawyers before the Warren Court,* pp. 147–48. Cox's personal position, stated in 1967, was that he could not see how to draw any line between desegregating a lunch counter and judicially invalidating "discrimination in employment, in admitting pupils to private schools and colleges, and in the sale and rental of housing."—Archibald Cox, *The Warren Court* (Cambridge: Harvard University Press, 1968), p. 36. If the police could not be brought in to take away a trespasser at a lunch counter, Cox feared they also could not be brought in to take away a trespasser from a man's backyard swimming pool. Even doctors and lawyers, Cox feared, might not be able to discriminate on any racial, religious, or otherwise arbitrary grounds.
28. Greenberg, "The Supreme Court," p. 1529.
29. Quoted in Grossman, "A Model for Judicial Policy Analysis," p. 432.
30. This represents, Kalven says, "once again our perennial issue of the limits of judicial realism."—Harry Kalven, Jr., *The Negro and the First Amendment* (Chicago: University of Chicago Press, 1965), p. 126.
31. Ibid.
32. Ibid., p. 127.
33. This paragraph draws heavily on a discussion with Carol Welch, May 29, 1973.
34. Kalven, *The Negro and the First Amendment,* p. 125.
35. Oral argument from 31 L.W. 3159–63 (1962).
36. Thomas P. Lewis, "The Sit-In Cases: Great Expectations," *The Supreme Court Review 1963,* ed. Philip Kurland (Chicago: University of Chicago Press, 1963), pp. 120–21.
37. Monrad G. Paulsen, "The Sit-In Cases of 1964: 'But Answer Came There None,'" *Supreme Court Review 1964,* ed. Philip Kurland (Chicago: University of Chicago Press, 1964), p. 149.
38. Thomas P. Lewis, "The Sit-In Cases," pp. 148, 144.
39. Ibid., p. 113.
40. Grossman, "A Model for Judicial Policy Analysis," p. 436.
41. For a story of the case, see Clifford J. Durr, "Sociology and the Law: A Field Trip to Montgomery, Alabama," *Southern Justice,* ed. Leon Friedman (Cleveland: World Publishing Co., 1965), pp. 43–56.

42. Oral argument in these cases and the subsequent *Griffin* case from mimeographed transcript, Library of the Supreme Court, October 1963 Term, Nos. 6, 9, 10, 12, and 60. Also at 32 L.W. 3145–48.

43. Grossman, "A Model for Judicial Policy Analysis," pp. 444–45.

44. Oral argument from 31 L.W. 3160.

45. For criticism of Goldberg's use of history, see Charles A. Miller, *The Supreme Court and the Uses of History* (Cambridge: Harvard University Press, Belknap Press, 1969), pp. 116–18.

46. Kalven, *The Negro and the First Amendment*, p. 168.

47. Grossman, "A Model for Judicial Policy Analysis," p. 443.

48. Philip Kurland has written about *Bouie* that "the Court distorted a statute with plain meaning into ambiguity in order to decide the case on the due process clause rather than the equal protection clause. . . . It would be helpful if these and other similar cases could be labeled 'good for use in sit-in cases only.' "—"Equal in Origin and Equal in Title to the Legislative Branches of the Government," *Harvard Law Review* 78 (November 1964): 143, 162. On the other hand, it may be noted that Kurland's view of the distinction between the Due Process and Equal Protection Clauses is not shared by others who think the relation between the two clauses is far from clear. The Court's own direction toward the mid-1970s has been away from Kurland's position and toward a far more complex view of the Due Process Clause in particular, for example, in the abortion cases. While a violation of equal protection would appear to be ipso facto a violation of due process—see *Bolling v. Sharpe*—the reverse clearly is not always true.

49. Paulsen, "The Sit-In Cases of 1964," p. 146.

50. Ibid.

51. In a reversal of roles, the NAACP Legal Defense and Education Fund filed an amicus brief in support of the government. This was to happen more frequently as the federal government began greater initiatives in the civil rights area, formerly almost an NAACP sanctuary.

52. Oral argument from 33 L.W. 3109–14.

53. In that case, 317 U.S. 111 (1942), the Court had sustained the validity of regulations limiting the quantity of wheat a farmer could grow for consumption on his own farm.

54. U.S. v. Sullivan, 332 U.S. 689 (1947), where the Court held that Congress had the power to forbid a small retail druggist from selling drugs without the form of label required by the Food, Drug and Cosmetics Act, even though the drugs were imported in properly labeled bottles from which they were not removed until put on the shelves of the local retailer.

55. Oral argument from mimeographed transcript, Library of the Supreme Court, October 1964 Term, No. 2.

56. Other questions concerned the coverage of restaurants by the 1964 act, congressional intent, and whether the Fourteenth Amendment as well as the interstate commerce clause was involved. As to the latter, Greenberg said Congress was not expanding the Fourteenth Amendment, but merely defining its scope more precisely. "Good point," Black granted.

57. See for example Daniel v. Paul, 395 U.S. 298 (1969).

58. Grossman, "A Model for Judicial Policy Analysis," p. 436.

59. Grossman, "A Model for Judicial Policy Analysis," lists *Edwards v. South Carolina*, discussed in the text below; *Heart of Atlanta Motel v. United States; Katzenbach v. McClung;* and *Burton v. Wilmington Parking Authority.*

60. Grossman, "A Model for Judicial Policy Analysis," p. 458.

61. Greenberg, "The Supreme Court," p. 1541.

62. Ibid., p. 1542.

63. Grossman, "A Model for Judicial Policy Analysis," pp. 436–37.
64. Ibid., p. 458.
65. Black's position here was not anomalous, although it may seem so to those who view him as a thoroughgoing civil libertarian. Even the most peaceful demonstration made him fearful and provoked extreme language, whether it was pickets outside a supermarket or schoolchildren wearing black armbands to schools. See S. Sidney Ulmer, "Parabolic Support for Civil Liberties: The Longitudinal Behavior of Hugo Lafayette Black, 1937–1971," *Florida State University Law Review* 1 (Winter 1973): 131–53.
66. *New York Times,* January 13, 1967, p. 26.
67. Freedman v. Maryland, 380 U.S. 51 (1965).
68. See Greenberg, "The Supreme Court," p. 1534*n*.
69. Grossman, "A Model for Judicial Policy Analysis," p. 438.
70. For example, in Schiro v. Bynum, 375 U.S. 395 (1963), the Court had affirmed per curiam a federal district court opinion granting injunctive relief to New Orleans Negroes against the city's segregation at public functions held in the city auditorium and its discrimination against the NAACP and similar organizations by denying use of the city auditorium to organizations advocating desegregation. The city had conditioned use of the building on the speakers' advocacy of views compatible with the municipal policy of segregation. The district court had held the law unconstitutional, 219 F. Supp. 204 (E.D. La. 1963).
71. Hillegas v. Sams, 349 F.2d 959 (5th Cir. 1965), *cert. denied,* 383 U.S. 928 (1966).
72. The other case decided from the Greenwood racial situation was Weathers v. City of Greenwood, 347 F.2d 986 (5th Cir. 1965).
73. The AFL-CIO, in an amicus brief, later asked the Court to reconsider its decision because of a fear that the ruling might help hostile local officials undercut established national labor policy regarding the right to picket or strike and the right to organize in general.—*New York Times,* July 11, 1967, p. 37.
74. Note, "Criminal Prosecutions Affecting Federally Guaranteed Civil Rights: Federal Removal and Habeas Corpus Jurisdiction to Abort State Court Trials," *University of Pennsylvania Law Review* 113 (1965): 793–912.
75. For a more recent example, see the holding of nonjusticiability in O'Shea v. Littleton, 414 U.S. 488 (1973), involving a class action claim of discriminatory treatment by state judges in Cairo, Illinois.

Chapter 9. "Freedom-of-Choice" and the End of "Deliberate Speed"

1. *New York Times Magazine,* October 13, 1963, pp. 56 ff.
2. Ibid., pp. 116–17. Robert L. Carter also feels that *Brown* did nothing to change basic racial patterns in America, although the ruling "completely altered the style, the spirit, and the stance of race relations." He feels "the pre-existing pattern of white superiority and black subordination remains unchanged." "The Supreme Court and Desegregation," *The Warren Court: A Critical Analysis,* ed. Richard Sayler et al. (New York: Chelsea House, 1969), p. 56.
3. In italics in original.
4. He noted later, "We summarize the Court's policy as one of encouraging the maximum legally permissible correlation between judicial standards for school desegregation and HEW Guidelines."—372 F.2d at 861.
5. See also Alabama NAACP State Conference of Branches v. Wallace, 269 F. Supp. 346 (M.D. Ala. 1967), striking an Alabama statute concerning the federal guidelines.
6. Oral argument in these cases from tapes obtained from the National Archives.
7. At one point, Tucker made the constitutional point that "the state is forbidden by the Fourteenth Amendment to extend such choice to parents and thereby permit parents

to accomplish the same thing the state is forbidden to do," but this was not the core of his argument.

8. Gray later distinguished *Reitman v. Mulkey,* the California fair-housing case raised in questioning, as involving a procedure which denied the individual the right to acquire what he was seeking; under freedom-of-choice, every child can go where he wants, with the Court instead being asked to take their choices away from them again.

9. Gray had said the *Brown* cases had been talked about for thirteen years with results similar to those in the game "Gossip." Chief Justice Warren was obviously not amused, and asked whether the game was comparable to the segregation cases and had accuracy or distortion as its aim. Gray, citing Frankfurter that the Court needed to use "fastidious accuracy" in its language, said that the Chief Justice had chosen precise language in *Brown* and that courts had not tried to distort but had tried to repeat as accurately as they could what the Supreme Court had said in *Brown.*

10. The precise argument was used by South Africa when its *apartheid* policy in South West Africa (now Namibia) was under attack before the World Court in 1965.

11. The lack of visibility of some of the dots on the charts the attorneys had prepared for use in the courtroom provoked some amused remarks over whether the use of bifocals was causing the problem, one justice adding, "I don't use bifocals and I can't see any dots, either."

12. "You didn't realize that a white citizen in Jackson, Tennessee, might not want to go to the Washington-Douglas School, did you, especially when it's named Booker T?" asked Marshall. He had already had some fun over the school name by asking Nabrit, "I didn't know whether it was Booker or George, I just wanted to know."

13. Said Greenberg later, "I did not know then what I know now and if I had known it, I would have stated matters somewhat differently." In response to the prod from the bench that he might not have written the book, he responded, "I might not have written that section," producing laughter, to which he added, "No, I think I would have written it but stated things differently."

14. His citation of Baltimore brought Marshall's remark, "Would it interest you to know, as an old Baltimorean, no one ever knew about it? It was there, but nobody ever knew until after the *Brown* case."

15. Whether by design or a slip, he had clearly said *for.*

16. During his rebuttal, Gray challenged the suggestion that the forms were complicated: "I don't know of a simpler way in the world to find out which children are going where than to ask them where they want to go. If you draw a zone line, you've got to take a census and find out where every child in that county lives . . . and you're still going to have to get a form from him to determine his age and all the other factors that school officials always get from children when they go to school."

17. See, among others, Conley v. Lake Charles School Board, 293 F. Supp. 84 (W.D. La. 1968).

18. See 1 R.R.L.S. 101 (1969) for summary and quotations from the statement. It also said that no one desegregation plan would be effective in all situations nor would a single "arbitrary" date for the completion of desegregation be appropriate for all districts.

19. Black stated, "So long as that phrase is a relevant factor, [dual school systems] will never be eliminated. 'All deliberate speed' has turned out to be only a soft euphemism for delay." Later in his statement, he remarked, "In my opinion there is no reason why such a wholesale deprivation of constitutional rights should be tolerated another minute. I fear this long denial of constitutional rights is due in large part to the phrase 'with all deliberate speed.' I would do away with that phrase completely."

20. Oral argument from tapes obtained from National Archives. Justice Brennan did not participate in oral argument but did participate in the case through listening to the tapes. See Chief Justice Burger's statement to Greenberg, 38 L.W. 3151 (1969).

21. Furthermore, Greenberg had found it very difficult to obtain the case record from Judge Cox. Finally a Supreme Court official had got Cox to send the record. As Greenberg remarked, "That's the history of this litigation. Judge Cox won't let you have the record and Mr. Satterfield says you don't belong in this Court because you don't have it."

22. The motto "Segregation Forever" had now become "Litigation Forever," Greenberg had said. Compare the statement that high stakes "are a strong incentive to litigate every doubtful issue in an enforcement proceeding." Daniel J. Gifford, "Communication of Legal Standards, Policy Development and Effective Conduct Regulation," *Cornell Law Review* 56 (February 1971): 447.

23. Frank T. Read, "Judicial Evolution of the Law of School Integration Since *Brown v. Board of Education*," *Law and Contemporary Problems* 39 (Winter 1975): 31.

24. Ibid., p. 32.

25. See "Time Stands Still in Integration Split," *Milwaukee Journal,* July 30, 1973, on Bowman, South Carolina.

26. B. Drummond Ayres, "Nearly 20 Years After Landmark Court Case, New Suit Charges Topeka Schools Still Discriminate Racially," *New York Times,* October 23, 1973, p. 24C.

27. See John Egerton, *"Adams v. Richardson:* Can Separate Be Equal?" *Change* 6, no. 10 (Winter 1974–75): 29–36. The opinions in the case are at 356 F. Supp. 92 (D.D.C. 1973) and 480 F.2d 1159 (D.C. Cir. 1973).

28. Alexander M. Bickel, "Desegregation: Where Do We Go From Here?" *New Republic,* February 7, 1970, pp. 20–22.

29. See Gary Orfield et al., "Replies to Alexander M. Bickel: The Debate Over School Desegregation," *New Republic,* March 7, 1970, pp. 32–38.

30. Christopher Jencks, *Inequality* (New York: Basic Books, 1972); David J. Armor, "Research Report: The Evidence on Busing," *Public Interest,* no. 28 (Summer 1972): 90–126.

31. Respectively *New York Times,* May 12, 1974, p. 1; Roger Wilkins, *New York Times Magazine,* May 12, 1974, p. 43.

32. Archibald Cox, "After Twenty Years: Reflections Upon the Constitutional Significance of Brown v. Board of Education," *Civil Rights Digest* 6 (Summer 1974): p. 44.

33. Arthur J. Goldberg, "An Appeal for Unity," *The Continuing Challenge: The Past and the Future of* Brown v. Board of Education (Evanston, Ill.: Integrated Education Associates, 1975), p. 77.

34. Joseph B. Robison, "Speeding Reforms," *The Continuing Challenge,* p. 34.

35. Constance Baker Motley, "Twenty Years Later . . .," *The Continuing Challenge,* pp. 20–21.

36. Derrick A. Bell, Jr., "Waiting on the Promise of *Brown,*" *Law and Contemporary Problems* 39 (Spring 1975): 345.

37. Ibid., p. 344.

38. United States Commission on Civil Rights, *Twenty Years After Brown: Equality of Educational Opportunity* (Washington, D.C.: Government Printing Office, 1974), p. 80.

39. Ibid., p. 84.

40. Bell, "Waiting on the Promise of *Brown,*" p. 344.

41 United States Commission on Civil Rights, *Twenty Years After,* pp. 73, 76.

42. Ruby G. Martin, "A New Look at *Brown,*" *The Continuing Challenge,* p. 56. She adds: "Many believe that . . . legal theories and the immediate and long-range goals were developed by whites as the first step in a giant, continuing well thought out and designed white conspiracy to maintain the status of black people as second-class citizens of this country."

43. Motley, "Twenty Years Later . . .," p. 20.

44. The cases are Milliken v. Bradley, 418 U.S. 717 (1974) and San Antonio School District v. Rodriguez, 411 U.S. 1 (1973). As Marshall charged in *Milliken,* the Detroit case, in responding to "perceived public mood," the Court was engaging in strategy, although with a different thrust than that of the Warren Court. It was trying to fit in more with the mood of the times, to align itself more with attitudes on busing held elsewhere in the government.

45. Motley, "Twenty Years Later . . .," p. 21.

46. Bell, "Waiting on the Promise of *Brown,*" pp. 345–46.

47. Walter F. Murphy, *Elements of Judicial Strategy* (Chicago: University of Chicago Press, 1964), pp. 29–30, 214*n*. Contemporary examples not involving race include Ginzburg v. United States, 383 U.S. 463 (1966), obscenity conviction based on advertising, and Stanley v. Illinois, 405 U.S. 645 (1972), rights of unwed fathers. See particularly Chief Justice Burger's dissent in the latter.

48. Dissenting, Paris Adult Theater I v. Slaton, 413 U.S. 49 at 83 (1973).

49. "The decision to remand becomes more difficult when the subsequent 'incident' raises questions of federal law."—Note, "Individualized Criminal Justice in the Supreme Court: A Study of Dispositional Decision Making," *Harvard Law Review* 81 (April 1968): 1273.

50. Ibid., p. 1274: "Dispositional problems often are submerged in the summary disposition with which an opinion traditionally concludes."

51. Commission on Revision of the Federal Court Appellate System [Hruska Commission], *Structure and Internal Procedures: Recommendations for Change* (Washington, D.C., 1975), p. 14.

52. Edelman v. Jordan, 415 U.S. 651 at 671 (1974). That the Court is not necessarily approving the reasoning of the lower court is also clear from Chief Justice Burger's statement that "When we summarily affirm without opinion the judgment of the three-judge District Court we affirm the judgment but not necessarily the reasoning by which it was reached."—Concurring, Fusari v. Steinberg, 419 U.S. 379 at 391 (1975).

53. David W. Rohde, "A Theory of the Formation of Opinion Coalitions in the U.S. Supreme Court," *Probability Models of Collective Decision-Making,* ed. Richard Niemi and Herbert Weisberg (Columbus: Merrill, 1972), pp. 167–68. Interestingly, very recently some members of the Court have been treating prior cases as having precedential weight according to the particular majority coalitions in those cases, and Justice Blackmun, in an extraordinary statement, has even intimated that the majority coalitions are entitled to less weight now if the coalition members are not presently on the Court.

54. Charles A. Miller says, "In the political as in the judicial world, it is not possible to determine the extent to which history is a source of policy and the extent to which it is only a source of argument in justification of policy."—*The Supreme Court and the Uses of History* (Cambridge: Harvard University Press, Belknap Press, 1969), p. 196.

55. More recently, in the area of housing, the Court avoided discussing race even though the case involved low-income housing a community did not wish to have.—James v. Valtierra, 402 U.S. 137 (1971).

56. Charles A. Miller, "Constitutional Law and the Rhetoric of Race," *Perspectives in American History,* ed. Donald Fleming and Bernard Bailyn (Cambridge: Harvard University Press, 1971), 5: 162.

57. See the trenchant argument by Matthew Holden, Jr., *The White Man's Burden* (New York: Chandler Publishing Co., 1973).

58. Charles A. Miller, "Constitutional Law and the Rhetoric of Race," p. 200.

59. See Glendon Schubert, *Quantitative Analysis of Judicial Behavior* (Glencoe, Ill.: Free Press, 1959), pp. 210–54, and Harold Spaeth, "Is Justice Blind?" *Law and Society Review* 7 (Fall 1972): 131.

Table of Cases Cited

Index

136922